MAIN LIBRARY

STO

ACPL ITEM
DISCARDED

W9-CTM-107

NEW SOUNDS

NEW SOUNDS

A LISTENER'S GUIDE TO NEW MUSIC

JOHN SCHAEFER

1817

HARPER & ROW, PUBLISHERS
New York
Cambridge, Philadelphia,
San Francisco, Washington,
London, Mexico City, São Paulo,
Singapore, Sydney

Allen County Public Library
Ft. Wayne, Indiana

NEW SOUNDS. Copyright © 1987 by John Schaefer. All rights reserved. Printed in the United States of America. No part of this book may be used or reproduced in any manner whatsoever without written permission except in the case of brief quotations embodied in critical articles and reviews. For information address Harper & Row, Publishers, Inc., 10 East 53rd Street, New York, N.Y. 10022. Published simultaneously in Canada by Fitzhenry & Whiteside Limited, Toronto.

FIRST EDITION

Designer: Abigail Sturges
Copyeditor: Brian Hotchkiss
Index by Brian Hotchkiss

Library of Congress Cataloging-in-Publication Data

Schaefer, John.
   New sounds.

   Includes index.
   1. Music—20th century—History and criticism.
I. Title.
ML197.S235   1987   780'.904   86–45695
ISBN 0-06-055054-6   87 88 89 90 91 RRD 10 9 8 7 6 5 4 3 2 1
ISBN 0-06-097081-2 (pbk.)   87 88 89 90 91 RRD 10 9 8 7 6 5 4 3 2 1

for ELLEN

7133964

CONTENTS

ACKNOWLEDGMENTS

Usually only one name goes on the cover. But any book of this size owes a great deal to a lot of people: first and foremost, to the "New Sounds" radio-program listeners for generating enough enthusiasm to make this book a necessity; and then to another group, only slightly smaller, for making it a reality.

My list of without-whoms must start with the musicians* who gave of their valuable time to take part in this project: William Ackerman, Laurie Anderson, Darol Anger, David Behrman, Pierre Bensusan, Glenn Branca, Chick Corea, David Darling, Michael Doucet, Michael Galasso, Philip Glass, Peter Gordon, Kip Hanrahan, Paul Horn, Richard Horowitz, David Hykes, Simon Jeffes, Scott Johnson, Ben Tavera King, Mark Kirkostas, Elodie Lauten, Margaret Leng-Tan, Daniel Lentz, Julie L. Lieberman, Ingram Marshall, Tom McVeety, Meredith Monk, Robert Moran, James Newton, Bill Ochs, Pauline Oliveros, Jim Palmer, Steve Reich, Terry Riley, L. Shankar, Ravi Shankar, Don Slepian, Vangelis, David Van Tieghem, Andreas Vollenweider, Carl Weingarten, Ransom Wilson, Paul Winter, Bernard Xolotl, Yas-Kaz, La Monte Young, and Marian Zazeela.

Keeping track of all the music would have been impossible without the help of collectors and record companies. Edward Haber graciously allowed me access to his impressive record collection time and again—special thanks for his help in compiling the discography in Chapter 8; Joseph Marcus introduced me to some electronic music that I would never have found otherwise. Thanks also to Dan Behrman of Immigrant Music; Una Johnston; Bob Hurwitz and Peter Clancy of Nonesuch Records; Ellen Lampert, Susan Spier; the staff at the Brooklyn Academy of Music; and IPA/Independent Production Associates.

And finally, my personal thanks for their interest and support to Yale Evelev of Icon Records and New Music Distribution Service, whose expertise in the field of ethnic music was terrifically helpful; Lee Townsend of ECM, for invaluable information and memorable margaritas; Eckart Rahn and Ruby McFarland of Celestial Harmonies, who were even more helpful than they probably realize; Dave Kanzeg, Tim Page, Ray Gallon, and the staff of WNYC; and of course, Mom and Dad.

*Many of the interviews quoted from in this book were broadcast and copyrighted by WNYC-FM, New York and are used here by permission. The interview with La Monte Young is copyright 1985 by La Monte Young and Marian Zazeela and is used by permission of the artists. The quote on page 11 from Peter Michael Hamel's *Through Music to the Self* is used by permission of the author. The diagram on page 145 is based on material used in *The New Grove Dictionary of Music and Musicians,* Vol. 9, (London: Macmillan Publishing Ltd., 1980).

Felicia Eth was the person who convinced me to write this book and was immeasurably helpful in its planning and execution; and Rick Kot was the editor every writer wishes he had. Without either of them, this book would not have been written. The manuscript was proofread by Ellen Shea who provided valuable editorial assistance, and took time out from her own writing schedule to do it.

INTRODUCTION
"NEW SOUNDS"—WHAT'S IN A NAME?

■ In Hollywood, a previously unheralded Greek composer receives an Academy Award for an electronic film score. Though he has labored in obscurity for over a decade, Vangelis suddenly becomes a household name.

■ In New York's Metropolitan Museum of Art, a visiting gamelan (Indonesian percussion orchestra) gives a performance in the room which houses the Temple of Dendur. The gamelan attracts so many people that it takes almost two hours for the crowd to squeeze into the performance space.

■ The Metropolitan Opera House agrees, with reservations, to allow a two-night production of Philip Glass and Robert Wilson's five-hour, nonstop "Minimalist opera," *Einstein on the Beach.* The opera is the surprise success of the season, selling out both nights, and the Met invites the artists to do a third performance.

■ In Palo Alto, building contractor and part-time record producer William Ackerman convinces a virtually unknown pianist to record an album for his Windham Hill label. The album, *Autumn* by George Winston, sells over a half-million copies in three years. At one point, three albums of Winston's lyrical, quasi-Impressionist piano solos appear simultaneously on the *Billboard* charts of best-selling jazz records.

■ Sax player and composer Paul Winter includes the songs of loons, wolves, and whales on his recordings. His albums also contain well-developed thoughts on conservation and ecology. The United Nations responds with an award for his environmental concerns, and invites him to give a concert, the first of its kind, in the General Assembly.

■ In North America, and Europe, and beyond, the phenomenal rise of "psychoacoustic" music is evident in the number of hospices, psychologists, and health therapists using carefully selected recordings to relieve stress. Bookstores and health-food shops begin to carry this music, especially that of artists like Kitaro, Steven Halpern, and Iasos, all of whom combine electronic music with the sounds of nature and acoustic instruments.

■ And, in New York City, WNYC radio quietly unveils its "New Sounds" program—devoted to various forms of "new music"—late at night on the weekends. Within three years, "New Sounds" has expanded to nine shows a week; close to 4,000 letters are received in a single year inquiring about the music; and National Public Radio agrees to broadcast a weekly edition of the program on its nationwide satellite network.

W hat's going on here? "Modern Music," to many people a forbidding term for some pretty forbidding listening, is now beginning to branch out in new directions and to reach new audiences. The idea of musicians making music for other musicians is giving way to music that communicates more directly. Composers are moving beyond the confines of well-defined styles and are developing a personal yet accessible means of expression instead. *New Sounds* is a survey of this new type of modern music: music that falls into the gray areas between classical and rock, ethnic and jazz, Eastern and Western, electronic and acoustic.

Along with every other form of communication, music has expanded its vocabulary and its horizons, and its unprecedented evolution in this century is a direct result of the technology of our time. New instruments, especially electronic ones, have changed the sound of music. Tape and recording techniques have fundamentally altered how music can be presented, and how we perceive it. And with the advent of recording has come easy access to a bewildering array of styles—from the most extreme atonal music to the exotic sounds of the world's ethnic traditions.

As music has expanded in so many different respects, categories for defining it have become increasingly useless. Unfortunately, we listeners seem to have a kind of built-in category reflex: Whenever we hear something new, our first thought is not, How does it sound? but What type is it? So the diversity of new music has resulted in a proliferation of unfortunate labels and improvised categories: new wave, no wave, New Age, new jazz, Minimalism, and perhaps most useless of all (at least as far as describing music goes), "performance art."

Categories, Minimalism and performance art included, tend to be self-perpetuating. Once members of the musical press decided that "performance art" would refer to only a minuscule fraction of the works actually being "performed," certain composers—Laurie Anderson, most notably—found themselves neatly pigeonholed. The Minimalist composers faced a similar problem: Through an accident of musical history they've been tagged with a name which poorly describes their music. Minimalism is often used to label repetitive music, yet music has in fact always employed repetition in some form. Perhaps no music is more repetitive than Erik Satie's *Vexations,* a purposely irritating composition in which a simple phrase is repeated over and over—theoretically, several hundred times by a relay team of pianists. Yet *Vexations* precedes the so-called Minimalists by fifty or sixty years, so no one thinks to call it Minimalism.

For the most part, in an effort to use as few of these uninformative labels as possible, *New Sounds* is organized according to how the music sounds, not according to how music critics file their records at home. (Naturally there are categories with some socially redeeming values: Even Minimalism usefully refers to a group of composers who have at least some recognizable similarities.) Those composers usually termed "performance artists," Laurie Anderson, Robert Ashley, or Meredith Monk, for example, appear separately in *New Sounds,* in the context of other musicians with similar styles and backgrounds. The title of the book itself reflects this wish to avoid categorization. In surveying the wide range of music being created today, it was obvious that any catchall term used in referring to the field would have to be fairly vague, yet manage to be descriptive in a general way. Although the elegantly simple "new music" did just fine, the radio series that spawned this book was called "New Sounds," a title that was loose enough to include a bit more material than "new music." Both terms are appearing with increasing frequency in the titles of major music festivals around the world (the annual New Music America festival, for instance, whose 1984 edition in Hartford, Connecticut was entitled "New Sounds U.S.A.").

At least one aspect of the new-music scene is in fact a direct result of the shrinking world of jet-age travel and global telecasts: the introduction of ethnic music to the West. If not really new, the traditions of Asian and African music are certainly "new sounds" to many ears. Elements of Indian, Indonesian, Japanese, and Near Eastern music have been common sources of inspiration and material for many contemporary composers, so it's not surprising that the music itself, performed in the authentic traditions of these lands, is now appealing not only to more musicians but to listeners as well.

Electronic instruments, another product of today's technology, have insinuated themselves into every field of music. At the same time, the considerably less exotic sounds of solo piano and guitar have left the confinement of the concert stage. Composers like George Winston and William Ackerman have been successfully resurrecting the idea of solo instrumental music outside the classical recital hall. An instrument as common as a six-string guitar can produce new sounds as well as the latest digital music computer or the most alien-sounding ethnic instruments.

The musicians who are tearing down the barriers between these musical forms have remarkably diverse backgrounds, ranging from jazz pianists like Keith Jarrett to classical flutists like Ransom Wilson to the rock renegade Brian Eno. Classically trained composers as markedly different as Morton Feldman and Steve Reich have cultivated simpler, almost mystical styles that bear little resemblance to the density and dissonance of contemporary classical music. Similarly, musicians in the jazz field—Chick Corea, Charles Lloyd, and others—have developed a lyrical style of improvisation in which frenetic displays of virtuosity have given way to creating or maintaining a mood. When Bob Dylan and Phil Ochs used electric instruments, they enraged folk music purists, but attracted new listeners and helped renew interest in the possibilities of folk. In rock music, Klaus Schulze has found inspiration for his synthesizer tapestries in the operas of Richard Wagner. And from the Beatles to Talking Heads, the influence of ethnic music has contributed to the cutting edge of rock.

Naturally, many composers still choose to work in one particular style or another; the jazz and classical avant-gardes are alive and well. But we're going to concentrate here on the musicians who work between the usual categories. Major twentieth-century figures like John Cage, the Beatles, and John Coltrane will be discussed, if regrettably only in passing, because of their historical importance and their legacy to today's musicians.

The "New Sounds" radio program started in 1982 as a way of showing people that the term "modern music" didn't necessarily mean the dry "honk-squeak" style of the music schools. For much of this century, and especially since the end of World War II, the trend in avant-garde music has been toward atonality, Serialism, and chance procedures. Since WNYC had recently made a commitment to twentieth-century music, our listeners had had some exposure to these styles, and it was easy to demonstrate on "New Sounds" how some composers had reacted to this trend —namely, by creating music that didn't share the avant-garde's real or imagined lack of concern for the audience. Here we don't have the luxury of making that contrast explicit, but a bit of background material will be helpful.

Aleatoric music is a style based on chance procedures: random decisions made by either the performer or composer. John Cage, one of the most influential musicians of this century, determined what went into his 1951 *Book of Changes* by tossing a coin. Even Heitor Villa-Lobos, a more traditionally minded Brazilian composer, once wrote a piece dictated by a drawing of the New York City skyline: he traced the skyline onto music paper and used whatever notes his pencil happened to land on as his score.

Atonality is also easily defined. It refers to music that is not in any specific key; there is no tonal center. While tonal music employs a number of related notes and usually revolves around one basic note, atonal music uses all twelve notes in the Western scale impartially. Atonality is often dated from Austrian composer Arnold Schoenberg's String Quartet #2 (1907). Atonal music eventually evolved into the twelve-tone system, wherein the twelve notes were still treated equally, but in a more or less rigorously ordered row. In the 1940s, atonality began to appear in jazz, and became an important ingredient in the music of the avant-garde in that field, too.

The next step in the history of modern music resulted from the work of Schoenberg's friend and pupil, Anton Webern who, in the 1930s and 40s, used a basic "series" of twelve notes to govern *every* aspect of a piece's development. Logical, mathematical rules were applied in structuring each work, so that even rhythms were eventually controlled by serial techniques.

Serialism remains one of the most influential styles of modern classical music —influential, but not popular. Melody and harmony, at least in their traditional forms, are nonexistent in serial music; rhythms are disjointed, and in later serial works they are difficult even to perceive. Lacking a concert audience, Serialism found a home in the academic world. At the conservatories, composers had a haven where they could teach the strict rules of Serialism, write bristling works to be played by ensembles connected with the school . . . and wait for the day when the rest of the world would catch up.

Of course, composers using the various avant-garde styles *have* created important music that has not been given due credit. At its best—say, in the music of Elliott Carter or Milton Babbitt—there's an undeniable excitement and even an appreciable beauty in the modern avant-garde. But since jazz and classical music appeal to relatively small percentages of the population to begin with, removing even their most fundamental aural framework—melodies, harmonies, keys—usually means that the audience for this music, at least when compared to more traditional styles, will unfortunately be a small one.

To draw on an obvious analogy, musical styles are like languages. All too many people speak only one language—in both a literal and figurative sense. Many Americans have an unfortunate chauvinism with respect to second languages: English is an international language, so why bother with anything else? A lot of people get locked into thinking about music the same way: The classical-music listener who thinks music died with Brahms, the jazz buff who thinks music started with King Oliver, the rock fan who can't listen to anything without a beat—they're all unwilling to hear anything but their own musical language.

To continue the analogy, new music is like an especially helpful foreign-language class, teaching a new language in the comfortably familiar terms of the old. Jazz fans who enjoy the quartet Oregon, which combines jazz with Western and Indian classical styles, will soon become accustomed to the sounds of the Indian sitar and tabla. When they hear authentic Indian music, their familiarity with its instruments may enable them to be more receptive to its traditions, and in turn, lead them to try the Eastern-influenced music of Terry Riley, or the microtonal scales of such contemporary Dutch composers as Henk Badings or Adriaan Fokker.

A constant theme running through this book is that music can still be adventurous and well-crafted, without resorting to what Laurie Anderson has called, only half in jest, the "relentless and impenetrable sound of Difficult Music." Most of the works we will cover are tonal, but not necessarily in the usual way. Simple folk melodies, complex chromatic lines, or exotic Eastern scales all use tonality in some way. This allows room for the composer to experiment while providing the listener with a point of reference that atonal music doesn't have.

Another factor accounting for the popularity of new music is that it has been able to attract an audience among the dissatisfied rock and jazz fans who have fled formula-bound commercial radio and recordings. While, on the one hand, radio has provided easier access to more music than was ever before possible, commercial stations have not used their potential for diversity. So music outside the mainstream is not usually heard. For fans of rock or pop music, this means the same two- or three-dozen songs are played repeatedly, while hundreds of others, which could be just as enjoyable, languish in the corners of record libraries because they don't "fit the format." What would happen if a rock or Top-40 station decided to try out something different? It happened at least once, in 1981, when London disc-jockeys gave Laurie Anderson's "O Superman" a shot on the air, and it became one of their Top-10 hits.

Jazz fans have even more of a problem. Across the United States—the country of its birth—jazz has proven to be an untenable format for commercial radio. Even in New York, the city's only commercial jazz outlet became a country-music station in 1980.

The solution for many listeners has been to turn to the hybrid ensembles and musical experiments of new music, where they can rediscover the novelty and sense of adventure that originally attracted them to classical, jazz, or rock music.

Of course, new music does present problems of its own. Musical works have always been used for extramusical purposes—to accompany dance or the visual arts, for example. But the recent trend toward music written for relaxation, meditation, massage, etc. has given rise to a utilitarian style that sometimes sacrifices content. To listeners who do not "use" the music in the way it was intended, the results veer dangerously close to Muzak. Even this style can't be dismissed out of hand, however. Some artists have already created fine music that also happens to be relaxing; this field shows a lot of promise and will be worth watching if it's allowed to discipline itself and mature.

New Sounds is not a textbook; nor is it a record catalog. A survey of twentieth-century classical, jazz, folk, or rock music would be far beyond the scope of a single book. But by concentrating on the many types of music that don't fall into these categories, we'll be able to examine a wide spectrum of new music. If you are familiar with the radio series, you will find here a complete discography of works from those shows right up to the time of writing, as well as an extensive list of sources to help in getting some of this music for yourself. Even if you've never heard of "New Sounds" though, this book should give you a running start toward finding out where today's most interesting sounds are. Note that the discography isn't necessarily a complete list of any given artist's work: Some recordings may not be listed, especially if they are the work of an artist who composes in a mainstream form. Also, a number of important figures are mentioned only briefly or not at all, but for the most part these are composers whose careers have been amply chronicled elsewhere. Most of the musicians in *New Sounds* have not had their work discussed in any kind of detail in a book before.

While the discographies include a bit of description or analysis—highly opinionated, but with at least a nod in the direction of fairness—I didn't want this book to become an extended discourse on "What I Like in New Music," so you'll find excerpts from various interviews with the artists themselves sprinkled here and there. As the great French essayist Montaigne once said, "I quote others only the better to express myself."

NEW SOUNDS

1
THE ELECTRONIC AGE

Will electronics dehumanize music? The computer is only a tool; it's always up to a human being to use a tool one way or another.
Bernard Xolotl

Lo! Men have become the tools of their tools!
Henry David Thoreau

Some months ago I awoke on the first day of a vacation with the inevitable flu. By evening, the combination of illness and medication had pretty well knocked me out, and I found myself half-dozing through a number of prime-time TV shows. One thing about watching TV while sick is that you tend to have your eyes closed a lot, so the audio compels more of your attention. As the closing credits for one particularly noxious program began, I looked up to see who had perpetrated the musical mess that served for a soundtrack and was a little horrified to see on the screen "Music by Tangerine Dream," the German electronic music group whose recordings are a staple on the "New Sounds" radio program. The credits for the next show featured another familiar name: Jan Hammer, whose electronic music has inspired mixed feelings in me, but who has nevertheless popped up on "New Sounds" occasionally.

Electronic music, once the province of people who liked "weird music," has obviously become big business. The move to American prime-time TV is a potentially lucrative one, so it's not surprising that electronic music's first steps in that direction are, to put it mildly, somewhat tentative. And, of course, one doesn't expect serious art to accompany network TV. But its appearance in the mainstream is a clear indication of the increasingly important and widespread role that electronics plays in contemporary music.

Strictly speaking, *all* recorded music for the past sixty years has been electronic. Inherent to the recording medium is the reproduction of sound by electronic means —whether by a hand-cranked 78-rpm phonograph, a radio, or a laser-decoding compact disc player. But the term "electronic music" has come to mean music composed with specific electronic media in mind: synthesizers, electronically altered instruments, tape, and modern studio processes. These first three chapters will

1

examine three related types of electronic music: first, works whose sound is predominantly, if not completely, electronic; next, electro-acoustic music in which acoustic and electronic sounds are treated as more or less equal partners; and finally, process music, where the electronic process itself is the instrument—more conventional instruments, if used at all, play second fiddle to the electronic or tape effects.

Like any other form of art, music cannot be divorced from the society from which it arises. The context of contemporary Western music is a society permeated by electronic technology on almost every level, so it's hardly surprising that electronics have had such an enormous impact on every style or genre of music being made today. While classical and popular music have been greatly influenced by electronic media, a sizeable amount of literature has already been written about its effects on both. Here we'll begin in classical circles, but focus on some of the more indefinable music being made with electronic instruments.

Electronic Music, From Genesis to Generation

The fact that electronic music was first developed before the turn of the century comes as a shock to many. Yet it was in 1895 that Thaddeus Cahill put together the massive bank of rotary generators and telephone receivers he called the "telharmonium." The instrument, played from a keyboard, debuted in Holyoke, Massachusetts before a small group of the inventor's friends and curious onlookers. That first performance featured a less than impressive amount of whirring and humming. The problem, quite simply, was that although Cahill had invented a feasible electronic-music instrument, he had done so before the invention of loudspeakers and amplifiers: The music had no way of getting out of the instrument. Cahill plugged away at his device, though, and in 1906 he gave it another try. The telharmonium was exhibited in New York, generating a great deal of excitement in the press and among some of the leading musicians of the day. But at a weight of two hundred tons, it was not the most convenient of instruments, and it disappeared by the end of the decade.

The next electronic instrument, and the first one to be used in "serious" performance, was the theremin. Invented in 1920 by the Russian Leon Theremin, this instrument's eerie, almost vocal sound is immediately familiar to anyone who has ever watched a 1950s B-movie set in a benighted Eastern European town or on a foggy moor. Despite its later clichéd uses, the theremin was initially popular among classical musicians. In 1929, the Russian émigré Joseph Schillinger wrote a piece called *The First Airphonic Suite* for the Cleveland Symphony Orchestra and theremin, with the inventor himself in the solo role. The concert at which it premiered appears to have been the first documented concert performance of an electronic work.

Like most early electronic instruments, the theremin was monophonic—that is, capable of playing only one note at a time—but unlike the telharmonium, it was small and relatively light. The odd-looking instrument functioned like a radio receiver: A small box received information from two antennae, and the sound was produced by changes in the beating, or oscillation, of the high-frequency circuits inside the box. One antenna was a metal rod in front of which the player moved his hand to change the pitch. Volume was controlled by the second antenna, a metal loop through which the player would pass his other hand.

Since the invention of the theremin, most electronic instruments have been keyboard oriented. An early example, invented in Germany in 1923 by Jörg Mager, was the sphaerophon, a kind of prototype electronic organ that used radio valves as the sound-production devices. The sphaerophon was reportedly a sophisticated instrument capable of many advanced effects, but all of the machines were lost during the Second World War.

The most important and successful early electronic instrument was the ondes martenot ("Martenot's waves"). Built in 1928 by French musician Maurice Martenot, the ondes martenot is a sort of keyboard theremin, with a range of five octaves and a number of possible tone colors. Its versatility inspired several of the most celebrated composers of the day to write works for it: Darius Milhaud and Edgard Varèse used the instrument in some of their scores during the 1930s. Arthur Honegger included the ondes martenot as early as 1934 in his stage work *Jeanne d'Arc au bûcher* ("Joan of Arc at the Stake"), and André Jolivet followed with a *Concerto for Ondes Martenot and Orchestra* in 1947. Olivier Messiaen was impressed enough with the instrument to write a purely electronic work for it in 1937. *Fête des belles eaux* used no less than six ondes martenot, and must be regarded as one of the earliest pieces to be composed specifically and exclusively for electronic instruments. Although it has since been supplanted, the ondes martenot was responsible for the first flowering of electronic music, and many of the works written for it are still in the concert repertoire today.

The development of electronic music began in earnest in the late 1930s and 40s. As long as electronic instruments remained incapable of playing more than one note at a time, their usefulness would be limited, so an early concern was to develop one that could play harmonies. In 1936 a pair of German designers developed the hellertion, a keyboard instrument similar in construction to the sphaerophon, but able to cover six octaves, simulate the sounds of voices and some instruments through foot pedals, and perform four-part harmony. Further musical developments were interrupted by World War II, but in the late 40s the advances in technology made during the war were put to use in civilian fields, and electronic music took great strides.

Experiments at Bonn University in West Germany led to a milestone demonstration of electronic music at Darmstadt in 1951. That year proved to be the real beginning of modern electronic music, for it was then that the first electronic-music studios were established, one at West German Radio (WDR) in Cologne, and another in New York, the famous Columbia–Princeton Electronic Music Center. These studios were an invaluable tool for composers in the medium. A piece of electronic music would generally start with a variety of tone generators (most of which were still monophonic) and would be built through a number of tape procedures: changing the speed of the tape, thereby changing the pitch; splicing different sounds together; overdubbing material from two separate tapes simultaneously onto a third tape with a mixer; playing a tape backwards; or playing the tape through a filter. This is obviously a tedious way to make music, and it could take weeks or months to assemble a five-minute piece. The resources of the studio made electronic-music creation a somewhat easier process, and the style soon became the province of composers associated with one or another of them.

In America, the Columbia–Princeton center was co-directed by Otto Luening and Vladimir Ussachevsky, who brought electronic music to the concert hall by using a completed electronic tape as an accompaniment to a live instrumental performance. Luening's *Fantasy in Space,* for example, uses a solo flutist performing with a prerecorded tape track. In Germany, Herbert Eimert, director of the WDR studio, and Karlheinz Stockhausen were also expanding the boundaries of electronic music, combining elements of electronics and live instrumental performance in their works. Eimert's *Fünf Stücke* ("Five Pieces") and Stockhausen's *Gesang der Jünglinge* ("Song of the Youths") are two of the most notable works of the mid-50s. Stockhausen's piece was especially remarkable, since it consists of a boy's voice singing and speaking, altered and multiplied in so many different ways that it sounds like a whole chorus of voices, with electronic effects that are as much a part of the work as the natural sound of the voice.

The notion of using prerecorded tapes as the basis of music had actually begun in France, where radio technician and composer Pierre Schaeffer had been experimenting since 1942 with music built in collage fashion. In 1948, he coined the term *musique concrète* to describe this form. "Concrete music"—as opposed to "abstract music," made by putting notes on paper—could be built from natural sounds (crowd noises, surf, etc.) or from man-made sources (musical instruments, radio programs, and such). Schaeffer's first example of *musique concrète* was called *Etude aux chemins de fer* ("Study on a Railway"), which is a collage of railway-track noises. In this area, too, Olivier Messiaen made an important contribution. Among his students was Schaeffer's collaborator, Pierre Henry, who became director of the Paris *musique concrète* studio in 1950. Messiaen produced a collaborative tape work with Henry in 1952 called *Timbres-durées,* thus becoming the first major composer to work in both electronic music and *musique concrète.*

For many years *musique concrète* was treated as a separate branch of music, since it is not, in its strictest form, electronically modified in any way. Over time, however, the techniques of tape collage and tape manipulation have merged with electronic processes, and today the term "electronic music" refers generally to any kind of tape or electronic work. Even during the early period, though, some similarities between the two styles were apparent. Both relied on tape recorders as the means of sound production and reproduction; live performances were usually impossible. *Musique concrète* differed mainly in its selection of source material.

Stockhausen's *Gesang der Jünglinge* was completed in 1956, and was one of the first pieces to blur the distinction between electronic music (which the composer had studied with Eimert) and *musique concrète,* which he had studied in Paris. Like most of the electronic music of the 50s, Stockhausen's style was thought by many listeners to be somewhat extreme. Working with a complete range of sounds instead of the usual twelve notes of the Western scale meant his music could be completely atonal. Traditional forms, recognizable melodies, harmonies and rhythms, even the usual method of presenting the music in public were all left behind—along with much of his audience.

By the early 60s, however, a few composers began to try to bring electronic music outside the avant-garde, out of the circuit of universities and music studios into a more public arena. Many of the key electronic composers of the 60s were Americans: Donald Buchla, Pauline Oliveros, and Morton Subotnick all worked at the influential San Francisco Tape Music Center. Buchla eventually devised one of the first commercial synthesizers, and to this day his instruments are among the few synthesizers that are not "keyboard-biased." Subotnick once set up a board of knobs and buttons in a New York City toy store which passing shoppers could press to create their own instant electronic compositions. Oliveros, who had been working with tape music, found that she preferred live electronic performances, feeling them to be more participatory and "human." "All through the 60s," she recalls, "I did a lot of electronic music—all of which was live, that's to say, performed. Even the pieces that were called tape pieces were really performances in the studio, so they could at least theoretically be done live for an audience."

The face of electronic music was changed completely by the introduction of the synthesizer. RCA had been working on a prototype model as early as 1953, but the instrument first became commercially available in 1964. Robert A. Moog in New York and Donald Buchla in California took advantage of the new transistor technology to make synthesizers that were more flexible and less bulky. The Moog synthesizer was the most popular model, since anyone with a knowledge of piano or organ could play its keyboard. The early Buchlas, controlled by sixteen touch-sensitive plates (though some models were also adapted for keyboards) were favored by West Coast musicians; Subotnick especially was responsible for some wild, colorful music made on a custom-designed Buchla.

With the advent of the synthesizer, electronic music could be created more easily, but more important it could be performed live, with the artist in control of the frequency (what note was played), amplitude (how loud or soft), envelope (the length of time), and timbre (what type of sound was used). Of course, the live performance capability of the early instruments was limited and required a good deal of preprogramming, and these first synthesizers still tended to be monophonic. But versatile instruments capable of polyphony were on the way. Not only did many composers in the university-centered studios begin creating music for the synthesizer, but electronics was about to reach into popular music as well.

By the early 1960s the electric organ had already become a familiar instrument on the rock and pop scenes, the result of experiments with electric keyboards that had been carried out by the Hammond Organ Company as early as the 1930s. While these organs were a far cry from synthesizers, they nonetheless produced a generation of pop musicians who had at least rudimentary keyboard technique and who were accustomed to mechanical means of sound production. These artists enthusiastically adopted the synthesizer once they realized its potential. In 1969 the Beatles, who had already used some fairly avant-garde tape effects in their music, added some very discreet synthesizer sounds to their album *Abbey Road,* and electronic rock was off and running. Credit for bringing the synthesizer to a wider audience, though, must go to Wendy Carlos who the year before released the album *Switched-On Bach,* a collection of Bach orchestral and keyboard pieces played on the Moog. Carlos was a true virtuoso performer, wringing out of the still-limited synthesizer an impressive array of subtle effects. Her album sold more copies than any recording by a classical musician ever had, and Robert Moog himself called it "the most stunning break-through in electronic music to date."

Carlos's own view is more pragmatic. "If I had had the technology then that I have now," she notes, "I wouldn't have needed to do *Switched-On Bach.*" While her work demonstrated the potential of the synthesizer, it also showed where work was still needed. Carlos talks of the "Three T's" of electronic music: timing, the synchronizing of musical elements and rhythms that wouldn't otherwise be possible, has long been exploited by electronic composers; tuning is a matter of individual taste, as we'll see in later chapters; but timbre was a strong concern. "The repertoire of sounds that everyone was so crazy about were actually quite boring once the novelty wore off," Carlos says. She has since worked at adapting new technology to create truly new sounds. "Now, with digital synthesis," she says, "there's an element of fun to it, which wasn't there for me earlier."

The 1960s, of course, also saw the beginning of the psychedelic movement in rock—swirling, hypnotic organs, exotic sitars, LSD, paisley and Peter Max every-where. Electronic instruments fit right in, but the synthesizer was not the only electronic medium used for making spacey, allegedly mind-expanding music. Organs were augmented with electronic gadgetry which allowed layers of music to be played by one musician; new studio techniques of tape manipulation and sound distortion were continually, sometimes accidentally, being discovered by imaginative or incom-petent young musicians; there was even a band called Lothar and the Hand People which featured the old theremin ("Lothar" being the instrument's name).

Besides adopting some of the sound-production techniques of the classical avant-garde, the rock avant-garde began to show a similar interest in atonality and —even more surprising for a style so concerned with "the beat"—nonmetric or arhythmic music. This was especially true in Europe, where many young French and German musicians followed the progress being made in electronic music by the likes of Schaeffer and Stockhausen. Bernard Xolotl, a French composer/performer who's been living in the San Francisco Bay Area for a number of years, also credits the importance of the elaborate, trancelike organ and tape pieces of the American "Minimalist" composer Terry Riley. "He was definitely a major influence," Xolotl claims. "It's not apparent now, but it was quite obvious earlier." Certainly people like Klaus Schulze in Germany had heard Riley's music; and the combination of avant-garde techniques with the psychedelic sounds that Terry Riley or rock bands like Pink Floyd were making triggered a new development in electronic music. Take the early albums by Tangerine Dream, for example. Here were three young German rock musicians (Klaus Schulze briefly among them) playing music that sounded as bizarre and self-indulgent to pop listeners as Eimert or Stockhausen sounded to much of the traditional classical audience. Often without any recognizable melodies or harmonies, early Tangerine Dream recordings, such as the two-record set *Zeit* ("Time"), took the listener on a flight through a chemical wonderland. Spacey, occasionally abrasive, at times completely adrift from conventional musical forms, electronic psychedelia lasted only a few years before burning itself out.

Since leaving Tangerine Dream, Klaus Schulze has been one of Europe's most successful electronic artists. He cofounded the group Ash Ra Tempel in 1970 with electric guitarist Manuel Göttsching. Their first, untitled album appeared in 1971, and Schulze, apparently deciding that two bands in three years was enough, took off on a solo career. Between 1971 and 1974 he released four albums of electronic music that gradually evolved out of psychedelia and into a more melodic, accessible style. He was searching for what he called "the music of the future"; everyone else called it simply "space music."

By 1974, this style had caught on in Europe. Tangerine Dream and Ash Ra Tempel underwent a few personnel changes and began their most creative periods; like Schulze they began producing lush, neo-Romantic electronic works. It was at this point, with psychedelia left behind and the popular sounds of electronic rock still ahead, that the electronic scene really began to mature. There were some inevitable lapses in taste. The most common, not only among the Germans but among the British and French composers as well, was a tendency to fall into a heavy, Teutonic, *Angst*-ridden quagmire. But some exciting music did emerge during this phase. Klaus Schulze revealed his enthusiasm for the music of Richard Wagner and led the development of a quasi-orchestral style that looked back to the classical tradition, yet maintained a new, original sound. Schulze's *Timewind*, released in 1975, was one of the finest albums of the period; each of the side-long works was inspired by a place in Wagner's life. "Wahnfried 1883" was the scene and date of Wagner's death, and "Bayreuth Return" refers to the site of the opera house built especially for Wagner's music-dramas. Tangerine Dream's *Rubycon* (1975) and *Phaedra* (1973), and Ash Ra Tempel's *Inventions for Electric Guitar* (1974) also feature lush tapestries of electronics that belie the rock origins of the respective musicians. Bernard Xolotl, meanwhile, left Europe in 1974. After making his way to the United States, he recorded an early album, *Music of Xolotl* (eventually released in 1977), using cyclic procedures à la Terry Riley, with electric guitar, organ, and tape loops. But Xolotl, too, soon began experimenting with a musical style that seemed to grow out of the European Classical/Romantic heritage.

What about Wendy Carlos? In 1972 she released the first album of her original compositions, the two-record set *Sonic Seasonings*. Although Carlos was a product of a completely different tradition, some of the music on *Sonic Seasonings* had a quality similar to that being developed by the Europeans. Using avant-garde electronic and *musique concrète* techniques with her own lyrical bent, Carlos created four seasonal landscapes. The sounds of nature, either on tape or simulated by the synthesizer, blend seamlessly with the ambient, brooding music. "Winter" especially displays Carlos's compositional gifts: With its howling wolves, crystalline electronics, and eerie vocalise by long-time collaborator Rachel Elkind, "Winter" evokes an icy, barren musical scene.

Carlos had begun exploring the expressive possibilities of electronics in 1971 while creating the film score for Stanley Kubrick's *A Clockwork Orange,* which turned out to be the last film music she would write until 1980, when she again collaborated with Kubrick on *The Shining.* During the 70s, though, many other filmmakers seized upon the pictorial quality of electronic music—and of course, many more were attracted by the thought of paying only one musician instead of an entire orchestra. One of the first, most prolific, and ultimately most successful of electronic film music composers was the Greek-born Vangelis.

Like Wendy Carlos, Vangelis has had an unusual career. He is a somewhat reclusive character, rarely appearing in public and frankly uncomfortable about the business that has grown up around music. "It's a basic problem that creation always happens and the business always follows," he claims. "There's tremendous pressure to repeat successes; but I try very hard to keep a low profile and avoid that pressure."

Vangelis began composing distinctive film music in 1970, two years after leaving his troubled homeland and settling in Paris. Using his full name, Vangelis Papa-thanassiou, he had become part of a Greek émigré rock band called Aphrodite's Child. The group was enormously popular in Europe (though their success never carried across the Atlantic), and Vangelis attracted attention for his atmospheric keyboard work, especially on the synthesizer. After the release of the band's psyche-delic album *666,* Vangelis withdrew from the world of popular music and concen-trated on his solo career. He began working with the renowned French television director Frederic Rossif in 1970; one of his earliest film scores, *L'Apocalypse des Animaux,* was recorded in Paris that year, and released as an album in 1973. Though an early work, *L'Apocalypse des Animaux* has the typical Vangelis sound—beautiful melodies, glowing orchestral textures, and acoustic instruments like the fluegelhorn all appear on the album. He has continued to work with Rossif well into the 80s, producing nine film scores for him to date.

In 1974 Vangelis left Paris and moved to London, dropping his tongue-twisting last name in the process. He set up a studio in his London home which has allowed him to pursue a highly personal style. "Whatever I've done, I've done in my own studio," he points out. "And because I can do what I want, that sort of freedom is possible. Otherwise, I couldn't see going to a record company and proposing even a tenth of what I'd like to record." The first album to be released during this period was 1975's *Heaven and Hell.* With its dramatic contrasts between the ethereal, angelic beauty of the "heavenly" sections and the demonic stamping of the infernal parts, this album of electronic keyboards, chorus, and solo voice* is vintage Vangelis.

Throughout the 70s and into the 80s, Vangelis has been able to maintain a consistent, recognizable sound without becoming a self-parody. Except for occa-sional misfires like *Spiral,* his musical instincts usually have been accurate. In 1978, Vangelis collaborated with the Greek actress Irene Papas on a collection of tradi-tional Greek folk songs arranged for electronic instruments and voice. Though the album, *Odes,* was released under Papas's name, Vangelis did the actual arrange-ments, played all the instruments, and produced the recording. "That was a coinci-dence," he says, "because Irene Papas is a friend of mine, and we happened to have the same idea. I always wanted to do something with Greek traditional music— which is not just bouzouki music as many people think—and she wanted to do the same." The result is one of Vangelis's finest, but least-known, recordings. Ironically, his "hit record," the score *Chariots of Fire,* is a more qualified success, and since it appeared he has turned down a number of film projects. "I'm not saying I won't do another one," he explains, "but I don't want to become a factory of film music."

*Guest vocalist on the album was Jon Anderson of the popular rock group Yes. They met when Vangelis was offered the keyboard spot in the band after Rick Wakeman's departure. Three weeks of rehearsal convinced Vangelis that his musical approach and that of the group were too far apart, but he and Anderson became friends, and have since released three albums together.

One of Vangelis's strong points is his versatility, and the fact that whatever he plays—a jam session on some dreadful pirate records aside—generally comes out sounding like Vangelis. The classical sound of his 1976 film score to Rossif's *Opéra Sauvage,* the pastoral, serene *Soil Festivities* (1984), and the dramatic, intense 1985 recording *Mask,* while very different in mood, are similar in style. One of the composer's rare forays out of character was 1985's *Invisible Connections,* an album of mostly atonal, arhythmic electronic music released on the prestigious classical-music label Deutsche Grammophon. The fact that he recorded such a defiantly uncommercial record shows that Vangelis is still capable of the unexpected, and is still exploring new types of music.

Despite the work of talented artists like Wendy Carlos, Vangelis, and a handful of others, the old problems of predictablity and formularization have hit electronic music particularly hard. The first synthesizers were capable of a limited number of sounds, and a certain "cold" or artificial quality was automatically associated with early electronic music. The development of the sequencer in the 70s compounded the trouble. This device allows rhythmic passages or harmonic lines to be repeated automatically, so that the musician only has to play the melodic parts. In the second half of the decade, Tangerine Dream started featuring the chugga-chugga-chug of sequencers in their music; lo and behold, their albums became increasingly popular with the large and lucrative rock audience. Not surprisingly, the sequencer grew to be electronic music's most overworked sound, with some compositions taking on an assembly-line aspect. An alarming number of musicians seemed to feel that, with the right equipment, they could sound just like Klaus Schulze or Tangerine Dream.

But the sequencer wasn't the only rock-oriented device gaining popularity, for synthesized drums and electronic percussion had appeared in the meantime. Led by Tangerine Dream and the popular German group Kraftwerk, many electronic-music composers abandoned their cosmic, lyrical styles for a driving, insistent form of music that soon became widely imitated. And when Kraftwerk actually broke into pop music's top twenty with their electronic song "Autobahn" in 1974, electro-pop was born. (Not all sequenced or heavily rhythmic music is second-rate, of course. Although their recent soundtracks, especially for American television, have been regrettable, some of Tangerine Dream's electronic rock albums, including *Exit* (1981) and *White Eagle* (1982), still have much to recommend them.)

For a while, it looked as if Klaus Schulze was developing a more popular, accessible sound as well. In 1976, he recorded two albums, *Moondawn* and *Body Love,* which leaned in the direction that Tangerine Dream was starting to explore. But Schulze was still interested (at least temporarily) in fashioning a more "serious" kind of electronic music, and in 1978 and 1979, he released a pair of projects, *"X"* and *Dune,* which retreated from the seemingly inevitable move toward a rock-oriented style; parts of these albums represent some of the best music Schulze and his many colleagues have done. *"X"* was a two-record set, the title being the Roman numeral ten (this was Schulze's tenth solo album), not the letter *X* as is often thought. It consists of six musical biographies of such figures as Ludwig II, Bavaria's "Mad King" and patron of Richard Wagner; German poets and writers like Heinrich von Kleist; and sci-fi author Frank Herbert. Despite the use of both live and sequenced percussion in several of the works, *"X"* was far removed from what Tangerine Dream or Kraftwerk was doing at the time. The follow-up disc, *Dune,* was inspired by Frank Herbert's book of the same name. On it, Schulze employed the talented cellist Wolfgang Tiepold, and on one side featured Arthur Brown reading some of Schulze's own futuristic poetry. But with the notable exception of 1983's two-record set *Audentity,* which is occasionally quite experimental, Schulze's music since then has been much more conventional.

French composer Jean-Michel Jarre is another musician who showed, at least in his early albums, that prudent use of synthdrums or other electronic percussion could actually add something to the music. His 1976 album *Oxygene* and 1978's *Equinoxe* were extraordinary electronic suites, with a wide variety of moods and styles. The sequenced portions were perfectly integrated, and acted as a kind of foil for the more cosmic excerpts. But even Jarre has begun to rely more heavily on a strong rock beat in recent albums; the "music of the future," as Schulze once called it, seems to have again gotten sidetracked by the money of the present.

Fortunately, not all the movement has been in one direction. Eberhard Schoener, a talented composer, orchestral conductor, synthesizer artist, and sometime rock musician, returned to the electronic music fold, after a few ill-conceived rock projects, with 1984's *Sky Music/Mountain Music.* This recording featured several unusual music-making techniques involving the combination of electronic and natural sounds. "Sky Music," in fact, uses a "sky organ," a musical curiosity made up of whistles and bells strapped to the chests of pigeons, which were then placed in a wind tunnel; the wind caused the whistles and bells to sound, while Schoener added some flowing synthesizer accompaniment.

Meanwhile, in California, Bernard Xolotl has continued making electronic music that grows out of the "space music" of the 70s. Although he has written music for purely electronic media, he has also produced works for synthesizers and acoustic instruments, including violin and cello. Probably his finest recording is *Procession* (1983), full of sweeping tapestries of synthesizers and violins, the latter played by the San Francisco Symphony's Daniel Kobialka. In contrast to the current trend, Xolotl prefers more offbeat percussion to drums, for example using inverted Japanese temple bells on his album *Last Wave* (1984).

Xolotl is also one of the few composers who writes about trends in electronic music, and his assessment of the current state of affairs is accurate if none too cheery. European electronic-music composers, Xolotl argues, have almost universally sold out to British electro-pop, and the blame rests squarely with the development of electronic or synthetic drums: "Drum machines are too mechanical; even if these expensive digital drum machines, which have become almost unavoidable on records now, had a beautiful drum sound, it would still be the usual snare-drum/hi-hat sound. That makes for a very simple-minded, mechanical type of music. To me it would be more interesting if you could put your own sounds in it." (Some drum machines can now be programmed for more exotic effects, but the majority of musicians who use these devices continue to stay with the traditional Western trap-drum sound.)

The second problem, Xolotl maintains, is that while Europeans and many others fell under the sway of pop music, many Americans (he singles out Californians particularly) went to the opposite extreme, creating what he winningly describes as "the mellow suburban vitamin supermarket muzak of New Age."

The term "New Age music" has become very common, although everyone seems to have a different idea of what it means. To some, it includes the solo piano and guitar music of the artists of the Windham Hill record label (see Chapter 9); but these musicians deny any involvement with the New Age movement. Many view the Swiss musician Andreas Vollenweider (see Chapter 2, page 37) and his electro-acoustic harp as a quintessential example of New Age music; he also disavows any connection, though he's on shakier ground than the Windham Hill crew with his denials. Even Xolotl has been characterized as a New Age musician.

Because a lot of New Age music—much of it electronic—has been composed in recent years, and not just in California, it's worth trying to find a satisfactory definition for the term. The name itself is based on the astrological premise that Earth is entering a new age—the "Age of Aquarius" as the musical *Hair* told us. The movement seems to believe that this new age will usher in an era of worldwide peace and harmony. The main objective of New Age music seems to be combining electronic and/or acoustic sounds in a way that is conducive to meditation, relaxation, etc.; the music sometimes reflects a concern with ecology, conservation, and occasional mysticism, especially in works with sung or spoken texts.

Paul Winter's music, with its strong environmental bent (see Chapter 6, pages 115–119) is one example of acoustic New Age music. Its electronic counterpart is almost exclusively designed for meditation or stress reduction—and therein lies its weakness: The quality of the music itself often suffers. In all too many New Age works, any compositional merit is of secondary importance to extra-musical concerns. The market is now so filled with this type of music that really important works have been lost in the crowd of cheap imitations. Look at the volume of New Age records to be found in alternative bookstores, mail-order catalogs, and larger record stores, and it seems as if everyone with a working wall outlet is making electronic music in this vein. The amount of relatively small, more-or-less independent record companies sprouting up is phenomenal. Normally, that's a welcome sign of diversity and growth in music, and it's something we'll see happening in other styles throughout this book. With this particular kind of music, however, where the product is meant to be passively heard rather than actively listened to, the diversity of records has not been the expression of a diversity of personal styles.

The best New Age music is that which concerns itself with music, and just allows people to do with it as they see fit. In his book *Through Music to the Self,* German composer Peter Michael Hamel states that:

Most of the music which is today categorised as "meditative" is merely a form of imagery recounting the musician's own spiritual experiences and visions, describing "the universal consciousness, the cosmic joy" and eagerly using it as an occasion for subjective music—music which, to the "uninitiated" outsider, can seem naive, rhetorical, intoxicated, or just rubbish. And with few exceptions the meditator . . . cannot "use" this music anyway. The only exception would be an improvisatory or contemplative music which is not *about* meditation at all, but which is itself capable of being a vehicle . . . a music which has *no predetermined function to perform.* (Italics mine)

As mentioned earlier, a number of talented artists who have written music that can stand or fall on its own merits have for better or worse become known as New Age musicians. These include underground favorite Kitaro, the most successful Japanese import not on four wheels; a host of Americans like Michael Stearns, Don Robertson, and Don Slepian; and British-born composer Brian Eno, whose "Ambient Music" series not only brought this type of music to many listeners for the first time, but also remains one of the most effective examples of New Age music to date.

Eno is one of a handful of musicians whose names will appear throughout this book, since his career has embraced a number of musical styles. His gradual move into the field of ambient, electronically processed works in the late 70s remains a milestone in the evolution of "space music" and its later offshoot, New Age. Eno's musical experiments began while he was a student in the 60s, when he was working with the possibilities of sound-taping facilities. This concern with methods of recording, treating, and manipulating sound is the foundation of Eno's art; he has become a master at using the recording studio as a sort of extended instrument or compositional tool.

His first real public exposure came with the rock band Roxy Music in the early 70s, though Eno states that his first performance was in 1967 or 68, when he played a work by American avant-garde composer La Monte Young. Eno remained with Roxy Music for their first two albums, leaving after 1973's *For Your Pleasure.* During this time he seemed to be a prime candidate for schizophrenia: On one hand, he was one of rock's most flamboyant figures, appearing in ostrich plumes and make-up, threatening to upstage lead singer Bryan Ferry as the center of attention in the group; at the same time he was pursuing his more sober, experimental projects with tape delays and sound treatments.

Eno's first two solo recordings were unabashed, intelligently crafted rock albums. In 1975, he moved closer to the British avant-garde, producing a set of records by such noted English composers as Michael Nyman and Gavin Bryars on his own Obscure label. In the same year, he released his watershed recording, *Another Green World.* With this album Eno began experimenting with moody, atmospheric music and what's-wrong-with-this-picture lyrics. On *Another Green World* and its follow-up, *Before and after Science* (1978), he developed a style in which the usual focus of interest—the "story" in the lyrics, or the basic melody—is replaced by the overall setting. The background is at least as important as the foreground, and often the two are virtually indistinguishable. Instead of complete stories or swooning love songs, his works on these records are like snapshots or paintings—some fully drawn, others tantalizingly incomplete. *Before and after Science,* in fact, is subtitled "Fourteen Pictures," referring to the ten compositions on the album plus the four prints by the late Peter Schmidt that were initially included with the record.

Another Green World and *Before and after Science* could hardly be called rock albums, but they were obviously a product of rock technology: Instruments were multitracked, their sounds were distorted or otherwise treated, and electric guitars and organs appeared alongside the synthesizers and tape effects. But Eno's next release, later in 1978, was a whole new type of music. *Ambient 1: Music for Airports* inaugurated the "Ambient Music" series, which now numbers four recordings. "I have become interested in the use of music as ambience," Eno wrote, "and have come to believe that it is possible to produce material that can be used thus without being in any way compromised." He went on to define ambience as "an atmosphere, or a surrounding influence: a tint"; the music's purpose is to induce calm and a space to think. Unlike the musicians who manufactured sounds specifically for stress reduction or contemplation, Eno recognized that his ambient music had to maintain interest on a musical level as well: "[It] must be able to accommodate many levels of listening attention without enforcing one in particular; it must be as ignorable as it is interesting."

The "Ambient Music" records are mostly electro-acoustic, but they had a significant impact on composers of electronic music, especially those working in the New Age field. Like Eno, some have succeeded in creating music that is atmospheric but challenging. Others have tried and failed. Many have not even made the attempt, settling instead for pieces that produce a calm, numbing effect that's hard to distinguish from boredom.

Current Trends

Ironically enough, as synthesizers have progressed from early monophonic analog instruments to digital polyphonic tools capable of almost endless varieties of tone color, the cry that electronics produce only "heartless" and "mechanical" sounds has become stronger. Obviously, the accuracy of these claims varies from artist to artist. The synthesizer is, after all, just another type of instrument, and many composers have come to treat it as such. Although best known for his electronic work, Vangelis maintains that acoustic and electronic instruments are equally important. "I don't have any preference," he says. "I like any sound. I'm not just a 'crazy synthesizer player.' I could play acoustic instruments with the same pleasure. I'm happy when I have unlimited amounts of choice, and to do that, you need everything from simple acoustic sounds to electronics."

One factor that has prevented people from accepting the fact that electronic instruments are no more and no less "musical" than any others is the computer. The music computer enables any kind of sound to be reproduced on any note of the keyboard, which facilitates composition and opens up new vistas in sound to the performer. But according to David Behrman, a pioneer electronic composer in the 60s and an artist who figures prominently in the following chapters, "there's a tradeoff between having a technological system respond in a way that's satisfying, and the feeling of a person having control. You can press a button and some wonderful music can come back, but you don't feel proud of what you've done." This is a curiously modest statement for Behrman to make, since some of his interactive pieces for acoustic instruments and music computer are both convincing and beautiful. But it's true that his concerns are no longer those of the "composer with a capital C"—a term that becomes almost obsolete in the face of computer-controlled music.

With the refinement of electronic instruments in the past ten to twenty years, electronic music has more versatility and more potential than ever before. A composer can now choose between three kinds of synthesizers: analog, digital, and computer sampling. Analog synthesis uses electric current, which vibrates in a way that's analogous to sound waves. The vibrations in the current are converted into sound waves by a loudspeaker system. Digital synthesis uses computer binary information, which it stores as a series of on and off pulses. Digital is a much more flexible process, allowing for a wide variety of sounds to be created by the composer.

Finally, the new programmable music computers can sample any sound—a violin, a spoken word, a door slam—and play that sound back at any pitch the artist desires. A sneeze on B-flat may follow a dog's bark on C, for example. Even sounds that don't exist as acoustic phenomena can be created, a tone halfway between a flute and an oboe, perhaps, or between a piano and a dulcimer.

"I'll use any of these three," Bernard Xolotl says, "anything that fits. What's interesting to me is developing an orchestration of the future: how all these different sounds and instruments can give you varied colors, timbres, and sonorities. And there *will* be different sounds and instruments, even if they're under computer control. It's how you put these sounds together, the orchestration, that's interesting."

The potential of music computers is unlimited, but not everyone is happy with their present state. "I enjoy the fact that they're like a library of sounds," Vangelis says, "but don't try to tell me they're a real instrument. The 'playability' is not correct today. Not because we don't know how, but because we don't think we need it. It's a matter of attitude, not technology." Computer sampling could do with a bit more spontaneity; much of it sounds canned, and for that reason is limited to special effects in most works.

Each new development in electronics has brought increased fears that electronic instruments will someday replace the more traditional acoustic ones. The possibility of a computer being able to sample and store the sound of a violin is now a reality. The possibility of that computer being able to play those sounds back with the same articulation as a human performer is remote. According to Xolotl, "we are not at that stage yet, and we will never get to that stage, exactly. There's no way that by pushing a button you can have the immensely fluctuating vibrato with the infinitely variable speed that you can get from a violin. That's only attempted with very simple-minded, mechanical types of music."

What then does the future hold for electronic music? Its development up to the present has closely paralleled the advance of modern technology, from telephone to loudspeaker to tape to digital programming. But in one respect electronic-music instruments themselves have not changed all that much since Cahill's telharmonium: They are still largely keyboard-controlled, with the Buchla synthesizers the notable exceptions. New developments in keyboard techniques are still appearing, however. Don Slepian, for example, specializes in little keyboards that make big noises. His modified Casio, which still looks like the child's toy it once was, is a good example of a recent advance: "Experiments are being made not just with sounds but with the keyboards themselves," he says. "Now, on two-and-a-half octaves of keyboard, I can generate over seven octaves of sound."

Important as it is, the keyboard is primarily a means of gaining access to and controlling the actual circuitry of the instrument, and it's in the circuitry itself that the greatest changes are taking place. If you ask the composers of electronic music what the next phase will be, most of them will probably give you an answer similar to Bernard Xolotl's: "It will all become computer. It's already happening; even the analog parts of the synthesizer, like the filters, are now computer controlled." The possibilities of using computers in music are obviously still being explored; David Behrman may calm some worries about the impersonality of computer music with his belief that it will develop in an unexpectedly old-fashioned way. "Computer programs are getting more scorelike," he points out. "As the programs get more complex, one starts to relate sections to each other and develop parts, just like in a traditional classical score."

Reactions to the spectacular growth of electronic instruments remain mixed, though, and many musicians continue to be somewhat defensive about it. "It's not a technology show," Don Slepian says. "It's a new aesthetic, striving for something new using the tools we have available. Instruments are all tools; the synthesizer is a tool, but as a composer I'm just as happy to use anything, including acoustic instruments."

Laurie Anderson, who takes an ironic, ambiguous stance toward electronics in her musical stage work, *United States,* says: "I don't have anything against hi-tech. I really like it. But I think you can do very powerful things with a cassette deck and a speaker that costs ninety-nine cents. I also think you can do very schlocky things with hi-tech equipment. A lot of my comments about technology in *United States* were fairly negative, but to make those comments I was using 15,000 watts of power and the latest in studio technology. So there were a couple of things going on there."

In at least one important respect, the spread of electronics may have tremendous value. As David Behrman explains, "One thing that seems to be happening is the development of very inexpensive musical instruments that are very easy to play, which should make it possible for a large number of people to enjoy the act of making music. That would be a wonderful thing, if that happens. I just hope the amateur tradition is helped along by all these developments."

Don Slepian agrees: "As synthesizers become portable and available, it's really going to change things. People will be able to bring music, and make music, almost anywhere. For fun, I play my portable synthesizer on the train. Or if I'm on the expressway I have it on the seat next to me for when I'm stuck in traffic. Wherever you can bring music, particularly live music, people lighten up. They love to hear it."

Electronic instruments, in the end, are simply a new means of expression. They control a work only to the extent the composer allows, so any criticism that an artist's electronic music has a hollow, mechanical sound reflects less on the instrument than on the composer. Synthesizers, like acoustic instruments, have limitations, and it's at least as important for a synthesizer player to know his or her equipment as it is for a violinist. Someone like Brian Eno, for instance, may not be a keyboard virtuoso, but he can wrestle an appropriate sound from even the most reluctant synthesizer because he knows the instrument's possibilities *and* its limits, and how to take advantage of both.

Electronics are no longer the province of the university-supported music studios. For better or worse, electronic instruments and techniques are everywhere. After gaining such widespread acceptance among musicians, it would seem likely that the next step in the development of electronics would be a combination with acoustic instruments. Many of the composers we've heard from so far mention using acoustic instruments as well as electronic; they are included in this chapter because their overall sound is predominantly, if not exclusively, electronic. In the next chapter, we'll examine the music made by composers for whom the distinction between electronic and acoustic instruments is not as clearly defined, and who use electronics as but one sound among many.

DISCOGRAPHY AND RELATED WORKS

ALEXANDROS
- *Antithesis* (Alexandros Audio-Video Research Inc., 250 Fifth Avenue #PH, New York, NY 10001). Well-produced electronics from a young Greek-American composer; some energetic electronic percussion as well. Digital recording.

AMERLAN
- *Ascendances* (Caeleste Arc 1-0985) FOR, EUR.* Michael Amerlan (he doesn't use his first name) plays synthesizers, and though he fits squarely into the New Age category at times, this is a pretty good record. A few works recall the moody musings of California's Harold Budd.

RUTH ANDERSON
- *"Points"* from the LP *New Music for Electronic and Recorded Media* (1750 Arch S-1765). An early work (1974) by a composer who was exploring the relationship between sound and meditation well before the New Age movement came about. This may be more of a study in sound than real music; it's comprised of sine waves, which are "pure" sounds. The results are somewhat naked and piercing.

THE ANDROID SISTERS
- *Songs of Electronic Despair* (Van. VSD-79453). The brainchild of Tim Clark and Tom Lopez, this album of electronically processed voices and synthesizers is so strange and so well made that it transcends the boundaries of "humorous" records—if, in fact, that's what it was originally meant to be. While the lyrics are totally off the wall, the music is often haunting and even a bit forlorn.

ANNA SJÄLV TREDJE
- *Tussilago Fanfara* (Silence SR-4646). One of the most effective albums of group electronics to come out of Scandinavia's surprisingly large "space music" scene. (O.P.)

NEIL ARDLEY
- *"Soft Stillness and the Night"* from *Harmony of the Spheres* (Decca TSX-R-133) WAY. This album-length suite is mostly jazz-rock fusion, but this piece, based on the conversion of the ratios of the orbits of the planets into musical intervals, is purely electronic and appropriately cosmic.

ASH RA TEMPEL
- *Inventions for Electric Guitar* (Cosmic Couriers KM 58.015)

ASHRA
- *New Age of Earth* (Vir. V2080) FOR, NAR
- *Blackouts* (Vir. V2091)
- *Correlations* (Vir. V2117)
- *Belle Alliance* (Vir. V202 284)
Manuel Göttsching is the leader, and on some of these discs the only member, of this German group. The first two albums are spacey, electronically derived guitar works. Later records turn toward a throwaway rock style with occasional looks back at their earlier material.

BAFFO BANFI
- *Hearth* (IC KS-80.008) SBMG
- *Ma, Dolce Vita* (IC KS-80.032) SBMG
Sunny, cheerful electronics from an Italian composer and engineer. The second album might be the better of the two, but the first album has a charming gimmick: It can be played at either 33- or 45-rpm.

THE BEATLES
- *The Beatles ("The White Album")* (Cap. SWBO-101). The Beatles experimented with all sorts of avant-garde techniques in their later studio albums. "Revolution #9" is a good example of *musique concrète.*

WILLIAM BENT
- *Sirius Lullabye* (Bentsounds, 151 Brighton Avenue, San Francisco, CA 94112). New Age–style

*See Appendix 2 for explanation of the two- to four-letter codes used throughout the discographies.

music for synthesizers and music computers, some of it quite beautiful.

JOHANNA M. BEYER

- *"Music of the Spheres"* from the LP *New Music for Electronic and Recorded Media* (1750 Arch S-1765). A 1938(!) work for "three electrical instruments or strings" with string-drum (or "lion's roar") and triangle. This German-American composer is almost completely unknown; she probably intended this work for the theremin or ondes martenot. Here, the Electric Weasel Ensemble plays instruments designed by Donald Buchla.

EASLEY BLACKWOOD

- *Twelve Microtonal Etudes for Electronic Music Media* (privately released LP). Blackwood's album is hard to find, but worth looking for. Each étude, or study, uses a flexible electronic system in a different tuning. Instead of our usual twelve notes to the octave, he uses thirteen- through twenty-four-note octaves. Some of these scales are quite unnerving; others are unusually colorful.

DAVID BORDEN

- *Music for Amplified Keyboard Instruments* (Red 002) NMDS. Electronic music, much of it in a Minimalist vein. See Chapter 4 for description.

KEVIN BRAHENY

- *Perelandra* (HS 001 T) HOS, NAR. Synthesizers, electronic winds, and the Computer Music Instrument are combined in a fine album of spacey, almost orchestral works.

RICHARD BURMER

- *Mosaic* (For. FOR-025) FOR, NAR. Short electronic vignettes. His own works are undistinguished, but Burmer does an unusual arrangement of the fourteenth-century "Lamento di Tristan."

RAY BUTTIGIEG

- *Compucircuit 0.008 m/s* (Cykx Cyr-1-6001) NMDS
- *Agriculture, Architecture, & Astronomy* (Cykxtapes 6042)
- *Etere* (Cykxtapes 6036)
- *Nearing the Millennium/Symphonic Poem #3* (Cykx 24-tcx-6048) NMDS
- *Music for Movies* (Cykxincorp 6072) NMDS
- *Quantum Mechanics* (Cykxincorp 6066) NMDS
  Often pretentious and self-indulgent, Buttigieg's recordings are at least professional quality. *Compucircuit* will appeal to fans of the German space music of the 70s, and although his "symphonic poem" is unfocused and disjointed, it still has its moments. *Music for Movies* is a varied album of short works, some of which are more concise and effective; *Quantum Mechanics* is in the style of recent Tangerine Dream records.

CAMERA OBSCURA

- *Camera Obscura* (Originalton West 006) EUR. A quite good German quartet using a lot of Eno-esque/ambient sounds, with dashes of vintage Schulze.

CAMERATA CONTEMPORARY CHAMBER ORCHESTRA

- *The Electronic Spirit of Erik Satie* (Deram DES-18066). This album does indeed include a chamber orchestra, but the featured instrument is an old Moog synthesizer. This last of a three-LP series is from 1972, so the sound is now quite dated. The idea, though, of recreating Satie's spare piano works and defiantly witty ensemble pieces electronically was inspired.

TOM CAMERON

- *Music To Wash Dishes By* (Bathing 1003) NMDS. Disarming, unpretentious electronics that are bubbly and energetic, except for an enchanting piece of space music called "Another Question."

CANADIAN ELECTRONIC ENSEMBLE

- *Canadian Electronic Ensemble* (Centrediscs 0181) CMC. A live electronic performance group—one of very few, even today. Formed in 1971, they've had several hundred works composed for them, including scores by all four members. The only standout here is David Grimes's *All Wounds,* for soprano, piano, and electronic ensemble.

WENDY CARLOS

- *Switched-On Bach* (Col. MS-7194)
- *The Well-Tempered Synthesizer* (Col. MS-7286)
- *Switched-On Bach II* (CBS KM-32659)
- *Sonic Seasonings* (Col. PG-31234, 2 LPs)
- *By Request* (CBS M-32088)
- *A Clockwork Orange* (CBS KC-31480)
- *"Main Title," "Rocky Mountains"* from the LP *The Shining* (Original Soundtrack) (War. 23449)
- *Switched-On Brandenburgs, Vol. I* (CBS HM-45950)
- *Tron* (Original Soundtrack) (CBS SM-37782)
- *Digital Moonscapes* (CBS M-39340)
- *Beauty in the Beast* (Audion SYN-200)
  Carlos's early recordings stand up quite well today. Recently, she has released a few more albums of her own compositions; of these, the last two are much the best, and prove that she is still one of the most sensitive musicians working in the electronic field.

SERGIO CERVETTI

- *Enclosed Time*
- *Wind Devil* (Rinker-Cervetti Dance & Music, 96 Park Place, Brooklyn, NY 11217).

Cervetti is from Uruguay, but now lives and works in New York, where his music is often used by choreographers. *Enclosed Time,* written for Nina Wiener, is a multiform suite that includes the sampled sounds of Cervetti's cat along with more conventional effects; *Wind Devil* is reminiscent of middle-period Tangerine Dream.

SUZANNE E. CIANI
■ *Seven Waves* (Finnadar 7-90175-1) NAR. Extremely high production standards and deft use of electronic effects all but overwhelm the music on this album. Definitely a recording for people who like beautiful sounds, regardless of content.

BARRY CLEVELAND
■ *Mythos* (Audion SYN-101) JEM. A tasteful album combining Robert Fripp–style electric guitars, synthesizers, and electronic percussion.

COLLECTIVE EGO
■ *Fragments of the Wall for Pasolini* (Collective Ego, no #). This is a real weird one. Lots of fragments and ideas that just never seem to gel. One moment you've got a vapid melody on bells or chimes, then some avant-garde-style twittering. Also occasional found sound and vocals.

COMPUTER EXPERIMENTS
■ *Volume I* (Audion SYN-104) JEM. Larry Fast, of Synergy fame (see below), presents perfectly accessible yet still genuinely interesting music.

CRYSTAL
■ *Rainbow Voyagers* (Crystal 1983) FOR. American synthesizer music from a duo who do a good job in the Tangerine Dream/Klaus Schulze tradition.

THOMAS DESISTO
■ *The Room of My Life* (Four Pie Are Music, 42 West 13 Street, New York, NY 10011). A bit of live flute joins the synthesizers in this music for a live theater piece. A student of Mario Davidovsky, DeSisto has a bit more musical grounding than many other young electronic composers.

DOUBLE FANTASY
■ *Universal Ave.* (IC KS-80.054) SBMG. Double Fantasy is Charly McLion on guitars and synthesizers, and Dreamstar (Robert Schröder), with rock-derived electronics typical of Schröder's later work (q.v.).

LASZLO DUBROVAY
■ *"Sonata for Computer," "Harmonics II," "Parte con moto"* from the LP *Computer Music/Dubrovay, Mandolini, Ungvary* (Hungaroton SLPX-12809). Dubrovay, one of Hungary's most respected electronic composers, works mostly in an avant-garde style; the "Sonata" and "Harmonics II" are his most tuneful scores currently on disc.

THE DUNCAN TRIO
■ *Baron Ochs* (Spooky Pooch, no #) NMDS. Important? Groundbreaking? Maybe not, but this is enjoyable synthesized music without pretensions.

ELECTRONIC ART ENSEMBLE
■ *Inquietude* (Gram. GR-7003) GRAM. Just what their name says: a group of talented performers who specialize in electronic instruments of various kinds.

▲ *Electronic Music: Caron, Perron, & Dawson* (McGill 80011) CMC. In Canada too, electronic music grew up in university-associated studios. Here's an idea what some of that music currently sounds like. A bit on the academic side.*

▲ *Electronic Music by Canadian Composers, Volume I* (Melbourne SMLP-4024) CMC. Includes a disappointing work by the usually interesting Ann Southam; a "free tonal" (sounds atonal) work by Violet Archer; and an excellent piece of *musique concrète* by Robert Daigneault.

BRIAN ENO
■ *Discreet Music* (EG EGS-303) JEM, NAR, FOR
■ *Music for Films* (EG EGS-105) JEM, NAR, FOR
■ *Apollo: Atmospheres and Soundtracks* (EG ENO-5), JEM, NAR, FOR, VB
■ *On Land* (EG EGED-20) JEM, NAR, FOR
■ *"Prophecy Theme"* from the LP *Dune* (Original Soundtrack) (Polydor 823 770-1)
■ *Thursday Afternoon* (EG EGCD-64) JEM
For a composer who has been so influential to many electronic musicians, Eno has relatively few recordings of electronic music. Of these, *Discreet Music* is the earliest, and is discussed in Chapter 3. The rest are impressive tone poems using the recording studio as a giant electronic processor. Even at his worst he's derivative of no one but himself.

EVERFRIEND
■ *Shoot To Kill* (Jazzical Records, 1 Wyndmere Road, Piscataway, NJ 08854). The title track is a dramatic electronic suite that attempts to depict the tragedy of Korean Airlines Flight 007, shot down over Soviet airspace in Asia. The second side is given over to some uninspired pop music.

ROBERT FAIR AND TERENCE THOMAS
■ *Forces* (Interface 303065X; Robert Fair Productions, 268 Elizabeth Street, New York, NY 10012). An unusual album: Instead of collaborating, each musician took a side of the album for himself.

*This symbol, ▲, indicates a new entry which should be read separately from the preceding entry.

Fair's side has some especially interesting synthesized textures.

LARRY FAST, *SEE* SYNERGY.

THIERRY FERVANT
- *Seasons of Life* (Ph. 6313 288). A few lyrical works —one with violin—are strong enough to make this Swiss album worth hearing.

EDGAR FROESE
- *Macula Transfer* (Brain 60.008)
- *Aqua* (Brain 1053) FOR
- *Ypsilon in Malaysian Pale* (Vir. V-2040) FOR
- *Stuntman* (Vir. V-2139) FOR
- *Kamikaze 1989* (Vir. V-2255) FOR
- *Pinnacles* (Vir. V-2277) FOR

Froese is the only original member of Tangerine Dream still with the group. Like his ensemble, Froese as a solo artist has come to rely in recent years on a heavily sequenced rock beat that often removes any element of surprise from the music. Fortunately, *Ypsilon in Malaysian Pale* is an exception: It evokes the steamy heat of a tropical jungle; some fine music can also be found on the earlier albums and *Stuntman.*

MICHAEL GARRISON
- *Eclipse* (Windspell 112882) FOR. Garrison is American, but his music is definitely in the Teutonic camp of electronics. Competent performances, though the singing seems superfluous.

MICHEL GENEST
- *Crystal Fantasy* (Sono Gaia 130) NAR. Kitaro fans should find a kindred spirit in Genest.

GHOSTWRITERS
- *No Man's Land* (Zero 0) NMDS. A Philadelphia duo. This EP has two works, of which "Sleepwalker, Sleepwalker" is easily the best. See Chapter 13.

PATRICK GLEESON
- *Beyond the Sun: An Electronic Portrait of Holst's* The Planets (Mer. SRI-8000)
- *Vivaldi's Four Seasons: Computer Realizations* (Varese-Sarabande VCDM-1000.100)

About eight years separate these two albums in the Carlos/Tomita vein. Gleeson's Holst performances are accurate, sincere, but in retrospect rather thin. Using computer technology, he has fleshed out the sound on the Vivaldi album, which is a tour de force of electronic sound programming.

- *Gothenburg '84* (Radium 226.05, RA-005). Mostly electronic, *musique concrète,* and electro-acoustic music from eight avant-garde composers living in Gothenburg, Sweden. All very industrial, though J. Söderburg and C. M. von Hausswolff contributed some genuinely musical pieces.

PETER MICHAEL HAMEL
- *Colours of Time* (Kuckuck 046) CH
- *Bardo* (Kuckuck 048) CH

Hamel is part of the group Between, and also a solo keyboardist. These two early recordings feature synthesizer and electric organ. See Chapters 4 and 6.

STEN HANSON
- *Secret Connection* (Radium 226.05, RA-007). "The Flight of Icarus," the album's featured piece, is an intriguing bit of computer-generated sounds on an otherwise blip-and-twittery LP.

MICHAEL HOENIG
- *Departure from the Northern Wasteland* (War. BSK-3152). Another former associate of Edgar Froese and Tangerine Dream. This is an excellent album, alternately exciting and serene. (O.P.)

REED HOLMES
- *"Moire"* from the LP *Computer Music from the Outside In* (Folk. 37465). "Moire" is a pattern, usually a watery or wavy design found in silk, and that title perfectly fits this complex weaving of different melodic patterns.

GARRY HUGHES
- *Sacred Cities* (Audion SYN-102) JEM. Well-recorded album of electronics that seems to draw on equal parts of Vangelis and the Germans.

INTERIOR
- *Interior* (Wind. WH-1047) WH. Pleasant music for various synthesizers, with occasional percussion and sax, but some of this Japanese quartet's music is mere fluff.

AKIRA ITOH
- *Inner Light of Life* (King SKS-38) NAR. Dismal, easy-listening music from a former associate of Kitaro.

JEAN-MICHEL JARRE
- *Oxygene* (Motors 77000) CH, NAR
- *Equinoxe* (Poly. PD-1-6175) CH, NAR
- *Magnetic Fields* (Poly. PD-1-6325) CH, NAR
- *The Concerts in China* (Dreyfus FDM-18110) CH, NAR

France's premier synthesist has been steadily moving closer to the rock style of electronics (except for the offbeat *Zoolook;* see Chapter 2). But his first two album-length works, and parts of the Chinese recording, still have much to commend them.

EDDIE JOBSON
- *Theme of Secrets* (Private 1501) PRI. The album notes maintain that it's all done on the Synclavier music computer. If so, it's an uncanny (and pointless) imitation of a piano. The compositions don't always meet the standards of keyboard program-

ming, virtuosity, and production, all of which are first-rate. Nevertheless, this recording will probably appeal to both rock fans (Jobson has played with Frank Zappa, Roxy Music, UK, etc.) and New Age listeners. See Chapter 10.

DARREN KEARNS
■ *Optimal Being* (Atmosphere 100) NMDS. Side one is above-average ambient music that doesn't sacrifice content for mood; side two is more rock-oriented and isn't half bad, either.

GERSHON KINGSLEY
■ *Much Silence* (Relativity TR-8061) IMP. Kingsley has been making electronic music since the 60s. In 1971, he wrote a quartet for Moog synthesizers and, in a less "serious" vein perhaps, penned the tune "Popcorn," which has appeared on countless radio and TV shows as theme music. This album is ample proof that electronics can be placid and lyrical without being trite or cliché.

KITARO
■ *Ten Kai* (Wergo SM-1021) CH, GRAM, VB, NAR, FOR
■ *Oasis* (Kuckuck 053) CH, GRAM, VB, NAR, FOR
■ *Silk Road, Volumes 1 & 2* (Kuckuck 051/052) CH, GRAM, VB, NAR, FOR
■ *Silk Road Suite* (Kuckuck 065/066) CH, NAR, FOR
■ *In Person, Digital* (Kuckuck 054) CH, GRAM, NAR, VB, FOR
■ *Ki* (Kuckuck 057) CH, GRAM, NAR, VB, FOR
■ *Ten Jiku* (Sound Design 1342-5) NAR, VB, FOR
■ *Silver Cloud* (Sound Design 1342-17) NAR
■ *Tunhuang* (Kuckuck 058) CH, GRAM, FOR, VB
■ *Full Moon Story* (Geffen GHS-24083) NAR, FOR
■ *Queen Millennia* (Geffen GHS-24084) NAR, FOR
■ *India* (Geffen GHS-24085)
■ *Asia* (Geffen GHS-24087)
Formerly associated with Klaus Schulze and the Far East Family Band, Kitaro has become something of a phenomenon. If you've heard his music, you know what these albums sound like; if you haven't, it's probably worth your while to hear at least one. Kitaro uses occasional acoustic-instrument effects, but his basic sound is the synthesizer; he particularly loves a program that sounds like bells or chimes. And when Kitaro finds something he likes, he sticks with it. With Kuckuck, Gramavision, Geffen, Sound Design, and Canyon Records all having sizeable Kitaro catalogs, you'll find considerable overlap between Japanese, German, and American pressings, with different cover art and often different title translations applied to the same record. And since they all, quite frankly, sound alike after a while, it becomes impossible to

keep track of them. Nevertheless, Kitaro *is* a phenomenon; his music really affects people. I'll never forget when, after a broadcast of a Kitaro album, a woman called the studio in tears and told me her autistic child, on whom the experts had all but given up, had begun to respond to the music coming over the radio. The thrill wears off more quickly for some than for others; but if you haven't heard him yet, try *Silk Road* (*not* the Suite, which is orchestral) and/or *Tunhuang*.

ESA KOTILAINEN
■ *Ajatuslapsi* (Love LRLP-196). Quite different from Kotilainen's work with the group Karelia (see Chapter 8): predominantly spacey electronics, with an icy, Nordic twist.

KRAFTWERK
■ *1* (Ph. 6305 058)
■ *2* (Ph. 6305 117)
■ *Autobahn* (War. 25326)
■ *Trans Europe Express* (Cap. 4N-16301)
Kraftwerk ("Powerplant"), in their earlier records, combined the Minimalist aesthetic (somewhat superficially, perhaps) with the burgeoning electronic rock scene to produce often flawed but usually pleasant music. *Trans Europe Express* is an example of Kraftwerk's later, pop style. The robotic sound is often too cold to be really popular, but the name-dropping title track became something of a hit.

RON KUIVILA
■ *Fidelity* (Lovely VR-1722) NMDS. A speech synthesizer that sounds close enough to human vocal sounds to be disturbing. See Chapter 3.

DAVID LANGE
■ *Return of the Comet* (DL-101) HOS, NAR. For the return of Halley's comet . . . "Space music," what else? Beautifully produced, this album has attracted a following.

PASCAL LANGUIRAND
■ *de harmonia universalia* (Minos 1002)
■ *Vivre ici Maintenant* (Minos 1003, Minos Ltée., C.P. 431, succ. Victoria, Montreal H3Z 2V8, Quebec).
Exotic cosmic music for keyboard and guitar synthesizers, with touches of percussion and quasi-vocal effects.

PAUL LANSKY
■ *"mild und leise"* from the LP *Electronic Music Winners* (Odyssey Y-34139). If there could be such a thing as avant-garde New Age music, this would be it. Lansky's notes tell us to "listen easily and slowly (hence the title)—this music takes its time," yet it is obviously "serious" music, and rewards active attention rather than passive reception. See also Chapter 3.

LARRY LEEDER

- *Uplift* (Unlimited Inspiration UI-8401) NAR, FOR
- *Views from the Summit* (Unlimited Inspiration UI-8402) NAR

The notes to the second LP claim that it was performed mostly on a single electronic instrument "which perfectly recreates the sound quality of a full orchestra of instruments." Don't you believe it. Both albums contain trite music in hackneyed arrangements.

K. LEIMER

- *Closed System Potentials* (Palace of Lights POL 03/3000) NMDS, WAY
- *Land of Look Behind* (Palace of Lights POL 06/2000; O.P.)
- *Imposed Order* (Palace of Lights 17/2000) NMDS, WAY

Kerry Leimer's first name is no longer a secret, but to many listeners, his music still is. And that's largely the fault of Leimer's own record company, which allowed *Land of Look Behind* to go out of print. At any rate, Leimer is one of the most talented electronic music composers in the United States. His first album is unabashedly based on Brian Eno's work and will certainly appeal to Eno fans. The later two records incorporate live, taped, and tape-loop percussion; using the Brian Eno/David Byrne album as a starting point (see Chapter 6), Leimer has developed his own voice.

CRAIG LEON

- *Visiting* (Thunderbolt ARB-1; O.P.)
- *Nommos* (Takoma 7096)

Except for "Ring with Three Concentric Circles," *Nommos* is not nearly as interesting as Leon's first, out-of-print album. Although independently produced, *Visiting* was a completely professional job.

JEAN-PAUL L'HEUREUX

- *Prelune* (Orandia, no #). Synthesizers and natural sounds blend together on this French-Canadian release. Not up to the standard of the following album, but still pretty good.

JEAN-PAUL L'HEUREUX AND MARC LAPERLE

- *Crepuscule* (Third Ear C-9532) VB. Despite the marginal sound quality, this has become one of the most popular recordings played on the "New Sounds" radio programs, conjuring up images of moonlit nights, or alien landscapes, with a minimum of deliberately spacey effects. One of the finest recordings of its genre—whatever that might be.

PÄR LINDGREN

- *"Elektrisk Musik"* from the LP *Festival of Electronic Music, Stockholm 1979* (Caprice CAP-3019) FYL. Sparkling, scintillating music from

Sweden. Not a lot of harmonic movement—the piece doesn't really *go* anywhere—but the textures are quite impressive.

- *"Det andra rummet"* *("The Other Room")* from the LP *Stockholm Elektronmusikfestival 1981* (Fylkingen FYLP-1026) FYL. Considerably more happens in this piece, yet it's not as successful as *Elektrisk Musik* as it seems to wander rather than develop.

BJÖRN J:SON LINDH

- *Atlantis* (Storyville SLP-4132, Moss Music Group, 48 West 38 Street, New York, NY 10018). Another Swedish musician, who often plays flute for Ralph Lundsten (see below), but who concentrates on Synclavier on this album. Some pop, some spacey material, and a lovely arrangement of the folk song "Calum Sgaire."

- *Liquid Sky* (Original Soundtrack) (Cinevista Inc, 353 West 39 Street #404, New York, NY 10018). Odd arrangements of music by Carl Orff, Marin Marais, and Anthony Philip Heinrich, as well as many less effective original compositions on this soundtrack to a cult film.

RALPH LUNDSTEN

- *Fadervår* ("Paternoster") Op. 67 (Swedish EMI E061-34608)
- *Suite for an Electronic Accordion "Pastoral"* (EMI E061-34873)
- *Nordisk Natursymfoni #2 "Johannes Och Huldran"* (Odeon E061-35200)
- *Universe* (EMI C062-35340)
- *Alpha Ralpha Boulevard* (EMI 7C 062-35666) Lundsten, Sweden's most popular electronic musician, lives in a pink fairytale castle which includes a complete recording studio. Stephen Hill and Anna Turner of the radio series "Music from the Hearts of Space" have aptly described some of Lundsten's music as "the corniest cosmic schlock ever devised . . . his concepts are pure Disneyland." I agree. Each of the albums listed above contains one or two excerpts worth hearing, but as albums they're all pretty hard to take.
- *Strömkarlen/Johannes Och Huldran* (EMI 7C 061-35777)
- *Cosmic Love* (EMI E062-35290)
- *En Midvinter Saga* (EMI 7C 061-35888)
- *Summer Saga/Pop Age* (Angel S-38108) Consistently better recordings than those listed above, mainly because the first two are compilations of some of Lundsten's better music, and because the second two consist of electronic symphonies that seem to hold together. Also, see Chapter 2 Psycho-Acoustical Laboratories listing.

ADRIAN MARCATOR

- *Imagination* (Trance 07) EUR. Marcator may be Germany's answer to Eno in that he tries to create refined, ambient soundscapes that are meditative *and* musical. He has also made recordings as part of the German electronic group Trance.

A. MASHAYEKI
■ *A Mashayeki* (Retro 2801) NMDS. Mashayeki, an Iranian, tries to meld the meditative qualities of Near Eastern Sufi music with Western computer technology. Not yet convincing, but promising.

MICHAEL McNABB
■ *Computer Music* (1750 Arch S-1800) NMDS. Proves that computer music doesn't have to sound inhuman: On "Orbital View," McNabb takes a single soprano voice and synthesizes an entire chorus from it. Elsewhere, the sounds of computer-stored acoustic instruments lend an almost familiar quality to what can at times be very way-out music. An important album.

PETER MERGENER AND MICHAEL WEISSER
■ *Beam-Scape* (IC KS-80.046) SBMG
■ *Phancyful-Fire* (IC KS-80.053) SBMG
■ *Electronic Universe* (IC KS-80.055/56, 2 LPs) SBMG
■ *Night Light* (IC KS-80.058) SBMG
SOFTWARE
■ *Chip Meditation* (IC KS-80.050) SBMG
Nothing particularly innovative about these Innovative Communication discs, but what Peter Mergener and Michael Weisser do, they do well. Light, accessible electronics with lots of sequenced and synthesized percussion. Their album under the name Software is a bit too upbeat for meditation, unless you're used to chanting "Om" while bopping around the house.

OLIVIER MESSIAEN
■ *"La Fête des Belles Eaux"* from the LP *Music for Ondes Martenot* (Musical Heritage Society 821-L). An entrancing work for an ensemble of ondes martenot, this must be one of the very earliest purely electronic ensemble pieces, and certainly the first by a composer of such stature. It's paired with works by Jacques Charpentier ("Lalita" for ondes martenot and percussion) and Darius Milhaud (Suite for Ondes Martenot and Piano). (O.P.)

ROGER MEYERS
■ *After "The Pond"* (Opus One #63) NMDS. Inspired by Charles Ives's song "The Pond," Meyers's piece is for computer-controlled synthesizer. Harmonically drifting electronics from an album which also features music by Ruth Anderson.

RICK MILLER
■ *Starsong* (The Art of Relaxation, no #) VB. Space music, a bit heavy on the sound effects and a bit thin on musical material, but quite nice in spots. Side two is in the Braheny/Stearns mold.

CLARA MONDSHINE
■ *Luna Africana* (IC KS-80.009) EUR
■ *Memorymetropolis* (IC KS-80.022) EUR, SBMG
"Clara" is a man who's put together a pair of whimsical albums of synthesizers and processed sounds that sound like Third World space rock. Brilliant sound, diverting music.

MOTHER MALLARD'S PORTABLE MASTERPIECE COMPANY
■ *Like a Duck to Water* (Earthquack 002) NMDS. See Chapter 4.

GORDON MUMMA
■ *Dresden/Venezia/Megaton* (Lovely VR-1091) NMDS. This album from Mumma—long an important figure among the American electronic music studios—is noisy and forbidding, employing all manner of electronic and concrete sounds.

▲ *Musique Concrète* (Candide CE-31025). Contains works by Pierre Schaeffer, Luc Ferrari, and several others. *Musique concrète,* at least as practiced in the 50s and 60s, rarely produced "pretty" music, but an exception would be Bernard Parmegiani's "Danse" from 1962, which uses only the sound of the human voice.

NEIL NAPPE
■ *July* (Audion SYN-103) JEM. Texture at the expense of any kind of thematic development, in the manner of the early Minimalists; if it isn't profoundly weighty music, it's still eminently listenable.

NEURONIUM
■ *Chromium Echoes* (Solaris 8201). A Spanish duo, Neuronium produces some exquisite electronic sounds that compete with very uninteresting vocals.

▲ *New Age Music* (IC KS-80.051/52, 2 LPs) SBMG. A compilation by some of the seminal figures in this alleged style, although if your definition of "New Age" is not IC's, it may seem like there's no New Age music in this set. Jean-Michel Jarre, Tangerine Dream, Klaus Schulze, Ashra, Robert Schröder, Mergener & Weisser, Baffo Banfi, and Kurt Riemann are included.

▲ *The Nonesuch Guide to Electronic Music* (None. NB-78007). Bernard Krause takes us through the ways of building electronic sounds: the basic wave forms, how to mold them, and how they're combined. Using an illustrated booklet, diagrams, scores, and clear, listenable musical examples, he has created an indispensable tool for electronic music enthusiasts and would-be composers. Krause's own composition, "Once below a Time," is a beautiful piece of music even considered apart from the rest of the album.

MARTIN E. O'CONNOR
- *Alterations* (Martech Music, 3605 Brush Hill Road, Nashville, TN 37216). Subtitled "New Music for Synthesizers," nothing here is all that *new:* Several cuts are in the Vangelis style, spacey but not completely static, one or two others cross over into the New Age sound.

BRUCE ODLAND
- *Chaco* (XO Records, Inc., 79 Eagles Drive, Boulder, CO 80302). Chaco Canyon in northwestern New Mexico contains some astounding ruins of a fairly advanced Indian civilization. Odland's work was commissioned as a dance score but was inspired by the canyon; using conventional and self-designed percussion instruments as a foil for the synthesizer, Odland creates a distinctive suite of works.

YASUHITO OHNO
- *Music in DNA* (Fontec FO-2057) EUR. This young Japanese musician draws on Kabuki music, electronics, and rock music; the synthipop isn't too original, but occasional pieces like the title track are more interesting.

PAULINE OLIVEROS
- *"Bye Bye Butterfly"* from the LP *New Music for Electronic and Recorded Media* (1750 Arch S-1765). Fans of Oliveros's later, more meditative music may be put out by this piece, with its unlikely combination of academia and humor.

ORCHESTRA SIDERAL IMPACT
- *Orchestra Sideral Impact* (Transtar OSI-1). Keyboards and computers are brought together on this cassette recording of lightweight electronics.

GALE ORMISTON AND CARL WEINGARTEN
- *Windfalls* (Multiphase WF-003) NMDS. This energetic album is almost universally and favorably compared to the Fripp and Eno recordings (see Chapter 3). Electronic keyboards and guitars are combined with enough pulsating effects to take this out of the realm of ambient music. Also, see Carl Weingarten below.

OSE
- *Adonia* (EGG 90.277). Ose is basically Hervé Picart joined by Richard Pinhas's group, Heldon. Tightly knit, often rock-inspired electronics.

IRENE PAPAS
- *Odes* (German Poly. 2417-343) NAR. See Chapter 8.

ÅKE PARMERUD
- *"Out of Sight."* from the LP *Stockholm Elektronmusikfestival 1981* (Fylkingen FYLP-1026) FYL.

Glittering electronics in a style that approaches avant-garde techniques. Probably the best piece on this recording.

PHILIP PERKINS
- *King of the World* (Fun 1003) NMDS. Splendid recording. Perkins divides the album into three suites, one for each of three different kings, each of whom could have been considered "King of the World" in his time. Using a Casio that makes deceptively natural sounds (thunder, for example), Perkins evokes the rituals of the Mayans, or the splendor of ancient Rome.

MARK PETERSEN
- *"Kokopelli the Flute Player," "Icy Worlds," "Memories of Mimas,"* other works (Loch Ness Productions, PO Box 3023, Boulder, CO 80307)

GEODESIUM
- *Double Eclipse* (Loch Ness Productions #MP-8112)
Petersen (see above) does a lot of music for planetariums, so his works have a cosmic, floating quality to them. Under the name of Geodesium, he recorded arrangements of *Pachelbel's Canon in D* and a Bach fugue, as well as some less successful originals. His other solo works, especially *Kokopelli,* can be much more effective.

PGR
- *The Flickering of Sowing Time* (RRRecords, no #) NMDS. Industrial-strength electronics with lots of *musique concrète,* including tapes of TV evangelists, an Indian sarod performance, choral music, etc. Not pretty, but absorbing.

ANTHONY PHILLIPS
- *1984* (Passport PB-6006) JEM. English guitarist Anthony Phillips, primarily an acoustic performer (see Chapter 10), occasionally does synthesizer pieces, and made this one recording of purely electronic music. Unlike the shorter works, this album-length composition doesn't compel attention.

RICHARD PINHAS
- *Heldon 2* (Disjuncta 000002)
- *IceLand* (French Poly. 2393 254)

HELDON
- *Heldon IV* (Aural Explorers AE 5001)
Pinhas is a French synthesist whose recordings, under the name Heldon or on his own, are characterized by an unrelieved gloom and oppressive atmosphere. *Heldon 2* may be his best, though it's certainly no walk in the sun. *IceLand* and *Heldon IV* each include one or two gripping passages and an overabundance of, and over-reliance on, sound effects.

RUSSELL PINKSTON

■ *"Emergence"* from the LP *The Dartmouth Digital Synthesizer* (Folk. 33442) NMDS. From a recording that's mostly academic in its musical approach, Pinkston's contribution deals with the emergence of lush, tonal music out of an initially dense concentration of sounds.

SANFORD PONDER

■ *Etosha—Private Music in the Land of Dry Water* (Private 1101) PRI. Is the music simply unpretentious tunes in beautiful settings? If so, then the recording works. But I can't help wondering if Ponder aspires to something more serious here. If that's the case, the album must be judged a gorgeous but hollow failure.

■ *Tigers Are Brave* (Private 2012-1) PRI. A more varied, and, in spots, more successful second release. Some violin and other acoustic instruments, but mostly CMI and synthesizers.

VITO RICCI

■ *Music with Memory* (Creation CC-1) NMDS. Runs the gamut from sparse, minimal drones and beeps, to heavy industrial-sounding noise, to slick synthipop. The combination is so strange that you have to be prepared for anything when listening to it.

KURT RIEMANN

■ *Electronic Nightworks* (IC KS-80.047) SBMG. Bach, Handel, Satie, Ravel's *Bolero,* "Carol of the Bells," and a couple of short originals.

STEVE ROACH

■ *Now* (private release) FOR, NAR
■ *Traveler* (Domino NO-101) FOR, NAR
■ *Structures from Silence* (Fort. FOR-024) FOR, NAR
■ *Empetus* (For. LP036) FOR, NAR
■ *Dreamtime Return* (due for release on Fortuna)
Roach's progress has been remarkable. His early recordings are cut from the same cloth as Tangerine Dream, with lots of technopop and some occasionally interesting works. *Structures* is a recording of space music, designed to induce calm and a sense of suspended time; it's really Roach's first mature album. *Empetus* is a driving, kinetic album with two shorter, reflective works, again tapping into the Tangerine Dream style. *Dreamtime Return* may be Roach's most well-rounded and successful album to date, synthesizing, if you will, both sides of his style.

DON ROBERTSON

■ *Spring* (DBR Music 1984) EUR, NAR
■ *Starmusic* (DBR Music 1982) EUR, NAR
Robertson has developed into a top-notch synthesizer programmer. *Starmusic,* "for intergalactic computer orchestra," has typically lush, brilliant sounds; *Spring* may have a bit more substance to

it, and is probably Robertson's best recording to date.

CLARA ROCKMORE

■ *The Moogs Present Clara Rockmore, Virtuoso Theremin* (Delos 25437). Rockmore is indeed a virtuoso theremin player, and at first you don't even realize that you're hearing an electronic instrument. It sounds like someone humming, or playing a violin with no vibrato, or anything but an artificially produced sound. Music of Rachmaninoff, Saint-Saëns, Falla, Stravinsky, Ravel, and Tchaikovsky is played with piano accompaniment. One note of interest: The Moogs had originally wanted to do this album with synthesizer accompaniment by Wendy Carlos.

DAVID ROSENBOOM

■ *Future Travel* (Street 002) NMDS. Somehow, Rosenboom has managed to maintain a fresh perspective on electronic music after being so closely involved with it for over fifteen years. From rock to Latin to Near Eastern sounds, this album is always surprising. Also see Chapter 3.

DAVID ROSENBOOM AND DONALD BUCHLA

■ *Collaboration in Performance* (1750 Arch S-1774) NMDS. Two old hands at electronic music get together for a recording of spiky, avant-garde electronics, using Buchla's computer-assisted 300 Series Electric Music Box.

SŌMEI SATOH

■ *"Mandala"* from the LP *Mandala/Sumeru* (ALM AL-26). A purely electronic work that cunningly simulates the sound of Shomyo (Japanese Buddhist chant). See Chapter 10, especially the Harmonic Choir and Tibetan Monks recordings, for an idea of what this work actually sounds like, as well as Chapter 5 for more on Satoh.

CONRAD SCHNITZLER

■ *Control* (Dys 4). Schnitzler helped found the German group Cluster, was an early member of Tangerine Dream, then took off on a solo career. This is often severe, bruising stuff.

EBERHARD SCHOENER

■ *Meditation* (Kuckuck 059) CH, NAR, FOR
■ *Trance-Formation* (EMI IC064-32526) CH, NAR, FOR
■ *Bali Agung* (CH CEL 002) CH, NAR, FOR
■ *Sky Music/Mountain Music* (Kuckuck 071) CH, NAR, FOR
Only *Meditation* is purely electronic; the rest of these albums probably belong in the next chapter, though their overall sound is certainly electronic. After traveling through Asia several times, Schoener has incorporated the sounds of Indonesian percussion and has become adept at recreating

the trancelike atmosphere of certain Asian religions.

JACK SCHRAGE AND LEW CORELIS
■ *Songs you've never heard before* (Musik Werks 1) NMDS. Another independent synthesizer release, this one from Moline, Illinois. Several very good, distinctive pieces of electronic music.

ROBERT SCHRÖDER
■ *Floating Music* (IC KS-80.001) SBMG
■ *Mosaique* (IC KS-80.016) SBMG
■ *Galaxie Cygnus A* (IC KS-80.021) SBMG
■ *Paradise* (IC KS-80.029) SBMG
■ *Harmonic Ascendant* (IC KS-80.033) SBMG
Schröder's earliest and most interesting recordings all dating from between 1980 and 1983; after that, his music becomes conventional rock-oriented electronics. Schröder occasionally builds the instruments he plays on these records, and certain pieces, especially on *Galaxie Cygnus A,* borrow gestures from the avant-garde. *Harmonic Ascendant* is probably the most musical of his recordings; it's a richly colored suite with bits of guitar and cello added.

KLAUS SCHULZE
■ *Irrlicht* (Brain 1077)
■ *Cyborg* (Brain 21078, 2 LPs)
■ *Picture Music* (Brain 40146)
■ *Blackdance* (Brain 1051)
■ *Timewind* (Brain 1075)
■ *Moondawn* (Brain 1088)
■ *Body Love* (Brain 0060.047)
■ *Mirage* (Brain 0060.040)
■ *Body Love Volume II* (Brain 0060.097)
■ *"X"* (Brain 0080.023, 2 LPs)
■ *Dune* (Brain 0060.225)
■ *Live* (Brain 0080.048, 2 LPs)
■ *DigIt* (Brain 0060.353)
■ *Trancefer* (IC KS-80.014) SBMG
■ *Audentity* (IC KS-80.025/26, 2 LPs) SBMG
■ *Dziekuje Poland* (IC KS-80.040/41, 2 LPs)
■ *Angst* (Inteam ID-20003)

KLAUS SCHULZE AND RAINER BLOSS
■ *Drive Inn* (Inteam ID-20002)
Given Schulze's beginnings as a drummer and the motoric pulsing of his earliest solo albums, his recent move into the area of electronic rock is not too surprising. Yet Schulze really seemed to be serious about his "music of the future" in the 70s, and almost each of the recordings listed above has something to recommend it. The 1971–1974 albums (*Irrlicht* through *Blackdance*) still reflect the influence of the psychedelic period. Parts of *Moondawn, DigIt,* and *Audentity* are good examples of electronic space music; but the two live collections (*Live* and *Dziekuje Poland*), *Trancefer,* and the *Body Love* albums are best left for real Schulze fans. Although Schulze's finest albums—which also happen to be some of the finest records in the entire field—are from the late 70s (*Dune, Timewind, "X,"* and *Mirage*), his 1984 *Angst* soundtrack has a few interesting moments and the album with Rainer Bloss from the same year is such a "feel good" recording it's hard not to enjoy.

JONN SERRIE
■ *Starmoods* (Future Music, PO Box 930096, Norcross, GA 30093). Another composer who specializes in music for planetariums. This cassette recording contains some fine music in a restrained celestial style.

MARK SHREEVE
■ *Thoughts of War* (Uniton 001) VB. A dark-hued, sometimes dense recording, similar to early Schulze in spots, and featuring an extended piece called "Dream Sequence" which is quite satisfying.

MICHAEL SHRIEVE, KEVIN SHRIEVE, AND KLAUS SCHULZE
■ *Transfer Station Blue* (For. FOR-023) FOR, NAR. Effervescent music for synthesizers, percussion, and electric guitar. Pop music for the New Age.

DON SLEPIAN
■ *Computer Don't Breakdown* (Don & Judy D-11028)
■ *Rhythm of Life* (For. FOR-009) FOR, NAR
■ *Sea of Bliss* (For. FOR-015) FOR, NAR
■ *Largos* (currently being re-mixed) FOR, NAR
■ *Reflections* (Audion SYN-106) JEM
Slepian is a young American musician who's a triple threat: as composer, performer, and programmer. Even a simple, early piece like "Sunrise," from *Rhythm of Life,* becomes interesting because of the unusual percussive program used in the keyboard. *Sea of Bliss* is skillfully produced ambient music, and his recent *Reflections* is a good example of more lightweight space music.

ANN SOUTHAM
■ *The Reprieve/Emerging Ground* (HS 290147) CMS. An important Canadian composer, Southam wrote this music for the Toronto Dance Theater. It combines an academic sensibility with almost Minimalist rhythms and musical patterns.

CHRIS SPHEERIS
■ *Gallery* (Epiphany 098301)
■ *Electric Europe* (Epiphany 118201)
Mostly electro-pop; some slower pieces as well.

CHRIS SPHEERIS AND PAUL VOUDOURIS
■ *Passage* (Epiphany 028201). Lots of electronic percussion joining the keyboards; quite well done, although it doesn't try to break any new ground.

LAURIE SPIEGEL

- *The Expanding Universe* (Philo 9003) PHI, NMDS
- *"Appalachian Grove"* from the LP *New Music for Electronic and Recorded Media* (1750 Arch, S-1765)

Two very different but entertaining works. "Appalachian Grove" is a bouncy computer-generated look at Appalachian banjo picking. *The Expanding Universe* is a serious album that nevertheless sounds as accessible as the lightest New Age music.

- *"Drums"* and *"Voices Within"* from the LP *The Capriccio Series of New American Music, Volume 2* (Capriccio CR-1002) NMDS. These works have to be considered because of their composer's importance. *"Drums"* has an interesting sound, but little else to commend it, while *"Voices Within"* is unfocused; both pieces sound like studies for future scores.

MICHAEL STEARNS

- *Morning/Jewel* (Sonic Atmospheres 208) SON, NAR, VB, FOR. "Morning" is simply electronic background music with natural ambient sounds. "Jewel" features the Eikosany vibes, an early example of Stearns's career-long interest in unusual instruments. See Chapter 12.
- *M'Ocean* (originally *Lightplay*) (Sonic Atmospheres CD-309) SON, NAR, VB, FOR. Electronic originals and one classic: Stravinsky's "Walking Song." Stearns created these pieces between 1980 and 1983, by the end of which time he had emerged as one of the best musicians in the New Age genre. Although this is New Age music, it still moves along at a good clip at times.
- *Planetary Unfolding* (Continuum Montage CM-1004) VB, NAR, FOR
- *Chronos* (Sonic Atmospheres 112) SON, NAR, FOR

Along with 1983's *Lyra* (see Chapter 10), these are Stearns's finest albums. They are also some of the best (i.e., most musical) New Age albums available. *Chronos* was a 1985 film score for a silent Omnimax film by Ron Fricke.

KARLHEINZ STOCKHAUSEN

- *Kontakte* (Wergo 6009)
- *Gesang der Jünglinge/Kontakte* (DG 2543 003)
- *Hymnen (Anthems for Electronic and Concrete Sounds)* (DG 2707 031, 2 LPs)

Contemporary electronic music, especially among avant-garde classical composers, would be unthinkable without this often radical German musician. For all the ear-bending and concentration Stockhausen's pieces demand, they remain crucial works. See Chapter 3.

PAULINE ANNA STROM

- *Trans-Millennia Consort* (Ether Ship 3289) FOR, NAR
- *Plot Zero* (TMCR 2002) NMDS, NAR
- *Spectre* (TMCR 2003) NMDS, EUR

Strom, a.k.a. the Trans-Millennia Consort, is a blind keyboardist from California. Her first album is full of empty electronic tinklings; the second album falls into the Tangerine Dream camp; the third's brooding, ghostly atmosphere is quite a welcome departure.

MORTON SUBOTNICK

- *Silver Apples of the Moon* (None. H-71174)
- *Four Butterflies* (Col. 32741)
- *After the Butterfly/A Sky of Cloudless Sulphur* (None. NS-78001)
- *Axolotl* (None. N-78012)
- *Ascent into Air/The Fluttering of Wings* (None. N9-78020)

This is just a partial list of Subotnick's major electronic recordings. In fact, *Silver Apples,* commissioned by Nonesuch in 1967, was the first electronic piece written specifically *for* a record. Few composers can match Subotnick's ear for color, and perhaps none are capable of such unbridled energy without either losing control or lapsing into self-indulgence. Most of Subotnick's works use the language of the classical avant-garde; there are a lot of blips and squeaks, so if you're looking for something electronic to veg out to, Subotnick is definitely not it.

- *Return (a triumph of reason)* (New Albion 010) NMDS. This 1985 piece celebrated the return of Halley's Comet and the triumph of reason over superstition that Halley's work represented. Using the Yamaha Computer-Assisted Music System, Subotnick created his first purely electronic score (as opposed to instruments with electronic "ghost" orchestras) since 1978, and it's easily his most lyrical, accessible work. He even dares to be pretty for much of the piece, which is no less brilliant in the subtlety of color and the idiomatic use of the instrument than any of his ground-breaking works of the 60s and 70s.

HENRY SWEITZER

- *Te Deum* (Nimbus N-100). The title work is a lovely, heartfelt composition for synthesizer. Also includes a bit of *musique concrète,* the self-explanatory "Study on a Waring Blender." May now be out of print.

SYNERGY

- *Electronic Realizations for Rock Orchestra* (Passport PB 6001) JEM
- *Sequencer* (Passport PB 6002) JEM
- *Games* (Passport PB 6003) JEM
- *Audion* (Passport PB 6005) JEM

There are people who think Larry Fast, the only member of this "band," is the finest synthesizer virtuoso today, at least in the rock world. His programming and keyboard prowess are undeniably great. These recordings are best for electronic rock fans.

- *Cords* (Passport PB 6000) JEM

■ *Jupiter Menace* (Passport PB 6014) JEM
These LPs are another story. *Cords* is a superb
album of electronics; in terms of both texture and
composition it's Fast's finest. The other is a soundtrack to a sci-fi film, and occasionally draws on
earlier albums.

TANGERINE DREAM
■ *In The Beginning* (Relativity EMC-8066, 6-LP set)
IMP. This six-record set is a retrospective of the
group's music, from 1970's *Electronic Meditation*
through 1972's *Atem.* Although this may not be
the most coherent music ever made, at least it's
unpredictable and capable of sporadic surprises.
■ *Phaedra* (Vir. VI-2010) NAR, FOR
■ *Rubycon* (Vir. VI-2025) NAR, FOR
■ *Ricochet* (Vir. VI-2044) NAR, FOR
■ *Stratosfear* (Vir. VI-2068) NAR, FOR
■ *Cyclone* (Vir. VI-2097) FOR
■ *Force Majeure* (Vir. VI-2111) NAR
■ *Tangram* (Vir. VI-2147) NAR
■ *Hyperborea* (Vir. V-2292) NAR
■ *White Eagle* (Vir. 204 563-320) FOR
■ *Sorcerer* (MCA 2277)
■ *Thief* (Elektra 5E-521) FOR
■ *Exit* (Elektra 557)
■ *Le Parc* (Relativity EMC 8043) IMP, NAR,
FOR
Despite all the personnel changes over the years,
Tangerine Dream's music has not changed much
since 1978's *Cyclone.* Of the later recordings, only
the *Sorcerer* soundtrack and the album *Exit* are
consistently good; the others contain interesting
moments but don't sustain them. Still, the trio
maintains a large and enthusiastic following, and
their middle-period recordings *(Phaedra, Rubycon,* and *Stratosfear)* were highly influential
works.

GREGORY TAYLOR
■ *The Logic of Possible Worlds* (ARTLevels, no #)
■ *Given Names* (ARTLevels, no #)
Offbeat, engaging electronics. The first cassette re-
cording is especially noteworthy for its use of In-
donesian gamelan tunings and patterns.

WHARTON TIERS
■ *Great Awakening* (from the audio-cassette magazine *Tellus,* Vol. 3) NMDS. A very short but radiant work for Korg synthesizer.

ASMUS TIETCHENS
■ *Nachtstücke* (EGG 91.040)
CLUB OF ROME/ASMUS TIETCHENS
■ *Endzeit Kino, Geheimspinst* (from the audio-cassette magazine *Tellus,* Vol. 8) NMDS. Tietchens's
album is an engaging, nocturnal collection in
which themes are constantly developed and
brought back in different form. The two shorter
pieces are less successful, spooky works for electronics, bells, and ambient tapes.

ISAO TOMITA
■ *Snowflakes Are Dancing* (RCA ARL-1-0488)
NAR
■ *Pictures at an Exhibition* (RCA ARL-1-0838)
■ *Firebird* (RCA ARL-1-1312)
■ *The Planets* (RCA ARL-1-1919) NAR
■ *Kosmos* (RCA ARL-1-2616) NAR
■ *Bermuda Triangle* (RCA ARL-1-2885)
■ *Bolero* (RCA ARL-1-4312)
■ *Greatest Hits* (RCA ARL-1-3439)
■ *Greatest Hits, Vol. 2* (RCA ARL-1-4019)
■ *Grand Canyon Suite* (RCA ARL-1-4317)
■ *Spacewalk* (RCA ARL-1-5037) NAR
■ *Canon of the Three Stars* (RCA ARL-1-5184)
NAR
■ *Live at Linz, 1984* (RCA ARL-1-5461)
Of all the synthesists doing classical music tran-
scriptions, Tomita is the best known and most
commercially successful. From the very beginning
Tomita has labored long hours to produce full,
intricate, and complex electronic orchestrations.
His best recordings are those where he more or less
sticks to the original notes: the Debussy works on
Snowflakes, parts of *Kosmos* and *Bolero,* and the
live album. It's when he begins to tinker with the
scores that he runs into trouble. *Pictures at an
Exhibition* and *The Planets* are both marred by an
indulgence in white noise and grade-B sci-fi sound
effects that can be quite annoying, and continue on
later albums too.

TAMAS UNGVARY
■ *"L'aube des flammes"* from the LP *Computer
Music/Dubrovay, Mandolini, Ungvary* (Hungaroton SLPX-12809). Interesting avant-garde electronics from another of Hungary's fine young composers.

VANGELIS
■ *L'Apocalypse des Animaux* (French Poly. 2393
058) NAR, FOR
■ *Opéra Sauvage* (French Poly. 2490 161) NAR,
FOR
■ *La Fête Sauvage* (EMI C-066-14276) FOR
■ *Ignacio* (EGG 900.531) NAR, FOR
■ *Beauborg* (Poly. NL-70010)
■ *Earth* (Poly. 6499 693) NAR
■ *Heaven and Hell* (RCA AFL-1-5110) NAR, FOR
■ *Albedo 0.39* (RCA AFL-1-5136) NAR, FOR
■ *Spiral* (RCA AFL-1-2627) NAR, FOR
■ *China* (Poly. US PD-1-6199) NAR, FOR
■ *Chariots of Fire* (Poly. US PD-1-6335) NAR,
FOR
■ *Antarctica* (Japanese Poly. 28MM-0290) NAR
■ *Soil Festivities* (English Poly. POLH-11) NAR
■ *Mask* (English Poly. 824245-1) NAR
■ *Invisible Connections* (DG 415 196-1) NAR
■ *The Dragon* (Oxford OX 3196, bootleg LP)
■ *Hypothesis* (Oxford OX 3162, bootleg LP)
At its worst, (albums like *Beauborg* and *Mask*),
Vangelis's music is full of sound and fury, signify-

ing nothing. At its best, his recordings incorporate many types of sound and may nod in the direction of a number of different musical styles without destroying an album's overall mood. The film score *Antarctica* is a good example, or the vastly underrated *China.* To many, Vangelis's soundtracks to the Rossif films *L'Apocalypse des Animaux* and *Opéra Sauvage* remain his least mannered and most beautifully effective recordings.

CYRILLE VERDEAUX AND BERNARD XOLOTL
- *Prophecy* (For., no #) FOR. A 1981 cassette by two expatriate Frenchmen, using only keyboard and prototype guitar synthesizers. Despite lapses into aimless repetition or mood music, it's generally a superior effort. See Xolotl, below, and Verdeaux, Chapter 2.

RICHARD VIMAL
- *Aquarhythmies* (Poly. France). Unlike Vimal's other electronic rock albums, this 1980 release has an almost classical, Satie-like feel to it, only with a much fuller, orchestral sound. (O.P.)

RICHARD WAHNFRIED
- *Tonwelle* (IC KS-80.006)
- *Time Actor* (IC KS-80.031)

Not a person, but a group: Klaus Schulze is joined by Manuel Göttsching on the first album, and by vocalist Arthur Brown on the second. Of interest primarily to Schulze fans, especially those who like his other works from this period (early 80s).

GARY WASHINGTON
- *Angel in the Northern Sky*
- *Beneath the River*
- *Annie in Africa* (G. Washington, 230-14 88 Avenue, Queens Village, NY 11427).

Three nicely recorded cassettes, played on the Seiko synthesizer. *Angel* consists of lots of very short pieces, which can sound somewhat disjointed; *Beneath the River* has much longer works. Their floating, spacey sound is like an electronic lullaby at times. *Annie* is a more varied collection, and is probably Washington's best effort to date.

DARRYL WAY
- *Concerto for Electric Violin* (Island ILPS-9550). Two former members of the group Curved Air put this together. Way plays electric violin, and Francis Monkman creates an orchestral accompaniment on a number of synthesizers. Not a consistently successful piece, but usually an enjoyable one.

CARL WEINGARTEN
- *Living in the Distant Present* (Multiphase CW-004) MULT
- *All Things Return* (Multiphase, not yet released) MULT
- *Pandora's Garage* (Multiphase, not yet released) MULT

CARL WEINGARTEN AND WALTER WHITNEY
- *Dreaming in Colors* (Multiphase WW-007) NMDS, MULT

CARL WEINGARTEN, GALE ORMISTON, AND PHIL NEON
- *Submergings* (Multiphase SUB-001) NMDS, MULT

Besides the recording with Gale Ormiston listed earlier, Weingarten also has a rock-oriented group called Delay Tactics (see Chapter 11) and these other projects. His solo material, for electric guitar and electronic processing, is in the ambient style, but there's too much obvious thought behind it to be dismissed as sonic wallpaper. *Dreaming in Colors,* from 1986, is a solid effort for processed guitars, synthesizers, and some sequenced percussion à la Tangerine Dream.

BROOKS WILLIAMS
- *Demented Folk Tune* (from the audio-cassette magazine *Tellus,* Vol. 12) NMDS. Fairlight CMI and Apple computer are the source materials for this charming piece in a nine-tone scale. It's just close enough to our usual eight-note diatonic scale (*do, re, mi,* etc.) to make all the notes sound out of tune. As with Easley Blackwood's music, you simply have to "retune" your hearing, at which point this becomes lovely and accessible.

BERNARD XOLOTL
- *Return of the Golden Mean* (Syntasy 1980)
- *Procession* (Pulse NP-007)
- *Last Wave* (Syntasy 1982)
- *Modulation* (not yet released)

Xolotl uses occasional splashes of acoustic color (e.g., violin, cello) to offset his grand, orchestral electronics. *Last Wave,* though, relies almost exclusively on Xolotl's own synthesizers and music computers; it's an exciting, vigorous recording. *Procession* is probably his best; Daniel Kobialka plays violins, which may or may not be amplified, and Xolotl produces a lush, shimmering tapestry of electronics.

ZANOV
- *In Course of Time* (Solaris SOL-8202). Pierre Salkazanov is this French synthesist's full name. He works in a cosmic style that can be enjoyable without being all that original.

FRANK ZAPPA
- *Francesco Zappa* (Barking Pumpkin ST-74202). There really *was* a Francesco Zappa in the eighteenth century, one of thousands of minor Baroque composers. Here he's snatched out of well-earned oblivion by a Synclavier arrangement of his music.

FRANK ZAPPA & THE MOTHERS OF INVENTION

- *Freak Out!* (Verve V6-5005-2X)
- *Lumpy Gravy* (Verve V6-8741).

As far back as 1966, Zappa was using classic *musique concrète* techniques, including "Return of the Son of Monster Magnet" from *Freak Out! Lumpy Gravy,* from 1967, is also tape music, using chorus and orchestral and rock instruments as source material.

2
ELECTRO-ACOUSTIC: MIXING OLD AND NEW

Electronic music as such will gradually die and be absorbed into the ongoing music of people singing and playing instruments.
Steve Reich, Some Optimistic Predictions About the Future of Music *(1970)*

It's easy to have 20/20 hindsight—or so the saying goes. But history often gives people credit for intentions they may never have had. For example, I like to imagine what Sir Alexander Fleming must *really* have thought on the morning he first saw the green mold that led to his discovery of penicillin. . . . Well, history tells us that Leon Theremin and Maurice Martenot were responsible for two crucial inventions in the development of electronic music, namely, the instruments which bear their respective names. History usually glosses over the fact that both machines were failures, as far as their creators were concerned. The theremin and the ondes martenot were not intended to help form a new type of music: They were supposed to join the ranks of orchestral instruments, adding a new family of sounds to the usual winds, strings, and percussion. The concept of electro-acoustic music, treating old and new instruments equally, is therefore probably even older than the idea of purely electronic music.

While composers like Vangelis, Bernard Xolotl, and Michael Stearns have used acoustic instruments with synthesizers, their work is still based primarily on electronic sounds. Many others, however, have greeted synthesizers and similar instruments as simply another color on their musical palette. It may have taken a while, but these composers have come full circle to the original notion behind the development of electronic instruments.

The difference between the music we'll now explore and the works in the first chapter lies in the way the instruments are combined. The emphasis is still on creating new sounds, but electronics are used to provide a contrasting background for traditional instruments or, in some cases, as a way of altering the acoustic instruments' natural sounds. As we've already seen, most early electronic music was in fact electro-acoustic: The ondes martenot and the theremin were most often featured in orchestral works by various French composers; purely electronic works were seldom encountered till the 1950s. With the boom in electronic music in the 60s and 70s, synthesizers and music computers became the center of attention, even when other instruments were involved. When, after a few years, the novelty wore off, musicians could finally begin treating the newer instruments the way they treated the more conventional ones, as integral parts of an ensemble.

A pioneer in this area was David Behrman, who in fact did more than just *combine* electronic and acoustic—he made them *interact,* so that neither one could perform without the other. The acoustic sounds generated by the composer and the electronic sounds generated by a computer formed a closed system, almost as if they were a single composite instrument.

Although Behrman began working with interactive music in the 60s, it was not until 1977 that two of his works for acoustic instruments and computer appeared on disc. *On the Other Ocean* featured flute and bassoon; *Figure in a Clearing* used a cello. "I also used what now seems like an ancient microcomputer from the mid-70s when they were first available," he explains. "I used the computer as an interface between some circuitry I had built that made electronic music, and a pitch-sensing device that listens for pitches made by acoustic instruments." The live performer improvised on a set of notes, which generated a response from the computer. Depending on the notes chosen and the order in which they were played, the computer would produce a series of harmonies to which the performer would in turn react. The new improvisation triggered a new set of changes, and the process would begin again.

These interactive works represent a kind of process music (discussed in the next chapter), but unlike most process pieces, the technical or systematic aspects of the composition are not the main attraction of Behrman's scores. Although a complicated process actually does help determine the outcome, the work itself sounds completely natural, as if the live musician were being accompanied by a synthesizer player instead of a computer.

Not all electro-acoustic music depends on such unusual ways of combining old and new instruments, and simply playing a synthesizer and acoustic instruments together is a very common approach. But Behrman is not alone in looking for more intriguing ways of merging the two. Composer Ingram Marshall, who has used pure electronics, *musique concrète,* and electro-acoustic techniques in the course of his career, finds that "more and more, electronically generated sounds aren't that interesting to me. I'm more attracted to instrumental sounds, but I still want to expand them and alter them." That means using electronic filtering and delay processes* to change the timbre of the acoustic instruments. In his 1976 work *The Fragility Cycles,* Marshall uses an Indonesian gambuh flute, falsetto vocals, an iron clanger, prerecorded tapes, synthesizer, and a four-channel delay system that ultimately determines how "natural" or transformed any of the instruments sound. He tends to use

*Tape delays work like this: The tape picks up the signal from a machine's recording head. A fraction of a second later, that tape moves past the machine's playback head. If the machine is fed into a mixing board so that you can hear both the tape *and* the live performance, you'll get a delay, or echo, of a fraction of a second. That delay can be lengthened by increasing the time it takes the tape to get from the recording head to the playback head. A common way to do this is to put two or more machines side by side and let the tape run from the recording head of the first one to the playback head of the others. Lengthy delays can be produced this way; a note played live may come back six or seven seconds later, by which time the performer may have moved on to something else. The digital delay, a relatively recent development, can produce delays of various lengths without cumbersome tape technology. One simply hooks the delay unit up to the output of the mixing board or the amplifiers. Both forms of delay have now become familiar ways of altering acoustic sounds.

the delays more for structure than for simply changing the instrumental sounds. "The architecture of the piece is how the delays are used; it can sound very lush or very dry. Delays, either tape or digital, are *usually* treated as an effect or an enhancement. *I've* used it structurally; it gives the piece its acoustical form and its texture." In his 1984 *Gradual Requiem,* for instance, Marshall's use of the delay system produces one of the most haunting sections of the work when he puts a recording of Corsican men singing a sixteenth-century Mass by Pierre de la Rue through a lengthy delay. The resulting sounds are completely abstract—the "vocal" quality almost completely disappears into a ghostly, electronic texture. At this point it becomes difficult to distinguish between "acoustic" and "electronic" music; the instruments may be flutes or pianos or voices, but the sounds of those acoustic instruments are now electronically produced.

Pauline Oliveros, who has done work in a similar vein, also believes the barrier between acoustic and electronic music is breaking down: "That's as it should be. As a composer, I want to be able to use anything that's effective." Many of her works for solo accordion use digital delay, adding an electronic dimension to the sound.

Oliveros was also one of the artists who saw that the potential of acoustic instruments themselves had broadened with the growth of electronics and tape processes. "Toward the end of the 70s," she recalls, "I began to get interested in voices and instruments again, because there was a change in attitude among young performers. The interest in playing in new ways and the level of performance is now incredibly high; it's amazing the things you can get performers to do that you never could've gotten twenty years ago." As an example, Oliveros cites her 1985 work *Tasting the Blaze,* premiered in Austin, Texas, by an ensemble of ten Gagaku instruments (from the Japanese court tradition), five accordions, a clarinet, trombone, cello, and percussion. Oliveros became a kind of electronic conductor for this offbeat orchestra; she amplified each instrument and, working from behind a mixing board, processed different instruments at different times and mixed the resulting sounds together.

In the works of David Behrman, Ingram Marshall, and occasionally Pauline Oliveros, the acoustic and electronic components of the piece are inseparable. Marshall, in fact, says he no longer considers himself an electronic music composer. "I used to, but I don't anymore because I've been doing a lot more ensemble music, though very frequently with electronics involved. My piece for the Kronos String Quartet, *Voces Resonae,* has digital delay processing, and in *Fog Tropes* it's a mixture of brass and sounds (mostly foghorns) on tape. So in a way it is electronic music, but it's more concerned with the interaction of the 'live' instruments and the 'canned' electronics."

That interaction takes different forms in different works. In *Gradual Requiem,* Marshall uses flute (gambuh), voice, piano, and mandolin along with electronics. The mandolin, at the start of the work, dictates the placement of the center frequencies of various filters. Normally a filter will selectively pass only *one* specific band of frequencies from a sound source. In *Gradual Requiem,* however, the notes played on the mandolin change the position of the center frequencies, so the filter is constantly passing *different* frequency bands. The result is a sweeping, whistling effect that a mandolin wouldn't normally produce.

"David Behrman's interaction is a lot more sophisticated," Marshall admits. "He sets it up so that a solo instrument can actually change the timbre and pitch of the computer. It's almost like artificial intelligence, and David handles it beautifully." Behrman's pitch-sensor technology has enabled him to write interactive music for violin, cello, and even two Japanese wind instruments, the hichiriki and the ryuteki. Since his compositions rely on similar technology and are not written down in the usual form of notes on a staff, an intriguing question arises—are these separate works in a related series, or all portions of one on-going piece? "It's hard to say," Behrman muses. "The pieces are in the form of computer programs and hardware."*

New developments in technology have enabled other composers to employ increasingly subtle and refined electro-acoustic effects. Like Ingram Marshall, Richard Horowitz has also combined a type of ethnic flute with synthesizer and unusual electronic processing. Horowitz learned to play the ney, a cane flute found in one form or another in every country between North Africa and northern India, while living in Morocco. Returning to California in the 1970s, he began writing music for ney, synthesizer, and sound processors—filters, for example. His 1981 album, *Eros in Arabia,* took advantage of a process that enabled him to keep the synthesizer in tune with the ney, which was naturally modeled on a non-Western scale. "The means may be hi-tech," Horowitz maintains, "but the result is that now, with a Western instrument, you can play those microtonal inflections that you couldn't get on, say, a piano. You can actually do a lot more with synthesizers now. They've opened up the possibility of reflecting the ancient modes and systems in modern technology."

Most of Horowitz's more recent works have also included vocals in the Persian folk style by Sussan Deihim. Both voice and flute are altered by the use of a Lexicon 224X which, as Horowitz explains, "splits the overtones of Sussan's voice with six faders that you can move in six different directions. It's like tuning the breath or voice—and it works well for flute, too. It breaks the sound into its component parts, six different harmonics, and reorganizes them." The overall effect is an odd sonic "shadow" surrounding the acoustic sounds, almost as if the vocals were coming through an electronic fog.

The prevalence of computers, as we've seen in Chapter 1, has elicited mixed reactions from many composers. Although computers, with their almost limitless sampling capabilities might seem at first to threaten the use of acoustic instruments, their still-limited capacity to reproduce the sounds of conventional instruments in a natural way has prompted some musicians to restrict their use of the computer to achieving special effects. "In fact," says pianist/composer Elodie Lauten, "it was *after* working with the Fairlight CMI [Computer Music Instrument] that I began writing for acoustic piano." Lauten takes advantage of a computer only for its

---

*Riddles of this sort are presented by other types of electro-acoustic music as well. Don Slepian, who composes primarily electronic music, uses flute sounds in his *Largos,* a collection of classical pieces (mostly slow movements—adagios, largos, andantes) that he arranged and played. Knowing Don as an electronic-keyboard player, I asked him if he used a real flute in the recording. "That's almost a philosophical question" was his reply. "It's a mellotron—thirty-two tapes lined up under a keyboard. It was really developed by Mike Pinder [of the Moody Blues; he used it in the 60s to imitate the sounds of a string orchestra]. It's not synthesized, but it's not a live performance either. It's transposed in time. There *was* a real flutist playing originally, but now that's on a tape recording and that tape is started by pressing a key."

"noise" capabilities; the processed sounds of modern life (radio, street noise, etc.) accompany most of her works. "The things you can't get on the computer are the subtleties that musicians do—maybe bowing a little stronger here, holding a note a little longer there. So after working with the computer, all I wanted to do was work with acoustic piano and sound effects with sequencers." That statement basically describes her first album, *Piano Works*. Her second and third recordings, *Concerto for Piano and Orchestral Memory* and the opera *The Death of Don Juan*, use other acoustic instruments (sometimes amplified) as well. *The Death of Don Juan* naturally includes voices. The "orchestral memory" of the second disc functions as a kind of "ghost orchestra," as Lauten describes it. The strange, not-quite-orchestral sound, like the lingering echoes of a departed philharmonic, consists of violin, viola, cello, trombone, tape, and computer processing.

So far, most of the music we've discussed has involved some form of electronic processing of acoustic instruments. This perhaps gives a false impression of the field: Much electro-acoustic music consists simply of an ensemble of acoustic and electronic instruments, without any complicated sort of interaction. This is the case with such composers as Harold Budd (who has recorded electro-acoustic music both with and without Brian Eno), Eugene Bowen, John Adams, and Daniel Lentz, among others. Like Ingram Marshall, all of these musicians are based in California, and since they're all writing tonal, lyrical works and they all seem to know each other, it's tempting to infer that they're all part of some kind of "California school."

"There's a much looser environment," Marshall says, "so a composer could more readily succumb to his or her hedonistic impulses in California, without worrying about whether he or she were falling into the proper niche of history or whatever. There's less demand to write something that's historically 'correct,' and that's the big difference between the so-called East Coast 'academic music' and the West Coast let-it-all-hang-out style. It has more to do with attitude than an actual style."

Nevertheless, the element of tonality *is* common to all of the California-based composers, who are concerned with beautiful melodies to a degree that no self-respecting academic composer could tolerate. "The tendency in California was toward 'pretty' music," Marshall explains. "Hal [Budd] used to call it 'lovely music,' but then of course the people in New York formed that record company [Lovely Music Records]. He was really into that aesthetic more than anyone else, even more than Lentz. Lentz was occasionally complex; but Hal just got to the point where he wanted to write pretty pieces—lush, simple music." Budd's recordings use both electric and acoustic pianos, often with very discreet, atmospheric wisps of synthesizer in the background. His two albums with Brian Eno, *The Plateaux of Mirror* and *The Pearl,* are full of evocative, nocturnal musings on the piano with understated electronic accompaniment; what they lack in structure is more than made up for by the beauty of the sound. This style is one that Budd has been developing since the early 70s, when he began to move away from the angular, aleatoric music that characterized his earlier works.

Echoes of Budd's lyricism can now be found in many other West Coast composers. "You can say there's a California school," Marshall admits. "I mean, I've given lectures in Europe on the whole 'California new music scene.' But," he adds with a chuckle, "I feel in a way I've fabricated it somewhat to make it more a historical reality than it really is." Determining who is and who isn't part of this alleged school seems like a difficult task. Harold Budd and Brian Eno's simple, melodically pretty music has been greatly appealing to the New Age crowd, and many New Age composers have tried to copy that sound.

But as we've already seen in Chapter 1, the term New Age is pretty vague, and a lot of the finest electro-acoustic music now found in New Age record bins and mail-order catalogs is not by self-professed New Age composers at all. Case in point: Ingram Marshall. "I've found my records lumped into the category of New Age or 'space music,' because a piece like *Gradual Requiem* is not standard, academic music," he says. "It's not written for people to meditate to, but if they want to, fine. You can't control how people will use the music. And I certainly don't expect people to sit around wringing their hands trying to figure out how I structured the piece." In addition to Marshall, Richard Horowitz, Pauline Oliveros, Harold Budd, Terry Riley, and numerous others have made unwitting forays into the New Age field.

Within the musical community itself, reactions to the New Age movement vary. For some, it's opened up avenues for their own music. As New York-based violinist and composer Julie Lyonn Lieberman says, "I've been ecstatic over the whole development of the New Age movement. The growing interest in the public for this kind of music has really increased mobility for artists who don't fit into one category." Lieberman's *Empathic Connections,* an electro-acoustic outing with zither player Laraaji, is a good example. It's neither rock nor jazz nor classical; its ambient sound fits perfectly under the New Age umbrella. But to other electro-acoustic composers, New Age has become an unfortunate catchall term. Amplify an instrument, maybe process it a bit, and above all keep it pretty, and the New Age label is instantly applied. While it's not fair to dismiss an entire genre out of hand, it's equally unfair to pigeonhole a piece of tonal music simply because it uses amplification or reverb.

Perhaps the most popular form of electronically altered acoustic sounds is the recent branch of New Age music called "healing music," in which acoustic instruments are phased, flanged, delayed, and otherwise toyed with in an attempt to make music that will soothe the savage breast of the modern Western listener. Like the New Age electronic works mentioned in Chapter 1, a good deal of "healing music" is accompanied by cloying, cliché, often inadvertently hilarious trappings. "A thousand crystal shards of sound spiral through the ether and devolve into the center of your awareness," sighs one record sleeve, while my favorite warns: "This recording may cause drowsiness. It is not recommended for use while driving or operating machinery."

One successful artist, California's Steven Halpern, goes so far as to proudly boast that his music "has no driving beat or compelling harmonic and melodic progression"! If it has no interesting harmonies, melodies, or rhythms, what's left? Halpern's "Anti-Frantic Alternative" series is typical of this genre: Although much of it is indeed devoid of any musical content, some of it is good despite itself. One suspects that Halpern could compose some interesting music if he were working in another genre; as it is, his recordings of flute, piano, violin, and electronics are probably the most widely heard and frequently purchased examples of this style. But "healing music" need not limit itself to a utilitarian level to be effective. Many of the works being composed in this area do have real musical value. *Elixir* (1983), by the Greek-born, California-based Iasos, is a fine example of this form, with acoustic and electronic instruments mixed into a veritable sonic bath. Like Brian Eno's Ambient Music, it's worthy of attention, and can engage a listener at several levels.

In the field of electro-acoustics, the quintessential New Age music would probably be the gentle tinklings of Andreas Vollenweider's "modified electro-acoustic harp." Using an amplified harp with a knee-operated damper, synthesizer, percussion, and other instruments, this phenomenally popular Swiss musician has created a kind of Easy Listening style for the younger generation. Like most "healing music," Vollenweider's compositions strive for a smooth, unobtrusive surface that's conducive to relaxation. Yet he insists, "I'm not a part of New Age, or anything else. There are so many people in New Age who are lost in spirituality; but you need both, the spiritual and the physical. My music starts with an idea, which is spiritual, but you experience it physically—you can feel it, dance to it."

It's hard to imagine, though, the kind of dance you could do to Vollenweider's music; the rhythms are there, but the energy's lacking. Vollenweider is a talented musician—by putting the harp up front and using the synthesizer sparingly, he has already avoided many of the clichés of electro-acoustic New Age music—yet the lack of any kind of dramatic moments limits his music; his albums, despite their excellent production, tend toward a sameness of mood. "Music doesn't have to be complete," he claims. "It does have to be true, honest, and seen in the context of all other things. I'm presenting a different way of looking at things, a more relaxed way. I like to build a free space for the listener where he or she can be assured there is no enemy—that would disturb their creative process." This attitude, which is also common among purveyors of "healing music," would not seem to give any credit to the audience's imagination; unless the music is as bland as oatmeal, the listener won't be able to take it in. Maybe people *are* so overloaded with external stimuli during the day that this type of sonic background provides a much-needed release. Certainly it's not a new phenomenon.

"North American Indian music is almost exclusively medicinal," Ingram Marshall points out. "There are many cultures where it plays an important role that way.* I see more people in New York City than anywhere else wearing headphones on the street, and I often wonder what they're listening to. It's obvious they're trying to get away from the pressures of an urban environment. And in a sense, *whatever* they're listening to is having a healing effect on them, at least for the time being."

Using music that has been electronically enhanced or altered specifically for meditation or relieving stress is a practice that has become more common among psychiatrists, as well. There are cases in which New Age–type music has had a proven benefit as a therapy. One of the most consistently successful organizations

*In parts of North Africa, for example, there are still tribes that believe certain intervals of notes played on a pair of reed instruments can cure fevers or hallucinations.

in this field is Psycho-Acoustical Laboratories in New York. Their tapes are created by mixing edited musical recordings (they've recently begun working closely with Sweden's Ralph Lundsten, for example) with the sounds of wind, water, and birds, which are then electronically altered, with certain tones enhanced and others suppressed.

This formula may be hard to distinguish from that used by most "healing music" artists, but the difference is that Psycho-Acoustical Laboratories' collages make musical sense—they can stand or fall as music, pure and simple. Yet their compositions are no less effective at reducing stress or inducing calm. In fact, in a University of Illinois study on the effects of one of their tapes, the music proved to be significantly effective in virtually every category tested (reducing noticeable stress, lowering blood pressure, etc.). The only catch is that their tapes are not commercially available, at least not at the present; they are designed for hospitals, music therapists, and similar clinical uses.

While music undeniably influences our mood, *any* sound can apparently have that effect. Michel Bayan, who assembles the sound collages for Psycho-Acoustical Laboratories, once did an informal study in New York's Grand Central Station. He noticed that commuters passing through the train terminal after work would invariably run across the floor even when not hurrying to catch a train. Commuters leaving work earlier or later in the day, however, didn't race through the terminal. The clue, he thought, was that the evening rush-hour crowd consisted of large groups of men and women walking together across a large, hard floor which provided a sharp, percussive sound when struck by boots or high-heeled shoes. Bayan's theory was this: The women, who are on the average shorter than men and thus have a shorter stride, would require more steps to keep up with the men; the striking of their heels on the floor would set up a rapid rhythm; and the men would naturally begin to fall in step with this rhythm, something that every army since the beginning of human history has instinctively understood. With the men now walking faster, the women (and the shorter men) would have to walk that much quicker to keep pace, establishing an even faster rhythm and creating an even quicker pace.

Bayan's conclusion has a certain elegant logic to it—if you've ever walked down the street while a radio is playing loudly, you may have found yourself subconsciously falling into the rhythm of the music. But that doesn't necessarily prove this theory. To do that, Bayan padded one area of the terminal, and again observed the rush-hour crowds. Without the audible pattern of shoes striking the floor, no rapid rhythms occurred in the padded section—and no one ran. In the other parts of the terminal, the running continued as always. Obviously, rhythm can be a very strong, yet subtle, stimulus—so making a strong case for the affective potential of music.

Commercially marketed recordings of "healing music" have yet to prove, though, that their over-reliance on echo, reverb, and electronic gadgetry is any more calming than other music. In the eighteenth century, well before the age of electronics, it was believed that feelings and emotions could be affected by *all* types of music. The German composer/harpsichordist/music theorist Johann Mattheson published a book early in the eighteenth century called *Die Affektenlehre,* the "Doctrine of Passions," in which he categorized the various keys and types of melodies according to which emotions they induced in people. Mattheson's writings were highly influential, especially among opera composers, at the time. Today, it's almost exclusively the droning, lightweight electro-acoustic style that has identified itself with this theory. "Healing music" does have its place, but in the end it's most effective—or affective—when it's concerned as much with "music" as it is with "healing."

DISCOGRAPHY AND RELATED WORKS

AEOLIAH
- *The Light of Tao* (Sono Gaia C-126) NAR. Asian and Western instruments are effectively blended in this New Age cassette.

ALLEN, BERNOFF, BELL & SMITH
- *Petals* (Rising Sun RSA-120). These four musicians, collectively, in duos, or as soloists, have recorded a large number of albums that include piano, lyricon (a synthesizer that imitates wind instruments), vibes, and guitar. All of them are long on mood, very short on musical substance.

WILLIAM AURA
- *Aurasound I* (For. FOR 007) FOR, NAR, VB
- *Aurasound II* (For. FOR 008) FOR, NAR, VB
Part of the healing music genre, Aura's music is supposedly used by therapists and hypnotists. At least he creates a nice sonic bath, using lovely blends of zither, synthesizers, and sundry others.

DAVID BEHRMAN
- *On the Other Ocean/Figure in a Clearing* (Lovely LM-1041) NMDS.
- *Circling Six/Interspecies Smalltalk* (scheduled for release on Lovely Music) NMDS
Behrman's first album is a delightful, hypnotic recording of two interactive pieces: one for flute, bassoon, and microcomputer; the other for cello and microcomputer. The second album, with solos for trombone and violin, works on the same principle. What really sets Behrman apart is his ability to combine acoustic instruments with electronics in a way that sounds completely natural.

BELL, BERNOFF, ALLEN & POWELL
- *Summer Suite* (Rising Sun RSA-130) RIS. Another work from the Rising Sun Records crew. Similar to *Petals,* listed above; some interesting textures early on side two.

THOMAS JOHN BELLINO
- *Star Gods of the Ancient Americas* (Blue Moose BMCA 1001; T. J. Bellino, PO Box 597 Ansonia Station, New York, NY 10023). Written for an exhibit produced by the Museum of the American

Indian, this cassette combines traditional native American ritual music played on wood, clay, and ceramic flutes with Bellino's own synthesizer music. An original, engagingly tranquil piece of work.

ERIK BERGLUND
- *Beauty* (Sono Gaia LP-139) NAR. Subtitled "Music for Harp," the Celtic harp is the only instrument here, but it's so heavily processed and altered that it's closer to Andreas Vollenweider than Turlough O Carolan—in fact, it sounds like what I imagine Vollenweider would sound like if he ditched the drum machines and other trappings. A pleasant record.

JON BERNOFF AND MARCUS ALLEN
- *Breathe* (Rising Sun RSA-110) RIS, NAR. Perhaps the most popular of the Rising Sun discs; if you like New Age music, you'll probably enjoy *Breathe.*

DAVID BORDEN & THE NEW MOTHER MALLARD BAND
- *Anatidae* (Cuneiform RUNE-4) WAY. See Borden in Chapter 4.

DAVID BOWIE
- *Low* (RCA CPL-1-2030)
- *"Heroes"* (RCA AFL-1-2522)
The popular rock singer went through a period in the late 70s, while living in Berlin and working with Brian Eno, where he experimented with ethnic and electronic music. The second side of each of these albums consists of some of the most innovative music to come from a commercially successful artist. "Moss Garden," from *"Heroes,"* has Bowie playing the Japanese zither or koto to a marvelous electronic accompaniment by Eno, and is perhaps the best example of the more unconventional Bowie/Eno music.

SPENCER BREWER
- *Shadow Dancer* (Willow Rose WRRC-1006) FOR, NAR. The talented guitarist Eric Tingstad is

wasted on this enervating, lifeless collection featuring synthesizer, piano, lyricon, harmonica, cello, and others.

MICHAEL BROOK WITH BRIAN ENO AND DANIEL LANOIS
- *Hybrid* (EG EGED-41) JEM. Hybrid indeed; this album mixes acoustic instruments from Africa, Europe, and South America with Eno's and Lanois's characteristic electronic processing. The overall sound is reminiscent of Eno's recent ambient records.

HAROLD BUDD
- *The Serpent (In Quicksilver)* (Crepuscule TWI-083) NMDS
- *Abandoned Cities* (Cryonic MAD-3015) WAY

HAROLD BUDD AND BRIAN ENO
- *The Plateaux of Mirror* (EG EGS-301) NAR, JEM
- *The Pearl* (EG EGED-37) NAR, JEM

With or without Brian Eno, Budd's music is drifting, cosmic, and often has an ominous undercurrent running through it. *Abandoned Cities* includes Eugene Bowen's electric guitar; the two albums with Eno feature ultra-Romantic piano musings followed by wisps of electronics. These recordings practically define the term "ambient."

STEPHEN CAUDEL
- *Wine Dark Sea* (Landscape NAGE-6) JEM. This British "New Age" music series describes its repertoire as a "development that appeals to those with modern values and taste from Eno to Elgar; . . .able to evoke atmosphere and emotions through the playing of instruments." This work, originally for rock instruments and orchestra, was arranged for guitars and synthesizers, all played by Caudel. It may not stand up over the long haul, but it has moments of real grandeur or energy, and is undeniably "music" as opposed to aimless improvising.

CLUSTER
- *Cluster II* (Brain 0060.402)
- *Curiosum* (Sky 063)
- *Sowiesoso* (Sky 005)

CLUSTER & ENO
- *Cluster & Eno* (Sky 010) IMP
- *after the heat* (Sky 021) IMP

Cluster is a duo, comprised of German keyboardists Hans-Joachim (Achim) Roedelius (see listing below) and Dieter (Möbi) Moebius. The three Cluster albums listed here are representative of different stages in the group's career; a complete list of their albums would be quite extensive. Their early recordings tried to avoid the clichés of electronic rock and went for a more avant-garde sound. Such albums as *Cluster II* and *Curiosum* seem to meander and never really come together. *Sowiesoso,* from 1976, is vintage Cluster: Short, repeating keyboard motifs, usually in slowly pulsing rhythms, create a pleasant atmosphere. The two albums with Eno tend to be more exotic.

- ▲ *Cold Blue Sampler* (Cold Blue L-10) NMDS. Music for various electro-acoustic combinations from a number of composers who have appeared on California's Cold Blue record label: Chas Smith, Ingram Marshall, Daniel Lentz, Rick Cox, Eugene Bowen/Harold Budd, Jim Fox, and Peter Garland (the latter not really electro-acoustic). A most impressive collection.

RICK COX
- *These Things Stop Breathing* (Cold Blue E-3) NMDS. Electric guitar loops with voice and reeds. Ambient, but won't dull your senses.

CLYDE CRINER
- *New England* (Terra/Van. T-4). Almost a Gospel flavor at times; Criner uses piano, flute, and Fairlight CMI. A little too soothing.

TIM CROSS
- *Classic Landscape* (Landscape NAGE-3) NAR. Mostly electronic arrangements of Bach, Mozart, Beethoven, Schubert, Elgar, and a Cross original. Some vocals, some acoustic instruments too. It's not up to the standard of Wendy Carlos, not as intricately colored as Tomita; still, you can't fault the music.

ALVIN CURRAN
- *Canti e Vedute del Giardino Magnetico* (Ananda #1) NMDS. Curran, a founding member of Musica Elettronica Viva, lived in Rome for many years. MEV was an early (mid-60s) experimental group that also included Frederic Rzewski and Richard Teitelbaum, both of whom are listed elsewhere in this book. Curran's title translates as "Songs and Views from the Magnetic Garden"; it is a haunting work for synthesizers, natural sounds, kalimba, plastic tubes, voice, etc. A luxuriant, exotic, and highly atmospheric work.

DANNA AND CLEMENT
- *A Gradual Awakening* (For. FOR-022) FOR, NAR. Nothing here that hasn't already been done often. But Danna and Clement, like Eno, try to make the music interesting on more than one level. They succeed only occasionally, but when they do they're capable of some handsome works.

PETER DAVISON
- *Selamat Siang* (Avocado AR-101) NAR. "Music on the Way" is the subtitle of this peaceful album of synthesizers, harp, cello, and sax. A good example of meditative music that's well done.

CONSTANCE DEMBY
- *Skies above Skies* (Gandarva, no #) NAR, FOR
- *Sunborne* (Gandarva, no #) NAR, FOR
- *Sacred Space Music* (Gandarva, no #) NAR, FOR

- *At Alaron, Live* (Gandarva, no #) NAR, FOR
Demby plays a wide assortment of instruments, including the "space bass" and "whale sail," large metal string instruments of her own devising. She has a lovely voice, which she uses on some bizarre texts in her first two cassettes. *Skies above Skies* includes a Tibetan chant, and St. Francis's Prayer; *Sunborne* is subtitled "A Symphonic Poem in 5 movements with lyrics from the Emerald Tablets, an ancient text by Hermes Trismegistus." Both feature hammer dulcimer, Asian instruments, and synthesizer. But her best recording is *Sacred Space Music,* which is instrumental. Using hammer dulcimer, piano, synthesizer, and viola, Demby plays a sparkling, personal brand of New Age music.
- *Novus Magnificat* (Hearts of Space 003) HOS. Demby's latest release is music first, New Age second. Sets a standard for the use of electronics against which future New Age albums should be judged.

BILL DESMOND
- *Trapezoid Stringway to Light* (Third Ear TE-301) VB
- *Sparkle String Discoveries* (Third Ear TE-302) VB
- *Sparkle Strings* (compilation of first two) (Vital Body/The Art of Relaxation) VB
- *Waterflow* (Vital Body/The Art of Relaxation) VB
Desmond's first two cassettes, now available only as a "best-of" compilation, are superlative recordings that feature the hammer dulcimer and the psaltery (a forerunner of the harpsichord), along with synthesizers, winds, guitars, and various unusual effects. *Waterflow* is pleasant and considerably more mellow. It includes several Irish and Hungarian folk songs, the influence of which can be felt throughout Desmond's music.

ROBERTO DETREE
- *Architectura Caelestis* (Wergo SM-1037) NAR. Detree, an Argentine guitarist who plays with the group Between (see Chapter 6), here creates slow, sustained, ethereal works on guitars and other instruments of his own devising.

CHAITANYA HARI DEUTER
- *D* (Kuckuck 017) CH
- *Celebration* (Kuckuck 2375 040) CH, NAR, FOR
- *Aum* (Kuckuck 009) CH, NAR, FOR
- *Silence Is the Answer* (Kuckuck 049/050) CH, NAR, FOR
- *Haleakala* (Kuckuck 2375 042) CH, NAR, FOR
- *Ecstasy* (Kuckuck 044) CH, NAR, FOR
- *Cicada* (Kuckuck 056) CH, NAR, FOR
- *Nirvana Road* (Kuckuck 068) CH, NAR, FOR
- *Call of the Unknown—Selected Pieces, 1972–1986* (Kuckuck 077) CH, NAR, FOR
Deuter's first albums were released in Germany under his original name, Georg Deuter. He later moved to India, where he spent several years as a follower of the Bhagwan Shree Rajneesh, and

has since developed a personal style that flows from active electronics to resonant mysticism. *Haleakala* will interest fans of electronic space music; *Cicada* and *Nirvana Road* (the latter done in the U.S., where Deuter now resides) are his best overall recordings.

ERIC DEVISSCHER
- *"With Hidden Noise"* from the LP *Lawalree/Oosterlynck/DeVisscher/Fesler* (#WLS-12/13, 2 LPs; Editions Walrus, Rue Beckers 16, B-1040 Bruxelles, Belgium). Pianos with electronic sounds on tape. The work is in three parts, with three different interactions between the "music" (from the keyboards) and the "noise" on tape. Surprisingly, the piece is not noisy; it's more of a new look at how ordered sound leaves an imprint on or changes the focus of unorganized sound.

DOCTOR WIZE
- *"Jah's Garden of Delight"* from the LP *American Music Compilation* (Eurock Eurlp-01) EUR. Catchy stuff for kalimbas, synth-bass, harp, and mellotron.

EARTH STAR
- *Atomkraft? Nein, danke!* (Sky 051). Synthesist Craig Wuest is the leader of this international lineup, whose record title translates as "Atomic power? No thanks!" From sunny acoustic works to experimental electronics, this album consistently presents interesting, agreeable music.

EMERALD WEB
- *Dragon Wings and Wizard Tales* (Stargate 4230) NAR, FOR
- *Valley of the Birds* (Stargate 10005) NAR, FOR, VB
- *Nocturne* (For. FOR-012) FOR, NAR, VB
- *Lights of the Ivory Plains* (For. FOR-026) FOR, NAR
- *Catspaw* (Audion SYN-100) JEM
Emerald Web consists of Kat Epple and Bob Stohl, both of whom play various flutes and synthesizers. Even the "natural" sounds—birds, insects, etc.—come from their digital synthesizers. Since the beginning of the 80s, Emerald Web has been a popular act in New Age circles, but they've never fallen into New Age complacency.

DANIEL EMMANUEL
- *Wizards* (North Star NSP-2003) NAR, VB
- *Rain Forest Music* (North Star NSP-2001) NAR
Fairly typical of the New Age/healing music style. "Visions during Movement" from *Rain Forest Music* isn't bad.

BRIAN ENO
- *Another Green World* (Island ILPS-9357) JEM
- *Before and after Science* (Island ILPS-9478) JEM
- *Music for Airports* (PVC 7908) JEM, FOR, NAR

With *Another Green World* and *Before and after Science,* Eno took a quantum leap beyond the world of rock music. Though they still contain singing, rock musicians, and some rock techniques, these two albums are "serious" music. (The opening theme for the "New Sounds" radio program is the beginning of "Julie With . . ." from *Before and after Science.*) *Music for Airports* was the first of Eno's Ambient Music Series releases. See also Chapters 1 and 11.

ROGER ENO
- *Voices* (EG EGED-42) JEM. Roger appeared on Brian's album *Apollo* in 1983, and in 1985 the younger Eno released his first solo album. Well, not really solo: Brian Eno treats the various instruments and Daniel Lanois produced it. The result sounds like another of the recent Brian Eno ambient albums.

DEAN EVENSON
- *Tropic of Paradise* (Soundings of the Planet, no #) NAR. At various times, if you can stay awake, you'll hear synthesizer, harp, strings, guitar, flute, and natural sounds. Peaceful and relaxing, if that's what you want.

FIRST AVENUE ENSEMBLE
- *Dream Again* (First Ave. Inc., 214 West 102 Street #1B, New York, NY 10025). C. Bryan Rulon (see Chapter 4) plays synthesizer, Matt Sullivan plays oboe, and Ted Mook cello. Nocturnal pieces, perhaps not what you'd expect: much of it is gentle without being soporific; some of it gets surprisingly chromatic, even ominous.

KEITH FOLEY
- *"Futures"* from the compact disc *The Pugh-Taylor Project* (DMP CD-448) DMP. Talk about unlikely ensembles, this work is for tenor trombone, bass trombone, and eight synthesizers. Pretty stuff, impeccably played; ravishing digital sound.

PETER GABRIEL
- *Birdy* (Geffen 24070). Gabriel is a well-known rock singer and a talented musician who has also been interested in non-Western music for several years. This is music used in the film *Birdy;* some of it was specifically written for the movie, but most of it is adapted from Gabriel's earlier albums of songs. The vocals are removed, and what's left is a strong album of moody instrumentals, some incorporating ethnic instruments.

HEARN GADBOIS
- *GAHT MAYH MOH8JOH3 WOYKIN* (from the audio-cassette magazine *Tellus*, Vol. 12) NMDS. Muddy Waters's classic blues, "Got My Mojo Working," is sung here by a Macintosh computer! Gadbois accompanies the computerized voice with

ethnic percussion in this lively, completely delightful piece.

EDWARD LARRY GORDON, *SEE* LARAAJI.

STEVE GORDON AND DAVID GORDON
- *Misty Forest Morning* (Earthlight ELC-204) NAR. Not much real music; this is meant as an environment, a room ambience . . . a goal it unquestionably achieves.

J. GREINKE
- *Cities in Fog* (Intrepid IN-04) NMDS. Ambient music for electronics, guitar, and tape. And fog, lots of fog, in the form of production work murky enough to obscure the music. It's an interesting idea, but it grates after a while. Imagine K. Leimer in a fit of depression and you'll get the idea.

GURUMANDER AND FRIENDS
- *Blue Star* (GRD, no #) FOR, VB. "Experimental" guitar, synthesizers, percussion, and lots of sound effects. Produced by Liv Singh Khalsa (see below) whose recordings have a similar tone.

HALPERN, STEVEN
- *Comfort Zone* (Gram. GR-7786) GRAM, VB, FOR, NAR
- *Zodiac Suite* (Gram. GR-18-7770) GRAM, VB, FOR, NAR
- *Timeless: Solo Piano* (Gram. GR-18-7833) GRAM, VB, FOR, NAR
- *Spectrum Suite* (Gram. GR-18-7771) GRAM, VB, FOR, NAR
- *Rings of Saturn* (Halpern Sound HS-797) GRAM, VB, FOR, NAR

The king of "healing music," Halpern has recorded a number of other projects, mostly cassettes, which can hardly be considered music; they are in fact not intended to be used as music. *Timeless*, as a solo piano disc, doesn't really belong in this chapter, except that it supposedly serves the same function as his other records. With its occasional chords that linger and die before the next one comes along, it's a pretty abysmal affair. *Spectrum Suite* and *Rings of Saturn,* however, can easily appeal to anyone who enjoys spacey electronics and some of the better New Age music. These albums contain some of Halpern's most "musical" material, and feature Iasos on electric flute on the former LP, electric violinist Tony Selvage and keyboardist Rasheed Horowitz on the latter.

STEVEN HALPERN AND PAUL HORN
- *Connections* (Gram. GR-18-7838) GRAM, NAR, FOR, VB

STEVEN HALPERN & GEORGIA KELLY
- *Ancient Echoes* (Halpern Sound HS-783) NAR, FOR, VB

STEVEN HALPERN & DANIEL KOBIALKA
- *Recollections* (Gram. GR-18-7823) GRAM, NAR, FOR, VB

STEVEN HALPERN AND DALLAS SMITH
- *Threshold* (Gram. GR-7301) GRAM, NAR, FOR, VB
- *Natural Light* (Gram. GR-7834) GRAM, NAR, FOR, VB

Halpern's collaborative records are generally spiritless. The album with Kobialka has some lovely moments of almost classical-sounding violin and keyboard interplay, and the Kelly/Halpern at least tries to be different, but these discs are best used in what seems to be their intended manner: as inoffensive background sound.

STEVE HILLAGE
- *Rainbow Dome Musick* (Vir. VR-1) NAR, FOR, VB. Very celestial music from a fine electric guitarist. Synthesizers, processed guitars, and Tibetan bells are featured.

HOMECOMING
- *Elevator Express* (Mirror Image Labs 2-1002) VB. Pretty works for electronic and acoustic instruments that ultimately sound like hi-tech elevator music.

RICHARD HOROWITZ AND SUSSAN DEIHIM
- *Eros in Arabia* (Ethnotech RH-777)
- *Memoir/Out of Thin Air* (private tapes)
- *Solo Ney Improvisations* (Shandar, out of print, and private tape).

Actually, these three recordings are mostly solo efforts by Horowitz, with Daniel Kobialka playing violin on *Memoir*. The ney is a cane flute which Horowitz processes to the point where it can no longer be considered a simple acoustic instrument. He also uses the technique of circular breathing (i.e., playing while exhaling *and* inhaling); the result is music that's plaintive and a little unsettling: You keep wondering when he's going to come up for air.
- *Theme 87, Jum Jum, Armour, Helix 1–3* (private tapes)
- *Azax/Attra* (not commercially released)
- *Desert Equations* (Crammed Discs MTM-8) NMDS. Flavored with the sounds of the Near East, this LP music combines voice, ney, keyboards, and percussion with various electronic gadgets. Whether for trance or dance, Horowitz and Deihim consistently present fascinating music.

IASOS
- *Elixir* (Wave #2) (Interdimensional Music W2-C-D) NAR, FOR, VB. Like so many New Age musicians, Iasos is primarily concerned with bathing the listener in beautiful sound. A conventional but well made recording.

MARK ISHAM
- *Vapor Drawings* (Wind. H. WH-1027) WH, NAR
- *Film Music* (Wind. H. WH-1041) WH, NAR

Isham is not only a top-flight musician, he's also a fine composer. Equally at home with trumpet or synthesizer, he's played with such diverse acts as Group 87, David Torn, and Art Lande. His works are tautly constructed without losing any of their spacious beauty; *Vapor Drawings* has more up-tempo numbers, while *Film Music* contains lovely ensemble pieces from three different soundtracks. Both are enhanced by careful production.

JEAN-MICHEL JARRE
- *Zoolook* (Dreyfus FDM 18118) CH, NAR. A 1984 recording that is unlike anything else Jarre has done. Using tapes of voices in dozens of languages as a sound source, Jarre has applied all sorts of tape and electronic processing to change the voices into musical material, which he then combines with synthesizers and other instruments. Adrian Belew and Laurie Anderson contribute guitar and vocal parts, respectively. See Chapter 1.

ALAP JETZER
- *Towards the Golden Shore* (USA contact: Shambhu Vineberg, 150–12 85 Avenue, Jamaica, NY 11432)
- *Eternity's Sunrise* (TE-401) VB

Jetzer is a Swiss multi-instrumentalist whose recordings are inspired by the compositions of Sri Chinmoy, who is apparently Jetzer's guru. Similar to Deuter's albums, these cassettes combine guitars, electronic drones and effects, winds, and occasional others.

ALEX JONES AND DOUG CUTLER
- *Awake and Dreaming* (X-7) NAR, VB. Electric piano and synthesizer drivel that is likely to lull one into a profound narcosis. See Chapter 9.

RYO KAWASAKI
- *Ryo* (Ph.-Japan 30PJ-5). Kawasaki plays guitar synthesizer and acoustic guitar. Despite the presence of arrangements of Manuel de Falla, Joaquin Rodrigo, Ernest Bloch, and Antonio Carlos Jobim compositions, it's Kawasaki's own "Twilight Song" that provides the high point of the album.

LIV SINGH KHALSA
- *Music of the Spheres* (Guru Ram Das Records) FOR, NAR. Khalsa plays a variety of instruments, and his cassettes have a very cosmic sound. Like his *Music of the Spheres, Vol. 2* (Chapter 6) this piece is based on an Indian raga scale *(Raga Bhairo)*.

BOB KINDLER
- *Music from the Matrix I* (Global Pacific GP-203) GP, NAR, FOR

- *Music from the Matrix II* (Global Pacific GP-209) GP, NAR
- *Music from the Matrix III: Waters of Life* (Global Pacific GP-309) GP, NAR.

Kindler is a cellist, and brother of violinist Steve Kindler (see Chapter 3). This series of cassettes uses cello, guitar, autoharp, flute, synthesizer, sitar, and others. It's really quite good, especially the second volume, which includes some unusual cello sonorities.

DANIEL KOBIALKA

- *Timeless Motion* (DK 102-LP) NAR, FOR, VB.

This is one of about a dozen New Age music recordings Kobialka has done. It contains a gently effective "Lullaby," which is probably the closest thing to real music that you'll find on any of his New Age albums. The real shame is that Kobialka can do better (his concert recordings are listed in Chapter 5).

GEORGE KOCHBEK

- *Hamlet Tagträume* (Ausfahrt 08-6108) SCA. A set of short pieces of incidental music for a performance based on Hamlet. Mostly moody electronics, but there's a tango and some avant-garde-style noises too, played on synthesizers and a sizeable ensemble of acoustic instruments.

JACK LANCASTER AND ROBIN LUMLEY

- *Marscape* (RSO RS-1-3020). All of the members of the fusion group Brand X, as well as Simon Jeffes of England's Penguin Cafe Orchestra, appear on this album, which goes through a wide range of moods and a surprising variety of instrumental combos.

LARAAJI

- *Celestial Vibrations* (SWN 52824) VB
- *Day of Radiance* (EG EGS-203) JEM, NAR, FOR, VB
- *Sun Zither* (Laraaji, PO Box 227, Cathedral Station, New York, NY 10025)
- *Live at WNYC,* 7/85 (see previous listing).

Laraaji is best known for the *Day of Radiance* album he did with Brian Eno for the Ambient Music Series, a splendid showcase for Laraaji's treated, amplified zither. One side is devoted to rapid, almost bluesy dances, which create a huge wave of sound; the other is a side-long meditation, full of highly evocative special effects, all created on the zither. *Celestial Vibrations* was done under Laraaji's real name, Edward Larry Gordon, and is similar to the meditative side of *Day of Radiance.* *Sun Zither* is a poorly recorded zither solo; and the live pieces which Laraaji improvised in our studios on an edition of "New Sounds" differ from the others in that they include piano, synthesizer drone, and occasional bits of thumb piano and chimes. Laraaji also has some cassettes of vocal music which are much inferior.

LARKIN

- *O'cean* (Narada C-8015) NAR, FOR, VB
- *Earth Light* (Sono Gaia 138) NAR
- *Moments Empowered* (Wind Sung Sounds 1005) NAR, VB, FOR

The bad news is that Larkin is one of the worst offenders when it comes to corny, smarmy notes and packaging. The good news is that he's one of the better New Age musicians, using flute, santur (a Near Eastern zither), bells, and synthesizers.

ELODIE LAUTEN

- *Piano Works* (Cat Collectors CKG-7000) NMDS
- *Concerto for Piano and Orchestral Memory* (Cat Collectors CKG-777) NMDS
- *The Death of Don Juan* (Cat Collectors CC-713) NMDS

Lauten is a pianist, composer, and synthesist who usually combines instruments with Fairlight CMI and tape processing. The first album is for piano and tape and is described in Chapter 4. The *Concerto* is actually a suite for piano, violin, viola, cello, trombone, and processing; the unusual blend of live and processed sound works better in some sections than in others, but as a whole the *Concerto* is an intriguing piece. *The Death of Don Juan* is Lauten's strongest work to date: an opera in two short acts dealing with a metaphorical, surreal version of the Don Juan story. Besides such oddities as taped voices, amplified harpsichords, and computer, Lauten also uses an electro-acoustic lyre of her own devising.

BENJAMIN LEW AND STEVEN BROWN

- *Twelfth Day: Speech, Adornment, Love* (Original Music OMG-301) NMDS
- *A Propos d'un Paysage* (Crammed Discs CRAM-038) NMDS
- *"A la Recherche de B."* from the LP *Made To Measure, Vol. I* (Crammed Discs CRAM-029) NMDS

Lew and Brown make murky, brooding music with lots of electronics (played by Lew) and keyboards and sax (played by ex-Tuxedomoon-member Brown). Marc Hollander of Aksak Maboul and Vini Reilly from Durutti Column also appear on clarinet and guitar, respectively. With bits of ethnic percussion, "fake oud," "pseudo-sitar," and similar noises, there's a surprising amount of variety beneath the apparently monochrome surface.

JULIE LYONN LIEBERMAN

- *Empathic Connections* (Harmony, no #) VB. Lieberman plays violin and occasionally sings. Laraaji appears on this cassette as well. The lovely combination suffers from bad production and recording.

RAY LYNCH

- *The Sky of Mind* (Ray Lynch Productions 101) NAR, FOR

■ *Deep Breakfast* (Ray Lynch Productions RLLP-102) NAR, FOR
Lynch's New Age electronics are mixed with lots of acoustic instruments and occasional vocals. Despite vacuous titles ("Celestial Soda Pop" is one) and limited ability on the synthesizer, Lynch has picked up a following, and his recordings aren't half bad.

MICHEL MAGNE
■ *La Terre* (EGG 90.187). A 1978 French release, now quite hard to find. Keyboards, electric violin, African and Indian drums, and sitar are thrown together here, and there are some effective moments.

ALAIN MARKUSFELD
■ *Contemporus* (Visa 7012) WAY. Another French release, this one from 1979. The music, while simple, has a Gallic charm and occasional echoes of Romanticism. Markusfeld plays synthesizer, guitars, and many other instruments.

INGRAM MARSHALL
■ *The Fragility Cycles* (IBU-101) NMDS
■ *Fog Tropes/Gradual Requiem* (New Albion NA-002)
■ *Alcatraz* (not yet released)
Marshall is an outstanding composer, and may well turn out to be one of the most important of his generation. All of these works combine keyboards with live processing, voices on tape, found sound, Indonesian flute, and occasional other instruments. *The Fragility Cycles* is not as immediately accessible as the second album, but it's an impressive achievement in the field of live electro-acoustic music. *Fog Tropes* is a stunning, award-winning piece combining brass sextet with processed tapes, and both *Gradual Requiem* and *Alcatraz* seamlessly blend the electronic and acoustic elements they contain. See *Cold Blue Sampler* listed above, as well.

SUSAN MAZER
■ *The Fire in the Rose* (Rising Sun RSA-160) RIS, NAR. Electric harp, lyricon (a wind-instrument synthesizer), flute, and lots of ethnic percussion. Comparisons to Vollenweider will be inevitable, but with more real percussion and a leaner sound, Mazer's diverting music is perhaps more interesting.

SAM MCCLELLAN
■ *Music of the 5 Elements* (Spirit 7007) NAR, VB. One of the better "healing music" albums, with tapes, instruments, and relatively restrained liner notes.

MUSIC FOR PROGRESSIVE RELAXATION
■ *Vol. I: Innerlight* (Yvonne YRH-81282) NAR
■ *Vol. II: Earthbeat* (Yvonne YRH-43083) NAR

■ *Vol. III: Gentle Harmony* (Yvonne YRH-43084) NAR
These records by Rudy Helm and David Kessner are not only supposed to be relaxing but, as the liner notes tell us, "music has real therapeutic value. Your purchases as such are tax-deductible." Wonder what the IRS thinks of that? All three records present listless muzak played on guitar, piano, and synthesizer; Vols. I and II include natural sounds, too.

NEW AGE
■ *Transformation* (Isis 30003) NAR, VB
■ *Transmission* (Isis 30004) NAR, VB
A German duo whose music is a little different from what their name might lead you to expect. Spare and repetitive, it contains some good ideas desperately in need of an editor.

TOM NEWMAN
■ *Bayou Moon* (Landscape NAGE-2) NAR, JEM. As you might expect from the former producer of Mike Oldfield, John Cale, and many others, this album has more rock in it than most other New Age records. What's surprising is the strong influence of deep Southern blues and Cajun music. The gumbo doesn't really work throughout, but some interesting textures develop, and "Moonrise" and "Voodoo de Bayou" are impressive compositions.

PATRICK O'HEARN
■ *Ancient Dreams* (Private 1201) PRI, NAR. Beautiful sounds, pristine production. Maybe *too* beautiful—the glossy synthesized textures often overwhelm the music itself.

PAULINE OLIVEROS
■ *Accordion and Voice* (Lovely VR-1901) NMDS. Like so much of Oliveros's recent work, the pieces on this album deal with drones and static effects. The accordion, paired with some of the subtlest electronic altering ever recorded, and sustained vocals create a truly contemplative music.

ORCHESTRA OF THE 8TH DAY
■ *Music for the End* (Fly. F. FF-292) FF. This Polish duo consists of Jan Kaczmarek, probably the world's only virtuoso on the Fischer Fidola (a turn-of-the-century German harp-zither which he's transformed into an electro-acoustic device), and Grzegorz Banaszak, who plays guitar. Ominous and intricately colored.

DANIEL PALKOWSKI
■ *Asterism* (no label or #) NMDS. Palkowski has studied composition with Elias Tannenbaum and teaches at the Manhattan School of Music. Not surprisingly, his music, even at its most cosmic and accessible, is likely to appeal to listeners with more traditional tastes. Most of the pieces use piano and electronics, very often in an interactive way.

DAVID PARSONS
- *Sounds of the Mothership* (For. 006) FOR, NAR, VB
- *Tibetan Plateau* (For. FOR-013) FOR, NAR, VB

Parsons is from New Zealand, and both cassettes not only combine Western electronics with instruments from India but also manage to make the blend sound convincing in at least several excerpts.

MAGGIE PAYNE
- *Crystal* (Lovely VR-2061) NMDS. Payne, the flutist on David Behrman's *On the Other Ocean*, here uses flute, synthesizers, digital delay, and other devices. Some dramatic, colorful music in a style similar to the mid-70s works of Morton Subotnick.

POPOL VUH
- *Hosianna Mantra* (CH CEL 004) CH, FOR, NAR
- *Tantric Songs* (CH CEL 006) CH, FOR, NAR
- *In the Gardens of Pharao/Aguirre* (CH CEL 008/ 009, 2 LPs) CH, FOR, NAR

Led by keyboardist/composer Florian Fricke, this German group combines Indian and Western music and creates an ancient-sounding type of space music. It is rich in images—forgotten moonlit rituals, the steamy heat of the Nile Delta—and director Werner Herzog has often used their music in his films. The group's name, by the way, is the name of the Mayan Book of the Dead.

PSYCHO-ACOUSTICAL LABORATORIES
- *Scandinavian Fantasy*
- *CIGNIA*
- *Midwinter Saga* (all private tapes; for information, contact Psycho-Acoustical Laboratories, 10–47 48 Avenue, Long Island City, NY 11101; 718-786-9498)

Using tape manipulation, filtering, and collage techniques, these cassettes are designed to be both healing and music. *CIGNIA* is a carefully constructed collage of natural sounds and prerecorded music; it became one of "New Sounds' " most requested pieces, despite the fact that it's not for commercial release. *Scandinavian Fantasy* uses the music of Ralph Lundsten (see Chapter 1) with natural sounds, and *Midwinter Saga* is a psycho-acoustical reworking of Lundsten's *En Midvinter Saga*. As music specifically designed for relaxation, this works better than most.

RAMANANDA
- *Song of the Golden Lotus* (Satsaya 1980) FOR, VB, NAR
- *Hymn to a New Age* (Satsaya 1981) FOR, VB
- *In the Garden* (Satsaya 1982) FOR, VB, NAR

Despite his name, Ramananda is apparently an American from Chicago. He is a fine bass flutist, also plays synthesizer and occasional bells or gongs, and sometimes constructs unusual scales on which his compositions or improvisations are based. Using avant-garde and Oriental flute techniques, Ramananda has developed a very expressive style. In the last cassette especially, one hears the influence of Japanese music, as the koto (the Japanese zither) joins the flutes and electronics. His music is always slow and attractive, but it's also unusual enough to stand out from most other New Age recordings.

SHEILA ROBERTS AND JIM REIDER
- *Moonflower* (Message Box 1001) VB
- *Moonflower Ascending* (Message Box 1002) VB

While these recordings of pretty piano and synthesizer tunes don't avoid the usual pitfalls of most similar music, they do show some promise: Obviously, a bit of thought went into "Intra Dawn" on the second album.

ACHIM ROEDELIUS
- *Durch die Wüste* (Sky 014)
- *Wenn der Südwind weht* (Sky 064)
- *Offene Türen* (Sky 072)
- *Flieg' Vogel, Fliege* (Sky 078)
- *Geschenk des Augenblicks/Gift of the Moment* (EG EGED-34) JEM, NAR

Roedelius is half of the group Cluster. His solo works are similar to the Cluster albums in their combination of acoustic and electronic keyboards and their simple, repeating melodies. The last album also includes violin and cello, and almost sounds like chamber music in spots. *Wenn der Südwind weht,* cheery but not intrusive, is great music for weekend mornings.

DAVID ROSENBOOM
- *"How Much Better If Plymouth Rock Had Landed on the Pilgrims"* from an LP by J. Jasmine called *My New Music* (AAFF #DR-001) NMDS. From an album of offbeat vocals, this instrumental track is a short version of one of Rosenboom's most variable compositions. This version is, like its title, quite engaging.

SCHAWKIE ROTH
- *Fortune* (Heavenly Music HM-0109) NAR, FOR.

"Healing music" by a musician who seems to know his way around all different kinds of wind and keyboard instruments. Taken simply as music, there's not much of interest here, but at least it's well played.

RYUICHI SAKAMOTO
- *Esperanto* (School MIL-1007). A leading Japanese musician, Sakamoto is at home in a number of styles: synthipop, Romantic-style piano music (see Chapter 9, page 218), and albums like this that combine Eastern and Western instruments and rhythms. Yas-Kaz plays percussion, Arto Lindsay handles electric guitar.

SIEGFRIED SCHWAB
- *Meditation* (Melosmusik 65701). Schwab has appeared as guitarist with Eberhard Schoener, and like Schoener has been inspired by the music and atmosphere of Asia, especially Tibet. Guitars, synthesizers, bass, and some percussion recreate the meditative ambience of Tibetan chant, but the sound is thoroughly Western.

SLAP
- *Slap* (Duotone DUO-4) NMDS
- *Pratique* (Duotone DUO-5) NMDS
- *Downtime* (Duo-6) NMDS

Slap is basically Stephen Nester, who plays synthesizer, percussion, tape, rhythm box, and especially sound effects. Mostly electronic rock, but each album contains one or two less conventional pieces; the most effective of these may be "Elegy" on the first LP, which combines violins and electronics.

GARY SLOAN
- *Harmonitalk* (Boogie-Til-Dawn, Gary Sloan, 17100 Feodosia, Anchorage, AK 95516)
- *Nightraid* (same as preceding)

Sloan plays a bizarre pair of instruments: harmonica and synthesizer. The harmonica is often synthesized, but Sloan occasionally takes a little bluesy solo on the unaltered instrument. *Nightraid* is an original, superior album; *Harmonitalk* is strange enough to be interesting, but may take some getting used to.

CHAS SMITH
- *Santa Fe* (Cold Blue E-7) NMDS. Pedal steel guitar, dobro, and banjo—instruments normally associated with bluegrass—are used to create a haunting musical cloud. The sound itself is so peculiar that it's almost impossible to identify the instruments involved without prior knowledge.

DALLAS SMITH
- *Stellar Voyage* (Rising Sun RSA-140) RIS, NAR. While Ali Akbar Khan's "Karuna Supreme" has some decent sax playing by Smith, the rest of this New Age album is very light on musical content.

LARRY SNYDER AND DENNIS MCCORKLE
- *Peaceful Fantasy* (Vital Body/The Art of Relaxation) VB, NAR. Guitar and synthesizers. Lush, spacey music that won't disappoint fans of ambient records.

DEBBIE SPITZ
- *Pipedreams* (Life Records 35903) LADY. Flute, violin, synthesizer, and voice. New Age with a hint of jazz here and there.

YOSHIO SUZUKI
- *Morning Picture* (IC KS-80.048) SBMG. Suzuki is a jazz bassist, now playing acoustic and electronic keyboards. His style is reminiscent of Andreas Vollenweider, or Pat Metheny's lighter moments. The album is mellow to the point of over-ripeness at times, but the pictures of New York City—"The Bagel" and "Meet Me in Sheep Meadow"—are quite charming.

JACK TAMUL
- *Electro/Acoustic* (Spectrum 134) NMDS
- *The Referee Has Vanished, The Parthenon* (private tape; for information, contact Becky Meagher Management, PO Box 121264, Nashville, TN 37212)

An uncommon blend of the academic and the mellifluous, which doesn't always sound convincing for all that it was a good idea. Tamul's tape pieces, though, are excellent. The first is for voice and electronics, the second pairs a cello with electronics. The mix of electronics and acoustics is cunning and seamless; in *The Parthenon*, particularly, the results are beautiful.

RICHARD TEITELBAUM
- *Blends* and *The Digital Pianos* (Lumina 005) NMDS. *Blends* features percussionist Trilok Gurtu and shakuhachi virtuoso Katsuya Yokoyama (Teitelbaum's teacher). More than a cross-cultural fusion of Western electronics and Eastern instruments, this piece explores aural phenomena like audible overtones and "beating." The piece works on many levels: as an experiment in musical color, an exploration of acoustics, or simply an engaging piece of music. *The Digital Pianos* features three computer-enhanced pianos. Through computer storage and foot pedals, all three can be "played" simultaneously, looping, delaying, fading, and inverting as needed.

TRI ATMA
- *Yearning & Harmony* (For. FOR-016) FOR, NAR. The most upbeat, pop-inflected New Age music released so far. The group records in Germany and combines guitar, synthesizer, and Indian tabla.

"BLUE" GENE TYRANNY
- *For the Record* (Lovely 1062) NMDS. Pieces by Robert Ashley, John Bischoff, Paul DeMarinis, and Phil Harmonic. Only intermittently interesting music for multiple keyboards, played by Tyranny (a.k.a. Robert Sheff).
- *Out of the Blue* (Lovely 1061) NMDS
- *The Intermediary* (Lovely 1063) NMDS

Sheff/Tyranny's own music: *Out of the Blue* is frankly pop-derived, played by a band that includes Peter Gordon, Maggie Payne, and Barbara Higbie (here playing fiddle). The lyrics are poor, but some of the music is fun to listen to. *The Intermediary*, an excellent record, pits a piano against computer-controlled electronics. It's a delightful mix of honky-tonk, barroom piano and infrequent

Impressionist musings with hi-tech computer sounds.

CYRILLE VERDEAUX
- *Moebius* (Soundings of the Planet) NAR
- *Offrandes/Offerings* (For., no #, may be out of print)

Piano and synthesizer, with occasional others, create an Indian-inspired contemplative mood. On *Offrandes,* Indian instruments and processed voices chanting/singing Indian drumming syllables create an alien but enchanting sound.
- *The Kundalini Opera* (Eurock EDC 07-12, 6 cassettes) EUR. A mammoth opus for keyboards and other instruments. It's probably the best music Verdeaux has done since *Offrandes;* it's also quite simply some of the most genuinely musical New Age music around.

CYRILLE VERDEAUX AND THE DELIRED CHAMELEON FAMILY (EMI 2C 066-13087).
This early Verdeaux record from the mid-70s leans toward the jazz-rock fusion of the day, but several works anticipate his later interest in Indian music.

ANDREAS VOLLENWEIDER
- *Behind the Garden ... Behind the Wall ... Under the Tree* (CBS MK-37793) NAR, FOR
- *Caverna Magica* (CBS MK-37827) NAR
- *White Winds* (CBS MK-39963) NAR
- *Pace Verde* (CBS 44-05008, extended play 45-rpm) NAR
- *Down to the Moon* (CBS FM-42255) NAR

To say that Vollenweider has become one of the most popular and successful New Age artists misses the point: Vollenweider has become one of the most popular and successful musicians in *any* style. His albums are big hits; his tours are always sold out; his audience includes high school students and retired doctors. And yet I find myself writing critically about him. It's obvious the man has talent: His production, his playing, his interest in ethnic percussion—they're all marks of a serious musician. And each album has at least one excerpt (but never more than two) in which he lightens up enough on the simpering choral effects and mechanical drumming to let some real music come through. But like Kitaro, Vollenweider has found something that works, and has allowed himself to fall into a rut. Try *Caverna Magica* if you want to hear a typical Vollenweider effort.

JOHANNES WALTER
- *Music Mantras* (For. FOR-017). Walter is not the composer, but simply the producer of this collection of muzak. When it tries to be tranquil, it's simply bland. When it aims for pathos, it succeeds only in being pathetic.

WOLFGANG WIGGURS
- *"Alluvium"* (from the audio-cassette magazine *Touch 33.4: "Land's End"*) NMDS. A sax solo over a catchy bed of synthesizers and electronic percussion. (*Touch* is a British cassette magazine featuring new, old, and sometimes terribly avant-garde music from rock, audio art, and new-music circles.)

MAURICE WRIGHT
- *Chamber Symphony for Piano and Electronic Sounds* (20th-Century Consort/Smithsonian Collection N-022) SM. Bristling and often atonal, this is nonetheless a clever blend of piano and electronics, à la "Blue" Gene Tyranny's *The Intermediary.*

CHRIS WYMAN
- *In the Andes* (C. Wyman, 25 East Sheffield Avenue, Englewood, NJ 07631). Despite the title, this music has at times a certain Asian tinge. A mature, evocative recording (cassette only) for synthesizers and synthetic effects, Bolivian flutes, and bells.

STOMU YAMASH'TA
- *Kukai* (JVC SJX-30227) NAR
- *Iroha—Ten/Chi* (RVC RPL-3026/27, 2 LPs) NAR
- *Iroha—Sui* (RVC RPL-8144) NAR
- *Iroha—Ka* (RVC RPL-8187) NAR, VB
- *Sea and Sky* (Kuckuck 072) CH, NAR, HOS

Yamash'ta began his career as one of the world's great percussionists. The list of major contemporary classical composers who have written works for him is long and impressive. But these albums, all dating from the early to mid-80s, feature Yamash'ta primarily playing electronic keyboards. Buddhist monks chanting, sounds of water, and some others also appear on these recordings. The Iroha series contains some immensely satisfying music; *Kukai* is a compilation of Iroha pieces and some apparently new works, put together for a film. *Sea and Sky* is described in Chapter 5.

STOMU YAMASH'TA AND GO
- *Go* (Island ILPS-9387)
- *Go Too* (Arista AB-4138)

Go was one of Yamash'ta's earlier bands (also see Chapter 6), dating from the mid-70s. It included Klaus Schulze on synthesizers, as well as a few well-known rock musicians (e.g., Michael Shrieve, Steve Winwood). Both albums are basically experimental rock, with a number of interesting electronic pieces.

MATTHEW YOUNG
- *Recurring Dream* (Full Moon #1) NMDS. Electronics, tape, log drums, piano, guitars. Muted recording of music in an Eno/ambient vein with a few more upbeat numbers.

3
PROCESS MUSIC

The end must justify the means.
Matthew Prior

We know that butter comes from cream, but how long must we watch the churning arm?
Charles Ives (on the music of Tchaikovsky)

"I am sitting in a room," says Alvin Lucier, "different from the one you are in now." Indeed it is. For one thing, *my* room isn't loaded with tape decks and recording equipment. Lucier, however, is knee-deep in electronic apparatus. He's recording his own voice, playing it back on one machine, and rerecording it onto another, again and again (and again and again) until, as he explains, "the resonant frequencies of the room reinforce themselves, so that any semblance of my speech, with perhaps the exception of rhythm, is destroyed. What you will hear then are the natural resonant frequencies of the room, articulated by speech." By the end of the piece, the ambience of the room has taken over, the spoken phonemes have broken down, and the phrase "I am sitting in a room" sounds instead like a choir of gongs and bells.

This is music? At the beginning of his recording *I Am Sitting in a Room* (1970), Lucier speaks for about ninety seconds—stuttering once or twice—to explain exactly what's about to happen on the piece the listener will hear. That's not music. But by the end of the recording, the room ambience and the recording process have not only smoothed away the stuttering, they've rendered Lucier's voice totally unrecognizable as human speech, and the series of ethereal, chiming notes we hear instead certainly *is* music.

Though obviously a product of the same technology as the music discussed in the first two chapters, this type of composition—generally known as process music —goes beyond even the purely electronic works in its reliance on the studio. Process music is any sort of piece where the technology is as much responsible for the final product as the performer. "Part of the idea is to make sort of gamelike situations for the performers," David Behrman asserts. "They might be experts or novices— the technology seems to work for both."

There are any number of methods for generating process music, and contemporary composers have been especially inventive in devising new ones. Probably the most common process used is the tape-delay/feedback system, in which a performer plays a single note or phrase, sends it into a closed electronic loop, and while the first phrase is repeating, adds a second and third layer on top. These repeating, additive loops are particularly useful in transforming such "nonmusical" sounds as people talking into something more recognizably musical. In works like *I Am Sitting in a Room,* the tape-recording process itself is transformed into a kind of musical instrument. Somewhat more bizarre are works that take natural phenomena as the basis for music, human brain waves for example. Even the movement of clouds across the sky has not escaped the clutches of the contemporary music maker.

The speed with which a process generates music varies with the type of operation being used. Tape loops allow a single performer to build up huge masses of polyphony within a few seconds. Lucier's piece, on the other hand, requires about fifteen or twenty minutes before the results of the process really become evident. *I Am Sitting in a Room* takes up an entire album; side one is comprised entirely of Lucier's voice in successive stages of decomposition, and it isn't until the second side of the album that the process begins to produce music. It's fascinating stuff the first time around, but once you know the premise, you begin to wish that first side was a good deal shorter. Herein lies the main problem in making process music, and in listening to it: It sometimes takes ten or twenty minutes of repetitions, computer blips, or whatever, before any recognizable music is produced. The question remains, *does* the end justify the means? And if it does, how much of the means do we have to listen to before we hear the end?

There are, as you might expect, a number of process works in which the process is, in fact, as intriguing as the music it produces. But even in cases where the process itself isn't inherently interesting, the end almost always justifies the means. The rich music produced toward the end of Lucier's piece *is* made even more remarkable when you've heard where it originated. (So am I violating the spirit of the piece if I choose to go straight to side two when listening to the record? Another of life's unanswerable questions . . .) Fortunately, many of the processes used in creating this kind of music are much quicker than the gradually cumulative effects of Lucier's tape piece.

The history of the origins of process music is somewhat confused. Like so much of the music discussed in this book, the form can ultimately be traced back to the American composer John Cage. One of the most important and influential avant-garde figures in twentieth-century music, Cage had composed a prototypical process work as early as 1939. His *Imaginary Landscape #1* called for frequency recordings, two record players whose speeds could be varied, as well as more conventional instruments—a muted piano and cymbal. Between 1939 and 1942, Cage composed three *Imaginary Landscapes,* employing audio oscillators and an amplified wire coil, among other sound-producing devices. In this one set of works, Cage anticipated both the electronic music developed by Eimert and the Germans in Cologne, and the *musique concrète* work of Schaeffer and the French in Paris.

A more immediate predecessor is Stockhausen's *Gesang der Jünglinge.* As we saw earlier (p. 4), this 1956 work was one of the first to bridge the gap between the previously separate schools of electronic and tape/concrete music. Through imaginative manipulation of the recording process, Stockhausen was able to produce a layered effect similar to the tape-loop results described above, but with infinitely more variety, since each layer could be sonically altered in any number of ways. Stockhausen continued to work with blends of electronic and tape processes throughout the 1960s: *Kontakte* ("Contacts"), completed in 1969, calls for piano, percussion, and four tracks of recorded electronic sounds. These pieces reached a relatively large audience, especially in Europe, although Stockhausen's application of serial procedure to every aspect of his composition led many listeners to equate process music with serialism and atonality. As the 60s progressed, however, other composers revealed that process music could take other forms.

Stockhausen had begun teaching some of Darmstadt's famous summer courses in 1957, and his renown as a teacher soon spread across Europe and America, Lucier himself being one of the many composers who studied at Darmstadt during his tenure. But Stockhausen's influence was widely felt even beyond Darmstadt. His work with altered layers of tape in *Gesang der Jünglinge* created a stir in the music studios of state-run radio throughout Western Europe. By 1962, when Terry Riley began working in the ORTF (French radio and television) studios, he found himself in an environment where he could experiment with sophisticated, state-of-the-art recording and tape equipment.

Riley had been familiar with the new works of Stockhausen and Italian composer Luigi Nono when he arrived in Paris in 1962, but once in the studio he began working in a somewhat different direction. "I had a chance to produce a couple of pieces," he explains. "One of them was *Music for the Gift,* in which I worked with jazz trumpeter Chet Baker. I didn't *play* with him, but I recorded Chet's group and individual solos, and looped them together into a whole new piece. It sounded like live music, but it was looped and put together in different ways."

Riley's other early works deal with short recorded fragments that are repeated continuously and layered on top of one another. As these pieces progress, the accented beat may shift gradually from one note to another; or one layer of the recording may slowly move out of alignment with respect to another, resulting in a sonically ambiguous "phase shifting" effect.

Returning to California in 1964, Riley joined the San Francisco Tape Music Center and began to experiment with having live instruments imitate these tape processes. *"Music for the Gift* worked quite well, since it was modal music," he recalls. "I found you could take the Dorian mode and chop it up in many different ways and it would still make sense, even looping it like that. So I decided to try to write an instrumental piece based on taking a mode and cutting it up." The method led to such historically important works as *Keyboard Studies* (1963) and *In C* (1964).

Another American composer working in San Francisco that year, Steve Reich, also began to create pieces with taped sounds and phase shifting. Reich applied the phase-shifting technique to human speech in two similar works: *It's Gonna Rain* (1965) and *Come Out* (1966). These are angry, aggressive works—the text for *Come Out* is a tape loop of a young black man who has been beaten by police; *It's Gonna*

Rain is a recording of a fire-and-brimstone preacher shouting apocalyptic messages, including the phrase "it's gonna rain." While the content of the source material is arresting and provocative in itself, the purpose of these works is to examine what happens when a recording goes in and out of phase with itself. Repeated recordings of the phrase "it's gonna rain" are layered and subsequently manipulated so that they move out of synch with one another by imperceptible degrees. The piece gradually takes on some unusual acoustic properties, sounding less like voices and more like music. Since the recordings are all identical, they all use the same frequencies. As these identical frequencies move out of phase, however, an acoustic phenomenon known as "beating" occurs. A similar effect occurs on a guitar that is not quite in tune: The first string is tuned to E; if you play that same E note sharply on the *second* string and then quickly release it, both strings will resonate in the body of the instrument. If they are slightly out of tune, you'll hear the note pulsing or "beating" as it dies away.

Once this point has been achieved in *It's Gonna Rain,* the process is reversed. The acoustic "beating" and audible harmonics disappear, the layered, cyclical recordings move back in phase, and the piece concludes in the same way it began. As with Lucier's *I Am Sitting in a Room,* the development is fascinating, but it is a process that demands an open mind and a bit of patience from the listener.

By introducing techniques of tape manipulation into instrumental performance, Terry Riley and Steve Reich laid the foundations for the repetitive, pattern-oriented sound that would characterize the musical style later known as Minimalism (which will be covered in depth in the next chapter). Both composers, however, continued to develop new musical processes throughout the 60s. Reich invented a "phase-shifting pulse gate" which he used in several compositions; it allowed him to explore the phase-shifting phenomena without resorting to difficult and unwieldy tape techniques. Terry Riley began to apply tape-loop technology to solo performance: His "time-lag accumulator" was a musical feedback device consisting of several tape recorders that played music back several seconds after it was recorded. In a work like *Dorian Reeds* (1965), Riley would play a series of notes—on a saxophone in this case—and feed them into the recorders. While that series was being repeated by the tapes, another line of music would be added on top, in "real time." This, in effect, allowed Riley to play duets and ensemble pieces with a single instrument. "We discovered that technology in Paris while I was working on *Music for the Gift,*" Riley says. "I'm sure it was the first time it was used in a musical application, because I've looked at a lot of older electronic music and I've never seen this technique used before."

The tape and feedback system has become one of the most important tools for making process music for the past twenty years; Brian Eno, Robert Fripp, Daniel Lentz, and Paul Dresher have all used variants of this method. Its major advantages are the speed with which it builds up layers of sound and the fact that it allows a single performer to produce an impressive amount of sound, in varied textures, either live or in the studio.

While Riley was developing new tape technologies, Alvin Lucier had begun experimenting in another area of process music. Lucier had joined the faculty of Brandeis University in 1962 and became director of their electronic-music studio;

he also helped form the Sonic Arts Union in 1966 with like-minded composers David Behrman, Gordon Mumma, and Robert Ashley. In 1965, his work with electronic apparatus resulted in *Music for Solo Performer,* the first piece in musical history to use brain waves as a source of sound. In this composition, electrodes are placed on the performer's scalp to pick up alpha brain waves. As the performer attains a meditative state, the alpha waves emitted from the brain are greatly amplified and filtered, and directed to a set of loudspeakers. These speakers are placed beneath or on top of various percussion instruments around the performance space. When the amplified alpha waves cause the loudspeaker cones to vibrate, they in turn cause the instrument they're touching to vibrate as well. The work can be performed with any assortment of percussion instruments. In the 1982 recorded versions of the piece, Alvin Lucier first performs it with a battery of Western classical and jazz percussion instruments, followed by Pauline Oliveros using four separate groups of ethnic percussion instruments—West African; Indian; Japanese, Chinese, Korean; and Javanese.

Obviously, no two performances of *Music for Solo Performer* will ever be the same, since the patterns of the brain waves will vary from day to day and from person to person. Although the work does produce an unusual array of sounds, especially from the more exotic percussion instruments, this is an instance where the conception is perhaps more interesting than the execution. Through biofeedback, a performer can control the way brain waves are produced to some extent, but not to the point where a constant rhythm is established. The piece therefore often sounds disjointed, as rhythmic passages dissolve into seemingly random bursts of loud percussion.

Lucier has gone on to create compositions based on many other unconventional sound sources. *Whistlers* (1967) is a musical depiction of magnetic disturbances in the Earth's ionosphere. A set of multimedia works that appeared between 1975 and 1977 used modified recordings of bird calls and electronic sounds. Since 1968, Lucier has been presenting a series of pieces dealing with the acoustical properties of natural or architectural spaces. *I Am Sitting in a Room* is perhaps the most successful of these works, although the most unusual and immediate work in the series is probably *Spinning,* which was installed at the 1984 New Music America festival in Hartford, Connecticut. In its simplicity of design and clarity of purpose it is certainly the most elegant of Lucier's compositions. The work is based on a phenomenon closely related to the "beating" used by Steve Reich in *It's Gonna Rain.* Two pure electric tones are broadcast through a pair of speakers installed at opposite ends of a room. They're tuned to *almost* the same wavelength so that, to the human ear, the two sound like a single tone. But the slight difference between them causes an unexpected motion by the sound: It quite literally moves through space, "spinning" from one side of the room to the other, without the aid of any technical effects like stereo panning, fading speakers in and out, etc. The sound "spins" at a speed determined by how close together the two component tones are.

Spinning can have a disconcerting effect at first, but the piece is quite easy to appreciate, and very clearly demonstrates the acoustic properties of the space in which it's housed. These types of music, Lucier says, "ask you to listen in a different way." Certainly you wouldn't approach *Spinning* as a concert-type work. The piece can be installed for any length of time, theoretically; it is not meant to be "performed" before an audience. One can simply walk in, walk around, and walk out —and have taken in the entire piece.

Although Lucier himself did not pursue the practice of generating music with brain waves, other musicians did. American composer David Rosenboom began a fairly rigorous study of neurophysics and biofeedback techniques in 1970. Although Rosenboom has continued to write music for conventional instruments, he has also presented a number of experimental works that incorporate his unusual research. In fact, these works, recorded under the general heading of "Brainwave Music," are notated as engineering blueprints rather than as traditional symbols on music paper. The liner notes for Rosenboom's recording *Brainwave Music,* now sadly out of print, are full of polysyllabic terminology that can best be deciphered with a physics textbook. In his 1972 *Portable Gold and Philosophers' Stones,* subtitled "Music from Brains in Fours," four performers are monitored via electrodes for brain-wave production as well as body temperature and skin response. Four frequency dividers, capable of different responses to the same sine-wave frequency, produce exact pitch ratios according to the voltage output of the monitors, which are then processed by a group of voltage-controlled band-pass filters (or Holophone), enabling the application of brain-wave analysis to the voltage control inputs of the filters. What could be simpler?

Translated into English, this means that the four performers and a technician are producing brain waves which are filtered in such a way that their frequencies suggest a certain mode or scale of notes. Both technician and performers have to be schooled in neurofeedback techniques in order to maintain control over the piece. However much it may sound like a medical experiment, *Portable Gold and Philosophers' Stones* works as a musical experience. The output of the bank of filters is vaguely similar to that of an electric organ or a softly played synthesizer. The work has a quietly flowing meditative sound that in truth is hard to reconcile with the intimidating neurophysical treatise that accompanies it.

Rosenboom's Piano Etude #1 is somewhat easier to grasp. Using a small amount of musical material from his piano-with-electronics composition *How Much Better If Plymouth Rock Had Landed on the Pilgrims* (1969), Rosenboom establishes a process whereby the performer's brain waves change the frequency of two filters, which in turn change the sound of the repeating piano fragments passing through those filters. The filters "carve a hole" in the music. They start at the lower end of the spectrum and by the end of the piece have moved to its uppermost register. Piano Etude #1 uses a motoric, repetitive sound as its basis; it would probably be immensely irritating by itself after a few minutes, and it is made only a bit less so by the filtering process.

One of the most impressive qualities of the composers of process music, besides their ingenuity in devising these pieces, is the technical expertise they display in making them work. Before the advent of digital synthesizers and music computers, an artist working in this field had to be as much inventor as composer. Lucier, Riley, and Rosenboom have all actually created the "instruments" with which they produce music.

In an era of digital synthesis and music computers that sample, store, and retrieve any sound and distribute it over any number of notes, however, process music is becoming increasingly a product of unusual interfaces, since the processes themselves are becoming more commonplace.

David Behrman, another member of Lucier's Sonic Arts Union, has also experimented with process music and has developed several computer interfaces that allow him to set up some unusual musical systems. As we saw earlier, his works *On the Other Ocean* and *Figure in a Clearing* are interactive pieces between live musicians and an early microcomputer. These compositions are a kind of process music: The computer acts as an interface between the electronics and the acoustic instruments, so a closed system is produced; once the system is set in motion, it determines the form of the piece—and even, to a degree, the soloists' improvisations.

A more striking example of Behrman's imaginative use of technology is *Cloud Music* (1978). "The idea was that light from the sky would trigger some kind of system," Behrman explains, "and make changes as clouds went by. So Bob Diamond, who is a brilliant designer of video, made a video system that would detect changes in light level on the screen, and I made a music synthesizer for it." Like much of Alvin Lucier's work, *Cloud Music* is an installation piece, and it appeared in several different settings before being consigned to Behrman's basement.

"In the 70s," Behrman says, "it seemed to make sense to build things. But now there's been such technical advance that there are things on the market that you couldn't possibly equal yourself. People now make interfaces between one system and another; for instance, take the *Cloud Music* idea. Say you want music to change when the clouds go by—you can't buy that in a store. You have to design the interface, in this case the sensor that tells the computer what's going on in the sky."

Just as technology has now caught up with the process music created by the former members of the Sonic Arts Union, it has also served the growing needs of composers who use tape-delay and tape-loop processes. Terry Riley's time-lag accumulator, a delay and feedback system, was both relatively easy to build and easy to use. As the 70s progressed, other composers began to use similar processes. Brian Eno had been experimenting with the musical possibilities of tape recorders during the 60s, and had become involved with the highly experimental music of Cornelius Cardew and the Scratch Orchestra, and Gavin Bryars. By 1972, when he joined the British rock group Roxy Music, Eno had already devised a tape-loop system similar to Riley's. Eno's innovation was to make a closed loop of the system: The output of a second machine was, in turn, fed back to the first machine, where it was rerecorded along with whatever new material was being fed into the system.

Eno's tape loops obviously provided a quick way to produce huge amounts of sound from one source; fortunately, material that is being rerecorded again and again tends to decay—as Alvin Lucier's *I Am Sitting in a Room* demonstrates—so that the sound on the tape does not degenerate into a monolithic block of noise. Eno's system was soon utilized by electric guitarist Robert Fripp, leader of the British "art rock" group King Crimson. Through the use of various foot pedals that changed the output of his instrument, Fripp developed one of the most distinctive sounds of any guitarist in the field. His sinuous, often harmonically advanced solos provided the input for the first recording using Eno's tape loops. "The Heavenly

Music Corporation" was recorded in 1972, and appeared on the Fripp and Eno album *No Pussyfooting* (1973). Although further modifications were later made by both Fripp and Eno, the system is basically intact and surprisingly refined on this first recorded outing. The other work on the *No Pussyfooting* collection, "Swastika Girls," uses two inputs: Fripp's guitar, and a synthesizer played by Brian Eno. Although it was recorded a year later, it is a bit rougher around the edges.

Not all of Fripp and Eno's music was a product of the tape process itself. One switch on Fripp's pedal board enabled the guitarist to route the instrument's output from the tape system to allow it to be heard in "real time"; that is, while the loops continued to repeat, the guitarist could reel off a solo, with his previous music acting as an accompaniment. In the late 70s, after disbanding King Crimson, Fripp used this method of producing music in his solo performances and recordings. The system came to be known generally as "Frippertronics," though Fripp himself has always credited Eno with introducing him to this technology. (In all fairness, it should again be pointed out that historically, Terry Riley was the first to use this process, but instances of simultaneous inventions or discoveries are certainly not unknown, especially when a field is burgeoning at the rate electronic music was in the 60s.)

The 1975 Fripp and Eno recording *Evening Star* contained several short works that proved the technology could do more than simply accumulate progressively denser layers of sound. The shimmering, atmospheric texture that characterizes the album as a whole is proof of the subtleties of which the tape loop system was capable. In the same year, Eno released the album *Discreet Music.* Originally intended as accompaniment for solo performances by Robert Fripp, the record was pure and simple process music. Using two synthesizer melodies of different lengths as the only input material, Eno allowed the tapes to create the music with minimal aid, or interference, from himself.

In the course of the 1970s ever more sophisticated tape-delay and tape-loop technology became a standard element of composition. In California, Daniel Lentz investigated the length of delay a system could withstand. Employing what he termed a "cascading echo system," he was able to create music that operated on a delay time of up to thirty seconds. The most immediately striking use to which Lentz put his system was on the human voice. "My main concern has been almost a textual concern," Lentz explains. "Not that the music is arbitrary or added on, but the forms of all my works come from textual devices and processes."

In 1971, Lentz used this system to build up short spoken phonemes into familiar speech patterns. "You Can't See the Forest . . . Music" begins with three performers making short vowel sounds and striking wineglasses. Consonants are added on when those vowels repeat, almost half a minute later. By the third repetition, words have been created. Eventually, sentences are formed and the piece ends. As a demonstration of a process, "You Can't See the Forest . . . Music" is effective not only because it shows clearly how the cascading echo system works, but also because it's relatively short.

In 1973, Lentz composed the *Missa Umbrarum,* or "Mass of Shadows," a work that may well prove to be his most important to date. The Mass uses the thirty-second tape delay to produce "sonic shadows" of earlier material, so that the syllables that make up the first cycle of the piece return and are combined with new material in the second cycle. The text of the Mass is built up through the addition of the various cycles; the performers sing only a few words or phonemes at any time, and accompany themselves with wineglasses. The glasses can be rubbed or struck, and the performers change the note of the glasses by drinking some of the wine, giving rise to a second "process" that continues through the piece—the performers getting progressively drunker. "The transformation from sobriety to something less than that was all very important," Lentz says. In recent years, Lentz's music has moved away from such concerns, and by the time the *Missa Umbrarum* was recorded, in 1985, it was performed by an apparently sober ensemble. True to its name, the *Missa Umbrarum* is a nebulous, shadowy piece. Dark and dramatic, it is a disturbing work to some ears, but it is also one of the most effective examples of process music on record.

Further refinements in technology led to an even greater variety of available delay processes. Composer Paul Dresher, also working in California, began experimenting with tape effects in the 1970s. His 1979 work *Liquid and Stellar Music* uses an electric guitar with a complex tape-processing system that is capable of producing up to twenty channels of music; a four-channel tape machine with three separate playback heads and a series of foot pedals controls the routing of the sounds.

Dresher's system used tape delay in conjunction with live electronic processing. The next logical step was to integrate electronic delays, which eliminated the need for bulky (and too often fragile) tape recorders. Electric-cello player Tom McVeety has combined tape echo from a small recorder with an electronic digital delay. As with the Frippertronics system, McVeety's gadgetry allows him to produce rich textures, especially since his instrument includes an additional upper string that reaches into the violin range, and an additional lower string, extending the range to that of the double-bass. The versatility of the digital delay, according to McVeety, "gives you a real orchestral ability. You can get all over the instrument, and still have the lower register sounding while the top notes are echoing. Meanwhile you're playing live in the middle register."

An unusual side effect of McVeety's consolidation of tape echo with digital delay is an ethereal, quasi-choral sound that appears when the delay is allowed to operate unattended. "Once you get beyond four or five cycles of the delay, and don't put new information on top," he says, "you'll find what sounds like a female choir in the background that I can only partially control. Part of it is from my tape echo or foot pedal, but part of it is from the digital delay, which is out of my hands. It surprises me each time, because it's always new, and usually quite beautiful."

Daniel Lentz has also discovered the benefits of electronic delays. "The old tape/analog technology limited one to additive means; and thirty seconds was the amount of all the delays we used because that was the limit imposed by the tape." But, Lentz explains, digital delay helped make his 1984 album, *On the Leopard Altar,* a more well-rounded achievement. "Now I can control and change the figures—one piece may repeat in two or three seconds while another cycle is twenty seconds long. And now I can subtract, as well as working in additive forms." In *On the Leopard Altar,* Lentz once again structures the music according to textual processes, but now the texts' manipulation is more varied. At the start of each section of the song "Is It Love," Lentz explains, "all the phonemes are present simultaneously, and then

I begin taking them away. I'm subtracting phonemes, and therefore the keyboard notes as well, until I uncover the complete line and complete melody." The rapidly pulsing keyboard notes and apparently nonsensical syllables don't slow down, but when they spread out words and melodies can be distinguished. On "Is It Love," and in many of his additive pieces, Lentz creates a jigsaw puzzle of voices and instruments with a surprising application of the delay technology.

Before concluding this chapter, there are two other composers worth mentioning. Both use tape technology, but neither, strictly speaking, writes process music. The first is the Englishman Gavin Bryars, whose work *Jesus' Blood Never Failed Me Yet* (1975) is an ineffable and powerfully moving combination of a tape loop with gradually accumulating music. The recorded tape is a London tramp singing a fragment of an old English hymn. As the loop repeats, Bryars adds his own stately, somber music, an instrument at a time; when the entire ensemble has entered and is accompanying the repeated loop, the piece fades out and ends. Bryars's music is harmonically simple, as it had to be, to avoid overwhelming the tape.

In some of his later recordings—*Hommages* (1981) for example—he occasionally mixes subtle tape parts with simple, though not simplistic, keyboard music. These taped segments in Bryars's pieces can be distinguished from true process music in that they repeat not through any kind of feedback, but because the tape is manually edited together. Similarly, the music in *Jesus' Blood Never Failed Me Yet* is performed live, not through any delay processes. Nevertheless, composing with "found sound" is a practice closely related to process music; Bryars's piece was recorded by Brian Eno for his Obscure record series, which included Eno's own *Discreet Music.*

Working along similar lines is New York composer Scott Johnson. With electric guitars (which add an unmistakable rock inflection to what is in fact rigorously structured music) as his primary instrument, Johnson has based several of his pieces on meticulously edited recordings of the human voice—talking, stuttering, crying, or laughing. Repeated in short fragments, the natural inflections of the voice begin to take on musical values. Johnson then uses musical instruments to "pin down" those values to specific notes and rhythms. In a work like *John Somebody* (1980–1982), the results are striking, as Johnson creates what he terms "involuntary songs."

"If you listen to most voices," Johnson says, "people tend to have a pedal point, a place where their voice 'rests.' If you listen to a repeated loop of somebody speaking, that point becomes almost like a tonal center—the implication being that that's one of the origins of tonality." Once the tonality, or key, of a fragment of speech has been established, Johnson can begin to assign approximate note values to other vocal inflections. In *John Somebody,* he explains, "I took the phrases I wanted and transcribed the pitches, or at least the *implied* pitches, and selected fragments for counterpoint, which goes from two voices to ten. After that was all edited together and layered on a multitrack machine, *then* I added the instruments."

The problems of synchronizing the approximate note values of human speech with the more or less precise notes of an instrument (in this work, electric guitars and wind instruments on tape, with live solo guitar) are monumental. "The material is 'dirty,' " he says, "that is, it *sounds* on the beat, it *sounds* on pitch—in truth it really isn't, though. The sense of 'normal music' is completely imposed."

Obviously, process music is the arena for some of the most provocative and, yes, bizarre sounds being made today. Critics of this style, though, look askance at the reliance on technology, attributing it to shortcomings on the part of its creators. "Often composers aren't all that aware of what processes they're using," says Ingram Marshall, "and when they are, they're *really* aware of it, and I don't think that's a very creative state of mind. I mean, you can say that Bach was a process composer. You can show where he followed processes, but you also have to say that that wasn't his main concern. Someone who's constantly thinking of what the process is and how the scheme or process will work is a long way from writing music. In my humble opinion." In some cases, that's true, but in general, this is one opinion with which I have to disagree. Intriguing and valuable music *has* been made by composers who have gone beyond purely electronic works, and beyond electronic manipulation of acoustic sounds, to setting up processes that—in a feat of technology which should not be underestimated—will make music themselves.

DISCOGRAPHY AND RELATED WORKS

CHARLES AMIRKHANIAN

- *Lexical Music* (1750 Arch S-1779) NMDS. Using three-machine tape delays, juxtaposed tape loops, filters, and his own voice, Amirkhanian creates unusual percussive and harmonic effects. Some of this takes a while to get going, and the results are uneven; but pieces like "Mugic" and "Muchrooms" are fascinating and relatively brief examples of what one voice and an imaginative composer can do.

DAVID BEHRMAN

- *On the Other Ocean/Figure in a Clearing* (Lovely LM 1041) NMDS. See Chapter 2.

GAVIN BRYARS

- *The Sinking of the Titanic* (Obscure #1). Side two is *Jesus' Blood Never Failed Me Yet*. A tape loop of a London hobo, gradually accompanied by strings, winds, harp, brass, guitar, organ, and vibes. An extraordinarily moving piece. Incredibly, it has been allowed to go out of print in the United States.
- *Hommages* (Crepuscule, TWI 027) NMDS. See Chapter 4.

JOEL CHADABE

- *Rhythms* (Lovely 1301) NMDS. A computer generates various percussive sounds and rhythms, to which live percussionist Jan Williams responds and upon which he improvises. African, Caribbean, and Indonesian rhythms are all explored in this witty, well developed, and slightly oddball collection.
- *Settings for Spirituals/Solo* (Lovely VR 1302) NMDS. Solo voice with computer-generated electronics on side one, and a solo computer-music piece on side two. The spirituals are distorted but not destroyed, owing to the simplicity of the settings.

NICOLAS COLLINS

- *Let the State Make the Selection* (Lovely VR 1712) NMDS

NICOLAS COLLINS AND RON KUIVILA

- *Going Out with Slow Smoke* (Lovely 1701) NMDS Collins has been associated with Lucier et al., and his own recordings are full of tape noise—rumblings, hisses, distortions, that sort of thing. Source materials, from electric guitars wired backwards to Grandmaster Flash recordings, are thrown into digital delays, computerized mixes, computer-assisted synchronizations, etc. Some interesting textures appear, though musically it's pretty hard to take.
- *Devil's Music* (Trace Elements 1013) NMDS. Side one is a broadcast of today's dance music, digitally sampled, looped, and otherwise disembodied and reassembled. Side two is similar, but uses easy-listening and classical music. It is witty, abrasive, and oh-so-strange. Side two, where inane muzak ditties take on unusual rhythmic properties through Collins's computerized scratch technique, is a bizarre but still genuinely musical (I think) experiment.

CHARLES DODGE

- *Earth's Magnetic Field* (None. 71250). Changes in the Earth's magnetic field are translated into electronic notes. Musically, the piece is of only occasional interest.
- *"Any Resemblance Is Purely Coincidental"* from the LP *Stockholm Elektronmusikfestival 1980* (Aberg/Fylkingen #FYLP 1025) FYL. The delightfully misleading title refers to the fact that an old Caruso recording of the famous aria "Vesti la Giubba" by Leoncavallo serves as the basis for this piece. Dodge creates what he calls a "synthetic song" through computer manipulation and synthesis, with a bit of live piano added. An "avant-garde" rarity—a piece that's actually a lot of fun.

PAUL DRESHER

- *Liquid and Stellar Music* (Lovely VR 2011) NMDS, FOR. Electric guitar and tape processing. Dresher takes the "Frippertronics" route a step further by incorporating Minimalist elements—repeating patterns of notes; studies in phase relationships—and comes up with an individual style and a fine recording. See Chapter 4.

BRIAN ENO
- *Discreet Music* (Editions EG EGS 303) FOR. Process music in its purest form. The second side features *Three Variations on Pachelbel's Canon* for an instrumental ensemble; see Chapter 5.

ROBERT FRIPP
- *God Save the Queen/Under Heavy Manners* (Poly. PD-1-6266)
- *Let the Power Fall* (Editions EG EGS 110)
Frippertronics, with the exception of side two of the Polydor disc, which features some disco bass-and-drum accompaniment and the voice of "Absalm El-Habib" (David Byrne of the group Talking Heads). Both albums are primarily ambient in nature.

FRIPP AND ENO
- *No Pussyfooting* (Antilles AN 7001)
- *Evening Star* (Editions EG EGS 103) VB, NAR
Eno's tape-delay system with Fripp as the main source of information; on *Evening Star* there's some very discreet keyboard music by Eno as well. *No Pussyfooting*'s first side, "The Heavenly Music Corporation," is fascinating as an early example of this kind of music.

SCOTT JOHNSON
- *John Somebody/No Memory* (None./Icon 79133) NMDS. The human voice becomes an instrument —without singing—through the manipulation and repetition of taped segments. Johnson plays electric guitars and isn't afraid to resort to dramatic gestures when appropriate; he uses a horn section to great effect as well. The last half of *John Somebody* is absolutely irrepressible; you'll find yourself grinning all the way through it.

STEVE KINDLER AND
PAUL LLOYD-WARNER
- *Lemurian Sunrise* (Waterfall, Cassette #105) VB, NAR. Kindler plays an electric violin sent through tape loops, similar to those used by Fripp or McVeety. Lloyd-Warner accompanies at the piano. An ambient recording, made on the slopes of Mt. Haleakala in Hawaii.

RON KUIVILA
- *"TI Intends . . . (to enforce its intellectual property rights to the fullest extent permitted by law)"* and *"Working Title Deleted"* from *Fidelity* (Lovely Music VR 1722) NMDS. Kuivila is on the fringe between music and noise. These two works explore an area where synthesized sound takes on almost vocal qualities. The "Frames" section of "TI Intends . . ." (an incomplete work so far) uses a speech synthesizer to produce drifting, unearthly

sounds, in marked contrast to the noisy, industrial *musique concrète* of the album's other works.

PAUL LANSKY
- *Six Fantasies on a Poem by Thomas Campion* (CRI 456) NMDS, CRI. An extraordinary and often lyrical work. A vocalist reads a Campion poem six times; the voice generates a sine-wave accompaniment in one section, in another the computer alters the tone and the timbre of the voice, in a third the voice is split up and provides its own ghostly accompaniment, etc.

DANIEL LENTZ
- *"You Can't See the Forest . . . Music"* from *Cold Blue Sampler* (Cold Blue L10) NMDS
- *After Images* (Cold Blue E4) NMDS
- *Missa Umbrarum* (New Albion 006) NMDS
First using a cascading echo system and now employing electronic delay devices, Lentz builds up music that usually deals with ways of combining words, phonemes, and their accompanying notes. *After Images* is lyrical music in the style of Harold Budd or Eugene Bowen. Unfortunately, the texts tend to be terrifically vapid, and since Lentz's music follows the text very closely, what sounds sweet at first is syrupy and saccharine by the end. *Missa Umbrarum,* on the other hand, is a work of considerable power and dramatic intensity. The Latin text of the Mass is broken down and built up in a kaleidoscopic fashion. The result is a hazy, shadowy vision of the Mass, with accompaniment of struck or rubbed wineglasses.
- *On the Leopard Altar* (Icon 5502) NMDS
- *Point Conception* (Cold Blue E11) NMDS
See Chapter 4.

ALVIN LUCIER
- *Music on a Long Thin Wire* (Lovely 1011/12) NMDS. In which an eighty-foot wire is driven by an oscillator, producing gradual, but not imperceptible, changes in timbre, volume, and color.
- *I Am Sitting in a Room* (Lovely 1013) NMDS. Lucier's voice is rerecorded until it breaks down into the harmonics of the room. Side two, when the process is well underway, is an exceptional experience.
- *Music for Solo Performer* (Lovely 1014) NMDS. The brain wave's connected to the amplifier. The amplifier's connected to the speaker cone. The speaker cone's connected to the percussion set . . . . Lucier's side of the record is quite cerebral; Pauline Oliveros's performance is more active, almost violent.
- *Still and Moving Lines of Silence in Families of Hyperbolae* (Lovely 1015) NMDS. Closely related to *Spinning*. A study in acoustical "beating," using one voice and three winds. Another instance where the idea is more intriguing than the music.

TOM MCVEETY

- *Electric Cello* (private cassette—Lynne Edelson, GPO 7060, New York, NY 10116; 212-243-0807). Using a six-string solid-body cello that he designed, McVeety creates a beautiful tapestry of sounds—spacey and exotic, spiced with an occasional bit of chromaticism. See Chapter 10, page 232.

D. L. MYERS

- *Electronic Guitar* (Presence Sound Productions, 228 Bleecker Street, New York, NY 10014). A 1985 cassette recording of Frippertronics. Some heavy industrial sounds on a few works show a side of this guitar system that's not often heard. Also, a lot of smoothly flowing ambient music.

MICHAEL PETERS

- *Sirius Sector* (Michael Peters, Am Wiesenplatz 3, 5067 Kürten-Eichhof, West Germany). Though not originally intended for professional or public release, this offbeat Fripp-and-Eno-style delay music for guitar and the old mellotron is good, moody material. Peters is part of Camera Obscura (see Chapter 1).

CLEVE POZAR

- *Solo Percussion* (CSP 125) NMDS. Well, not quite solo. Pozar uses Echoplex and other delay devices, including tape, to create a wide assortment of moods. "Changes" and "Cosmic Piece" are quite good; the rest are interesting or irritating—sometimes both.

STEVE REICH

- *"Come Out"* from *New Sounds in Electronic Music* (CBS Odyssey 32-16-0160) (O.P.)
- *"Violin Phase"* and *"It's Gonna Rain"* from *Live/Electronic Music* (Col. MS 7265) (O.P.) See Chapter 4.

TERRY RILEY

- *Poppy Nogood and His Phantom Band/A Rainbow in Curved Air* (Col. MS 7315)
- *Persian Surgery Dervishes* (Shandar 83.501/502) And others. See Chapter 4.

DAVID ROSENBOOM

- *Brainwave Music* (ARC, ST 1002). Fascinating. Unless you spend your free time devising artificial intelligence systems, though, give the liner notes up as a bad job. (O.P.)

REMKO SCHA

- *Machine Guitars* (Kremlin KR-006). Using one or two electric guitars and sabre saws, Scha has developed a process that makes sound without any human control or interference. And there's the problem: some fascinating sonorities, but no real music. Each piece simply presents a different

sound for a few minutes and then ends. The exception is "Stroke," where one vibrating bar across two guitars produces a cascade of delicate harmonics that keeps changing in the background.

KARLHEINZ STOCKHAUSEN

- *Gesang der Jünglinge, Kontakte* (DG DG 138 811). Two of the earliest works to bridge the gap between *musique concrète* and electronic music. Both are seminal works, and *Gesang der Jünglinge* has aged well.
- *Hymnen: Anthems for Electronic and Concrete Sounds* (DG DG 2707 039). A later work, not process music in a strict sense, but one that carries on the tradition of *Gesang der Jünglinge* and *Kontakte.*

CARL STONE

- *Woo Lae Oak* (Wizard 224) NMDS. Part of a set of works by this California broadcaster whose titles are the names of favorite Oriental restaurants. This is the only one recorded so far, and it features the most basic of instrumental noises: blowing over a bottle, and a vibrating string. Through various studio techniques and the use of tape processes he creates a work that spans dozens of moods. It demands some patience, but is well worth the effort.
- *Shibucho* (Electro-Acoustic Music, Inc., PO Box 38176, Los Angeles, CA 90038). Using a digital audio processor, Stone creates an intriguing work using excerpts from such 60s Motown hits as "My Girl," "Just My Imagination," and others. Clever, witty, and daring, this exercise in musical cubism walks a tightrope between irritating and brilliant.
- *Tellus, Vol. 9: "Music With Memory"* NMDS. This edition of *Tellus*, the audio-cassette magazine, is devoted to process music, especially various applications of microcomputers and computer storing. Nicolas Collins, Ron Kuivila, Paul DeMarinis, Brenda Hutchinson, and John Driscoll contribute; pieces range from random-sounding bleeps and burps to outright danceable rock.

JAMES TENNEY

- *Saxony* (CRI SD-528) NMDS, CRI. David Mott plays a solo sax with a cumulative delay system that rapidly turns the sax into something that could pass for the world's most beautiful synthesizer program. The music is based on the harmonic series (see pages 225–228).

DAVID TUDOR

- *Pulsers/Untitled* (Lovely 1601) NMDS. Tudor has been John Cage's right-hand man since the 50s, and is an important composer in his own right. Multiple feedback loops, phase-shifting amplifiers, and random selection: Once again, the processes and the actions by which the music is created are more interesting than the result.

4
MEET THE MINIMALISTS

One of the most exciting things you could do is to discover the art of your own time.
Philip Glass

If that's art, I'm a Hottentot!
Harry S. Truman

From Beethoven's *Eroica* to Schoenberg's *Pierrot Lunaire,* from Elvis Presley's gyrating pelvis to the antics of Johnny Rotten and The Sex Pistols, music has never lacked for controversy. Perhaps the most heated musical debate of the last twenty years revolves around a group of composers known, for better or worse, as the "Minimalists."

There's probably as much debate over the term *Minimalism* itself as there is over the music it purportedly describes. I should make it clear at once that the words *Minimalism* and *Minimalist* are used throughout this chapter purely for convenience's sake. I don't believe the term is an accurate one, but it is unfortunately one that both listeners and composers have to live with. So before we begin to discuss the musicians themselves, let's first take a look at the label.

Despite its pejorative connotations, the category Minimalism actually originated in the 1960s in circles in which the repetitive, pattern-oriented music of La Monte Young, Terry Riley, Steve Reich, and Philip Glass was appreciated.* While to some of its early audience Minimalism implied minimal creativity, minimal talent, its supporters believed the term somehow legitimized this back-to-the-basics style by linking it with the Minimalist movement in the visual-art world, likewise centered in New York during that era.

Some listeners took the word Minimalism at face value, as an accurate characterization of music built up from limited means. They welcomed the stripped-down

---

*Steve Reich attributes the label to British composer/author Michael Nyman. Philip Glass claims that Tom Johnson is the culprit. Johnson, himself a composer *(Nine Bells, An Hour for Piano),* was for many years a respected music critic for *The Village Voice.* "He's the one who coined that word; and I'll never forgive him for it," Glass says with a wry grin. "Then, just before leaving the *Voice,* he wrote another piece saying he was wrong—it was never Minimalism to begin with."

musical approach, shorn of the intellectual pretensions of the classical avant-garde. Minimalism was probably as good a way as any to describe early works like Riley's *In C* or Steve Reich's *It's Gonna Rain* (1965). *In C* took the principles of the tape processes Riley had worked with in the early 60s (see Chapter 3) and applied them to instruments in an actual performance. "I was really trying to make *Music for the Gift* in a live form," he explains. "I was playing piano in a bar in San Francisco for a living at that time, but I kept working on the idea. I was riding the bus to work one night, and really, just in a flash, the idea for *In C*—the sounds, the motifs, everything—hit me on the bus." Each member of a group of musicians is presented with fifty-three short, numbered fragments to be played in numerical order; but each figure may be repeated for a different period of time, at the discretion of the individual musicians. Once all the players have played all the fragments at least once, the piece ends. Any combination of instruments can be used, and performances may vary widely in duration; but the work always includes the same patterns. And it's always quite repetitive.

Reich's early work grows out of the same experiments with tape loops and phase shifting that led to *In C*. His tape pieces, as we saw earlier, transform speech into music or, at least, into something musical. Reich also applied these techniques to early instrumental works; in fact, the effects possible with phase shifting have been the source of much of his music over the years: the out-of-phase pianos in *Piano Phase* (1967) led to the sudden shifts in rhythmic position in *Six Pianos* (1973), which in turn reappears in such later works as *Sextet* (1985).

If the label "Minimalism" was appropriate for works like *In C* and *It's Gonna Rain,* it became less so when this music began to grow in complexity. Nevertheless, the term persists even today, and continues to plague any composer who uses additive or cyclic structures in his or her work. John Adams, Daniel Lentz, David Borden, and many others have absorbed some influence from the early Minimalists, and consequently often find themselves included in this involuntary composers' club.

"Everybody seems to need categories," asserts Daniel Lentz. "If you're used to listening to Lawrence Welk and think he has a fast beat, you're going to make that reference when you hear music with a pulse or fast beats, because that's the only reference point you have. But if you're used to the pulse of the contemporary Minimalists then you're going to refer to that."

"One of the worst things about the term," according to Philip Glass, "is that it poorly describes what you're going to hear . . . Once I began working on large-scale music/theater pieces with *Einstein on the Beach* in 1976, it was pretty much the end of that period for me. I just don't think the aesthetic of Minimalism and the demands of music/theater go together very well." Nevertheless, Glass's music has that signal pulse, and since his name is attached to it, the average concertgoer regards it as Minimalism, whether Glass intended it that way or not.

To take a more extreme but illustrative example, let's look at that classical warhorse, Ravel's *Bolero.* If that's not "Minimal," what is? No development, no counterpoint—just a theme repeated over and over, in unvarying rhythm, without even a key change until the very end. "Orchestral tissue paper," Ravel himself called it. But try calling it Minimalism in polite company and watch the reaction.

Despite the fact that Philip Glass, Terry Riley, La Monte Young, and Steve Reich recently have been trying to distance themselves from this confining classification, that they were initially lumped together is perhaps understandable since there are undeniable similarities in their careers.

Because they are almost exact contemporaries—less than two years separate the oldest of the four (Riley, born in June, 1935) from the youngest (Glass, born in January, 1937)—these composers' musical training came at a time when atonal, cerebral, avant-garde styles of music were beginning to dominate the academic field. All four studied in America's most illustrious music schools, eventually deciding that the avant-garde was, for them at least, a musical dead end. Each then returned to the most basic elements of music and evolved a tonally based style of often deceptive simplicity.

All four have also explored different forms of non-Western music: Riley, Young, and Glass have made extensive studies of the classical tradition of north India; Reich has found inspiration in West African drumming, Indonesian gamelan music, and traditional Hebrew cantillation (chanting).

And a final, important similarity: Each took it upon himself to become the main performer of his own music. Glass and Reich went the route of jazz and pop musicians, putting together their own ensembles and taking them on the road. That ground-breaking practice has created many new opportunities for younger artists. By the time the next generation of composers began to appear in the 1970s, the concert halls had opened up, however reluctantly, to Minimalist works. John Adams, for example, has had his music played by major symphony orchestras, chamber groups, and the like.

The evolution of Minimalism from a cult style, heard primarily in New York's seedy lofts and San Francisco's small galleries, to a tolerated (if not always respected) part of mainstream twentieth-century music has not been easy. Tracing the origins of the style and its subsequent growth is no easy task, either. The first problem is in deciding precisely where Minimalism actually began. Terry Riley's *In C?* La Monte Young's *Trio for Strings?* There are well-reasoned arguments supporting each piece's claim. But I would nominate an even earlier work: The first Minimalist piece, and arguably the most "Minimal" work ever created, is the 1952 composition *4'33",* by John Cage. *4'33"* calls for any instrument or combination of instruments, and lasts for four minutes and thirty-three seconds. During that time, the performer makes no sound.

The use of silence and the participation of an audience during a performance have always been foremost concerns in Cage's iconoclastic view of music. Indeed, without an audience, *4'33"* cannot exist: The "music" of the piece consists of the audience's reaction, which may range from baffled whispering to angry catcalls. Of course, *4'33"* is not music, at least not in the conventional sense. But by introducing people to silence as an important part of music (and by doing it in so uncompromising a fashion), Cage paved the way for La Monte Young's *Trio for Strings,* which appeared six years later.

Stylistically, Young has been the most consistent of the four original Minimalists. His explorations of tuning and the various ways of perceiving simple harmonies were an important element of the early Minimalism of the 60s. (Echoes of Young's work, either direct or indirect, can still be heard in the music of Yoshi Wada, Phill Niblock, and the Harmonic Choir, among others.) While expressing some reservations about the term, he acknowledges his own continuous relationship with (and responsibility for) the Minimalist style: "There are certainly Minimalist elements in my music. I founded the movement with such early works as the *Trio for Strings,* written in 1958 and composed entirely of long sustained tones and silences. But the complete scope of my music is very broad; it includes many types of work."

The influence of John Cage continued to be felt, and even more strongly, in some of Young's later pieces, and it was in fact Cage and his long-time collaborator David Tudor who first introduced Young's music in New York and Europe. His *Composition 1960 #2* consisted of building a fire in front of an audience. The written score for *Piano Piece for David Tudor #1* (1960) reads, "Bring a bale of hay and a bucket of water onto the stage for the piano to eat and drink. The performer may then feed the piano or leave it to eat by itself. The piece is over after the piano has been fed, or after the piano eats or decides not to." Cage once said that everything we do is music, and everywhere is the best seat. By this singularly bizarre definition, Young's early performance pieces are indeed music.

More accessible are *The Second Dream of the High-Tension Line Stepdown Transformer* (1962) for two violins and optional other instruments, and *The Overday* (1963) for sopranino sax, drones, and hand drums. The "minimal" elements present in the earlier *Trio for Strings* are developed more fully in these works. At this point, drones, whether electronically or acoustically produced, begin to figure prominently in Young's compositions, as does repetition, though not in the insistent, rhythmic fashion that other composers would later use.

The year 1964 was a critical one in the development of all four of the original Minimalists. La Monte Young began work on his two most important works: *The Tortoise, His Dreams and Journeys,* which eventually became the musical subject matter of his "Dream House" music-and-light installation series; and his magnum opus, *The Well-Tuned Piano,* which would occupy much of his creative energy right up to the present. Terry Riley composed *In C* and had it performed in San Francisco, making it the first publicly performed work to employ the repeated patterns that would come to characterize Minimalism. Among the performers who took part in the premiere of *In C* were composer/accordionist Pauline Oliveros; reed player and composer Jon Gibson (who later became part of the Philip Glass Ensemble), and Steve Reich. "I met Terry in 1964," Reich recalls. "Believe it or not, I had an improvisation ensemble at the time, and I offered to help him put this piece on with some members of the group. The work made an enormous impression on me." Reich and Gibson subsequently formed an ensemble together, and by 1967 they were performing seminal works in the Minimalist style in the art galleries of New York.

In 1964 Philip Glass found himself in Paris on a two-year Fulbright Scholarship to study with Nadia Boulanger, who had taught several generations of American classical composers, including some of America's most distinguished musical figures: Aaron Copland, Virgil Thomson, Elliott Carter, and Walter Piston, to name just a few. Despite the scholarship, Glass had found that he still needed to support himself, and in the course of doing so met up with an unusual musical influence: Indian sitarist Ravi Shankar. "To earn money," says Shankar, "he [Glass] used to play session music wherever he could. It happened that I was recording music for the film *Chappaqua* at that time, and he came in as a session artist." Glass still claims that Shankar and his accompanist, tabla player Alla Rakha, were the formative influences on his art. While working on the written notation of Shankar's music, Glass became absorbed in the structure of Indian ragas and talas, the cyclic rhythm patterns of north Indian music. "In a period of six or seven sessions, I told him as much as I could," Shankar says, "and I'm very happy—and amazed at the same time, because he has become almost a superstar—that he does still acknowledge that."

Many of the Minimalist pieces of those early years are built around repeating fragments that change in very slow, subtle fashion. One point of these repetitive works was to draw out the process of musical change to such an extent that the listener could practically "see" as well as hear the process taking place. Unlike the arcane structural methods used by serial composers, Minimalist procedures strove for simplicity and clarity. Simplicity they achieved; clarity proved to be more of a problem. The first Minimalist works demanded a large amount of patience and perseverance from the audience, for, like process music, these lengthy compositions required almost heroic feats of listener concentration. And some Minimalist works are lengthy indeed. Philip Glass's *Music with Changing Parts* is over an hour long; La Monte Young's *Well-Tuned Piano* once clocked in at just over five hours.

The Minimalists might have become the lunatic fringe of modern music had they continued down such an inaccessible path, but fortunately the following years saw a great deal of growth and development in the form. When, by the mid-1970s, Glass and Reich were able to attract a good number of young fans to their concerts, the musical establishment began to launch a barrage of hysterical invective against them, and the Minimalists, Glass and Reich in particular, became a *cause célèbre*. "If anything, the publicly negative criticism allowed our work to be controversial way beyond its time," Glass maintains. "If the people who had hated the music had simply ignored it, they might have achieved more of their goals."

Rock clubs and other unusual venues, generally in the crumbling lower reaches of Manhattan, seemed to be the most likely places to hear music by the fledgling Philip Glass Ensemble during these years. New York music critics seized the opportunity to draw battlelines between the so-called "uptown" and "downtown" styles: the former was the product of some of America's most respected, established composers (Milton Babbitt, Elliott Carter, and the Columbia–Princeton Electronic Music Center); the latter referred to the upstart Minimalists. The Minimalists broke all the rules. They used cheap-sounding electric organs; they amplified the sounds of wind instruments and voices; they employed strong, pulsing rhythms; and horror of horrors, they wrote *tunes.*

Although antagonism between younger composers and the musical establishment is almost a time-honored ritual in the history of music, the level of polemics reached during the 70s was extraordinary. "There was a review in a St. Louis newspaper in 1972," Glass recollects, "and the headline read 'Glass Invents New Sonic Torture.' " Glass especially seems to have taken a large number of pot shots from enraged critics; but it's the sort of reaction a composer has to learn to live with. "I don't think it's a personal thing—I don't think they're mad at *me.* They're mad at what the music represents." The popularity of the so-called Minimalists, with their "artistically trivial" music, was perceived as a slap in the face by some supporters of the academic community. Glass adds, "I never asked their permission to be a successful composer; there's a certain amount of posturing and power-playing involved. Clearly, they see themselves at the barricades of Culture, beating back the barbarians. I happen to be the barbarian."

Minimalism was not, despite the many composers living there, strictly an East Coast phenomenon. Simon Jeffes, now the leader of England's Penguin Cafe Orchestra, found himself in a situation not unlike that of his American counterparts while studying with the European avant-garde in the late 60s. "It became too complex and difficult," he says, "so I started looking elsewhere." Like the Minimalists in the States, Jeffes turned to ethnic music. "I found I was responding more to a mbira player from Zimbabwe than to avant-garde figures like Stockhausen."

Meanwhile, on America's West Coast, Daniel Lentz and Harold Budd were moving in a similar direction. "I was doing very eccentric kinds of activities," says Lentz.* "Doing bizarre pieces from airplanes, and so on. Harold [Budd] had been doing something similar, though at the time [1970] he was much closer to La Monte Young—long, sustained sounds on a particular chord or one interval. I felt I had to change, so I wrote *Canon and Fugue,* which was very pretty, with long sustained melodies, and just came out of nowhere in a way." Budd, Eugene Bowen, and Ingram Marshall likewise began writing tonal, melodic music in California around that time, but of the four, only Lentz became generally associated with Minimalism.

Any doubts about the seriousness of the Minimalist trend were shattered with the 1976 productions of *Einstein on the Beach,* a landmark Minimalist "opera" (without conventional plot, arias, or scenes) by Philip Glass and dramatist Robert Wilson. After a debut at the Avignon Festival in July, the opera toured Europe, and in November received its American premiere at New York's Metropolitan Opera House. Could a five-hour, intermissionless work from a downtown composer succeed in such a decidedly uptown venue? Incredibly, it did. Both performances were completely sold out. Critical response, however, was split down the middle: Some hailed it as the musical event of the decade; others were dismissive of what they considered a formless, ill-conceived, and pretentious evening of irritating music. *"Einstein* was a much more controversial piece than people seem to remember now," Glass says. "It was a work that made people take a stance one way or another."

Composer Laurie Anderson recalls going to the Met to see *Einstein* "with a lot of other downtown people; and a lot of the thrill was in thinking, at last! People up here are getting what we're doing downtown! And of course, they didn't really."

If *Einstein* didn't put money in Philip Glass's pocket,† it did put the composer, and Minimalism, permanently on the musical map. *"Einstein on the Beach* left a real

---

*This is in fact quite an understatement. One of Lentz's more startling pieces was a 1969 "Sonata" called *Love and Conception,* in which a young man and woman, both naked, are instructed to crawl under the lid of a grand piano and simulate sexual intercourse. According to the *Baker's Biographical Dictionary of Music and Musicians,* the piece was actually "performed" at the University of California in Santa Barbara, but as a result, Lentz was fired from his teaching job there.

†The vagaries of American opera houses are such that, according to Glass, they are in effect built to lose money. And since Glass and Wilson didn't have an opera company, they had to absorb a $10,000 *loss* for each of the sold-out evenings. When the Met asked them to do a third performance, they were forced to refuse; they simply could not afford another.

mark on the art world," says Anderson. "Everyone I saw after that was working on an opera. You'd walk down the street—'Hey, how's your opera?' 'Fine, how's yours?'" Even composers and musicians who had previously disliked Minimalism were forced to re-examine their opinions. Flutist Ransom Wilson, a Jean-Pierre Rampal protégé and one of the most popular flutists on the classical concert circuit, remembered his reactions swinging from one extreme to the other during the performance.

"At first, I couldn't believe it. I felt I had been taken in by some musical practical joke; it was like listening to an orchestra imitating a broken needle. I considered walking out, but there were no intermissions and I decided to sit it out a while longer. And about an hour or so into the piece—I don't recall exactly when—an amazing thing happened. I suddenly found I was being caught up and carried away by the music. It had a hypnotic effect, and whenever it changed, you could almost *feel* it, physically. It was a tremendous experience." Wilson has since become an active and vocal supporter of the music of Steve Reich, Philip Glass, and John Adams.

Since *Einstein,* music with interlocking instrumental patterns, pulsating rhythms, and recognizable melodies has become one of today's most often heard styles. In the late 70s and early 80s, large numbers of young composers began to compose, perform, and record music directly influenced by Glass, Reich, Riley, and Young. To be called a Minimalist was suddenly an advantage. The Philip Glass Ensemble filled Carnegie Hall while Steve Reich received commissions from the San Francisco Symphony and Radio Frankfurt. La Monte Young held a ten-year commission from the Dia Art Foundation that allowed him to create his "Dream House," a continuous light-and-sound environment, in a six-story building in lower Manhattan. John Adams began to make a name for himself on the West Coast with works like *Shaker Loops,* a pattern-based piece for string septet, which, in a later arrangement for string orchestra, was recorded by the San Francisco Symphony.

Tortuous though its development has been, Minimalism has by now entered the working vocabulary of composers in almost every branch of music. Saxophonist John Surman and cellist David Darling, who are often associated with "new jazz," have both used some features of Minimalism, especially repetitive patterns of notes, in their music. Brian Eno has acknowledged the influence of La Monte Young; Bernard Xolotl, as we saw in Chapter 1, was strongly influenced by Terry Riley. Rock star David Bowie has written several songs whose inspiration he attributes to Philip Glass's music. George Winston, known primarily for his lyrical, almost Impressionistic piano solos, incorporates a number of interlocking rhythms, à la Steve Reich, into his concert performances and informs his audience that Reich's music has had a great influence on his own. Even Lukas Foss, a well-known conductor and composer of both traditional and aleatoric music, employs Minimalist elements in his 1981 piece, *Solo Observed.*

The extreme reactions of the press and public to Minimalism served a useful purpose: It brought this style—if indeed it ever was a coherent "style"—to the attention of a lot of people who otherwise might not have been exposed to new music. But regrettably, the sharp division between the two sides of the debate remains. One hundred years from now, this uptown/downtown controversy may seem as unnecessary as the nineteenth century's Brahms/Wagner debate. "The animosity is unfortunate," says La Monte Young. "I don't think it has to be, nor should it be, since I see myself coming out of the Webern tradition." Although he died in 1945, Austrian composer Anton Webern is considered by many to be the most influential composer of postwar serialism, and, indeed, of an entire generation of postwar music. "I became absorbed with Webern; I felt he was the epitome of clarity. I see Minimal aspects in many parameters of Webern's music—in the sparse textures, the short orchestral pieces, the static characteristics. Webern's work in general leads to the static quality of my *Trio for Strings*. That's one of the lines of origination of Minimalism."

Young's *Trio for Strings* is organized in strict serial fashion; Karlheinz Stockhausen, the dean of the European avant-garde, has in turn used some techniques in his works *Aus dem Sieben Tagen* and *Stimmung* (both 1968) that derive from La Monte Young's work with voice-and-drone combinations. Cross-fertilization like this has been important throughout musical history; perhaps we do contemporary composers a disservice with such terms as "uptown," "downtown," "reactionary," and "avant-garde."

When viewed with the benefit of hindsight, musical styles tend to follow much the same course. Some works will be produced that are absolute rubbish, a large group of pieces will range from mediocre to somewhat interesting, and a small body of works of real value will endure. Such will undoubtedly turn out to be the case with both the complex styles of academia *and* Minimalism.

Now that we've traced, however briefly, the development of Minimalism, let's look at the composers themselves. Because of publicly perceived similarities in approach or temperament, one often sees Young and Riley discussed together; Glass and Reich are usually paired as well. It's a useful convention that we'll follow here.

La Monte Young and Terry Riley

A number of unfortunate rifts have appeared among the four original Minimalists —the result, perhaps, of the pressures of their individually burgeoning careers. In the late 60s, Philip Glass and Steve Reich were not only friends but close collaborators; now they give widely different accounts of that period and have little to do with each other. Glass and Young also don't see eye to eye. Young claims to have influenced Glass, while Glass points out that when Minimalism was just beginning to make its presence felt with *The Tortoise, His Dreams and Journeys* and *In C,* he was in Paris working with Ravi Shankar. La Monte counters by maintaining that even if his influence on Philip wasn't direct, he had still so charged the musical atmosphere of the time that the influence came from second-generation sources, specifically Riley and Reich. And so forth. Even the Borgias look like a happy family by comparison.

La Monte Young and Terry Riley, though, have kept up a close relationship over the years. They first met in 1959 while students at Berkeley. There Riley heard

Young's *Trio for Strings,* which impressed him deeply; in fact, Terry acknowledges
La Monte's work as his primary musical influence. Young had studied briefly with
Stockhausen in Darmstadt, where he became interested in the music of John Cage.
On returning to California, he involved Riley in Cage's music as well. Cage's
strangely skewed musical vision had a strong effect on some of their early pieces.
The two often performed together, using "friction sounds" in place of more traditional instruments. Young's *Poem for Chairs, Tables, Benches, etc.* (1960) consisted
of the sounds of those objects being scraped across the floor. Terry Riley wrote a
similar piece in which he and La Monte produced friction sounds on various parts
of a piano.

By 1960, Young had moved to New York, where he organized and directed a
historic series of concerts in the loft of Yoko Ono who, in those pre-Lennon days,
was part of the artistic ferment in downtown Manhattan. These events, and Young's
An Anthology (a collection of extreme avant-garde works including Young's own
1960 compositions), became associated with the Fluxus movement. Fluxus, a group
that often stretched the definition of "art" or "music" to the breaking point, attracted some of the city's most unusual artists, including Yoko Ono and Nam June
Paik, the Korean-born composer who was already notorious for a "composition"
that consisted of "cutting off John Cage's necktie, and shampooing him without
advance warning." Paik (who, when he wasn't grooming John Cage, was also a
pianist), vocalist Simone Forti, pianist Robert ("Blue" Gene Tyranny) Sheff, and
Fluxus's founder George Maciunas performed Young's earliest conceptual pieces in
New York and Europe.

In 1962, Young formed his own performing group, the Theatre of Eternal
Music. The group originally included violinist and bowed-guitarist Tony Conrad,
violist John Cale, percussionist Angus MacLise, and vocalist Marian Zazeela. Cale
and MacLise soon went on to form the seminal rock band The Velvet Underground,
which would unleash both John Cale *and* Lou Reed on an unsuspecting public; Cale,
however, continued to perform with Young into the mid-60s. As for Marian Zazeela,
she and La Monte Young were married in 1963, and they've continued to collaborate
closely on all of his subsequent projects, for which she also creates the visual and
light environments.

In the early 60s Terry Riley began his work with the ORTF studios in Paris;
by 1966 he was also performing with the Theatre of Eternal Music. Inspired by
Young's early saxophone playing, Riley took up that instrument for a while too.
Both composers were interested in jazz, especially the music of John Coltrane and
Eric Dolphy. They experimented with melodies consisting of quick series of notes
played in four- or five-second bursts over sustained drones. The sound of a rapid-fire
sax was bound to remind listeners of contemporary jazz, but the music's modal
quality also strongly suggested the music of India. "Playing with La Monte and the
Theatre of Eternal Music, I felt I was doing the kind of music that is very similar
to what Indian musicians do," says Riley. "There's something in the spirit of that
music that is very mystical. It's not 'entertaining' music. It goes inside and gets
deeply into the tones. My association with him really brought out this mystical
quality."

Terry Riley's ground-breaking work was, of course, 1964's *In C.* This was a harmonically static piece, to be sure, but while La Monte Young used electronic drones to provide the stasis in his music, Riley created a kind of musical pointillism. "The work," Riley explains, "uses C as a base, and the notes which are outside the mode, for instance, the F-sharp, still are really coming out of that C-major tonality. I called it *In C* because I wanted a powerful, high-energy title. And it seemed to fit, instead of trying to call it 'Dewdrops in the Sun' or something." The *texture* of *In C* derived from Riley's tape works, but the *mood* was trancelike, and in an unusual way, still mystical. For all its busy sounds, *In C* never "goes anywhere."

In 1964 La Monte Young also began two major works. One was *The Well-Tuned Piano.* The other was *The Tortoise, His Dreams and Journeys.* The latter was a huge, unfolding composition; not only were new sections periodically added on, but the continuous electronic drones that ran through all of *The Tortoise* were intended to be permanently installed in a room or space (the "Dream House") along with a slowly changing light environment designed by Marian Zazeela, which Young's group(s) of musicians would occasionally enter to perform. When the musicians left, after up to eight hours of performance, the piece would continue as long as the drones were hooked up—theoretically forever. The drones were actually installed at various lofts, galleries, and museums in New York and Europe, usually for several days at a time, though some installations lasted for weeks and one, at 6 Harrison Street in New York, ran from 1979 to 1985. The music itself consisted of long, sustained chords with Indian-sounding vocals done by Young and Zazeela; several instrumental drones were added to the electronic ones to accentuate the rich acoustic and harmonic effects. John Cale and Tony Conrad were frequent performers; Terry Riley, trumpeter Jon Hassell, sometime violist David Rosenboom, trombonist Garrett List, and reed player Jon Gibson (who has the unique distinction of having played with all four of the original Minimalists) have also performed parts of *The Tortoise.*

The first part of *The Tortoise, His Dreams and Journeys* was performed in October of 1964, and was entitled *The Tortoise Droning Selected Pitches from the Holy Numbers for the Two Black Tigers, the Green Tiger and the Hermit.* One year later, Young introduced *The Ballad of the Tortoise or Pierced Earrings/Drone Ratios Transmitting the Manifestations of the Tortoise Center Drifting Obsidian Time Mists through the Synaptic Stepdown Barrier.* But the main section of *The Tortoise* produced so far is a piece begun in 1966 and lasting well into the 70s. It is entitled simply *Map of 49's Dream the Two Systems of Eleven Sets of Galactic Intervals Ornamental Lightyears Tracery.* ("49" referred to a pet turtle.) The work was introduced to the public as a "Dream House: a continuous frequency environment in sound and light with singing (and other instruments) from time to time."

The basis for *The Tortoise,* as well as for Young's *Well-Tuned Piano* and for much of Terry Riley's recent music, is the study of natural frequencies and tone relationships. Indeed, without the tuning system known as "just intonation," their work would not be possible, at least not in its present form. Western music is founded on the tuning system known as "equal temperament," which artificially forces notes away from where they naturally occur. In equal temperament, B-flat and A-sharp, for example, become the same note, represented by the same key on a piano, or the same fret on a guitar. Just intonation leaves the tones in their natural state as two separate and distinct sounds.

Every musical note actually consists of a series of vibrations, called the "harmonic series," which we hear in combination, not individually. But just intonation will, under proper conditions, enable some of the normally inaudible components, known as overtones or harmonics, to be heard. (For a further discussion of this concept, see pages 225–228.) These audible harmonics are a fundamental element of Young's and Riley's music.

In *The Well-Tuned Piano*, Young's master work, a piano (which is by design an equal-tempered instrument) is carefully retuned, and placed in a complete environment of humidity, temperature, etc., necessary to keep it precisely on pitch. Because of the tuning, the piano produces some unaccustomed music in the piece. The natural harmonics of each note are reinforced, resulting in what Young terms "clouds."

" 'Clouds' are when I set up a very strong acoustical array of harmonics that fill the air in such a way that it sounds as though there's a cloud." But these aren't the only acoustical oddities produced: "If you play two tones that are closer together than a half step (C to C-sharp, for example, is a half step), you produce a phenomenon known as 'beating.' When you have an array of harmonics, many of them happen to be very close to each other. As a result, you get interesting 'beat patterns' in these clouds; and when I play the rhythms, I synchronize them to some of these beat patterns. That sets up a series of resonances where everything is reinforcing everything else."

A performance of *The Well-Tuned Piano* can range from its shortest version —"I had the flu in Rome and could only play for three hours [!]" says Young—to its longest, just over five hours. Like Indian raga, *The Well-Tuned Piano* is almost a living thing—it grows and changes with each performance, according to how Young puts the individual pieces together and which ones he chooses to elaborate.

Obviously, a lot of careful research into the acoustical and scientific properties of music underlies La Monte Young's work. But out of this scientific grounding emerges what is essentially a mystical style, and words like "hypnotic" and "trance music" appear frequently when his music is discussed. Once the listener gets past the fact that *The Well-Tuned Piano* actually sounds *out* of tune, because of the just intonation, it becomes easy to enjoy the sonic bath that Young produces. Its daunting length, however, means that the piece is not for everybody. That, combined with Young's absolutely uncompromising way of dealing with record companies, kept *The Well-Tuned Piano* from being recorded for over twenty years.

As the 60s progressed, Terry Riley found himself the most visible of the Minimalists, mainly because a farsighted producer at CBS—none other than David Behrman, as it happens—gave him a recording contract. Behrman also attempted to record La Monte Young and Marian Zazeela singing into the surf of the Atlantic Ocean. After Young determined the fundamental pitch of the surf, he had Zazeela sing a drone on that pitch while he then sang some of the thematic material from "Dream House" over the drone. "David was very happy with the singing," Young recalls. "He said, 'This is the definitive La Monte Young.' But the surf was really bad; it was windy and choppy." CBS decided the project had already been too expensive to rerecord and proposed instead to edit in a new surf track. Young, however, insisted on a live, "real-time" recording, and when the two sides couldn't come to terms the album was never made.

Terry Riley, on the other hand, has recorded throughout his career. His early recordings for CBS put him at the forefront of mainstream Minimalism, and made him one of the most influential composers of the late 60s. *In C* was released in 1968, followed by *Poppy Nogood and His Phantom Band* (1968) and *Rainbow in Curved Air* (1969). The latter, in particular, is a classic example of early Minimalism. *Rainbow* is scored for electric keyboards, layered on top of one another; one provides a sort of drone, while the others improvise in modal patterns reminiscent of north Indian music. But while Young's music was performed in "real time," Riley began experimenting with "time-lag" and feedback systems, so that Poppy Nogood's "Phantom Band" actually consists of the various layers of Riley's own music. He also began to work with keyboard instruments tuned in just intonation. By using a Yamaha electronic organ and employing his tape/feedback devices, Riley produced a highly original and instantly identifiable sound, one he would continue to use right up to the 1980s.

In 1970, both Young and Riley met the great Indian vocalist Pandit Pran Nath, with whom they began to study Indian raga and vocal techniques. It's tempting to attribute Riley's mystical keyboard pieces of the 70s to that apprenticeship, especially the swirling textures and the almost vocal quality of the melodies in *Descending Moonshine Dervishes* (1975). But the composer points to an additional influence: "When I was living in Spain," he says, "I used to listen to the radio a lot, and I'd get the stations from Tangiers and the cities right across the Mediterranean. That's the first music that really sank in. Those *maqams,* the Middle Eastern scales, have always attracted me. Even though I'm a student of Indian classical music and that's my main love as far as ethnic music goes, when I write my own music it tends to have a Middle Eastern flavor. There's always been a kind of dream world for me there."

The effect of Riley's studies with Pandit Pran Nath is most clearly pronounced in the 1982 *Songs for the Ten Voices of the Two Prophets.* In this collection of three works, Riley abandoned the electronic organ in favor of two Prophet-V synthesizers (hence the title), and sang, using the traditional techniques of Indian raga. The synthesizers give this recording a depth and a brilliance that a single organ couldn't produce, though Riley himself has mixed feelings about them. He spent a year working on synthesizer technique, then rigged the two Prophets up like a double-manual organ. "It was a lot more awkward and a lot more knob-twiddling," he admits. "And it eventually resulted in my putting all my electronic equipment in boxes, and taking 1985 off as an acoustical year."

In 1983, Riley began working with North Indian sitar and tabla player Krishna Bhatt. Their first tour saw Riley playing synthesizer, but they soon developed a style of playing piano and sitar together, and in 1984, Riley began working with the muted piano. By using only one string for each piano key rather than the traditional three, he was able to produce strong harmonic and subtle percussive effects. The piano, of course, was tuned in just intonation and had to be amplified to make up for the reduction in volume. Riley's 1984 piano work, *The Harp of New Albion,* offers a baffling array of sounds that one normally doesn't associate with the piano. It is also structured differently—instead of cyclic forms, much of *The Harp of New Albion* is in spiral form. "Something spins off a little motif," he explains, "and gets larger and more arpeggiated, more embroidered. It cycles back to a certain note, but it's very irregular; it takes a circuitous route."

Since 1980, Riley has also been working closely with the Kronos String Quartet, an ensemble that plays everything from traditional string quartets to jazz and blues. The Kronos has performed a number of works written for them by Riley, and late in 1984 recorded several of his pieces. "My work in the 80s is taking on a new character," he says. "The quartets and the piano works both exhibit something new —I feel I'm working differently now. In some ways, I'm going back to the place I was before I started using loops and repetition."

Meanwhile, La Monte Young has remained the most elusive of the Minimalists. He continues to study with Pandit Pran Nath, but he rarely sings publicly. His music is equally difficult to find. For financial reasons he was unable to perform *The Well-Tuned Piano* publicly since between 1981 and 1987, and when the building in which the "Dream House" was installed for six years was sold in 1985, the "Dream House" itself had to be dismantled. Now, at least, *The Well-Tuned Piano* will finally be recorded, apparently in a full five-hour format. In any event, both Young and Riley have asserted their influence over a large number of composers during the past quarter century, and if Philip Glass and Steve Reich have appeared more often in print, that should in no way diminish their colleagues' stature.

Philip Glass and Steve Reich

For many years, the names Glass and Reich were inextricably linked in the musical press. To discuss one without the other was, depending on your point of view, like talking about Lennon without McCartney, Laurel without Hardy, or Scylla without Charybdis. Contrary to popular belief, however, Glass and Reich are *not* the Bobbsey twins of new music. In recent years, especially, the two have taken very different approaches in their work. Yet it is unarguable that, since the early 70s, Glass and Reich have been the most visible composers associated with the label Minimalism.

The two composers first met in 1958 while studying at New York's Juilliard School. Although they both worked with some respected teachers, it's virtually impossible to detect any influence from those early years of academic training in their subsequent music. Gradual changes in time and rhythm were characteristic of most of Reich's music in the middle to late 60s; 1964's *Music* for piano(s) and tape, *Piano Phase* (1967) for two pianos, and *Violin Phase* (1967) for violin and tape all deal with musical patterns going in and out of phase with one another. Parallels to Terry Riley's music are discernible in these early compositions, though Reich has never been interested in the Eastern-influenced exoticism that was found even then in Riley's music. While Riley used tape processes like delay and feedback as the means to an end, Reich used the manipulation of taped material as an end in itself. The exploration of the effects created when two identical lines of music are played in gradually diverging time frames even extended to works that don't use tape— *Piano Phase* uses a pair of instruments that are treated in much the same manner as one piano with a tape. If the music sounds harmonically and melodically simple, it still takes impressive concentration from the performers to play it properly.

Meanwhile, Philip Glass's career also veered off the path of academic "respectability." After working with Ravi Shankar on the *Chappaqua* score in Paris, Glass went to India in 1966 to study further with Alla Rakha. During this period Glass composed infrequently, but the repeating rhythmic cycles he was now discovering would soon become the basis for his new style. In 1967, one year after Steve Reich formed his New York group, Philip Glass began to put together his own ensemble, which gave its first concert in New York in 1968. Early Glass works like *Strung Out* (1967), for solo amplified violin, or *Piece in the Shape of a Square* (1968), for ensemble, are based on a technique completely different from that used by Reich, but the resulting music is surprisingly similar. The melodies are spare, the rhythms changing only gradually. Given their comparable styles, and the indifference they encountered in many musical circles, it was perhaps inevitable that Glass and Reich would become associated. Performances by the Philip Glass Ensemble and Steve Reich and Musicians were often poorly attended; twenty-five people was considered a successful night, Glass recalls. But the two continued to work with each other's ensembles, and in 1970 recorded Steve Reich's *Four Organs* for the French Shandar label. This was the first and only time that Glass and Reich appeared together on disc.

It's no surprise that the term *Minimalism* was affixed to the music Reich and Glass were composing as the 1970s began. It is highly repetitive, changes are stretched out over lengthy periods, and works that were designed to be simple and direct occasionally verge on the simplistic. "I don't think I could write that music today," Glass says, "but I enjoy playing it today." Glass means that seriously: The current repertoire of the Philip Glass Ensemble extends back to the 1969 work *Music in Similar Motion.* "There's no way for me to rewrite *Music in Similar Motion,*" he maintains. "It doesn't need updating. For one thing, people still like it. In a way, it crystallizes a moment in my musical career."

Steve Reich continues to perform his earlier works as well. As recently as 1985, he performed his 1968 *Pendulum Music,* in which microphones are set swinging over amplifiers. As they pass the amps, feedback results. Eventually the mikes come to rest over the amps, the feedback becomes continuous, and the piece ends. "The best way to do it is with the crummiest material," Reich quips. "That way it has a certain charm and humor. If you use good hi-fi equipment, you can actually hurt people."

After 1969, however, Glass and Reich went their separate ways. In that year, Steve Reich says, "we both did concerts at the Whitney Museum. The group was then Jon Gibson, Arthur Murphy, James Tenney, Dickie Landry, myself, and Philip Glass. In 1970, we went to Europe, and that got a bit tense—one ensemble and two composers. So the group basically split and it became clear that this was going to be difficult, but look, these things happen and it's understandable. We were working with the same concert promoters and touring the same places, after all."

The Philip Glass Ensemble recorded its first album shortly after the split— *Music with Changing Parts,* on Glass's own Chatham Square label. The record sold poorly, and Glass continued to work at odd jobs to support himself and his music. Steve Reich fared somewhat better. In 1970 he received a grant that enabled him to travel to Ghana to study West African drumming, and the following year wrote a major work based on those studies: *Drumming* calls for four pairs of tuned bongos, three marimbas, three glockenspiels, and voices. The expanding and contracting rhythmic cells in *Drumming* grow directly out of his earlier "Phase" series, but here they are fully notated in the score and are played by live musicians instead of being produced by tape processes or the "phase-shifting pulse-gate" that Reich invented and used in the late 60s.

If the tuned percussion and mallet instruments, which became an identifying trademark of Reich's music, tended to be disarmingly offbeat, Glass's instrumentation was, to many ears, just plain nasty. With an ensemble of electric keyboards, amplified voices, and amplified wind instruments, Glass seemed to be cultivating a more rock-oriented synthesis, whose dominant sound was the Farfisa organ. As a result, Glass's concerts attracted an enthusiastic younger audience. But more traditionally inclined listeners, and record companies, shied away from his music.

During the course of the 70s, both composers began moving away from the stripped-down Minimalism of their early works. Although Steve Reich still wrote pieces that employed the barest minimum of means, such as *Clapping Music* (1972) or *Music for Pieces of Wood* (1973), he also started composing for the larger ensembles that would soon occupy most of his attention. *Music for Mallet Instruments, Voices, and Organ* (1973), included with *Drumming* on a three-album Deutsche Grammophon recording, is a lush, appealing work for a group of eleven musicians. While still based on the augmentation and diminution of rhythms, it is much more melodic and almost orchestral in its rich texture.

Reich's music follows a consistent pattern of growth, from early works for limited instruments and performers, to the chamber-sized pieces of the early 70s, to the 1976 composition *Music for 18 Musicians,* which requires a far larger ensemble than any previous work by a so-called Minimalist, and ultimately to the choral and orchestral works of the 1980s. Philip Glass, in contrast, gave little indication during the early 70s of the dramatic leap in scope and substance his music would take with the 1976 productions of *Einstein on the Beach.* His compositions of this period—including *Music in Fifths* (1970), *Music for Voices* (1972), and *Music in Twelve Parts* (1974)—seemed rather to continue in the style he had developed in his earlier works.

Music in Twelve Parts is a huge piece, and in retrospect, one can detect hints of the grandeur and excitement of *Einstein* in it. But *Music in Twelve Parts* was only a qualified success; its length makes it difficult to perform, and even more difficult to record. (In fact, only parts one and two, taking up an entire album, ever appeared on disc.) In 1975, Glass released the album *North Star,* containing music he wrote for a film about sculptor Mark Di Suvero. It seemed to be an obvious retrenchment: Each part of the score was short, self-contained, and performed by a very small group of musicians. A few copies of *North Star* appeared in the rock bins at record stores, and an occasional excerpt from it even aired on the more adventurous rock radio stations.

As it turned out, though, it was *North Star* that was the anomaly, not *Music in Twelve Parts.* That Philip Glass could compose on a grand scale, and could do so with an intensity to which the shorter pieces of *North Star* didn't aspire, was demonstrated by the *Einstein on the Beach* collaboration with Robert Wilson. "The most successful collaboration of the avant-garde" is the way Laurie Anderson has described it. "The thing that's striking is the incredible speed of the music, just ripping along, and the incredible slowness of the images. That's an unbearable, wonderful tension."

Einstein was a truly dramatic work. While the music did indeed go ripping along, some passages had a slow, haunting beauty. The work was based on Glass's additive rhythms, and built around a fairly constant set of chords, but the range of tempos and dynamics far exceeded anything he had done before. The role of Albert Einstein, who in reality played the violin, was taken by a solo violinist dressed as the scientist. The character spent a fair amount of time as a spectator on the side of the stage, watching Wilson's surreal images unfolding. The singers were alternately onstage and in the pit with the instrumentalists; they sang numbers or solfège syllables (*do, re, mi,* etc.) rather than a conventional text. The instruments were basically those of the Philip Glass Ensemble: electric keyboards and amplified wind instruments. *Einstein on the Beach* was not only a radical opera, it was a radical departure for Glass, and for Minimalism.

Steve Reich's *Music for 18 Musicians* predates *Einstein* by two months, and although it is a less celebrated work it, too, represents a turning point. In 1978, when it was being recorded, Reich stated, "There is more harmonic movement in the first five minutes of *Music for 18 Musicians* than in any other complete work of mine to date." The piece is based on a cycle of eleven chords; the series is played at its beginning and end. In between are eleven sections, each built up from one of those eleven chords. *Music for 18 Musicians* is a rhythmically subtle piece; it contains echoes of Indonesian gamelans, which Reich studied in 1973 and 1974, and the twelfth-century organum, or sacred chanting, of the Notre Dame composers Leonin and Perotin.

After 1976, Reich began working with increasingly larger forces. The aptly named *Music for a Large Ensemble* (1978) called for thirty musicians, representing each of the orchestral families—winds, brass, strings, percussion—as well as female voices. *Octet* was premiered in 1979 by ten musicians, though no more than eight lines of music appear at any one time. These compositions have in common an almost hypnotic density of rhythms—they present a glittering surface, affording an occasional glimpse at the unexpected emotion beneath, as well as a melodic strength not evident in Reich's earlier scores.

The works that followed *Octet* completed the development of Reich's symphonic style. "Even back in 1970," he says, "Michael Tilson Thomas [the conductor and pianist] became aware of my music, and we did *Four Organs* at a Boston Symphony concert. Boulez [then conductor of the New York Philharmonic] was interested in my music, too. I could've probably made overtures then but I didn't want to. After *Octet,* though, I began thinking that I didn't want to keep writing for just the instruments in my ensemble, and touring with ever larger groups. By the end of the 70s, I was genuinely interested in doing orchestral music. *Variations* was a move in that direction."

Variations for Winds, Strings, and Keyboards was written in 1979 for the San Francisco Symphony and eventually recorded by it. Like most previous works by Minimalist composers, *Variations* is definitely tonal, but it contains an unusual amount of chromaticism. This tonal ambiguity, further testimony to the complexity developing in Reich's music, appears again in *Tehillim* (1981) and *The Desert Music* (1984). *Tehillim,* a setting of excerpts from the Book of Psalms, was written after Reich had begun studying ancient Hebrew cantillation. The work was written in two versions, one for Reich's own ensemble, and one for symphony orchestra. The ensemble version was premiered in Cologne, West Germany in 1981; the orchestral premiere was by the New York Philharmonic during the opening concerts of their 1982–1983 season. Since then, many of Reich's scores have been orchestral. *The Desert Music* is a grand symphonic setting of texts by William Carlos Williams, for full orchestra and chorus.

The problem of maintaining musical interest on a large scale while not disregarding the concentration of means and ideas that made his ensemble pieces so effective is one that Reich has confronted in each of these orchestral works. *Tehillim* is more coherent and more strikingly colored in the performance by Steve Reich and Musicians than in the orchestral version, which, in its New York premiere, had a more generous but less spirited sound. ("I warned them they had too many strings," he says.) *The Desert Music,* while even richer in texture, generally holds together as well as any of Reich's smaller works. "It's really my first work to engage the orchestra fully," he explains. "In *Variations,* the strings simply laid down the harmonic groundwork, like a rug on the floor. Here, strings join in idiomatic pulses and then subdivide into the rhythmic patterns that I often use."

While in his recent music Steve Reich has strived for a more traditional, classically oriented sound, Philip Glass has pursued a colorful, dramatic style that has made him one of the most successful composers for theater, dance, and film in the past decade. In 1980, Glass unveiled his second opera, *Satyagraha,* in Rotterdam. With a Sanskrit text pieced together from the *Bhagavad-Gita,* a Hindu scripture, the opera deals (somewhat obliquely at times) with the life of Mohandas Gandhi. It is also much more conventional in its scoring and its format than *Einstein* —it even has an intermission between each act. The Philip Glass Ensemble is replaced by a truncated orchestra, with Glass's trademark electric organ added. *Satyagraha* is hypnotic, dreamy, and highly symbolic; it is a work of surreal, almost *un*real beauty. Although the glowing orchestral sound was dismissed by some critics as too cloying, *Satyagraha* proved that *Einstein* was no fluke, and Glass's reputation as a composer of dramatic stage works was ensured.

In 1984, Glass produced *Akhnaten,* an opera loosely based on the life of an Egyptian pharaoh who espoused monotheism. Sung in a hodgepodge of ancient languages, it is a tightly constructed score that, like its predecessors, has a ritualistic, surreal quality about it. At its premiere in Stuttgart, the work received a fifteen-minute ovation but, although eight years had passed since the debut of *Einstein on the Beach,* the critical response to Glass's work was still highly polarized. "I *never* expected to be in such a storm of controversy," Glass professes. "*Akhnaten* had extremely positive and extremely negative reviews; I haven't read anything in between. What surprises me is that the music has remained controversial. It's not *new,* in the sense that the way I'm writing began almost twenty years ago—it shouldn't be a surprise to anyone by now."

In a sense, the continuing debate over the merit of Glass's music is understandable: He has become one of the most visible "serious" composers in America. For many tastes his vocabulary remains too limited, and as he has been asked to write so many works some have inevitably begun to sound like others. Even so, Glass continues to produce many distinctive scores. For example, in 1985 he completed a film score for Paul Schrader's *Mishima* involving a new type of instrumentation —an unusual grouping of strings and percussion. "There is a tremendous pressure to repeat successes," he explains. "So what I've done is to create new problems. I wrote the score for strings and percussion because I'd never done that before, and I figured, one way to have a new solution is to change the problem."

Glass has also collaborated with composer Robert Moran on an opera entitled *The Juniper Tree,* based on a Grimm fairy tale, and again with Robert Wilson on a mammoth opera entitled *the CIVIL WarS: a tree is best measured when it is down.* This work was to be performed in six parts, one in each of six cities, and each part was to have music by a different composer. (Glass wrote music for the Cologne and Rome sections.) Financial and logistical problems forced some changes in that plan, and if the opera is ever successfully staged, it will be in a completely different form.

Today both Philip Glass and Steve Reich have made the transition from little-known cult figures to highly regarded composers whose music is much in demand: Reich has received enough commissions to occupy him for several years, while Glass has already written another opera, based on one of Doris Lessing's futuristic allegories, and a set of songs, based on texts by some of his songwriting friends, including Laurie Anderson, David Byrne, and Paul Simon. The influence that the two composers have had is almost incalculable; echoes of both can be heard in the fields of rock, jazz, and new music.

Perhaps their greatest contribution, though, has been to provide the impetus for an entire generation of younger composers now working in a related style. John Adams's orchestral works and Daniel Lentz's pieces for ensemble with delay/feedback are very different examples of the spread of Minimalism on the West Coast. Although the new music in Britain often seems to be less an offshoot of American Minimalism than a parallel development, composers like Gavin Bryars, Michael Nyman, and John White have developed a peculiar, British version of the style, while their countryman Simon Jeffes draws on ethnic, pop, and classical forms to make simple, melodic music. And in Germany, Peter Michael Hamel's compositions for solo keyboards, either acoustic or electronic, echo the works of Philip Glass and Terry Riley.

As this style has matured, it has created new goals and problems. Having outgrown the term *Minimalism,* these composers are now threatening to outgrow the economy of means and directness of expression that made their works so distinctive. But their expansion into the realm of orchestral music is a welcome sign of growth, even if it has produced the occasional bombastic finale or ungainly orchestration. Several larger pieces that have the same excitement as the smaller, more concentrated scores have already been written: John Adams's *Harmonielehre* (1985) is a massive, dramatic affair, but it has the same intensity as his septet, *Shaker Loops.*

Whether these larger works will have the lasting significance and historical impact of the earlier Minimalist pieces is unclear. But this phase does represent a logical development. Having explored a basic vocabulary, the Minimalist composers are now using their early pieces as building blocks for a new type of concert music. According to Terry Riley, "We need a real integrity in our musical approach. And in some ways, to do that you just have to tear everything down and begin again. I think whatever Minimalism is, its real value is going to be that—taking away a lot of complicated musical movement to examine what the effects of simple processes are. It's a kind of re-education in music, and I think it's the beginning of the development of a new music."

DISCOGRAPHY AND RELATED WORKS

JOHN ADAMS
Ten years younger than the first generation of Minimalists, Adams has become one of the most highly regarded composers of his generation. He has worked in larger forms, especially orchestral music, for much of his career, and as the New Music Adviser to the San Francisco Symphony since 1978, Adams has been a major force in bringing all kinds of new music to public attention.

- *Shaker Loops/Phrygian Gates* (New Albion 007) NMDS. An excellent, completely individual pair of works. *Shaker Loops* is a pattern-based work for seven strings; *Phrygian Gates* is a pulsing piano solo.
- *Shaker Loops* (de Waart, San Francisco Sym./Ph. 412 214-1). An arrangement for string orchestra, paired with the Reich *Variations.* Sumptuous sound, but a lot remains to be said for the smaller version.
- *Grand Pianola Music* (R. Wilson, Solisti NY/Ang. DS-37345). Paired with Reich's *Eight Lines.* A terrifically misunderstood work: Funny, sarcastic, snarling, and at times rude, it's a serious work that can't afford to be taken seriously.
- *Harmonium* (de Waart, San Francisco Sym. Orch. & Chorus/ECM 1277) ECM. Alternately sinister and ecstatic, this is about as far from Minimalism as you can get. Some friends whose musical opinions I respect have nothing good to say about this score. There's no accounting for taste, I guess.
- *Light over Water* (New Albion 005) NMDS. A work for synthesizer (played by Adams) and brass, deployed so subtly that it's hard to tell where one leaves off and the other begins.
- *Harmonielehre* (None. 79115)
- *Nixon in China*
Two recent projects: The first, a work for large orchestra, is a wonderful, emotion-laden piece that avoids melodrama. The second is an opera, scheduled to debut in 1987. See Chapter 5.

FRANK BECKER
- *Stonehenge* (R. Wilson, flute, with tape and percussion/Ang. DS-37340). Lovely work from an American composer who lived in Japan through-

out the 70s, and whose music sounds more Asian than Minimal.

DAVID BORDEN
- *Music for Amplified Keyboard Instruments* (Red 002) NMDS. The founder of the Mother Mallard group (listed below), Borden in the 60s developed a style similar to Glass or Riley. Some Impressionist works, and some contrapuntal exercises.
- *Anatidae* (Cuneiform RUNE-4) WAY. Parts of this record, credited to the "New Mother Mallard Band," are influenced by New York's downtown art-rock crowd, but most of it is in Borden's cyclic, melodic style, alternating between kinetic pieces and more reflective electronics.

GAVIN BRYARS
- *Hommages* (Crepuscule 27) NMDS. Trancelike works for piano with discreet mallet instrument and percussion accompaniment. See Chapter 5.

MICHAEL BYRON
- *Tidal* (Neutral 5) NMDS. Performers on the steadily pulsing title track include Shem Guibbory of Reich's ensemble, and Peter Gordon. Builds up to a fairly large ensemble sound. The album's other work, "Entrances," is an opaque work for multi-tracked pianos.
- *"Marimbas in the Dorian Mode"* from the LP *Cold Blue Sampler* (Cold Blue L-10) NMDS. Soft, almost ambient music for marimbas.

JAY CLAYTON
- *"7/8 Thing"* from the LP *All Out* (Anima 1J35) NMDS. A gifted vocalist who's sung with Reich, Cage, Muhal Richard Abrams, and others. This is the only work on the album that shows the influence of her work with Reich; the rest use jazz, avant-garde, and World Music techniques.

PAUL DRESHER
- *Liquid and Stellar Music/This Same Temple* (Lovely VR 2011) NMDS. The first piece, as mentioned in Chapter 3, is a guitar work with live mixing and processing which results in a huge tap-

estry of sounds. The other score employs cyclic material on two pianos; the phrasing constantly evolves as the cycles progress at different rates. Dresher is one of America's most versatile composers: see Chapter 5 for his concert works; he has also done some music/theater pieces that use the language and technology of rock.

ARNOLD DREYBLATT AND
THE ORCHESTRA OF EXCITED STRINGS
■ *Nodal Excitation* (India Navigation 3024) NMDS.
■ *propellers in love* (Kunstlerhaus Bethanien ST-09) Dreyblatt's music, like La Monte Young's, is based on harmonics and just intonation. Since the instruments used are adapted or invented ones, these discs are listed in Chapter 10.

ELLIPSIS
■ *Ellipsis* (Fly. F. 339) FF, ALC. Imagine Philip Glass growing up in the hills of West Virginia or Kentucky. What would his music sound like? Probably like Ellipsis. Using banjos, mandolins, guitars, and other instruments, they perform additive, cyclic works that still recall the sounds of bluegrass, old-timey, or country music. Possibly the strangest album of Minimalism yet recorded.

LUKAS FOSS
■ *Solo Observed* (Foss, Chamber Music Society of Lincoln Center/Gram. 7005) GRAM. Despite Foss's claim that "this is not twelve-tone music . . . nor is this minimal music, in spite of insistent repetitions," the spiraling piano solo ("observed" by cello, vibes, and electric organ till the end of the piece) certainly echoes the Minimalist style.

MICHAEL GALASSO
■ *Scenes* (ECM 1245) NMDS. This 1983 release was, quite simply, one of the finest albums of the year. Each "Scene" is played by Galasso himself, on one or more violins. The multitracked pieces are never too busy, the solos never too spare. Despite some added delay effects, this album owes more to Vivaldi in spots than to Riley or Reich.

MICHAEL GALASSO AND
JOHN VAN RYMENANT
■ *Scan Lines* (Igloo 025). Galasso has worked with dance and performance groups since the mid-70s. *Scan Lines* features violin and delay music, along the lines of *Scenes.*

JON GIBSON
■ *Two Solo Pieces* (Gibson, organ, flute/Chatham Square 24) NMDS. Like the composers he's worked with for the past twenty-odd years— Young, Riley, Reich, and Glass—Gibson's music can range from the irritating to the inspired. This album is a fine recording of two Minimal but reflective solos. In general, Gibson's work remains very close to the original Minimalist aesthetic.

PHILIP GLASS
■ *"Strung Out"* (Zukofsky/CP² 6) NMDS. Paul Zukofsky, virtuoso violinist, performs Xenakis, Scelsi, and this primeval Glass work, a simple violin line that demonstrates the slow additive process that characterizes his later music.
■ *Music with Changing Parts* (Chatham Square 1001/2) NMDS
■ *Music in Fifths/Music in Similar Motion* (Chatham Square 1003) NMDS. Early ensemble works —repetitive, brash, and probably out of print.
■ *Solo Music* (Vir. 83515)
■ *Music in Twelve Parts—1 & 2* (Vir. 2010)
■ *North Star* (Vir. 2085)
More developed works; in the case of *Music in Twelve Parts,* a refinement of the explorations into repetition and change that the Chatham Square albums displayed.
■ *"Two Pages"* from the LP *New American Music, Vol. 2* (Folk. 33902) NMDS. Music for two keyboards.
■ *Einstein on the Beach* (CBS M4 38875). Three cheers to CBS for reissuing this four–LP set with its indispensable illustrated booklet, featuring a thoughtful essay by Robert Palmer and a useful musical exegesis by Glass himself. A fantastically powerful piece, though one wishes the visual imagery were somehow captured on tape as well.
■ *Violin Solo Music* (New World 313). The solo violin music from the "Knee Plays," the short connecting works between the separate acts of *Einstein.*
■ *Soho News Album* (Soho News, no #) NMDS. Originally pressed as a fund-raising premium for the now-defunct *Soho Weekly News.* This album contains two minor works composed around the time of *Einstein,* to which they are melodically and harmonically related. Both are very short (this is a 45-rpm disc); Glass and two vocalists are the only performers.
■ *"Modern Love Waltz"* from the LP *The Waltz Project* (None. D-79011). A catchy piano solo which encapsulates Glass's style in just about two minutes.
■ *"Modern Love Waltz"* arranged by Robert Moran (Da Capo Chamber Players/CRI 441). The piano work extended and arranged for chamber ensemble.
■ *"Secret Solo"* from the collection *Big Ego* (Giorno Poetry Systems GPS 012/13, 2 LPs) NMDS. The secret is, this is the same piece as "Dressed Like an Egg, Part 6," from the *Soho News Album.* Glass's contribution to a bizarre, eclectic compilation of New York's "downtown" music/poetry/art-sound scene.
■ *Dance 1 and 3* (Tomato 8029). Some of Glass's most accessible music; colorful works in his mature style.
■ *Glassworks* (CBS 37265). His most popular record to date. Lyrical, exciting, and deftly scored, this is probably the record to get if you're getting only one.

- *Facades* (Wilson, flute/Ang. DS-37340). An arrangement for flute and strings of the sax and strings original, which appears on *Glassworks*.
- *Koyaanisqatsi* (Antilles ASTA-1) NAR. Compelling music from an otherwise silent film. One of his best scores.
- *The Photographer* (CBS 37849). Act I's music has text by David Byrne; Act II has a violin solo played by Paul Zukofsky; Act III provides a grandiose, even bombastic finale to this music/theater production.
- *Mishima* (None. 79113)
- *Satyagraha* (CBS I3M-39672, 3 LPs)
- *"Company"* from the Kronos Quartet album *Sculthorpe / Sallinen / Glass / Nancarrow / Hendrix* (None. 79111)
These three works show Glass to be an effective colorist in a variety of forms. *Mishima* is a film score; dark, athletic music for strings, harp, and percussion. *Satyagraha* may sound like other Glass works, but Gandhi's closing aria is one of Glass's most powerfully moving compositions and is worth the price of the three-LP set. "Company" is a four-part working out of a single phrase into a series of typically lyrical transformations.
- *Songs from Liquid Days* (CBS FM-39564). Neither art songs nor pop songs, these are settings of texts by David Byrne, Paul Simon, Laurie Anderson, and Suzanne Vega. Linda Ronstadt, Douglas Perry, and the Roches are among the singers, and the Kronos Quartet appears, too. An unusual but ultimately unsuccessful recording.
Recent works:
- *Akhnaten* (1984) Scheduled for release by CBS in 1987.
- *the CIVIL warS* (Rome and Cologne sections; 1984)
- *The Olympian* (1984)
- *The Making of the Representative for Planet 8* (1986)
These are all operatic works, except for *The Olympian*, which was written for the 1984 Summer Olympics in L.A.

PHILIP GLASS & ROBERT MORAN
- *The Juniper Tree* (not commercially available). Based on the Grimm fairy tale, this collaborative work is full of black humor (grisly arias sung to lovely, angelic melodies) and some first-rate music. It's not too difficult to tell who wrote what, but the collaboration is never forced or jarring.

PATRICK GODFREY
- *Ancient Ships* (Apparition 280) NMDS. A Canadian pianist whose second album, *Bells of Earth*, was almost universally compared to Keith Jarrett (see Chapter 9, page 191). This first album consists of simple melodies on piano, harpsichord, marimba, bells, and others. Played separately or in ensemble, they produce light, pattern-based music.

PETER MICHAEL HAMEL
- *Aura* (Wergo SM-1009) CH
- *Nada* (CH CEL-001) CH
- *Transition* (Kuckuck 063/064) CH
Three albums of solo keyboard (piano, organ, synthesizer, prepared piano) from this multitalented German musician, one of Europe's leading proponents of the Minimalist style. See Chapter 5.

▲*Harmonia* (Brain 1044). Harmonia is the two members of the German duo Cluster with Michael Rother of the group Neu. One of the few primarily electronic groups (Cluster is another) whose music can really be considered "Minimal."

CHRISTOPHER HOBBS
- *"Aran"* from the Hobbs/Adams/Bryars LP *Ensemble Pieces* (Obscure 2). Hobbs, Bryars, and John White play toy pianos, triangles, reed organs, and other instruments in a charming but all too short piece from the early 70s. Also see Chapter 8. (O.P.)

TOM JOHNSON
- *An Hour for Piano* (Rzewski, piano/Lovely VR-1081) NMDS. A hypnotic work of gradually evolving piano patterns that somehow maintains an almost Romantic sensibility.

GUY KLUCEVSEK
- *"Oscillation #2"* from the Relache LP *Here and Now* (Callisto CAL 1) CAL. An accordion virtuoso, Klucevsek has shown a continuing interest in cellular music. Here, he creates an additive work for solo piano.

JONATHAN KRAMER
- *The Canons of Blackearth* (Blackearth Perc. Ens/ Opus One 31) NMDS. This piece for four-channel tape and percussion is not Minimalism; the musical language is different and often surprising, even jarring; but it does echo Reich's work in its working out of a canonic process and in its glittering web of mallet instruments.

KATRINA KRIMSKY AND TREVOR WATTS
- *Stella Malu* (ECM 1199) ECM. Krimsky has recorded Riley's *Rainbow in Curved Air* (see below). Here, she teams up with sax player Trevor Watts in a number of original compositions for piano and saxophone, several of them cyclic in form.

ELODIE LAUTEN
- *Piano Works* (Cat Collectors 7000) NMDS. Insistent rhythmic passages on the piano complement, coincide, or conflict with various processed-tape environments. See Chapter 2.

DANIEL LENTZ
- *On the Leopard Altar* (Icon 5502) NMDS. A brilliant album. The processes used are an extension of

those discussed in Chapter 3, but the music itself is of primary interest here. Rapid keyboards, cascading vocals, haunting wineglass effects—all the earmarks of Lentz's sound are expertly combined.

- *Point Conception* (Dunlap, pianos/Cold Blue E-11) NMDS. A work for nine pianos, or piano and tapes. A nice wash of sound at times.
- *Time's Trick, The Crack in the Bell* (Angel, scheduled for 1987 release). As usual, deliciously witty music, though *The Crack in the Bell* can provoke serious thought as well. May be his most important album to date.

ALLAUDIN WILLIAM MATHIEU

- *Streaming Wisdom* (Cold Mountain 008) NMDS
- *In the Wind* (Cold Mountain 009) NMDS
- *Second Nature* (Vital Body/The Art of Relaxation) VB

Mathieu has had a long, varied career: He wrote or arranged music for Stan Kenton and Duke Ellington; studied with Easley Blackwood, Hamza El Din, Pandit Pran Nath, and Terry Riley; directed California's Sufi Choir; and has released several solo albums of piano and prepared piano. His music is downright pretty at times; the Riley influence is apparent but not overpowering. Some works feature wordless vocals, and some are in just intonation. See Chapter 9, page 217.

LASZLO MELIS

- *Etude for Three Mirrors* (Group 180/Hungaroton SLPX 12545). This work for four pianists at two pianos and improvising ensemble is a complicated, disjointed exploration of tonal, atonal, pulsing, and syncopated music.

WIM MERTENS AND SOFT VERDICT

- *At Home/Not at Home* (Crepuscule 45-rpm TWI-047) NMDS
- *Vergessen* (Crepuscule TWI-092) NMDS
- *Struggle for Pleasure* (Crepuscule TWI-189) NMDS
- *Usura* (compilation of previous two; Crepuscule TWI-296) NMDS
- *Maximizing the Audience* (Crepuscule TWI-480, 2 LPs) NMDS
- *A Man of No Fortune and with a Name to Come* (Crepuscule TWI-748) NMDS, IMP

Mertens is a Belgian composer whose earlier records owe a lot to *Einstein*-period Glass: Electric and acoustic keyboards and wind instruments abound. The first five albums, from 1980–1984, alternate between propulsive rhythmic sections and poetic interludes. *Maximizing the Audience* includes a work for piano and voice (both Mertens) which points in the direction of his recent solo work. Mertens's innovative later pieces are obsessively beautiful: simple, repetitive chord patterns underlying his surprising countertenor vocals (most of which use random or nonsemantic syllables).

ROGER MILLER

- *No Man Is Hurting Me* (Ace of Hearts 10002) IMP. Side one is rock, from a member of Birdsongs of the Mesozoic (Chapter 13). Side two is Minimal piano music, with touches of toy piano, electric guitar, and others. Forceful, unpolished stuff; shows a lot of promise.

PIERRE MOERLEN'S GONG

- *"Ard na Greine"* from the LP *Time Is the Key* (Arista 4255). Beautiful work with some Reichian percussion, from a fine jazz-rock fusion group.

STEPHEN MONTAGUE

- *Slow Dance on a Burial Ground* (Lovely VR-2041) NMDS. "Romantic Minimal?" That's how Montague's work has been described. The tradition of late nineteenth-century music is melded with that of Minimalism. Using unusual performing techniques on piano, trombone, and other instruments, Montague has composed intriguing scores in an idiosyncratic style.

ROBERT MORAN

- *Juniper Variations* (Relache/currently unreleased). Moran's arrangement of some of the music written for the opera *The Juniper Tree* (see Glass and Moran, above), and premiered almost a year before the opera. An appetizing sample.
- *Ten Miles High over Albania* (Falcao, harps/not yet released). A marvelous work for eight multi-tracked harps. Moran has managed to use the diatonic, Minimalist language without sounding derivative. See Chapter 5.

MOTHER MALLARD'S PORTABLE MASTERPIECE COMPANY

- *Like a Duck to Water* (Earthquack 002) NMDS. Don't let the title fool you. This is David Borden, Steve Drews, and Judy Borsher playing electric pianos and synthesizers in articulate examples of aquatic art. Modular counterpoint for the post-psychedelic 70s.
- *Mother Mallard's Portable Masterpiece Company* (Earthquack 001). The group's first effort, not quite as strong as the second. (O.P.)

MICHAEL NYMAN

- *Decay Music* (Obscure 6). Music from an important British composer and author (*Experimental Music: Cage and Beyond,* et al.) who, until recently, has not been well-represented on disc. This album does not make a good case for his music. Both works on it are derived from interesting compositional procedures, but like much process music, they could stand to be much shorter. (O.P.)
- *The Kiss, and other movements* (EG EGED-40) JEM. Nyman's band on this 1985 LP is almost a chamber orchestra. The music is an appealing blend of Reich's motoric rhythms and Glass's easy

melodiousness. Tight ensemble playing and strange vocals make this a very colorful album.
- *A Zed and Two Noughts* (That's Entertainment TER-1106)
- *The Draughtsman's Contract* (DRG SL-9513)

These typically unorthodox film scores combine Baroque-style string work with irresistibly propulsive rhythms from horns and electric bass.

DAVID OLIVER
- *Lizard Grows on You* (Damiana 111) NMDS. A fine record of Minimalist works for piano and mallet percussion.
- *Hope for La Roo* (Damiana 122) NMDS. A similar album, also well-played, with some exotic percussion and bass added.
- *Marishka* (Damiana 133) NMDS. A superior album of pattern-based music and jazzy works.

PENGUIN CAFE ORCHESTRA
- *Music from the Penguin Cafe* (Editions EG 27) NAR, JEM
- *Penguin Cafe Orchestra* (Editions EG EGM-113) NAR, JEM
- *Broadcasting from Home* (Editions EG EGED-38) NAR, JEM

Simon Jeffes's strange, indefinable, delightful band of merry musicians has developed a style so spare, so unaffected, and so simply melodic that you'd swear you'd heard all the tunes before. Drawing on classical music; folk traditions of Britain, Africa, and South America; and contemporary popular styles, the PCO is unlike anything else on record. In keeping things simple, and in repeating themes instead of developing them, this group is perhaps ultimately more "minimal" than Glass, Reich, and company.

RICHARD PINHAS
- *"Claire P."* from the LP *Rhizosphere* (Cobra COB 37005). Dedicated to Philip Glass. Pinhas's electric guitars are modified to sound like Glass's Farfisa organ. Nice break from this typically brooding, disturbing album. See Chapter 1.

REGULAR MUSIC
- *"Music for Film"* (from the audio-cassette magazine *Touch 33.4: "Land's End."*) NMDS
- *"Purcell Manoeuvres"* (from the audio-cassette magazine *Touch 33: "Ritual."*) NMDS

Exciting, chromatic music that has a bit of a harder edge to it, but still uses the relentless progression of patterns of Minimalism. The interplay of lines is often complex, and the melodies are looser, almost improvisatory.

STEVE REICH
- *"It's Gonna Rain," "Violin Phase"* from the LP *Live/Electric Music* (Col. MS-7265)
- *"Come Out"* from *New Sounds in Electronic Music* (Odyssey 32 16 0160)

Process works dealing with parallel lines of sound gradually moving in and out of phase.
- *Four Organs/Phase Patterns* (Reich, Glass, Gibson, Chambers, Murphy/Shandar 10005). Slowly unfolding works that translate the phase-shifting process to live musical performance.
- *Four Organs* (Thomas, Grierson, et. al./Ang. S-36059). Paired with Cage's *Three Dances* for prepared pianos. A fine album.
- *Drumming, Six Pianos, Music for Mallet Instruments, Voices, and Organ* (DG 2740 106, 3 LPs). *Drumming* and *MMIVO* are still two of Reich's most important compositions, though *Drumming*, because of its length and almost imperceptible movement, still seems to be Reich's most irritating work for many listeners. Briskly energetic performances by Steve Reich and Musicians.
- *Music for Pieces of Wood* (Group 180/Hungaroton SLPX-12545). Hungary's Group 180 performs Minimalist works from Hungary and the U.S., including this work by Reich. By shifting rhythmic relationships, he sustains interest in a piece built from minimal means.
- *Music for 18 Musicians* (ECM 1-1129) ECM
- *Octet, Music for a Large Ensemble, Violin Phase* (ECM 1-1168) ECM
- *Tehillim* (ECM 1-1215) ECM

Except for the rerecording of *Violin Phase*, these works mark the progress of Reich's music through chamber ensembles to orchestral music, and present the quintessential Steve Reich.
- *Vermont Counterpoint* (R. Wilson, flutes/Ang. DS-37340). From Ransom Wilson's first "Minimalist album." Music for eleven flutes, overdubbed by one musician, though live performances by a flute ensemble have also been done.
- *Eight Lines* (Wilson, Solisti NY/Angel DS-37345). A version of *Octet* for chamber orchestra.
- *Variations for Winds, Strings, and Keyboards* (de Waart, San Francisco Sym./Ph. 412 214-1). Paired with John Adams's *Shaker Loops*, this is a good example of the new orchestral Minimalism. *Variations* is in the style of *Octet*, colorfully scored and accurately performed.
- *The Desert Music* (Thomas, Brooklyn Phil./None. 79101). A five-part setting of texts by William Carlos Williams, *The Desert Music*, for chorus, orchestra, and Steve Reich's ensemble, is a grand work and certainly his finest score on this scale to date. Although synthesizers and amplification are used, the textures are almost completely acoustic.
- *Sextet, Six Marimbas* (None. 79138). *Sextet* is more along the lines of Reich's great middle-period works: a smaller, tightly constructed, colorful score for four percussionists and two pianists doubling on synthesizers. The astral sounds of bowed vibraphones dominate the central parts. *Six Marimbas* is a reworking of *Six Pianos*, and sounds much clearer in this version.

Recent works:
- *New York Counterpoint*

- *Three Movements for Orchestra*
- *Electric Counterpoint* piece for electric-guitar player Pat Metheny.
The orchestral piece, from 1986, was written for the St. Louis Symphony. *New York Counterpoint* (1985) pits clarinetist Richard Stolzman against still more Stolzman on tape. The forthcoming work for Metheny will work along similar lines.

- *Repercussion Unit* (Robey 1) NMDS. An album of percussion music, one side recorded live, the other in the studio. The studio side is much better, but both feature works for dozens of percussion instruments, including such things as sewer pipes, hubcaps, and more. The styles of the pieces vary, but several use the interweaving rhythms associated with Minimalism.

TERRY RILEY

- *Reed Streams* (1966 Mass. Art recording; O.P.).
- *In C* (Col. MS-7178). The classic Minimalist piece. The liner notes of this late 60s recording are charmingly dated, but the music's still a "trip," as the notes say; you can still "dig it" twenty-odd years later.
- *Rainbow in Curved Air, Poppy Nogood and His Phantom Band* (Col. MS-7315). By 1969, Riley's solo style had essentially matured. Rich textures from solo keyboard or sax plus "time-lag accumulator."
- *"Rainbow in Curved Air"* from the LP *Katrina Krimsky* (Transonic 3008) NMDS. Krimsky's reading of the work is excellent, though it's only seven minutes long. She uses multitracked pianos to create some interesting effects.
- *Persian Surgery Dervishes* (Shandar 83.501/502, 2 LPs). Electronic organ and tape delay. One of several collections recorded in Europe in the 70s and used in one film or another.
- *La Secret de la Vie: Lifespan* (STIP ST-1011). Hard-to-find soundtrack material; organ and delay.
- *Descending Moonshine Dervishes* (Kuckuck 047) CH. Concert recording from Berlin's 1975 Metamusik Festival. A trancelike work for organ with stereo two-channel output and delay.
- *Shri Camel* (CBS M-35164). The last of Riley's solo organ discs. Four shorter works, using a versatile electronic delay system. One of his most exotic, mystical, and effective albums.
- *Songs for the Ten Voices of the Two Prophets* (Kuckuck 067) CH. Indian-style vocals and two Prophet-V synthesizers. The vocals may take some getting used to, but the combination is truly enchanting. Side one's "Embroidery" is a terrific piece; the singing on side two is less assured, but this LP is still capable of some real surprises.
- *Cadenza on the Night Plain and Other String Quartets* (Kronos Qt/Gram. 18 7014-4) GRAM. The ubiquitous Kronos turns in precise performances; the music has the same other-worldly aura

as Riley's keyboard music, though the string quartets are not as immediately colorful. This is a two-record set of very subtle beauty; it may take several hearings for the full impact of the music to be felt. The title work has thirteen movements, drawing on folk, classical, and raga styles.

- *No Man's Land* (Plainisphere PL 1267-17) NMDS. A film score, with Riley playing piano or synthesizer, and Indian musician Krishna Bhatt playing sitar and tabla. These short works are some of Riley's most energetic, and often seem to use jazz elements.
- *The Harp of New Albion* (Kuckuck 077/078) CH. A two-LP set for solo piano, using special dampers or mutes on the strings and just-intonation tuning. As with La Monte Young's *Well-Tuned Piano*, this piece includes a dazzling array of harmonic and percussive effects. The serene chorale sections complement and contrast with the knuckle-busting ornaments Riley improvises during the more rapid passages. A first-rate work in both structure and performance.

Recent works:

- *"The Ethereal Time Shadow"* from the LP *Music from Mills* (Mills College-1) NMDS
- *The Medicine Wheel*
- *The Song of the Emerald Runner,* others

The first piece, from 1982, is for voice and synthesizers, and is similar to the *Songs for the Ten Voices* album. The other works, from the early and mid-80s, include Krishna Bhatt and are similar to the *No Man's Land* LP. *The Medicine Wheel* is part of a cycle of works based on native American mythology. Other works from this period include tabla player Zakir Hussain.

TERRY RILEY AND JOHN CALE

- *The Church of Anthrax* (Col. M-30131). A real oddity. By the late 60s Cale had become a well-known figure in rock circles; Riley's influence in the European music scene was also growing. The two of them played over a dozen instruments in a style between rock and true, repetitive Minimalism. "The Hall of Mirrors in the Palace at Versailles" is particularly effective. (O.P.)

DAVID ROSENBOOM AND J. B. FLOYD

- *"Is Art Is"* from the LP *Suitable for Framing* (A.R.C. 1000). Trichy Sankaran joins these two keyboardists with a mridangam, or South Indian drum. The album is mostly thick atonal piano duels, but this work comes from the *In C* school, in which pattern A is played for a while, then pattern B, etc. (O.P.)

MIKEL ROUSE

- *Jade Tiger* (Crepuscule TWI-220) NMDS. The Mikel Rouse Broken Consort includes keyboards, sax, bass, and percussion. Good album from a promising young composer inspired, though not too obviously, by Steve Reich.

- *A Walk in the Woods* (Club Soda CSM-002) NMDS. Some beautiful melodies proceeding at a relaxed pace join with the more rhythmic style of the previous album. Rouse has developed his own voice, and may represent the next step beyond Minimalism: his music draws on elements of jazz, classical, and Minimal music, without being simply one or the other and without resorting to a self-conscious attempt at "fusion" music.

MIKEL ROUSE AND BLAINE REININGER
- *Colorado Suite* (Crammed Discs MTM-3) NMDS. Vigorous but less-developed music for synthesizers, drumulator (a percussion machine), and violin. Reininger, the violinist/synthesist for the group Tuxedomoon (see Chapter 13), contributes a kind of Minimalist rock piece; Rouse's three works are more like rock-laced Minimalism.

C. BRYAN RULON
- *Matt Sullivan's Momentum I, the running tape* (CBS cassette, RMT-39243). This curio was released as music for runners to listen to on their Walkmans. Though the tape is not in Rulon's name, it is his music, played on synthesizers, and employs a rock-steady beat to keep you fleet on your feet. Sounds good to more sedentary folks, too. Both Sullivan and Rulon are members of the First Avenue Ensemble; see Chapter 2.

RZEWSKI, FREDERIC
- *Coming Together/Attica* (Group 180/Hungaroton SLPX-12545)
- *"Moonrise with Memories"* from the LP *David Taylor Bass Trombone* (TLB-1409) NMDS
Although he occasionally uses Minimalist elements, Rzewski (pronounced Zhef'-skee) writes in a wide variety of styles. Of these two, *Moonrise*, with its kazoo, dulcimer, and other odd instruments, is the more lyrical and brightly colored.

STEPHEN SCOTT
- *New Music for Bowed Piano* (New Albion 004) NMDS. Scott met Reich in Ghana. Some influence is apparent, but this fascinating disc is like no other. See Chapter 10, page 230.

SEIGEN
- *Seigen* (IC KS-80.049) SBMG. Seigen Ono's debut LP is a collection of works for a large ensemble. "Mallets" and "5/8 RP" are well-crafted short scores; best of all is "Shikaruni Pt. 1," an excellent work for string ensemble reminiscent of Glass but with more development of thematic materials. The album is almost ruined by some muzak-style noodling for strings and keyboards.

PAUL SMADBECK
- *Music for Marimba* (Mallet Arts 101) NMDS. The marimba, from Bach to Reich and beyond. Nice selection of works; fine performances.

BRADLEY SOWASH
- *Near Miss* (Unicorn Productions, 156 Luquer Street, Brooklyn, NY 11231). Electronic music played only on the white keys of the keyboard. The use of digital delay makes it sound like Bryan Rulon's work, listed above; *Near Miss* may be derivative at times, but it's still a generally successful, energetic piece.

JOHN SURMAN
- *Upon Reflection* (ECM 1148) ECM
- *The Amazing Adventures of Simon Simon* (ECM 1193) ECM
- *Such Winters of Memory* (ECM 1254) ECM
- *Withholding Pattern* (ECM 1295) PSI
Minimalism, with its repetitive tendencies, and jazz, which is based on improvisation, would seem to be irreconcilable styles. English reed and keyboard player John Surman nonetheless tries to combine the two, with often quirky but enjoyable results. Keyboard textures à la Terry Riley beneath some fierce improvising on sax and bass clarinet make "On the Wing Again," from the third disc, a good example of Surman's approach. All four have weak links, but they're highly individual, creative efforts, and well worth hearing.

TIBOR SZEMSZÖ
- *Water-Wonder* (Group 180/Hungaroton SLPX-12545). Overdubbed piccolo, flute, and alto flute with tape feedback. An elegant work, the best from this recording.

SU TISSUE AND ARSPENLIAN REEVES
- *Salon de Musique* (Adversity, no #) NMDS. These 1982 works for piano, with occasional vocals or other instruments, are similar to the Bryars *Hommages* record, except the sound quality is not *quite* as dull. The insistent piano is always up front; the other instruments are buried deep in the mix.

LA MONTE YOUNG
The long-awaited full-length recording of *The Well-Tuned Piano* should be available as a five-LP set on the Gramavision label by the time you read this. At the time of this writing, however, most of Young's music is not available on disc. He maintains a large personal library of tapes which are the only current documentation of his major works, but to the general public, his music is simply not available except through infrequent live performances. His discography, aside from *The Well-Tuned Piano*, consists of two discs:
- *Dream House* (section of *The Tortoise, His Dreams and Journeys*), *Drift Study* (Shandar 83.510). A 1973 French release, with La Monte Young and Marian Zazeela, voices and sine waves; Jon Hassell, trumpet; Garret List, trombone.
- *31 VII 69* (from *Map of 49's Dream the Two Systems of Eleven Sets of Galactic Intervals Ornamental Lightyears Tracery*), *Studies in the Bowed Gong*:

The Volga Delta (Edition X, limited edition of 2,800 copies). A 1969 German album, issued privately and now virtually unobtainable. Side one features voices and sine-wave drones. On side two, Young and Zazeela play an amplified gong with double-bass bows. Side two can be played at 33 1/3-rpm, 16 2/3-rpm, or 8 1/3-rpm. At each speed, different harmonic structures become audible.

Selected works:
- *for Brass* (1957)
- *Trio for Strings* (1958)
- untitled works for piano (1959-1962) ("a rhythmic, chordal drone, piano style of my own development")
- *2 sounds* (1960)
- *Piano Piece for Terry Riley #1* (1960)
- *Piano Piece for Terry Riley #2* (composed 8:31 AM, Nov. 12, 1960; rejected by the composer 9:57 AM, Nov. 12, 1960)
- *Poem for Chairs, Tables and Benches, etc.* (1960)
- *Compositions 1960 #s 2–6, 9, 10, 12, 13, 15*
- *Death Chant* (1961) for male chorus or carillon
- *The Second Dream of the High-Tension Line Stepdown Transformer* (1962) for bowed strings or other precisely tuned drones
- *The Overday* (1963) for sax, drones, hand drums
- *B♭ Dorian Blues* (1963)
- *The Tortoise, His Dreams and Journeys* (1964–present)
- *The Well-Tuned Piano* (1964—1973—1981—present). These dates refer to the years of major changes or developments in the piece.

ZEITGEIST
Now almost a decade old, this ensemble from Minnesota has four albums to its credit, each one better than the last. The characteristic sounds of Zeitgeist are keyboards and percussion, especially mallet instruments. Though not all of the works written for the group are Minimalist, many of them are based on rhythm patterns and cycling pulses.

- *Zeitgeist* (Sound Environment TR-1015) NMDS. The aptly titled "Pattern Study #2" by Stacey Bowers is the center of attention on this first album. "Premonitions of Christopher Columbus" by James De Mars is based on the Moroccan *nuba* tradition, and evolves from an exotic wandering melody to a pulsating rhythmic conclusion.
- *Duplex* (Time Ghost Z-1002) NMDS. Tristan Fuentes contributes the excellent "Spinngewebe," a tightly structured musical exercise; and Homer Lambrecht's glowing "Signature One: A Mendelssohn Fantasy" closes the album by transforming Mendelssohn's "Adieu," one of the *Songs without Words*, into contemporary rhythmic and harmonic patterns.
- *Zephyr* (Time Ghost Z-1003) NMDS. The most overtly Minimalist album of the lot. Works draw on the language of Minimalism in different ways, depending on the formal concerns of each piece. The level of musical excitement and proficiency is consistently high in this collection.
- *Too Many* (Time Ghost Z-1004) NMDS. Subtitled "Zeitgeist Plays Fuentes." Tristan Fuentes handles all of the compositional chores, coming up with two superior works: "Risas de los Incas," based on a Bolivian folk melody and inspired by Gabriel García Marquéz's *One Hundred Years of Solitude;* and "Pan Am," a collage of Latin American folk songs. Obviously the music is much less Minimal, though the hazy, dreamlike mood of "Risas" may have Minimal elements.

A fifth album, Time Ghost Z-1005, is scheduled to include *Wails* by Frederic Rzewski, the featured work in many of the group's recent concerts.

5
NEW MUSIC FROM THE CONCERT HALL

I occasionally play works by contemporary composers for two reasons: first, to discourage the composer from writing any more, and secondly, to remind myself how much I appreciate Beethoven.
Jascha Heifetz

Nothing requires more courage than to applaud the destruction of values we still cherish. If a work of art or new style disturbs you, it is probably good work. If you hate it, it is probably great.
Leo Steinberg

Can music be both conservative and revolutionary at the same time? In recent years, such tradition-laden ensembles as the string quartet and the chamber orchestra have begun to play works by new-music composers, and visionary groups like the San Francisco Symphony, the Kronos Quartet, and the Ensemble Intercontemporain have even commissioned concert music from sources as unlikely as Keith Jarrett and Frank Zappa. Like the Minimalists of the preceding chapter, these composers have also created highly personal styles, many of them in reaction to the insular confines of academic music, and in the process have developed a more direct, straightforward idiom. Yet the music they've wound up producing is as radical in its way as the most impenetrable avant-garde scores.

As I stated in the Introduction, our concern here is with composers who have strayed from the musical mainstream and have produced music that is not easily categorized. Artists as diverse as Béla Bartók, Krzysztof Penderecki, and Hans Werner Henze have all written some pieces that would appeal to new-music fans, though these works generally remain in the traditions of twentieth-century classical or avant-garde music. A survey of the contemporary classical scene would require a book in itself—a project at which several authors have already taken a shot.

The new concert music discussed in this chapter does not adhere to any of the "schools" of composition that make up the kaleidoscope of twentieth-century classical music. Rather, it has grown out of, or parallel to, the Western classical tradition, and includes works as diverse as John Adams's frolicking *Grand Pianola Music,* Morton Feldman's ambient music landscapes, and Joseph Schwantner's curious amalgam of unusual effects and romantic sensibility. "New music" composers often draw inspiration from musical principles and philosophies that are foreign to the classical heritage. This can take many forms: the Eastern-derived spirituality of Alan Hovhaness or Pauline Oliveros; the so-called "New Simplicity" that Feldman represents; the Asian scales and instruments used by Lou Harrison or Henry Cowell. And of course, composers with backgrounds in jazz (like Keith Jarrett), rock (David Bedford), or electronic music (John Adams) have drawn on their own experience in these styles. The concern today is less with theoretical "correctness" or academic approval than with communicating more directly to listeners.

New music's move onto the concert stage has met with mixed reviews, for like most listeners who favor one particular genre, concertgoers are slow to welcome intrusions of the unfamiliar into their domain. Ransom Wilson recently has been trying to combine both old and new styles in the concert programs of his chamber orchestra, Solisti New York. Along with standards by Stravinsky, Ravel, and Mozart, the ensemble also plays works by Reich, Adams, and Schwantner. "We're getting a lot of flak," Wilson states flatly. "The traditionalists in the classical music scene are just not ready for this new music. They've been slowly brought around to the Schoenberg school, and all of its disciple schools; and that's a kind of music that's very complicated, and I think very difficult to listen to. Suddenly, we're asking them to listen to something that's tonal, or has regular rhythms."

The return to tonality has been a distinctive feature of many contemporary works (even the harmonically ambiguous works of George Crumb and Morton Feldman present at least the illusion of tonality), and not only in the area of new music: American David Del Tredici and expatriate-Pole Andrzej Panufnik, for example, have both composed beautiful tonal works that reside very definitely within the classical tradition. But even music that *isn't* actually tonal has become less complex and rigorously structured. Composers like Morton Feldman or Japan's Sōmei Satoh have not resolved the tonal/atonal question—they have simply ignored it. A languorous pacing and reflective surface mark Satoh's *The Heavenly Spheres Are Illuminated by Lights* (1979), a work clearly influenced by Gagaku, the stately, almost stationary court music of Japan. *Heavenly Spheres* is scored for soprano, piano, and percussion with variable echo and feedback devices, and is based, quite simply, on a single chord. "It's a sort of Japanese *Liebestod*," says pianist Margaret Leng Tan, who has given the American premiere of this and several other Satoh works. Like Wagner's *Liebestod,* Satoh's piece is a study in suspended tonality; although based on one chord, none of the twelve notes would sound out of place in the floating world he creates. Feldman's *Rothko Chapel* (1972) or *Chorus and Instruments II* (1967) don't concern themselves with serial technique (though Feldman is well-versed in the music of Webern), but they don't inhabit a particular tonal realm, either. Feldman's interest is in different timbres and degrees of density, not in the notes per se. In commenting on his piece *For Frank O'Hara* (1973), the composer neatly sums up his musical aesthetic: "My primary concern is to sustain a 'flat surface' with a minimum of contrast." The only criterion for selecting the notes, instruments, and durations seems to be how well they satisfy his ear. The result is a series of uniquely personal works, often characterized by a congenial stillness. The compositional process Feldman uses is so radically different from avant-garde methods that it has often been misunderstood; what is simple and intuitive has been perceived as simple-minded and naive.

Non-Western and non-classical traditions had, of course, made their way into the concert hall long before new music had appropriated them. John Cage (who else?) and Olivier Messiaen—both completely independent of any compositional schools—have often experimented with exotic forms. Cage's study of Asian music and Zen philosophy has profoundly affected his music, and Messiaen has displayed an even more transcendental-religious bent. Messiaen's musical tendencies are catholic—in both senses of the word; his works include bird songs, ancient Greek and Hindu rhythms, elements of ancient liturgical chant, and postwar Serialism.

Actually, one can trace the lineage of today's new-music composers back even further. Franco-American composer Edgard Varèse anticipated Cage's concern with rhythm, and his view of composition as the organization of blocks of sound has had a strong impact on later composers. Charles Ives used American hymn tunes as an important part of his musical language, and his programmatic notes for his second String Quartet (1913), *The Unanswered Question* (1906), and the proposed *Universe Symphony* betray Ives's cosmic, mystical leanings, often hidden behind the gruff, difficult, or clownish exterior of much of his music. Henry Cowell, whose pupils included John Cage, invented such unusual piano techniques as plucking the strings inside the instrument or muting them with cardboard or metal. Cowell studied Persian, Japanese, and Indian music, incorporating Eastern instruments like the Indian tabla in his works, and even wrote a pair of concertos for Japanese koto and orchestra.

In France, Claude Debussy had also developed an interest in Asian music, especially in the gamelans of Java, which he first heard in 1889, and in the scales used in Chinese and Japanese music, which he incorporated into some of his piano works. Erik Satie, another important figure, wrote piano works whose simplicity remains as fresh and daring today as it was a hundred years ago. Whether the unresolving harmonic structure of Satie's works influenced Debussy or vice versa is still unclear, but the two Frenchmen were both interested in deviations from conventional tonality.

Stepping back still further we reach, of course, Wagner, who in many respects is the father of modern music, a composer whose daring use of chromaticism and shifting tonalities changed the course of musical history. Wagner also studied Buddhism and wrote a treatise called *Religion and Art* in 1880. His brilliant but megalomaniac music dramas seemed, by the end of his career, to be heralding the advent of a new musicoreligion, where Wagner, if he couldn't be its god, would at least be its high priest.

These composers all wrote works whose concerns are very similar to those of many contemporary artists. Today young listeners are discovering that Ives's *Unanswered Question,* Debussy's *"La Cathédrale engloutie,"* and Satie's *Trois Gymnopédies* (all of which have been recorded within the last decade by artists working in new music) can be just as much a part of the new music "scene" as Philip Glass or Kitaro.

Cage and Messiaen, though, are the direct forerunners of new concert music, and for that reason it's worth considering each of their careers briefly. In a sense, it's unusual to discuss these two composers together, because their work is significantly different. But Cage's study and practice of Zen, and Messiaen's symbolic numerology, relating to the Holy Trinity and other tenets of his Roman Catholic faith, have given their works a comparable mystical dimension that has been further enhanced by their studies of Oriental music. (Both men have incorporated Indian rhythms in at least some of their pieces—Cage's *The Seasons* (1947), for example, and Messiaen's *Cinq Rechants* (1949)).

Olivier Messiaen's role in the development of electronic music was discussed earlier. But the compositions that featured the ondes martenot comprise only a small portion of Messiaen's work; he has also composed important orchestral pieces, vocal works, and many volumes of organ music. In this latter field, Messiaen is probably the most significant composer of the century. He has held the post of organist at the Trinity Church in Paris since 1930, a tenure that has spanned many decades and many changes in musical fashion, interrupted only by the two years he spent in a German prisoner-of-war camp, from 1940–1942. In Messiaen's music for the organ, even more than in his orchestral and vocal pieces, the transcendental, almost ecstatic quality that characterizes his best work is given full play.

Like Debussy's piano music, Messiaen's organ works are not confined to classical harmonies. Debussy used Oriental modes or scales; and he stretched the idea of Western tonality so far that the usual rules of harmony often don't seem to apply to his music. Messiaen likewise has experimented with Eastern modes and an idiosyncratic tonality; in addition, his musical vocabulary includes atonality and Serialism. As if that isn't enough, he has studied Hindu, Greek, and pre-Columbian American music. But despite its advanced language, his music eloquently and successfully communicates his uniquely personal vision. During the three and a half decades that separated *La Nativité du Seigneur* ("The Birth of the Lord," 1935) and *Méditations sur le Mystère de la Sainte Trinité* ("Meditations on the Mystery of the Holy Trinity," 1971), two organ works of understated beauty, Messiaen also attempted to establish some form of relationship between colors, numbers, and music.*

Messiaen has become a model not only for many of the new-music composers but also for the avant-garde figures who have worked within and extended the classical tradition. His students have included Pierre Boulez, Karlheinz Stockhausen, and Iannis Xenakis. Also influential have been his writings, which examine his own music as well as that of other composers, from the sixteenth century's Claude le Jeune to Stravinsky's *Rite of Spring*. And yet, like Wagner's or Scriabin's, his is finally a solitary genius; it's the spirit, not the letter, of his musical approach that has usually been followed.

John Cage, on the other hand, has spawned a horde of imitators—many of them cheap ones. Mercifully, though, the ranks of pseudo-Cageians have thinned since the anything-goes period of the 60s and early 70s. (Groups of young composers imitating the "sound" of Cage works like *4'33"* would be a frightening thought.) One John Cage is essential, but one is plenty; there is no need for anyone to recreate Cage's own performance of his 1962 work *0'0",* for any number of players using any sounds

*Messiaen apparently has synesthesia: He sees colors when composing, and colors figure prominently in some of his written scores.

at all. His interpretation of that work consisted of seeding, slicing, and pureeing various vegetables, and then drinking the resulting mess, while loudspeakers amplified the noises of the process to the delight or disgust of the assembled listeners.

Not all of Cage's "music" is so *outré*. His earliest works, from the mid-30s, are based on various ways of organizing the twelve tones of the Western scale. Cage had studied twelve-tone music with Schoenberg in Los Angeles, and some of that influence is apparent in his first compositions. His revolutionary step came in 1938, when he introduced the prepared piano in *Bacchanale*. The idea for the prepared piano was derived from two main sources: the percussion orchestras of Indonesia, and the unusual piano techniques devised by Henry Cowell. Cage had planned a percussive piece to accompany a dancer in Seattle, but he didn't want the logistical headaches of setting up and touring with the requisite large group of musicians. His solution was to transform the piano into a one-man percussion orchestra; in so doing, he created a new sound and a new school of piano playing that is often used in today's music. "Prepared piano" simply means that an unsuspecting grand piano is set upon by musicians armed with nuts and bolts, electric cable, rubber erasers, and other bits of debris which are inserted between the strings of the instrument. The resulting sounds are strikingly similar to West African drum ensembles or Javanese gamelans; each key of the piano has not only a different note, but also a different timbre. In fact, depending on what material was used and where it was inserted along the strings' length, one could conceivably have several keys playing the same note, but each one sounding a different "color."

In 1939, Cage began giving concerts of percussion music with the young American composer Lou Harrison. Since the notes of many percussion instruments—and much of the prepared piano—are indeterminate (one generally can't assign a particular note to the sound of a triangle or drum), Cage's focus during these concerts was on rhythmic organization instead of the usual Western concerns with melody, harmony, or other pitch organizations. Thus, like Messiaen, he found Indian and other non-Western rhythmic structures useful in his work, especially throughout the 1940s.

Cage's music became more extreme in the 1950s. He had begun studying Zen Buddhism in the late 40s, and in 1951 launched a series of compositions based on the *I Ching,* the Chinese Book of Changes. Instead of structuring these works himself, he tossed coins, or threw dice, or performed some other chance operation as directed by the oracles of the *I Ching*. The first piece in this style was *Music of Changes* (1951) for piano; Cage's avowed aim was to free the music from the "literature and 'traditions' of art." In subsequent years, Cage brought out the aforementioned *4'33"*, as well as many other pieces whose organization and sounds flew right in the face of accepted musical practice. After the Zen-inspired simplicity of his works of the 1940s, his music in the 60s and 70s became ever less accessible and more extreme, consisting of several complex collages of prerecorded sounds, both musical and nonmusical, in sections arrived at by chance procedures. While the most recent Cage works have rediscovered conventional instruments, they continue to inhabit a sparse, indeterminate musical space where chance still applies. In the absolute freedom he allows performers in many of his compositions, the distinction between Cage the composer and Cage the philosopher (or Cage the charlatan, some would say) becomes increasingly blurred. British composer Michael Nyman, author of the book *Experimental Music: Cage and Beyond,* has assessed Cage's career as that of an artist who "attempted—and succeeded—in removing the glue from musical relationships." In so doing, Cage opened the door for the "New Simplicity," whether one uses the term to refer to the early Fluxus material of La Monte Young, the floating soundscapes of Morton Feldman, or the early works of Steve Reich and Philip Glass.

Whatever else could be said about Cage's music, it was certainly direct; though he himself has not specifically criticized serial technique, many of the composers Cage has influenced feel that he enabled music to break out of the confines of Serialism. The result has been that dodecaphonic music is now approached in a wide variety of ways. Peter Gordon is one of the younger American composers who acknowledges Cage as a musical forebear, and while Gordon sometimes uses a twelve-tone row, he doesn't feel bound to manipulate it according to the rules of Serialism. His ballet suite *Secret Pastures* (1984), for example, starts with a twelve-tone pitch system, but as he points out, "I use the pitch system in my own way; I'm a bit looser about the harmonic implications." Gordon's tone row was constructed for its inherent harmonic qualities, so there is a certain tonal nuance in the piece even before it moves into more directly tonal areas.

Cage's success in "removing the glue" from musical structures has also led a number of composers to take a second look at tonality itself. Morton Feldman's radical approach to music—using sounds simply *as sounds,* not as part of an overall structure—is a response to the limitations of both serial *and* tonal techniques. A lot of our music relies on how notes are related to each other, melodically or harmonically. In the rarefied atmosphere of Feldman's best works, or those of Sōmei Satoh, the tone-colors themselves are the primary element; any relationship the notes may have to one another seems purely incidental. "What is so interesting about all of Satoh's music," says Margaret Leng Tan, "is that it all takes place within an Asian framework of suspended time." However, she adds, a piece like *The Heavenly Spheres Are Illuminated by Lights* really is a concert work: "It's the epitome of unadulterated, Romantic lyricism," even if it doesn't employ the usual Romantic harmonies.

While several other composers are working in this "nontonal" or "pan-tonal" style, a larger number have found that directness is still best achieved by working within the good old major and minor keys. Robert Moran, who has been part of the avant-garde for over twenty-five years, has produced a number of works in the past decade which are not only tonal but, as he puts it, "disgracefully pretty." As cofounder of the San Francisco New Music Ensemble, Moran was involved in numerous post-Cageian extravaganzas in the 60s and early 70s. *39 Minutes for 39 Autos,* written for the city of San Francisco, featured the sounds of synthesizer, theater groups, and airplanes, as well as the thirty-nine auto horns implied by the title; the work also used dancers, spotlights playing off thirty skyscrapers, two radio stations, and a TV station. The lights in various homes and offices in the city were turned on and off at cues from the radio, while the TV station provided live coverage. It all took place in August 1969 (during an intermission of the theater production

Hair) and epitomized the trend toward the gigantic multimedia "happenings" that debuted in that decade.

Moran, who has also studied Eastern music and has written pieces for Javanese gamelan, moved toward a more ingratiating style in the later 1970s. By the time of his 1975 "city-work," *Pachelbel Promenade,* written for Graz, Austria, the music had already become inherently tonal. ("What else could it be," Moran asks, "when one is given a Gothic *Altstadt* to deck out in music? It's shockingly Romantic.") Ensembles of various sizes, using orchestral and folk instruments, perform the music in different parts of the old city; the actual "composition," which will never be the same twice, is comprised of the ways in which the music of the groups is heard by people walking through the city or, in radio performance, how the different versions are mixed together.

Moran's more recent work still tends toward deploying large groups of unusual instruments, but he has also composed in smaller forms. The graceful "Waltz in Memoriam Maurice Ravel" (1976) for solo piano led to the celebrated "Waltz Project," which appeared on a Nonesuch recording in 1981. Moran was quick to point out that the waltz was in no way related to any of his previous compositions, but it has certainly affected his later work: It was through the Waltz Project that Moran and Philip Glass first met, leading to their lovely collaborative opera, *The Juniper Tree,* nine years later.

In more conventional "concert music" circles, George Rochberg and David Del Tredici have likewise written glowing, tonal scores after working with serial or atonal techniques for many years, and it's no coincidence that they have become two of America's most sought-after classical composers. Lou Harrison is another who has moved away from the more academic styles he employed in the 40s and 50s, although since he has been interested primarily in melody, it's tough to apply the word "difficult" to even the densest of his scores. Harrison was one of the first to experiment with Asian pitch systems and instruments. After developing an interest in Indonesian gamelan techniques from Cage, Harrison has worked throughout his career with large groups of percussion instruments, and like Cage has found rhythmic organization more important than the usual harmonic structures. During the 1970s, Harrison, dissatisfied with works that merely imitated the sounds of the gamelan, bought himself the real thing—a small gamelan for which he has written several pieces of great charm.

Since his studies in Korea and Japan in 1961, most of Harrison's compositions have been perceptibly tonal, although they are not based on Western harmony and draw liberally from non-Western music for both melodies and rhythms. Naturally the gamelan works are performed in a tuning determined by the instruments themselves, but Harrison has also employed Korean scales, ancient Babylonian modes, medieval European rhythms, Mongolian folk songs—in short, anything he can use in the pursuit of his primary interest, which he describes as the search for "a transethnic, a planetary music." In keeping with that goal, Harrison has written Esperanto texts for his vocal works in the past and has given some of his compositions Esperanto titles, as in the *Koncherto por la violino kun perkuta orkestra* (1959).

Although in the 60s Eastern-influenced music enjoyed a brief vogue, especially on the West Coast, Harrison's work with just intonation and other microtonal scales found in the Orient was years ahead of its time, and even today the possibilities of Eastern modes remain largely untapped in the concert hall. That situation is beginning to change somewhat with the Kronos Quartet playing pieces in just intonation by Terry Riley, with the North African-inspired wailing of the soloist in John Corigliano's colorful *Oboe Concerto,* and with the quarter tones and indefinite pitches used in George Crumb's scores. Riley believes this trend will continue to grow: "It'll be the biggest revolution in our music, because microtones are so fascinating. If you were painting with red, yellow, and blue all your life and suddenly somebody introduces green and orange and colors you haven't seen, you're going to use them. And that's essentially what we've been doing with the even-tempered scale, just painting with red, yellow, and blue."

Though influenced by Debussy, Bartók, and perhaps Webern and Mahler, George Crumb has often used microtones and Eastern instruments in his music. His works make extreme demands on the players, and on the instruments, while whole programmatic stories or images lie behind their musical development; like Messiaen, Crumb has applied symbolic numerology as a major structuring device. In addition, he requires a number of outlandish effects—whispering, shrieking, applying chisels to piano strings, "preparing" harp strings, etc.—that, in the hands of a less disciplined composer, could easily turn into a musical zoo.

Disregarding the fact that some people think Crumb's music *does* sound like a zoo, it's hard not to be impressed with his uncanny talent for devising new musical colors. This he does not for freakish effects, but to create and sustain a mood. In the tightly structured, highly symbolic form (or "plot" might be more appropriate) of his works, there is a reason for each sound. What keeps Crumb's music from being incomprehensible to listeners who don't have the written score in hand is that every element, no matter how bizarre, "fits" into that musical moment. His *Madrigals, Book IV* (1969), one of many works set to the poetry of Federico García Lorca, contains a song entitled "La muerte me está mirando desde las torres de Córdoba!" ("Death is watching me from the towers of Córdoba!") In this finely wrought musical nightmare, the soprano vocalist approaches the brink of hysteria; the accompaniment—tortured flutterings from a flute, an implacably droning bass, and flute-like peals of a bowed vibraphone—threatens to push her over the edge. And yet the piece is not noisy; its aim is not to overwhelm the listener with oppressive amounts of sound, but to portray an eerie, enchanted scene in which something is very wrong. Not a single effect is out of place. And not a single one would fit into Crumb's later *Dream Sequence* (1976) for violin, cello, piano, and percussion. Here, an ethereal shimmer is maintained by the continuous soft rubbing of four tuned wineglasses. Again, unusual instrumental effects are called for, especially from the percussionist, but they are of a completely different order from those used in the *Madrigals. Dream Sequence* has the pensive atmosphere of a Morton Feldman work, and like him Crumb seems to have an intuitive sense of what sounds good where.

While Crumb has been able to successfully combine an array of disparate elements into a coherent musical texture, other composers have met with mixed results. One of the major pitfalls facing new music, both in and out of the concert hall, is a concern with sound *at the expense of* structure. Some electronic music and other works which use novel effects or unusual processes have proven themselves especially vulnerable to what Scott Johnson calls "the gee-whiz effect," in which the listener—and the composer, apparently—is so taken with the sound or technique involved that he or she doesn't look for any real musical content. But the best new-music composers, however idiosyncratic their approach, never sacrifice the message for the medium. Pauline Oliveros's concert works are an excellent example: Her performances have an Eastern, ritualistic atmosphere, rather than a Western academic one. Oliveros, however, doesn't see the ritual aspects and the Western traditions as incompatible: "That sets up a polarity I'd rather avoid. I'd rather have a kind of tolerance for all approaches, because there's a valuable approach in academia, which tends toward the analytical. I'm involved in certain analytical processes in my music, as well as direct sensual processes. The integration of those is a great concern of mine: to produce the most complete kind of music." The results range from the rollicking 1983 work *The Wanderer* (for accordion orchestra) to the gamelan work *Lion's Eye* (1984). Oliveros's music is multifaceted; but through it all runs one concern. "What is primary," she explains, "is the sound itself, and the way it *feels.*"

John Adams is another composer of enjoyable music. Influenced by both Steve Reich and electronics, he has been hailed by many critics as one of America's finest young talents. But some concertgoers balk at Adams's work, leery, perhaps, of his so-called Minimalist background. There's nothing Minimal, though, about his *Grand Pianola Music.* With its Gospel tunes, "Sousa" marches, and big, raucous climaxes, *Grand Pianola Music* is a musical burlesque—pompous doggerel to some, a romping good time to others. Adams considered withdrawing the piece after the initial sharply divided reactions to it, but eventually allowed it to be recorded by Ransom Wilson. "I said in an interview once that with *Grand Pianola Music,* John Adams may have written his *Bolero,*" Wilson relates. "And I thought, God, maybe John's going to hate me forever for that . . . but he was flattered, as it turns out."

Robert Moran's *Leipziger Kerzenspiel* (1984–1985), or *Singspiel* as he refers to it, was written for the three-hundredth anniversary of the births of Bach, Handel, and Scarlatti. Like Adams's work, the *Singspiel* is not only tonal, it's also quite a lot of fun. "Some people may find it enjoyable," Moran adds, "particularly the part where Bach, Handel, and Scarlatti, accompanied by Anna Magdalena and the 229 children plus cats and dogs, get into a Baroque blimp to fly to Nova Scotia for a fiddling contest."

With sections like "Bach's Sewage Aria," "Arrival of the Guests from Florida," and "The Spoon Suicide Story," Moran's *Singspiel* may seem to belong to the same breed of zany, quasi-Baroque ingenuity that spawned Peter Shickele and his hilarious PDQ Bach creations. But *Singspiel* is also genuinely good music. Inspired by the shadow-puppet tradition of Cambodia, Moran has written an operalike piece that, even without its clever story and amusing titles, can still be appreciated as a fine neo-Baroque work, though the electric keyboards and occasional pattern-based musical sections might take a bit of explaining.

Though most of the composers discussed so far are American, there are similar developments abroad. Cornelius Cardew brought John Cage's musical philosophies to British music circles; when he became interested in Maoist and Leninist thought in the 70s, his music began to include more traditional harmony. By the time of his tragic death in a hit-and-run accident in 1981, he was considered somewhat of an eccentric, but nonetheless a major influence on such important British composers as Michael Nyman, Christopher Hobbs, Gavin Bryars, and Brian Eno. His Scratch Orchestra, formed in 1969, was an ensemble of variable size, usually thirty to fifty members, which played controlled or uncontrolled improvisations, collages, and more conventionally structured compositions, and proved a fertile breeding ground for talented young British musicians. The orchestral scores of another British composer, David Bedford, employ a wide range of styles, reflecting his work with children, his studies with Luigi Nono of the Italian avant-garde, and his longstanding association with rock musicians like Mike Oldfield and Kevin Ayers.

In West Germany, too, new music of more direct expression is being heard in the concert halls. Besides such home-grown talents as Wolfgang Rihm, West Germany has benefited from an influx of foreign composers, like the remarkable Estonian Arvo Pärt.

Nevertheless, the United States has established itself as the center of new concert music, due not only to its composers but also to its outstanding performers —foremost among them the Kronos Quartet, which has been steadily commissioning, premiering, and playing literally hundreds of new works since 1975. "I consider them the best string quartet playing modern music," says La Monte Young. "I just can't believe their repertoire." That repertoire extends from the standard string quartet fare to the music of Terry Riley, Paul Dresher, Morton Feldman, Wolfgang Rihm, Lou Harrison, and Dane Rudhyar, as well as blues, ragtime, rock, and country music. The chamber ensemble Relache has also proven to be an important source of new works, including pieces by Gavin Bryars, Pauline Oliveros, Guy Klucevsek, and many other composers in its repertoire.

Groups like the Kronos and Relache provide an irreplaceable service to new music by bringing virtuosic and sympathetic performances of experimental works to chamber audiences, who, like their orchestral counterpart, have been attending concert halls in ever larger numbers. Needless to say, though, skeptics remain, and as has always been the case with "serious music," there has been great resistance to the new styles. "I wonder why it's so threatening?" Ransom Wilson asks. "I think it's because the music is saying, let's *enjoy* something for a change. That's something we haven't seen in the concert hall in a long time—at least, not taken seriously. The idea that someone could take this music seriously is heresy to some."

"In a sense," says Peter Gordon, "it's a subversive music, because you *think* it's going to behave in a certain way, but it doesn't behave that way at all." Although that is an apt description of Gordon's own work, it also characterizes almost all of the music in this chapter—and in this book. People go to concerts with certain expectations, and when you consider that there are still segments of the audience that walk out on Stravinsky's *Rite of Spring,* it becomes apparent that some listeners just don't like being surprised. If John Q. Public goes to the weekly subscription concert of the local symphony to get a regular diet of Mozart, Beethoven, and Schubert, then by golly you better give him Mozart, Beethoven, and Schubert. At the opposite end of the spectrum is the Very Important Music Critic, who isn't happy unless he's dissecting terribly complex musical structures for the edification of other Very Important Music Critics.

Fortunately, most critics and listeners fall into the middle ground, and while retaining an open mind, sensibly acknowledge that new music doesn't automatically mean *good* music. There is, and should be, plenty of room for criticism in this area. Isn't Adams's *Grand Pianola Music* just a little overblown? Does Morton Feldman really expect us to set aside four or five hours to watch the Kronos Quartet sawing through his 1984 String Quartet? On the other hand, intelligent appraisal can certainly recognize the merits of these works. Critics and listeners alike breathed a collective sigh of relief in the early 80s when it became apparent that more accessible musical concepts were again being heard in the concert hall. Whatever the merits or faults of the individual composers or pieces might be, the return of more directly communicative work has brought new audiences to contemporary music, and that can only be beneficial.

DISCOGRAPHY AND RELATED WORKS

JOHN ADAMS
- *"American Standard"* from the Hobbs/Adams/Bryars LP *Ensemble Pieces* (San Francisco Conservatory New Music Ensemble/Obscure 2). Now out of print, this early (1973), non-Minimal piece can be played by any combination of instruments, with the performers adding any "extra materials" they feel are appropriate. As the title suggests, the work is not without humorous moments. It shows the same concern with Sousa marches, Gospel, and pop music that appear in the later *Grand Pianola Music.* It's not a major work, and it may not hold your interest throughout, but it's an interesting picture of where Adams was at an early point in his career.
- *Shaker Loops/Phrygian Gates* (New Albion 007) NMDS
- *Shaker Loops* (de Waart, San Francisco Sym./Ph. 412 214-1)
- *Grand Pianola Music* (R. Wilson, Solisti NY/Ang. DS-37345)
- *Harmonium* (de Waart, San Francisco Sym./ECM 1277) ECM
- *Harmonielehre* (de Waart, San Francisco Sym./None. 79115)

The last work has now been performed by major orchestras around the country; it may well be the finest orchestral work to come from a Minimalist composer. See Chapter 4.

JOHN ADAMS
- *A Northern Suite/Nightpeace* (Opus One 88) NMDS. No, not *that* John Adams. This one is from Alaska, and his music is appropriately icy, distant, and spacious. The suite is an Impressionist work for the Arctic Chamber Orchestra with percussion (bells, chimes, etc.) tellingly used to create a cold, northern landscape. The real beauty though is *Nightpeace,* a choral work with harp and a very busy percussionist.

THOMAS ALBERT
- *A Maze with Grace* (Relache live performance, not yet released). It's hard to believe that a work of

such simple beauty hasn't been commercially released yet. Based on the spiritual "Amazing Grace," it is set up like a musical maze, with instruments wandering in and out, hinting at the well-known melody; you don't actually hear the theme in its entirety until the end of the piece. Haunting, sad, and somehow comforting as well, it is impeccably performed by Relache.

NEIL ARDLEY
- *Kaleidoscope of Rainbows* (Gull 1018) WAY. A 1975 recording by a British composer who has written and orchestrated a number of works that feature leading European rock and jazz artists. This one is a series of musical "Rainbows" based on Indonesian gamelan scales, but it retains a Western orchestral sound. Really quite good in spots, if you can find it. See Chapter 1.

DAVID BEDFORD
Bedford's music is fairly well represented on discs. Some of them *(The Odyssey, The Rime of the Ancient Mariner,* and *Instructions for Angels)* are discussed in Chapter 11 (pages 244–245). Others, like *Music for Albion Moonlight* or *Tentacles of the Dark Nebula* (both Argo recordings), are in a more conventional avant-garde idiom.
- *Star's End* (Vir.) For rock instruments and orchestra, a soft, symphonic piece in Bedford's mature style. (O.P.)
- *Two Poems by Kenneth Patchen* (DG 137 004). Much of Bedford's music uses texts by this American author and poet; these early works, from 1963, are choral pieces, reminiscent of some of Gyorgy Ligeti's cosmic vocal work in later years.

BETWEEN
- *"Dharana"* from the LP *Dharana* (Wergo SM-1011) CH. A composition by German composer Peter Michael Hamel (see below) for his new-music group Between and symphony orchestra. A mystical, Indian-inspired piece, its modal development and drones never degenerate into cheap exoticism. See Chapter 6.

▲*Blackearth Percussion Group* (Opus One 22) NMDS. Percussion music by John Cage, Lou Harrison, Peter Garland, William Albright, and Mario Bertoncini. Precise performances and intriguing scores, especially the Garland work, make this an album worth hearing.

GAVIN BRYARS
■ *"1, 2, 1–2–3–4"* from the Hobbs/Adams/Bryars LP *Ensemble Pieces* (Obscure 2). In which a group of musicians, each wearing headphones, hears music that he or she must try to reproduce in performance. An amusing idea; the work just barely escapes falling apart. Cornelius Cardew plays cello; Brian Eno, vocals; Christopher Hobbs, piano; Andy Mackay (of the rock band Roxy Music), oboe; Bryars himself on bass.
■ *Three Viennese Dancers* (ECM 1323) ECM. This recording and the following tapes contain some of the most important music now being made in Great Britain. Having worked through his process- and Minimal-music periods without completely discarding the ideas he developed then, Bryars has emerged as a truly distinctive and gifted composer. This album includes a Romantic, appealing string quartet, played by the Arditti Quartet on electronic strings or RAADS, though it can also be played on conventional instruments; and an exquisite piece for French horn and percussion.
■ *Effarene*
■ *Medea*
■ *Les Fiançailles* (scheduled for later release)
Effarene is a gentle but by no means motionless score for soprano, four pianos, and six percussionists. *Medea* is one of the projects that Bryars and Robert Wilson have collaborated on. This almost-grand opera is sung in French and Greek; the orchestra has no violins and lots of percussion; and the chorus in Act 3 is a kind of Wagner pastiche. The last piece combines a frankly sentimental, almost mawkish string quartet with propellant, interweaving lines from a quartet of pianists (playing on two keyboards)—a strange but enchanting mix.

HAROLD BUDD
■ *The Pavilion of Dreams* (EG EGS-301) FOR, NAR. A reissue of a gorgeous set of chamber works by this important Californian. "Bismillahi 'Rrahman 'Rrahim" is a concerto for sax and an ensemble of mallet and keyboard instruments. "Two Songs" (based on music by Pharoah Sanders and John Coltrane), "Juno," and "Madrigals of the Rose Angel" are all quietly luminous scores.
■ *"In Delius' Sleep"* from the LP *Marty Walker/clarinets* (Advance FGR-13) NMDS. A ravishing work for clarinetist doubling on percussion and pianist. Written in 1974 for Walker; with Barney Childs, piano.

JOHN CAGE
■ *Sonatas and Interludes for Prepared Piano* (Maro Ajemian, piano/CRI SRD-199E). Probably the finest recording of these important Cage works. An early (1946–1948), but complete, compendium of the possibilities of this instrument, taking full advantage of its quasi-Indonesian or quasi-African sounds.
■ *Three Dances* (Grierson, Tilson Thomas/Ang. S-36059). A work for two prepared pianos; the most complex and virtuosic of Cage's prepared piano works.
■ *String Quartet* (LaSalle Quartet/DG 2530 735)
■ *Keyboard Music* (Kirstein/CBS M2S-819)
■ *6 Melodies for Violin and Keyboard* (Gratovich, Flynn/Finnadar 90023-1)
■ *In a Landscape* (Susan Allen, harp/1750 Arch S-1787) NMDS
■ *In a Landscape/Experiences #1* (R. Bernas, piano/Antilles 7031)
In these melodically simple pieces the chief interest lies in the evolving rhythms and phrase lengths, but the last movement of the quartet (1950) and *In a Landscape* (1948) are notable for their quiet, almost inadvertent beauty.
■ *Music of Changes* (Herbert Henck, piano/Wergo 60099) CH. A fine, sensitive performance of a crucial 1951 work, the first to use the *I Ching* as a structural tool. Melody, harmony, and rhythm, in their usual senses, are totally absent, resulting in a completely abstract sound piece. Like most of Cage's work after 1950, it's not easily accessible music, but Henck's recording is very sympathetic.
■ *Etudes Boréales, Ryoanji* (Pugliese, Uitti, Ganz/Mode Records, PO Box 375, Kew Gardens, NY 11415). Two recent scores. *Ryoanji* is an introspective work for voice and drum. The other is a moody, almost shrill work for piano or cello, or piano *and* cello. *Very* spare works, in both cases.

▲*Composers in Red Sneakers* (Northeastern NR-220) NOR. A group of six Boston-based composers whose purpose, stated in the album notes, is "to regain the broader public some of their predecessors voluntarily abandoned. . . ." The half-dozen works here are straightforward, charming scores. Christopher Stowens's "Anemocorde" for amplified harp and electronic tape, is exceptionally beautiful. Michael Carnes's *"Fantasy Music I"* for flute and tape employs avant-garde techniques in an accessible setting; Robert Aldridge's *"Combo Platter"* for violin, sax, and marimba is a colorful mélange of cabaret jazz, Minimalism, and other influences.

CHICK COREA
■ *Lyric Suite, for Sextet* (ECM 23797-1) ECM
■ *Septet* (ECM 1297) ECM
This highly touted jazz pianist has also performed some of his classical favorites—Mozart, Bartók, etc.—and his own chamber works on the concert

circuit. These albums feature a top-drawer ensemble of string players in a series of lyrical, jazz-inflected works.

CHICK COREA AND
NICOLAS ECONOMOU

■ *On Two Pianos* (DG 410 637-1). A recording which features excerpts from Bartók's *Mikrokosmos* as well as some duets by Corea and Economou themselves. Economou is a Cypriot pianist and one of the composers chosen by Robert Wilson for his production *the CIVIL WarS*.

CHICK COREA AND FRIEDRICH GULDA

■ *"Fantasy for 2 Pianos," "Ping Pong"* (Corea, Gulda/Teldec 6.42691). These partly structured, partly improvised pieces form the second side of a disc containing the Mozart Double Piano Concerto #10, K.365. Corea has moved from jazz improvisation to classical forms, while Gulda, a renowned Beethoven and Mozart interpreter, has devoted most of his resources in recent years to improvised music. The combination here is really quite exciting.

JOHN CORIGLIANO

■ *The Naked Carmen* (Mer. SRM-I-604). An album that went out of print about a week after it came out—when the record company was sold. This arrangement of Bizet's *Carmen* includes the Detroit Symphony, members of the cast of *Hair,* and artists from the Metropolitan Opera and the Newport Folk Festival. It's definitely a period piece, like *Hair* or *Jesus Christ Superstar,* but it still has its moments. Best are John Atkins's "Carmen Fantasette," in which a concert pianist embarks on a brilliant set of variations on a Bizet aria—only he can't remember how the original melody goes; and William Walker's "Toreador Song," a swinging, Dixieland arrangement with updated male-chauvinist-pig lyrics.
■ *"Rheita Dance"* from the *Oboe Concerto* (Bert Lucarelli, American Sym. Orch./RCA AGL-1-4926). Each movement of this vibrant, colorful score features a different characteristic of the oboe. (The opening of the piece is the oboe tuning the orchestra!) The most unusual movement is the last, where the oboist imitates the sound of the raita, or rheita, a nasal, microtonal, North African oboe. And unless my ears deceive me, there's a kazoo lurking in the orchestra as well. A lot of fun and a fine performance, too.
■ *Altered States* (Christopher Keene, cond./RCA ABL-1-3983). Soundtrack to the 1981 film; wild, orchestral psychedelia.
■ *Fantasia on an Ostinato* (not yet released). Corigliano wrote this work for the 1985 Van Cliburn International Piano Competition, and later orchestrated it. It takes a theme from Beethoven's Seventh Symphony and puts it through some static, repetitive paces which could easily be mistaken for

Minimalism (and probably will be, if the piece is ever recorded), despite the subtle, intricate differences between one moment and the next.

HENRY COWELL

■ *Persian Set* (Stokowski/CRI 114) CRI, NMDS. One of Cowell's works celebrating the sounds and forms of the East, though in a Western, orchestral guise. A fine piece, paired with Harrison's *Violin Suite* (q.v.).
■ *Piano Music* (Doris Hays/Finnadar 9016) NMDS. Nineteen pieces showing the unusual, often noisy techniques Cowell developed early in this century, including playing on the strings within the piano, smashing the forearm across whole clusters of notes, etc.

GEORGE CRUMB

Some of the most outlandishly colorful works in contemporary music come from this American composer. His ear for unusual sonorities and instrumental combinations is simply astonishing. The poetry of Lorca, the sounds of Asian percussion, and the appearance of such oddities as musical saw or amplified sitar, are integral parts of Crumb's work.

■ *"Dream Sequence," "Lux Aeterna," "4 Nocturnes"* (Odyssey Y-35201). *"Dream Sequence"* is perhaps Crumb's most effective piece. The Aeolian Chamber Players do a wonderful job with all three scores.
■ *Night of the Four Moons, Voice of the Whale* (CBS M-32739). The Aeolians again, with two more haunting, or haunted, works.
■ *Black Angels* (Concord Quartet/Turnabout 34610; or Gaudeamus Quartet/Ph. 6500 881). An "electric string quartet." Music depicting the struggles between God and the Devil, with suitable shifts in mood.
■ *Music for a Summer Evening,* for two pianos and percussion (None. 71311)
■ *Makrokosmos I,* for piano (None. 71293)
Crumb's treatment of the piano completely disregards convention; the pianist(s) sing, shout, play on the strings, rap on the body of the instrument, insert paper on the strings, and so forth. The result is weird, dramatic music, surprisingly rich in texture.
■ *Apparition* (de Gaetani, Kalish/Bridge 2002)
■ *Ancient Voices of Children* (de Gaetani/None. 71255)
■ *Madrigals* (Suderburg/Turnabout 34523)
Song cycles in which the voice is treated in much the same fashion as the pianos above. The hissing and shrieking, though, takes some getting used to.

ALVIN CURRAN

■ *For Cornelius* (scheduled for release in 1987). A solo piano work, written in 1981 after the death of Britain's Cornelius Cardew. Known primarily as an electronic-music composer, Curran has composed an emotionally charged work that is as moving a tribute as one could wish for.

SHAUN DAVEY
- *The Brendan Voyage* (Tara 3006) SHAN. A suite based on the legend of Irish St. Brendan's voyage to America in the sixth century. The orchestral writing is competent, but what makes the album a success is the playing of Liam O Floinn (or O'Flynn), one of the two or three greatest Irish pipers today.

DAVID DEL TREDICI
Del Tredici's music is something of a phenomenon. Developing out of the twentieth-century classical tradition, he has nevertheless transcended the boundaries between classical, avant-garde, and new music with his series of tonally based orchestral pieces, set to texts by Lewis Carroll. *Happy Voices, Adventures Underground,* and several others have not yet been recorded, though a complete cycle of the "Alice works" seems inevitable. Recorded so far are:
- *Final Alice* (Hendricks, Solti/London LDR-71018), and
- *In Memory of a Summer Day* (Bryn-Julson, Slatkin/None. 79043)
Almost extravagant in their beauty, these works are a far cry from Del Tredici's earlier atonal or twelve-tone pieces.
- *Acrostic Song,* for guitar (Starobin/Bridge 2004). A recent piece, transcribed from part of the Alice series.

PATRICK DI VIETRI
- *Invocation* (Teresiana TR-1984) NAR. Besides solo guitar performances of Satie and S. L. Weiss, this album highlights Di Vietri's own Romantic, delicate guitar works, often based on religious themes.

PAUL DRESHER
- *Channels Passing/Night Songs* (New Performance Group, Cornish Institute/New Albion 003) NMDS. Excellent, pattern-based chamber works from a talented young composer.
- *Casa Vecchia* (Kronos Quartet, not yet released). A 1982 commission, extending the techniques used above to string quartet music.
Other works listed in Chapters 3 and 4.

WILLIAM DUCKWORTH
- *The Time Curve Preludes* (Lovely VR-2031) NMDS. Superb collection of solo piano preludes, played by Neely Bruce on a specially tuned piano. Each work has its own character, yet the set hangs together quite well. Romantic, ominous, serene . . . this is a consistently subtle and well-constructed opus.

KEITH EMERSON
- *Piano Concerto #1* (Emerson, Mayer, London Phil./Atlantic SD2-7000). From the album *Works* by the rock group Emerson, Lake and Palmer. Considering that Emerson is often more of a baker than a composer (half a cup of Bartók, a tablespoon of Prokofiev, maybe a dash of honky-tonk), this isn't half bad. The orchestration is a bit dense at times, but the piece covers a variety of moods and styles.

BRIAN ENO
- *"Three Variations on the Canon of Johann Pachelbel"* (Obscure/EG 303). From the record *Discreet Music,* three works based on various ways of tearing apart and putting back together the famous (or infamous, depending on how often you've heard it) Pachelbel *Canon.*

DONALD ERB
- *"The Devil's Quickstep"* from the LP *Composers' Consortium* (Spectrum SR-195) NMDS. Like Crumb or Schwantner, Erb specializes in novel coloristic effects, including electronics.

MARIO FALCAO
[Untitled] (Canadian Music Centre MC-20485) CMC. Falcao plays three excerpts from the Waltz Project (listed below) arranged for harp, R. Murray Schafer's *The Crown of Ariadne* for harp and percussion, and several Baroque works.

MORTON FELDMAN
Feldman has been a determined individualist and a prolific composer for over three decades. His works are too numerous to mention, but some personal favorites include:
- *Rothko Chapel, For Frank O'Hara* (Col. M 34138). A pair of handsomely sculpted works for small ensemble. Both of them are completely characteristic of Feldman's music: low dynamic levels, nondramatic, abstract expression, and deep textures. *Rothko Chapel* (1972) features a chorus and is somewhat of an extension of the next piece.
- *"Chorus and Instruments II," "Christian Wolff in Cambridge"* both from the LP *Extended Voices* (Odyssey 32-16-0156). The first piece, from 1967, uses tuba and chimes. The second, from 1963, also vocal, was inspired by American avant-garde composer Christian Wolff.
- *"Piece, for 4 Pianos,"* from the LP *The Early Years* (Odyssey 32-16-0302). A 1957 work that marked the beginning of the rich simplicity of his later music. Four pianists play from a single part; that original source is obscured by shifting, repetitive layers of piano music.

ROBERT AND SARAH FEUERSTEIN
- *Transmutations* (Columbia Masterworks/Canada MST-80030). A remarkable guitarist, Feuerstein is joined by his wife Sarah on keyboards for a collec-

tion of original (in both senses of the word) compositions. Though there's some filler on this recording, it may appeal not only to classical guitar fans, but to anyone who enjoys lyrical but not mushy music.

EUGENE FRIESEN AND PAUL HALLEY
- *New Friend* (Living LM-0007) WH. Two members of the Paul Winter Consort perform gentle, lyric chamber works for cello and keyboard. Halley plays piano for the most part, but switches to pipe organ on occasion. Friesen has a full, warm cello tone that serves this music quite well.

KAY GARDNER
- *A Rainbow Path* (Ladyslipper LR-103) LADY, VB. A collection of meditative works for chamber ensemble—with a few differences. Besides the usual winds, strings, and occasional percussion, Gardner uses the Indian tamboura (a drone instrument), Celtic harp, and a small women's chorus.

PHILIP GLASS
Glass's orchestral and operatic scores are listed in Chapter 4.

DANIEL GOODE
- *The Thrush from Upper Dunakyn* (Pete Rose, bass recorder/Opus One 71) NMDS. A strangely forlorn yet pastoral piece based on bird songs, transcribed by Goode while spending some time in Nova Scotia.

PETER GORDON
- *Secret Pastures* (Love of Life Orchestra/Artservices recording) NMDS. Music from the popular ballet, premiered at the Brooklyn Academy of Music's Next Wave Festival in 1984, and featuring the Love of Life Orchestra. Some sections are closer to New York's downtown, rock-influenced sound, while others, the beginning parts especially, have a formal, chamber orchestra quality.

HENRYK M. GORECKI
- *Symphony #3—Symphonie des chants plaintifs* (Woytowicz, Bour, SWF Sym. Orch./Erato ERA-9275). A dazzling work for orchestra and soprano from a Polish composer. Apparently this piece was used as a film score, but don't be deceived by the wretched cover art: This fine score combines the cyclic form of Arvo Pärt's work with the power and emotion of late nineteenth-century Romanticism. The finale in particular will stay with you long after hearing it.

GURDJIEFF/DE HARTMANN,
SEE DE HARTMANN.

PAUL HALLEY
- *Nightwatch* (Gram. GR 7004) GRAM. This limited edition release is mostly tranquil music, excep-

tionally played on the organ of the Cathedral of St. John the Divine. See Friesen and Halley, above.

PETER MICHAEL HAMEL
- *Organum* (Kuckuck 074) CH. Unlike Halley's, this organ record includes a touch of Tibetan cymbal and Vedic conch (a mouth-blown shell from India). A little Riley/Glass-type ostinato work soon gives way to an expressive, powerful performance that synthesizes the colorings of Messiaen with the hypnotic, trancelike character of Asian music.

LOU HARRISON
Harrison's is some of the most accessible, charming music on the concert stage today. His finest works are those in which he allows free rein to his interest in non-Western scales and rhythms, as in:
- *Three Pieces for Gamelan* (Gamelan Sekar Kembar/CRI 455) CRI, NMDS. A sparkling, melodic trio of works, pairing the small gamelan (percussion ensemble) with retuned French horn, viola, and suling (flute). On the other side of the disc, the Kronos Quartet turns in a solid performance of Harrison's *String Quartet Set*. A delightful recording throughout.
- *Double Concerto for Violin, Cello, and Javanese Gamelan* (Goldsmith, King, Mills College Gamelan/TR 109) NMDS
- *Concerto for Violin and Percussion Orchestra* (Glenn, Beck/Turnabout 34653)
- *Concerto in Slendro* (Kobialka, Hughes/Desto 7144)
- *Gending Pak Chokro for Gamelan* (Berkeley Gamelan/Cambridge 2560)
- *Pacifika Rondo, 4 Pieces for Harp, 2 Pieces for Psaltery, Music for Violin with Various Instruments* (Desto 6478)
- *Suite for Violin, Piano, and Small Orchestra* (Ajemian, Stokowski/CRI 114) CRI, NMDS
- *"At the Tomb of Charles Ives"* from the LP *Brooklyn Philharmonic Symphony Orchestra* (Gram. 7006) GRAM
- *"Suite #1, for Guitar"* from the LP *Sonic Voyage* (Wager-Schneider/El Maestro 8004) NMDS
All of these works use the melodies, rhythms, and/or instruments of Asia. Although it's quite short, "At the Tomb of Charles Ives" is a fairly typical work: hammered dulcimer and psaltery (another zitherlike instrument) join the orchestra in playing a piece based on a Mongolian folk song. The Double Concerto is the most recent and perhaps the most effectively realized of these cross-cultural works.

THOMAS DE HARTMANN AND
G. I. GURDJIEFF
G. I. Gurdjieff's early years are shrouded in mystery; it is known that he was born in Armenia, perhaps in 1872. He wandered through Central Asia and the Middle East while still a young man,

absorbing the religious and philosophical ideas, both widely accepted and obscure, of those regions. He then made his way to the West, where he began presenting his own synthesis of what he had learned, using as part of his teaching a series of sacred dances or movements which were accompanied by music. His pupils included author P. D. Ouspensky, architect Frank Lloyd Wright, Einstein's student J. G. Bennett, and *musique concrète* composer Pierre Schaeffer. Gurdjieff died in 1949, but his teaching has attracted younger musicians as well, including Robert Fripp, Keith Jarrett, David Hykes, and Alain Kremski.

■ *Music of Gurdjieff and de Hartmann* (Henck/ Wergo SM 1035/36, 2 LPs) CH. Herbert Henck once again provides an extraordinarily sympathetic performance, this time in several piano cycles (one with percussion by Trilok Gurtu) written by Russian composer Thomas de Hartmann, based on melodies devised or collected by Gurdjieff. De Hartmann was already a well-known musician when he became a Gurdjieff disciple. Gurdjieff's themes were often Central Asian in origin, and these modal works were intended as accompaniment for his sacred dances. The music tends to be rather dark, even gloomy if the performer gets carried away. But it has attracted a sizeable following. To many ears, this is the finest recording of the Gurdjieff/de Hartmann music.

■ *Music of Thomas de Hartmann* (de Hartmann/Triangle 1001, 4 LPs) TRI. A historic set of recordings by de Hartmann himself, made within several years of Gurdjieff's death. See Appendix listing of Triangle for more.

■ *"Sacred Hymns" G. I. Gurdjieff/Thomas de Hartmann* (Jarrett/ECM 1174) ECM, VB, NAR, FOR. Keith Jarrett's highly personal interpretation of these piano works serves as a good introduction to the music.

■ *Music of Gurdjieff/de Hartmann Vol. 1* (Kremski/Auvidis 4721) CH

■ *Music of Gurdjieff/de Hartmann Vol. 2* (Kremski/Auvidis 4725) CH

Frenchman Alain Kremski is a composer, arranger, pianist, and percussionist. Here he gives a thoughtful reading of the Gurdjieff/de Hartmann work.

■ *Meetings with Remarkable Men* (Rosenthal, London Phil., Ambrosian Singers/Varese-Sarabande 81129) VB, NAR, FOR. Soundtrack to the film about Gurdjieff's life, with de Hartmann's music orchestrated—over-orchestrated in spots—by Lawrence Rosenthal, who adds some of his own music. There is some inspired music here: The choral "Great Prayer" is particularly powerful.

CHRISTOPHER HOBBS

■ *"Recitative"* from the LP *Marty Walker/clarinets* (Advance FGR-13) NMDS. Poetic 1979 piece for clarinet and celesta, paired with Budd's *In Delius' Sleep* (see above) which it complements nicely.

ALAN HOVHANESS

As with Lou Harrison, Hovhaness has drawn upon many Asian musical traditions, Japanese, Armenian, Indian, and Persian being the most prominent. A composer of incredible fecundity, Hovhaness has probably written more music than anyone alive today.

■ *Fantasy on Japanese Woodprints, Sunrise, Meditation on Orpheus, Floating World, And God Created Great Whales, The Rubaiyat of Omar Khayyam* (Kostelanetz/CBS 34537). The quintessential Hovhaness collection. *Fantasy* and *Floating World* evoke the spirit of Japan. *And God Created Great Whales* combines actual tapes of humpback whale songs with orchestra in one of Hovhaness's finest works.

■ *Symphony #2: "Mysterious Mountain"* (Reiner, Chicago Sym./RCA AGL-1-4215). An unrestrained lyrical work for orchestra.

■ *Khaldis Concerto for Piano, 4 Trumpets, and Percussion* (Masselos/Heliodor 25027). A colorful work using an odd combination of instruments, with Indian and other non-Western rhythms.

■ *Lousadzak Concerto, for Piano and Strings* (Ajemian/Heliodor 25040). The piano is called on to imitate the sounds of various Arabic instruments in a piece that occasionally uses aleatoric procedures.

■ *Talin* (Sobol, Flagello/Peters International PLE-071). A typical Hovhaness work; exotic melodies for clarinet and strings.

CHARLES IVES

■ *The Unanswered Question* (Bernstein, New York Phil./CBS 38777). Written in 1906, this haunting work for trumpet, flutes, and strings is "New Age" music written six or seven decades before there was such a thing. A pinnacle to which most New Age music doesn't even aspire.

KEITH JARRETT

■ *The Celestial Hawk,* piano concerto (Jarrett, Keene/ECM 1175) ECM

■ *In the Light* (Jarrett, Towner, others/ECM 1033/ 34, 2 LPs) ECM

■ *Luminescence* (Garbarek, Gutesha/ECM 1-1049) ECM

■ *Arbour Zena* (Jarrett, Garbarek, Haden, Gutesha/ECM 1-1070) ECM, NAR

In the Light is a collection of concert works for brass, guitar, strings, solo harpsichord, etc. The last two albums use string orchestra and soloists. The hushed, lyrical works on *Arbour Zena* are exceptionally good. Jarrett's scores outside the realm of piano improvisation have been sharply criticized by some, but *Arbour Zena* and *Celestial Hawk* both deserve to be heard more often.

ROGER JOHNSON

■ *Music for Two Pianos* (Garth, Liepa/Opus One 102) NMDS. Though he has impressive academic credentials, Johnson's piano works are complex without being totally obscure; at once melodic and athletic.

DANIEL KOBIALKA

- *Echoes of Secret Silence* (Nagano, Oakland Sym. Youth Orch./1750 Arch S-1792) NMDS. Kobialka is a talented violinist, and a talented composer, though you'd never guess it from his New Age records. This reflective, subtle concert work for strings is easily his best.
- *Autumn Beyond,* for biwa, violin, and Japanese bells (Kobialka/1750 Arch S-1795) NMDS. A somewhat more daring (i.e. less "pretty") piece. The biwa is a Japanese lute; the work has a suitably exotic sound.
- *Pachelbel Canon* (extended version) (Li-Sem DK-102 LP) VB, NAR, FOR. Extended indeed: This side-long piece of drivel is an exercise in stretching out poor Pachelbel's greatest hit until it collapses under its own weight.

THE KRONOS QUARTET

- *In Formation* (Reference Recordings 9) REF. Not what you'd expect from this celebrated group. Titles include "The Funky Chicken" (by David Kinchley), "Blues" (Derek Thune), "Junk Food Blues" (John Whitney), and others. Who said string quartet music couldn't be fun?
- *Sculthorpe/Sallinen/Glass/Nancarrow/Hendrix* (None. 79111). That last name is Jimi Hendrix, in case you were wondering. The quartet does the rock guitarist's "Purple Haze" in questionable intonation; this one just doesn't work. Sculthorpe's Quartet #8 is based on Balinese rhythms and is the strongest work here. Sallinen's Third Quartet has been recorded by the Voces Intimae Quartet on the Swedish Bis label (BIS-64), and though their recording is more idiomatic (the piece is based on a Finnish fiddle tune known throughout Scandinavia), the Kronos's ensemble playing is first-rate. The Glass work is listed in Chapter 4.

TANIA LEON

- *Haiku* (Lear, et.al./Opus One 101) NMDS. Japanese Haiku in English translations; for narrator, five Western instruments, Japanese koto, and five percussionists. Leon, whose credits include music for Robert Wilson's *The Golden Windows,* successfully synthesizes the Japanese sound of the "floating world" with contemporary techniques.

GYORGY LIGETI

In the 1960s, this marvelous Hungarian composer produced a series of works, especially choral ones, that defy easy classification. Even before his music appeared in the soundtrack of *2001: A Space Odyssey,* it was being described as "spacey."

- *"Lux Aeterna," "Atmospheres"* from the *2001* soundtrack (Bernstein, New York Phil./CBS 7176)

- *Lux Aeterna* (Franz, NDR Chorus/DG 2543 818)
- *Lontano* (Bour/Wergo 60045)

JON LORD

- *Sarabande* (EMI PPSA-7516). A colorful suite of works for orchestra with some rock and ethnic instruments from a well-known British rock musician. Arabic-sounding music and updated courtly dances make this a diverting record.

COLIN MCPHEE

- *Tabuh-Tabuhan* (Hanson, Eastman Sym./Mer. 75116). McPhee lived in Bali for part of the 1930s, and wrote this classic gamelan-inspired piece in 1936.

LUBOMYR MELNYK

- *The Lund-St. Petri Symphony* (Melnyk/Apparition 781) NMDS. A Canadian pianist, organist, and composer; Melnyk's "Symphony" is a collection of three album-length displays of keyboard pyrotechnics that at times threaten to overwhelm the actual music. It all gets pretty dense, and the muddy recording doesn't help. Which is regrettable—Melnyk's style, a sort of pan-tonal Minimalism, would probably be quite interesting if more clearly presented.
- *KMH: Piano Music in the Continuous Mode* (Melnyk/Music Gallery Editions 18) NMDS. A solo piano work, with the same pluses and minuses as above.
- *The Song of Galadriel* (Melnyk/Bandura BAN 19 B-84) NMDS. At last, a recording where you can actually hear all the music. Inspired by J.R.R. Tolkien's *Lord of the Rings,* this pair of side-long piano compositions is an impressive achievement. Try it.
- *TTOCJ/TAHIE "To the Living, the Dead, and to Those Yet Unborn"* (Melnyk et. al./Bandura BAN 19 A-83) NMDS. The Cyrillic title (pronounced "Poslyaniye") was the rallying cry of nineteenth-century Ukrainian patriot and poet Taras Shevchenko. Melnyk sets his texts for soprano, piano, violin, viola, French horn, English horn, and percussion. The vocals are overwrought, and will appeal primarily to opera fans. But the piano is typical Melnyk and the other instruments are added via chance procedures, making for a gently arresting sound.

OLIVIER MESSIAEN

- *Das Orgelwerk* (Roessler/Schwann 7-LP set, #350) CH. Although some of the works here have received better performances, there's really no need to look any further than this lavishly annotated, impeccably recorded set of the *complete* Messiaen *oeuvre* for organ. The performances by Almut Roessler are generally excellent, and were done under Messiaen's supervision.

MOONDOG (LOUIS T. HARDIN)

- *Selected Works* (Moondog, et. al./Musical Heritage Society 3803) MHS. Hardin is a blind keyboardist and composer whose music has attracted a cult following. The "Heimdall Fanfare" for brass and some of the short organ works are original, amiable scores. Others sound curiously anachronistic.
- *Moondog* (Col. MS-7335)
- *Moondog 2* (Col. AL-30897)
Both LPs feature insistent, almost medieval-sounding percussion; elements of jazz, Baroque, and pop music are apparent, too. The second disc has lots of weird Swingle Singers–type vocals which can be amusing one moment and irritating the next. (O.P.)

ROBERT MORAN

- *"Waltz: In Memoriam Maurice Ravel"* from the LP *The Waltz Project* (None. D-79011). A short, lyrical piano work.

GALESHKA MORAVIOFF

- *Piano Solo, Vol. I* (BSR-1001) NMDS
- *Piano Solo, Vol. II* (Cryonic MAD-3020) WAY
"Musiques Plastiques" is a two-album series of piano solos. Elements of Melnyk-style repetition, exotic modes, and angular, dissonant lines make this an uncategorizable and immensely satisfying collection.

NEW MUSIC CIRCLE OF ST. LOUIS

- *Reflections* (NMC 1985) NMDS. Michael Colgrass is probably the best-known composer here. His *Night of the Raccoon* is for soprano, alto flute, harp, percussion, and keyboard. The best piece on this album is Michael Hunt's *Other Realities,* for alto flute, bells, crotales, vibes, chimes, and piano strings.

NEXUS

- *Music of Nexus* (NE 01) CMC
- *Changes* (NE 05) CMC
Virtuoso percussion music by Canada's premiere new-music group. Composers include several Canadians, as well as such international stars as John Cage and Steve Reich.

KIRK NUROCK

- *"Creature Memory"* from the compact disc *The Pugh-Taylor Project* (Digital Music Products, Rockefeller Center Station, PO Box 2317, New York, NY 10185; DMP-CD448). Jim Pugh plays tenor trombone, David Taylor plays bass trombone, and their ensemble varies from piece to piece. This work uses elements of Minimalism and jazz, with one trombone desperately trying to be light and chirping, while the other has some apparent problems with flatulence. A funny, delightfully rude score.

MIKE OLDFIELD

- *The Killing Fields* (Schoener, Oldfield, et. al./Vir. V2328). Soundtrack to the film, and an all-star cast of musicians. The music ranges from lush hyper-Romanticism to invigorating rhythmic pieces that imitate Southeast Asian percussion ensembles.
- *The Orchestral Tubular Bells* (Bedford/Vir. VR 13.115). David Bedford's 1975 orchestration of Oldfield's hugely successful *Tubular Bells,* which sold over ten million copies after it became the theme for the film *The Exorcist.* Effective, but the original (see Chapter 11) is still better.

PAULINE OLIVEROS

- *The Well* (Relache, Oliveros/Hat Hut 2020, 2 LPs) NMDS
- *The Wanderer* (Springfield Accordion Orch./ Lovely VR 1902) NMDS
Oliveros describes *The Wanderer* as "great fun"; the performers, mostly high school age, "played the daylights out of the piece." *The Well* is a dramatic multimedia event that demonstrates the angelic/demonic quality of her music, as quiet harmonies give way to loud, aggressive passages. Oliveros's solo parts, done in an empty underground reservoir in Cologne, have to be heard to be believed. With a solo accordion and a forty-five-second echo from the space itself, she creates an amazing sonic experience. (See *Vor der Flut,* Chapter 12.)

HANS OTTE

- *Das Buch der Klänge/The Book of Sounds* (Kuckuck 069/70, 2 LPs) CH. Twelve exquisite piano solos from a former pupil of Paul Hindemith and highly regarded German radio producer. Though touching upon a number of styles, this collection is predominantly quiet and thoughtful.

ANDRZEJ PANUFNIK

- *Sinfonia Sacra* (Panufnik, Monte Carlo Opera Orch./Unicorn RHS-315). Admittedly, this is not a new-music score, but a personal favorite—a ravishing, emotional work composed in 1963, two years after Panufnik settled in Great Britain.

ARVO PÄRT

- *Tabula Rasa* (Kremer, Jarrett, Schnittke, others/ ECM 1275) ECM. An outstanding set of works for various ensembles: a violin/piano duet; a prepared piano, two violins, and string orchestra; and others, all done in a cyclic style. One of the best recordings of 1985.

EINOJUHANI RAUTAVAARA

- *Cantus Arcticus—Concerto for Birds and Orchestra* (Finlandia FA-328) PSI. Just what it says: Finland's Rautavaara takes tapes of Arctic bird songs and uses them as basic melodic material, occasionally changing the tape speed to bring the songs to the required pitch. The orchestral winds play counterpoint, while the strings have that typically open, brilliant sound we associate with Sibelius and other northern composers. A wonderful piece.

STEVE REICH
See Chapter 4.

RELACHE
- *Here and Now* (Callisto CAL-1) CAL. Works by Guy Klucevsek, Joseph Franklin, and others. Minimalism, highly chromatic music, and electronic pieces all receive excellent performances, leaving the individual compositions to stand or fall on their own merits. About half are still on their feet when all's said and done.

AMIRAM RIGAI
- *Piano Music from the Middle East* (Folk. FM-3360) NMDS. Iran's Andre Hossein provides "Prelude #1" and "Legende Persane," both with the modal sounds of Persian music. Also, from Israel, works by Paul Ben-Haim and Rigai himself; Greece's Manolis Kalomiri; Lebanon's Anis Fuleihan; and the Turkish-born Ilhan Mimaroglu.

TERRY RILEY
See Chapter 4.

GEORGE ROCHBERG
- *Electrikaleidoscope* (20th-Century Consort/ Smithsonian Collection N-022) SM. Dating from 1972, this is one of the first completely nonserial works Rochberg composed, scored for flute, clarinet, strings, piano, and electric piano.
- *Ukiyo-E*, for harp (S. Allen/1750 Arch S-1787) NMDS. An inward-looking, Japanese-flavored harp solo; superb performance.
- *Slow Fires of Autumn*, for flute and harp (Wincenc, Allen/CRI-436) CRI, NMDS
- *Violin Concerto* (Stern, Previn/CBS 35149) Later, tonal works; like Del Tredici, Rochberg has been able to compose charming tonal pieces of considerable popularity without disregarding the formal concerns of his earlier music.

DANE RUDHYAR
- *Stars* (Masselos, piano/CRI 247) NMDS, CRI
- *Tetragram #4* (Mikulak, piano/CRI 372) NMDS, CRI
The late Dane Rudhyar (born Daniel Chenneviere in Paris, 1895) took his Sanskrit name half a century before such things became fashionable. He wrote these works in the 1920s, after which he became known chiefly as an astrologer, with over a dozen books on the subject in print. This may help to explain the recent rediscovery of his work, especially among the New Age crowd, despite the fact that his music tends to be rather knotty.

FREDERIC RZEWSKI
- *The People United Will Never Be Defeated* (Oppens, piano/Van. 71248)

- *Coming Together/Attica* (Group 180/Hungaroton SLPX 12545)
- *Coming Together/Attica* (Rzewski et. al./Opus One 20) NMDS
- *Song and Dance* (None. 71366)
Rzewski's music is often politically motivated. Although occasionally self-indulgent, these are all affecting works.

MICHAEL SAHL
- *Music from the Exiles' Cafe* (Sahl, et. al./MHS 7097F) MHS. The man who brought you Nonesuch's *Tango Project* now brings you some of his own music—a rich, diverting amalgam of pop, classical, jazz, and folk styles, in colorful, witty presentations.

SŌMEI SATOH
- *"Sumeru,"* from the LP *Mandala/Sumeru* (ALM AL-26). *Mandala* is listed in Chapter 1; *Sumeru* is a soft, almost static piece for chamber orchestra.
- *Litania: Margaret Leng-Tan Plays Sōmei Satoh* (New Albion NA-008) NMDS. This superlative recording of several of Satoh's chamber works includes "The Heavenly Spheres Are Illuminated by Lights," "Birds in Warped Time" for violin and piano, and a contemplative, almost New Age–style piano solo called "Incarnation II." The title work is a thornier piece, in a sort of Penderecki-meets-the-Minimalists style. A highly recommended album.

R. MURRAY SCHAFER
- *Ra, excerpts* (Forrester, et. al./Centrediscs CMC 1283) CMC. Portions of a dusk-to-dawn epic, drawing on the mythology and symbolism of ancient Egypt. A fascinating, multimedia event from the dean of Canadian composers, with alto, soprano, occasional Arabic instruments, and ensemble.
- *East* (Radio Canada International RCI 434). A 1972 work; an orchestral meditation inspired by one of the Hindu Upanishads. The instrumentalists are asked to vocalize in spots, and the piece has an otherworldly aura.

JOSEPH SCHWANTNER
- *And the Mountains Rising Nowhere* (Hunsberger, Eastman Ensemble/Merc. 75132)
- *Magabunda* (Shelton, Slatkin, St. Louis Sym./ None. 79072)
- *Modus Caelestis* (New England Conservatory Repertory Orch./CRI 340) CRI, NMDS
- *Aftertones of Infinity* (Effrom, Eastman Phil./ Merc. 75141)
- *Wild Angels of the Open Hills*, texts by Ursula K. LeGuin (Jubal Trio/CRI 497) CRI, NMDS
- *Wind, Willow, Whisper* (da Capo/CRI 441) CRI, NMDS
All display Schwantner's prodigious gift for eccentric but effective orchestrations. As with Crumb's

music, the vocal works are an acquired taste, owing to the strange vocal effects.

RAVI SHANKAR
- *Concerto #1 for Sitar and Orchestra* (Previn, London Symphony/Ang. S-36806)
- *Raga-Mala, Sitar Concerto #2* (Mehta, London Phil./Ang. DS-37935)
- *West Meets East, Vol. 3* (Y. & H. Menuhin, Shankar, Rakha/Ang. S-36418)

Shankar's familiarity with Western classical music makes each concerto more than just an orchestral raga or a showpiece for sitar with simplistic accompaniment. The sitar is best suited to intimate forms, though, so the Shankar/Menuhin album is the best of the three. See Chapters 6 and 7.

▲ *The Shining* (War. HS 3449). Moody, atmospheric soundtrack that was as much responsible for the movie's tension and suspense as the action on the screen. Original music by Wendy Carlos is combined with perfectly appropriate excerpts by Bartók, Ligeti, and Penderecki.

ANN SILSBEE
- *"Go Gentle"* from the LP *Sleepers* (Finnadar 90266-1) NMDS. A modern lullaby on an album that collected new lullabies from a number of composers. Some of them are less soothing than you might expect. This gentle work for three strings or winds is played here on three flutes.

TORU TAKEMITSU
- *Raintree* (not yet recorded). Once considered ultra-avant-garde, Takemitsu's music has now become part of the mainstream of contemporary classical music. Yet some of his finest works haven't appeared on disc, as of this writing at least. They include this utterly bewitching work for three percussionists, playing mallet instruments and crotales (antique cymbals). The work is performed on a darkened stage, with the musicians controlling small lights near their instruments according to cues written into the score.
- *Ran* (Original Soundtrack) (Koinume, *shinobue;* Iwaki, Sapporo Symphony Orchestra/Fantasy FSP-21004) Glorious score to Akira Kurosawa's film. Blends an orchestra with the piercing Japanese *shinobue* flute and some ethnic drums. A real beauty.

CHARMAIN TASHJIAN
- *"Resan"* from the LP *New American Music, Vol.1* (Capriccio 1) NMDS. A pleasant work for chamber ensemble that uses Indonesian rhythmic patterns yet manages to come up with an original sound.

TUI ST. GEORGE TUCKER
- *Indian Summer* (Poulos, Solomon, Tucker/Opus One 107) NMDS. Subtitled "Three Microtonal Antiphons on Psalm Texts." Composed in 1983 and sung in Latin with a small ensemble of musicians, this is one of the most exquisite, impressive collections of microtonal music I've heard. Tucker uses quarter tones—notes exactly halfway between the twelve notes of our Western scale—that add a plangent quality to the music without making it dissonant. The smooth, sustained accompaniment has a nocturnal quality that may owe something to the music of the Far East.

VIENNA ART ORCHESTRA
- *The Minimalism of Erik Satie* (Hat Art 2005) NMDS. Satie never sounded like *this* . . . but he might have, had he been part of the avant-garde jazz/symphonic scene in Europe in the 70s and 80s. A truly strange recording.

▲ *The Waltz Project* (None. D-79011). The brainchild of Robert Moran and Robert Helps. Besides the Glass and Moran waltzes listed elsewhere, the collection includes Lou Harrison's lulling "Waltz for Evelyn Hinrichsen," Zygmunt Krause's tuneful "Music Box Waltz," Tom Constanten's bluesy "Dejavalse," Helps's lush "Valse Mirage," Ivan Tcherepnin's motoric "Valse Perpetuelle ('The 45 RPM')," and works by Peter Gena, Joan Tower, Virgil Thomson, John Cage, Milton Babbitt, and Roger Sessions. An amazing overview of today's American music.

ANDREW LLOYD WEBBER
- *Requiem* (Maazel, Domingo, et.al./Ang. DFO-38218). In which the composer of *Cats, Evita, Jesus Christ Superstar,* etc., applies his not inconsiderable talents to symphonic/choral music. Webber has an undeniable flair for dramatic gestures and catchy tunes. The orchestration ranges from sparkling to cliché; but despite some lovely moments and a spirited performance, the work is ultimately less than the sum of its parts.
- *Variations* (J. L. Webber, et.al./MCA 3042). This series of variations on the Paganini A-minor violin caprice was written for Webber's cellist brother Julian Lloyd Webber, and a group of noted jazz/rock musicians. The intention seems to be to have a good time playing with a venerable old theme. As such, it's a generally successful work. It has recently been reworked into the score for the Broadway hit *Song and Dance.*

STOMU YAMASH'TA
- *Sea and Sky* (Yamash'ta, Buckmaster/JVC 30221) CH. A lush, romantic work for synthesizers, percussion, and orchestra, with music similar to that on Yamash'ta's electronic albums (see Chapter 2), but this is perhaps his best, and certainly his most popular, recording.

GHEORGHE ZAMFIR AND MARCEL CELLIER
- *Flute de Pan et Orgue, Vol. 1* (Festival FLD-550)
- *Flute de Pan et Orgue, Vol. 2* (Festival FLD-617)

Imported and hard to find. The Rumanian pan-pipes virtuoso has put out some corny albums that border on easy listening, but these are early works with organ accompaniment, beautiful and not at all trivial.

FRANK ZAPPA

- *The Perfect Stranger and other works* (Boulez, Ensemble Intercontemporain/Ang. CDC-47125)

- *"Sad Jane"* from the LP *Zappa Vol. 1* (Nagano, London Symphony/Barking Pumpkin 38820) Genuinely interesting concert music from the enigmatic rock star; Zappa is a versatile musician, though his warped sense of humor can be annoying to some listeners.

6
WORLD MUSIC

Those contemporary musicians that have incorporated mystical-magical, spiritual, and metaphysical elements in their music, could be the founding fathers of an entirely new form of world-music, now in its earliest infancy.
Peter Michael Hamel, Through Music to the Self

Last is East and West is West . . . but sometimes the twain *do* meet. The merging of Orient and Occident, one of the most consequential developments in new music, is a direct product of the technology of recordings and jet-age travel. The results, depending on to whom you talk, are known by such labels as "World Music," "One-World Music," "Fourth World Music," "Earth Music," or any number of other terms.

The music discussed in the next several chapters is closely interrelated in that it is all derived from traditional forms—the "folk music" of its respective countries of origin. Chapter 8 will look at the re-emergence of the sounds of the Western folk traditions, Chapter 7 the traditional music of Asia and the Third World, and this chapter the contemporary artists who are perhaps creating a new tradition—that of Marshall MacLuhan's "global village." This hybrid form has evolved during the second half of our century, as the musicians of one culture have been exposed to the sounds and instruments of another. The influences are mutual, so that while Western pop is now heard in virtually every corner of the globe, some elements of non-Western traditions have been absorbed by jazz, folk, rock, classical, and avant-garde musicians.

Historically, one could point to the Crusades as the earliest important meeting of Eastern and Western music. Between the tenth and the thirteenth centuries, Europeans came in contact for the first time with a foreign, highly developed system of music. They were introduced by the Muslims to the 'ūd, later to become the lute; the rebec, the first bowed string instrument to be used in Europe; and other unfamiliar instruments, scales, and techniques. Reconstructing the music of that time is a tentative effort at best, but the recent practice among ancient-music groups of using Arabic modes and instruments in performance seems to be an appropriate one, as Middle Eastern sounds must have been fairly well established in Europe by the medieval era. Leading this search for a more historically correct but exotic sound are Thomas Binkley's Early Music Quartet and Joel Cohen's Boston Camerata.

Jumping ahead to the late nineteenth and early twentieth centuries, we have already seen the influence that Indian and Indonesian music had on the works of Debussy, Messiaen, Cage, and many others. The Americans Henry Cowell and Lou Harrison also studied the traditions of the Orient extensively, but their music was often considered outside the mainstream, and similar studies made by La Monte Young and Terry Riley were virtually unknown outside of a small circle of musicians. These and other isolated cases of cross-cultural music in both classical and jazz circles did set the stage for what was to come; but it remained for the most popular musicians of our time to give Eastern music the push it needed to start a new trend.

Would the World Music movement have gotten off the ground without the Beatles? Of course. It had to happen eventually; our rapidly shrinking world would have seen to that. But the Beatles, or George Harrison to be more specific, almost singlehandedly introduced the music of North India to the general public, and in so doing created a new *lingua franca*. Harrison had first displayed his interest in the sitar, the long-necked Indian lute, in the 1965 Beatles song "Norwegian Wood." The success of that experiment led him to approach the great Indian sitarist Ravi Shankar with the intention of studying the instrument formally.

"At that time," Shankar remembers, "I had never heard of the Beatles. But someone told me they were very famous, and I met them at a party, and George especially said he would like to learn sitar. So I said, you have to work very hard, and he agreed." Harrison went to India for a short while—"a very short while, only six weeks," Shankar says with a chuckle, "but in that time I did as much as I could." Though Harrison could hardly have mastered the sitar or even the fundamentals of raga in such a short time, his visit did have one powerful, unexpected effect: The rock world latched on to the sitar as fervently as it had embraced controlled chemicals and bellbottoms. "I really had no idea it would end—or rather, *begin*—as it did, with a whole new phase," Shankar continues. "It was like a sitar explosion, because George Harrison had taken me as his guru."

Indian music soon became one of the earmarks of the 60s counterculture, and Ravi Shankar, under contract at that time to several opportunistic managers, was booked into some of the decade's biggest rock festivals. "Monterey I'm not sorry about," he reflects. "My concert was in the afternoon, completely separate from that all-night jam session. After that, though, I was very unhappy, because by then I knew it was out of my control. Woodstock was the climax. That's where I saw half a million people in the rain and mud. No one was really in their right mind, and the music was just a background. That was the end; I promised I would never do that again."

In the 1970s, as Shankar extricated himself from the rock scene and the Beatles broke up, the cross-cultural fertilization in other musical circles began to come to the fore. Explorations of non-Western sounds by folk and jazz musicians had actually preceded those of the rock world, but had developed in relative obscurity. The sounds of ethnic Latin music were certainly familiar to jazz musicians as far back as the 30s and 40s, when Cuban and Brazilian rhythms became a part of the popular music of the day. By the late 50s, the modal scales that characterize much of the music of the Third World (and Western folk music as well) were being used by Miles Davis, most notably in his classic 1959 recording *Kind of Blue.*

Taking part in that session was the legendary saxophone player John Coltrane, whose own quartet was formed the following year. Coltrane's work in the early 60s was deeply personal, for his interest in Third World modes had blossomed into an intense period of study of African music and religion. Lionized by the avant-garde, his music was still incomprehensible to much of the general public. The ferocious dialogues he conducted with drummer Elvin Jones didn't sound like African music to most ears (though the combination of horns and drums is quite common in West Africa), and the mystical/ritual trappings appeared to be confined to the song titles and the album liner notes. But by drawing attention to African culture as the ancestor of jazz, Coltrane encouraged other jazz musicians to reconsider the ethnic roots of their tradition. McCoy Tyner (Coltrane's pianist for a spell in the 60s), trumpeter Don Cherry, and the Art Ensemble of Chicago are just a few of the jazz figures who have incorporated non-Western scales, ethnic instruments, and often a kind of ritualistic approach in their music.

The folk world, too, had by this time already discovered ethnic music. Several members of the steadily growing London folk circuit had become aware of the music of Ravi Shankar in the late 50s, when he began playing in England. In 1963, guitarist Davey Graham arranged the traditional folk ballad "She Moves through the Fair" as a "guitar raga." Using an Indian raga scale (*Raga Khammaj,* in case you're interested), Graham produced an exotic, brilliantly effective new version of that song —and did it almost two years before the Beatles' "Norwegian Wood."

While the Beatles may have had the greatest impact in introducing the combination of musical traditions to a large public, other factors were contributing to the development of this style. Music often draws on some pretty unlikely sources, but few musical sources have been as unusual, or as effective, as the U.S. State Department. In the 1960s, the State Department sent musicians on "goodwill" tours through developing countries—trips that often produced dramatic changes in those musicians' compositions. One of the artists thus affected is a man who has since taken a place among the most popular and acclaimed figures in the World Music field—Paul Winter, whose Consort has provided the springboard for several of the most accomplished musicians in this style.

Winter's first professional group was a jazz sextet, formed in 1961 at Northwestern University. Only a short time later, the group entered and won an intercollegiate jazz festival in Washington; one of the judges was the great jazz impresario John Hammond, and one of the prizes was a recording with Columbia. "The first thing we did," Winter recalls, "was approach the State Department about sending us on a goodwill tour. We wanted to go either to the Far East or the Iron Curtain. After going through the standard procedure, they wrote back and said they were sending us to Latin America for six months!"

Early in 1962, Paul Winter's group finished its first album for John Hammond and Columbia, and took off for a tour of twenty-three countries in Latin America. As Winter recalls, "it absolutely exploded our conception of what the world was."

Upon returning to the States, his band performed in the White House at the request of President and Mrs. Kennedy. That was November of 1962, and it marked the first time a jazz group had ever played there.* The ensemble then moved to New York and recorded a few more albums, but the influence of the music Winter had heard in South America, especially in Brazil, had gradually asserted itself, and in 1967 he decided to put together the first Paul Winter Consort.

"The sextet, the bebop group, began to evolve towards the Consort," he recounts, "partly through the influence of classical guitar, which we fell in love with in Brazil, and partly because I went back to Brazil several times to hear Afro-Brazilian percussion." Besides seeking an alternative to the usual trap drums, Winter wanted "to make a band with a wholly new instrumentation, and to interweave all of the instruments I loved, like cello and English horn—instruments that I rarely got to hear in a really soulful, solo way, in the way that jazz instruments are heard." The first Consort used a hybrid array of jazz instruments, including Winter's own saxophone, "concert" instruments like the cello, and ethnic percussion. Although the personnel and the precise makeup of the ensemble would constantly change, the combination of jazz, classical, and ethnic instruments has remained a characteristic feature of the Paul Winter Consort for some twenty years.

Even before the Consort had its first performance, though, at least one other important musician had already begun tearing down the walls between Eastern and Western styles. David Amram, a French-horn player by trade, had composed over a hundred orchestral and chamber works, and was, in fact, the first composer-in-residence with the New York Philharmonic in 1966. But Amram also played jazz —with his own quartet and with some of that field's brightest stars—and traveled via the State Department's goodwill tours to Brazil, East Africa, and the Near East. As the 60s progressed and the exoticism of ethnic music began to have wider appeal, Amram got right into the spirit with works like the *Tompkins Square Park Consciousness Expander* (1966). Despite the title, this is *not* a paean to the wonders of LSD, but a work which combines Western instruments with the North African bendir (a drum), the 'ūd, and the Pakistani flute, the latter played by the versatile Amram himself.

Amram also found inspiration in the music of Brazil, which he first visited in 1969 in the dual roles of classical conductor and jazz musician. As with Paul Winter, the influence of Brazilian music is most evident in Amram's use of percussion: Latin rhythms appear not only in works like *São Paolo* (1969), but also in the Triple Concerto (1970) for woodwind-, brass-, and jazz-quartets with full orchestra. This piece also uses Arabic rhythms and Armenian melodies, which are an even more prominent feature of this composer's work.

While Amram's explorations may have prepared the way for Winter's, they differed in some major respects. While Winter's music is fairly removed from straightahead jazz, Amram, by contrast, has many irons in the fire: His classical and jazz scores are still recognizable as such, however many ethnic instruments he uses. And he uses quite a few—besides the Pakistani flute, he also plays the shanai (a

---

*Some twenty-two years later, Winter's group became the first "jazz" ensemble to play in the United Nations General Assembly. The invitation came along with a U.N. award for his longtime efforts at putting environmental concerns before the public.

Central Asian type of oboe), numerous other ethnic flutes, and percussion instruments like the dumbeg, a Near Eastern jar drum.

An Israeli jar drum figured in the earliest incarnations of the Paul Winter Consort, the first of many strange percussion instruments from virtually every corner of the globe to appear in that group. "I've loved percussion as long as I can remember," says Winter. "My first memories of jazz were going to various dances with my parents when I was four or five, and standing behind the trap drummer, just watching with fascination. The first instrument I played was drums, and the percussion thing's always been there in the background." Actually, there were times in the group's history when the background threatened to take over the whole show. "At one point, in the mid-70s, the Consort had grown to be a kind of circus; we had six tons of gear and truckloads of percussion. I still have a barn full of different percussion instruments [Winter lives on a farm in Connecticut], and once in a while I'll go in and grab various things, and put them on the truck for a tour."

To many listeners, the finest percussionist to play with the Consort was Collin Walcott who, before leaving the group in the early 70s, introduced it to the sounds of the Indian tabla, and later to the sitar. It was at this time, around 1970, that the Paul Winter Consort reached its highest level of musicianship. One of its members, classically trained guitarist Ralph Towner, wrote a piece of music, originally with a strong bossa nova flavor, called "Icarus." The song became the "signature tune" for the Consort, appearing on at least four of Winter's albums. The bossa nova aspect was not discernible in early recordings of the piece; in its classic performance on the 1972 album *Icarus,* the song is propelled by Walcott's tabla and gets radiant solo work from reed player Paul McCandless and cellist David Darling.

Icarus was produced by George Martin, the former producer of the Beatles. In his 1979 autobiography, Martin called the record "the finest album I have made," and it is probably the finest album the Consort has made as well. By this point, not only had the group's style matured but Winter had also brought together a particularly impressive group of musicians: Herb Bushler, the bassist from David Amram's quartet, joined Winter, Towner, Walcott, McCandless, and Darling in the lineup. The Consort attracted a surprising amount of attention, and with it the inevitable question: What kind of music was this? "I really gave up trying to categorize my music about fifteen years ago," Winter states. "Agents and record companies want to have some kind of words to put on promotional materials, so there've been all kinds of labels from 'Whole Earth Music' to 'Earth Jazz.' My most flippant reply to the question is to just call it Contemporary Contrapuntal Connecticut Country Consort Music—and I usually don't get asked again."

On a more serious note, Winter describes his style as American music in the broadest sense: "It's really celebrating the convergence of both roots of American culture—European and African." The European influence is evident in Winter's use of cello, oboe, and guitar; he has also arranged music by Bach for Consort performance. The African influence came to the fore in two excerpts from *Icarus,* "Whole Earth Chant" and "Minuit," in which African percussion was included not as an exotic coloristic effect, but as the central sound of the pieces.

"African music is something I love very much," says Winter. "We've learned a bit from some Africans we met here, and Brazil is really an African offshoot, musically, so that's where that influence originally came from. We also studied the music of Uganda, especially the amadinda, which is a big log xylophone that lies on the floor, and two or three people play it at once." An arrangement of a traditional amadinda song appears on the album *Road* (1970), under the title of "Africanus Brasileiras Americanus."

Although the core instrumentation of the Paul Winter Consort has remained fairly constant—sax, oboe, guitar, percussion—the actual personnel have changed frequently. Winter thinks of the Consort as a kind of school, its purpose one of "learning and exploration." As with any school, the musicians eventually graduate and pursue their own projects. "I fully support that and encourage it," Winter says, "though it's sometimes hard to see your long-time colleagues and friends leave. But we always play together again eventually, on one project or another. We have a remarkable extended family."

Remarkable indeed. The quartet Oregon, perhaps the most talented group of its kind, consists of former Consort members. Oregon's Ralph Towner and Collin Walcott pursued solo careers as well, and made recordings of cross-cultural music with other musicians, the most notable being the collaborations between Walcott, trumpeter Don Cherry, and Brazilian percussionist Nana Vasconcelos released under the name Codona. Cellist David Darling, another Consort "graduate," has also had a successful solo career. "There are a lot of things I learned through the Consort," he acknowledges. "One was ethnic music, finding out that Indian and African music was totally mind-blowing; to try to play it on the cello was as exciting as trying to play classical music. There's something about it that's very challenging and very beautiful." Alumnus Jim Scott has recorded solo guitar material and, with other Consort musicians, has put together an ensemble called Radiance, with a number of recordings to its credit.

Perhaps as much a component of Paul Winter's music as the actual sound is its explicit concern for wildlife and ecology, an element that has appeared in all of the Consort's albums since the early 70s. Winter began investigating the music of other animals in 1968 when he heard a tape of humpback-whale songs. "That was astounding to me," he asserts. "To learn what went on in those songs and the obvious intelligence behind them, and then to learn what was happening with the very efficient extermination of those species—that stirred me very much.

"As I spent more time with those tapes, and began to hear recordings of wolves, it turned me on in the way that Charlie Parker did when I first heard him in the early 50s. After experiencing many human cultures, I suddenly realized that there's a greater world out there, of which we really are a part, and we've forgotten that."

In searching for ways to incorporate the themes of animal songs into the Consort's music, Winter found that whale songs and the cries of the loon could be assigned to a certain key; a piece written in that same key could use the taped animal sounds as part of its melodic material. Winter even went so far as to record a duet between himself and a wolf in a California wildlife preserve.

Even more than such electronic favorites as Kitaro or Steven Halpern, Paul Winter has become one of the leading figures in "New Age" music. His combination of ethnic traditions with Western classical and jazz styles represents an intentional disregard for cultural, racial, and geographic boundaries, an attitude that appealed early on to the nascent New Age movement. His work on behalf of wildlife conservation and protection of the environment has the distinction of being both important and widely recognized. As with the electronic New Age or "healing" music discussed earlier, Winter's work is meant not simply for listening; it has a stated purpose, or usefulness, that often seems at least as valid as the notes themselves. In Winter's case, however, the excellence of his musicians generally keeps the music from becoming a secondary concern. It's quite possible for someone to listen to a Paul Winter Consort recording, enjoy it thoroughly, and then go out and wreak ecological havoc.

Today, World Music has caught on with literally hundreds of musicians. We've seen how all four of the original Minimalists studied and used non-Western techniques; while their style may *sound* Western, it actually represents a parallel evolution from the same sources used by World Music ensembles. The influence of non-Western traditions has also extended to electronic music, where Cyrille Verdeaux, for example, includes Indian instruments as a foil for his synthesizers.

Given the interest in Eastern music on the part of such early West Coast composers as Lou Harrison, John Cage, and La Monte Young, it shouldn't be surprising that so many of the groups now playing cross-cultural music come from California. The seeds of the style had actually been planted in the West long before Amram and Winter began to popularize it. "California is the most remote part of the Western world from the tradition of European classical music," maintains Bernard Xolotl. "In many ways, California is closer to Oriental music: There are excellent schools of Indian music; many people practice gamelan. Ethnic music is closer to the California way of thinking about music than the Western classical tradition." The works of Cyrille Verdeaux, Ingram Marshall, and groups like Ancient Future and Mickey Hart's defunct Diga Rhythm Band all show the pervasive influence of Eastern music on the West Coast.

Ethnomusicology, the study of non-Western music, has for many years been a frequently appearing course in California schools. Ingram Marshall recalls travelling as a Cal Arts graduate student to Indonesia in 1971. "Charlemagne Palestine and I were the only composers in that group," he says, "the rest were ethnomusicologists. That's when we really got interested in Indonesian music. My electronic music up to that point had been modeled on the Columbia–Princeton studios—very tightly structured, where every little sound had a place and a reason for being there. One of the things about the Javanese influence was that my sense of timing relaxed. I realized that you could stretch time out almost indefinitely." Thus were born Marshall's gradually unfolding scores for gambuh flute and electronics, and Charlemagne Palestine's extended piano compositions.

Also part of the artistic ferment in California in the 60s and early 70s was Pauline Oliveros. Her approach to music is likewise an Eastern one, involving mystical elements like the mandala, a circular drawing used in Hindu and Buddhist traditions to represent the universe. "A mandala, or circle, implies an infinite number of points," Oliveros notes, "so there's always room for something else. I like to think of that as a way of looking at World Music." Strongly influenced by the music of Tibetan Buddhist ceremonies, Oliveros has developed a ritual style of vocal and accordion performance that is in the end more Eastern in spirit than in sound.

Of the genuinely talented West Coast groups that have appeared in the World Music field, perhaps the most ambitious and exciting is the quartet Oregon. As an offshoot of the Winter Consort, the group was already familiar with a wide variety of styles. Guitarist Ralph Towner, bassist Glen Moore, and oboist Paul McCandless were adept at classical music and jazz; Towner had already proven himself a fine composer. But the unique, immediately identifiable sound of Oregon's music was the contribution of gifted sitar and tabla player Collin Walcott. Walcott had studied tabla with Alla Rakha and sitar, briefly, with Ravi Shankar. "Collin Walcott was really very serious in the short time he trained with me," Shankar remembers. "But the situation arose where I was away and he had to do something else, so he started this group, Oregon, and he really went in another, very different direction." Walcott played not only Indian instruments, but also those of every other continent except Antarctica, in an idiosyncratic, often untraditional way. No matter what instrument he used, though, it blended perfectly with the forces of the rest of the quartet.

Although it mixed classical, jazz, Indian, and African styles, nothing in Oregon's music sounded forced or gratuitous. Their album *Music of Another Present Era,* released on Vanguard in 1972, already displayed the maturity and depth of the ensemble's sound; the compositional duties were split among all four members—though Towner's writing even then stood out from the rest—and over a dozen instruments were employed.

Oregon began attracting critical attention almost immediately. By the time the group left Vanguard Records for the larger Elektra label in the mid-70s, they had built a large and enthusiastic audience. Despite his classical training, Ralph Towner was highly regarded by jazz buffs, and as a solo artist developed a long, productive relationship with the "jazz" label ECM (see pages 186–195). The other members of Oregon produced solo albums as well; Walcott kept especially busy, producing and playing on several albums by vocalist Meredith Monk, and in 1979 formed the trio Codona.

Codona's music was even more radically exotic than Oregon's. The name comes from the first two letters of each musician's first name: *Co*llin Walcott played a large assortment of ethnic percussion and string instruments; *Do*n Cherry played trumpet, flutes, and the doussn'gouni, an African instrument that looks like a cross between a banjo and a garden hoe; and Brazilian percussionist *Na*na Vasconcelos added still more ethnic noisemakers. The level of composition in the group wasn't as high or as consistent as in its members' other projects—Codona's pieces often seem more like experiments in musical color than finished products—but its sound was extraordinary. The untitled first album includes several Walcott pieces, and some weird, hybrid arrangements of music by Ornette Coleman and, believe it or not, Stevie Wonder; it remains the strongest of the three Codona records.

Despite their various other projects, the members of Oregon continued to tour and record together. They made several fine albums for Elektra; the albums sold well and their concerts usually sold out, in spite of the fact that many listeners were puzzled by their music and couldn't easily categorize it. In 1983, Oregon made its almost inevitable move to ECM, releasing an untitled album that in many ways was the most unorthodox of their long, unorthodox career. Towner introduced the sounds of the synthesizer to the group; McCandless appeared on one piece with an eighteenth-century French bagpipe known as a musette. The music ranged from dark improvisations that verged on atonality to buoyant, striding jazz. This mixture of different musical traditions was accomplished without a trace of self-conscious-ness, and the various instruments and styles were integrated to such a degree that the music transcended its hybrid roots. Only when you saw it listed on paper would you realize that the tin whistle, tongue drum, and synthesizer were not instruments one heard together every day.

The album *Crossing,* issued in 1985, continued with the developments begun on the previous disc. It was a lyrical, well-knit collection—and it was, unfortunately, the last recording Oregon made, at least with its original personnel. In November 1984, while touring through East Germany, Collin Walcott was killed in an automo-bile accident. *Crossing* was completed just a few weeks before his death, and with the possible exception of earlier unreleased material, will be the last word from this memorable musician. Oregon has toured since then, with percussionist Trilok Gurtu taking Walcott's place, so further Oregon recordings are not out of the question; but the tragic loss of Collin Walcott deprived new music of one of its most distinctive voices.

Even while Oregon was just forming, an international ensemble in West Ger-many was beginning its own explorations of cross-cultural music. The group Be-tween, formed in 1970, released its first album *Einstieg* one year later. Though the personnel has changed somewhat, the core of the group has remained consistent: German author, keyboardist, and composer Peter Michael Hamel has been the ensemble's central figure, joined by American oboist Robert Eliscu and Argentine guitarist Roberto Detree, who have also composed and performed on all the Between recordings. Like the Paul Winter Consort, Between has a large extended family. Eliscu has been a part of the New York Kammermusiker, a chamber music ensem-ble, and of the German group Popol Vuh. Tom van der Geld, a vibraphonist who appeared in a later edition of Between, has had a notable solo career. And in the first Between lineup was a young Irish flutist, James Galway (or Jimmy, back then), who was part of the Berlin Philharmonic at the time of *Einstieg.* He didn't stay with Between very long, and quite frankly, he wasn't very effective while he was with them, but the "man with the golden flute" has since become one of classical music's most popular soloists.

Because of Hamel's many commitments—he composes contemporary classical scores, appears as a solo artist, and writes on music frequently—Between has not recorded a great deal. *Einstieg* is a tentative album, a bit of musical psychedelia that succeeds only in spots. The later Between recordings, on the other hand, are gener-ally excellent, blending Western classical music, jazz, Indian-inspired keyboards and scales, and percussion from Africa, South America, and Asia. *Contemplation, Dharana, And the Waters Opened,* and *Silence Beyond Time* represent some of the finest World Music to come from Europe to date.

The development of World Music across the globe is not really a surprising phenomenon. In our rapidly shrinking world, it's easier for a musician to travel halfway around the Earth than it was for Mozart to tour the capitals of Europe. Today music reaches any part of the planet as easily as Stephen Foster's songs entered the parlor of the average American home a century ago. Today the work of an artist as culturally distant as V. V. Lakshminarayana, a South Indian violinist, can be heard on disc and even in concert in the West. Meanwhile, one of his violin-playing sons, L. Shankar, has grown up on Western pop.

"When I was young," he says, "we'd always hear the Beatles and Elvis Presley." Shankar (not related to Ravi, who is North Indian) now lives in New York and is an example of cross-cultural music in reverse. A number of Eastern musicians—including Shankar, his brother L. Subramaniam, and Japan's Yas-Kaz—have begun to incorporate Western idioms into their own traditions. Shankar cofounded one of guitarist John McLaughlin's groups, Shakti, in 1976 after the breakup of McLaughlin's Mahavishnu Orchestra. Both McLaughlin ensembles combined jazz-rock fusion with Indian music, and since Shakti's inception Shankar has been closely involved with Western music.

"Music is like painting," he observes. "There are so many colors to choose from, and so many things to do with them. I like to combine different traditions, because I love a lot of different kinds of music." His recordings bear out that interest. *Who's To Know?* (1981) is a unique cross-cultural fusion of northern and southern Indian styles. *Vision* (1984) and *Song for Everyone* (1985) feature jazz saxophonist Jan Garbarek, and *The Epidemics* (1986) is an album by his pop group. Shankar has also played with such notable figures as Frank Zappa, George Harrison, Peter Gabriel, Talking Heads, and the Quebec Symphony. Even his instrument is a fusion of East and West. Using a double-necked, ten-string electronic violin of his own design, Shankar can create elaborate musical effects and a wide variety of moods, yet whether he's playing classical Indian music with his father or a solo for a Phil Collins album, he uses the traditional south Indian fingerings and techniques.

For the average listener, the real value of World Music is ultimately the exposure it gives to non-Western sounds. Most of us have little contact with the music and instruments of Brazil, or India, or Ghana, as part of our daily routines. But like the Europeans in the time of the Crusades, many Westerners are now discovering, to their considerable surprise, that a number of other highly developed musical cultures do exist, and that some of them are more ancient and, in the case of rhythm, even more complex than Western music. In addition to fostering interest in ethnic traditions (see Chapter 7), the rise of World Music may also bring new listeners to other musical forms: L. Subramaniam's concerto-style works for violin and orchestra bring jazz afficionados to the concert hall; and listeners who've grown to appreciate the sounds of the Near East are now attending concerts by such early music groups as Anonymus [sic] and the Boston Camerata. Of all the new styles that have appeared recently, World Music is perhaps the most successful at crossing—or ignoring—musical and cultural boundaries.

DISCOGRAPHY AND RELATED WORKS

MAHMOUD AHMED
- *Ere Mela Mela* (Crammed Discs CRAM-047) NMDS. Ethiopia's Frank Sinatra and Beatles all rolled into one. This album, Ahmed's first to be released outside Ethiopia, has energy and *joie de vivre* and sounds like a bizarre cross between southern blues and Indian or Indonesian popular music. An abundance of Western instruments, too.

AILANA
- *Archipelago* (Hannibal 1314) HAN. A remarkable if uneven effort: Traditional African ensemble drumming and spacey electronics are heard back to back, and are combined with jazz on the title track. Some of the attempts at jazzy riffing fall flat, but the production is quite good and the piece has some enticing passages.

DAVID AMRAM
- *At Home around the World* (Fly. F. FF-094) FF
- *No More Walls* (FC-27752) FF
The first includes recordings of Amram playing with musicians in the Near East and Central Asia, as well as Latin and jazz pieces. The second is a varied album of Latin, Near Eastern, jazz, and classical influences, with several Latin American and Near Eastern musicians performing.

ANCIENT FUTURE
- *Visions of a Peaceful Planet* (Beauty AF-79) NAR. Using Indian sarod (a lute), tabla, and sitar with guitars, flutes, harps, etc., this California ensemble gamely tries to fashion a sort of cross-cultural jazz. Interesting moments, but their second effort is far better.
- *Natural Rhythms* (Philo 9006) NAR, PHI, FOR. This 1981 recording was made partly on the island of Bali, and features Balinese musicians. There are also some works exploring the by now familiar fusion of Indian music and jazz, but it's the trio of works combining Balinese bamboo percussion with guitar, beer cans, and frogs on tape that really stands out. In all, this is one of the finest albums in this genre.

- ▲ *Asian Journal* (Music of the World J-101) MOW. Cross-cultural music blending Indian, Brazilian, and jazz elements, among many others. The all-star lineup includes Nana Vasconcelos, percussion; Steve Gorn, bansuri flute; Badal Roy, tabla; and Mike Richmond, bass. Sound quality is not the best.

SHLOMO BAT-AIN
- *Acacia Wood* (Trikont US-08-0123; Neran Productions, 55 Old Field Road, Huntington, NY 11743, 516–673–7297). This Israeli composer now works in New York. His album is based, he tells us, on "Indian ragas, Moroccan concepts of rhythm and melody as well as Western harmonics." Bat-Ain successfully captures the infectious sound of Near Eastern pop song orchestrations on a couple of tracks; a neat recording of synthesizer, guitar, bass, flute, lots of percussion, and only a bit of superfluous vocals.

BENGT BERGER
- *Bitter Funeral Beer* (ECM 1179) PSI. Based on and including the funeral music of the Lo-Birifor, Sisaala, and Ewe tribes of Ghana. Members of the Swedish jazz community, trumpeter Don Cherry, and an Ewe drum ensemble appear here.

BETWEEN
- *Einstieg* (Wergo SM-1001) CH
- *Dharana* (Wergo SM-1011) CH, FOR
- *Contemplation* (Wergo SM-1012) CH, FOR
- *And the Waters Opened* (Wergo SM-1014) CH, FOR
- *Stille über der Zeit/Silence Beyond Time* (Wergo SM-1023) CH, FOR
The core of this German-based group has been keyboardist Peter Michael Hamel, whose works are listed in several chapters; Argentine guitarist Roberto Detree (see Chapter 2); and American oboist Robert Eliscu, a member of the New York Kammermusiker (see below). With a number of guest artists from various countries, they mix Western jazz and classical forms with Indian, African, and Minimalist ingredients. Well-crafted

music that doesn't (usually) resort to cheap exotic effects.

BIG BLACK
- *Ethnic Fusion* (1750 Arch S-1790) NMDS. A Caribbean tumba and conga player whose best works are those with guitarist Anthony Wheaton, who appears on several tracks.

CARLA BLEY
"A.I.R." from the three-LP set *Escalator over the Hill* (JCOA EOTH) NMDS. There's little point in trying to describe this mammoth, ambitious work unless you're familiar with the Jazz Composers' Orchestra, *Devotion*-period John McLaughlin, Albert Ayler, and all of Carla Bley's early work. "A.I.R." is probably the most accessible piece here; Don Cherry and a number of others help out in some breezy Eastern-sounding jazz.

ANTONIO BRESCHI
- *Linguaggio dei Luoghi* (General Music GM-30712). Italian pianist/composer Breschi has had a long love affair with Celtic folk music (see Chapter 8), and while that influence is among the many felt here, this film score includes Indian and perhaps North African components, too. Breschi's most colorful album.

SANDY BULL
- *E Pluribus Unum* (Terra/Van. T-3). A reissue of a 1969 album. Bull plays electric guitar, Arabic 'ūd, bass, and percussion. The sound is badly dated, with cheap echo effects and loud, distorted reverb. Real 60s acoustic psychedelia.

DAVID BYRNE AND BRIAN ENO
- *My Life in the Bush of Ghosts* (Sire SRK-6093). Byrne (see Chapters 9 and 11) is singer and songwriter for the group Talking Heads, a group that Eno was closely involved with for several years. Around 1979–1980, these two began weaving African rhythms and other Third World ingredients into their music. This album is a powerful, arresting example of how the sounds of rock and ethnic music can be blended until the resulting music is neither one nor the other.

SHEILA CHANDRA
- *Quiet* (Indipop SCH-2)
- *The Struggle* (Indipop SCH-3) LADY
- *Nada Brahma* (Indipop SCH-4) LADY
Quiet is an excellent album-length piece based on Indian *sargam* (the equivalent of Western sight-singing), using Western instruments in the ensemble. It's unfortunately very hard to find. The title track of *Nada Brahma* is a similar work, again with an interesting combination of accompanying instruments. The rest of *Nada Brahma* and *The Struggle* are aptly described by the name of the record label.

DON CHERRY AND ED BLACKWELL
- *El Corazon* (ECM 1230) ECM. American trumpeter and African music enthusiast Don Cherry plays keyboards and doussn'gouni on this album; Blackwell plays drum kit, wood drum, and cowbell. A spare but energetic album of World Music.

DON CHERRY AND LATIF KHAN
- *Sangam* (Europa JP-2009) NMDS. Here, Cherry teams up with a young Indian tabla player. Cherry overdubs many instruments, and the result is some intricately colored music. "One Dance" may be the prettiest tune Cherry has written.

SRI CHINMOY
- *Flute Music for Meditation*
- *Existence—Consciousness—Bliss*
- *Victory's Dance* (all from Sri Chinmoy Centre, PO Box 32433, Jamaica, NY 11431)
Sri Chinmoy is a religious, athletic, and musical guru to people around the world. Originally from Bengal, he plays Indian instruments like the esraj, a type of cello. He also uses the flute and Western delay or echo techniques. Very mystical and meditative without being overtly New Ageish.

CODONA
- *Codona* (ECM 1132) ECM
- *Codona II* (ECM 1177) ECM
- *Codona III* (ECM 1243) ECM
The mixture of Walcott's Indian instruments, Vasconcelos's Brazilian percussion, and Cherry's African music didn't always work, but it was almost always interesting, occasionally brilliant, without exception well-played.

LARRY CORYELL
- *"Spiritual Dance"* from the LP *Standing Ovation* (Arista AN-3024). Most of the album is a solo guitar record, but on this piece L. Subramaniam joins Coryell on violin and drone. A fiery work for two dueling virtuosi, but with enough musical content to keep it from being an empty showcase for rapid scale work.

STEPHEN COUGHLIN
- *The Song of the Reed* (For. FOR-010) FOR, NAR, VB
- *Night Music* (Fortuna Records, scheduled for release in 1987)

EAST WINDOW (COUGHLIN AND FUNK)
- *Music of East Window* (EW-001) FOR, NAR, VB

STEPHEN COUGHLIN AND MOULABAKHSH FUNK
- *Archways* (For. FOR-028) FOR, NAR. Coughlin moved from R&B to Indian-inspired flute and sax improvisations after hearing Pandit Pran Nath in 1970, and often uses zither, percussion, and occasional electronics on his solo recordings. Both solo

albums are predominantly quiet and nocturnal, but some of the more rhythmic sections have a gentle swing to them; both are fine collections. The Coughlin/Funk recordings are for flute or sax and piano. Western classical elements are a bit more noticeable, and even if they're not quite as exotic, both recordings are just as well-played.

DÄFOS
- *Däfos* (Reference Recordings RR-12) REF. Däfos is Mickey Hart, percussionist for the Grateful Dead and an avid collector of ethnic instruments; Airto Moreira, the talented Brazilian percussionist/composer; and his wife, the vocalist Flora Purim. Steven Douglas adds some flute occasionally, but the amazing variety of percussion sounds makes any other instruments unnecessary. Some Latin jazz with vocals, some tribal drumming, and excellent production.

DAVID DARLING
- *Cycles* (ECM 1219) ECM. Electric and acoustic cellist David Darling is joined by Collin Walcott, saxophonist Jan Garbarek, guitarist Steve Kuhn, and others. Lyrical, swinging music. See Chapters 9 and 10; pages 231–32.

DIGA RHYTHM BAND
- *Diga* (Round RX-LA 600/RX-110). A 1976 album by Mickey Hart, tabla player Zakir Hussain, and *nine* other percussionists. A high-spirited celebration of drumming and rhythms from Africa, India, Indonesia, and the West.

DJURDJURA
- *Djurdjura* (Kondo Ra KRA-3003). This Algerian trio of female vocalists does a group of songs that are strongly influenced by Western pop music. But the backing ensemble includes the 'ūd, the raita, and North African percussion as well as strings, guitar, bass, and drums. The singing is beautiful, and except for a few overdone arrangements, this is a fine album.

DO'A
- *Light upon Light* (Philo PH-1056) PHI, NAR, VB, FOR
- *Ornament of Hope* (Philo PH-9000) PHI, NAR, VB, FOR
- *Ancient Beauty* (Philo PHDG-9004) PHI, NAR, VB, FOR
- *Companions of the Crimson-Coloured Ark* (Philo PH-9009) PHI, NAR, VB, FOR
Do'A is an Arabic/Persian call to prayer or meditation. Flutist and percussionist Ken LaRoche and guitarist/percussionist Randy Armstrong have been the steady members of Do'A, which was a duet until the last album, when they suddenly became a quintet. The first three albums feature instruments from virtually every continent. Soft flute and mandolin/harp duets alternate with stirring

feasts of percussion. The fourth album leans heavily on Western trap drums, catchy sax breaks, and jazzy ensemble playing, while still incorporating dozens of ethnic instruments.

EDIKANFO
- *The Pace Setters* (EG EGM-112). This "African Super Band" is a good example of West African "highlife" or pop music, with electric bass, guitar, keyboard, and brass over lots of traditional and Western percussion.

STEVE ELIOVSON AND COLLIN WALCOTT
- *Dawn Dance* (ECM 1198) ECM. Duets, with Eliovson on guitar and Walcott handling tabla. Simple, tasteful stuff.

- *Eternal Wind* (Fly. F. FF-348) FF. Reeds, horns, piano, guitars, and *lots* of percussion. Several works draw on West African Yoruba mythology, and most combine jazz with ethnic drums, rattles, and such.

JOHN FAHEY
- *The Voice of the Turtle* (Takoma Records C-1019). An important American guitarist (see Chapter 8) and a precursor to the popular Windham Hill label who's listed here because this album incorporates tapes of Indonesian percussion and Tibetan chant in his two-part piece "A Raga Called Pat." A 1968 album that is perhaps still ahead of its time.

PIERRE FAVRE
- *Singing Drums* (ECM 1274) PSI. Favre's ensemble, which includes three other percussionists (Paul Motion, Fredy Studer, and Nana Vasconcelos) in an album of unrestrained tympanophilia, drawing on several musical traditions.

GAMELAN SON OF LION
- *Gamelan in the New World* (Folk. 31313) NMDS
- *Gamelan in the New World, Vol. 2* (Folk. 31312) NMDS
Barbara Benary, Daniel Goode, Peter Griggs, and others perform quasi-Indonesian music on instruments they've built themselves. Western composition techniques are used, especially on the second album, and the result is a sophisticated blend of East and West.

RICHARD GARNEAU
- *Sunwheel* (Global Pacific JM-213) NAR. After an annoying opening piece, this cassette settles down to an enjoyable mix of sitar, cello, flute, tabla, and orchestra. Not terribly important, but not completely mindless either.

MICHAEL WILLIAM GILBERT
- *The Call* (Gibex 002) NMDS
- *Moving Pictures* (Gibex 001) NMDS

■ *In the Dreamtime* (Palace of Lights 02,2000)
NMDS
Gilbert, based in Massachusetts, has developed a
catchy style that combines jazz and electronic
music with a large dose of ethnic percussion. All
three albums have effective tracks, with the first
side of *The Call* and most of *In the Dreamtime*
representing his best work.

DAVID GILDEN
■ *Kora*
■ *Kora II*
■ *Ancestral Voices* (all from David Gilden, Kora
Productions, 165 Prospect Park West, Brooklyn,
NY 11215-5256)
Gilden plays the West African kora, a twenty-one-
string lute-harp with a fascinating delicate tone.
His cassette recordings are a curious blend of West
African music, British or Celtic folk music, and
original melodies. *Ancestral Voices* includes the
African thumb piano and quite a bit of synthesizer
as well. Immediately charming, accessible music.

EGBERTO GISMONTI
■ *Dança das Cabeças* (ECM 1089) ECM
■ *Sol do Meio Dia* (ECM 1116) ECM
■ *Solo* (ECM 1136) ECM
■ *Sanfona* (ECM 1203/04, 2 LPs) ECM

EGBERTO GISMONTI AND NANA VAS-CONCELOS
■ *Duas Vozes* (ECM 25015-1) ECM
A Brazilian musician whose specialty is the eight-
string guitar, Gismonti also plays piano, African
thumb piano, flute, and many others. Vasconcelos
usually accompanies on percussion and berimbau,
a Brazilian instrument that looks like an archery
bow with a gourd attached. For the most part,
Gismonti's music shows a keen awareness of the
music of the Afro-Brazilian culture and the traditions of the Xingu and other aboriginal South
American Indians. A brilliant musician, he's also
a fine composer. "Bianca," from *Duas Vozes,* and
all of *Sol do Meio Dia*'s first side are among the
best examples of World Music.

STU GOLDBERG
■ *Solos, Duos, Trio* (Pausa 7036). 1978 album from
a keyboardist associated with John McLaughlin.
L. Subramaniam and Larry Coryell appear on violin and guitar, and the music is an excellent example of jazz-meets-Indian-music. A fine recording,
now probably out of print.

GONDWANALAND PROJECT
■ *Terra Incognita* (Hot 1005) EUR. This Australian
duo combines the sounds of the traditional aboriginal didjeridoo with the Western synthesizer. An
effective combo, however bizarre it might look on
paper or sound on vinyl.

DAVEY GRAHAM
■ *Large as Life and Twice as Natural* (London PS-
552)
■ *Dance for Two People* (Kicking Mule SNKF-158)
KM

DAVEY GRAHAM AND SHIRLEY COLLINS
■ *Folk Roots, New Routes* (Righteous GDC-001)
Graham was probably the first member of the London folk circuit to adopt instrumental techniques
from Morocco, India, and Turkey. His early recordings include several "guitar ragas," and guitar
versions of North African music. Later albums
have Irish or British folk songs played on Indian
sarod, Greek bouzouki, or the Arabic 'ūd. See
pages 166 and 167, and discography for Chapter
8.

THE HABIBIYYA
■ *If Man But Knew* (Island HELP-7). Some of this
1972 recording is now a bit dated, but the smaller
works, "Koto Piece" and "Two Shakuhachis,"
have a nice Zenlike quality.

PETER MICHAEL HAMEL
■ *Aura* (Wergo SM-1009) CH
■ *Nada* (CH CEL-001) CH, NAR, FOR
Yet another listing for this multitalented musician
(see Chapters 1, 4, and 5) and leader of the group
Between. These works use Indian scales, pianos
prepared to sound like Indonesian gamelans, and
other World Music effects.

HART/WOLFF/HENNINGS
■ *Yamantaka* (CH CEL-003) CH. Mickey Hart here
teams up with Henry Wolff and Nancy Hennings
of Tibetan Bells fame. An album of ringing, resonant percussion that defies you to believe it's not
electronic. (See Wolff and Hennings, below.)

JON HASSELL
■ *Earthquake Island* (Tomato 7019)
■ *Vernal Equinox* (Lovely LML-1021) NMDS
■ *Aka/Darbari/Java—Magic Realism* (EG EGED-
31) JEM, NAR
■ *Power Spot* (ECM 1327) ECM

JON HASSELL AND BRIAN ENO
■ *Possible Musics* (EG EGS-107) JEM
■ *Dream Theory in Malaya* (EG EGM-114) JEM,
NAR
Hassell has studied Indian music with Pandit Pran
Nath, and has developed an almost vocal style of
trumpet playing, giving an otherworldly texture to
this familiar instrument. Ethnic instruments and
influences color virtually every work Hassell has
done. *Possible Musics,* a blend of African, Asian,
and Western forms, has some truly magical moments on it.

R. I. P. HAYMAN

■ *Nightsongs, et.al.* (New Wilderness Audiographics, 325 Spring Street, New York, NY 10013). Haunting music for Chinese instruments, including the gu qin, or lute. After five years of study in China, Hayman has succeeded in capturing the spirit of Chinese music in a truly international way.

PAUL HORN

■ *Cosmic Consciousness: Paul Horn in Kashmir* (WPS-21445). Much of flutist Paul Horn's recorded material, including most of his famous "Inside" series, deals obliquely with ethnic musical influences. (See Chapter 9, pages 187 and 208) This album was recorded in India with a number of Indian virtuosi, and is Horn's least Western-sounding album. Also see Shankar listing below.

RICHARD HOROWITZ AND SUSSAN DEIHIM

■ *Eros in Arabia* (Ethnotech RH-777)
■ *Desert Equations* (Crammed Discs MTM-8) NMDS
Although the Horowitz/Deihim works are all listed in Chapter 2, they are all examples of World Music as well. Since Deihim is from Iran and Horowitz lived for several years in Morocco, the Near Eastern quality of their music is entirely convincing.

DAVID AND AMANDA HUGHES

■ *Flowers from the Silence* (VRI 1980) VB
■ *Dreams of Immortality* (VRI 1981) VB
A pair of cassettes featuring flutes and zithers, with a little bit of Indian tamboura or similar sounds here and there. Pleasant recordings with an Oriental, contemplative cast to them.

LUCIA HWONG

■ *House of Sleeping Beauties* (Private 1601) PRI. Hwong plays zither, kayagum (a Korean zither), pipa (a Chinese lute), and synthesizer. The rest of the ensemble includes shakuhachi, percussion, hichiriki, and more synthesizers. Hwong's lush, exotic tapestries cross between East and West, and between electronic and acoustic, with no apparent effort.

INCREDIBLE STRING BAND

■ *Be Glad for the Song Has No Ending* (Island ILPS-9140)
■ *"U"* (Elektra 7E-2002)
A pair of 1970 recordings—and it shows. Acoustic, folk-derived psychedelia, using Indian instruments or Western imitations thereof. Mike Heron and Robin Williamson are both excellent musicians, so you can still find one or two good tracks on either of these albums. (O.P.)

MAURICE JARRE

■ *Shōgun* (Original Soundtrack) (RSO RX-1-3088). The popular film composer wrote parts for several Japanese instruments into this score. Osamu Kitajima (see below) and his colleague Kasuo Matsui play Japanese strings and flutes; even when they're not playing, though, the music has an appropriately Asian tinge to it.

HENRY KAISER, CHARLES K. NOYES, AND SANG WON PARK

■ *Invite the Spirit* (OAO/Celluloid CELL-5008/09) NMDS. Avant-garde guitarist Kaiser and similarly minded percussionist Noyes join Korean kayagum master Sang Won Park. The combination is evocative, intimate, and occasionally violent —just like the Korean music that inspired it. An acquired taste and a fine album.

LIV SINGH KHALSA AND RAHUL SARIPUTRA

■ *Music of the Spheres, Vol. 2* (Guru Ram Das GRD-98) NAR, FOR. Khalsa's other recording is listed in Chapter 2. On this one, he combines with noted Indian sitarist Sariputra for a cosmic, raga-based performance. The whole cassette is based on *Raga Kalyan,* and includes synthesizer, tabla, and other instruments, as well as sitar.

STEVE KINDLER

■ *Automatic Writing* (Global Pacific GP-303) NAR, GP. Excellent violin work on several tracks; "Dawn in Varanasi" is absolutely exquisite. But the album flits from style to style, and ultimately doesn't go anywhere.

MARK KIRKOSTAS

■ *Mwashahat, Taxim, Penar Olsam, Habaytak B'Saif, Ramshi Aynak* (private tapes). Kyrkostas transcribes and arranges music of the Middle East for piano. *Penar Olsam* and *Habaytak B'Saif* are played by his Jazz Quartet, comprised of flute, bass, piano, and derbeki (hand drum). In both his arrangements and his improvisations, Kirkostas displays a real sensitivity to the original music and accurate instincts as to how to present this music to a Western audience.

OSAMU KITAJIMA

■ *Osamu* (Island ILPS-9426)
■ *Benzaiten* (Island/Antilles AN-7016)
■ *Masterless Samurai* (Headfirst HF-9706)
■ *The Source* (Electric Bird K28P-431) NAR
Kitajima grew up on Elvis Presley and Western pop. After forming his own pop group, he became dissatisfied with the guitar and started studying Japanese instruments, the biwa, or lute, especially. His first two records are tentative but interesting; in the later two he confidently fuses Japanese music

with Western pop and light jazz. Unfortunately, only *The Source* is still in print.

ALAIN KREMSKI
- *Musiques pour un Temple inconnu* (Auvidis AV 4702, 2 LPs) CH
- *Musiques rituelles pour Cloches et Gongs* (Auvidis AV 4704) CH
- *Vibrations* (Auvidis AV 4727) CH
As noted in Chapter 5, Kremski is one of the many pianists who've been influenced by the Gurdjieff/de Hartmann music. The first two albums are played on Kremski's collection of ancient Iranian bells, Tibetan cymbals, gongs, etc. *Vibrations* combines the Tibetan singing bowls with the piano for a truly unusual-sounding record.

RILEY AND GABRIEL LEE
- *Satori* (Sono Gaia 101) NAR, FOR
- *Oriental Sunrise* (Sono Gaia 112) NAR, FOR
Riley Lee is one of the few true virtuoso shakuhachi players living outside Japan. Gabriel Lee plays guitar on his solo albums (see Chapter 9, page 216), but here he switches to Japanese koto. Original compositions with a reflective, Zenlike atmosphere.

CHARLES LLOYD
- *Pathless Path* (Unity UR-708) VB. A classic recording of cross-cultural music, combining flutes, electronics, koto, and percussion. Lloyd is a well-known jazz figure, but this is hardly a jazz record.

CARLOS LOMAS
- *From Malaga to Cairo* (Music of the World J-102) MOW. Lomas is a fine flamenco guitarist; his original compositions combine guitar with a large and surprising ensemble. Bass, drums, cello, sitar, 'ūd, nay, and ethnic percussion are just a few that appear on one track or another.

LOTHLORIEN
- *Lothlorien* (private release) NMDS, VB
- *Spaces* (private release) NMDS, VB
Not just another ensemble combining jazz and Indian music, Lothlorien includes two musicians, sarodist Jim Palmer and tabla/santur player Larry LeMasters, who have studied North Indian classical music and who play those Indian instruments on almost every track they've recorded. Flute and bass round out the group, adding bits of jazz and Western classical music to the mix. Production quality is just fair, but both albums present an agreeable, offbeat type of chamber music.

YO-YO MA
- *Japanese Melodies* (CBS FM-39703). The renowned cellist Yo-Yo Ma performs with the Pro Musica Nipponia, an ensemble that plays traditional Japanese instruments, and other musicians playing flute, harpsichord, bass, and percussion.

Some of the melodies are traditional, some are well-known classical works. All are impeccably performed; despite some pasteurized arrangements, this is a good album for Western ears.

JOHN MCLAUGHLIN/MAHAVISHNU ORCHESTRA
For recordings by McLaughlin, with or without the Mahavishnu Orchestra, see Chapter 9, page 209. See also Shakti, listed below.

PEPE MAINA
- *Il canto dell'arpa e del flauto* (Ascolta 20004). This rarity includes flute and harp (as the title says), both in their natural state and filtered through a synthesizer. Ethnic instruments from India, Japan, Indonesia, Pakistan, and Africa join them in a vibrant recording that somehow blends all these disparate influences with easy grace.

MANDINGO
- *Watto Sitta* (Celluloid CELL-6103) OAO. Led by Foday Musa Suso, who sings and plays doussn-'gouni, talking drum, thumb piano, and kora, this ensemble blends pop and jazz with West African rhythms.

HERBIE MANN
- *Gagaku & Beyond* (Finnadar SR-9014) NMDS. One of the very best albums in this entire chapter. Mann's jazz group teams up with Minoru Muraoka's New Dimension, a Japanese new-music collective that plays traditional instruments. They're joined by a quartet of Buddhist monks for a work based on the Shomyo chanting of Japan. The combination is so effective you have to keep referring to the liner notes just to keep track of which group's playing what: the two flutes, Mann's C-flute and Muraoka's shakuhachi, complement each other especially well.

MANU DIBANGO
- *Abele Dance* (Celluloid CELL-171) OAO. Another album that shows the influence of Western music in West Africa. Sax, vocals, and a sizeable ensemble make this recording even jazzier and funkier than the Mandingo album.

CHARLIE MARIANO AND THE KARNATAKA COLLEGE OF PERCUSSION
- *Jyothi* (ECM 1256) PSI. Mariano is a flute and saxophone player, but this album highlights the vocal and drumming styles of South India. Given the chance, this energetic, tightly woven collection of ensemble pieces can be hard to resist.

STEPHAN MICUS
- *Implosions* (JAPO 60017) CH, PSI, NAR
- *Till the End of Time* (JAPO 60026) CH, PSI, NAR
- *Behind Eleven Deserts* (WIND 001) CH, NAR

- *Koan* (ECM SP-2305 804) CH, PSI, NAR
- *Wings over Water* (JAPO 60038) CH, PSI, NAR
- *Listen to the Rain* (JAPO 60040) CH, PSI, NAR
- *East of the Night* (JAPO 60041) PSI, NAR
- *Ocean* (JAPO 60042) ECM

Micus is a German musician who has traveled around the world and absorbed the sounds of many different traditions. His last two records have concentrated on guitars (some of which he designs himself) and flutes, with tamboura on some cuts. The other albums present some of the wildest instrumental combinations on record, as Micus plays Bavarian zither, Japanese shakuhachi, Afghani rabab (a fiddle), and assorted others from Ireland, Spain, North Africa, India, and Southeast Asia. Rather than trying to imitate the form of any ethnic tradition, Micus plays all these instruments in a personal style that even at its most rhythmic has something contemplative about it. *Koan* and *Wings over Water* are probably the best albums to start with.

TIM MORAN AND TONY VACCA
- *Wizard's Dance* (Fretless 163) PHI, ROU
- *City Spirits* (Philo 9007) PHI, ROU

First-rate performances on flutes and percussion, with lots of African instruments and rhythms. The second album features Don Cherry and Tom Wolf, who also plays the African doussn'gouni.

PATRICK MORAZ
- *Patrick Moraz* (Charisma 2201). A well-known keyboardist in progressive rock circles, Moraz employs a group of Brazilian percussionists on this colorful, well-intentioned, but poorly executed album.

MICHAEL MOSS AND FOUR RIVERS
- *Live at ACIA* (Fourth Stream ERG-031) NMDS. Jazzy flute improvs backed by several percussionists and bass. Poor sound, but some interesting music.

▲*Music and Rhythm* (PVC 201) JEM, WAY. A benefit double-LP for an organization devoted to cross-cultural music, arts, and dance. This compilation is a truly impressive achievement: Peter Gabriel with L. Shankar, Holger Czukay, Jon Hassell, David Byrne, and Morris Pert appear alongside British pop bands like XTC, calypso great Mighty Sparrow, drum ensembles from Burundi and Ghana, and numerous others. Complete liner notes are a real plus. Warning: The American pressing is condensed to one album, with some excellent material unavoidably deleted.

THE NAIROBI SOUND
- *Acoustic & Electric Guitar Music of Kenya* (Original Music 101) NMDS. When African musicians play guitar, it often becomes an African instrument, as the music here proves. Folksy, unique,

and appealing. See The Sound of Kinshasa, below.

JOHN KAIZAN NEPTUNE
- *Dance for the One in Six* (For. FOR-LP030) FOR, NAR. Japanese, Indian, and jazz elements, reminiscent of Osamu Kitajima's *Masterless Samurai* in its blend of styles, and despite frequent lapses into easy listening, it contains a couple of enchanting works.

JAMES NEWTON
- *Axum* (ECM 1214) ECM
- *Echo Canyon* (CH CEL-012) CH, NAR, FOR

At first listen, the ethnic influences on Newton's flute solos are hard to detect, except on tracks like "Ise" and "Kamakura" from *Echo Canyon*. But he has been inspired by several ethnic-flute traditions. See pages 187–188 and 210 for more.

NJA LJUDBOLAGET
- *Nja Ljudbolaget* (MNW 110P). Aside from one Minimalist work, most of this album is devoted to various types of jazz-rock. Several pieces use rhythms from the Middle East and are among the album's most effective tracks.

ROBERT NORTHERN (BROTHER AH)
- *Key to Nowhere* (Divine 52134) NMDS. A member of the Jazz Composers' Orchestra, Brother Ah uses flute, harp, thumb piano, bass, and lots of unusual African and Near Eastern instruments. The instrumental excerpts are worth hearing.

OREGON
- *Distant Hills* (Van. 79341)
- *Friends* (Van. 79370)
- *In Concert* (Van. 79358)
- *Our First Record* (Van. 79432)
- *Music of Another Present Era* (Terra/Van. T-1)
- *Winter Light* (Van. 79350)
- *Violin* (Van. 79397)
- *Out of the Woods* (Elektra 6E-154)
- *Roots in the Sky* (Elektra 6E-224)
- *In Performance* (Elektra 9E-304, 2 LPs)
- *Oregon* (ECM 23796-1) ECM
- *Crossing* (ECM 25025-1) ECM

Operating from 1970 to 1984 without a personnel change, Oregon became one of the most distinguished ensembles in the U.S., equally at home with jazz, classical, or World Music. Records like *Out of the Woods*, *Roots in the Sky*, and the two ECM discs are among the finest albums of their kind and may remain classics for many years.

MICHEAL O SUILLEABHAIN
- *Cry of the Mountain* (Gael-Linn CEF-079) SHAN. An Irish composer and keyboardist, O Suilleabhain (the English equivalent would be O'Sullivan) has compiled several film collages—suites of excerpts from soundtracks he has written, using

Irish, classical, African, and Indian instruments. The record also includes a few unusual arrangements of Irish folk music.

OTHER MUSIC
- *Prime Numbers* (Other Music OMJ14) NMDS
- *Incidents out of Context* (Fly. F. FF-302) FF, NMDS

Two superb records from an American ensemble that builds its own instruments and often plays in the just intonation tuning system. The first album, mostly inspired by Balinese gamelan music, features lots of mallet instruments. The second is more diverse, incorporating dulcimer, French horn, and many others.

OXYMORA
- *Thundering Silence* (Fretless FR-164) PHI. An oxymoron is a pairing of apparently contradictory words, like this album's title. Oxymora blends classical, jazz, Latin, and Asian traditions, and manages to retain the intimacy of chamber music or a small jazz combo.

FRANK PERRY
- *Deep Peace* (CH CEL-007) CH, NAR, FOR
- *New Atlantis* (CH CEL-011) CH, NAR, FOR

Perry is an English percussionist who plays Tibetan, Burmese, and other Asian instruments (mostly bells, gongs, and chimes), and occasionally invents his own percussion devices. Both albums are slow, spacey collections of ringing harmonics and constantly reverberating bells.

POPOL VUH
- *Sei still, wisse Ich bin* (IC KS-80.007) MED
- *Das Hohelieds Salomons* (UA 529-7811)
- *Affenstunde* (IC KS-80.159) MED

Synthesizers, hand drums, and guitars are combined with occasional incantatory choruses. These are all early albums, with the influence of Tibetan chant and other Asian mystical rituals not as seamlessly absorbed as in the albums listed in Chapter 2.

RADIANCE
- *Inverness* (Invincible 113) VB, LADY
- *Lake unto the Clouds* (Invincible 114) VB, LADY
- *A Song for the Earth* (Invincible 115) LADY

Another offshoot of the Paul Winter Consort, featuring guitarist Jim Scott, oboist Nancy Rumbel, cellist David Darling, and others. Some vocals, but mostly fine ensemble playing, especially on the second recording.

- *Radio Iceland* (Music of the World H-102) MOW. Peter Griggs (from Gamelan Son of Lion) plays lute, guitar, and computer; Iris Brooks plays flute; and Glen Velez adds his usual array of frame drums and other exotica. A distinctive recording of World Music, beautiful and accessible without being pandering.

VASANT RAI
- *Spring Flowers* (Van. VSD-79379)
- *Autumn Song* (Van. VSD-79414) VB

The late Vasant Rai was a gifted sarod player, and also performed on guitar, flute, and piano. These albums of jazz-Indian fusion feature all-star lineups and several excellent performances. See Chapter 7.

DINO SALUZZI
- *Kultrum* (ECM 1251) PSI
- *Once upon a time—Far away in the south* (ECM 1309) ECM

Saluzzi plays what is, in effect, the national instrument of Argentina: the bandoneon. On *Kultrum,* this accordionlike instrument is combined with flute, voice, and percussion on a solo outing that runs from South American folk music to tango. On the second album, the combination of instruments is inspired: trumpeter Palle Mikkelborg, bassist Charlie Haden, and percussionist Pierre Favre join Saluzzi. The level of playing is consistently high; the music itself is occasionally uneven.

MICHIRO SATO AND JOHN ZORN
- *Ganryu Island* (Yukon 2101) NMDS. A very spare, rarefied collection of works for shamisen (a Japanese lute) and Western reeds, which Zorn plays in various unusual ways. Not "pretty" by any means, but true to the spirit of Japanese classical music.

TIM SCHELLENBAUM
- *"Tarantela"* (from the audio-cassette magazine *Tellus,* Vol. 3) NMDS. Based on the traditional medieval tarantella dance, this Arabic-sounding piece features mouth harp, piano, violin, and percussion.

EBERHARD SCHOENER
- *Bali Agung* (CH CEL-002) CH, NAR, FOR. Of all of Schoener's albums (see Chapter 1), this displays the most obvious ethnic influence. Balinese gamelan musicians join Schoener's own group throughout this record, which has not only the sound but also the energy of Balinese music.

TONY SCOTT
- *Music for Zen Meditation* (Verve V6-8634) VB, NAR, FOR. With Shinichi Yuize, koto, and Hozan Yamamoto, shakuhachi. Recorded in 1964, this early set of clarinet/koto/shakuhachi improvisations still sounds completely contemporary. In fact, it's only with the recent rise of New Age, World Music, and genuine interest in Asian musical forms that this recording is getting the attention it deserves.

SHADOWFAX
- *Shadowfax* (Wind. H. WH-1022) WH, NAR
- *Shadowdance* (Wind. H. WH-1029) WH, NAR

- *The Dreams of Children* (Wind. H. WH-1038) WH, NAR
- *Too Far To Whisper* (Wind. H. WH-1051) WH, NAR

This group's been around for a while, but in the late 70s they decided to change their sound from progressive jazz to a festive blend of electronics and ethnic instruments. Literally dozens of instruments from East and West appear on each record. Each disc contains some fine cross-cultural music as well as a number of tracks of harmless filler, all of it beautifully produced.

SHAKTI

- *Handful of Beauty* (Col. PC 34372). The best of the Indian/jazz fusion groups. John McLaughlin's guitar and L. Shankar's violin were accompanied by tabla whiz Zakir Hussain and south Indian drummer T. H. Vinayakram. All four had worked in cross-cultural music before, and this 1975–1976 band hit real peaks of virtuosity without sacrificing form and structure.
- *Shakti with John McLaughlin* (Col. PC-34162). Except for the haunting, delicate "Lotus Feet," this live recording has more energy, but also more indulgent soloing, than Shakti's studio efforts.

L. SHANKAR

- *"Windy Morning,"* from the LP *Touch Me There* (Zappa SRZ-1-1602). A graceful melody played on violin(s) by Shankar, with electric piano, bass, and percussion providing very discreet accompaniment. The rest of this early album sounds like a sub-par Frank Zappa disc.
- *Vision* (ECM 1261) ECM
- *Song for Everyone* (ECM 1286) ECM

These appealing albums all feature Shankar's double-necked electronic violin. Jan Garbarek appears on *Vision* and *Song for Everyone;* Zakir Hussain and Trilok Gurtu add live percussion on the latter album. See Chapter 7.

RAVI SHANKAR

- *West Meets East* (Ang. S-36418)
- *West Meets East, Vol. II* (Ang. S-36026)
- *Improvisations* (with Paul Horn and Bud Shank, flutes; Alla Rakha and Dutta, tabla; RSMC-6) FOR
- *Chappaqua* (Original soundtrack) (Col. OS-3230)
- *East Greets East* (with Hozan Yamamoto, shakuhachi; and Susumu Miyashita, koto; (DG 2531 381)
- *Gandhi* (Original Soundtrack) (RCA ABL-1-4557)

While the master sitarist has recorded other cross-cultural works (see Chapter 5), these are closer to the spirit of Asian music in that most of the pieces are not thoroughly composed; even Shankar's parts in the two soundtracks leave room for traditional improvisations. The *Gandhi* score includes a list of musicians that reads like a Who's Who in northern India. Probably the most unique and innovative recording here is *East Greets East*, in which Shankar and Rakha traveled to Japan and improvised with a pair of Japanese musicians. This charming album is World Music without any trace of Western elements.

- ▲*Solar Plexus* (Evidence, Exhibit-A). A sizeable ensemble of horns, bass, and percussion; Afro-Caribbean rhythms figure prominently, along with some jazzy riffing. (O.P.)

THE SOUND OF KINSHASA

- *Guitar Classics from Zaire* (Original 102) NMDS. An important stylistic development in African popular music. John Storm Roberts, author of *Black Music of Two Worlds,* provides excellent liner notes.

STRUNZ AND FARAH

- *Mosaico* (Ganesha 4004)
- *Frontera* (Milestone M-9123)

Jorge Strunz is Costa Rican; Ardeshir Farah is Iranian. With their numerous cohorts they create a melting pot of jazz, Latin, and Middle Eastern styles. Both musicians are acoustic guitarists, and there's blistering fingerwork aplenty on these albums, as well as works that follow traditional Central Asian rhythms, often using traditional instruments.

DAVID SYLVAIN

- *Alchemy—An Index of Possibilities* (Vir. SYL-1). The basic group here is Sylvain on guitars and keyboards, percussionist/keyboardist Steve Jansen, and coproducer Nigel Walker. But side one was mostly cowritten with Jon Hassell, side two was cocomposed with Ryuichi Sakamoto. Robert Fripp, Steve Nye, Seigen Ono, Kenny Wheeler, Percy Jones, and Holger Czukay also appear. Nor does this impressive crew disappoint: This is a good recording.

PER TALLEC AND TRIO

- *Mannawyddan* (TAL 33001). Tallec is a Breton flutist—a one-handed flutist, by the way—who combines violin, bass, and hand drums with wood flutes, creating music that sounds traditional even if you can't figure out *which* tradition it's part of. Inconsistent but quite intriguing.

OKAY TEMIZ AND SAFFET GÜNDEGER

- [Untitled] (Organic Music OM-5) SCAN. Two traditional Turkish melodies and a number of original tunes from a pair of Turkish musicians. Temiz is a first-rate percussionist; Gündeger plays the 'üd and the violin and clarinet in a Near Eastern style.

CHARLES THOMPSON AND DOUGLAS SCOTT

- *Heartspeak* (Full Circle FC-501) NAR. New Age World Music. This album is pleasant and won't tax too many listeners, but it probably won't lull them to sleep either. Nicely produced and competently played on keyboards, guitar, and percussion.

RANDY TICO

■ *Soundscapes One* (Inner Circle SS-31185R) NAR. Some jazzy items, some more laid back; Strunz and Farah appear on one of the LP's finest pieces; and Dick Dunlap's piano-harp, along with Tom McBride and Anton Korb's Tibetan percussion, turn the two "Constant Change" pieces into magical, atmospheric works. On the whole, a good album.

▲ *Touch 33: "Islands in Between"* (audio-cassette magazine) NMDS. This edition is devoted to Balinese and Javanese music, and British musicians influenced by the traditions of Indonesia and Africa. N.B.: The "33" is not an edition number, but occasionally appears as part of this "magazine's" name.

▲ *Touch 33.4: "Travel"* (audio-cassette magazine) NMDS. A musical travelog with brief excerpts of Balinese swastika bells, a pig slaughter in Nepal, a Venezuelan shaman, etc. Music from Frank Ricotti and Brian Gulland, whose "Journey" sounds like a cross between Aksak Maboul (Chapter 9, pages 193–94) and gamelan music; a pair of works called "Bam/Tsifteteli" by 3 Mustaphas 3, which have a Near Eastern pop sound; and a simply ravishing pair of piano works, one with synthesizer, by Ireland's Eithne Ni Bhraonain.

TOURE KUNDA

■ *Amadou Tilo* (Celluloid CELL-6104) OAO
■ *Casamance au Claire de Lune* (Celluloid CELL-6102) OAO
More African music inspired by Western pop and jazz, done better than by most anyone else. Strong West African drumming supports the electric guitars, vocals, and horns.

▲ *Troubadours & Trouvères* (T. Binkley, Studio der Frühen Musik/Telefunken, 6.35519, 2 LPs). The original cross-cultural music. Using Near Eastern instruments, as well as whatever early European instruments were around at the time of the Crusades, Binkley and his ensemble have put together one of the most convincing albums of ancient music. This set will remind you of the profound impact this early fusion of East and West had on the development of Western music. "Chanterai pour mon coraige," by late twelfth-century composer Guiot de Dijon, blends an Arabic mode with a medieval European melody; the two scales clash periodically, only to be beautifully resolved as the different musical lines come to rest on the same note. Now *that's* World Music.

NANA VASCONCELOS

■ *Saudades* (ECM 1147) ECM. Solo and accompanied percussion and berimbau. Highlights include the title track, a concerto of sorts for berimbau (again, a Brazilian single-string instrument)

and string orchestra, and "Cego Aderaldo," written by Egberto Gismonti who accompanies on guitar.

GLEN VELEZ

■ *Internal Combustion* (CMP Records CD-23). Velez is a regular in Steve Reich's and Paul Winter's groups. Here he collaborates with Layne Redmond, another drummer, on a collection of works for frame drums and otherworldly vocals.

NIKOS VEROPOULOS

■ *Las Momias de Guanajuato* (Liquid Gongs of the Universe, 21–79 Steinway Street, Astoria, NY 11105). Music inspired by the Mummies of Guanajuato, a Mexican city that decided late in the last century to exhume bodies whose crypt rights hadn't been fully paid. Owing to the climate and soil, the bodies didn't decompose, and these fascinating, gruesome mummies are now displayed in a museum there. Veropoulos plays dozens of instruments, from Central American percussion to Indian and Middle Eastern strings. Tibetan bowls, violin, bassoon, and others also appear with recordings of natural sounds. The music is occasionally evocative, and sometimes merely indulges in sound effects.

COLLIN WALCOTT

■ *Cloud Dance* (ECM 1062) ECM
■ *Grazing Dreams* (ECM 1096) ECM
The first album, with guitarist John Abercrombie, bassist David Holland, and drummer Jack DeJohnnette, has strong performances but only a few really notable works. *Grazing Dreams,* on the other hand, is more consistently successful. Abercrombie, Don Cherry, bassist Palle Danielsson, and percussionist Dom Um Romao help produce a heady brew of Indian, South American, and jazz ingredients.

PAUL WINTER AND CONSORT

■ *The Winter Consort* (A&M SP-4170) NAR
■ *Something in the Wind* (A&M SP-4207)
■ *Road* (A&M SP-4279)
■ *Earthdance* (A&M SP-4653) NAR, VB
■ *Icarus* (Living LMR-4) NAR
■ *Common Ground* (A&M SP-4698) FOR, NAR
■ *Callings* (Living LMR-1) FOR, NAR
■ *Missa Gaia/Earth Mass* (Living LMR-2) FOR, NAR, VB
■ *Sun Singer* (Living LMR-3) NAR, VB, WH
■ *Concert for the Earth* (Living LMR-5) NAR
■ *Canyon* (Living LMR-6) NAR, WH
Winter's music has something for everybody. Jazz fans will appreciate the ensemble playing on the early A&M records; New Age fans will enjoy the soothing yet celebratory music of the later discs; classical music lovers may find the chamberish quality of *Sun Singer* and *Canyon* congenial. Of course, jazz buffs may grow impatient with the

overwrought arrangements on *Missa Gaia* or the *Concert for the Earth* disc made at the U.N., and fans of the slower, later works may not enjoy being awakened by the vigorous early music, but then, you can't please everyone all the time. Winter stayed true to the original ideas behind his initial formation of the Paul Winter Consort in the 60s, and has built up a large and enthusiastic following.

▲ *Wise/Magraw* (Red House Records RHR-05) NAR. Music for guitar and tabla from a Minnesota-based duo. An uncluttered album that's quite well played.

HENRY WOLFF AND NANCY HENNINGS
■ *Tibetan Bells Vol. 2* (CH CEL-005) CH, NAR, FOR
■ *Tibetan Bells Vol. 3* (CH CEL-016) CH, NAR, FOR
These recent albums allow the full, mysterious sound and the amazing resonance of the Tibetan bells to come through clearly. (Volume 1, O. P.) Also see Hart/Wolff/Hennings, above.

XOCHIMOKI
■ *New Music Ancient Sources* (Xochimoki, no #) NAR. American Jim Berenholtz and Mexican Cesar Galindo, using authentic instruments from Central America, have produced a fascinating cassette of original works which often conjure up images of ancient Mayan rituals.

STOMU YAMASH'TA AND COME TO THE EDGE
■ *Floating Music* (Island HELP-12) WAY. This early (1972) group wasn't as successful as later Yamash'ta ensembles, but the piece "One Way" represents an interesting blend of avant-garde percussion and Japanese Gagaku, or court music.

YAS-KAZ
■ *Jomonsho* (Gram./Gravity 18.7013) GRAM, NAR
■ *Egg of Purana* (Gram. GR-7015) GRAM, NAR
Jomonsho features music written for the Japanese Butoh troupe Sankai Juku. Performed completely on acoustic instruments (some of them homemade) and toys, it is a surprisingly rich and varied album, though it has an ancient, pan-Asian sound throughout. *Egg of Purana* includes not only Yas-Kaz's homemade instruments, but also guitar synthesizers, violin, nay flute, and many others.

ZHOU LONG
■ *Valley Stream* (China Records RL-29). Zhou is a Chinese composer who writes for traditional Chinese instruments, but uses Western compositional techniques. Finely crafted, intimate works.

ZULU JIVE
■ (Carthage CGLP-4410) HAN. Like West and Central Africa, the southern regions of that continent have developed their own popular styles. This is some of most upbeat, joyful pop music you're likely to hear; the native influence is muted but discernible.

7
ETHNIC MUSIC: NEW SOUNDS FOR WESTERN EARS

If one does nothing but listen to the new music, everything else drifts, goes away, frays.
Donald Barthelme, "The New Music," from the collection Great Days (1979)

Its range is limited to one note. Its sound is somewhere between a frog croaking and a horse snorting. It's called a didjeridoo, and it has been the primary instrument of the Australian aborigines for thousands of years. Sounds unpleasant? You bet— but then, its origins are equally unpleasant. A didjeridoo is formed when termites attack the branches of a eucalyptus tree. When they've eaten away its interior, a branch is lopped off, coated with raw beeswax (presumably the termites have been cleaned out by now), and played as a wind instrument.

While the didjeridoo—along with other holdovers from the Pleistocene Era like the duckbill platypus and the dingo—has evolved in Australia in almost complete isolation, the ethnic traditions of most other countries of the world have experienced the benefits of cultural cross-pollination. Their more highly developed musical language, including unusual scales, appealing melodies, and instruments made by people instead of vermin, makes these traditions more accessible and lends them an exotic beauty and charm.

Even with the proliferation of World Music ensembles using musical instruments and styles from other cultures, real ethnic traditions, whether of the outback or of the islands of Indonesia, are still new sounds to many Westerners. "New music" they're not; but they can be as fascinating as anything presented by the avant-garde. World Music groups have done much to ease the listener's passage into ethnic music by introducing unfamiliar instruments into a familiar context. Someone who has heard Collin Walcott's sitar and tabla work with Oregon has at least some point of reference when approaching a Ravi Shankar raga performance. Although the techniques may be very different, the sound of the instrument will be recognizable—one need not be put off by the twangy, jangling noise of what seems to be an out-of-tune guitar.

The importance of ethnic traditions to new music as a whole can hardly be overstated, as almost every region of the world has provided inspiration for today's composers. Stephan Micus and Frank Perry have used instruments from Burma and Thailand; Egberto Gismonti has studied the Xingu Indian music of Brazil; the flute and vocal music of various Central African pygmy tribes has been cited as an influence by James Newton, Jon Hassell, and Paul Dresher.

Among the most highly developed regional musical traditions are those of the Middle East, China, and Japan, all of which have been taken up in various degrees by Western composers. In order to keep this chapter at a manageable length, however, we'll focus on the three regions that to date have had the greatest effect on World Music: India, Indonesia, and West Africa.

India

Perhaps no country's music suffers from as many misconceptions as that of India. While many musicians have studied it or are at least conversant with it, much of the general public remembers it as the background music for hippies dropping acid. Or at least that's how the northern Indian tradition is viewed—its southern equivalent is even more of a mystery. Yet both traditions are highly sophisticated, the result of over two thousand years of evolution from Vedic times.* Throughout India, music has always maintained a central role in society; relatively few of its citizens grow up without some training in dance, singing, or at least one instrument. But, just as in the West, the classical music of India appeals to a smaller, mostly elite audience —the majority of the population listens to popular or regional-folk music.

If the classical music being played in India today is only distantly related to its earliest Vedic form, its style has remained fairly constant since perhaps the sixteenth century. (For comparison's sake, consider the same period in Western music: Western would have been completely incomprehensible to even the most advanced musician four hundred—or even forty—years earlier.)

Ravi Shankar and Ali Akbar Khan, who have been known in the West for thirty years, are both masters of the northern, or Hindustani tradition. But the southern, or Carnatic tradition, is just as venerable; in fact, two instruments of southern India, the vina (a long, fretted fingerboard fitted between two resonating gourds, plucked like a guitar) and the mridangam (a barrel-shaped, two-headed drum), are thought by many to have been the prototypes for the northern sitar and tabla.† Other important instruments in the south include the voice, and the violin, adopted from the West and adapted for Indian use. In the north, the sarod, a kind of lute, the bansuri flute, the santur or dulcimer, the voice, and the sarangi, a kind of box cello, are most common.

*Vedic refers to the period between 1500 and 500 B.C., after the Aryan invaders in northern India set about compiling the four Vedas: three books of Hindu scripture (the Rig-Veda being the most celebrated) and one book of magic spells.

†Sitar derives from the Persian seh-tar, meaning "with three strings," despite the fact that the instrument has six or seven main strings and many subordinate, or "sympathetic," strings. Tabla is an Arabic word brought by the Persian invaders of medieval times. The Persian influence in the north has led some observers to conclude that the Hindustani style is somehow less pure than the more conservative and insulated southern style. There is, in fact, more than a superficial resemblance between the construction of north Indian ragas and their Middle Eastern counterparts, the Persian dastgah and the Arabic maqam.

The basis for both northern and southern Indian music, whether instrumental or vocal, is the raga, and its rhythmic counterpart, the tala. Although ragas and talas vary considerably from region to region and from performer to performer, the essential principles of both forms remain the same. "Raga," observes Ravi Shankar, "is really the most difficult thing to explain in a few words. I always make it a point to say what raga is *not*. It's not a scale, nor is it a melody or tune, nor just a key. It's a combination of all of these; plus, it has to belong to one of the 'parent scales.' We have seventy-two of these full-octave scales, and each raga must belong to one." The codification of these parent scales seems to have taken place between the sixteenth and eighteenth centuries, and was basically established by 1800.

"There are thousands of ragas," Shankar continues. "They're classified as early or late morning, early or late evening, and so on. Then there are seasonal ragas of spring or the rainy season; and there are others for special occasions." If Shankar's description applies in theory to both Hindustani and Carnatic music, southern musicians are generally less rigid about playing morning ragas in the morning and so forth, even though they accept these formal classifications. And, due to the prominent use of shakes and ornaments of various notes in the south, it is often difficult to determine from which parent scale a Carnatic raga is derived; one raga may have characteristics of several parent scales.

How does one raga differ from another? Since thousands of ragas exist, there must be some way to tell them apart besides the notes in their scales, since only a limited number of scales exist. To answer that question, let's look at how a parent scale is constructed, and how a raga might be derived from it.

The parent scales consist of seven notes, and the location of the first and fifth notes (corresponding to *do* and *sol,* or C and G) never varies, but is common to all seventy-two scales. The fourth note, which divides the scale in half, may be either F or F♯, and is otherwise not altered. That leaves only two notes in each half of the scale that *can* be altered. So the construction of a parent scale is really quite simple.

Figure 1 shows the thirty-six possible combinations, as used in the southern tradition, that result when F is used as the fourth. As you can probably guess, the other thirty-six parent scales are the same as these, except that F♯ replaces F.*

This looks fairly straightforward and may leave the reader wondering why Indian music has such a reputation for microtonal complexity. Early writers thought that the Indian traditions used scales with twenty-two notes to the octave. As you can see, that's inaccurate, but Indian musicians *do* have twenty-two possible ways of inflecting or shading the notes in a scale. These are called *sruti* (pronounced shroo' tee). To understand this fundamental aspect of Indian music, let's look at one of these scales. If you read the chart four rows down and four rows across, you will find this scale: C D E♭ F G A B♭.

---

*This does not mean all the scales are in the key of C; if you read across the fourth row and down the second, you'll find a scale equivalent to the Western E-flat. The C and G are invariable, but they are not necessarily the key notes in many ragas.

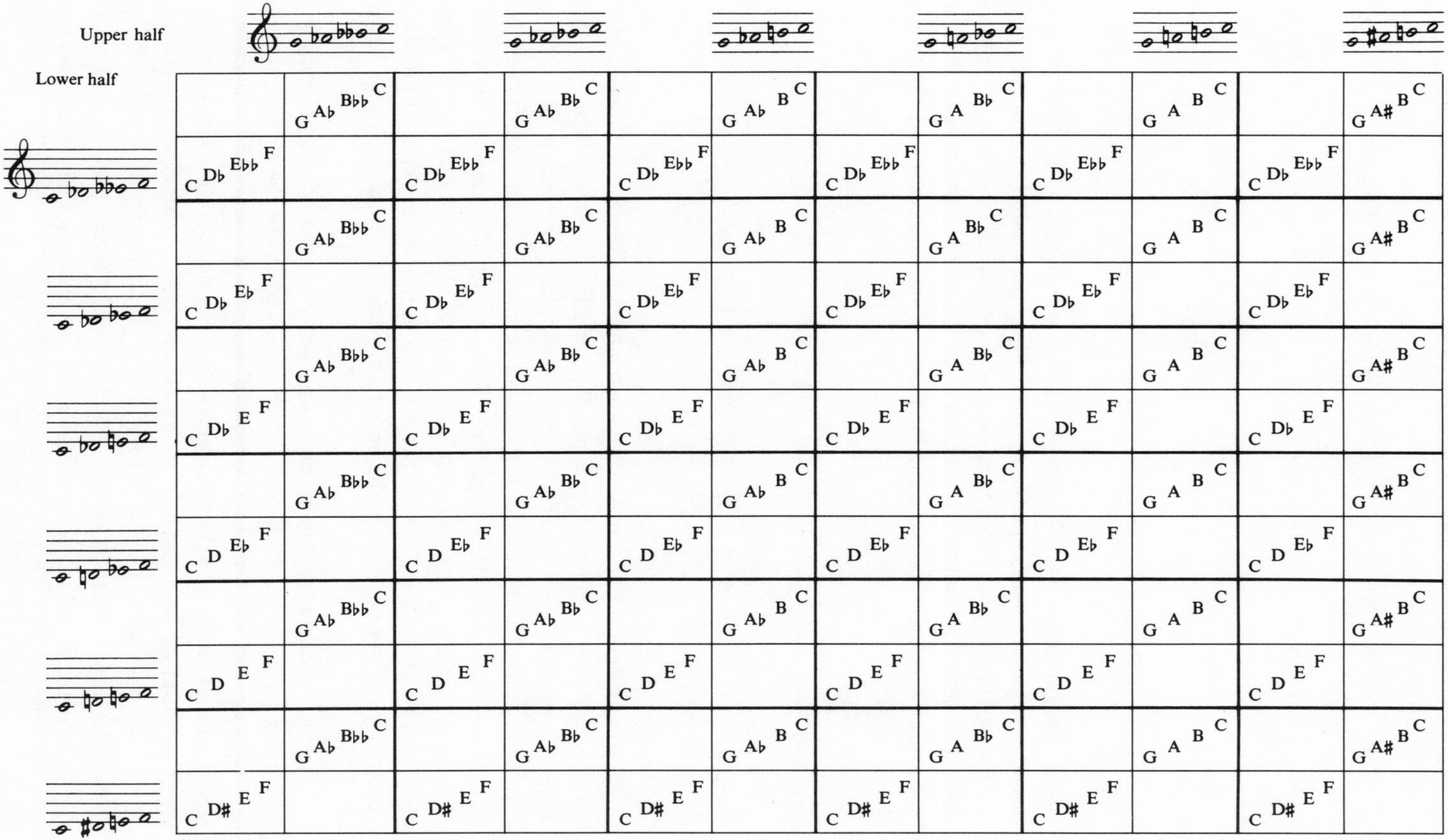

	G A♭ B♭♭ C		G A♭ B♭ C		G A♭ B C		G A B♭ C		G A B C		G A♯ B C
C D♭ E♭♭ F		C D♭ E♭♭ F		C D♭ E♭♭ F		C D♭ E♭♭ F		C D♭ E♭♭ F		C D♭ E♭♭ F	
	G A♭ B♭♭ C		G A♭ B♭ C		G A♭ B C		G A B♭ C		G A B C		G A♯ B C
C D♭ E♭ F		C D♭ E♭ F		C D♭ E♭ F		C D♭ E♭ F		C D♭ E♭ F		C D♭ E♭ F	
	G A♭ B♭♭ C		G A♭ B♭ C		G A♭ B C		G A B♭ C		G A B C		G A♯ B C
C D♭ E F		C D♭ E F		C D♭ E F		C D♭ E F		C D♭ E F		C D♭ E F	
	G A♭ B♭♭ C		G A♭ B♭ C		G A♭ B C		G A B♭ C		G A B C		G A♯ B C
C D E♭ F		C D E♭ F		C D E♭ F		C D E♭ F		C D E♭ F		C D E♭ F	
	G A♭ B♭♭ C		G A♭ B♭ C		G A♭ B C		G A B♭ C		G A B C		G A♯ B C
C D E F		C D E F		C D E F		C D E F		C D E F		C D E F	
	G A♭ B♭♭ C		G A♭ B♭ C		G A♭ B C		G A B♭ C		G A B C		G A♯ B C
C D♯ E F		C D♯ E F		C D♯ E F		C D♯ E F		C D♯ E F		C D♯ E F	

Figure 1. Possible Parent Scales with F as the Fourth Note

This is an important scale, particularly in North India, where it is known as *kafi.* Although there are seven notes, there are two possible forms—one slightly higher than the other—for each note except C and G. So the scale has twelve possible note locations:

	D	E♭	F		A	B♭
C				G		
	D	E♭	F		A	B♭

Notice that the upper D, for example, is still represented as a D, not a D♯. Both forms are regarded as acceptable ways of filling the second step in this scale.

Each of these upper variants can be raised even further, in this example creating a note that actually sounds like our Western D♯ but is still considered an altered D. Each of the lower variants can be flatted a bit, thus forming the twenty-two *sruti:*

Sharped variants	D↑	E♭↑	F↑		A↑	B♭↑
	D	E♭	F		A	B♭
C				G		
	D	E♭	F		A	B♭
Flatted variants	D↓	E♭↓	F↓		A↓	B♭↓

So far we have seventy-two scales, each made of seven notes, chosen from twelve possible locations, with twenty-two possible inflections or *sruti.* Where do the thousands of ragas then come from? A raga, as Ravi Shankar explains, is more than just a scale. The characteristics of a raga include not only which scale is used, but how that scale is arranged: Many ragas have the same set of intervals, but in a different order. Some ragas have the same scale in the same order, but with different predominant notes or phrases. (Although the first and fifth notes are constant in the parent scales, they are not necessarily the important notes of a raga; each raga has its own key notes.)

A raga's scale need not be the same going up the octave as coming down; sometimes notes are omitted, or repeated, or taken out of the normal ascending or descending order, resulting in a "crooked" scale. Other ways of distinguishing one raga from another include the particular inflections or *sruti* associated with the scale, the ornamentation or *gamaka* of an individual note or notes,* and even the tempo, or whether the raga is played or sung in a high or low register. Most ragas use a seven-note scale, but there are six- and five-note scales, and at least one raga,

*The use of *gamaka* varies from north to south. The notes of Hindustani music are often steady and sustained; purity of tone is highly prized. The Carnatic musician can hardly allow a note to sound for any length of time without a shake or slur of some kind. The *gamaka* is more than an ornament: It's a way of "pronouncing" a note, and can vary that note over a whole step of the scale.

malashri, which breaks the rules by containing only three notes. *Malashri* is rarely heard, since it takes an extraordinary musician to maintain interest in a work whose melodic base is so limited.

In the face of such a large number of variables, the existence of many thousands of ragas not only looks plausible, but inevitable. In practice, however, only a few hundred ragas are commonly heard; several dozen popular ragas make up the lion's share of classical Indian performances.

In both north and south, songs serve as the melodic base upon which the singer or musician improvises—even in nonvocal performances—and are the only fixed compositions in raga. It is tempting to draw an analogy to jazz here, but the comparison would be misleading. While the Indian musician is allowed to improvise within the raga, the motifs and characteristic phrases of the song *must* be alluded to or returned to or combined. "It's almost scientific," Ravi Shankar says, "but at the same time, you're free as a bird." The features of most Indian vocal music— contrasting verses and refrains, end-of-section rhymes, and a return to the opening material—also feature prominently in a raga performance.

There are many songs, some associated with specific ragas, and an Indian musician's training, no matter what his instrument, begins with the voice. L. Shankar, the South Indian violinist, commenced his training with his father, noted violinist V. V. Lakshminarayana, in the traditional manner. "I started singing lessons with him when I was two," he says. "We come from a vocal tradition, so all the tunes, even the ones played on violin or other instruments, come from that, and that's what I learned. You see, in India we don't have instrumental music, really. We adapt the lyrics of the songs to our instruments."

The number and type of songs a performer knows help determine his reputation. Individual compositions have often been jealously guarded family secrets, and it was not unusual for a traditional wedding dowry to include some of the family's songs. "It's very important to learn many songs in different ragas," states Ravi Shankar. "When Baba Allauddin Khan started teaching me, he taught me a lot of songs, because all of our music is based on vocal music."

The structure of a raga is not as difficult as it may seem: If one is aware of when a song melody is being presented, the direction of the improvisations can usually be followed. In both traditions, the raga usually begins with the exposition of the notes of the scale and indicates the way they've been altered. If the scale is different in its ascending and descending modes, this is when you'll find out. This *alap,* or *alapanam* in the Carnatic style, is slow, reflective, and usually unaccompanied by drums. It is considered the most difficult and important part of the raga in the north. The emphasis is not on showy displays of virtuosity, but on expressive playing that will bring out the "soul" of the raga and establish its mood.

The second part of a classical raga is a more rhythmic development of the musical material introduced earlier, either with or without drum accompaniment, and is known as *jod* in the north and *tanam* in the south. Here the soloist may begin to show off his technique, always reserving his most rapid playing for the last part of the raga. Finally, we hear the fixed compositions, the songs themselves if the soloist is a singer, or the adapted melody for an instrumentalist. These songs are called *gats* in the Hindustani tradition; in the Carnatic style the most common song is the *kriti,* a three-part composition which offers a lot of possibilities for improvisation. The two-part *varnam* and the "light-classical" *tillana* are also used in the south.

While performances with one *kriti* seem to be the rule in Carnatic music, the Hindustani performer may use several *gats* in succession, and each may be in a different rhythm. In either case, the songs' possibilities are fully explored, and both soloist and accompanist take part in a display of increasingly brilliant musical pyrotechnics intended to drive both artists and audience to a fever pitch of excitement. The breakneck speeds of the final part of the raga are achieved in two ways: In the north, the drummer continually increases the tempo until the desired pace is achieved; in the south, the tempo remains the same, but more notes are played for each beat. The effect is the same: the soloist and drummer go careening through the climax of the raga, somehow manage to arrive at the same place at the same time, and the performance ends.

In the south, the *kriti* is the most important part of the work, and as in Western classical music, is often attributed to a specific composer (when necessary—usually the audience will recognize a famous composer's work). Tyagaraja, who lived from 1767 to 1847, is thought to be the originator of the modern Carnatic style. His songs went far beyond previously accepted limits of mood and subject, and today they remain the core of the southern repertoire, both for singers and instrumentalists. The works of two of Tyagaraja's contemporaries, Syama Sastri and Muttusvami Dikshitar, are also staples of Carnatic music.

The southern *alapanam* is often a mere formality or memory aid; the composition is the focus of attention. By contrast, detailed study and practice of the rules of raga structure and improvisation are a necessity in the north, where the *alap* is all-important; Hindustani song compositions play a relatively limited role.

Hindustani music actually has three styles. The first is *dhrupad.* The oldest *dhrupad* music still extant is that of Tan Sen, a sixteenth-century composer whose stature in the north is on a par with Tyagaraja's in the south. *Dhrupad* is an old, severe form of music which has been almost completely supplanted by *khayal,* a more diverse style that is not restricted to the old devotional songs. Besides *gats,* this style also uses compositions based on religious or nonsensical texts (sometimes both!) called *tarana.* These have been enthusiastically appropriated in the south, where they've become the light-classical *tillana. Khayal* is a colorful style that is by far the most popular on the concert stage.

The final type of Hindustani music is its own light-classical style, known as *thumri.* The texts are usually short, amorous, often erotic; elements of different ragas are mixed in performance. Only a small number of ragas are considered suitable for *thumri,* and there is usually no *alap.*

One feature that is common to all the classical and folk traditions throughout the Indian subcontinent is the central role played by rhythm. The cyclical rhythm pattern of Indian music is called the *tala,* and is usually established by the hand drums. To take an example, the tala known as *tintal* is a sixteen-beat cycle, each beat known as a *matra.* Each *matra* can contain a number of drum strokes; in fact, adjacent *matras* may have different numbers of strokes. The tala is set up like this:

	1st Phrase				2nd Phrase				3rd Phrase				4th Phrase			
Matra #:	1	2	3	4	5	6	7	8	9	10	11	12	13	14	15	16
Counts	One				Two				———				Three			

Notice the third phrase is not counted. If this cycle is played on the tabla, the first, second, and fourth phrases contain strong, resonant strokes. The third is played with the drummer muting the loud resonance of the left-hand drum.

Although *tintal* appears to be equivalent to Western 4/4 time (four beats, a quarter note each, to a bar), in practice, the parallel isn't valid. Where do the bar lines go? Do we have four bars of 4/4 time? Or one bar divided into sixteenth notes? The latter is plainly inaccurate, since each *matra* may contain not one, but two, three, four, or up to eight drum strokes. The former proposal also doesn't work because it doesn't take into account the "empty" third phrase; the relationship between the four phrases, which are constructed in a sort of mirror image (the first and third sections contain similar drum strokes, so do the second and fourth); or the fact that each pair of phrases can be put together and the whole thing repeated in this fashion:

Matra #	1 2 3 4 5 6 7 8	9 10 11 12 13 14 15 16	1 2 3 4 5 6 7 8	9 10 11 12 13 14 15 16
Counts	One	Two	———	Three

Remember, each of the *matras* may contain a different number or combination of strokes: Since Indian rhythms are additive, there's no dividing the *matra* into its component parts. The number and type of strokes that go into each *matra* depend entirely on the artist and the composition he's performing. These compositions, or *kaida,* serve the drummer in the same way a song serves the soloist: They are vehicles for elaboration and improvisation.

As if all this weren't confusing enough (and this is an *easy* tala!), the drummer, whether playing the two tabla drums side by side or the two heads of the barrel-shaped mridangam, uses polyrhythms as well. Some strokes call for both hands in combination while some require only one. Since the left drum of the tabla and the left head of the mridangam have a deeper, more variable pitch than the right, an audible pattern of polyrhythms—one hand playing a different phrase than the other —is established.

The drums of India are among the most difficult and advanced percussion instruments in the world. The south Indian mridangam is held in the lap, one hand beating each end. Somewhere along the way, the north seems to have split the mridangam into two separate drums, or tabla. The left drum is the larger of the two, and both are placed on the floor before the musician. An Indian drummer's right hand can produce many different sounds, by striking either the rim of the head, the central patch of black paste (its makeup is a closely guarded secret since it controls precise tuning of the drum), or the area of skin within the circumference. Strokes can be muted or resonant, soft or loud, and formed with finger(s) or palm. The left hand can also use resonant or nonresonant strokes. If the stroke is resonant, the pitch can be varied up to an octave (especially on the tabla) by sliding the left wrist across the drumhead right after the stroke. This is what gives the tabla its characteristic "wobbly" sound.

The study of Indian music is intense and time-consuming. To learn all the songs in the various ragas, or the many talas, from three-beat cycles to an incredible 108-beat cycle, takes years of study with a guru or master. The traditional means of passing on the music to the next generation is the *gharana*—another of those hard-to-translate Indian terms. A *gharana* is a school, but it also carries connotations of a family tradition; even if the student is not part of the family, he lives with the guru as if he were his son. The word also refers to a specific body of compositions and means of expression. When a student goes to a guru to learn music, he does just that: He learns the music itself, not necessarily the guru's instrument. Sitarist Ravi Shankar's guru was a sarod player, Baba Allauddin Khan. (The sarod, another string instrument, is held and played like a guitar.) Khan's son, and Shankar's brother-in-law, is the great sarod player Ali Akbar Khan. "I wanted to study sarod too, in the beginning," Shankar remembers, "but he [Khan] insisted that I continue with sitar."

Ravi Shankar's early training in music was actually quite unorthodox. "I grew up in music and dance. When I was fifteen, I was traveling with my brother's troupe." Uday Shankar was a renowned dancer, and a pioneer in bringing not only the dance but also the music of India to the West in the 1930s. "I was playing sitar, sarod, flute; I was dancing, I was singing—I was doing anything I could. When Baba Allauddin Khan joined my brother's troupe as a soloist for a year, he found out quickly that I had a lot of talent. But he was very angry, seeing me do so many things, so he began by rebuking me! He told me, you are like a butterfly, you do too many things. In spite of that, he started teaching me. After he left, I had to decide: should I continue as a dancer, or take up music seriously. It took me another year, but I left everything else and went to him, when I was almost eighteen. It was long, rigorous work, up to sixteen hours a day."

Ali Akbar Khan's training was a bit more traditional: twenty years with his father, and then a spell as a court musician. With India's independence, however, most court musicians were suddenly on their own, and in 1955 Ali Akbar Khan accepted an invitation from the visionary violinist and ethnic music enthusiast Yehudi Menuhin to visit the West and make a recording. His album of *Ragas Piloo and Sindhi Bhairavi* was the first record of Indian music available in North America or Europe. In 1956, Ravi Shankar followed his brother-in-law to the West.

"In the beginning," he says, "no one knew anything about Indian music. Here and there you'd find one or two people with an ear for it, so I had to start from the very beginning—playing small halls, doing lecture demonstrations, and so on. It took me until about 1959 before I played larger halls: Royal Festival Hall in London, Paris's Salle Pleyel, Carnegie Hall in New York. In the large cities, there was always a small group of people who were immediately interested. In the U.S. I found the jazz musicians and jazz buffs to be the first group really interested in Indian music."

Its recent visibility in the West has led to some concern that India's classical traditions are dying or becoming tainted. Such worries are premature; since no satisfactory system of notating its music has yet been devised, India's musical heritage will remain an oral one for years to come. While the institution of the *gharana* is in some jeopardy, no immediate threat has been posed to the country's musical culture. The north Indian violinist V. G. Jog, for example, does not adhere to any single *gharana* (perhaps because violinists in northern India have always been a rarity), and claims to be a freer musician because he can draw on many styles. His outstanding performances bear him out.

In the end, neither technique nor which *gharana* he is part of determines a musician's stature as an artist. In Indian music, technique is merely a means to an end, a tool, as Ravi Shankar describes it, "to get to the point where you can perform a raga in a chosen tala and improvise freely, without being cramped by all the do's and don't's." Elaborating on this idea, La Monte Young, who has studied with singer Pandit Pran Nath since 1970, explains, "One of the things Pandit Pran Nath used to tell us about raga is that you practice it for twenty years, until you can do it in your sleep; then you go on stage and you don't think—you forget everything you know and you just let it happen. That's called *uppaj.* It means imagination, or flying like a bird. You let go of all this knowledge you've accumulated and you take off."

This ideal has indeed survived Indian music's journey west. While some Western musicians have appropriated elements of the Indian tradition, it has managed a feat that no other ethnic tradition has yet matched: It has maintained an audience outside its native region without sacrificing its identity.

Indonesia

To most listeners Indonesian music means one thing—gamelan. These orchestras of percussion instruments have captivated Western composers since Debussy first heard one in 1889 at the Paris Exhibition. In the 1930s Colin McPhee went to Bali and became well-versed in gamelan music; Francis Poulenc quoted a gamelan melody in the second movement of his Double Piano Concerto (1932); the gamelan influence for John Cage and Lou Harrison has already been discussed. Yet Western audiences continue to have almost as many misconceptions about Indonesian music as they do about raga.

For one thing, a number of different traditions coexist among the 13,000 islands which make up Indonesia. The gamelan is only one of a large number of percussion ensembles that can be found throughout that region, and the gamelan itself has developed over the centuries into a number of distinct variants. Most Westerners associate gamelan exclusively with the orchestras of Bali and central Java, which are, in fact, the most commonly heard styles. But Madura, Sumatra, and Sunda (western Java) have developed notable traditions as well.

Just as one can draw fairly accurate inferences about Persian music from the heritage it has left in North India, so too can one gain a picture of the "gong-chime" cultures of Southeast Asia by examining Indonesian music. The music of Vietnam,

Thailand, Burma, and the southern Philippines all springs from the same source as the Indonesian gamelans, namely, the Bronze Age percussion instruments of the gong-chime family. These instruments, which usually took the form of kettle-shaped gongs as well as larger disc-shaped instruments, probably originated on the mainland. Because of their military and religious significance, they were eventually carried by various invading emperors or petty kings from the mainland to the islands. There, specifically on the island of Java, the gong-chime tradition developed in earnest. Later, as the tide of invasion reversed, the Javanese brought their music back throughout Southeast Asia, though that influence subsequently took very different forms in different areas.

The term *gamelan* refers specifically to the orchestras of Java, Madura, and Bali; the form developed, particularly on Java, around 2,000 years ago as a local form of gong-chime ensemble. Because its instruments were carefully cast in metal, and because they were considered a reflection of a court's prestige and status, many gamelans and related ensembles have survived for hundreds of years, and much of their repertoire is just as ancient. The earliest variety of gamelan was a three-note set of gongs and metal kettles, known as *gamelan munggang.* A few of these ensembles, dating back to the fourth century, still exist and are considered the most sacred gamelans of all. Although the repertoire of *gamelan munggang* now consists of a single piece (actually a fragment), that four-note theme has been memorable enough to last through many centuries.

The prototype gong-chime music probably used the same interlocking rhythm patterns that are characteristic of modern gamelan music, for the simple reason that the large, often unwieldy instruments could not produce lively music otherwise. In fact, size is a very simple, very effective way to judge the relative age of a gamelan: The smaller and more numerous the instruments, the more sophisticated the casting technique and, therefore, the younger the ensemble. Older gamelans have fewer and larger instruments.

Over the centuries a number of forms of gamelan have evolved. These include the old *gamelan gambuh,* a soft ensemble using four gambuh flutes; the much louder *gamelan semar pegulingan* ("gamelan of the love god"), originally played outside the royal bedroom in a manner calculated to be, shall we say, invigorating; the stately *gamelan gong gede;* and its explosive, relatively recent offshoot, *gamelan gong kebyar.* All are organized in a basically similar fashion. Each group of instruments, whether mallet percussion, drums, or gongs, has a particular function such as stating the melody, embroidering on the melody, providing the rhythmic form, or filling in gaps between the beats.

By the year 800 the first of Indonesia's two scales, the five-note *slendro,* had been established. The seven-note *pelog* followed in the twelfth century. With two different tunings, two sets of instruments are required by many gamelans, though some choose to perform exclusively in one scale only. In gamelans that contain both *slendro* and *pelog* instruments, the two groups are arranged in performance at right angles to each other. Only the set of instruments appropriate to a given piece is used; the two sets never play together. The structure of gamelan music is often compared with the structure of a sentence, and that analogy is quite useful. While the melodic instruments state the theme—the basic thesis of the sentence, so to speak—a second set of instruments embellishes or paraphrases it, serving a correlative function to that of adjectives and adverbs in a sentence. Meanwhile the gongs mark off the form of the piece in much the same way that punctuation defines the form of a sentence.

Gamelan compositions are generally known as *gending*. Each *gending* is built up from a fixed, precomposed melody known as a *balungan*. The traditional repertoire contains several thousand *balungan*, with new ones being added by contemporary composers, but only a thousand or so are used regularly. The *balungan* is played by a group of metallophones called saron. Each saron has six or seven large keys struck with a mallet, and the whole group usually plays in unison. The saron are accompanied by one slentem, which is simply a kind of bass saron. Because the basic melodies are often slow, two other groups of instruments ornament them with elaborate filigrees and standard countermelodies: the gender, which is almost identical to the Western marimba, except that it has bronze keys instead of wood; and the bonang, a row of gong-chimes resembling inverted tea kettles that rest on a frame and are struck with padded sticks. The gender and the bonang not only give the gamelan its characteristically bright, metallic sound, they also contribute to its visual appeal since both instruments tend to be cast with beautiful, ornate frames.

Like the *balungan* melodies, the rhythmic patterns of a gamelan composition are limited by the traditional repertoire. While the saron play the theme and the gender and bonang amplify it, the family of gongs establishes the piece's structure. The largest is the gong agung, actually a pair of huge gongs, which mark off the main musical phrases. Secondary beats, usually one-fourth or one-half of the main beat, are provided by the kempur or the higher-pitched kenong. If both are used, they strike alternate beats. These beats are further subdivided by the smallest gongs, the ketuk. A simple example would be the rhythm pattern known as *lancaran*, which, like the Indian *tintal*, is comprised of sixteen beats. Figure 2 shows how it would look if you broke it down:

Figure 2.   Lancaran Pattern

	1	2	3	4	5	6	7	8	9	10	11	12	13	14	15	16
Notes of the melody	1	2	3	4	5	6	7	8	9	10	11	12	13	14	15	16
Strokes on the ketuk	*		*		*		*		*		*		*		*	
Strokes on the kenong				+				+				+				+
Strokes on the kempur						x					x				x	
Strokes on the gong-agung																X

The leader of the orchestra, who is responsible for keeping the rhythms, cueing the musicians, moving the ensemble from one part of the work to the next, and varying the tempo and volume, is the drummer. The kendang, a long cylindrical drum struck at both ends, is the "leading" instrument in the gamelan, and comes in various forms depending on the style of music being played.

Rounding out the gamelan are the somewhat autonomous suling (flute), rebab (two-string fiddle), and singers. Occasionally, a type of zither is used as well. These instruments provide a counterpoint to the main melody. In the case of the suling, especially, the part is exceptionally intricate.

This basic organization is common to all the gamelan traditions, but only in

Java are all of the instruments, in both *pelog* and *slendro* tuning, commonly found in a single ensemble. In Bali, where gamelans are used mostly as accompaniment for dance or shadow-puppet theater, a gamelan is tuned to only one system, usually *pelog.* Balinese instruments are also tuned in pairs, with one instrument slightly higher in pitch than its partner. The result, as we've seen in Chapter 3, is that, while the two notes are close enough together to sound like one tone, the differences in their vibrations set up an acoustic "beating." The further the two notes are from each other, the more rapid the beating. Each ensemble is tuned differently, according to local preference.

In Bali and in the older Javanese ensembles, one finds the spectacular interlocking figures known as *kotekan.* These virtuoso passages are entrusted to the gender and the other mallet instruments, and are most often featured in the modern style called *gamelan gong kebyar,* which has swept through Bali in this century and is now the major form of gamelan there.

In Sunda (western Java), smaller gamelan ensembles have evolved. One style, *gamelan pelog salendro,* is close to the traditions of the early Javanese gamelans and is used as accompaniment to dance. The most individual gamelan style is the *gamelan degung.* In its usual form, it features the suling, two or three variants of the saron family, one bonang, a set of gongs, and a pair of kendang drums. The suling has uncommonly florid countermelodies, and the ensemble produces a sound that is refined and intimate, yet still exciting. *Gamelan degung* is based on a five-note scale derived from the seven-note *pelog* system. These ensembles were decimated during World War II, when the occupying Japanese melted down many of the bronze instruments for military use.

Other important Indonesian styles, outside the gamelan tradition, include the misnamed gamelan angklung, the kacapi ensemble, and the famous Monkey Chant, or *kecak.* * The angklung is a bronze or bamboo set of tuned rattles, and the angklung ensemble usually consists of several angklung, a suling flute, a gong, and at least one metallophone. It is used for festivals, processions, and funeral rites, as well as for dance performance. The kecapi ensemble is a courtly style of chamber music, featuring the kecapi suling, a long version of the gamelan flute; the kecapi indung, a large zither; and the rincik, a smaller zither. This versatile group can accompany poetry and folk song, or can stand in for a larger gamelan ensemble. The kecapi ensemble is usually found in Sunda.

The dramatic, exciting Monkey Chant is one of Bali's greatest attractions. At night, around the light of a huge torch, over a hundred men sit together and, raising their arms and shaking their shoulders, begin to cry "chak, chak . . ." Meanwhile, silent actor/dancers perform the Hindu epic, the *Ramayana.* The repetition of the "chak" sound, in its various interlocking rhythms, is designed to induce a hypnotic state in one of the young dancers, who in the context of the Ramayana story is supposed to aid the god Rama and the monkey general Hanuman in frightening off the demons who've abducted Rama's wife Sita. The monkey army is represented by the barking chorus of men. The Monkey Chant is almost certainly a stylized de-

*Indonesian spelling has only recently been standardized; the official language, Bahasa Indonesia, contained several holdovers from Dutch spelling which have now been eliminated. Thus, *ketjak* still appears on many recordings of the Monkey Chant. Both spellings are pronounced ké-chak.

scendant of an ancient exorcism rite, and it remains a powerful ritual today. It also represents virtually all of the choral music to be found on Bali.

The gamelan influence on Western composers has been mentioned earlier, but Indonesian gamelans have also had a unique impact in the field of ethnomusicology. As a result of the longstanding Dutch interest in Indonesia, performances of gamelan music began to take place in the Netherlands after the Second World War and by the 1950s spread to the rest of Europe, as well as to Japan and North America. The success of these concerts gave rise to an important trend called "bimusicality," in which study of a musical culture takes the form of actually participating in that heritage. The rhythmic energy in the gamelan traditions continues to attract new listeners in Indonesia and abroad; that, combined with the longevity of the instruments and repertoire, has made this one of the strongest, most durable ethnic styles in the world.

West Africa

To use the term "African music" to refer to a specific style is even more inaccurate than the analagous use of "Indian music." There is no *one* tradition of African music; even dividing the continent, as is often done, into North, West, Central, East, and southern Africa results in forcing together distinct, very different cultures. Much of the music of North Africa shows the influence of Arabic and Persian music and is best examined in that context. Eastern and southern Africa have so many contrasting styles—ranging from the Ethiopian music of the Coptic church, which has a written tradition (unique in Africa) spanning many centuries, to the primitive music of the nomadic tribes of Botswana, trying to eke out an existence in the Kalahari Desert—that trying to apply any sort of generalities to them is fruitless. Indian and Indonesian traders have left their mark on the culture of Africa's east coast in the form of both instruments and tuning systems.

While Central and West Africa also contain a variety of tribes, each with its own music, certain general trends can be found in those regions. Central Africa, home to most of the pygmy tribes, is the source of some of the most fascinating music on the continent, but it is West African styles that have had the strongest influence in the West.

Of the West African countries, Nigeria has recently become the most visible, owing to the strength of its pop music, or Highlife. The phonograph and radio have brought a heavy Caribbean and Afro-American influence to countries like Nigeria and Ghana where one finds large cities and, for better or worse, a strong Western urban character. The recent success of King Sunny Ade, Fela Kuti, and other West African musicians has in turn introduced Nigerian styles like Juju music and Afrobeat to North American and European audiences. In terms of "new sounds," though, Ghana seems to be the place to go; Brian Eno, Steve Reich, and Stephen Scott number among the Western musicians who have been attracted to its music. Ghana's ethnic traditions are particularly rich—richer, in fact, than its still-developing pop styles.

In African culture music is not a "leisure" activity, but part of the daily fabric of life. Ritual of almost any sort—whether manual labor, religion, or the dramatic arts—is particularly associated with music. According to Paul Winter, "That's why African music has so much magic—they've found timeless elements, the universals, in that music. Somehow, after improvising ages ago on instruments created to imitate the sounds of nature, they arrived at some amazing polyrhythmic forms that are as intricate in their own way as Bach. Yet that music still has that ancient 'Earth Magic' in it."

In Ghana the most common musical rituals are those associated with birth, puberty, marriage, and death. Although some tribes will not celebrate all of these occasions, one event is honored universally with music: the funeral. Often the most elaborate and expressive drumming is done at funeral rituals, especially those for a chief or other leading citizen. Religious festivals, national holidays, and even the weekly outdoor market are among the other affairs that usually have musical accompaniment.

Besides the characteristic African use of polyrhythms, Ghanaian music shares a number of structural elements with much West African music. The first of these is the leader/chorus form, which is especially common in vocal music. One of Ghana's traveling professional musicians, or *griots,* may sing verses that recount a historical event or praise an important leader, while the chorus is sung by the local folk. Work songs often fall into this category, and not just in West Africa but around the world: Most sea-shanties have a leader/chorus form, for example.

A related style is the call-and-response. Instrumental music often uses this device, in which a leader or small group states the melody and rhythm, and a second, larger group responds in like fashion. In those parts of Africa where the language is a highly rhythmic or percussive one, call-and-response can be executed by a singer and a drummer, with the instrument imitating the rhythm and even the inflection of the voice.

Another standard formal device is the hocket. Hocket was common in early Western music, and you can hear brief experiments with it in some of Duke Ellington's pieces, but for the most part it was not a technique used in the West until the recent work of Steve Reich and others. Basically, a hocket is a melodic line played by two or more musicians who alternate notes: If two are performing, they play every other note of the melody; three musicians will play every third note. Hocket is particularly suited to instruments that are difficult to play quickly or have limited range, as it allows them to be used in interweaving patterns of rhythms and notes that would not otherwise be possible. The Balinese *kotekan* and the layered rhythms of some Minimalist music are similarly constructed.

In Ghana, wind instruments are most often played in hocket; a very simple example of hocket (see Figure 3) shows two groups of wiik (flute) players alternating between roughly C and D, while two groups of namuna (trumpet) players accompany with notes that approximate E and F.

Drums often play in hocket, too, producing quick runs that one player could not perform alone. While vocal music is also constructed in hocket form, it is more often encountered in Central and southern Africa where the hocket yodeling of the pygmies is found.

African music is often considered to be essentially percussive music, with the interplay of rhythms as its most fundamental feature. This is, however, an overstate-

Figure 3. Example of Hocket

ment: Although it's more difficult for Western ears to pick out, melody is just as important an element as rhythm. We don't normally think of drums or other percussion instruments as carrying melodies, but in parts of Africa the relationship between music and speech is so close that drums are often used as melodic, almost "singing" instruments. Since many of the languages in West Africa are based on the inflection or pitch of the voice as well as on the particular configuration of vowels and consonants, a drum can "talk" by imitating the speech patterns of the language. When one pitch pattern can apply to several words, the drummer will add another phrase to clarify which word is being imitated. As Ghanaian melodies are also based on these speech inflections, the pattern of the talking drum can serve both as rhythm and melody.

Ghanaian music includes a variety of these so-called "talking drums." One of the most common and effective is the donno, shaped like an hourglass with strings or wires connecting the two heads. The player holds the drum under the crook of the arm and strikes one head with a stick. By squeezing the wires between the elbow and his side, the player can change the tension on the head, pulling it tighter to raise the pitch, or loosening it to get a lower note. A second type of talking drum functions by changes in the size of the space inside the instrument where the sound resonates. By inserting his hand inside the open end of a single-head drum, a player can vary the pitch; the farther in he sticks his hand, the higher the note.

Another standard African instrument is the thumb piano, which is familiar throughout the continent and is known by hundreds of names, sanza, kalimba, and mbira being the most common. A thumb piano basically consists of a number of thin strips, usually metal, attached to a small wooden board. The strips are played by the thumbs while the instrument is held between the palms; it may or may not be played into a large gourd resonator. Like the drum, the thumb piano carries a tune *and* can show off the player's rhythmic skill, since each thumb can play in a different meter.

The West African battery of instruments also includes a number of fixed-pitch drums, xylophones, log drums capable of different notes depending on where they are struck, literally dozens of different types of rattles, and string instruments like Ghana's gonje (a type of lute). The most exciting music, though, is played with the drum ensemble, where the West African rhythmic sense can be heard at its most developed. The rhythms are built from types of phrases; short phrases that match up with the music's basic pulse are common, but longer phrases that cover several beats of the pulse are also used, as are phrases that don't necessarily line up with the pulse at all. The most complex drumming in West Africa uses all three phrase styles in different parts of a piece.

The polyrhythms that result from these practices can sometimes obscure the form of a piece, which generally consists of three levels. The first level introduces the piece's basic pulse, and indicates how long the sections are, whether the piece is in call-and-response form or not, etc. The second level contains the standard phrases associated with that structure. Finally, the foreground material is the ornamental work of the master drummer, which can be as intricate and vigorous as he wishes, but which does not really affect the structure of the piece, any more than the Indonesian suling flute affects the form of the gamelan music playing behind it.

The drumming of Ghana varies from tribe to tribe, with the most sophisticated forms having developed in the Ga and Ewe tribes in the southeastern part of the country. Like the classical music of India and the gamelans of Java, these West African drum ensembles were originally attached to royal courts. The Ghana Empire began sometime between 300 and 600 A.D.; its successor, the Ashanti Empire, lasted until the European invasion and the arrival of the slave trade. But, as in India and Indonesia, the musical tradition in West Africa has proven strong enough to withstand years of external pressure.

This resilience must account for at least part of the allure these traditions have for Western musicians—our music seems to change drastically with every generation, but the musicians of Ghana, Java, and the Indian subcontinent have maintained a rich and lasting heritage. While that heritage may have changed somewhat over the years, the basic underpinnings—instruments, techniques, and the view of music as both an art and as a living part of the culture—have survived. And, of course, the sound itself has attracted Western listeners to these traditions. The music of these regions is not only exotic, it is often stimulating and vital. For that reason as well, these ethnic traditions are worth investigating.

DISCOGRAPHY AND RELATED WORKS*

AFRICA

WEST AFRICA

OBO ADDY
■ *Kukrudu* (Cascade 5540) NMDS. A master drummer of the Ga tribe from Ghana, Addy plays with a group of Portland, Oregon jazz musicians. A vocal group substitutes effectively for the tribal singing that would normally appear with the drums, and there's lots of brass throughout. Far from authentic, but energetic and fun.

▲ *Africa: Ancient Ceremonies—Dance Music and Songs of Ghana* (None. Explorer H-72082). Just what the title says; includes some wind hockets and fascinating xylophone duets.

FRANCIS BEBEY
■ *Akwaaba* (Original OMA-105) NMDS. Much of Bebey's music uses Western instruments like the electric guitar, but this LP features the sanza, or thumb piano. It includes some strange, growling vocals; otherwise, the combination of sanzas, bass, pygmy pipes, and percussion is a happy one.

YA YA DIALLO
■ *Nangape* (Onzou OZ-001) NMDS. Diallo is from Mali, and plays balafon (a wooden xylophone), talking drum, and others. Canadian flutist Sylvain Leroux provides a nice foil for the percussion on two works, but mostly this is an album of lively, melodic percussion.

▲ *Mali: Ancient Strings* (Bär. BM 30 L2505). Traditional music played on West African lute-harps.

▲ *Mandinka Kora par Jali Nyama Suso* (Oc. OCR-70) HM. Music from Gambia. Jali is the name the Manding people of West Africa give to their *griots,*

or professional musicians/teachers/historians. Suso's album is an enticing collection of songs and instrumentals played on the kora, or lute-harp. An easy recording for Western ears to appreciate.

▲ *Musique Gouro de Cote d'Ivoire* (Oc. OCR-48) HM. The Gouro are one of the largest tribes in the Ivory Coast, and one of the most musical. Especially good are the percussion duets, featuring mallet instruments like the balafon.

▲ *Touch 33: "Drumming for Creation"* (audio-cassette magazine) NMDS. This edition of *Touch* is devoted to drums, balafon, kora, and iseze (another string instrument, with either nine or thirteen strings) from Gambia, Nigeria, Niger, and the eastern country of Tanzania. Neat ensemble drumming, questionable sound.

CENTRAL AND SOUTHERN AFRICA

▲ *Angola—Mukanda Na Makisi* (Museum Collection, West Berlin MC-11, 2 LPs) CH. Profusely illustrated and annotated collection of music and dance associated with circumcision rites and other masked ritual performances.

▲ *Anthologie de la Musique des Pygmées Aka—Centrafrique* (Oc. 558 526-27-28, 3 LPs) HM. Without dismissing the music of the Aka pygmies—whom both Jon Hassell and James Newton, among others, claim as a musical influence—this might have been more effective as a single album. Most of the tracks are group songs or chants, accompanied by some very intricate hand claps. Drum and flute make cameo appearances, and there's a lovely lullaby done in the pygmy yodeling style by two young girls.

*Recordings of ethnic music have become more widely available in recent years. Entire series of ethnic music albums have been put out by Radio France (the Ocora series), Nonesuch (the Explorer series), UNESCO (several collections, including one for the German Bärenreiter label and one for the Dutch Phillips label), the Museum Collection of West Berlin, Lyrichord, and others. What follows here is just a representative sampling of ethnic recordings; for further listings, consult one or more of the catalogs listed in Appendix 2.

▲ *Burundi: Musique Traditionelle* (Oc. 558 511) HM. A lot more instrumental work and considerably fewer vocals than most other ethnic African recordings. The instrumental solos, particularly the drumming excerpts, are short and easily digested.

▲ *Centrafrique: Musique Gbaya* (Oc. 558 524) HM. Voices, sanzas, rattles, and shakers. Catchy and amiable music, even if you don't usually like ethnic vocals.

▲ *Instrumental Music of the Kalahari San* (Folk. FE-4315). In the barren Kalahari Desert, the nomadic San not only eke out a living, they improvise on crude instruments and produce music that contains no hint of the oppressive environment from which it comes. (O. P.)

▲ *Madagascar: Valiha* (Oc. OCR-18) HM. Like the West African kora, the valiha is a harp-zither, or lute-harp, played by plucking the strings on either side of the instrument with alternating left and right hands. Valihas differ in shape and number of strings. We get a good sample of them here. Some of the tunes are catchy enough to be pop melodies.

▲ *Music of Africa: Guitars I* (Kaleidophone 6). Is the guitar an African instrument? Historically no, but musically, it has become one of the most widespread and enthusiastically played instruments on the continent. Some great ethnic African guitar solos. (O.P.)

▲ *The Music of the Ba-Benzele Pygmies* (Bär. BM 30 L2303). Flute music and rhythmic pounding of found objects can be found here; but the real gems are the tracks of soft, breathy yodeling done in hocket form by the Central African pygmy tribe. Curiously and surprisingly beautiful.

▲ *Musique Malgache* (Oc. OCR-24) HM. A companion to *Madagascar: Valiha,* this album presents some of Madagascar's other forms of music making: singing, drumming, solos of flutes and stick-zithers. It's primarily a vocal album, with the singer(s) often providing the musical accompaniment as well. Especially appealing and somehow touching is one track of a blind singer who wanders from place to place accompanying himself with an empty gasoline can.

▲ *The Soul of Mbira—Traditions of the Shona People of Rhodesia* (None. Explorer H-72054). Mbira is just another name for the thumb piano. This album, for voice and mbira, at times sounds like a hoax: Some of the pieces are so bluesy they sound like they came from the Mississippi Delta instead of Zimbabwe.

NORTHEASTERN AFRICA

Egypt

OM KHALSOUM
■ *El Hob Kollo* (Sono Cairo SC-22 132). This great Egyptian popular-music singer made many recordings throughout her lifetime; this one has some lengthy instrumental excerpts that display her orchestra's versatility and virtuosity, using Western strings played in Near Eastern fashion, kanun (a zither), and a sizeable group of percussion instruments.

ALI JIHAD RACY
■ *Ancient Egypt* (Lyrichord LLST-7347) NAR. Of course, no one really knows what ancient Egyptian music sounded like, but Racy, an ethnomusicologist and performer, attempts at least to recreate the mood and spirit of that culture. He uses Near Eastern instruments like the tar (drum), 'ūd (or oud), mijwiz (clarinet), and buzuk (lute), whose metal strings he often bows instead of plucking. Whether it's authentic or not, it's haunting music that is rich in imagery.

Ethiopia

▲ *The Music of Ethiopia: Music of the Ethiopian Coptic Church* (Bär. BM 30 L2304). Africa's only longstanding written musical tradition. The sound is almost a cross between Near Eastern Christian chants and the sounds of Islamic Sufism.

▲ *Musik der Hamar/Südäthiopien* (Museum Collection, West Berlin MC-6) CH. The Hamar are a nomadic tribe of southern Ethiopia whose music is mostly vocal, with simple percussion (hand claps, scraping stones) and occasional lyre or flute.

Sudan

HAMZA EL DIN
■ *Eclipse* (Pacific Arts PACR-7-119)
■ *Escalay: The Water Wheel* (None. Explorer H-72041) El Din is from the Sudan, though he has lived in the U.S. for many years. He is one of the world's great 'ūd players, and also sings and plays percussion. *Eclipse* includes a fine *mwashah,* the traditional North African/Near Eastern improvisation, but seems now to be out of print. *Escalay* features a side-long work for 'ūd and voice, a Nubian song for voice and tar (the Sudanese drum), and a voice-and-'ūd arrangement of one of Om Khalsoum's songs.

▲ *Dikr und Madih/Sudan* (Museum Collection, West Berlin MC-10, 2 LPs) CH. Music derived from Sufi rituals (see the Halvetti-Jerrahi Dervishes, listed under Near and Middle East, below). These village performances, though not as polished as the traveling Dervish troupes, are still good examples of how expressive the combination of rhythmic chanting and increasingly frenzied (but always precise) percussion can be.

▲ *Musik der Nubier/Nordsudan* (Museum Collection, West Berlin MC-9, 2 LPs) CH. The first record of this set, with its folk melodies, surprisingly intimate lyre work, and energetic foot stomps and hand claps, has a quiet, almost naive charm. You can even sing along with it.

ASIA

CENTRAL ASIA

▲ *Afghanistan—Music from the Crossroads of Asia* (None. Explorer H-72053). Both geographically and culturally, Afghanistan is midway between Iran and India. Indian drums, Iranian strings, and Afghani vocals all appear on this disc.

▲ *Armenie: Chants Liturgiques du Moyen-Age* (Oc. OCR-66) HM. The sacred chanting of the Armenian church. Much of this music dates from the fifth through twelfth centuries, and it's probably safe to assume that this is not so much a strict performance of a liturgical tradition as an attempt at re-creating the spirit of that ancient music.

▲ *Kashmir—Traditional Songs and Dances* (None. Explorer H-72058)
▲ *Kashmir—Traditional Songs and Dances Vol. 2* (None. Explorer H-72069)
The sound here is very similar to the Afghanistan recording, with a bit more of the North Indian influence. Each record has a santur (zither) improvisation by Muhammed Tibetbaqal which is marred only by its brevity.

CHINA

▲ *China/Musik für Ch'in* (Museum Collection, West Berlin MC-7) CH. Perhaps the finest album of Chinese music available in this country, this collection features complete technical information; crystalline sound; slow, deeply felt performances; and detailed liner notes—you can even follow along with the music in the drinking song "Wine Madness," as the ch'in portrays the protagonist's inevitable journey through inebriation, nausea, and slumber. The ch'in is one of the Chinese zithers, similar to the Japanese koto. *This* is what music for meditation should sound like.

▲ *Eleven Centuries of Chinese Classical Music* (Everest 3427). From 600 to 1600 A.D. Several ch'in

solos, one pipa solo, and a duet for pipa and hsaio (a flute). All are quiet, intimate, and graceful.

▲ *Floating Petals . . . Wild Geese . . . The Moon on High—Music of the Chinese Pipa* (None. Explorer H-72085). Lui Pui-Yuen plays this Chinese lute in a set of pictorial, programmatic pieces that include graphic portrayals of battles, dances, and nature scenes.

▲ *Little Sisters of the Grasslands* (China Record Company M-2387). Music for pipa and orchestra, featuring the Central Philharmonic Symphony Orchestra, led by Seiji Ozawa. This contemporary Chinese music combines Chinese and Western instruments, using traditional *er-hu* fiddle techniques on violins and cellos. It's not bad, thanks to Ozawa. The title work is a pipa concerto, part four of which is subtitled "The Party's Love Will Always Be Remembered."

INDIA (NORTH)

NIKHIL BANNERJEE
▪ *Sitar, Vol. 1* (Oriental BGRP-1042) ORI
▪ *Sitar, Vol. 2* (Oriental BGRP-1043) ORI
Bannerjee is a gifted sitarist, accompanied here by tabla player Anindo Chatterjee. Both albums were recorded live in Stockholm; volume one is an album-length performance of *Raga Piloo,* while the second volume is *Raga Desh.*

JAGDEEP SINGH BEDI
▪ *Soft and True* (Music of the World T-108) MOW. One side features surbahar, or bass sitar; the other is a set of flute/sitar duets with tabla.

HARIPRASAD CHAURASIA
▪ *The Mystical Flute of Hariprasad Chaurasia* (Oriental BGRP-1025) ORI
▪ *Charm of the Bamboo Flute* (Oriental BGRP-1058) ORI
The North Indian bamboo flute, or bansuri, has a soft, engaging tone, making it an ideal instrument for Westerners looking for a way to approach Indian music. Chaurasia is one of the best bansuri flutists around.

SUBROTO ROY CHOWDHURY
▪ *Calcutta Meditation* (ENJA 4054) CH. Digital German pressing of two ragas, performed on sitar with tabla accompaniment. Chowdhury's style is considerably less florid than that of many other sitarists.

STEVEN GORN
▪ *Bansuri Bamboo Flute* (Music of the World T-103) MOW
▪ *Yantra* (Music of the World T-102) MOW

Although he lives in New York, Gorn has studied the bansuri flute in India and seems to be completely at home in the North Indian tradition. The first cassette is unusual in that it doesn't include tabla; Badal Roy adds the hand drums in the second recording.

PANDIT JASRAJ
- *Vocal* (Oriental BGRP-1029) ORI. Two vocal raga performances *(Darbari* and *Ahir Bhairav)* by a master singer, accompanied by Zakir Hussain (Alla Rakha's son) on tabla.

BRIJ BHUSHAN KABRA
- *Indian Slide Guitar* (Celluloid CELL-5102) NMDS
- *The Golden Guitar of Brij Bhushan Kabra* (Oriental BGRP-1049) ORI

Kabra has spent two decades or more studying and playing Hindustani music on his chosen instrument, the slide guitar. The idea is not as bizarre as it might sound: By using a metal slide on the left hand, the guitarist is no longer constrained by the frets of the instrument, and can achieve the delicate microtonal shadings, the shakes and slides that Indian musicians revel in. The first album is only the *alap* section of *Raga Puriya;* it's a long, slow solo for guitar with no drum accompaniment, only tamboura. The second is a more conventional album: one full-length raga and a short, stylish *Dhun.*

ALI AKBAR KHAN
- *Pre-Dawn to Sunrise Ragas* (Connoisseur Society CS-1967). Khan's discography is far too extensive to list here. This is a 1967 album of two ragas performed before sunrise: *Bairagi* and *Aheer Bhairow.* (Compare this last name with the second raga in the Jasraj listing and you'll get an idea of one of the things to watch for when buying Indian records: Despite the different spellings, *Ahir Bhairav* and *Aheer Bhairow* are the same raga. On the other hand, ragas like *Bhairavi* or *Sindhi Bhairav* are completely different.) This is a beautiful LP, though now difficult to obtain.
- *Music for Meditation* (Connossieur Society CS-2063)
- *Half Moon* (Metalanguage 122) NMDS
- *Soul of the Sarod* (Oriental BGRP-1041) ORI

More solo recordings from the greatest sarodist alive today. *Half Moon* is particularly interesting because of its unusual raga selections: *Chhayanat* is a "combination" raga, in a restrictive style that borders on *dhrupad;* and *Malashri* is a raga with only three notes in its scale. *Soul of the Sarod* is a more immediately colorful and accessible recording. See Shankar/Khan, below.

ALI AKBAR KHAN AND L. SUBRAMANIAM
- *Ethereal Duet* (Ganesh 4002)
- *Master Musicians* (RSD/Bainbridge RSD-27) NAR

The *jugalbandi,* or duet, has become more common in recent years, and with it has come the idea of combining northern and southern musicians. L. Subramaniam, the South Indian violinist, joins Ali Akbar Khan in two lengthy raga performances. Each soloist brings his own drummer to the performance, so besides the sarod/violin interplay one also hears fascinating rhythmic duels between tabla and mridangam.

AROOJ LAZEWAL AND BADAL ROY
- *Songs for Sitar and Tabla* (Music of the World C-101) MOW. Short compositions by Lazewal himself. An innovative, decidedly untraditional cassette that even includes a duet, "Flamenco Sitar," with guitarist Carlos Lomas (see Chapter 6).

LATA MANGESHKAR
- *Marathi—Devotional* (Odeon India). An early recording by a phenomenally popular Indian singer: Hardly a soundtrack has been released in the past three decades that doesn't have her voice on it somewhere. The most recorded voice in human history is, however, dreadfully tired and cliché now. But this album of sacred songs shows why Mangeshkar reached this position in the first place. It's superbly performed and quite beautiful. (O.P.)

PANDIT RAM NARAYAN
- *Sarangi: The Voice of a Hundred Colors* (None. Explorer H-72030)
- *Master of the Sarangi* (None. Explorer H-72062)
- *Inde du Nord: Ram Narayan* (Oc. OCR-69) HM

Ram Narayan almost single-handedly turned the sarangi from an instrument used exclusively to accompany the voice into a wonderfully expressive solo instrument. A kind of short, box-shaped cello or fiddle, the sarangi is one of the Indian instruments with many sympathetic strings that are not usually played but rather vibrate when the main strings are bowed. The result is a rich, silvery tone.

PANDIT PRAN NATH
- *Ragas Punjabi Berva and Yaman Kalyan* (Shandar 10007). A classic recording of North Indian vocal music, highlighting Pandit Pran Nath's highly flexible, delicately embroidered technique. Liner notes by La Monte Young. (O.P.)
- *Ragas of Morning and Night* (Gram. 18-7018-4) GRAM. A late issue of a 1968 recording of *Ragas Todi* and *Darbari.* Accompaniment consists of sarangi, here paralleling the vocal part (in itself no mean feat), and tabla.

VASANT RAI AND ALLA RAKHA
- *Play Ragas of Meditation and Happiness* (Van. SRV-73013). *Ragas Bhairav, Kafi,* and *Misra Pahadi* are played in the alternately serene and flashy style that both of these musicians have become known for.

DOCTOR N. RAJAM

- *The Magical Fingers of Dr. N. Rajam* (Oriental BGRP-1048) ORI. Zakir Hussain accompanies on tabla while Rajam performs *Raga Mian-ki-Malhar* on violin. North Indian violinists are somewhat rare, and Rajam is an excellent representative of the Hindustani violin style.

G. S. SACHDEV

- *Memories* (Music India 2393 905) NAR, VB
- *In Concert* (Unity UR-600)
- *Bansuri: The Indian Flute* (Ph. 6405 611)
- *Romantic Ragas* (Chandi CP-104) NAR, VB

Sachdev is a bansuri flutist who has built up a sizeable following among Western listeners. He specializes in gentle, nocturnal pieces, often quite short by Indian standards; and his albums may well be the best introduction to Indian music for Western listeners.

RAVI SHANKAR

- *Sitar* (Odeon/GCI EALP-1273)
- *Ravi Shankar* (Odeon/GCI EALP-1307)
- *Sitar—Pandit Ravi Shankar* (Odeon/GCI EALP-1261)
- *India's Master Musician in London* (Odeon/GCI EALP-1251)
- *India's Master Musician* (World Pacific WPS-21248) NAR
- *In Concert* (World Pacific WPS-21421)
- *The Sounds of India* (Col. CS-9296)
- *The Genius of Ravi Shankar* (Col. CS-9560)
- *Ravi Shankar, Portrait of Genius* (World Pacific WPS-21432)
- *The Sound of the Sitar* (World Pacific WPS-21434)
- *Three Ragas* (World Pacific WPS-21438)
- *Live at Monterey* (World Pacific WPS-21442) NAR
- *A Morning Raga; An Evening Raga* (World Pacific WPS-21464)
- *Theme From Pather Panchali and Gat Kerwani* (World Pacific WPS-77871)
- *Two Raga Moods* (Cap. ST-10482)
- *Raga Parameshwari* (Cap. SP-10561)
- *Ravi Shankar's Festival from India* (Dark Horse SP-22007) NAR
- *Ragas Hameer and Gara* (DG 2531 216)
- *Raga Jogeshwari* (DG 2531 280)
- *Homage to Mahatma Gandhi and Baba Allauddin* (DG 2531 356)
- *The Genius of Pandit Ravi Shankar* (Oriental BGRP-1051) ORI

Like Ali Akbar Khan, Ravi Shankar's discography is too extensive to list here; these are some of his best recordings. The *Ragas Hameer and Gara* are personal favorites, and certainly give the lie to those critics who claim that Shankar's music is showy and lacks substance. Alla Rakha is the only accompanist (aside from the ubiquitous tamboura drone) on most of these albums, though the *Music Festival from India* album on George Harrison's

Dark Horse label is an exception, featuring dozens of musicians, including L. Subramaniam, sitarist Kartick Kumar, and Shivkumar Sharma (see below).

RAVI SHANKAR AND ALI AKBAR KHAN

- *Ravi Shankar & Ali Akbar Khan* (Odeon/GCI EASD-1296)
- *In Concert* (Apple SVB-3396)
- *Raga Mishra Piloo* (Ang. DS-37920)

In a *jugalbandi,* or duet, the focus of the music seems to change a bit: Instead of losing himself in the music, the performer now has to worry about another musician on stage. The result is shorter *alap* sections and extended, sizzling duets in the later parts. Shankar and Khan don't neglect the *alap,* but their duets are still flashier and a bit less substantial than their solo efforts.

SHIVKUMAR SHARMA

- *Purple and Gold* (EMI/India ECSD-2868)
- *Santoor* (Ravi Shankar Music Circle RSMC-2) NAR
- *Scintillating Sounds of the Santoor* (Oriental BGRP-1026) ORI

Shivkumar Sharma (also spelled Sivakumar Sarma) is the finest Indian santur (also spelled santoor or santour) player around. Since he plays a hammered string instrument, there is a rhythmic excitement inherent in his music; but Zakir Hussain (on the third album), Alla Rakha (second disc), and Shafaat Khan (first LP) add their intricate tabla patterns to provide a complex interplay of rhythms.

SHIVKUMAR SHARMA AND HARIPRASAD CHAURASIA

- *Jugalbandi* (Ravi Shankar Music Circle RSMC-42) NAR. A flute and santur duet. Since the two instruments are from completely different families, this *jugalbandi* seems to work better than most.

PARWEEN SULTANA

- *Sings Jogeshwari and Three Enchanting Bhajans* (Oriental BGRP-1034) ORI. *Bhajans* are devotional songs, usually much shorter than a raga performance. A good record for fans of Hindustani vocals.

INDIA (SOUTH)

S. BALACHANDER

- *Divine Veena Sings the Praise of Lord Krishna* (Oriental BGRP-1053) ORI
- *Immortal Sounds of the Veena* (Oriental BGRP-1020/21, 2 LPs) ORI

The vina (or veena) is a stick-zither like the North Indian sitar. It is an ancient, delicate-sounding instrument capable of almost vocal effects. Balachander is an accomplished virtuoso who benefits from the digital recording process used in the first album. Both collections include mridangam accompaniment; the two-LP set also uses kanjira (a tambourine) and ghatam (clay pot).

SRI ANAYAMPATTI S. DHANDAPANI

■ *The Art of Jalatharangam* (Oriental BGRP-1036/37, 2 LPs) ORI. The jala-tarang (or jal-tarang, or jalatharangam) is one of India's most unusual instruments. It consists of goblets of water, tuned by varying the amount of liquid each holds. The sound is completely captivating; accompaniment is by the usual violin, mridangam, and ghatam.

KADRI GOPALNATH

■ *South Indian Classical Music for Saxophone* (Oriental BGRP-1056/57, 2 LPs) ORI. The sax could easily become, like the violin, a completely integral part of Carnatic music. Southern Indians have long been familiar with the piercing, reedy nadasvaram, "India's most ancient instrument," and the saxophone does an admirable job of expanding upon that instrument's capabilities.

NAMAGIRIPETTAI KRISHNAN

■ *Haunting Melodies of the Nadhaswaram* (Oriental BGRP-1063/64, 2 LPs) ORI. The nadasvaram is often used for outdoor performances. It's probably not the kind of thing you want blaring in your living room. Energetic stuff, though.

▲ *Music of India: V. V. Subramaniam and Vadya Ghoshti* (Decca DL-75102). A *vadya ghoshti* is a South Indian "orchestra," usually comprised of violin, venu (flute), clarionet (the clarinet, adopted for Carnatic use), mridangam, kanjira, and tamboura. The sound is kind of busy—as with northern music, the Carnatic tradition is most effective when the ensemble is small.

▲ *Musik für Vina/Südindien* (Museum Collection, West Berlin MC-8, 2 LPs) CH. Beautiful collection with illustrated book, containing everything you could want to know about Carnatic music: scale structure, performance techniques, construction and playing styles of the instruments, etc. Performances are all first-rate, ranging from short *kriti* to a full-length raga.

L. SHANKAR

■ *Who's To Know?* (ECM-1195) ECM. Subtitled "Indian classical music," this isn't completely authentic Carnatic music because it includes North Indian percussion as well as mridangam and it's played on Shankar's electronic violin. Nevertheless, it is an album of serious and effective raga performances.

MASTER U. SRINIVAS

■ *The Adorable Child Prodigy* (Oriental BGRP-1054/55, 2 LPs) ORI. Srinivas is responsible for introducing the mandolin to Carnatic music, some-

thing he did at an early age. His accompaniment includes violin, mridangam, ghatam, and morsing (mouth harp). A congenial recording, though a bit overlong.

▲ *M. S. Subbulakshmi* (EMI/India ECLP-2293). Subbulakshmi is one of the greatest South Indian singers; she possesses an incredibly expressive voice that makes the unaccompanied rhythmic chanting of side one quite hypnotic. (Unaccompanied, that is, except for tamboura and a second, identical track of overdubbed voice.) More conventional but equally enchanting is the *Bhavayami*, a song that travels through seven ragas, on side two.

DOCTOR L. SUBRAMANIAM

■ *Magic Fingers* (Ganesh DRLS-4003)
■ *Indian Classical Music* (Sonet SLP-1595)
■ *The Creative Genius of Dr. L. Subramaniam* (Oriental BGRP-1012) ORI
■ *Enchanting Melodies of the Violin* (EMI/India ECSD-2789)
■ *Le Violon de l'Inde du Sud* (Oc. 558 585) HM
■ *Incredible Maestro* (Ganesh DRLS-4001)
Like L. Shankar, Subramaniam will occasionally use North Indian percussion (Alla Rakha appears on *Magic Fingers*). He has devoted much of his time (too much, for some tastes) to his jazz-fusion projects, but when he does play Carnatic music, he does so with great intensity. See Khan/Subramaniam, above, and *Two Musical Traditions of India*, below.

▲ *Two Musical Traditions of India* (Ganesh DRLS-4008). L. Subramaniam and percussionist Palghat Mani Iyer represent the South; vocalist Lakshmi Shankar and tabla player Zakir Hussain represent the North. A virtuoso performance by all four musicians.

INDIAN FOLK STYLES

▲ *Indian Street Music: The Bauls of Bengal* (None. Explorer H-72035). The Bauls are wandering folk musicians from the northeastern states of India who often travel in families. Their texts are weird combinations of the devotional and the erotic, and their instruments include stringed drums, cymbals, ankle bells, and a small sarod. Buoyant, appealing music, obviously meant for dancing.

▲ *Music from South India: Tavil-Nadasvaram Group/Madras* (Moers Music 01090) NMDS. Loud, almost martial outdoor music for drum and reed instruments. Proves that Indian music is not exclusively intimate and well-behaved.

▲ *Rajasthan: Vielles et Guimbardes* (ChM LDX 74. 639) HM. An album of folk music from western India. Earthy, unrefined music for jal-tal (jala tarang), swarmandal (zither), iron jew's harps, and fiddles. Quite a bit of singing, too.

INDONESIA

Bali

▲ *Bali—The Celebrated Gamelans* (Musical Heritage Society MHS-3505) MHS. Excellent LP of various styles of Balinese gamelan. Also an excerpt from the *kecak,* or Monkey Chant.

▲ *Bali—Golden Rain* (None. Explorer H-72028). Includes several examples of *gamelan gong kebyar.* This album's main claim to fame is its side-long *kecak* excerpt, which could use a little editing but which is still an important aural document.

▲ *Bali: Le Gong Gede de Batur* (Oc. 558 510) HM. An older gamelan with larger instruments and a larger number of players. Somewhat more martial and regal-sounding than the *kebyar* style that has replaced it.

▲ *Bali: Joged Bumbung* (Oc. 558 501) HM. Metal is expensive—too expensive for many small villages. These people displayed their resourcefulness by making a gamelan out of bamboo, which is plentiful and cheap. The resulting style is much more rapid, with more attacks on the instruments, to make up for the lack of volume and sustaining power that only metal instruments have.

▲ *Bali—Musique et Theatre* (Oc. OCR-60) HM. Shorter excerpts, some of them vocal, presenting music for the live theater productions of Bali. Not as consistently interesting as the gamelan records.

▲ *Gamelan Semar Pegulingan—Gamelan of the Love God* (None. Explorer H-72046). One of the most famous Balinese gamelans, this ensemble was reorganized and maintained by Colin McPhee. There is also one older *gambang* piece on this album.

▲ *Music of Bali: Gamelan Gender Wayang* (Lyrichord LLST-7360). A dramatic, dynamic Balinese gamelan style, often used for theater performance.

▲ *Panji in Bali: Gamelan Semar Pegulingan* (Bär. BM 30 L2565). Another album displaying the not inconsiderable charms of this well-known gamelan.

Java

▲ *Java—Palais Royal de Yogyakarta* (Oc. 558 598) HM. Excellent record of one of Java's most celebrated court gamelans. Grand, stately music and reasonably good sound.

▲ *Javanese Court Gamelan Vol. 1* (None. Explorer H-72044)

▲ *Javanese Court Gamelan Vol. 2* (None. Explorer H-72074)

▲ *Javanese Court Gamelan Vol. 3* (None. Explorer H-72083)
Each of these albums explores the style of a particular court. Each contains several vocal works, especially Volume 3, and at least one extended piece. Volume 2, featuring a twenty-minute rendition of *Babar Layar,* one of the most dignified and dramatic works in the gamelan tradition, is the finest of the set.

▲ *Musical Atlas—Java* (EMI/Odeon 3C 064-18369). Includes some of the less known but still intriguing angklung music. A fairly good recording, but very hard to find.

Sunda

S. BURHAN
■ *Arum Bandung* (Hidyat, no #). Burhan is probably the best suling player in western Java. This album of flute and gentle percussion is a typically graceful effort.

H. IDJEH HADIDJAH
■ *Tonggeret* (Jugala, no #; an American release is planned for 1987 on Icon Records/NMDS). Hadidjah is a popular Sundanese singer who possesses a marvelous voice. The title song has a seductive melody and muted accompaniment that almost makes it sound like vocal *degung* music. Much of her other material is closer to the style known as *jaipong,* or *jaipongan,* which is more energetic and danceable.

KECAPI SULING
■ *Sunda Jaya* (Gita/FM, no #). Lively, ornate chamber music for suling, kecapi (zither), and rincik (smaller zither).

E. KOESTYARA AND GROUP GAPURA
■ *Sangkala!* (Icon 5501) NMDS. One of the most delightful, infectious albums of ethnic music available. S. Burhan plays suling and is accompanied by a Sundanese all-star ensemble. In the usual *degung* manner, the group includes a drummer and five mallet percussionists.

RINEKA SWARA
■ *Daun Pulus Adu Manis* (Jugala, no #). A classic example of *jaipong.* Like ragtime, this style started in the brothels and is primarily rhythmic. Unlike ragtime, though, it hasn't yet been prettified. This is raucous, sensual music that never stands still.

SASAKA DOMAS
■ *Mangsa Padeukeut* (Jugala, no #). Normally, male and female vocalists do not perform together in Sunda, but this cassette does on occasion com-

bine the two. Another nice recording of simple melodies and intricate interplay between the musicians.

▲ *Sunda: Musiques et Chants traditionels* (Oc. 558 502) HM. His name is listed as Burhan Sukarma, but this is obviously the same suling wizard who appears in several of the preceding collections. Music for flute and zithers, with some folk-style vocals.

Other Regions

▲ *Lombok, Vols. 1 & 2/Panji in Lombok* (Bär. BM 30 SL2560/2564). Lombok is the next island to the east as you travel from Java to Bali toward New Guinea. It has developed a related style of orchestral music, but the island also has smaller forms of music-making. These LPs give an overview of Lombok's instrumental styles.

JAPAN

▲ *Flower Dance: Japanese Folk Melodies* (None. Explorer H-72020). Folk tunes for shamisen (lute), koto, shakuhachi, and percussion. Easily accessible ensemble and solo pieces.

▲ *Japan: Traditional Vocal and Instrumental Music* (None. Explorer H-72074). A first-rate album, though traditional Japanese vocals take a lot of getting used to. The Ensemble Nipponia and leader Minoru Miki perform the gentle "Edo Lullaby" and several other Japanese favorites.

▲ *Japan: Unesco Collection I* (Bär. BM 30 L2012)

▲ *Unesco Collection II* (Bär. BM 30 L2013)

▲ *Unesco Collection III* (Bär. BM 30 L2014)

▲ *Unesco Collection IV* (Bär. BM 30 L2015)

▲ *Unesco Collection V* (Bär. BM 30 L2016)
Japan is home to a multitude of musical styles: the old court style, Gagaku, is characterized by a timeless feeling, usually suggested by long notes on the mouth organ, or sho, and violent outbursts of oboe or percussion; the traditional koto and shakuhachi repertoires are more intimate; the Buddhist chant, or Shomyo, is derived from Central Asian music; and the music of the theater has developed a highly stylized tradition of its own. The Unesco series covers all of these. Not all of this music will appeal to Western tastes, but the set as a whole is quite useful to anyone seriously interested in Japan's various musical traditions.

MASAYUKI KOGA
■ *The Distant Cry of Deer* (For., no #) FOR, NAR. Solo music for shakuhachi, including the popular "Shika No Toone" (the title track) and a shakuhachi arrangement of the famous koto melody "Rokudan."

RALPH SAMUELSON
■ *Music of the Shakuhachi* (Music of the World T-104) MOW. Samuelson is an American who plays the shakuhachi as his primary instrument, not simply as an exotic coloristic device. These pieces are all drawn from the Japanese Zen music repertoire.

WATAZUMIDO SHUSO
■ *The Mysterious Sounds of the Japanese Flute* (Everest SDBR-3289). Shuso plays a long, heavy wooden flute only distantly related to the shakuhachi. The music is quite peaceful, and as the title says, somewhat mysterious.

TOSHA SUIHO
■ *Die Vier Jahreszeiten in Kyoto* (Denon WB-7097/7100, 4 LPs) CH. Beautifully produced set of flute music recordings, one album for each of the four seasons. Most of the pieces are solos, but there are a few flute duets and some ambient natural sounds mixed in. A recording that really creates its own space.

TOMOKO SUNAZAKI
■ *Spring Night (Haru No Yo)* (For. FOR-020) FOR
■ *Sound of Silk Strings* (For. FOR-021) FOR
Music for solo koto, the national instrument of Japan. Sunazaki performs both classical and modern Japanese works.

GORO YAMAGUCHI
■ *A Bell Ringing in the Empty Sky* (None. Explorer H-72025). Another album of solo shakuhachi music; a bit better than most.

KATSUYA YOKOYAMA
■ *ZEN—Classical Shakuhachi Masterworks* (Wergo SM-1033/34, 2 LPs) CH. Yokoyama is one of Japan's most respected shakuhachi players. He has also become interested in contemporary music; see Richard Teitelbaum, Chapter 2.

KOREA

SAMUL-NORI
■ *Drums and Voices of Korea* (None. Explorer H-72093). Exciting, aggressive music for several gongs and drums, with some rhythmic vocals. "Youngnam Nong-ak" gives you an idea why this ensemble's concerts in the West met with high praise from the critics.

SOUTHEAST ASIA

Burma

▲ *Birmanie: Musique d'art* (Oc. 558 555–57, 3 LPs) HM. This set presents Burma's court traditions, which range from the loud and primitive to the graceful and refined. Instruments include typical gong-chime percussion, flute, and a fragile-sounding harp.

Cambodia

■ *The Music of Cambodia* (Bär. BM 30 L2002). An album of folk and court music; the folk pieces are generally performed on solo winds or voice, while the court music includes the local representatives of the gong-chime, flute, and fiddle families.

Laos

▲ *The Music of Laos I* (Bär. BM 30 L2001). Like Cambodia, Laos was part of the ancient Khmer Empire, which affected and was affected by the cultures of India, China, and Java. Elements of all three survive there today, in both the court music and the folk styles. This colorful LP includes several fine works for khene, the mouth organ.

▲ *Musique pour le Khene* (Oc. 558 537/38, 2 LPs) HM. Lam Saravane plays the Southeast Asian mouth organ. Not unlike its Chinese and Japanese counterparts, the sheng and the sho, it has a plaintive tone, even when playing celebratory music. Two records of it are a bit much, though; the previous album is a sufficient introduction to the instrument.

Solomon Islands

■ *Fataleka and Baegu Music* (Ph. 6585 018). These two tribes inhabit the Solomon Islands, in the Southwest Pacific to the east of New Guinea. The selections of panpipe music are the most appealing on the album.

Vietnam

■ *Musique Mnong Gar du Vietnam* (Oc. OCR-80) HM. The Mnong Gar live in the hills and jungles of southwestern Vietnam. Their music uses voice, drums, and primitive gong-chime instruments. But the real point of interest on this album is a track that features a prehistoric lithophone—a stone xylophone of sorts—which may well be the oldest surviving complete instrument in the world.

TRAN QUANG HAI
■ *Landscape of the Highlands* (Music of the World, C-103) MOW. The Vietnamese zither, or Dan

Tranh, has sixteen strings and a delicate sound. All of the works are original compositions by Tran, but done according to traditional methods.

▲ *Viet-Nam: Nouvelle musique traditionelle* (Oc. 558 512) HM. Tran Van Khe plays local lutes, zithers, and drums, to the accompaniment of spoons, clappers, and other percussion. The instruments and modes are traditional, but Tran's compositions are original.

TIBET

■ *Cho-Ga: Tantric and Ritual Music of Tibet* (Dorje Ling DLP 76965) NAR. Includes the Gyütö and Gyüme monks, perhaps the most celebrated proponents of Buddhist overtone chanting in the world. But this album puts more emphasis on the noisy clatter of Tibetan instruments than the beauty of the voices. Lots of *very* short excerpts make this useful as a demonstration, but keep the album from maintaining any musical continuity.

▲ *Heart Dance, River Flow: Folk Music of Tibet* (Dorje Ling DLP-07903) NAR, FOR. Tibetan folk music is as closely related to the better known ritual chanting as Western pop music is to Beethoven. While some of the instrumental works sound Chinese, other songs and dances sound amazingly like the music of northeastern and eastern Africa.

▲ *Tibetan Buddhism/Tantras of Gyütö: Mahakala* (None. Explorer H-72055)

▲ *Tibetan Buddhism/Tantras of Gyütö: Sangwa Düpa* (None. Explorer H-72064)
Despite problems with the sound of these two recordings, they are indispensable to anyone interested in ancient *or* avant-garde vocal techniques. The Gyütö monks chant in almost impossibly deep, throaty tones, and can make a second or third note from the overtone series audible as well, in effect singing two or three notes simultaneously. See Chapter 10.

▲ *The Music of Tibetan Buddhism Vol. 1* (Bär. BM 30 L2009) FOR

▲ *The Music of Tibetan Buddhism Vol. 2* (Bär. BM 30 L2010) FOR

▲ *The Music of Tibetan Buddhism Vol. 3* (Bär. BM 30 L2011) FOR
Each volume is devoted to a pair of Tibetan Buddhist sects. As with most Tibetan ritual music, the vocal works are of primary importance here: The racket the monks raise with their instruments is

often designed to scare away demons, and is enough to frighten off all but the most determined Western listener.

▲ Tibetan Ritual Music: Lamas and Monks of Tibet (Lyrichord LLST-7181). More rich choruses of basso-profundo voices. Another old recording, but still serviceable.

THE NEAR AND MIDDLE EAST*

THE HALVETTI-JERRAHI DERVISHES
■ Journey to the Lord of Power (ITI 1001) NMDS. The dhikr is the Sufi ritual remembrance of God, and often involves the highly rhythmic chanting of His many names. Accompaniment consists of ney, kemanche (violin), and percussion like the kudum or bendir.

▲ Iran: Anthologie de la musique traditionelle (Oc. 558 540) HM. Dariush Tala'i plays two string instruments from the Persian tradition, the tar and sehtar. These unaccompanied solos are naturally rather spare, but they're good examples of what are held to be two of the most important instruments in the tradition.

▲ Iran: Art of the Persian Santur (Musical Heritage Society MHS-4877F) MHS. Djalal Akhbari plays the santur, the Persian zither, with tombak (hand drum) accompaniment, in two suites. One is based on a dastgah (the seven dastgah-ha are roughly the equivalent of the parent scales in Indian raga), and the other on one of the five other modes central to Persian music.

▲ Iran: Musique Persane (Oc. OCR-57). Two side-long dastgah performances by a group of Iranian soloists.

▲ Iran/Santur par Majid Kiani: Radif (HM/France HM391) HM. Radif is the name given to the entire arrangement of the seven dastgah-ha and the melodic sequences, or gousheh, that derive from them. Kiani plays two side-long improvisations with zarb (drum) accompaniment. Excellent liner notes not only tell you which dastgah the pieces are based on, but which gousheh are being played and in what order. A concise but reasonably complete essay also explains the structure of the twelve Avaz (the seven dastgah-ha and the five auxiliary modes mentioned above).

▲ Iran: Unesco Collection, Vol. 1 (Bär. BM 30 L2004). An album of shorter pieces, featuring solos for kemanche, sehtar, and voice.

▲ Iraq: Makamat (Oc. OCR-79) HM. Makamat is the plural of makam (or maqam) which is the Arabic and Turkish equivalent of Indian raga. (Before the nineteenth-century, Persian music was also based on the maqam system.) These works for vocalist and ensemble—fiddle, santur, tabla, def—are more colorful than a solo performance but are less easily accessible: Like South Indian music, Iraqi ensemble music can be loud and biting, to some ears abrasive.

▲ Iraq: 'ūd classique arabe par Munir Bashir (Oc. OCR-63) HM. Expressive performances of several demanding taqsim (the traditional system of improvisation), each based on a maqam that is popular throughout the Arabic world.

▲ Turquie: L'Art Vivant de Talip Ozkan (Oc. 558 561) HM. Ozkan plays Turkish lutes—the saz, tambura (not to be confused with the Indian drone instrument), and others—in a set of pleasant, folk-tinged improvisations.

▲ Turquie: Chants sacrées d'Anatole (Oc. 558 577) HM. Ashik Feyzullah Tchinar performs a set of sacred songs in a highly rhythmic chanting style. It's an unusual sound, though an entire album of it may be a bit too much.

▲ Turquie: Musique Soufi (Oc. 558 522) HM. For an LP of ethnic vocals, this is quite accessible. Softly sung devotional texts with ney flute and drum.

SOUTHEASTERN EUROPE

▲ Ancient Turkish Music in Europe: 16th–18th Centuries (Hungaroton SLPX-12560). Buoyant, charming music from the era of Turkish rule in southeastern Europe, performed by Hungary's Kecskes Ensemble. The instrumentation is a blend of East and West; the relation between Persian, Arabic, and Turkish music is highlighted by the appearance of the Persian santur and tombak in the European music of this time. There are also some vocals, sung in a strange hybrid language, part Hungarian and part Turkish.

▲ Grèce: Chants sacrées de la tradition Byzantine, Vol. 1 (Oc. 558 521) HM
▲ Grèce: Chants sacrées de la tradition Byzantine, Vol. 2 (Oc. 558 530) HM

*The terms Near East and Middle East are often used interchangeably, but in theory, at least, the two are different. The Middle East lies between Central Asia and the Mediterranean (Iran, Pakistan, Iraq, Syria, Saudi Arabia, etc.); the Near East includes those countries that either were part of the Ottoman Empire (Greece, Turkey, Rumania, etc.), or those that border on the eastern Mediterranean (Egypt, Lebanon, Israel, etc.). Because the two regions are quite similar musically—Arabic, Persian, and Turkish traditions are closely related in structure and instrumentation—all of these traditions are placed together here, with the more distantly related music of southeastern Europe listed separately.

▲ *Grèce, Vol. 3 & 4: Liturgies anciennes orthodoxes* (Oc. 558 545/46, 2 LPs) HM Since we don't often think of Gregorian chants or other Early Christian singing as "ethnic music," these splendid recordings by Theodore Vassilikos and his Vocal Ensemble are covered in Chapter 10, page 236.

HALKIAS FAMILY ORCHESTRA
■ *Songs and Dances of Epiros* (Ethnic Folks Arts Center BA-US-1003; Ethnic Folk Arts Center, 325 Spring Street #314, New York, NY 10013). Epiros is an area of Greece with a folk tradition that sounds as if it came from the Far East. This group plays traditional works, with perhaps too much singing. But the almost vocal uses of the clarinets and violin are amazing, and the rhythms are irresistible. Laouto (lute) and santoori (zither) round out the ensemble.

▲ *Musik der Pontosgriechen* (Museum Collection, West Berlin MC-5) CH. The Pontic Greeks are originally ethnic Greeks who lived in northwestern Turkey, on the Black Sea near Armenia. They were expelled in the 1920s and settled in Greece. Their music obviously sounds more Turkish than Greek, and includes catchy bits of dance music for lyra, bagpipe, voice, clarinet, drum, and others.

ORIENTEXPRESSEN
■ *Andra Resan* (Sam URS-7) SCA. Traditional dances and songs from Turkey, Greece, Yugoslavia, Bulgaria, and Rumania, played by a Swedish group. Ney, bagpipe, panpipes, fiddle, and others are all used, as are some traditional vocals. Bulgarian songs can be charmingly nasal; aside from that, this excellent album is readily accessible to Western ears.

▲ *Orient/Okzident—Musik aus Südost-Europa* (Museum Collection, West Berlin MC-3, 2 LPs) CH. Comprehensive survey of music from all the countries ruled by the Osmanli Turks. After the Turkish withdrawal in the nineteenth century, Central European instruments were adopted and added to the Near Eastern instruments already in use. The results, as this nicely produced two-record set shows, were often energetic, likeable songs and dances.

▲ *Yugoslavie: Les Bougies du Paradis* (Oc. 558 548) HM. Although no one will admit to believing in vampires today, the people in Yugoslavian villages will still play or sing the "Melody to Drive Away Vampires" whenever someone is buried, to prevent the deceased from returning. It is played here on a flute, and quite frankly, the story is more interesting than the music. Most of this album is simple folk singing and playing, with little of the exotic influence heard in the preceding records.

NORTH AND SOUTH AMERICA
THE ANDES

LOS CALCHAKIS
■ *La Flauta India a Través de los Siglos* (Arion/ Gamma GX-01-660). This Mexican group plays traditional South American instruments—flute, guitar, drums. The instrumentals are best; the vocals are pretty awful.

▲ *Flight of the Condor* (BBC 22440) NAR. A soundtrack to a BBC film, featuring two Chilean ensembles (Inti Illimani is one of them, and the album is sometimes listed under their name). Using panpipes, flutes, charango (a small guitar), and percussion, these bands have recorded an album that effectively and consistently evokes the mystery and simplicity of life in the Andes.

INCANTATION
■ *Music of the Andes* (PVC 8945) JEM. Five British musicians play traditional South American music, including "Cacharpaya," (which became a surprise hit-single in Britain), the well-known "Papel de Plata," and "Dance of the Flames." The album is just as authentic and enjoyable as those done by South American bands.

▲ *Musik im Andenhochland/Bolivien* (Museum Collection, West Berlin MC-14, 2 LPs) CH. A lavishly annotated set of music of the Aymara and Quechua people, whose languages are still spoken in the higher altitudes of the Andes where Spanish hasn't yet established itself. Lots of flute ensembles and panpipes, with some guitar-style instruments, often accompanied by small or large drums.

▲ *Musiques du Perou* (Oc. OCR-30) HM. A fascinating glimpse into the seldom heard music of the Peruvian highland Indians. Lots of flutes, some harp, occasional vocals or drums, and even a piece played on an early-seventeenth-century organ wheezing away in a village church.

UNA RAMOS
■ *Poupée de Porcelaine* (ChM. LDX-74683) HM. Ramos plays a number of South American flutes; the back-up ensemble includes charango, guitar, bombo (drum), harp, and cello. Like the instrumentation, the music is a blend of traditional and contemporary South American styles. "Rocotito" is one of the most melodic, irresistible pieces of Andean music on record.

TAHUATINSUYO
■ *Music of the Andes* (Adelphi AD-3001). Instrumentals played on the usual flutes, charangos, etc. Not particularly well produced, unfortunately.

▲ *Urubamba* (War. BSK-3553). Infectious pre-Columbian music from a very talented South American ensemble.

CARIBBEAN

NORTH AMERICA*

▲ *Under the Coconut Tree: Music from Grand Cayman and Tortola* (Original Music OMC-201) NMDS. Music from these small islands has apparently not been recorded before. It has a strong British flavor, especially in the fiddle tunes. Naturally, other Caribbean forms, including reggae and Calypso, have made their presence felt.

▲ *Inuit Throat and Harp Songs* (Canadian Music Heritage WRC-1-1349) NMDS. Near the Hudson Bay in Canada, Inuit Eskimo women shout into one another's throats. It may not be the most hygienic means of making music, but it produces some strange and actually quite musical sounds. One person's throat acts as a resonator for the other's voice, and the hocket-style breathing and chanting is fun to hear. Several works for metal mouth-harp round out this intriguing collection.

*Along with that of Europe, the folk music of the U.S. and Canada is listed in the next chapter. Although recordings of some American Indian music do exist, there don't seem to be any good, sympathetic ones.

8
UNUSUAL FOLK SONG ARRANGEMENTS

The notion that there is such a thing as "folk music" as distinct from other kinds of music is widespread in Europe and America. It is an ambiguous term that has different meanings and shades of meaning.
The New Grove Dictionary of Music and Musicians

They're all folk songs—I ain't never heard a horse sing.
Big Bill Broonzy

If you own a record collection, chances are that somewhere among your albums you'll find the phrase "trad./arr."—traditional, arranged by whomever. Although the folk traditions of both Europe and North America have a long history, by the 1950s many Westerners had grown so estranged from them that the appearance of early "revivalist" recordings had as much surprise value, and as much exotic appeal, as the ethnic records that were beginning to appear at the same time. While some musicians subsequently turned to the Third World for inspiration and source material, others were drawn to the equally rich (and to some, equally obscure) heritage of Western folk music. Today, unusual arrangements of folk songs have become a popular means for musicians to produce works that are highly individual and innovative yet still firmly rooted in tradition.

Our focus here is on the use of folk music *outside* the classical field, where folk themes have long been used to add "local color" to the music. The real development of folk song as a source for new music began after the folk revival had taken hold in the 1950s. Once musicians on both sides of the Atlantic rediscovered the folk legacies of their countries, it was only a matter of time before someone thought of playing a Celtic folk song on Indian instruments, or on a synthesizer. (Oddly enough, it seems to have taken a bit longer for them to realize that playing Celtic songs on their original instrument, the Celtic harp, would be an equally novel idea.)

Many folk purists regard these unusual arrangements as simply a bastardization of traditional folk forms, but a more commonly held view is that the use of traditional music, even in the most *un*traditional guises, helps keep interest in, and respect for, folk songs alive. In this chapter we'll limit our discussion to how new music has treated two traditions, the British and the Celtic (the latter including the music of Brittany in northwestern France). Without slighting the folk music of North America and continental Europe, it seems safe to say that these insular styles are remarkably well-preserved and have inspired a large number of contemporary artists.

On the surface, a culture so reliant on technology and so concerned with what's new and modern seems an unlikely one for folk music to thrive in. Yet the revival of interest in folk song that we have seen in the last twenty years or so has origins that go back as far as the nineteenth century. At that time, when it seemed that the industrialization of the West was going to make folk music obsolete, musicologists attempted to capture that heritage for posterity by traveling into the countryside to notate the songs they heard. In England, for example, Francis Child collected 305 folk songs, and published them in 1898 as *The English and Scottish Popular Ballads.* Across the Atlantic, John A. Lomax, his son Alan, and Charles Seeger made equally significant contributions to American folk song research. And Cecil Sharp, founder of the English Folk Dance Society, traveled during the second decade of this century through the Appalachian mountains in the eastern United States, where he discovered many British folk songs, some of them preserved in a "purer" form than were their counterparts in England.

This turned out to be a useful exercise, but not for the reasons these scholars intended. First of all, folk music proved to be an exclusively oral tradition: It was often not easily notated, and even when it could be, the rigid codification which resulted from the setting of notes on paper contradicted the way folk music is passed on—by memory, in many variant forms. In England, Ralph Vaughan Williams, Gustav Holst, and Benjamin Britten all made classical arrangements of British folk songs; almost without exception, they're beautiful, sympathetic settings. But they're not folk music. Preserving folk music in print, even with a number of variants, is like trying to save an endangered species by placing its collective members in formaldehyde. You may have all the pieces, but the life has gone out of it.

"It's still an oral tradition," explains Bill Ochs, who plays the Irish uilleann pipes. "The music is written down and a huge percentage of Irish musicians are musically literate—they can read music and they can transcribe it; but the transcriptions are looked at as just a skeleton of the tune, a memory device, and if you played it exactly as it was written down people would not regard that as very good playing."

On the other hand, the early musicologists and folk song collectors *did* provide a valuable service by drawing attention to folk music and in some cases adding rough field recordings to their written output. These recordings—wax cylinders in the first decade of the century, acoustic discs in the second—were the beginning of the real revival of folk music. If notation inhibited growth and change, both essential to the folk tradition, recordings in the early years of this century and radio broadcasts starting in the 1920s encouraged them. Since that time the written works of Sharp, Seeger, the Lomaxes, and others have proven to be important less for the preservation of folk music than for providing source material and acting as a kind of catalog of folk songs. The songs in Child's *The English and Scottish Popular Ballads* are still referred to today by their number in Child's book: "The Gallows Pole," for example, is Child No. 95. This song exists in arrangements as diverse as those by the Kingston

Trio and Led Zeppelin, and versions of it have also been found in almost every country in Europe. With so many variants around, it's convenient to have a basic reference work available.

Catalogs of American folk song also exist, but here we come to an important distinction between American folk music and that of the British Isles, and a key reason why this chapter deals primarily with the latter. Folk music evolves slowly, over centuries. European folk traditions, which have a long history behind them, contain a large body of works that are appropriate for just about any occasion or situation. A European musician needs only to adapt, arrange, and perhaps update the traditional material. America's folk music, in contrast, is quite young; it is just over a century since the emancipation of the slaves and the development of the blues, the major influence on the American folk tradition. Lacking a large group of pre-existing songs, American folk musicians have had to write their own.

This American folk heritage was given a real shot in the arm in the 1930s when musicians discovered folk music's usefulness as a vehicle for popular, protest-oriented lyrics. The union songs of the 1930s injected a note of political protest into American folk music that has remained ever since. Previously, the folk songs heard in America had been brought from Europe, but over the next twenty years, a native folk scene developed, mainly as an extension of the blues, with elements of European-based bluegrass and early country styles added. The music was nurtured by artists like Big Bill Broonzy, a Chicago-based musician who performed in the 1940s in a style that was both traditional and popular; Huddie Ledbetter, better known as Leadbelly, and Woody Guthrie, both of whom developed a gripping style of performing work songs and other original tunes; and Pete Seeger, Charles's son and founder of the Weavers. These artists built up both a repertoire of songs and a small but loyal audience.

These were the origins of the American folk revival, but the music in this chapter really grows out of the developments of the 1950s. This was the decade of the "skiffle" style, a type of music ordinarily consisting of a simple American folk tune played over a shuffling rhythm section. Skiffle acts like Lonnie Donegan topped the pop charts in both Britain and America, and represented an early effort at using folk melodies in settings that could hardly be called "folk music." Then, in 1958, an American pop group, the Kingston Trio, hit it big with "Tom Dooley," a Carolina folk song in an arrangement of calculated appeal. The Kingston Trio were not folk singers; they were pop musicians looking for an angle, and folk music fit the bill. But despite its compromises, works like "Tom Dooley" helped bring folk music to an entirely different audience. And it demonstrated to Britain's quietly growing folk circuit that this music had the potential to reach a great number of people.

When in the early 1960s pop music in both North America and the British Isles went into one of its periodic comas, younger artists turned toward forms like jazz, avant-garde, and folk. The trickle of (mostly American) folk songs that had reached the musical public through skiffle and pop groups like the Kingston Trio had already proven that folk could be adapted in a popular way. But in London and Dublin, efforts began to create native music to compete with the popularity of American songs, folk-derived or otherwise. Both England and Ireland had a great heritage of traditional works to choose from, and it didn't take long for these to attract the attention of the pop audience. The Clancy Brothers and Tommy Makem, who had left Ireland for America in the late 50s, became quite popular in the 60s with arrangements of Irish folk music that paralleled what the Kingston Trio did with American folk song.

Beyond this pop transformation of folk, though, was another group of artists who took this new interest in folk arrangements and used it as the basis for serious music. Foremost among them were Sean O Riada in Ireland and Davey Graham in England. Neither man was interested in pop music; each hoped to draw on his respective tradition to develop a new approach that could bring folk music out of the closed circle of clubs in which it had been growing during the 1950s.

Neither O Riada nor Graham was originally a folk musician: O Riada, born John Reidy in 1931, was a classical composer, a student of Messiaen, while Graham was a blues guitarist. Both had been influenced by Indian raga and other types of Eastern music. O Riada began working for Radio Eireann and its Symphony Orchestra in the late 50s, producing several works for orchestra that combined traditional Celtic themes and Western classical instruments in an entirely new way. He Gaelicized his name and in 1959 produced the soundtrack for the film *Mise Eire*. In this score, traditional Irish tunes were not simply dressed up in orchestral clothing; they were the basis of the music itself, varied, inverted, and developed in a classical, symphonic style. O Riada's passion for Irish folk music prompted him to create in 1961 an innovative folk ensemble he called Ceoltoiri Chualann ("The Musicians of Cuala").

Ceoltoiri Chualann was the first group of its kind; although its roots were in folk, it played with the precision of a classical ensemble. Several of the group's musicians were from the Dublin folk scene, and kept the music from straying too far from the tradition. Even so, the ensemble was revolutionary in several ways. Aside from the *ceilidhe* (pronounced kay'-lee) bands used for dancing, Irish folk music was customarily performed solo. Ceoltoiri Chualann combined traditional solo instruments—pipes, whistles, and fiddles—with one another and with O Riada's harpsichord; while the various members of the group still took solos, much of its music was performed by the entire ensemble. O Riada himself used the harpsichord because he disliked the sound of the modern, nylon-strung harp and because almost no one could make or play the old wire-strung Celtic harp at that time.

In selecting the repertoire of Ceoltoiri Chualann, O Riada used not only Irish folk songs but also the music of Taordhealbhach O Cerabhallain—better known as Turlough O Carolan, an Irish harpist of the eighteenth century. O Carolan was part of the Celtic harp tradition, but he had also absorbed the Italian classical styles of the day—Vivaldi, Corelli, etc. In resurrecting O Carolan's music for Ceoltoiri Chualann, O Riada bridged a gap of two hundred years during which there had been little or no contact between Celtic and other Western styles.

Meanwhile, in London, guitarist Davey Graham was working the folk club circuit, playing blues and developing, along with guitarist and singer Alexis Korner, a style known as "folk-blues." Korner, who helped bring together the Rolling Stones and who played "da blooz" with Mick Jagger, Jack Bruce, Ginger Baker, and many others destined for stardom, released an album with Graham called *3/4 A.D.* (1961); although it seems to have disappeared without a trace, it was considered a prime example of folk-blues.

As we have seen in Chapter 6, Graham next went on to experiment with various other influences, including Indian raga. His 1963 arrangement of "She Moves through the Fair" as a guitar raga was one attempt to place the folk style into a surprising context. This experiment came to be known as "folk-baroque," and it proved to be a major inspiration to most of the figures—Bert Jansch, John Renbourn, their group Pentangle, and Fairport Convention, among others—who would make unusual translations of folk so popular in the late 60s and 70s.

In 1965 Graham released *Folk, Blues, and Beyond,* an album on which he performed raga-based themes, North African music, a Leadbelly tune, some jazz, and some folk music. It was the first LP of folk-baroque, and it had some wonderful moments as well as some unfortunate singing. It has not aged well, but it was a revelation to many. Later in 1965 Graham followed it with *Folk Roots, New Routes,* with folk singer Shirley Collins mercifully taking over the vocal chores. The sheer audacity of the concept—pure folk singing against the Oriental exoticism of Graham's guitar—made it unique, and the guitar work would be widely imitated over the next several years.

While Graham was busy establishing himself in London, O Riada had already attracted a good deal of attention in Dublin. His Ceoltoiri Chualann made a number of albums on which it managed to walk a fine line between tradition and innovation. At this point, several members of the group decided to form a band of their own, while continuing to play with O Riada. Led by uilleann piper Paddy Moloney, they believed that the music would be better served with less singing, and with the accordion and harpsichord being replaced by the more authentic sounds of the concertina and harp. Given that the Celtic harp was still an instrument that could be found only behind a glass case in a museum, Moloney and his ensemble contented themselves with a concertina and a bodhran, a large tambourinelike drum, along with pipes, whistle, and fiddles. They called themselves The Chieftains, and they became the most famous of the contemporary traditional bands. Despite the change in instrumentation, The Chieftains' music continued to reveal O Riada's influence; even today their performances have an almost classical accuracy and grace, especially when compared to later groups like Planxty or the Bothy Band, whose lineups, while often just as traditional, played in a more energetic, even rock-oriented style.

By 1966, O Riada and The Chieftains had so successfully tested the waters that several other traditional groups were now ready to jump in. Ceoltoiri Laighean was another splinter off O Riada's ensemble. Sweeney's Men was a band very popular in England, both with the Irish workers there and with the English folk musicians. Emmet Spiceland recorded a new version of an old song that became the first piece in Gaelic to hit the pop charts. (Emmet Spiceland was the first of Donal Lunny's ensembles; the ubiquitous Lunny later helped form both Planxty and the Bothy Band.)

As so often happens, the originators of the new folk style were eventually overshadowed by their successors. As the folk scene grew, both Graham and O Riada suffered from health problems. While Graham survived his, he never really got beyond the folk club circuit to achieve the wider acclaim of some of the newer bands. O Riada died in 1971 at the age of forty. He kept his Ceoltoiri Chualann going until 1969, but that group had been pretty well replaced in popular favor by ensembles like The Chieftains and Sweeney's Men.

Although most of the major developments in folk music during the late 60s occurred in England, one important step was taken in the United States—the introduction of electric instruments to the folk ensemble. Bob Dylan had used an electric guitar on his 1964 album *Freewheelin'*, and had scandalized most of the audience at the annual Newport music festival in 1965 when he plugged in his electric guitar. Electric instruments were eventually used by many folk artists, including Fairport Convention and Alan Stivell, but the full potential of this approach wouldn't really become apparent for several years.

The key figures on the London scene in the 60s remained acoustic musicians, of whom the two most notable were guitarists Bert Jansch and John Renbourn. Like Davey Graham, both had begun their careers as blues singer/guitarists, and had released recordings of American blues. In 1966, Jansch began to apply Graham's techniques of folk-baroque to English folk song. The result was the album *Jack Orion,* which featured Renbourn on several tracks; the two guitarists collaborated on the *Bert and John* collection later that year. These records showed Jansch and Renbourn to be prodigiously talented musicians, and fine arrangers as well. In 1967, they founded an ensemble called Pentangle, the first London-based group to draw on the folk tradition while not staying directly within the tradition itself. Pentangle was primarily an acoustic band, combining folk song with elements of jazz and blues. The band lasted until 1972, releasing six somewhat uneven albums during that period. Renbourn, meanwhile, continued to record solo projects, including 1968's *Sir John Alot Of Merrie Englandes Musyk Thyng & Ye Grene Knyght,* reissued about a dozen years later under the title *Sir John Alot Of,* and the brilliant 1970 album *The Lady and the Unicorn.*

At about the time Pentangle was forming, bassist and folk enthusiast Ashley Hutchings was putting together the first edition of the now legendary Fairport Convention. Fairport was an exceptional collection of musicians: Problem was, it was almost impossible to keep track of *which* musicians were playing with the band at any given time. By 1971, not a single member of the original 1967 lineup was still with the group. Hutchings, guitarist Richard Thompson, fiddler Dave Swarbrick, and vocalist Sandy Denny were probably the finest of the Fairport crew, and it is they who are responsible for Fairport Convention's best music—including the band's second album, *What We Did on Our Holidays* (reissued in the U.S. as *Fairport Convention*), and the landmark 1969 release *Liege and Lief.*

Fairport Convention practically defined the style known as folk-rock. Using electric guitars and drums along with a traditional singer and fiddler, they produced some of the most creative arrangements of folk songs available on disc. *Liege and Lief* was the first really successful attempt at performing traditional music in a contemporary way. "Reynardine" and "Matty Groves," two perennial folk song favorites, appear on the album; "Reynardine" is given an ominous, chilling treatment, with psychedelic-style reverb and moaning electric guitar sounds; while "Matty Groves" is transformed into an energetic, stomping piece that sounds folksy even with the electric instrumentation. Sandy Denny's incomparable vocals and Swarbrick's fiddling kept the other musicians honest, and helped maintain some degree of continuity through the band's first few personnel changes.

Fairport Convention built up a large following over the years. But the constant uncertainty over who would or wouldn't show up for the next tour or recording session took its toll. One result of all these comings and goings was that almost every major English folk ensemble in the 70s was in effect a Fairport Convention spinoff. Sandy Denny's Fotheringay and her own solo career, tragically cut short by her death in 1978, are two examples; Richard Thompson went on to become a brilliant soloist as well. After leaving Fairport, Ashley Hutchings attempted to recruit Andy Irvine and Johnny Moynihan from Sweeney's Men to form a band. That didn't pan out—both Irvine and Moynihan later wound up in Planxty—so Hutchings went on instead to put together Steeleye Span. (The group's name came from a character in —what else?—an old English folk song.) Although the group's entire repertoire was traditional, and the voice/guitar team of Maddy Prior and Tim Hart gave the music at least an occasional folksy twang, for the most part Steeleye Span was a very thinly disguised rock band, and not surprisingly, the most commercially successful of the contemporary folk groups.

After two albums of rock stylizations of folk songs, Steeleye Span released *Ten Man Mop or Mr. Reservoir Butler Rides Again* (1971), proof that it was capable of producing effective folk arrangements that could, in one song at least, rival those of vintage Fairport Convention. The song, "When I Was on Horseback," uses the electric instruments to provide dramatic coloristic effects and to complement the traditional vocals and fiddle. "Skewball" and "Wee Weaver" were also given genuinely faithful, but unusual treatments.

Ashley Hutchings, however, was still not satisfied, and he left Steeleye Span to team up with ex-Fairporters Thompson and drummer Dave Mattacks for a recording entitled *Morris On* in 1972. As the title implies, traditional dance music was the basis for the album, and a group of Morris Dancers actually appears on a couple of tracks. Hutchings next founded the Albion Dance Band, another folk-dance ensemble, which featured a number of medieval and Renaissance instruments—crumhorns, rebecs, and such—played by members of London's renowned Early Music Consort, as well as traditional and electric instruments. Like Hutchings's earlier groups the Albion Dance Band has been disbanded and resurrected several times over the past several years.

Despite their instability and inconsistency, these early English groups had a considerable impact on the British music scene. Steve Winwood's popular rock group Traffic, for example, recorded an acoustic, very traditional-sounding version of the ancient ballad "John Barleycorn," and took the title of the album on which it appeared, *John Barleycorn Must Die!*, from a line of the song. Traffic found "John Barleycorn" in a Cecil Sharp collection, not the usual source for material for a rock band, certainly, but by this time the folk idiom had become a pervasive part of the musical language in England.

The next important wave of folk musicians in the early 1970s came out of the Celtic tradition, from Ireland and from the French province of Brittany. Alan Stivell Cochevelou had been playing Celtic harp music, both from Ireland and from his native Brittany, as early as 1965. Under the name Alan Stivell, he began to build upon the work of his father, Jord Cochevelou, who had spent some twenty years trying to redevelop the techniques of constructing and playing the traditional wire-strung Celtic harp. Inspired by the success of The Chieftains and other Celtic revivalist groups, Stivell became the first to perform publicly the music of the harp repertoire on its original instrument. In 1967, Stivell assembled his own band and started touring in France and the British Isles. The ensemble consisted of acoustic and electric guitar, bass, and percussion, with Stivell himself singing and playing the harp, Irish flute, and bagpipes. The group's success in France established Stivell as the early leader of the French folk scene, and paved the way for other contemporary folk musicians such as Gabriel Yacoub and his group Malicorne, Dan Ar Bras (who played guitar with Stivell for several years and briefly joined Fairport Convention), and guitarist Pierre Bensusan.

"Alan Stivell and Malicorne were the real leaders," Bensusan asserts. "At that time, people in France were very keen on Irish music. A lot of musicians would not play French music at all; they'd rather play Irish jigs and reels." Of course, as Breton musicians, Stivell and Ar Bras had a natural affinity for Irish music; the language and the music of Brittany are also Celtic.* But the French enthusiasm for Irish folk music, often at the expense of their own tradition, is a bit harder to explain. "There was a lot of French traditional musical culture lost in the two world wars," Bensusan suggests. "That happened in Germany as well. So people came to think that French music wasn't rich enough—which is neither true nor false; it's just subjective."

Contemporary Irish groups, with over a decade of groundwork laid by O Riada, The Chieftains, and others, also began to blossom in this period. In 1971, Donal Lunny, Christy Moore, Andy Irvine, and the remarkable piper Liam O Floinn formed what would become one of the finest bands of the contemporary folk revival. Planxty was the name they gave the group, and it soon developed a reputation for outstanding musicianship (with Lunny, Irvine, and Moore playing guitars, bouzoukis, mandolins, and other "adopted" folk instruments) and for innovative programs. Traditional songs and dances were mixed in with original compositions, and all were sung or played with an energy that appealed to younger listeners while not veering too far from folk standards. Planxty also featured songs that most folk singers wouldn't perform, such as the title track of its second album, *The Well below the Valley*. The song is loosely based on the fourth chapter of the Gospel of John, in which Jesus meets a woman at a well, tells her the sins she's committed (she's had five husbands and is shacking up with another man), and eventually saves her. "The Well below the Valley" is a good deal more specific in its retelling—for many tastes, too specific.

The song unfolds slowly in the classic folk style: at first the woman speaks, then the refrain appears, then Jesus speaks, the refrain follows, and back we go to the

---

*There are actually two families of Celtic peoples: the Goidelic, or Gaelic, comprises the people of Ireland, Scotland, and the Isle of Man; the Brythonic branch includes Brittany, Wales, and Cornwall. Although the languages of the two branches vary, their music is similar.

woman, and so on. This simple, ancient means of building up suspense is the framework for Jesus' revelation, piece by piece, of the woman's sordid past. Her activities have apparently included incest with several family members and the murder of the resulting progeny, two of whom are buried, as it happens, beneath the well itself. In Planxty's version of this controversial song the simple, repeating accompaniment becomes more intricate and more insistent as the story develops, the singing is in true folk style, the beating of the bodhran is completely traditional, but although the arrangement is one of the band's most conservative, the piece has an absolutely contemporary sound.

Like England's folk scene, its Celtic counterpart was an intramural affair: From one group to another the same names keep appearing. In 1975, another fine group, the Bothy Band, was formed; it included Donal Lunny, the brother/sister team of Micheal O Domhnaill and Triona Ni Dhomhnaill* from the group Skara Brae, Paddy Glackin from Ceoltoiri Laighean, and Matt Molloy, a flute and whistle player who eventually became the only musician to play with all three of the major Irish bands. While the Bothy Band's sound was reminiscent at times of Planxty, the ensemble was somewhat larger and, if anything, even more energetic. Lunny's instrumentation, always on the edge as far as traditionalists were concerned, expanded to include synthesizer and dulcimer. Triona Ni Dhomhnaill's clavinet and harpsichord may have recalled O Riada's Ceoltoiri Chualann, but the Bothy Band played with an intensity very far removed from the almost courtly style of O Riada. The Bothy Band's range of music was as impressive as Planxty's. The tunes were mostly traditional, but they varied in style from speedy jigs to the Gaelic "mouth music" known as *puirt a beul*. The song "Fionnghuala" (from the second Bothy album, delightfully entitled *Old Hag You Have Killed Me*), is a splendid example of *puirt a beul:* Each musician sings nonsense syllables, usually in rapid succession, without instrumental accompaniment. The resulting textures made "Fionnghuala" an unlikely favorite among Bothy Band audiences. Although rumors that the group was going to switch to an all-electric lineup proved untrue, the Bothy Band did release five albums with hybrid instrumentation before its various members went their separate ways.

While Planxty and the Bothy Band were gradually changing the sound of Celtic music with new instruments, others were doing the same with old ones. By the mid-70s, Alan Stivell had experimented at various times with the Indian sitar and tabla, synthesizers, an Algerian women's choir, a symphony orchestra, rock instruments, and several varieties of bagpipes, whistles, and frame drums—yet he remained associated in the public's mind most with the Celtic harp. Though Stivell himself later moved on to works like the *Symphonie Celtique*—a ninety-minute bit of megalomania involving seventy-five musicians and very little harp—he had already opened the door for a number of other artists who wanted to bring the Celtic harp back to Celtic music. The Chieftains, who had originally wanted a harper in the group, finally hired Derek Bell in the mid-70s, and Scotland's Charles Guard, the American Patrick Ball, and Bell himself all recorded solo harp albums. Ironically, like the ethnic music of the previous chapter, Irish harp music from the

*Traditionally, male and female versions of a Gaelic surname are spelled differently. Both spellings are approximately pronounced dun'-ul.

traditional and the O Carolan repertoires has come full circle: Played on instruments modeled after those of the sixteenth or seventeenth centuries, it has become among the most appealing of new sounds to contemporary audiences.

The late 70s was a peak period for Celtic musicians in Ireland, Scotland, and France, but in England the folk scene had reached something of a plateau. Fairport Convention supposedly broke up for good in 1976, but then began a series of "reunion tours" that have continued into the 80s. Hutchings's Albion Dance Band released a few albums, including a fine 1977 recording *(The Prospect before Us)*, though sales were less than spectacular. John Renbourn formed a group in 1977 with an Indian tabla player and a few of his ex-Pentangle cohorts. And, while Davey Graham appeared back on vinyl, his 1978 album *The Complete Guitarist* hardly qualifies as part of the English folk revival, since over half the album is devoted to traditional Irish jigs and reels.

If the use of unusual folk arrangements has not actually disappeared in the 80s, it has dispersed a bit, and artists who ten years ago were playing primarily folk are now branching off into other fields. After releasing several albums in the 70s derived from folk traditions (mostly Celtic), Pierre Bensusan began to incorporate jazz, classical, and ethnic sounds into his music.

"Folk was very important to me," he says, "but it was one step, not an end." He cites the late 70s as a turning point in his development. "At that time, the folk circuit was thinking too much about itself and ignoring other musical expressions. It was just too closed in. What I wanted had a lot to do with the fusion of my influences—ethnic, folk, classical—and my very first influence, the North African. [Bensusan was born in Algeria.] But I'm not trying to imitate any tradition; I feel I have something of my own to say."

This appears to have become a common trend among the musicians who originally helped bring the sounds of folk traditions to new music circles. Without betraying their association with folk music, Dan Ar Bras, Richard Thompson, Bert Jansch, and others have in their recent work been concerned almost exclusively with original compositions in increasingly personal styles. Of course, the traditional music still has its adherents, many of whom are now in the United States. After the demise of the Bothy Band, several of the group's musicians moved to America: Triona Ni Dhomhnaill based her group, Touchstone, and her solo career, in Chapel Hill, North Carolina; while singer/guitarist Micheal O Domhnaill and fiddler Kevin Burke relocated in Portland, Oregon, building a studio there from which they have released several albums of folk music arrangements. In New England, a long-standing heritage of instrument building has resulted in access to Celtic harps for American artists who have become interested in Irish music.

In the 1980s reasonably straightforward acoustic arrangements of folk music have become more commonplace—the revived interest in the music having led naturally to a revived interest in the original instruments—though electric guitars and synthesizers have also proven adaptable to folk songs. The successful explorations of the traditions of the British Isles have also encouraged many other European and North American musicians to investigate their own heritage. Vangelis's arrangements of Greek folk songs for Irene Papas is one example; Malicorne's work with

French and Quebecois folk music is another. In the United States, new-music audiences have welcomed the reappearance of some of the older, less-known folk traditions. Michael Doucet and his group Beausoleil have revived the irrepressible sounds of Louisiana's Cajun heritage and have made several exciting albums. Ben Tavera King has taken the Tex-Mex tradition and updated it with bits of jazz and flamenco.

Of course, the verbal warfare continues over whether this music is authentically "folk" or just a corruption. Folk music, as the purists would have it, will continue to exist as long as people live out its classic themes—love, love lost, war, work, and death. Because these themes aren't likely to change, it's probably not an overstatement to say that there will always be people who sing the traditional songs in the traditional way; hence, there should be little objection to musicians bringing this music in altered forms to listeners who would otherwise not get to hear it. Ideally, of course, their interest will be piqued, and they will be lured into seeking out "the real thing." As with any style, the use of folk music in unusual arrangements may have produced some bad to mediocre material, but it has also been responsible for a body of excellent, imaginative works—which should be all the justification it needs.

DISCOGRAPHY AND RELATED WORKS

ALBION COUNTRY BAND
- *Battle of the Field* (Carthage CGLP-4420) HAN

ALBION DANCE BAND
- *The Prospect before Us* (Harvest SHSP-4059)

ALBION BAND
- *Rise up Like the Sun* (Harvest SHSP-4092)
- *Light Shining* (Albino ALB-001) KM, SHAN

ALBION DANCE BAND
- *Shuffle Off* (Spindrift SPIN-103) ROU

ALBION BAND
- *Under the Rose* (Spindrift SPIN-110) ROU, ALC
- *A Christmas Present* (Fun 003)

Despite the different names, these recordings, listed chronologically, are all the work of Ashley Hutchings and his most recent group. All of the Albion discs deal with British folk dances in rocking arrangements. Ancient instruments often join the electric guitars, bass, and drums, and the Albion Band albums include a number of vocals as well. *The Prospect before Us* is a strong series of dances that will appeal to both folk and rock fans; *Under the Rose* sounds like middle-period Fairport Convention with its easily melodic folk-rock tunes. Special mention should be made of the Christmas album, which includes Christmas songs from England, an American shape-note or Sacred Harp hymn, and a German carol.

AN TRISKELL
- *Kroaz Hent* (ChM LDX-74.613) HM
- *Harpe Celtique* (ChM LDX-74.640) HM

One of the many Breton ensembles using their Celtic heritage as a musical point of departure. An Triskell is a family affair, with Hervé and Pol Quefféléant playing the Celtic harps, Yann Quefféléant playing flute, and other regional musicians helping out. Their first album is the less polished, but is still enjoyable. The second LP is mostly instrumental, and ranges considerably further afield in terms of instrumentation and mood. Both albums combine traditional and original compositions, the second including some slow, atmospheric pieces along with the usual dances and reels.

DAN AR BRAS
- *Douar Nevez (Terre Nouvelle)* (W.E.A.-Hexagone 883009). Dan Ar Bras is a brilliant guitarist and a gifted composer. He's played with Alan Stivell, Malicorne, and Fairport Convention, but despite his long association with the folk revival, his albums mostly contain original works, drawing on his Celtic heritage and often dealing with the culture and mythology of his native Brittany. This album, his first, is a musical depiction of the legendary city of Ys. Ar Bras plays both acoustic and electric guitars, and is joined by synthesizer, piano, bass, percussion, uilleann pipes, flute, and vielle (a Renaissance string instrument).
- *Allez Dire à la Ville* (W.E.A.-Hexagone 883021)
- *The Earth's Lament* (W.E.A.-Hexagone 883034) Two albums that feature the electric guitar and some vocals by Ar Bras. The first includes a rendition of the Beatles song "Rain"; the second is in the electric folk-rock style, without actually quoting from folk music.
- *Acoustic* (Gr. L. SIF-3035) GLT. Probably Ar Bras's finest album. Most of the works are acoustic guitar solos; several have vocals, and there's a bit of piano accompaniment, too. Beautiful, deeply felt playing.
- *Musique pour les silences à venir* (Keltia RS-3063) SHAN. The title translates as "Music for the Silences To Come." It's another lovely album, with the electric guitar imitating the cry of the whales on "Les Lamentations de la Mer," and atmospheric use of the instrument elsewhere. Some typically idiosyncratic acoustic-guitar work as well.
- *Anne de Bretagne* (FLVM 45104, 7-inch 45-rpm single). Four songs for a stage production in France. Guitar, piano, and bagpipes.

Ar Bras *has* recorded some actual folk tunes as well: see *Irish Reels, Jigs, Hornpipes, and Airs,* listed below.

PATRICK BALL

- *Celtic Harp—Music of Turlough O Carolan* (For. FOR-005) FOR, NAR
- *Celtic Harp 2—From a Distant Time* (For. FOR-011) FOR, NAR
- *Secret Isles* (For. FOR-029) FOR, NAR

Ball, an outstanding musician, is perhaps the finest Celtic harper currently recording in America. His albums include most of the standards in the harp tradition: "Si Bheag Si Mhor," for example, which he spells phonetically "Sheebeg Sheemore"; and of course, numerous O Carolan works. The crystalline sound of the instrument is well captured on these discs.

BARE NECESSITIES

- *English Country Dances* (Varrick VR-013) ROU. Rustic dances, in mostly acoustic arrangements that resemble the Albion Dance Band without the electric guitars.

BEAUSOLEIL

- *Michael Doucet Dit Beausoleil* (Arhoolie C-5025) ARH, ROU
- *Parlez-Nous à Boire* (Arhoolie 5034) ARH, ROU
- *Allons à Lafayette* (Arhoolie 5036) ARH, ROU

It's hard to resist Cajun music when Beausoleil plays it. Whether they're doing jigs, reels, slow waltzes, haunting ballads, or the gritty Zydeco music of the region west of the delta, Michael Doucet's outfit always seems to have a good time, and the feeling's contagious. Doucet is aware of avant-garde jazz trends, and grew up with rock'n'roll, but his music is always true to the Cajun culture. Beausoleil's finest album to date is *Parlez-Nous à Boire* (the albums's title track translates as "let's talk about drinking, not about marriage"); the album's other standout track, "Mercredi Soir Passé," is a real rip-your-heart-out blues ballad. The latest album features Cajun oldtimer Canray Fontenot on fiddle and has several instrumental tracks.

DEREK BELL

- *Carolan's Receipt* (Shanachie 79013) SHAN
- *Musical Ireland* (Shanachie 79042) SHAN

Very good albums from The Chieftains' harper. The first LP includes the obligatory "Sidh Beag agus Sidh Mor" ("Si Bheag Si Mhor" in yet another spelling), and many other favorites. The second features "She Moves through the Fair" and an excerpt from Sean O Riada's Folk Mass. Other Chieftains help out, lending a classical, chamberish quality to these traditional works.

PIERRE BENSUSAN

- *Près de Paris* (Roun. 3023) ROU. First LP from this talented Algerian-born, French guitarist. Acoustic works, some with mandolin, show the

influence of Alan Stivell, Planxty, and some of the British and French folk song arrangers.

- *2* (Roun. 3037) ROU. Some ensemble pieces with strings or winds, and a number of guitar solos. Bensusan adds some original compositions to the traditional French and Irish pieces.
- *Musiques* (Roun. 3038) ROU. Excellent, surprisingly eclectic album. Several originals join an impressive lineup of traditional Irish, Turkish, and Argentine pieces. *Definitely* worth hearing.
- *Solilai* (Roun. 3068) ROU. Original works, many with vocals. Sort of jazzy, folk-derived music.

BOTHY BAND

- *1975* (Gr. L. SIF-3011) GLT
- *Old Hag You Have Killed Me* (Gr. L. SIF-3005) GLT
- *Out of the Wind into the Sun* (Gr. L. SIF-3013) GLT
- *Best Of* (Gr. L. SIF-3001) GLT

During the years of the first Planxty breakup, Donal Lunny occupied much of his time with this first-rate ensemble. The band lasted from 1975 to 1979, and besides these albums, also released *After Hours,* a live recording which is considerably more rock-oriented. The *Best Of* collection is one of the few such albums that really deserves the title; a good place to start. But all of this group's recordings have something to recommend them.

LIONA BOYD

- *Live in Tokyo* (CBS M-39031). Boyd is one of today's most successful classical guitarists. This album has several of her own arrangements of folk songs from the British Isles, including a version of the lovely "Brian Boru's March."

ANTONIO BRESCHI

- *Ode to Ireland* (Pick 100-265). Though he's Italian, Breschi has long been fascinated by Irish folk music, and this album of original tunes sounds uncannily like traditional Irish material. Breschi plays piano, and is accompanied by a large ensemble of often unusual instruments, including the Australian didjeridoo.
- *Linguaggio dei Luoghi* (General Music GM-37012). See Chapter 6.
- *Mezulari* (Elkar ELK-101). An album with Basque singer/guitarist Benito Lertxundi. While this is not consistently good, its combination of Celtic musical styles and legends with Basque, Old Basque, ancient Greek, and ancient Egyptian texts is certainly unique.
- *Land, Seas, and Memories* (Shanachie, scheduled for release in 1987) SHAN. More music for piano and a variable ensemble, continuing Breschi's exploration of Celtic styles.

MARC BRIERLEY
- *"Dragonfly"* from *The Electric Muse: The Story of Folk into Rock* (Island FOLK-1001, 4 LPs plus booklet). Brierley's Impressionistic guitar solo is one of the great surprises on this impressive collection. The title may put off listeners who don't like rock, but it shouldn't. With its complete notes (and companion book), this set would be absolutely indispensable to anyone interested in the recent folk revival in England, if only it were still available. It also includes excerpts from Davey Graham, Fairport Convention, Albion Country Band, and Martin Carthy's original version of "Scarborough Fair," which Simon and Garfunkel closely followed in their own recording.

KEVIN BURKE
- *Up Close* (Gr. L. SIF-1052) GLT. Except for the harmonica quartet, which ends up sounding like a cross between a Jew's-harp and an accordion, this album consists of fairly straightforward folk arrangements. Perhaps it's of less interest to new-music fans, but if you love folk music, it's a great record. Includes "The Maids of Mitchelstown," paired with "The Bunch of Green Rushes" in a medley that's so seamless you have to wonder if one tune isn't simply a variant of the other.

KEVIN BURKE AND MICHEAL O DOMHNAILL
- *Portland* (Gr. L. SIF-1041) GLT. Two ex-Bothy Band members made this album in Portland, Oregon, but musically, they've never left Ireland. A wide array of tunes, including a delightful bit of mouth music (which they chose to accompany with instruments).

CEOLTOIRI CHUALANN, *SEE* SEAN O RIADA.

CEOLTOIRI LAIGHEAN
- *An Bothar Cam* (Gael-Linn 035) ROU, SHAN. The title means "The Crooked Road." As you might expect from an offshoot of O Riada's group, this ensemble has a certain formal or classical sound.

THE CHIEFTAINS
- *The Chieftains* (Shanachie 79021) SHAN
- *2* (Shanachie 79022) SHAN
- *3* (Shanachie 79023) SHAN
- *4* (Shanachie 79024) SHAN
- *Barry Lyndon—Music from the Soundtrack* (War. 2903)
- *5* (Shanachie 79025) SHAN
- *Bonaparte's Retreat—6* (Shanachie 79026) SHAN
- *Live!* (Shanachie 79027) SHAN
- *7* (Col. JC-35612)
- *8* (Col. JC-35726)
- *Boil the Breakfast Early—9* (Col. JC-36401)
- *Cotton-Eyed Joe—10* (Shanachie 79019) SHAN
- *The Year of the French* (Shanachie 79036) SHAN
- *The Grey Fox—Music from the Soundtrack* (DRG SL-9515)
- *In China* (Shanachie 79050) SHAN
- *Ballad of the Irish Horse* (Shanachie 79051) SHAN

The best-known group of Irish musicians; while other groups have been splitting up and re-forming in various configurations, The Chieftains have remained consistent. Their sound still has the precision and, when appropriate, the gentility of a classical ensemble. They continue to do fine arrangements of traditional songs and dances, but they've also begun adding original works in recent years.

CLAIRSEACH
- *Ann's Harp* (Clairseach 2381). A Minnesota-based duo, performing traditional and original works on Celtic harp and other string instruments. A good album if you can find it.

SHIRLEY COLLINS
- *Amaranth* (Harvest/EMI SHSM-2008). Includes the 1968 "Anthems of Eden" suite; David Munrow's Early Music Consort of London appears throughout. Collins's voice, which even folk purists loved, is in fine form on the album, especially on "Edi Beo Thu Hevene Quene," a thirteenth-century hymn sung in Old English with vielle and recorder accompaniment. ("Anthems of Eden" and several other works have been reissued on the See-For-Miles label (SEE-57) ROU.) Also see Davey Graham and Shirley Collins.
- ▲ *The Compleat Dancing Master* (Carthage CGLP-4416) HAN. 1974 album of folk dances from Ashley Hutchings, John Kirkpatrick, and a sizeable cast of characters. Similar to the Albion Dance Band's sound.

ANDREW CRONSHAW
- *The Great Dark Water* (Waterfront WF-009) ALCA. This is a great album, one of the best recordings of unusual folk song arrangements around. Cronshaw plays electric zither, concertina, electric flute, and other odd instruments. Ric Sanders, violin, and June Tabor, voice, are among the other featured musicians. They perform some jigs and dances, but the LP's high points are the moody, dramatic folk songs that English musicians occasionally produce. Spacey production throughout.

JOHN CUNNINGHAM
- *Thoughts from Another World* (Shanachie 79029) SHAN. A member of the Scottish folk band Silly Wizard, John Cunningham turns in an album of straightahead folk tunes with one exception: The title track uses fiddle, guitars, and mandolins, but employs some very atmospheric production techniques.

PHIL CUNNINGHAM
- *Airs and Graces* (Gr. L. SIF-3032) GLT. John's brother in a standout collection of airs and dances and other tunes, gracefully performed on traditional instruments and the occasional synthesizer.

MARTY CUTLER
- *"Blackberry Blossom," "Angeline the Baker"* from the LP *Charged Particles* (Gr. L. SIF-1046) GLT. Two folk songs performed by banjo master Marty Cutler. On the first, he plays two "stranjos"—a combination electric guitar and banjo; the second is a banjo/fretless-electric-bass duet with Jeff Ganz. The remainder of this album consists of that mixture of bluegrass, country, and jazz called "New Acoustic Music," see page 212.

MALCOLM DALGLISH AND GREY LARSEN
- *Banish Misfortune* (June Appal 016) ROU
- *The First of Autumn* (June Appal 026) ROU
- *Thunderhead* (Fly. F. FF-266) FF, NAR
Dalglish plays hammer dulcimer and has a solo recording listed in Chapter 9, page 214; Larsen is a flutist and fiddler. They perform Irish folk music, some original tunes, and traditional works from America, France, Belgium, and Greece. Some of their larger ensemble pieces sound like the Bothy Band with a dulcimer added—not surprising, considering that Kevin Burke, Micheal O Domhnaill, and Triona Ni Dhomhnaill appear on several works.

DAL RIADA
- *The Magician Upstairs* (Eagle SM-4189) ALCA, KM. Competent LP of Irish music by an American group, in the O Riada/Chieftains mold.

SANDY DENNY
- *Sandy* (A&M SP-4371). A 1972 solo outing by this extraordinary singer. Some of the arrangements are pretty sappy, but there is a wonderful version of "The Quiet Joys of Brotherhood" for multi-tracked voice and a bit of fiddle at the end.
- *Who Knows Where the Time Goes?* (Hannibal HNBX-5301) HAN. The several other Sandy Denny albums pale beside this lovingly compiled four-LP retrospective of her career, taken from old unreleased Fairport tracks, live performances, solo records, even a rare track from the original Strawbs. They're not all good, but even those tracks of less interest still have her expressive vocals.

SUSAN DRAKE
- *Echoes of a Waterfall* (Hyperion A-66038) CH. An album of mostly classical harp music, but it contains a number of beautiful arrangements of traditional Welsh tunes by John Thomas.

LASSE ENGLUND
- *Drakväder* (Alternativ ALP-6). Englund is a Swedish guitarist; his countryman Thomas Almqvist, also a guitarist, joins him here. Besides the Irish tune "Caitlin Triall" and some Swedish folk dances, the LP includes a number of original works derived from the Irish, English, and Swedish traditions. Good album of skillful guitar playing.

JOHN FAHEY
Along with Robbie Basho and Leo Kottke (see pages 214 and 216), Fahey is one of America's most influential and talented acoustic guitarists. Although all three base their music on American blues and folk styles, only Fahey has consistently retained a traditional, even anachronistic sound, which includes occasional arrangements of American folk and Gospel songs. With his simple Impressionistic playing and his pungent, twangy blues alternating from piece to piece, and even from moment to moment, he was perhaps the first artist to combine folk and blues with classical, ethnic, and avant-garde elements. His discography is extensive, and includes the following:
- *Guitar* (Takoma C-1008)
- *Days Are Gone by* (Takoma C-1014)
- *The Yellow Princess* (Van. VSD-79293)
- *The Voice of the Turtle* (Takoma C-1019)
- *The New Possibility: Christmas Album* (Takoma C-1020)
- *Requia* (Terra/Van. T-2)
These LPs all date from the mid-to-late 1960s. *The Voice of the Turtle* is listed in Chapter 6; both it and *Requia* feature classic *musique concrète* techniques. In *Requia*, at least, these can be quite jarring, but Fahey's guitar makes them worth hearing. Most of these recordings include other musicians (don't be fooled by the credits for "Blind Joe Death"—that's Fahey himself). The title track of *The Yellow Princess*, by the way, is an improvisation on a theme from Camille Saint-Saëns's *Yellow Princess Overture*.
- *Of Rivers and Religion* (War. /Reprise MS-2089)
- *After the Ball* (War./Reprise MS-2145)
- *Old Fashioned Love* (Takoma C-1043)
These early 70s discs include often sizeable lineups; the first two are credited to "John Fahey and his Orchestra." They all have an old-time, vaudevillian sound, though the third LP also includes a country/blues arrangement of a traditional Hindu chant.
- *Christmas with John Fahey, Vol. II* (Takoma C-1045)
- *1959–1977: The Best of John Fahey* (Takoma C-1058)
- *Live in Tasmania* (Takoma TAK-7089)
- *Railroad I* (Takoma TAK-7102)
- *Christmas Guitar, Volume One* (Varrick 002) ROU
Dating from 1975 through 1982, these albums concentrate mostly on what Fahey does best: play the

guitar. Christmas seems to bring out some of his finest music, but these are all worthwhile recordings.

FAIRPORT CONVENTION

Many groups played what came to be known as folk-rock. In fact, many of them were Fairport Convention. But despite the personnel changes and the years of inconsistency after Sandy Denny left, when Fairport was good, few bands could match them.

- *Fairport Convention* (Poly. UK 583-035; British release, only available in the U.S. as an import)
- *Fairport Convention* (originally released in the U.K. as *What We Did on Our Holidays*) (Island ILPS-9092)
- *Unhalfbricking* (A&M SP-4206)
- *Full House* (A&M SP-4265)
- *Liege and Lief* (A&M SP-4527)
- *House Full* (Hannibal HNBL-1319) HAN
- *Expletive Delighted* (Woodworm WR-009) ROU

If I had to pick a favorite Fairport album, I would not hesitate to pick *Liege and Lief,* which is one of the finest albums of this genre. The worst? *Gottle O'Geer* and a couple of other 1970s LPs and singles not listed here. Each of the above records, though, contains a number of folk arrangements. *House Full* is a live album, minus Sandy Denny; Dave Swarbrick's fiddle is sometimes the only traditional sound you'll find here, despite all the trad./arr. markings, but then, Fairport was a pretty good rock band, too. *Expletive Delighted* is a departure for the group—an album of instrumentals with Ric Sanders replacing Swarbrick, and only one traditional tune.

FEAST OR FAMINE

- *Brecon Beacon* (Fretless 159) PHI. This acoustic ensemble does an arrangement of the English folk standard "Matty Groves," as well as a lovely rendition of Ralph Towner's "Icarus." A good album for folk fans.

PADDY GLACKIN AND JOLYON JACKSON

- *Hidden Ground* (Tara TARA-2009) ROU. Fiddler Glackin and keyboardist Jackson actually play quite a few instruments, and several of this album's best works incorporate electronics. Good album of interesting arrangements.

DAVEY GRAHAM

- *Folk, Blues, and Beyond* (Decca LK-4649)

DAVEY GRAHAM AND SHIRLEY COLLINS

- *Folk Roots, New Routes* (Righteous GDC-001)

Of these two early albums, the one with Shirley Collins singing beats the one with Graham himself singing by a country mile. "Pretty Saro" and the guitar solo "Rif Mountain" are classic Graham pieces, both off the second LP.

DAVEY GRAHAM

- *Large as Life and Twice as Natural* (London/ Decca PS-552). You have to pick and choose here. This 1968 release has lots of second-rate covers of other people's songs, second-rate singing, and second-rate ensemble works. But it does have two more guitar ragas and the Moroccan-based "Jenra."
- *All That Moody* (Eron 007)
- *The Complete Guitarist* (Kicking Mule KM-138) KM
- *Dance for Two People* (Kicking Mule SNKF-158) KM

All good albums. The first is a limited edition with lots of solos and a bit of tabla. *The Complete Guitarist* is mostly Irish music, while the last disc features Graham the 'ūd, sarod, and bouzouki player more than Graham the guitarist. Music from Ireland, England, North Africa, India, and the Middle East—all played on a string instrument from another country.

STEFAN GROSSMAN AND JOHN RENBOURN

- *Stefan Grossman & John Renbourn* (Kicking Mule KM-152) KM
- *Under the Volcano* (Kicking Mule KM-162) KM

Grossman is an American guitarist; Renbourn is listed below. These guitar duos include original works in a folk-jazz style, and jigs, Irish airs, and Fahey-style Americana.

GRYPHON

- *Gryphon* (Transatlantic TRA-262)
- *Midnight Mushrumps* (Transatlantic TRA-282)
- *Red Queen to Gryphon Three* (Bell 1316)

This band's first two records, from 1973 and 1974, include some excellent folk-derived instrumentals, with medieval European instruments like the crumhorn featured. The third album, from 1974, is the beginning of a less interesting period, as the band evolved toward a derivative progressive-rock sound.

CHARLES GUARD

- *Avenging and Bright* (Shanachie 79014) SHAN, NAR. Celtic harp music, which means some O Carolan; but this beautifully played, wide-ranging collection also includes tunes from Ireland, Scotland, and the Isle of Man.

KENNY HÅKANSSON

- *Springlek* (Silence SRS-4645). Håkansson plays traditional Swedish dance tunes, originally for two fiddles in many cases, on electric guitar. The guitar's volume seems to be up too high: the instrument is always threatening to feed back, but it never does. The resulting sound, gritty and forceful, will not be to everyone's taste, but it seems to suit the music.

DIANE HAMILTON

- *Green Autumn* (Greenhays GR-711) FF. Hamilton plays the harpsichord in a set of Celtic and English songs. Donal Lunny helps out on synthesizer, bouzouki, and harmonium; Indian instruments also appear on one track.

HICKORY WIND

- *Crossing Devil's Bridge* (Fly. F. 074) FF. This American bluegrass outfit is joined by drummer Dave Mattacks for a set of American, Irish, and Rumanian works. It's a well-knit ensemble, and the album as a whole should have appeal.

CHRISTOPHER HOBBS

- *"McCrimmon Will Never Return"* from the Hobbs/Adams/Bryars album *Ensemble Pieces* (Obscure #2). This work, played on two reed organs by British composers Gavin Bryars and Christopher Hobbs, is based on a Scottish *piobaireachd* (or *pibroch*) tune. Several variations are played simultaneously over a drone, and the piece is slowed down to the point where those quick bagpipe skirls, or grace notes, can be heard clearly as individual notes in the melody.

- ▲ *I'm on My Journey Home: vocal styles and resources in folk music* (New World NW-223) ROU. An incredible document of American folk music, especially on side one, which includes examples of hollerin', an African-derived falsetto shout that instantly calls to mind the yodeling of Central African pygmies; tobacco auctioneering (actually quite musical, believe it or not); and tunes like "Bold McCarthy" which are obviously Celtic and don't sound American at all. "Barbara Allen" is on this record—a 1936 recording made in a cave in North Carolina with some involuntary overtone effects that are quite amazing. But the real treat is the liner notes: How else would you learn that "Risselty Rosselty" is a variant of "The Wife Wrapt in Wether's Skin," Child #277?

INCREDIBLE STRING BAND

- *"U"* (Elektra 7E-2002). See Chapter 6; and Robin Williamson, listed below.

- ▲ *Irish Reels, Jigs, Hornpipes, and Airs* (Kicking Mule SNKF-153) KM. Davey Graham, Dan Ar Bras, Duck Baker, and Dave Evans play Irish tunes, each of them playing four or five pieces. The album doesn't always deliver what followers of these guitarists might hope for, but it's worth a listen.

BERT JANSCH

- *Jack Orion* (Van. VSD-6544)

BERT JANSCH AND JOHN RENBOURN

- *Stepping Stones* (Van. VSD-6506)

Two early albums in the folk-baroque style. Renbourn appears on both, lending a hand on "Henry Martin" in the *Jack Orion* set.

BERT JANSCH

- *A Rare Conundrum* (Kicking Mule KM-302) KM, ROU
- *Conundrum* (Kicking Mule KM-309) KM, ROU
- *Best Of* (Kicking Mule KM-334) KM, ROU

BERT JANSCH AND MARTIN JENKINS

- *Avocet* (Kicking Mule KM-310) KM, ROU

These are later, more mature albums containing a good deal of original material, much of it folk-derived and some of it incorporating jazz and traditional American ingredients. In the album with Martin Jenkins some of the guitar/mandocello interplay gets very tricky, and it sounds like they're using quarter tones at times, too.

MARC JOHNSON

- *"Black Is the Color of My True Love's Hair"* from the LP *Bass Desires* (ECM 1299) ECM. This LP by bassist Marc Johnson spotlights two of the best electric guitarists in the business: Bill Frisell (who also plays guitar synthesizer) and John Scofield. It's an album of electric jazz, except for this brilliant folk arrangement. Elegant, restrained, and spacey, it's well worth hearing.

KARELIA

- *Maanitus* (Bluebird BBL-1021) SCA. This Finnish group plays native folk music on dozens of acoustic, ethnic, and electronic albums. Esa Kotilainen plays synthesizers (see Chapter 1), but the sound is primarily acoustic. A bit off the beaten track, but a first-rate recording.

DOLORES KEANE AND JOHN FAULKNER

- *Sail Og Rua* (Gr. L. SIF-3033) GLT. Mostly traditional Irish music—mostly for fans of same. Contains a stunning vocal duet on "The Wee Weaver."

BEN TAVERA KING

- *Border Crossings* (Folk. 37458) NMDS. Subtitled "New Directions in Tex-Mex Music," this 1984 album first introduced King to the general, or at least to a wider, audience. King is a great guitarist, and the weave of jazz, flamenco, classical and Tex-Mex forms is seamless. This was easily one of the best and most unusual albums of 1984.
- *Southwestern Scenarios* (Terra/Van. T-5)
- *Desert Dreams* (Global Pacific GP-301) GP, NAR

These two later discs are at their best when King is allowed to cut loose. But his guitar work is often reined in by sax or synthesizer, bass, and drums. Neither album is bad, but the arrangements are not as energetic as the first album.

MARK KNOPFLER

- *Cal* (Original Soundtrack) (Mer. 822 769-1-M-1). Lovely, atmospheric work from the leader of the

rock band Dire Straits. No rock music here, just moody, Irish-sounding pieces for guitars and Irish instruments, the latter played by Paul Brady.
- *Local Hero* (Original Soundtrack) (War. 23827-1). Similar to the preceding, rustic and moody, but with less of an Irish flavor.

KORNOG
- *Premiere* (Gr. L. SIF-1055) GLT. Another Breton ensemble. Mostly vocal music, but there are a few instrumentals. The slow dances, "Dans An Dro" and "Laride/An Dro," are particularly beautiful.

SAKARI KUKKO
- *Will o' the Wisp* (Kerberos 605). Like his compatriots in Karelia, Kukko plays some Finnish folk songs in very strange arrangements. A few of his own compositions are dead ringers for Finnish folk music, too. Almost impossible to find.

BJÖRN J:SON LINDH
- *"Marion's Dream"* from the LP *Atlantis* (Storyville SLP-4132). An arrangement of the folk song "Calum Sgaire," played on Synclavier and given an English title. (See Chapter 1.)

- ▲*Lutunn Noz: Celtic Music for Guitar* (Musical Heritage Society MHS-3577) MHS. I could never figure out why his name doesn't appear on the cover, but this top-flight album of folk-inspired compositions is by Breton guitarist Bernard Benoit. Other musicians sometimes help out on guitar, pipes, flute, etc. From lively jigs to lovely airs, the tracks are consistently strong, and the variety of styles makes it an attractive album even to people who never thought they'd be interested in folk music. Oh, and the title apparently means "Leprechaun of the Night" (thanks to Dan Ar Bras for the translation).

MAGICAL STRINGS
- *Spring Tide* (Fly. F. FF-282) FF
- *Above the Tower* (Fly. F. FF-360) FF
Philip and Pam Boulding build and play Celtic harps, dulcimers, and a few others. The music consists of Irish folk tunes and Celtic-sounding originals. Both albums have a warmth often missing in solo harp records.

MALICORNE
- *Malicorne* (Disques Hexagone/W.E.A. 883002)
- *Malicorne* (W.E.A.-Hexagone 883004)
- *Almanach* (W.E.A.-Hexagone 883007)
- *Malicorne* (W.E.A.-Hexagone 883015)
- *Quintessence* (W.E.A.-Hexagone 883018)
- *En Public* (Ballon Noir BAL-13010)
- *Le Bestiare* (Elektra 52271)
- *L'Extraordinaire Tour de France d'Adelard Rousseau* (Elektra 52272)
- *Balançoire en Feu* (Elektra 52280)
The leaders of the French folk revival, Malicorne

had its greatest strengths in the voices of Gabriel and Marie Yacoub and in Gabriel's penchant for experimental arrangements. The first of the three untitled albums has several almost medieval-sounding pieces, especially the "Bourrée" and "Dame Lombarde." Many of the arrangements, especially on the last album, are very close to rock music, but they in large measure stay true to the spirit of French folk songs. And if you like new music, or folk music, or any music, you owe it to yourself to check out "La Blanche Biche" from the fourth, also untitled, album. It is one of the most arresting, foreboding folk song arrangements on record. See Gabriel Yacoub, below.

JOHN MARTYN
- *"Eibhli Ghail Chiuin in Chearbhaill" and "Beverly"* from the LP *Inside Out* (Island ILPS-9253). The first title means "the fair and charming Eileen O'Carroll"; the second piece is one of Martyn's own. It's also the best work on this uneven album of electric and acoustic guitar works by the British guitarist and cult figure.

JOHN McCUTCHEON
McCutcheon, a master of the hammer dulcimer, usually surrounds himself with good musicians. His musical interests are diverse, but you have to watch him sometimes. One of his albums comes with a coloring book inside, is full of childish sing-along-type pieces, and is just *too* cute. Fortunately, he has put out some good records:
- *Fine Times at Our House* (Greenhays GR-710) FF, ROU. Some shape-note hymns (so called because the notes are shaped like circles, squares, and triangles to facilitate sight-reading), American folk, bluegrass, old-timey music, cowboy songs, and Irish tunes. Real foot-stompin' stuff.
- *The Wind That Shakes the Barley* (June Appal 014) ROU. May be his finest album. Bach, the Dallas String Band, O Carolan, the Carter Family, and Alan Stivell go into the musical stew here. All convincingly performed.
- *Winter Solstice* (Roun. 0192) ROU. Beautiful collection of Christmas carols, New Year's songs, and an exquisite Chanukah song by Israel's Josef Hader. Traditional American, Huron Indian, and Irish songs share the bill with originals and a Handel work.

RALPH McTELL
- *"Willoughby's Farm"* from the LP *The Electric Muse: The Story of Folk into Rock* (Island FOLK-1001, 4 LPs and booklet). Beautiful guitar solo from an early (1968) London folk recording, reissued on the same set that includes the Marc Brierley piece, q.v.

LES MENESTRIERS
- *Chanson Legère à Entendre* (Cavalier/RCA FTL-1-0133). Includes traditional and medieval Euro-

pean music, with an especially long and delightful version of "Lamento di Tristan e Rotta."

MATT MOLLOY, PAUL BRADY, AND TOMMY PEOPLES

- [Untitled] (Gr. L. SIF-3018) GLT. Three well-known Irish musicians, playing flute, guitar, and fiddle respectively. As you might expect from an album of dance tunes, it's full of Celtic exuberance.

▲ *Morris On* (Carthage CGLP-4406) HAN. From 1972, the original LP of electric folk dances. The personnel is similar to that of the Albion groups and *The Compleat Dancing Master,* above.

MOVING HEARTS

- *Dark End of the Street* (W.E.A. 58 718). Another group featuring Donal Lunny, with vocalist Christy Moore and others; basically a rock band, though, with an Irish twist. On this album, "Downtown" and "Half Moon" are the closest in spirit to the Bothy Band or Planxty.
- *"Static Music/May Morning Dew"* (Tara 020, 45-rpm 7-inch single). Side A is more Celtic rock. Side B is a handsome arrangement of a traditional Irish tune.

MYRDHIN

- *Harpe Celtique* (Velia 22310)
- *Hollaika* (Velia 22333)
- *An Delen Dir 3* (Velia 22363)
- *Merlin l'Enchanter* (Velia 22376)
- *Emersion* (Velia 22373)
- *Harpeges* (Velia 20121)
- *An Delen Dir 7/Courir le Guilledou* (M&A 30123) Myrdhin is a Breton bard/harpist/composer. His albums include voice, Indian tabla (an increasingly common accompanist to the harp—the two sound good together), and some others. "Ancient and modern music from the Celtic traditions" is how he describes it. If you can find any of these albums, they're worth hearing, even if they all seem to lag in spots. The later LPs are better than the earlier ones.

ANDY NARELL

- *"Jig"* from the LP *Stickman* (Hip Pocket HP-101) WH. He doesn't tell us *which* jig this is (an unforgivable crime in folk circles), but after a bit of musical sleuthing, I'm now certain it's "Port Ui Mhuirgheasa." It's played on the Caribbean steel drums, on an album otherwise devoted to light, unavoidably Caribbean-sounding jazz.

TRIONA NI DHOMHNAILL

- [Untitled] (Gr. L. SIF-3034) GLT. Arrangements of Irish tunes, especially "O Carolan's Farewell to Music," and a set of Breton dances are highlights of this album by vocalist/harpsichordist Ni Dhomhnaill. Good lineup of accompanying musicians.

NIORIN NI RIAIN

- *Caoineadh na Maighdine* (Gael-Linn CEF-084) SHAN. Ni Riain has a clear, crystalline voice, and here she's accompanied by the monks of Ireland's Glenstal Abbey, directed by her husband, composer Micheal O Suilleabhain. The works are all old Irish hymns, and these performances, recorded inside the abbey with its impressive resonance, achieve a rare, timeless quality.

▲ *The Old and New Kantele* (Finnlevy SFLP-8578) PSI. The *kantele,* or Finnish folk harp, is reputed to be two thousand years old. On this disc, three separate players demonstrate the 5–, 9–, 25–, 32–, and 36–string versions of this versatile, intimate-sounding instrument.

SEAN O RIADA AND CEOLTOIRI CHUALANN

- *Reacaireacht an Riadnigh* (Gael-Linn CEF-010) SHAN
- *The Playboy of the Western World* (Soundtrack) (Gael-Linn CEF-012) ROU
- *Ceol na nUasal* (Gael-Linn CEF-015) SHAN
- *O Riada sa Gaiety* (Gael-Linn CEF-027) ROU
These recordings share a restrained sound that some might find stodgy. But O Riada was a real pioneer, and even when his own efforts were unsuccessful, he still paved the way for the wave of musicians who were to follow. The first album, with Darach O Cathain singing in the Irish *sean-nos* style, and the 1962 soundtrack LP use many of the improvisatory techniques of Irish music. *Ceol na nUasal* includes O Carolan's music and other works from the harp repertoire. The last album is probably the best; it's a live recording at the Gaiety Theater in Dublin in 1969.

SEAN O RIADA

- *Mise Eire* (RTE Sym. Orch., O Riada/Gael-Linn CEF-080) ROU
- *Ceol Is Cibeal* (Gael-Linn CEF-074) ROU
Two later releases; the first album is a reissue of some of O Riada's film music. They are stylistically very close to the albums listed above.

BILLY OSKAY AND MICHEAL O DOMHNAILL

- *Nightnoise* (Wind. H. WH-1031) WH. Oskay is a well-known Irish fiddler; O Domhnaill was a member of the Bothy Band, who with Kevin Burke moved to Portland, Oregon. These pieces are all original compositions, pretty but lacking the fire and drive of the Bothy Band. See *A Winter's Solstice,* Chapter 9, as well.

MICHEAL O SUILLEABHAIN

- *Cry of the Mountain* (Gael-Linn CEF-079) SHAN. A 1981 album of collages of film scores and folk arrangements. Sitar and thumb piano join Irish and Western instruments on this often fascinating album.

IRENE PAPAS WITH VANGELIS

- *Odes* (Poly. 2417 343) NAR. Superb record of Greek odes and laments, arranged, produced, and performed by synthesizer player and multi-instrumentalist Vangelis. Irene Papas's expressive singing makes this as much her album as his. A long-overdue followup album is expected soon.

DAVE PEGG

- *The Cocktail Cowboy Goes It Alone* (Woodworm WR-003) ROU, ALCA. Another former Fairport member, Pegg plays electric guitar and bass, and occasionally adds percussion and other instruments. This is a good album that in spots aspires to brilliance; Pegg's multitracked electric guitar rendition of the Irish tune "Lord Mayo"—two guitars echoing the theme and the rest providing a solid wall of chords in the background—is really marvelous. Some originals and a few fair-to-middling vocals appear elsewhere.

PENTANGLE

- *The Pentangle* (War./Reprise RS-6315)
- *Sweet Child* (War./Reprise 2RS-6334)
- *Basket of Light* (War./Reprise RS-6372)
- *Cruel Sister* (War./Reprise RS-6430)
- *Reflection* (War./Reprise RS-6463)
- *Solomon's Seal* (War./Reprise MS-2100)
- *Open the Door* (Varrick 017) ROU

With the exception of the last record, these albums date from 1968–1972, and spotlight the guitar work of John Renbourn and Bert Jansch. *Open the Door* is a 1985 album from a re-formed lineup that doesn't include Renbourn. At the risk of dismissing an important ensemble, this group never seemed to equal the sum of its parts; but each album has at least one or two cuts which stand out —"The Lyke Wake Dirge" from the third LP, for example.

PLANXTY

- *Planxty* (Shanachie SH-79009) SHAN
- *The Well below the Valley* (Shanachie SH-79010) SHAN
- *Cold Blow and the Rainy Night* (Shanachie SH-79011) SHAN
- *The Planxty Collection* (Shanachie SH-79012) SHAN
- *After the Break* (Tara TARA-3001)
- *The Woman I Loved So Well* (Tara TARA-3005)
- *Timedance* (W.E.A./Ireland IR-28207)
- *Words and Music* (Shanachie SH-79035) SHAN

One of the very finest of the traditional-based Irish bands. *The Planxty Collection* is compiled from the first three LPs, and includes an otherwise unreleased track, "Cliffs of Dooneen." These records are from 1972–1974. *After the Break* dates from 1979, when Planxty re-formed after the dissolution of the Bothy Band. *Timedance* is an extended single with only one track per side. *Words and Music* features an even wider array of instruments than the earlier albums, including synthesizer. The piece "Taimse Im' Chodladh" ("I Am Asleep"), pairing synthesizer with uilleann pipes, is from that LP.

PYEWACKETT

- *7 to Midnight* (Familiar FAM-47). Pyewackett plays five hundred years of pop music: from medieval *brawls* to original works. Violin, dulcimer, recorders, synthesizers, drums, and others are involved but the unimaginative use of the electronics and drums give the music a rather conventional sound.

JOHN RENBOURN

- *John Renbourn* (U.S. reissue of two U.K. releases: *John Renbourn* and *Another Monday*/War. 2RS-6482)
- *Sir John Alot Of* (Wind. H./Lost Lake Arts LLA-0084) WH
- *The Lady and the Unicorn* (Wind. H./Lost Lake Arts LLA-0087) WH
- *Faro Annie* (War./Reprise MS-2082)
- *The Hermit* (Kicking Mule/Transatlantic TRA-336) KM
- *The Black Balloon* (Kicking Mule KM-163) KM
- *The Nine Maidens* (Transatlantic, scheduled for 1986–1987 release)

THE JOHN RENBOURN GROUP

- *A Maid in Bedlam* (Shanachie SH-79004) SHAN
- *The Enchanted Garden* (Kicking Mule KM-312) KM

Renbourn's solo efforts contain original works and guitar arrangements of folk music from the British Isles. They also include some jazzy or blues-style riffing, medieval tunes, and guest appearances by other musicians. *Sir John Alot Of* and *The Lady and the Unicorn* are still excellent discs—neither one sounds like a product of the late 60s. The group albums include a stronger ethnic influence, partly because of the presence of tabla player Keshav Sathe.

THE ROCHES

- *The Roches (War. BSK-3298)*. The first of several recordings by this vocal trio. Maggie, Terre, and Suzzy (rhymes with "fuzzy") Roche have been singing in the New York City folk circuit for years, and though they write all their own music, their wry delivery has a definite folk twang. Robert Fripp produced this album and adds a splendid guitar solo to the "Hammond Song."

STEELEYE SPAN

- *Parcel of Rogues* (Chrysalis CHR-1046)
- *Hark! The Village Wait* (Chrysalis CHR-1120)
- *Please to See the King* (Mooncrest CREST-8)

More rock than folk-rock (and not especially good rock, either), this group brought many traditional melodies to a large rock audience.

- *Ten Man Mop or Mr. Reservoir Butler Rides Again* (Mooncrest CREST-9, scheduled for reissue on Shanachie Records). The best album, and arguably the folkiest, by this English band. Along with their usual rock arrangements are "When I Was on Horseback" and a set of jigs. Bassist Ashley Hutchings is joined by vocalist Maddy Prior; guitarist Martin Carthy; Tim Hart on dulcimer, voice, guitar, and others; and fiddler Peter Knight.

ALAN STIVELL

- *A Longonnet* (Polygram 6325 332) PSI
- *Chemins de Terre* (Polygram 9729 038) PSI
- *"Grands Succes"* (Poly. 6680 004) PSI
- *Reflets* (Fontana 6325 340)
- *Trema'n Inis/Vers l'Ile* (CBS-France 82977) Some of these early albums are pretty dated now. The latter two, though laboring under a late-60s-early-70s psychedelic folk sound, also contain some beautiful harp instrumentals and songs.
- *Journée à la Maison* (Roun. 3062) ROU
- *Renaissance of the Celtic Harp* (Roun. 3067) ROU
- *Celtic Symphony/Symphonie Celtique* (Roun. 3088/89, 2 LPs) ROU *Journée* and *Renaissance* represent Stivell at his formidable best. The former has a number of lovely songs as well as colorfully scored instrumentals; "An Try Marrak" ("The Three Knights"), sung in Cornish, is just one of many excellent cuts. The latter is *the* classic album of Celtic harp music. The *Celtic Symphony,* though, gets a bit out of hand: The ethnic performers don't really add anything except trivial coloristic effects, and at close to ninety or so minutes in length, it takes a lot of patience to listen to.
- *Harpes du Nouvel Age* (Roun. 3094) ROU. The harp as percussion, the harp as experimental-sound source, and the harp as harp. Though I think he's asking for trouble with the title ("Harps of the New Age") Stivell has recorded a very good album that displays the versatility of the Celtic, electro-acoustic, and purely electric harps. Some original tunes, and a lot of Celtic folk music, even a bit of Scottish *pibroch.*

DAVE SWARBRICK AND SIMON NICOL

- *Close to the Wind* (Woodworm WR-006) ROU. Fairport's long-time violinist and guitarist, respectively. Dave Pegg on bass and Dave Mattacks on percussion also appear. Includes lively interpretations of "The Young Black Cow," "The Dark and Slender Boy" (all the parts played by Swarbrick), and of course, "Si Bheag Si Mhor."

RICHARD THOMPSON

Since leaving Fairport Convention, Thompson has pursued a career as a singer/songwriter, with and without Linda Thompson. While his folk roots have always been apparent, much of his music is rock. His most acoustic, folk-oriented albums are:

- *guitar, vocal* (Carthage CGLP-4413) HAN. Features rare tracks, unreleased versions of previously recorded songs, etc. Only a few pieces, like the short guitar solo "Flee as a Bird," are really effective.
- *Strict Tempo!* (Carthage CGLP-4409) HAN. Jigs and reels, Irish airs, even a couple of North African melodies, all impeccably performed by Thompson.

TOUCHSTONE

- *The New Land* (Gr. L. SIF-1040) GLT
- *Jealousy* (Gr. L. SIF-1050) GLT Triona Ni Dhomhnaill's band. Spirited, bluegrassy versions of Irish dances, some vocal material, and on the second LP, a lovely trio of Breton tunes (one written by Dan Ar Bras).

TRAFFIC

- *"John Barleycorn"* from the LP *John Barleycorn Must Die!* (United Artists UA-5504). A great arrangement of a folk classic from Steve Winwood's forward-looking rock group. (O.P.)

GERALD TRIMBLE

- *First Flight* (Gr. L. SIF-1043) GLT. American-born Trimble plays the "cittern," but not the original Renaissance cittern. His instrument is a cousin of the Greek bouzouki, which is now a fixture in Celtic music. John Cunningham (fiddle) and Micheal O Domhnaill (guitar) are part of his ensemble here. The jaunty pieces are nicely balanced by slow ballads, and the cittern solos are especially effective.
- *Heartland Messenger* (Gr. L. SIF-1054) GLT. Another good record, with a similar ensemble. Colorful arrangements, well conceived and well played. Curiously, the lengthy title track is mostly American tunes, played by a very large group, and is less successful.

ROBIN WILLIAMSON

- *Music for the Mabinogi* (Fly. F. FF-340) FF
- *The Dragon Has Two Tongues* (Towerbell TVLP-001)
- *Legacy of the Scottish Harpers* (Fly. F. FF-358) FF Williamson plays many instruments, and usually confines himself to short (under five minutes) pieces. The first album consists of works written for a production of the Mabinogion, the book of Welsh legends. The second, a soundtrack to a film about Wales, has lots of unfortunate electro-pop numbers. The third is basically an update of some early Scottish harp pieces.

SYLVIA WOODS

- *The Harp of Brandiswhiere* (Tonmeister 1213) NAR, ROU. Woods is a harper who not only plays the Celtic variety, but also a number of other members of the harp family. One very ominous-sounding piece uses a wind harp. Other struck stringed instruments and winds are featured, too. Imaginative arrangements and clean production.

JOHN WRIGHT AND CATHERINE PERRIER

▪ [Untitled] (Gr. L. SIF-1011) G GLT. Folk music of France, Ireland, and England. Mostly vocal material; the choice of songs is often unusual, the instrumentation is bizarre (including the épinette des Vosges, a French plucked string instrument, along with Jew's harp and harmonica), and the liner notes are excellent.

GABRIEL YACOUB

▪ *Trad./Arr.* (Gr. L. SIF-3035) GLT. The leader of Malicorne, Yacoub sings some haunting ballads here with minimal (as opposed to Minimal) accompaniment: "Honore mon enfant" is the French version of the old English poem "Lord Randall." Other works are boisterous and sometimes bawdy, in the best folk fashion.

▪ *E.L.F.* (Shanachie, scheduled for release in 1987). The title stands for "Elementary Levels of Faith." This album consists of original material, with a good deal of digital sampling, Emulator (a voice synthesizer), and a little bit of help from Hungary's Ivan Lantos.

▲ *The Young Tradition* (Van. VSD-79246). If you don't like real earthy British vocal styles, this album of three unaccompanied vocalists may grate a little. But the trio's performance of "The Lyke Wake Dirge," though spare and lean in the extreme, may be more appealing.

ATAHUALPA YUPANQUI

▪ *La Guitare des Andes* (ChM. LDX-74.439) HM. More a folk record than an ethnic one, this is a fine album of solo guitar music. Yupanqui is a masterful guitarist, and performs persuasive arrangements of traditional Andean melodies as well as contemporary compositions from South America in a similar folk style.

9
ECM AND WINDHAM HILL: A TALE OF TWO LABELS

I'll play it first and tell you what it is later.
Miles Davis

*I don't know where the term jazz belongs anymore. It doesn't really lead you
anywhere except to want to know what the person who said the word meant when he
said jazz.*
Chick Corea

All that Windham Hill stuff—it's just music for the hot tub!
unidentified (and irate) listener, radio call-in show, WNYC, 11/84

*I've seen this music communicate with people—bright, discerning people. There's
nothing rational in that kind of charge; it speaks more of the inevitable backlash that
comes with popularity than anything else.*
William Ackerman, founder of Windham Hill Records

Iime was when you could look at the jazz bestseller charts and see names like
Art Blakey, Tony Williams, Dexter Gordon, and of course, Miles Davis. Miles is
still there, but look at some of the other artists who have hit those charts in recent
years: Andreas Vollenweider, George Winston, Bob James. Is *this* jazz? Louis
Armstrong once answered that question by saying, "Man, if you gotta ask, you'll
never know." Well, anyone developing an interest in jazz these days *has* to ask,
because this genre of music, always a makeshift one anyway, is now coming apart
at the seams.

As I've mentioned before, it's often good to see the boundaries between categories falling away, but in this case, there's some cause for concern. Jazz isn't disap-
pearing as a musical label; instead, it's being stretched out to include a whole
spectrum of musical styles, from Keith Jarrett's inspired piano solos to the limp,
washed-out California jazz that CBS Records tried foisting upon us in the late 70s.

In this chapter, we'll examine two "jazz labels" that are not really *jazz* labels.
Although their records often appear on the jazz charts, in jazz periodicals, and in
the jazz sections of record stores, neither ECM nor Windham Hill can accurately

be described as a jazz label, in the sense that Blue Note or Black Saint might be. We've already looked at new music that grew out of the folk tradition but was not itself folk; similarly, a lot of new music has grown out of jazz, to which it is now only obliquely related. Many such artists happen to record for ECM, so it is appropriate to discuss this label in the context of jazz-derived music. Windham Hill label has followed ECM's lead in areas like packaging and production, but although there are elements of jazz in some Windham Hill albums, and although people who've played jazz have recorded for them, the Windham Hill sound owes as much to American folk and French Impressionism as it does to jazz. It will be treated separately, in the final part of this chapter.

ECM and All That "Jazz"

Much of the confusion about the music being discussed here results from the ambiguities of the term jazz. The two earmarks of jazz are syncopation and improvisation. Even the big bands, with their regular rhythms and written parts, used both of these traits. However, ethnic music is usually improvised, too, and it is often syncopated. Bach was an inveterate improviser; Beethoven not only improvised but also wrote a highly syncopated, jazzlike conclusion to his Piano Sonata #31. On the other hand, a number of contemporary jazz musicians have recorded music that is not syncopated or even particularly rhythmic at all. And a good deal of new music is being created today by musicians who use improvisation and syncopation, but don't consider themselves to be part of the jazz tradition.

Of course, jazz has long been open to other styles of music. In the late 1950s, composer Gunther Schuller coined the term Third Stream to describe the confluence of jazz and classical elements that was then taking place in musical circles. Schuller himself was the most effective and convincing of the Third Stream composers, and the Modern Jazz Quartet the style's foremost practitioners. For a while, it seemed that orchestral jazz, twelve-tone jazz, or jazz sonatas and fugues would be the next big movement in music.

But jazz developed in other directions that have proven to be at least as important: the development of World Music, for one, and more recently, the growth of a highly emotional, less emphatically virtuosic style, characterized by musicians like Pat Metheny or Eberhard Weber, who record for ECM.

Jazz-inflected new music was already being improvised more than twenty years ago. In 1964, the prominent jazz clarinetist Tony Scott went to Japan, where he induced two extraordinary Japanese musicians to record a set of improvised meditations with him. Scott played with koto master Shinichi Yuize and shakuhachi virtuoso Hozan Yamamoto in a gentle, reflective style; the album that resulted, *Music for Zen Meditation,* proved that the breeding ground between jazz and ethnic music could be a fertile one.

In the years since the Scott recording, many jazz musicians have looked beyond their own heritage for inspiration. (Gunther Schuller eventually modified his definition of Third Stream to mean a style that synthesized Western art music—whether composed, improvised, or both—with various types of ethnic music.) Even without actually using exotic instruments, such jazz figures as Anthony Davis, James Newton, and Paul Horn have produced improvised works that echo the sounds of Japan, Africa, Bali, or the Near East.

Paul Horn has played or recorded with Duke Ellington, Chico Hamilton, Miles Davis, and many others, but his best-known works remain the exotic solo flute recordings he made in the domed chamber of the Taj Mahal and inside the Great Pyramids at Gizeh. *Inside the Taj Mahal* (1968) and *Inside the Great Pyramid* (1976) are magical albums; they capture not only the music, but the ambience of the location in which they were recorded. Both discs feature the beautiful tone of Horn's flute bouncing around these incredibly resonant spaces; one flute makes such a rich sound that any studio tricks—added reverb, multitracking, etc.—would have been superfluous.

"I've always rebelled against categories," Horn asserts, "and I still do. In a traditional sense this music isn't jazz: There's no rhythm section and all that. But in the broadest, truest sense it is jazz, because it's improvised, and the basis of jazz is improvisation." Jazz, in Horn's very general view, is simply the most practical word to describe the revival in this century of the art of improvisation, which has been overshadowed by the tradition of composed art music for much of the past four hundred years.

Horn credits his attitude toward improvisation to a specific recording session in 1965. The recording was with Ravi Shankar; it was less than a year after the release of Tony Scott's *Zen* album, and Shankar was not yet the unexpected hero he would soon become. "It was the first time I ever saw someone show up at a record date and not have anything down on paper," Horn remembers. "He started to create everything right there at the session. That just blew my mind, because I always felt, be prepared, and if I have a record date I'm gonna come in and the music's going to be right there. And here was a man who used the last-minute pressures or energies to stimulate his creative process, and there it was, happening real quick."

In both his solo outings and his performances with the preeminent bassist David Friesen, Horn has adopted something of that approach. "The feeling of a space, its history, becomes a part of the music when you improvise, because you're open to the spirit of the moment." Over the years, Horn has continued to perform in large, resonant spaces, pioneering a type of improvised music whose mood depends not only on the mixture of Eastern and Western styles but also on the quality of the space itself. The presence of Friesen at many of these performances lends a great deal of the interplay between musicians that makes straight jazz so enjoyable, especially since Horn and Friesen can each produce a wide array of sounds. Horn plays several sizes of flute, including the Chinese ti-tzi, while Friesen's Oregon bass, a collapsible, solid-body electric instrument, is capable of sustaining notes far longer than a regular double bass. Friesen has also recorded with shakuhachi player Hozan Yamamoto and has learned how to play that instrument, as well. And since both Horn and Friesen can draw on their varied backgrounds in classical, jazz, fusion, and more lyrical, meditative styles, it is small wonder that their music is not easily categorized.

Another flutist who has moved into the gray area between genres is James Newton. Newton won his first *Down Beat* critics' poll in 1982, and in the next two years was named top jazz flutist in both the critics' and the readers' votes. His work with Lester Bowie and Cecil Taylor, and even his contribution to the somewhat chamberish *I've Known Rivers* (1982) with Anthony Davis and Abdul Wadud certainly qualify him as a jazz flutist, but like Horn, Newton has an eclectic training in music and has not been content to play in just one style. His album *Echo Canyon* (1984) and the proposed *In Venice* are solo flute projects in the tradition of Horn's *Inside* series. An earlier album, *Axum* (1982), is also for solo flute, though one that took place in and utilized the possibilities of a recording studio.

In all of these collections, Newton's improvisations are colored by his keen interest in ethnic music and his background in 1960s R&B, which he played while growing up. "The challenge was to create *new* music," he says. "I started thinking about how elements of the world's folk music affected aspects of my playing. I dealt with how the shakuhachi has affected my playing, and tried to deal with certain things I learned from folk music of several parts of Africa, especially the pygmies, as well as certain Afro-American things, coming from the church. I tried almost to take a non-Western approach to a Western instrument."

Newton's unerring instinct for phrasing is a clear indication of his accomplishment as a jazz musician, but the ethnic influences are equally apparent. In one work from *Echo Canyon* entitled "Kamakura," Newton produces a sound uncannily like that of a bamboo flute (a Bolivian kena, perhaps, or the Indian bansuri flute) on a Western C-flute, an effect he accomplishes by using techniques borrowed from non-Western music.

"When you have the north and south Indian traditions," he explains, "or the shakuhachi tradition, and the flute traditions of New Guinea, Africa, and South America, you really have to deal with bamboo. But a lot of people approach it like dilettantes." Newton avoids a superficial approach to ethnic flutes by performing mostly on the Western flute; but this has involved a rethinking of his approach to the instrument, Newton says, so he can "recreate something respectful of those traditions, and not just a poor imitation of a lot of ideas that have developed over centuries."

It's hard to overestimate the impact ethnic music has had on jazz musicians. Given jazz's long association with black Americans, it's not surprising that African music became a particularly strong inspiration to jazz artists in the 60s. By the time of John Coltrane's untimely death in 1967 at the age of forty, his colleague Pharoah Sanders and several others had already begun to incorporate Coltrane's African influences into their own works. Sanders often recorded exotic repetitive pieces that were as much a product of North African mysticism as they were displays of saxophone dexterity; his sources were reflected in titles like "Upper Egypt," "Karma," "Hum-Allah-Hum-Allah-Hum-Allah," and "Thembi" (all dating from the 1966–1970 period).

By the mid-70s, Sanders developed a style of playing sax that featured the usual shrill dissonances of avant-garde jazz, but also included a soft, whispering intonation that sounded almost vocal. Many of his works were set to devotional lyrics, and most of them used lots of African percussion. In pieces like "Harvest," from the 1976 album *Pharoah,* he created hypnotic music that just barely touched upon the jazz idiom.

The Art Ensemble of Chicago has been similarly engaged in making music that combines jazz with elements of African culture. Since 1969, they've formulated a dramatic, almost theatrical style that's sometimes funky, sometimes brooding; they often perform in colorful quasi-tribal robes and makeup, and the presence onstage of close to thirty or forty ethnic percussion instruments gives the AEC's concerts a visual exoticism that perfectly complements their unique sound.

Since trumpeter Lester Bowie and reedmen Joseph Jarman and Roscoe E. Mitchell are also accomplished composers, the AEC's music always has a distinctive formal coherence—not that its improvisations are any less spirited than those of other ensembles. But the AEC is able to take a melting pot of musical styles—jazz, composed works, African music, urban funk, Latin American instruments, and electronics—and combine them in ways that make sense musically.

In addition to African music, jazz musicians have been drawn to the sounds and rhythms of Bali. Pianist Anthony Davis, for example, has absorbed the Balinese influence and uses it as part of a highly personal style that combines both composed and improvised music, often inspired by the Yoruba mythology of West Africa.

Davis is perhaps the quintessential Third Stream composer. He uses jazz inflections even in his composed works, which range in scale from solo piano pieces to a full-scale opera called *X* (1986), based on the life of Malcolm X. His album *Episteme* (1981), played by his ensemble of the same name, fuses Balinese rhythms and ideas from the Balinese shadow-puppet theater with contemporary jazz. On his solo piano disc *Lady of the Mirrors* (1980), rhythmic drones in the left hand and rhythm patterns reminiscent of Indonesian *kotekan* occur alongside some rigorously structured improvisations.

Artists like the AEC or Anthony Davis are not alone in their juxtaposition of composed, improvised, and ethnic music. This Third Stream style, in Schuller's revised definition, has now become what the original Third Stream could not: a major force in new music.

One of the most striking directions taken by jazz in the past fifteen years is represented by the so-called "ECM sound," referring to the German ECM record company. No one can define precisely what that sound is, but everyone seems to know it when hearing it. Typified by such performers as Keith Jarrett, Chick Corea, Pat Metheny, and Ralph Towner, the "ECM sound" is lush, lyrical, and often recorded in a way that produces a spacious effect.

As with any generalization, this one can be refuted with plenty of counterexamples. But the fact remains that ECM records have led the development of an appealing, tonally based, improvised music where virtuosity is subordinated to emotional impact and musical content. Pianist Chick Corea, who has released a dozen albums on ECM since the earliest years of the company, claims that "ECM is a very easy thing to describe in terms of anatomy, because it's essentially the vision of Manfred Eicher. I can't think of any other record producer or record company as successful as he has been, using the operating basis he does: Basically he records music according to his own taste. It's definitely what gives their catalog a particular quality and a particular sound."

Like most good things, ECM started small. At the outset it was primarily a basement industry in Munich, originally known as Jazz by Post, or JAPO (the JAPO label, by the way, still exists as one of the more esoteric branches of the company), and it wasn't until Eicher arrived on the scene around 1970 that the present company began to take shape. ECM stands for "Editions of Contemporary Music," a purposely noncommittal phrase that describes the label's talent roster more accurately than any name including the word *jazz*. Although many jazz artists have recorded on the label, ECM has featured the work of more uncategorizable improvisers, as well as composed music.

Violinist Michael Galasso's brilliant album *Scenes* (1983) is representative of the breadth of the ECM catalog. Although his works begin as violin improvisations, they are eventually written out. The discreet use of delay effects means that some element of improvisation is involved in the actual performance, but this music is not jazz. "Manfred has a real classical background," Galasso offers by way of explanation. Eicher was briefly a double bassist for the Berlin Philharmonic, "so he's always had this involvement with different types of contemporary music, and he started doing things with Steve Reich and Meredith Monk. Some of the more jazz-oriented people have done things, too, that get a little more classical-sounding than straight jazz.

"He told me he's trying to do more in that area, because you worry about getting boxed in and, well, 'labeled' as a label too much. Now, it's really hard to describe ECM; they've got the Art Ensemble of Chicago and Arvo Pärt, and I'm working on another one for them, too."

The common perception remains, however, that ECM is primarily a label devoted to quirky, arcane, and offbeat material by jazz luminaries who have saved their weird stuff for Eicher's sessions. No doubt this view started in 1971–1972, when Keith Jarrett and Chick Corea first appeared on ECM with solo piano improvisations while playing in straightahead group formats on other labels. Jarrett, for example, was still recording conventional jazz for the Impulse label when his ECM album *Facing You* (1972) came out.

Chick Corea is a multitalented musician who is comfortable in several fields of music, whether they be classically composed works, solos and duets with the great vibraphonist Gary Burton, or electric jazz-rock fusion bands like Return to Forever. Characteristically, ECM has for the most part ignored lucrative projects, the fusion band, for example, and has concentrated on that area of Corea's music that it sees as more serious.

Corea describes his works for ECM as "tending toward more chamberlike music, with smaller groups, and definitely toward the acoustic piano, though not exclusively, since my first Return to Forever album is actually on ECM." That first album, *Return to Forever,* is the closest the group has come to jazz and features a stellar cast: Corea on electric piano, Airto Moreira playing all manner of percussion, Flora Purim adding vocals and percussion, Joe Farrell on flute and sax, and Stanley Clarke on acoustic and electric basses.

Jarrett, Corea, and guitarist Pat Metheny must rank among the most successful artists in the field of jazz or near-jazz in the past decade, because they have all achieved some degree of commercial success and have developed large followings without compromising their music. Other key musicians who have been ECM regulars since the early 70s include German bassist Eberhard Weber, American guitarist Ralph Towner, Brazilian guitarist Egberto Gismonti, and sax player Jan

Garbarek and electric guitarist Terje Rypdal, both from Norway. Together, they have shaped a new kind of jazz-derived style. Cellist David Darling, who has recorded for ECM on his own and with Towner and Rypdal, describes it as music "that doesn't have the busyness of progressive jazz, that has a meditative quality." He's quick to add, though, that these are not records aimed at the New Age market.

Ironically, the questing, transcendent piano solos of Keith Jarrett, the nocturnal ambience of Rypdal's albums, and the easy lyricism of Metheny and Weber might very well be taken for New Age music—albeit in a much more accomplished form. It's introspective without being mushy; Jarrett's *The Köln Concert* (1975) is a contemplative work, but it's invigorating too. And the brooding, atmospheric guitar and synthesizers in "Rumours of Rain," from Towner's *Blue Sun* (1983), don't hide the fact that there's real music being played; this is not meant as a sonic pacifier.

Of course, others take a much dimmer view. In a 1981 review of a Barre Phillips album, one critic described the ECM label as a "massive musical mush-making machine, run by one Manfred Eicher, whose avowed purpose it appears to be to turn us all into blanc-mange." The "ECM sound" is described in another pithy phrase: "as bland as a Ford Pinto full of Cream of Wheat." Worth a chuckle, but not really a fair assessment.

Many ECM artists not only improvise, they also compose—which is to say they do more than just write out the "charts" for themselves or other musicians; they actually have a written score, notes on a staff, to perform from. Even these composed works, however, leave some sections looser than others, to allow for improvising. And so we come back to the principles of the Third Stream.

Keith Jarrett's incomparable piano solos have always seemed to generate at least as much enthusiasm among classical music circles as among jazz fans. As a result of invitations to work with conductors and concert-music festivals, he began a series of composed or semicomposed scores. His *Celestial Hawk,* recorded by ECM in 1980, might be the most classically structured of these. Written in a stylish, lyrical manner, it is a three-movement concerto for piano, percussion, and orchestra. Jarrett has also composed works for brass, concertolike pieces for sax player Jan Garbarek, and a solo piano score that conductor/pianist Dennis Russell Davies recorded in 1977.

Ralph Towner, a classically trained guitarist, has written a large body of concert music and has performed widely with some of America's leading orchestras. Chick Corea has probably been the most successful in this area, having created works for the Chamber Music Society of Lincoln Center and the classical chamber group Tashi. He has worked closely with cellist Fred Sherry and violinist Ida Kavafian, two justly renowned classical musicians, and has also composed a Piano Concerto, which debuted early in 1986. Despite such efforts, Corea rejects any characterization of himself as a Third Stream composer.

"A lot of it simply has to do with the musicians I like to work with," he says. "When Gary Burton and I were thinking of expanding our duet, the string quartet had already become a classical ensemble I felt comfortable with; so I got together with Fred Sherry again, with the idea of adding a string quartet to our work. The result was the *Lyric Suite for Sextet.*

"It wasn't a conscious attempt to mix styles of music. I just knew what I had to work with was Gary and myself and what we do, and what I knew the Tashi players could do and how much of the jazz side I could get them to work with."

Like so much of Corea's music, the *Lyric Suite* is a work of understated virtuosity. Both Corea and Burton are immensely talented, but their albums consistently focus on the music and not the musicians. It has been said that a good novelist does not call attention to his style: The technique becomes almost transparent, and the story is what holds a reader's attention. The Burton/Corea discs, with or without other musicians, are much the same. Both vibes and piano are handled so well that the musicians practically disappear, and the music seems to play itself.

ECM was the first record company to devote itself seriously and successfully to new music that grew out of the jazz field. And it is still the most prominent in terms of presenting music that straddles the line between composition and improvisation. But Eicher's outfit has by no means cornered the market. Just as Corea, Jarrett, and others have begun to move into the classical field, classical musicians have developed an interest in improvisation, and some of the major classical music labels have responded to that trend. Two such prestigious companies, Phillips and Deutsche Grammophon, have released duo-piano albums featuring Chick Corea with the Austrian Friedrich Gulda or the Cypriot Nicholas Economou. Both Gulda and Economou were classically trained pianists and composers, familiar in recital halls well before they became known as improvisers. Gulda, in particular, was a celebrated interpreter of Mozart and Beethoven for many years; his interest in jazz was thought to be merely a sideline. In 1970, however, he was awarded the Beethoven Bicentennial Ring by the Vienna Academy of Music, and later returned it as a protest against a musical-education system he considered too conservative. The Corea/Gulda albums thus present two musicians with similar views, who arrived at them from opposite directions.

Despite its public image, ECM has not limited its roster to artists who typify the "ECM sound": violinist L. Shankar has recorded Indian classical music on the label; Steve Reich has several albums on ECM; and the Codona albums, David Byrne's brass-band works from Robert Wilson's *the CIVIL warS,* and recognizably straightforward classical and jazz performances are all part of the catalog. Somehow, though, Eicher's outfit has been able to present all this diversity, including dozens of crossover styles, without being relegated to the "fusion" category. The "ECM sound" may not appeal to everybody, but *fusion* has been a dirty word among many jazz fans for quite a few years.

Fusion music usually refers to the style that resulted when rock elements—electric instruments, high volume, and repetitive rhythms—were introduced into a jazz setting in the late 60s and early 70s. Miles Davis opened the floodgates with his 1970 album *Bitches Brew,* and within a few years, jazz-rock had swept through the music industry. John McLaughlin's Mahavishnu Orchestra, the group Shakti which he cofounded with L. Shankar, and Chick Corea's Return To Forever were only a few of the groups that came to prominence during this period.

Although jazz-rock fusion attracted a wide following, it failed to satisfy the critics and could not sustain the enthusiasm of many listeners. Impressive exhibitions of technical expertise were the rule; tight ensemble playing and dueling solos played at breakneck speed were highly prized. But the musical material on which these solos were based was often flimsy. Fusion became synonymous with empty displays of virtuosity, and by the mid-70s the movement had greatly subsided. A few groups did continue successfully through the decade—most notably Weather Report, thanks to the solid musical content of Wayne Shorter's and Joe Zawinul's compositions.

The union of jazz and rock, and occasionally other ingredients, was not a bad concept in itself, though, and in the late 70s and the 80s, fusion music began to reappear, this time with more attention paid to structure and content. "Certain technical elements of the fusion era are still valid," Chick Corea maintains. "I think the musicians who have been through that, including myself, are already correcting and changing things that didn't work and keeping things that did work." While one of the things he has kept in the Chick Corea Elektric Band, formed in 1985, is a respect for technique—"I'm a player as well as a composer," he points out, "and I like to keep in my performances a certain level of technical expertise"—the Elektric Band is not simply a return to Return To Forever. "The spirit I formed RTF with is the spirit of the band. It's my desire to reach people more broadly and to put my music in a form that's an accepted common language. In that way, it's like Return To Forever. Otherwise, it's very different in the kind of music we're playing and the sound we're getting."

L. Shankar is another artist who has reevaluated fusion. His 1985 album *Song for Everyone* combined jazz and pop styles with the sounds of Indian percussion and Shankar's own Indian-style violin playing. Jan Garbarek's sax was the main melodic instrument, but the focus was less on the musicians' skill at their instruments than on catchy tunes and the overall upbeat mood.

"For me, structure is important," Shankar explains. "Sometimes, someone will really master an instrument and just play solos, but if there's no composition, it has nowhere to go. That's probably why jazz-rock died so quickly, within ten years. It's amazing the first time you hear it, these great techniques and electric instruments. But you need a composition; you need a reference—what does that have to do with this? In *Song for Everyone,* there are free improvisations, and even within the compositions the players have their own variations. But they're definitely structured."

The concern with form and structure is perhaps best seen in some remarkable new European groups, who have developed a completely different style of fusion. Occasionally called "chamber jazz" or even "symphonic jazz," this music uses electric and electronic instruments alongside reeds, brass, and percussion, a jazz approach to ensemble playing, and forms ranging from the simple A–B–A of popular songs to the more extended suites of classical music. A prerequisite also seems to be having an unusual name for the group: France's Art Zoyd and Belgium's Univers Zero and Aksak Maboul are some of the finest ensembles working in this style.

Aksak Maboul was the brainchild of Marc Hollander, a multitalented instrumentalist and composer. The group's last record was issued in 1979; their first album, *Onze Danses pour Combattre la Migraine,* was originally released in 1977. The eleven dances mentioned in the title consist of Hollander originals, arrangements of folk song and a Duke Ellington standard, and compositions by members of the band. Aksak Maboul drew upon aspects of cabaret, jazz, Minimalism, rock, and classical music, but unlike the better-known fusion ensembles, it didn't go in for long flashy solos and rapid-fire syncopations. *Onze Danses* sounded like the result of a group of musicians getting together and playing in whatever styles they wanted, producing some lyrical, swinging music along the way.

Art Zoyd's double album *Phase IV* (1982), in contrast, presents a much darker, more intense set of works. The more dissonant avant-garde sounds that Aksak Maboul uses only sparingly are incorporated into some of Art Zoyd's pieces at great length. At times, the music degenerates into violent noise, but more often, a surprising harmonic twist here and there keeps it interesting and gives it a real emotional depth.

Avant-garde rock and classical techniques color much of the music of Art Zoyd and Univers Zero. Each group has a pair of very capable composers who incorporate ideas from those styles, but in both ensembles, free and structured improvisations determine to a large extent how the music finally sounds. As with Aksak Maboul, the range of their compositions is often surprising; they run from beautiful, nocturnal melodies to dramatic, pulsing ensemble pieces to out-and-out musical chaos. Although none of these bands are household names, either at home in Europe or on this side of the Atlantic, they do demonstrate that the fusion movement is capable of producing exceptional music as well as exceptional musicians.

By now it should be apparent that the new music that has grown out of the jazz tradition has simultaneously drawn on many other sources as well. The final artist we will mention here is one of the best illustrations of this crossover phenomenon.

New Yorker Kip Hanrahan has released several acclaimed albums, beginning with 1981's *Coup de Tête,* which absolutely transcend any attempt at classification. The extensive personnel lists on his recordings include jazz artists like bassist Steve Swallow and sax player Chico Freeman in the company of New York's brightest avant-garde instrumentalists—guitarist Arto Lindsay and drummer Anton Fier, for example—and a group of Caribbean musicians like Haitian guitarist Elysee Pyronneau or Cuban-born percussionist Daniel Ponce. What the listener hears is a vibrant style with a strong Afro-Caribbean flavor, though the instruments are used in nontraditional ways. It might best be described as avant-garde pop, however much that seems a contradiction in terms. "If avant-garde means you're given a tradition and taking the next step or inverting it," Hanrahan says, "then what I'm doing is avant-garde . . . but not necessarily in a formal way."

Hanrahan's pursuits were initially nonmusical. Since the 70s, he has been an experimental filmmaker, and though he names Miles Davis as a favorite, he also mentions Cage, Stockhausen, and avant-garde filmmaker Dziga Vertov as musical influences. When *Coup de Tête* was released, it was not aimed at the jazz market, nor was it intended as a jazz-fusion effort, but jazz fans were the ones who sat up and took notice. In 1983, when his album *Desire Develops an Edge* appeared, Hanrahan was receiving five-star rave reviews in the jazz press, while more mainstream and pop music critics largely ignored him.

Despite the attention he has attracted in the jazz media, Hanrahan regards jazz as being somewhat cliquish, and tries to maintain a certain distance from it. "Sometimes I think of myself as a pop musician," he says. But it's worth noting that while Hanrahan's music is not jazz (not intentionally, at least), it's not quite pop, either. "That word 'pop' comes apart in a big way," he agrees. "I'm sure Elysee considers himself the main Haitian pop guitar player, and in a sense he is. But that's Haitian pop; there's an audience in the French-speaking Caribbean and West Africa that would understand it as pop. [Percussionist] Milton Cardona is definitely a Latin pop musician, but in this context, in my music, they're not pop musicians if they're playing to a jazz audience."

Besides creating an idiosyncratic sound on his albums, Hanrahan has also begun to investigate the possibility of applying experimental film techniques—like those of Vertov or Jean Rousch—to making recordings. He hopes to use his studio musicians in the same way that Rousch used native Africans in the physical production of his films on Africa—his subjects were both the image *and* the means of presenting it. "In following one creative idea," he says, "a Puerto Rican born in New York would react in one way, a Scotsman would react another. Regardless of the actual music, those different creative answers to the same question would create the recording process itself.

"The studio is always treated as a way of simply recording a document of that music at that time. But there could be a million other possibilities—how come no one moves the microphones around? In film, you can move the camera around, but the space between the musician and the mike always remains the same. Any differences are corrected in the mix. Wouldn't it be great to hear a record in which the mike moved?"

While Kip Hanrahan's relationship to jazz is an almost incidental one, he may, ironically, be closer to the spirit of conventional jazz than many of the other musicians in this chapter, especially in the lively rhythms and finely meshed ensemble playing that appear on his albums. If this section has drawn one conclusion, it is that the classification of what is or is not jazz is finally an arbitrary one. Newton claims that *Echo Canyon* has little to do with his earlier jazz records; I find it full of the spontaneous inventions that you'd expect from a jazz musician, and have included it here. Feel free to cut it out and paste it on another page if you disagree. Many people consider pianist George Winston and his colleagues on the popular Windham Hill label jazz artists, but their approach differs significantly from that of the artists mentioned above. Although ECM certainly paved the way for Windham Hill, it's probably best to avoid drawing too many parallels between the younger label and the music discussed so far. In fact, in its early years, Windham Hill was associated more with one or two instruments than with a genre of music. We'll look at this unlikely but phenomenal success story next.

Windham Hill and the New Impressionism

Acoustic music, solo or otherwise, has always been a staple of the classical concert hall and the jazz club, but the preponderance of electronics in the 60s and 70s created a void in other branches of music; acoustic forms were apparently being swept away by the eager acceptance of the new technology. Bob Dylan and Phil Ochs had already undertaken the electrification of folk. Miles Davis's "fusion" experiments paved the way for an invasion of electric and electronic instruments into jazz. And, of course, modern rock and pop music would be unthinkable without the electric guitar and bass and the various electronic keyboards. It seemed there was little place for something as old-fashioned and understated as a fellow plunking away at a six-string acoustic guitar. But a few musicians resisted the electric onslaught. Some mistrusted the whole business of electronics; others simply believed that there were still techniques and sounds to be explored on the older instruments. One of these was guitarist William Ackerman.

Ackerman's Windham Hill label is a quintessential case of someone being in the right place with the right stuff at the right time. The company's first album was released in 1976, a time when disaffection with amplified pop music was becoming widespread. The next five years would be bleak ones for much of the record industry: Many independent labels were swallowed up by the larger corporations, marginal acts (a term that seemed to include most jazz artists) were cut, and sales were, in terms of the record companies' profit margins, distressingly low. Yet it was during this same period that Windham Hill, on the strength of its solo guitar and piano recordings, not only grew and prospered but came to define its own sound, much in the same way as ECM had. In fact, the two have been compared quite often; it is an analogy that neither firm is happy about, but an early Windham Hill ad using the phrase "an American ECM" did little to help matters.

Whatever their differences, Ackerman will admit to ECM's stylistic inspiration: "The continuity, the taste, and the quality that I perceived in the early ECM catalog were very influential to me." And indeed, the simple graphics and striking cover photography that are the signature of Windham Hill's albums certainly *look* like ECM's style of artwork. Musically, though, the two labels are worlds apart. Acker-man lists *fin-de-siècle* French composer Erik Satie and guitarists John Fahey and Robbie Basho as his central influences. The Windham Hill label was, at least in its early days, much closer in sound to Fahey's old Takoma label, devoted primarily to folk- or blues-derived guitar music, than to anything ECM did. Ackerman de-scribes the early Windham Hill sound as "a more or less hi-tech, quality-oriented, Takoma-type sound coming out of two generations of guitarists."

Even that statement tends to give the wrong impression, however. Ackerman didn't start out with a plan to create an updated Fahey/Basho approach. In fact, he claims, he didn't start out with any musical plans at all. Ackerman's involvement with music occurred in a roundabout way. He was born in Germany, adopted by American parents, and raised in California. By the time he began attending Stanford University, he was playing guitar as a hobby and occasionally writing music for a local theater group. During his senior year, Ackerman left Stanford to become a building contractor. The company he founded was called Windham Hill Builders.

"I was working as a carpenter/house builder," he recalls, "and only by virtue of the fact that during the winter it would rain and I'd have to do something indoors did I have any sort of audience at all. People would request that I come over to their houses and play into their cassette decks. That was fun and novel for a while, and then it got a little old. So I came upon the brilliant idea of doing a record. My friends all chipped in about five bucks and said, OK, go do a record. So the initial concept with Windham Hill was nothing more than one privately released record that didn't even bear the name Windham Hill."

Ackerman soon found that a name was necessary when a few West Coast radio stations began playing the album. "Distributors that found my record via the airplay it was receiving started asking, well, what's coming out next on your label? The light went on in my head, and I said, you mean if I release something else you'll distribute it? And they said yes." Ackerman took the name of his building company, put it on his album, and Windham Hill Records was born. That 1976 disc, *The Search for the Turtle's Navel,* became its first release.

Ackerman maintains that even at this point he was hesitant—especially when he learned that the minimum number of albums he could obtain from the record pressers was three hundred. "If there was any vision in my head at all, it was of 223 discs sitting in white paper sleeves, warping and turning to dust in my closet."

The second Windham Hill album was a vocal project which was less than enthusiastically received and was soon dropped from the catalog. William Ackerman's own followup album, the beautiful *It Takes a Year* (1977), began the real development of the label, as the care and technical expertise devoted to both the recording and the pressing became as important as that given to the graphic design and the music itself. Ackerman's solos blended American folk and blues styles with a simple, almost Impressionistic mood. Alternately whimsical and bittersweet, *It Takes a Year* was the most successful of the early Windham Hill releases.

"Somehow a sense of continuity was born with the release of my cousin Alex de Grassi's record *Turning: Turning Back* (1978), which was the fourth album in the catalog," Ackerman says. "Then we did Robbie Basho, which made sense historically and musically. Number six in the catalog was my *Childhood and Memory,* and number eight was the Erik Satie album."

The Satie album, by pianist Bill Quist, was a surprise to most observers. "At that time," Ackerman says, "we were regarded as a modern evolution of the Takoma catalog, and everybody was content with that. Throwing in something regarded as classical repertoire really threw people for a loop." In retrospect, the Satie recording not only fit right in—it was, after all, a solo acoustic piano album—but it provided a clue to the origins of the Windham Hill style. The music of Satie is spare, lyrical, and suggestive, a perfect complement to the equally Impressionistic musings of Ackerman, de Grassi, and company.

The addition to the company roster of guitarists David Qualey from Germany and Daniel Hecht from Vermont reinforced the classical sound (Qualey even gave his pieces opus numbers), and it no longer seemed feasible to call the music "folk," or to consider Windham Hill an outgrowth of the American folk guitar tradition. The real anomaly, however, proved to be George Winston, whose completely personal, highly evocative piano solos debuted on the 1980 recording *Autumn.* Because Winston's instrument was solo piano, which at that point was the province of Keith Jarrett, comparisons between the two were constantly being made. This did not please the jazz community at all; Jarrett himself appeared a little miffed that so many listeners couldn't distinguish between the two very dissimilar styles. Finally, because

Winston appeared on the Windham Hill label, some people began calling his style "folk piano," which, if not completely accurate, at least was pointed in the right direction.

If the Windham Hill label must be considered a phenomenon in the music industry, then George Winston must rank as the label's most phenomenal artist. His first three Windham Hill records have all "gone gold," meaning they have sold over half a million copies each. And at one point in 1983, all three albums appeared simultaneously among the top dozen bestselling jazz releases. Winston's style has been blithely copied by literally hundreds of pianists, but Winston himself has evolved his musical language carefully over a period of twenty years. He describes it as "Impressionistic"—a characterization almost everyone would agree with—and falling "somewhere between folk and jazz."

Winston began playing the organ and, later, electric piano after leaving high school in Miami, taking his inspiration from such mid-60s pop acts as Booker T and the MGs, Dave "Baby" Cortez, and others. In 1971, he first heard the music of Fats Waller, the giant of the 1920s style known as "stride" piano. The organ and electric piano were replaced with an acoustic piano, and Winston began writing stride and blues piano pieces. Like Ackerman, he also admired the guitar works of John Fahey, and in 1972 he released his first album, *Piano Solos,* on Fahey's Takoma label.*

The story of how Winston became a Windham Hill artist illustrates the diversity of his talent and musical interests. Although he records only as a pianist, in concert he plays (and plays well) the guitar and the harmonica. "But his greatest instrument is the phone," states William Ackerman. "George wrote me a letter in 1978, telling me how much he liked my tune 'Processional' and demonstrating a remarkable knowledge of the tunings I was using and those of Alex de Grassi. In subsequent letters and phone calls—I spent hours and hours on the phone with George—we talked about everything in the world of music. Everything except for the fact that he was a musician. He knows as much about a number of different fields of music as anyone possibly could; he has a record collection larger than many radio stations'. Finally, I was playing in LA with Alex, and he came and introduced himself after the concert, and asked if I'd like to come over to his house and play a bit.

"Now this was a revelation—but it was as a guitarist that I first heard him. To be honest, after hearing his slide-guitar work, I was insisting that evening on doing an album of slide guitar with George Winston! It was about two A.M., I was dead tired, and I was going to crash there when he said, you mind if I play a little piano while you go to sleep? I thought, how marvelous, he plays a little piano too. And he launched into a transcription of three of my pieces, did a note-for-note transcription of one of Alex de Grassi's pieces, which are incredibly dense—the transcription alone was a work of art—and then he played Bola Sete's 'Ocean Waves.' *Then* he launched into the music that comprised *Autumn.* I was completely floored. And when I got up in the morning, I said, George, I think we're going to do a piano album first."

*This album soon went out of print, but was reissued in 1981 on Windham Hill's Lost Lake Arts label, under the title *Ballads and Blues: 1972.*

To anyone who's only heard Winston's albums, his concerts can come as a surprise. In addition to the dreamy, quasi-Impressionistic solos that he (and Windham Hill in general) has become associated with, Winston performs works that reflect the influence of Fats Waller, the New Orleans blues pianist Professor Longhair, the Minimalist works of Steve Reich, and the late Vince Guaraldi who wrote music for the "Peanuts" TV shows (most notably "A Charlie Brown Christmas," from which Winston usually plays several excerpts).

With the dramatic increase in the popularity of Windham Hill's records, especially those of George Winston, came the inevitable question from critics and the public: What kind of music is it? "I spent years trying to answer that," Ackerman says. "I would string words together like 'Contemporary Impressionism' and it really began to sound like a German schizophrenic disease or something, so I gave up." Then a funny thing began to happen. Record stores were getting more customers asking when the next Windham Hill album was due—not necessarily the next Winston, or the next de Grassi, but the next Windham Hill album. For that reason, most major record stores now have a Windham Hill bin. While its records are usually also cross-filed under folk or jazz, Windham Hill has effectively created a new style that the label itself defines.

This is not to claim, however, that this type of music represents a remarkable innovation: Guitarist Anthony Phillips, for example, a musical maverick who left the art-rock group Genesis after only one album, began making Windham Hill–style records in 1970, five years before the label was even conceived. Phillips's albums feature an engaging combination of Impressionism, Renaissance music, and occasional tape or electronic effects, along with extraordinarily witty cover art.

What Windham Hill has accomplished, rather, is to produce music by talented artists and package it with an extraordinary degree of confidence and creativity. Needless to say, their formula has inspired a host of imitators. Some are quite good; many are obvious attempts to catch a ride on Windham Hill's not inconsiderable coattails. The proof that a large audience for new music exists has not gone unnoticed by the larger companies, either. As Ackerman puts it, "With Polygram having gotten involved with Kitaro and CBS with Andreas Vollenweider, the major corporations—let alone the many independents springing up—are taking a cue from the success of Windham Hill, both graphically and stylistically."

A related phenomenon has been the development of what is being called "New Acoustic Music," a term general enough to include Windham Hill and its clones as well as more folk-, jazz-, or bluegrass-oriented musicians. Violinist Darol Anger has been a leading voice in this movement. Anger has recorded two duet albums with pianist Barbara Higbie for Windham Hill, but he's better known for his work with the David Grisman Quartet. Along with the DGQ's Mike Marshall, Anger and Grisman work in a style that lies somewhere between bluegrass and jazz, with elements of classical and rock added. Their instruments include fiddles, mandolins, and guitars, along with Anger's "octave violin," which uses thicker strings to produce a tuning an octave lower than normal. ("It has a peculiar sound," he says, "sort of like an old man hacking and wheezing—but with great soul.")

In an article for *The Black Sheep* entitled "What Is New Acoustic Music?"

Anger described the genre as follows: "Rather than be constrained by unwieldy pejoratives such as 'grassy-jazzy-confusion' or 'plucko-funko-string jazz' bestowed upon us by bewildered journalists, we can at least find a semiuncolored, not too specific (or stupid) name of our own choosing. Some room to breathe, please!" Two potential problems plague this classification, however: One is that *some* New Acoustic Music is actually electric. On a less dogmatic level, the term seems not to have caught on except as a way of describing the Grisman/Marshall/Anger contingent. During the years when Windham Hill was seeking to establish its identity, the company seemed to encourage the use of weighty-sounding labels like Neo-Impressionism, so it's hardly surprising that this sort of terminology has tended to stick as a general classification despite the fact that Anger, Marshall, et. al., have recorded New Acoustic Music on the label. Even so, Windham Hill itself has progressed beyond strict categories, having gone on to record electronic music (Mark Isham) and World Music (Shadowfax); at the time of this writing, plans are in the works for an album of Gregorian Chant.

While a backlash against electronics may account to some extent for Windham Hill's popularity and the resurgence of acoustic instruments (whether in a solo, duet, or even larger format), the very prominence that the company has achieved has made it the target of two different critical contingents.

One group consists of those who simply find the music of Windham Hill artists too aimless or empty—this is usually the reaction of critics who equate George Winston and William Ackerman with New Age music. Ackerman has never considered Windham Hill part of the New Age trend, even though it was that segment of the marketplace where his company first caught on. As to the criticism itself, it's certainly too much to expect that everyone will respond favorably to the work of an artist like George Winston. But Winston's sincerity is obvious, both in his music (and his complete lack of pretension in presenting it) and in his work as a record producer, repaying old debts to those who inspired him by reissuing their albums (he has supervised the rerelease of records by Professor Longhair and Brazilian guitarist Bola Sete) and recording underrated artists. On a purely technical level, even detractors of Windham Hill would have to admit that Alex de Grassi is a superior musician—"the *Guitar Player* poll has him right after Chet Atkins every year," claims Ackerman—and that Michael Hedges has evolved an impressive new style of playing the guitar. Clearly, some Windham Hill albums are better than others, and while the crystalline, audiophile sound quality never varies, the musical content does.

The second part of the critical backlash is more pervasive. "Recently," says Ackerman, "I read an absolutely scathing article on Windham Hill, in which we were described as bloodthirsty capitalists, out to pillage and plunder and create this yuppie lifestyle and exploit it." Calling these accusations "fantastic," he claims that, in the mid-70s, "no one in his right mind would have created Windham Hill Records as a profit-making entity." Still, among many large retailers and in other music-business circles, the label has built up a reputation for a sort of quiet ruthlessness, despite its low profile in the advertising field. Much of this is undoubtedly just sour grapes, though Ackerman himself admits that, once George Winston was signed, "the evolution from that point on was a bit more calculated. Once you have some momentum going and you have a little time to objectify what's going on, you begin to see and create trends or patterns."

In response to those trends, Windham Hill has built itself into a hydralike entity with its arms reaching in several directions. The company now includes a reissue label, Lost Lake Arts; a jazz label, Magenta; a label produced by George Winston called Dancing Cat; a vocal branch, Open Air; and a fusion-directed label called Hip Pocket.

With the success of Windham Hill, the market has been flooded with albums of lyrical, Impressionist-type music from guitarists, pianists, harpists, flutists, and others. But like the New Age music with which it is often compared, this style is threatening to succumb to the effects of oversaturation. Already the "not-another-solo-piano-album syndrome" has set in; the market simply cannot support such a glut of second-rate releases. Once this music becomes more familiar to the general record-buying public—as it shows every sign of doing—listeners will be able to exercise a bit more discrimination, and the frantic rush to get as many similar-sounding albums as possible into the stores should abate.

Meanwhile, the popularity of solo acoustic music, or small acoustic ensembles, continues to grow. A George Winston album is equally likely to be found among Dad's classical music records as it is with Junior's rock collection. Perhaps the most remarkable aspect about the renewed popularity of acoustic music, however, is its understatement. As Ackerman explains, the companies involved "are not bludgeoning the marketplace with brilliant marketing. It's the result of word-of-mouth advertising—one friend playing it for another. And that more than anything is what's phenomenal about this music."

DISCOGRAPHY AND RELATED WORKS

PART ONE: ECM AND ALL THAT "JAZZ"

JOHN ABERCROMBIE
- *Timeless* (ECM 1047) ECM
- *Characters* (ECM 1117) ECM
- *Current Events* (ECM 1311) ECM

Solo efforts from an outstanding guitarist and, on the last release, guitar synthesist. The first album has a couple of uninspired Jan Hammer compositions, but the title track is nothing short of terrific. All three LPs vary in mood from funky to subdued. *Characters* features solo guitar, electric guitar, and electric mandolin. *Current Events* includes bassist Marc Johnson and drummer Peter Erskine.

JOHN ABERCROMBIE, DAVE HOLLAND, AND JACK DEJOHNETTE
- *Gateway* (ECM 1061) ECM
- *Gateway 2* (ECM 1105) ECM

These records are more concerned with chops. The slower, bluesy pieces, somewhat less flashy, are quite striking.

JOHN ABERCROMBIE AND RALPH TOWNER
- *Sargasso Sea* (ECM 1080) ECM. The first of two duet albums; the other is listed as Towner and Abercrombie (below). Challenging guitar works, both for the listener and the performers.

MUHAL RICHARD ABRAMS
- *Spiral* (Arista Novus AN-3007). An important figure in jazz/new-music circles. "String Song," with its unpredictable textures from piano strings, gongs, and percussion, is the most intriguing work here.
- *Afrisong* (India Navigation 1058) NMDS. A rare sampling of accessible, *almost* pretty music for piano. Try it.

AKSAK (OR AQSAK) MABOUL
- *Onze Danses pour Combattre la Migraine* (Crammed Discs 011) NMDS
- *Un Peu de L'Ame des Bandits* (Crammed Discs 002) NMDS.
Onze Danses ("Eleven Dances") is one of the very

best albums of eclectic jazz/new music/World Music: From the "improvised Minimalism" (as leader Marc Hollander puts it) of "Mastoul Alakefak" to the mock-cabaret "Milano per Caso," the LP produces one surprise after another. The second album is, by Hollander's own admission, a less interesting, more rock-oriented work; but it contains a delightful Near Eastern–style arrangement of the Italian tune "I Viaggi Formano la Gioventu."

THOMAS ALMQVIST
- *Nyanser* (Mistlur MLR-6). Pensive, lyrical music for guitar, ethnic percussion, reeds, and keyboards from an unjustly neglected Swedish guitarist.
- *The Journey* (Mistlur MLR-12). Some electric works, more moody soundscapes, and a stunning cover photo by Ansel Adams.
- *Unknown Tracks* (Breakthru BRS-8) SCA. Side one shows Almqvist's typical flair for combining instrumental colors, with some hi-tech electronics included. Side two is facile jazz and probably should have stayed unknown.

COSTE APETREA, STEFAN NILSSON, AND JUKKA TOLONEN
- *Vänspel* (Love SLLP 02) SCA. Nilsson is a Swedish keyboardist; the other two are Finnish guitarists (see Tolonen, below). This album has some fine ensemble work, mostly acoustic, but with restrained (and thus effective) electronic touches.

ART ENSEMBLE OF CHICAGO
- *Nice Guys* (ECM 1126) ECM
- *Full Force* (ECM 1167) ECM
- *Urban Bushmen* (ECM 2-1211, 2 LPs) ECM
- *The Third Decade* (ECM 25014-1) ECM

The album titles from these mature, mid-70s to mid-80s recordings tell the AEC's whole story. The music is full of vigor and a sense of fun; but it's certainly not trivial. The entrance of the Irish-sounding theme in the "Prayer for Jimbo Kwesi," from the last LP, is a powerfully moving moment. And they can wail with the best of the avant-garde, too.

ART ZOYD

- *Musique pour l'Odyssée* (Cryonic 1253)
- *Les Espaces Inquiets* (Cryonic 1153)
- *Le Mariage du Ciel et de l'Enfer* (Cryonic 3009) NMDS

Uncompromising, Expressionistic jazz-rock, often harsh and loud, and infrequently gentle and tuneful.

- *Phase IV* (Recommended RR-14/15, 2 LPs) NMDS. Without losing the harder edge of their music, the five members of this group have put together a musical blend of jazz, classical, and jazz-rock elements.

SERGIO AND ODAIR ASSAD

- *Piazzolla/Ginastera/Brouwer/Pascoal/Gnattali* (None. 79116). A must-have for guitar fans. The music is composed, but the Assad brothers have a quasi-improvisatory style that combines folk, samba, tango, and jazz techniques.

AZIMUTH

- *Azimuth* (ECM 1099) ECM
- *The Touchstone* (ECM 1130) ECM
- *Depart* (ECM 1163) ECM
- *Azimuth 85* (ECM 1298) ECM

John Taylor—piano, organ, and some synthesizer; Norma Winstone—voice; Kenny Wheeler—trumpet and fluegelhorn. While the serene yet emotional second album remains their best, the other LPs each contain exquisite music. And of course, all of it is performed by as unlikely a trio of instruments as you can find.

ALVIN BATISTE

- *Musique d'Afrique Nouvelle Orleans* (India Navigation 1065) NMDS. Avant-garde and old-style New Orleans jazz get mixed together on this LP by one of New Orleans' most talented, but still underrated clarinetists. Along with the straightforward jazz you'll find the "Endochrine Song," which is supposed to enhance meditation by containing every audible sound between 20 and 20,000 Herz. Don't know about that, but it's an offbeat, entertaining piece anyway.

TIM BERNE AND BILL FRISELL

- *Theoretically* (Empire EPC72K) NMDS. Except for one or two aimless improvised duets, this is an excellent album of music on the edge: both Berne and Frisell have completely original voices on their respective instruments (sax and guitar). See Frisell, and Reid and Frisell, listed below.

CARLA BLEY

It's hard to overstate Bley's importance to fringe jazz acts and record companies. As the prime mover behind the Jazz Composers' Orchestra and the New Music Distribution Service, she has done a great deal for small, independent jazz labels and musicians. Most of her own records definitely belong to the jazz camp, but a few are tougher to categorize.

- *Social Studies* (ECM/Watt 11) NMDS, ECM
- *Night-Glo* (ECM/Watt 16) NMDS, ECM. Hard to know what to make of these. The synthesizers, electric piano, and shuffling rhythms of the latter LP flirt with banality—as if Bley were daring us to accuse her of "going commercial." But she isn't—not with titles like "Rut" and "Sex with Birds." The catchy first disc is no less whimsical, though it may be in better taste.

DUSAN BOGDANOVIC

- *Early to Rise* (Palo Alto Jazz PAJ-8049) PAJ. Bogdanovic is a guitarist, and his quartet—James Newton on flute, bassist Charlie Haden, and percussionist Tony Jones—is a strong one. Classically trained Bogdanovic effectively combines the formal concerns of classical music with an undeniable flair for improvisation.

LESTER BOWIE

- *All the Magic* (ECM 1246/47, 2 LPs) ECM. The eccentric trumpeter from the Art Ensemble of Chicago leads his own big band on the first album of this double-album set in some post-bop pieces; on the other disc he plays solo trumpet, including a couple of works that use an opened piano with the sustaining pedal depressed as a natural echo chamber.

LESTER BOWIE'S BRASS FANTASY

- *I Only Have Eyes for You* (ECM 1296) ECM
- *Avant Pop* (ECM 1326) ECM

As the titles indicate, Bowie's colorful brass band plays melodies you probably know, but may never recognize in these versions.

DOLLAR BRAND

- *African Piano* (JAPO 60002) ECM
- *Ancient Africa* (JAPO 60005) ECM

Dollar Brand (now known as Abdullah Ibrahim) is a South African pianist who recorded these early discs in 1969 and 1972. Listen to "Bra Joe from Kilimanjaro," recorded on both albums, and you'd think Kilimanjaro was just west of New Orleans. Tinny sound, unpolished performances, but infectious stuff that swings.

- *African Portraits* (Sackville 009) ROU. One of his finest LPs. Deeply felt solo piano music, with folksy melodies and insistent left-hand ostinatos.

ABDULLAH IBRAHIM

- *Autobiography* (Plainisphare 1267-6/7, 2 LPs) NMDS. Dollar Brand captured live in a 1978 performance, only recently released. Weaves his own music with fragments of Duke Ellington, Thelonius Monk, and others.

RAINER BRÜNINGHAUS

- *Freigeweht* (ECM 1187) ECM
- *Continuum* (ECM 1266) ECM

An associate of Eberhard Weber, this German keyboardist teams up with musicians including

Azimuth's Kenny Wheeler on the first album, Markus Stockhausen on the second. "Stille," on the second LP, comes closest to the so-called "ECM sound," as typified by Weber et. al.

GARY BURTON AND CHICK COREA
- *Crystal Silence* (ECM 1024) ECM
- *Duet* (ECM 1140) ECM
- *In Concert, Zurich, October 28, 1979* (ECM 1182/83, 2 LPs) ECM

All too often, duets can disappoint fans of one artist or another. Not here. These albums helped define the ECM style. Fine performances by two highly influential musicians; Corea on piano and Burton on vibes. (See Corea and Burton, as well.)

GARY BURTON AND STEVE SWALLOW
- *Hotel Hello* (ECM 1055) ECM. Duet from two members of Burton's quartet. Swallow plays bass and piano; Burton plays vibes, marimba, and organ. Well-crafted throughout. (See Towner and Burton, listed below.)

THE GARY BURTON QUARTET, WITH EBERHARD WEBER
- *Ring* (ECM 1051)
- *Passengers* (1092) ECM

The first album no longer seems to be in print. Burton's group included guitarist Pat Metheny, whose lyricism is echoed in parts of these records.

DAVID BYRNE
- *Music for "The Knee Plays"* (ECM 25022-1) ECM. One of the things that has made Byrne one of the most consistently fascinating artists to come out of the rock field is his refusal to sit still. After working with Philip Glass and Brian Eno, he collaborated with Robert Wilson on "The Knee Plays," or short, self-contained interludes, of the gargantuan stage work *the CIVIL WarS*. And he came up with a totally unexpected album of brass music (with some narration by Byrne himself) that draws inspiration from New Orleans brass bands, Bulgarian folk music, and spirituals. Artistically, he took a real chance; and the record, by Talking Heads standards, was a commercial failure. But it's a typically witty, energetic, perhaps naive album—and a unique accomplishment.

C'EST WHAT?!
- *Kyting* (Lissenclose LM 82001) NMDS. An acoustic quartet that comes up with one excellent cut, "Maggie's Movie," on an album of above average, independently produced new jazz.

NELS CLINE AND ERIC VON ESSEN
- *Elegies* (9 Winds 0105) NMDS. Guitarist Cline and double bassist von Essen are half of Quartet Music (see below). This haunting collection of elegiac duets is improvised, but it's only tangentially related to jazz (and so completely in line with what

this chapter is about). A beautiful album that bears repeated listening.

ALICE COLTRANE
- *Transcendence* (War. BS-3077) LADY. Coltrane plays meditative improvised music for several instruments, including organ and piano, but her best works are the harp pieces.

JOHN COLTRANE
Like Stockhausen in earlier chapters, Coltrane is listed here for completeness's sake. His music is an important part of the development of jazz in the last quarter-century, and since so much has been written about him elsewhere, it will serve our purposes merely to list a *few* of his pivotal recordings.
- *Greatest Years, Vol. 1* (Impulse 9200, 2 LPs)
- *Greatest Years, Vol. 2* (Impulse 9223, 2 LPs)
- *Greatest Years, Vol. 3* (Impulse 9278, 2 LPs)
- *Ballads* (Impulse 32)
- *Impressions* (Impulse 42)
- *A Love Supreme* (Impulse 77)
- *Ascension* (Impulse 95)
- *Kulu Se Mama* (Impulse 9106)
- *Meditations* (Impulse 9110)
- *Selflessness* (Impulse 9161)

CONTREVENT
- *Jeu de Paume* (CTV-1985; Contrevent, 1465 de Villars, Sillery G1T 2C1, Quebec, Canada). Good album combining classical instruments (cello, classical guitar) with a jazz quartet format; vibes and guitar stay up front. Mellow without being vapid.

CONVENTUM
- *"Commerce Nostalgique"* from the *Recommended Records Sampler* (Rec. RR8/9, 2 LPs) NMDS. Chamber jazz-rock from a Montreal quintet. Neatly sidesteps the clichés of the genre.

CHICK COREA
This is only a partial list of Corea's albums. He has recorded a lot of mainstream discs and some frankly ill-advised pop-jazz albums (*Secret Agent* for Polydor, for example). His more uncategorizable records include:
- *Piano Improvisations Vol. 1* (ECM 1014)
- *Piano Improvisations Vol. 2* (ECM 1020)
- *Return to Forever* (ECM 1022) ECM
- *Children's Songs* (ECM 1267) ECM
- *Septet* (ECM 1297) ECM

CHICK COREA AND GARY BURTON
- *Lyric Suite for Sextet* (ECM 23799-1) ECM

CHICK COREA AND NICOLAS ECONOMOU
- *On Two Pianos* (DG 410 637-1)

CHICK COREA AND FRIEDRICH GULDA
- *The Meeting* (Ph. 410 397-1)
- *Mozart: Piano Concerto #10 in E-flat/Corea: Fantasy/Gulda: Ping Pong* (Teldec 42961)

CHICK COREA AND STEVE KUJALA
- *Voyage* (ECM 25013) ECM

CHICK COREA, MIROSLAV VITOUS, AND ROY HAYNES
- *Trio Music* (ECM 1232/33, 2 LPs) ECM
This last album is the closest to the traditional notion of jazz and jazz ensembles, but Corea has also become respected outside jazz circles. The albums with Economou and Gulda are some of the finest displays of his versatility and talent.

LARRY CORYELL
Another musician who has done a lot of straight jazz; again, this list represents his more offbeat work.
- *European Impressions* (Arista Novus AN-3005). Solo acoustic guitar, uneven but with moments of brilliance. Side one, recorded at the 1978 Montreux Jazz Festival, is excellent.
- *Standing Ovation* (Arista Novus AN-3024). See Chapter 6 for the track "Spiritual Dance," with L. Subramaniam. Rest of this LP is solo guitar, much of it based on classical themes.
- *The Lion and the Ram* (Arista AL-4108). Julie Coryell sings on a few tracks. The "Improvisation on Bach Lute Prelude" is the best work on the album.

LARRY CORYELL AND PHILIP CATHERINE
- *Twin House* (Elektra 6E-123). Superior disc of duo-guitar works. "Nuages"—which looks back to gypsy guitarist Django Reinhardt—and "Ms. Julie" are especially inventive.

LARRY CORYELL AND BRIAN KEANE
- *Just Like Being Born* (Fly. F. FF-337) FF. What's like being born? Whose idea was this? Lackluster guitar duets that waffle between jazz and New Age.

DAVID DARLING
- *Journal October* (ECM 1161). Darling plays electric and acoustic cellos here, along with bells and gongs and such. An enjoyable collection, now somewhat difficult to find. See Rypdal and Darling, below.

ANTHONY DAVIS
- *Variations in Dream Time* (India Navigation IN-1056) NMDS
- *Lady of the Mirrors* (India Navigation IN-1047) NMDS
Solo piano music with hints of ethnic music and allusions to Duke Ellington and others; one of the strongest facets of Davis's work.

- *Episteme* (Gram. GR-8101) GRAM, NMDS
- *Hemispheres* (Gram. GR-8303) GRAM, NMDS
Ensemble pieces, featuring Davis's group Episteme. The first album uses Indonesian elements; the second, a collaborative work with dancer/choreographer Molissa Fenley, is forceful and loud, with only one slower section.
- *Middle Passage* (Gram. GR-8401) NMDS, GRAM. Three works by Davis using various degrees of improvisation and composition, plus a work for piano and tape by Earl Howard. An important album by one of the most promising musicians of his generation.

ANTHONY DAVIS, JAMES NEWTON, AND ABDUL WADUD
- *I've Known Rivers* (Gram. GR-8201) GRAM. As you might expect from these three, an album of lyric, engaging, yet still challenging music.

MILES DAVIS
- *Kind of Blue* (Col. PC 8163)
- *Sketches of Spain* (Col. PC-8271)
Jazz, whatever that may or may not be, wouldn't be the same without Miles. Given his pivotal role in that field, he's only obliquely related to this chapter; yet, like Coltrane, he must be included here. These early albums, from 1959 and 1960, are classics, and are among the most influential from this influential figure.
- *In a Silent Way* (Col. PC-9875). Restrained and languorous, especially "Shhh/Peaceful."
- *Circle in the Round* (Col. KC-2-36278). Unreleased tracks. Especially good are "Sanctuary" by Wayne Shorter, given a much more controlled reading than the previous version from *Bitches Brew,* and "Guinnevere," by David Crosby, which includes one of Miles's most eclectic lineups: Wayne Shorter, Joe Zawinul, Chick Corea, and others, with a prominent role for sitar. Not particularly Eastern-sounding, but a colorfully exotic piece.

PACO DELUCIA
- *Castro Marin* (Polygram Imports 6301 025) PSI. With fellow guitarists John McLaughlin and Larry Coryell: blistering fretwork and occasional romantic interludes.
- *Meister der Spanischen Gitarre* (Poly. Germany 6695 001) PSI
- *Motive (Best Of)* (Polygram Imports 6358 085)
Good examples of DeLucia's Spanish, sometimes Impressionistic guitar improvs.

AL DI MEOLA
- *"Mediterranean Sundance"* and *"Lady of Rome, Sister of Brazil"* from the LP *Elegant Gypsy* (Col. 34461)
- *"Fantasia Suite for Two Guitars"* from the LP *Casino* (Col. 35277)
Acoustic works with some overdubbing, off of two

albums otherwise devoted to electric jazz-rock. The "Fantasia Suite" alone is worth the price of the second album: It's an incredible display of guitar virtuosity at the service of some Spanish-flavored improvising. Di Meola adds mandolin, hand claps, and foot stomps, too.

DR. JOHN
- *The Brightest Smile in Town* (Clean Cuts CC707) CC
- *Dr. John Plays Mac Rebennack* (Clean Cuts CC705) CC
Dr. John (who, by the way, *is* Mac Rebennack) chucks the band, for the most part chucks the singing, and gets down to basics: buoyant, striding New Orleans-style boogie'n'blues.

DOUBLE IMAGE
- *Double Image* (Inner City 3013)
- *Dawn* (ECM 1146) ECM
- *In Lands I Never Saw* (CH CEL-015) CH
Double Image is David Samuels and David Friedman, playing vibes, marimba, and some other percussion. Other musicians help out on the earlier discs, but the third LP is just the two of them. With help or without, they create a mesmerizing, shimmering wash of percussion. All are beautifully played, but *In Lands* and *Dawn* are best.

MARK EGAN
- *Mosaic* (Hip Pocket HP-104) WH. Pristine production showcases Egan's considerable talents. Using a double-neck, four- and eight-string electric bass, he creates a wide range of moods. A neat Matti Klarwein painting adorns the cover.

MARK EGAN AND DANNY GOTTLIEB
- *Elements* (Philo 9011) PHI. An earlier album, not nearly as mature or well-produced as *Mosaic*, but with a few interesting cuts.

FLAIRCK
- *Variations on a Lady* (Poly. PD-1-6243). Only American release by this Dutch group. They use guitars and other strings (a sitar, for example), violin, and flutes; they combine jazz, classical, Celtic, and ethnic sounds. They keep you waiting for something to happen, but it never really does. But while you're along for the ride, the LP can be quite charming.

FREE FLIGHT
- *The Jazz/Classical Union* (Palo Alto Jazz PAJ-8024) PAJ. Ouch. Discs like this could give (and may have already given) the jazz-classical fusion style a bad name.

DAVID FRIESEN
- *Amber Skies* (Palo Alto Jazz PAJ-8043) PAJ. Stellar cast includes Chick Corea, Airto Moreira, and Paul Horn. "Sitka in the Woods" remains a favorite at the Horn/Friesen concerts. See Horn and Friesen, below.

BILL FRISELL
- *In Line* (ECM 1241) ECM. One of the most original and proficient guitarists now playing, in any genre. This mostly solo outing has some prepared guitar (similar to a prepared piano in that the strings are stopped or deadened with things like alligator clips or chopsticks), electric and acoustic guitars, and a little electric bass. Atmospheric works that can really draw you in.

FRED FRITH
- *Guitar Solos* (Caroline C-1508). An early (1974) solo disc, released only in the U.K. Frith was one of the first masters of the prepared guitar (see Frisell above); his improvs can be angular and dissonant or, less often, melodic. See Chapter 11.

FRED FRITH AND HENRY KAISER
- *With Friends Like These . . .* (Metalanguage 107) NMDS
- *Who Needs Enemies?* (Metalanguage 123) NMDS
Two guitarists who have specialized in some pretty far-out free improvising. The second album is one of the most tuneful—Dare I say accessible? No, probably not—LPs either of them has done.

GALLERY
- *Gallery* (ECM 1206) ECM. David Samuels, vibes; Michael Di Pasqua, drums; Paul McCandless, reeds; David Darling, cello; and Ratzo Harris, bass. Manfred Eicher, Mr. ECM, actually cowrote one of the tracks. You might guess that this would be a good example of the "ECM jazz sound"—and you'd be right.

JAN GARBAREK
- *Dis* (ECM 1093) ECM. Striking album of sax and some wood flute, with Ralph Towner accompanying on guitar. The Norwegian Brass Sextet appears on one track, and a large wind-harp provides an alien drone in several others.
- *Places* (ECM 1118) ECM. A fine quartet album, with Bill Connors's guitar and John Taylor's organ adding nice textures and unusual colors.
- *Aftenland* (ECM 1169) ECM. With church organ; a beautiful combination. Soulful, dark music.
- *Eventyr* (ECM 1200) ECM. John Abercrombie (guitar) and Nana Vasconcelos on percussion help out. Garbarek's sax playing is somewhat restrained here; this is his most songful, underrated LP.
- *Paths, Prints* (ECM 1223) ECM. With Bill Frisell on guitar, Eberhard Weber on bass, and Jon Christensen on drums, there was little chance of this album being a dud. Christensen has never sounded more versatile, and Frisell's accompaniment is often so subtle it's almost invisible.

JAN GARBAREK/BOBO STENSON QUARTET
- *Witchi–Tai–To* (ECM 1041) ECM
- *Dansere* (ECM 1075) ECM
Early quartet albums. They have a more mainstream lineup and sound, but they still sound good today.

JAN GARBAREK, EGBERTO GISMONTI, AND CHARLIE HADEN
- *Magico* (ECM 1151) ECM
- *Folk Song* (ECM 1170) ECM
Sax, guitar, and bass. Even without the usual drums, these albums swing. Ethnic, Latin, and jazz ingredients are used.

JAN GARBAREK GROUP
- *Wayfarer* (ECM 23798-1) ECM. With a group similar to the *Paths, Prints* lineup, Garbarek gets considerably more jazzy. Some of the tracks will appeal to fans of his more eccentric records, though.

FELIU GASUL
- *"*"* from the LP *Recommended Records Sampler* (Rec. RR-8/9) NMDS. From Barcelona, Gasul is part of Recommended's network of avant-garde rock and jazz-rock musicians; but on this (untitled?) piece he gives us some delicate, intricate guitar work with vaguely Spanish-sounding accompaniment. *Not* typical of this label's sound.

EGBERTO GISMONTI
- *Dança Das Cabeças* (ECM 1089) ECM
- *Solo* (ECM 1136) ECM
- *Sanfona* (ECM 1203/04, 2 LPs) ECM

EGBERTO GISMONTI AND NANA VASCONCELOS
- *Duas Vozes* (ECM 25015-1) ECM
These two Brazilian musicians, a guitarist and a percussionist, appear together on most of their "solo" albums, though *Solo* is just that. The first and last albums highlight their engaging blend of Latin, Afro-Brazilian, and jazz forms. *Sanfona* has one solo disc and one with a Brazilian dance ensemble. (See Chapter 6.)

PATRICK GODFREY
- *Bells of Earth* (Apparition 0982-3) NMDS
- *Small Circus* (Apparition 1085-6) NMDS
Two more LPs from a Canadian keyboardist who appears in Chapter 4. The first was widely compared to the work of Keith Jarrett (a superficial comparison, but it gives you an idea what the album sounds like). *Small Circus* is similar for half its length; the other half is odd, almost childlike music for harpsichord.

OLIVER GRIFFITH
- *Pictures* (Red House RHR-002). Some straightahead jazz and a couple of haunting, Impressionistic

pieces ("Moon over Destroyed Castle" and "Evening Song"). A solid album.

FRIEDRICH GULDA
- *Gegenwart* (ERP-1) CH, NMDS. Gulda plays piano, electric piano, and recorder. Ursula Anders adds some percussion. Spare, often atonal pieces with some lyrical moments.
- *Gulda Plays Gulda* (Ph. 412 115-1). Piano improvisations. Some are quite fetching, but the album is ultimately little more than a momentary diversion.

GUNTER HAMPEL
- *Dances* (Birth 002) NMDS. Solos on various instruments by one of the leaders of the European avant-garde jazz community. Hampel's music is an acquired taste, but it's worth trying.

GUNTER HAMPEL AND BOULOU FERRE
- *Espace* (Birth 006) NMDS. An ear-catching disc with Ferre's gypsy guitar work compared and contrasted with Hampel's vibes, winds, etc.

HERBIE HANCOCK AND CHICK COREA
- *An Evening With* (Col. PC-2-35563, 2 LPs). Concert recording of some originals and some chestnuts ("Someday My Prince Will Come"). No gimmicks, just basic piano from two musicians who are at their best in this sort of format.

FREDERIC HAND
- *Jazzantiqua* (Musical Heritage Society MHS-4887) MHS. Original works and arrangements of medieval music. Hand plays lute and guitar, and his ensemble plays ancient and very modern instruments. A convincing and appealing album.
- *Trilogy* (Musical Heritage Society MHS-4692) MHS. Original works, dedicated to folks like Gary Burton, Chick Corea, Bill Evans, and Dave Brubeck. Composed works with a strong improvised feel.

KIP HANRAHAN
- *Coup de Tête* (American Clavé 1007) NMDS
- *Desire Develops an Edge* (American Clavé 1008/09) NMDS
- *Conjure* (American Clavé 1006) NMDS
- *Vertical's Currency* (American Clavé 1010) NMDS
- *A Few Short Notes from the End Run* (American Clavé EP, 1011) NMDS
Hanrahan's blend of Caribbean, Western, and Afro-Cuban forms makes for some of the most vibrant, intelligent music to come out of this field. The vocals on the first album have an intentionally amateurish sound that takes some getting used to. The same goes for all the other albums if you're not enamored of Jack Bruce's voice. But Kip's ear for novel combos and undiscovered talent is impressive: Anton Fier, Bill Laswell, Jamaladeen

Tacuma, Elysee Pyronneau, Daniel Ponce, Chico Freeman . . . the list goes on. *Desire* contains some of Hanrahan's finest ensemble writing/arranging, but *Conjure*, based on poems by Ishmael Reed, is his most ambitious project. Mostly vocal, it will appeal primarily to jazz and blues fans. With Taj Mahal, Allen Toussaint, and Lester Bowie in the cast, this disc really swings, especially on Toussaint's "Skydiving." The EP is sparer, with clearly defined percussion and tight ensemble playing.

JONAS HELLBORG
- *Elegant Punk* (Relativity 8063) IMP. Don't know about the "punk" part, but "elegant" is exactly the word for this solo bass album. Miles Davis's "Blue in Green" is attributed here to Bill Evans, but the arrangement is right on. Jimi Hendrix's "Little Wing" sounds surprisingly good as an electric bass solo, too. The rest are skillful performances of originals.

HENRY COW
- *Legend* (Red V-2005)
- *Unrest* (Red V-2011)
Two records from the early 70s. Henry Cow, featuring Fred Frith and most of what later became Art Bears (see Chapter 11), was one of the most influential avant-garde jazz-rock fusion bands. How many avant-garde jazz-rock fusion bands are there, you ask? Not many before Henry Cow, dozens after. (O.P.)

HUGH HOPPER AND ALAN GOWEN
- *Two Rainbows Daily* (Europa JP-2003) NMDS. Hopper plays bass, Gowen keyboards. Outstanding collection of unorthodox, surprising, but always musical duets; one of the last recordings Hopper made.

PAUL HORN
- *Inside the Taj Mahal* (Kuckuck 062) CH
- *Inside the Great Pyramid* (Kuckuck 060/061, 2 LPs) CH
- *Inside the Powers of Nature* (Golden Flute GFR-2006) NAR
- *Inside the Cathedral* (Kuckuck reissue of GFR-2008) CH
Some of Horn's famous solo recordings. Mostly flute, some piccolo, alto flute, bass flute, and soprano sax. The *Powers of Nature* record, ironically, was recorded entirely in a studio, using tape and artificial echo to create some unique effects. Uses overdubbing of a number of flutes, some of them processed, to create otherworldly pieces. The others are ambient or space music, in the best sense.

PAUL HORN AND DAVID FRIESEN
- *In Concert* (Golden Flute GFR-2009) NAR
- *Heart to Heart* (Golden Flute GFR-2002) NAR
The first album isn't credited to Horn and Friesen

(it's simply another Horn album), but it is a concert recording of the two of them, with organist Ralph Hooper, in St. Mary's Cathedral in San Francisco. It's okay, but much better is the second LP, from 1983. Horn and Friesen both take solos using delay effects; prerecorded tapes of guitar and kalimba are used on some pieces, too.

ABDULLAH IBRAHIM, *SEE LISTINGS UNDER* DOLLAR BRAND.

KEITH JARRETT
Jarrett really has created a whole new genre of music with his solo piano improvisations. Despite hundreds of similar recordings in recent years, too many would-be imitators remain just cheap imitations. Jarrett is the real thing. With all of his solo recordings, his organ works, his composed scores, and his concert appearances playing works by Lou Harrison, J. S. Bach, and numerous others, Jarrett is much more than a jazz musician. I once asked him if he still considered himself a jazz artist; after a moment's thought, he replied, "It depends on who's asking the question. If my old high school principal asked me that, I'd say no. But if it were Bud Powell asking, I'd probably say yes." The albums listed here present Jarrett at his most unconventional.
- *Facing You* (ECM 1017) ECM. His first ECM album, and still a classic.
- *Solo Concerts—Bremen and Lausanne* (ECM 1035–37, 3 LPs) ECM
- *The Köln Concert* (ECM 1064/65, 2 LPs) ECM
- *Staircase* (ECM 1090) ECM
- *Concerts—Bregenz/München* (ECM 1227–29, 3 LPs) ECM
- *Concerts/Bregenz* (ECM 1228, single LP from preceding set) ECM
- *G. I. Gurdjieff/Sacred Hymns* (ECM 1174) ECM
- *Sun Bear Concerts* (ECM 1100, ten-LP set) ECM
Yes, that's right: *Sun Bear* is a ten-record set of Jarrett in Japan. Transcendent, as usual, but you have to be a real fan—preferably a fan with lots of time and money—to spring for this. The other albums, also solo piano, vary from good *(Bregenz)* to superb *(Köln, Bremen)*.
- *Invocations/The Moth and the Flame* (ECM 1201, 2 LPs) ECM
- *Hymns, Spheres* (ECM 1086/87, 2 LPs) ECM
The Moth and the Flame is solo piano, but its companion disc is pipe organ and/or soprano sax. *Hymns, Spheres* is played on a Baroque organ; Jarrett gets strange, almost electronic effects from unusual combinations of organ stops and by playing with the stops only partially opened. Provocative music on both recordings.
- *Treasure Island* (ABC AS-9274)
- *Best Of* (ABC IA-9348)
- *Nude Ants* (ECM 1171) ECM
- *Changes* (ECM 25007-1)
- *The Survivor's Suite* (ECM 1085) ECM

These five albums lie somewhere between his mainstream and more eccentric works. The last one ranges furthest afield of this group.

■ *Spirits 1 & 2* (ECM 1333/34, 2 LPs) ECM. Jarrett describes this remarkable set as a "musical diary," chronicling the months after a breakdown brought on by the pressures of constant touring. He claims to have reached in this set of "basement tapes" the goal toward which his searching piano solos were aimed. *Spirits* is indeed a special album. It is Jarrett's most personal document, consisting of improvisations on various wind instruments, ethnic percussion, guitar, and only a little piano. See Chapter 5 for Jarrett's concert works.

KEITH JARRETT AND JACK DEJOHNETTE
■ *Ruta + Daitya* (ECM 1021) ECM. Fine album of duets, some with an ethnic flavor.

ANDRÉ JAUME AND RAYMOND BONI
■ *Pour Django* (C.E.L.P. 2). Interesting textures in this French LP. Jaume's reeds stand out against Boni's highly processed guitar sound. Without bass and drums, it doesn't swing, but it does hold your attention.

STANLEY JORDAN
■ *Magic Touch* (Blue Note 85101). Jordan has been widely praised for his two-handed fretwork, which turns the guitar into a quasi-keyboard instrument and sounds like two or three musicians playing. This is supposed to be Jordan's debut LP; so most of the reviews said. But it isn't.
■ *Touch Sensitive* (Tangent 1001) is his debut. It's similar to the preceding.

ART LANDE AND JAN GARBAREK
■ *Red Lanta* (ECM 1038) ECM. Piano and reeds. Both musicians are in good form here.

ART LANDE, DAVID SAMUELS, AND PAUL MCCANDLESS
■ *Skylight* (ECM 1208) ECM. Piano, vibes, and reeds; a colorful ensemble, and a well-made record.

EVAN LURIE
■ *Happy? Here? Now?* (Crepuscule TWI-574) NMDS. If Lurie's probing questions don't bring on a fit of depression, you'll find some intriguing stuff here. A member of New York's avant-garde band The Lounge Lizards, Lurie plays solo piano; lounge music it's not—it's a bit too spicy. Maybe Thelonius Monk in a cabaret would have sounded like this.

JOHN LURIE
■ *Music for* Stranger Than Paradise *and* The Resurrection of Albert Ayler (Crammed Discs MTM-7) NMDS. Evan's brother and co-Lounge Lizard. Side one is lean, angular music for string quartet; side two is closer to the Lizards' sound, and closes with a burst of violence reminiscent of Ayler's "Ghosts."

MICHAEL MANTLER
■ *Movies* (WATT 77) ECM, NMDS
■ *Something There* (ECM/WATT 23786-1) ECM Mantler likes big ensembles; these are eccentric but effective recordings with all-star casts.

GEORGE MARSH AND JOHN ABERCROMBIE
■ *Drum Strum* (1750 Arch S-1804) NMDS. Percussion and guitar. Some of the duets don't go anywhere, but the album has some intriguing, often surprising sounds.

JOHN McLAUGHLIN
■ *My Goal's Beyond* (Elektra-Musician E1-60031). Hard to say too much in praise of this early solo disc. Actually, only side one is solo: McLaughlin has a Mahavishnu-type group backing up on side two. By eschewing both the electric guitar and the clichés of jazz-rock, he comes up with perhaps his finest album.
■ *"My Foolish Heart"* from the LP *Electric Guitarist* (CBS 82702). Remember Tony Bennett and Bill Evans's recording of this song? McLaughlin's solo electric guitar version is in the same league. The rest of the album is typical fusion.

JOHN McLAUGHLIN AND MAHAVISHNU ORCHESTRA
■ *The Inner Mounting Flame* (Col. PC-31067)
■ *Birds of Fire* (Col. PC-31996)
Not too many people listen to these any more, but they seemed kind of important ten years ago. Each album still has a few good moments, though.
■ *Mahavishnu* (War. 25190)
■ *Adventures in Radioland* (Relativity 88561-8081-1) IMP
These are recent (1985–1986) albums featuring a re-formed lineup and electronics; with only a few melodic exceptions, they're still conventional jazz-rock.

PAT METHENY
■ *Bright Size Life* (ECM 1073)
■ *Watercolors* (ECM 1097) ECM
■ *New Chautauqua* (ECM 1131) ECM
■ *American Garage* (ECM 1155) ECM

PAT METHENY GROUP
■ *Offramp* (ECM 1216) ECM
■ *Travels* (ECM 1252/53) ECM
■ *First Circle* (ECM 1278) ECM
■ *The Falcon and the Snowman* (EMI SV-17150)

PAT METHENY AND LYLE MAYS
■ *As Falls Wichita, So Falls Wichita Falls* (ECM 1190) ECM
Metheny's flowing, precise guitar style has until

recently been one of the identifying trademarks of the ECM sound. Whether playing acoustic guitar, electric guitar, harp guitar, or guitar synthesizer, Metheny has demonstrated musical gifts obvious enough to gain him a commercial success that eludes many others in this area. Among his finest albums are *New Chautauqua,* a solo disc of acoustic works; *Watercolors,* with Lyle Mays on keyboards and Eberhard Weber on bass; and *Wichita Falls,* with Nana Vasconcelos on percussion. In all of his work, melody reigns supreme; it's that, more than the tight ensemble playing or Metheny's virtuosity, that has made his music so popular.

JAMES NEWTON
- *Axum* (ECM 1214) ECM. Studio recording, using some overdubbing. Several works inspired by the music and history of northeastern Africa, especially Ethiopia.
- *Echo Canyon* (CH CEL-012) CH. If you ever wanted to know what it felt like to be out in New Mexico's Echo Canyon on a clear September night, with only the birds and crickets and frogs for company, but couldn't actually arrange to go there, this album is the next best thing. Newton's improvs echo the traditions of many ethnic cultures, and the canyon provides all the accompaniment he needs.
- *In Venice* (CH CEL-017) CH. Another ambient album of flute solos, scheduled for release in 1987.

CLAUS OGERMAN, FEATURING JAN AKKERMAN
- *Aranjuez* (Jazzman JAZ-5015). Hyperromantic arrangements of classical and original works, for guitar and orchestra. Hard to find, and not worth the bother.

OREGON, SEE CHAPTER 6.

JACO PASTORIUS
- *"Continuum"* from the LP *Invitation* (War. 23876-1). One of jazz's premiere electric bassists performs this cool solo on an album otherwise closer to the fusion sound.

JIM PEPPER
- *Comin' and Goin'* (Europa 2014) NMDS. Of "Witchi–Tai–To" fame. That song appears here, too, along with a cast including all three Codonas, John Scofield and Bill Frisell on guitars, and Pepper himself on sax. He's in typically buoyant, joyous form. Don Cherry all but steals the show with some of the most melodic, restrained trumpeting he has put on disc.

BARRE PHILLIPS
- *Three Day Moon* (ECM 1123) ECM. Bassist Phillips employs guitarist Terje Rypdal, percussionist Trilok Gurtu, and Dieter Feichtner on synthesizer in a spacey, sometimes atonal album that effectively sustains a nocturnal mood.

PEKKA POHJOLA
- *Harakka Bialoipokku/"B" the Magpie* (Love LRLP-118) SCA
- *Visitation* (Digit DGLP-4) SCA
- *Everyman* (Breakthru BRS-2) SCA
- *Urban Tango* (Breakthru BRS-1) SCA
Pohjola is a terrific bass player and composer who combines jazz with some genuinely interesting orchestral writing (*Visitation*), with electronics (*Everyman*), and with the sounds of a rock band (all of them, especially *Urban Tango*).

PATRICK PORTELLA AND JOSEPH RACAILLE
- *Les Flots Bleus* (Rec. RR-16) NMDS. A 45-rpm, full-length album of composed pieces and improvisations for clarinet (Portella) and keyboard (Racaille). Side two, a collection of over a dozen instrumentals, has a pleasant, Gallic charm. See also ZNR, below.

KEVIN POSTUPACK
- *Release* (PRM 1020)
- *Voice of Silence* (PRM 1030; PRM Records, Box 210, New Brunswick, NJ 08903)
Postupack writes music for guitars, recorders, percussion, and some others, and dedicates these pieces to folks like Keith Jarrett and John McLaughlin. His works are not just imitations, however; they stand fairly well on their own.

QUARTET MUSIC
- *Quartet Music* (9 Winds 0106) NMDS
- *Ocean Park* (9 Winds 0113) NMDS
Nels Cline and Eric von Essen (see above) join Alex Cline, percussion, and Jeff Gauthier, violin. Each album has a work or two with a strong ethnic feel, but mostly this quartet plays straight, melodic jazz.

VERNON REID AND BILL FRISELL
- *Smash and Scatteration* (Rykodisc RCD-10006; Rykodisc, 400 Essex Street, Salem, MA 01970). Compact disc of electro-acoustic guitar music. Frisell's lyricism is tempered by Reid's jazzy funk—or is it funky jazz?—and the result is a multifaceted disc touching on many styles. Besides the acoustic, electric, delayed, and synthesized guitars, they use banjo and programmed percussion. Some of it just sounds like two guys having a good time jamming, but their solos are distinctive, ear-opening examples of virtuosity. Incredible production.

FRANK RICOTTI AND BRIAN GULLAND
- *"Pillow Under"* (from the audio-cassette magazine *Touch 33.4-"Lands End"* (see Chapter 6)) NMDS. Cocktail-style improvs on reeds over Minimalist patterns on vibes. Similar to John Surman with more of a cabaret feel.

NED ROTHENBERG

- *Portal* (Lumina L006) NMDS. Spare, neatly sculpted solos for sax, bass clarinet, soprano double ocarina, et.al., many of them inspired by Greek myths. Rothenberg really extends the limits of possibilities on these instruments.
- *Trespass* (Lumina L011) NMDS. More solos, and again, it's hard to believe he does all this without overdubs. Most of it, though, is more interesting for its virtuosity than its musicality.

TERJE RYPDAL

- *What Comes After* (ECM 1031)
- *Whenever I Seem To Be Far Away* (ECM 1045) ECM
- *Odyssey* (ECM 1067/68, 2 LPs)
- *After the Rain* (ECM 1083) ECM
- *Waves* (ECM 1110) ECM
- *Descendre* (ECM 1144) ECM
- *Chaser* (ECM 1303) PSI

Rypdal, from Norway, has developed an instantly recognizable voice on the electric guitar. By masking the initial sound of plucking the string and then raising the volume on his guitar, he creates a smooth legato sound while creating the impression that he's strangling his instrument. *Whenever I Seem To Be Far Away* has an electric-guitar concerto on one side; that, along with most of *Odyssey* and all of *After the Rain*, share an Impressionism that's competely genuine. The latter album is probably his best. The last three albums listed demonstrate Rypdal's guitar in a more energetic jazzy style.

TERJE RYPDAL AND DAVID DARLING

- *Eos* (ECM 1263) ECM. Between Rypdal's electronic guitar and Darling's eight-string electric cello, there are some pretty wild sounds here. Not that the music is wild, though. After an inexplicable opening that sounds like a bad rip-off of Jimi Hendrix, the album settles down to a mostly nocturnal set of pieces.

TERJE RYPDAL, MIROSLAV VITOUS, AND JACK DEJOHNETTE

- [Untitled] (ECM 1125) ECM. Hard to miss with a trio like this. One of the relatively few ECM albums that you can really say has that "ECM sound."

GEORGE SAMS

- *Nomadic Winds* (Hat Music 3506) NMDS. Distinctive jazz with Sams on trumpet and piano, accompanied by bass, violin, and percussion. This strange ensemble really comes together on "The Path with a Heart for Africa," an exotic piece that includes Indian tabla.

PHAROAH SANDERS

I'm surprised that more New Age fans haven't latched on to Sanders's work. Sure, it gets pretty shrill at times, but it's also meditative, devotional, and has lots of ethnic percussion. Some of his most compelling music includes:

- *Pharoah* (India Navigation IN-1027) NMDS. Especially the side-long track "Harvest Time."
- *Best Of* (Impulse 9229). This really *is* a best-of collection. Two-LP set includes his all-time classic, "The Creator Has a Master Plan."

TONY SCOTT
See Chapter 6.

L. SHANKAR

- *Vision* (ECM 1261) ECM
- *Song for Everyone* (ECM 1286) ECM

Palle Mikkelborg, trumpet, and Jan Garbarek, sax, appear on *Vision* along with Shankar's ten-string violin. It's the closest he comes to the sound one expects from an ECM disc. See Chapter 6 for more.

STEVE SWALLOW

- *Home* (ECM 1160) ECM. An album of poems by Robert Creeley set to music. If the vocals don't bother you, this can be a most rewarding album. Almost like a nonethnic Hanrahan LP.

JUKKA TOLONEN

- *Mountain Stream* (Sonet SLP-2636). Brilliant album of acoustic-guitar solos and one piano solo. "East Meets West" has a modal, Indian quality; the rest are well-balanced displays of virtuosity and a strong musical gift. (O.P.)

JUKKA TOLONEN AND COSTE APETREA

- *Touch Wood* (Terra/Van. T-6). A compilation from several of Tolonen's albums, some of them with Apetrea adding his own acoustic guitar. A fine album; not as good as the preceding, but the only one in print right now. See Apetrea/Nilsson/Tolonen, above.

RALPH TOWNER

- *Diary* (ECM 1032) ECM
- *Solstice* (ECM 1060) ECM
- *Batik* (ECM 1127) ECM
- *Old Friends, New Friends* (ECM 1153) ECM
- *Solo Concert* (ECM 1173) ECM
- *Blue Sun* (ECM 1250) ECM

Diary, Solo Concert, and *Blue Sun* are excellent solo albums. The others are jazz ensemble discs, occasionally straying into less-definable areas. *Blue Sun,* in which Towner plays a number of guitars, keyboards, horns, and percussion, is probably the most colorful and appealing of all.

RALPH TOWNER AND JOHN ABERCROMBIE

- *Five Years Later* (ECM 1207) ECM. Follow-up to their first album; see Abercrombie and Towner, above. Similar in mood and sound.

RALPH TOWNER AND GARY BURTON
- *Matchbook* (ECM 1056) ECM
- *Slide Show* (ECM 25036-1) ECM

Towner's guitar and Burton's vibes make a beautiful pair. The first album is a solid group of duets, but the second is even better. Ten more years of experience and ideas go into it, and some tracks even outshine the Burton/Corea material.

RALPH TOWNER WITH GLEN MOORE
- *Trios/Solos* (ECM 1025) ECM. And with Paul McCandless, and with Collin Walcott. All four members of Oregon are here, but it's still Towner's show, and they never all appear together on one piece. Still, the sight of these four names together raises certain expectations, which this LP only occasionally meets.

UNIVERS ZERO
- *Ceux de Dehors* (Rec. RR-10) NMDS. These guys get filed with Art Zoyd and Henry Cow. The musicians have backgrounds in jazz and contemporary music, and it shows. Pretty dense stuff, for the most part.

TOM VAN DER GELD
- *Path* (ECM 1134) ECM. Bill Connors, guitar; Roger Jannotta, reeds and winds; and Van der Geld, vibes. Sparkling, subdued virtuosity makes this a likeable recording.

TOM VAN DER GELD AND CHILDREN AT PLAY
- *Patience* (ECM 1113) ECM. An earlier album, with some fine excerpts. Not as consistently good as *Path.*

GREGG WAGER
- *Adjacent Lines and Equal Parts* (MF MFLP-001) NMDS. Solo piano. An odd combination of repeating fragments, continuously developed à la Lubomyr Melnyk, with a gritty jazz inflection, reminiscent of Jarrett's more rhythmic flights.

EBERHARD WEBER
- *The Colours of Chloe* (ECM 1042)
- *Yellow Fields* (ECM 1066) ECM
- *The Following Morning* (ECM 1084) ECM
- *Fluid Rustle* (ECM 1137) ECM
- *Later That Evening* (ECM 1231) ECM

Weber, an electric bassist, has been one of the mainstays of the ECM roster. Several albums use a string orchestra *(Colours of Chloe, Following Morning, Later That Evening),* and all feature musicians like Charlie Mariano, Rainer Brüninghaus, and Bill Frisell. Weber's rich bass sound always manages to stay up front, though, and he's penned some beautiful tunes on each of these records. The last two albums are excellent throughout.

EBERHARD WEBER AND COLOURS
- *Silent Feet* (ECM 1107) ECM
- *Little Movements* (ECM 1186) ECM

Ensemble pieces, mostly quartets. Without the surprising textures of the other albums, these discs lose something; but they're still worth hearing.

HAJO WEBER AND ULRICH INGENBOLD
- *Winterreise* (ECM 1235) PSI. Two guitars and some flute. Their delicate musings contain fleeting echoes of other guitarists—Towner; perhaps Coryell—but this album ends up sounding like no one else's. Just the thing for a snowy day in winter.

DENNY ZEITLIN AND CHARLIE HADEN
- *Time Remembers One Time Once* (ECM 1239) PSI. Understated bass/piano duets. Haden and Zeitlin originals, some Ornette Coleman, Coltrane, etc. These two musicians can impress you without (apparently) even trying.

ZNR
- *Barricade 3* (Rec. RR-7) NMDS. Hector Zazou and Joseph Racaille, with Patrick Portella on several tracks. See their individual or duo listings above and in Chapter 12 for more. Works range from abrasive, chaotic improvisations to almost classically melodic songs and instrumentals.

PART TWO: NEW ACOUSTIC MUSIC*

DAROL ANGER
- *Fiddlistics* (Kaleidoscope F-8) ROU. NAM's leading spokesman performs good-natured works with almost incidental virtuosity. Includes David Balakrishnan, another NAM fiddler.

DAROL ANGER AND BARBARA HIGBIE
- *Tideline* (Wind. H. WH-1021) WH. With Mike Marshall on a few tunes. Higbie plays piano, Anger handles violin, octave violin, mandolins, and cello. Fine album of substantial music that fits nicely with the mood of most Windham Hill albums.

*New Acoustic Music, or NAM, forms a convenient musical bridge between the jazz-derived sounds of the ECM contingent and the folk Impressionism of the Windham Hill crew. Although several of the artists listed here record for Windham Hill, their music also has a healthy dose of jazz and bluegrass, with bits of classical, Celtic, and ethnic music.

Remember comedian Steve Martin's routine about the banjo—how you couldn't sing a *sad* song on the banjo because the instrument has such a *happy* sound? Well, bluegrass music is like that too, and that style's sense of fun pervades most of the NAM albums. Some of the key figures of this relatively small field are listed in this section.

DAROL ANGER/BARBARA HIGBIE QUINTET

■ *Live at Montreux* (Wind. H. WH-1036) WH. Mike Marshall, mandolin and guitar; Todd Phillips, bass; Andy Narell, steel drums. Excellent blend of instrumental colors and styles: Higbie's lyricism, the Anger/Marshall brand of down-home funk, and Narell's Caribbean sound somehow mesh without stepping on one another's toes. This album and the Marshall/Anger album (see below) led to the formation of one of the most promising new-music ensembles, the group Montreux.

DAROL ANGER AND MIKE MARSHALL

■ *The Duo* (Roun. 0168) ROU. While not as good as the Marshall/Anger album *Chiaroscuro* (see below), this earlier effort is a typically enjoyable example of NAM.

DAVID GRISMAN

■ *Dawg Grass/Dawg Jazz* (War. 25804)
■ *The David Grisman Quintet* (Kaleidoscope 5) ROU
■ *The David Grisman Rounder Album* (Roun. 0069) ROU

Grisman's combination of bluegrass and jazz has proven to be a most influential development, to say the least. Darol Anger, Mike Marshall, Earl Scruggs, and Stephane Grappelli are just a few of the names you'll find on his albums. Although closer to either bluegrass or jazz than to new music, Grisman's records are important NAM contributions.

DAVID GRISMAN AND ANDY STATMAN

■ *Mandolin Abstractions* (Roun. 0178) ROU. Now this *is* a new-music LP. Duo music for mandolins, with some mandola or mandocello (two larger members of the mandolin family). Completely improvised, but with a surprising formal quality. Ultimately, a whole album of mandolins is best for fans of these musicians and their instruments.

KENNY KOSEK AND MATT GLASER

■ *Hasty Lonesome* (Roun. 0127) ROU. Kosek and Glaser are fiddlers, and they're joined by Andy Statman (mandolin and clarinet), Russ Barenberg (guitar), Tony Trischka (banjo), etc. The title track, with its insistent, repetitive fiddle lines, recalls the Minimalist sounds of Ellipsis (see Chapter 4). Other works are much closer to the sounds of bluegrass.

MIKE MARSHALL

■ *Gator Strut* (Roun. 0208) ROU. Although Marshall plays guitars and mandolins instead of fiddle, this record is similar to Darol Anger's solo album.

MIKE MARSHALL AND DAROL ANGER

■ *Chiaroscuro* (Wind. H. WH-1043) WH. This 1985 release may be the finest album of NAM released

so far, and proves that the "Windham Hill sound" isn't exclusively laid back and mellowed out. It includes some relaxed works that do more than just set a mood, as well as some kinetic ensemble pieces, and even a couple of enchanting Bach arrangements.

MARK O'CONNOR

■ *False Dawn* (Roun. 0165) ROU. If it has strings, O'Connor can play it—and well.
■ *Meaning Of* (War. 25353-1). The ex-Grisman Quartet and former Dixie Dregs violinist on a major label. And certainly it's a commercial effort, though I wouldn't call it a "sell-out." Except for "Irish Maiden," there's little that's really acoustic.

ANDY STATMAN

■ *Flatbush Waltz* (Roun. 0116) ROU. Excellent album by a mandolin virtuoso who's equally at home with jazz improvising, bluegrass picking, Near Eastern modes, and the energy of Klezmer music. With strings (both bowed and plucked), percussion, and others. He has also recorded bluegrass and Klezmer LPs.

TONY TRISCHKA

■ *"A Robot Plane Flies over Arkansas"* (Roun. 0171) ROU. This album, and Trischka's other recorded work, remains very close to the traditional sounds of American bluegrass, old-timey, and Appalachian folk styles.

▲ *Turtle Island String Quartet* (scheduled for release by Windham Hill). Turtle Island is Darol Anger and David Balakrishnan, violins; Laurie Moore, viola; and Mark Summer, cello. So they're set up like a classical string quartet—but there the similarity ends. Classical elements are all but submerged under a blend of jazz, funk, folk, and bluegrass. The quartet does, however, play with what you might call classical precision. The music includes arrangements of some of Balakrishnan's violin quartet music, which really comes to life in this setting, and some jazz numbers. Really *new* acoustic music.

PART THREE: WINDHAM HILL AND THE NEW IMPRESSIONISM

PHILIP AABERG

■ *High Plains* (Wind. H. WH-1037) WH. Well, since everyone else will be comparing him to George Winston, so will I . . . though I prefer Aaberg. Far from being imitative, Aaberg has put together an individual blend of the folk and Impressionist elements that made Winston so popular. These piano solos positively reek of the wide open spaces of the West (Aaberg is from Montana), and his experiences touring with Peter Gabriel and studying composition with Leon Kirchner give his music a breadth that's missing in most similar albums.

WILLIAM ACKERMAN

- *The Search for the Turtle's Navel* (Wind. H. 1001) WH
- *It Takes a Year* (Wind. H. 1003) WH
- *Childhood and Memory* (Wind. H. 1006) WH
- *Passage* (Wind. H. 1014) WH
- *Past Light/Visiting* (Wind. H. 1028) WH
- *Conferring with the Moon* (Wind. H. 1050) WH

Ackerman is not only CEO of Windham Hill, he's also one of their best artists. The first three albums, all solo guitar, defined what the label would generally sound like. The blues and folk roots are never far from the surface in the early releases, and all of his records have a tinge of melancholy. The last three LPs are ensemble collections. The last is the best; it contains a genial work for charango (South American guitar) and zampoña (a flute), as well as appearances by Philip Aaberg, Eugene Friesen, and others.

MARGIE ADAM

- *Naked Keys* (Pleiades 2748) LADY. Likeable piano music, with a sense of whimsy. Good performances, decent sound.

MARCUS ALLEN

- *Quiet Moments* (Voyager V-7101) RIS, NAR
- *Solo Flight* (Voyager V-7102) RIS, NAR
Solo piano tinklings; very New Agey.

JOEL ANDREWS

- *Violet Joy* (Vital Body C-9515) VB. Pulls out every cliché in the harp manual. Still, it should appeal to fans of Vollenweider.

ROBBIE BASHO

- *Art of the Acoustic Steel String Guitar* (Lost Lake Arts LLA-83) WH
- *Best of Basho, Vol. 1* (REP Master Series REP-1001) VB
- *Twilight Peaks* (Vital Body/The Art of Relaxation) VB
- *Visions of the Country* (Third Ear 2013) VB

With his fusion of American folk, Near Eastern, North Indian, and classical guitar music, Basho has been an original voice for over twenty years. The first of these recordings is an excellent collection of guitar solos. *Best of Basho* is good, but it's more a set of live or unreleased performances from the 60s than a real "best of" album. On *Best Of* and *Visions*, Basho indulges in a bit of singing which is strictly for his very loyal fans.

BLAIR & BERG

- *Happy Medium* (Binney 454-442; Binney Records, 386A Great Road, Suite 1, Acton MA 01720). Blair is Jeffrey B. Young; Berg is John Eisenberg; both are acoustic guitarists. Their album incorporates classical and jazz elements in a nice set of duets. Classy performances and reasonably good sound.

STEVEN BROWN

- *Solo Piano Music* (Crepuscule 8405) NMDS. Part of Tuxedomoon and collaborator with Benjamin Lew (see Chapter 2), Brown is joined by Blaine Reininger on violin. So it's not solo piano after all. Brooding music, only average production.

BRUCE COCKBURN

- *"Water into Wine"* from the LP *In the Falling Dark* (Island ILTN-9463). 1976 album from a Canadian folksinger and cult figure. (The name's pronounced Coe'-burn.) This piece is a guitar instrumental, brilliantly done.

BILL CONNORS

- *Swimming with a Hole in My Body* (ECM 1158) ECM. What's an ECM record doing here? Connors's beautiful brand of guitar Impressionism fits right in. It is music of elegance and substance, played on acoustic guitar by one of that instrument's most underrated talents.

SCOTT COSSU

- *Wind Dance* (Wind. H. 1016) WH. Produced by Winston, Cossu's album of piano works also includes Alex de Grassi's guitar on one work, along with some percussion. Has a strangely Caribbean feeling at times.
- *Islands* (Wind. H. 1033) WH. A large ensemble comes and goes on this release. The smaller groups (solos, duets) are generally much better than the large pieces.

SCOTT COSSU AND EUGENE FRIESEN

- *Reunion* (Wind. H. WH-1049) WH. Piano and cello, of course, but also some violin, English horn, guitar, and percussion. Friesen's cello has a warm, singing tone, and these autumnal, contemplative works sound like a kind of nonclassical chamber music.

- *Country* (Original Soundtrack) (various artists/ Wind. H. 1039) WH. Charles Gross wrote most of the music, but the performers are all members of the Windham Hill crew. Anger and Marshall, George Winston, Mark Isham, and others lend their talents, and the album, despite some obvious background music, has a number of fine excerpts.

GEORGE CROMARTY

- *Wind in the Heather* (Dancing Cat 3001) WH. From G. Winston's own division of Windham Hill, this album of solo guitar is about what you'd expect.

MALCOLM DALGLISH

- *Jogging the Memory* (Wind. H. 1046) WH. Solo hammer dulcimer, except for "Rivulets," where an almost Reichlike pattern of overdubbed dulcimers, amplified or processed somehow, is set up. "Bell Pump" uses prepared strings; the rest of the album has a more traditional dulcimer sound. A nice change from the usual solo guitars, pianos, and harps. (See Chapter 8.)

HAROLD DANKO
- *Ink and Water* (Sunnyside 1008) NMDS. Solo piano works, spontaneously improvised on and inside a piano; a far cry from the complacent prettiness of many such records. Danko tries to, and often succeeds in, creating a musical equivalent to *suibokuga,* the spontaneous brush painting/calligraphy of Japan. Sometimes icy, or harsh, or contemplative, this album is not for all tastes, but it deserves to be heard.

GINO D'AURI
- *Passion Play* (Sonic Atmospheres 103; compact disc 303) SON, NAR. "Spatially enhanced flamenco guitar channeled via electro-crystals thru [sic] deep digital reverb into the spaciousness of a thousand and one reflections." Excuse me? Well, there's some decent flamenco guitar here—D'Auri has a well-developed technique—and if you don't mind the artificial echo effects, you might like this album.

ALEX DE GRASSI
- *Slow Circle* (Wind. H. 1009) WH
- *Turning: Turning Back* (Wind. H. 1004) WH
- *Clockwork* (Wind. H. 1018) WH
- *Southern Exposure* (Wind. H. 1030) WH
De Grassi's guitar wizardry is well known to fans of that instrument. On *Clockwork* it is less obvious because of the other instruments used, but on all of his recordings, he subordinates technique to establishing and maintaining a mood.

LAR DUGGAN
- *From "The Lake Studies"* (Philo 9002) PHI, ROU. "The Lake Studies" are a set of solo piano works, excerpts of which are played here. Very slow and atmospheric music.

DAVID FLIPPO
- *New Age Variations* (Inner Light IL-1001) IMP, FOR, ROU
- *Winter Sketches* (Inner Light IL-1003) IMP, FOR, ROU
Solo piano from a classically trained composer. The second album is easily the better of the two, despite being derivative of Debussy.

PAUL GREAVER
- *Returning* (Global Pacific GP-305) GP. One or two good works for guitar, one with tabla accompaniment. The rest are overly sweet and fluffy.

SYLVAN GREY
- *Ice Flowers Melting* (For., no. #) FOR, NAR. Music for kantele, the Finnish folk harp. Delicate original works, melodic and appealing.

DANIEL HECHT
- *Willow* (Wind. H. 1013) WH. Music for six- and twelve-string guitars in a style typical of early Windham Hill albums.

MICHAEL HEDGES
- *Breakfast in the Field* (Wind. H. 1017) WH
- *Aerial Boundaries* (Wind. H. 1032) WH
Hedges, like Stanley Jordan (see Part One) and a handful of others, has developed a keyboard-style approach to the guitar. This incredible virtuosity is always subordinate to his engaging music. His more balanced second album includes a version of Neil Young's "After the Gold Rush," with Michael Manring on bass, and a bit of *musique concrète* called "Spare Change," in which Hedges's guitar sounds are put on tape and manipulated in various unusual ways. Beware of his third album, *Watching my life go by:* It is a collection of songs, with Hedges doing the vocals. Unfortunately, his singing is not as advanced as his guitar technique.

EDDIE JOBSON
- *"The Dark Room" "Disturbance in Vienna,"* and *"Ballooning over Texas,"* from the LP/CD *Piano One* (Private Music 1401) PRI. Effective solo piano music, almost Romantic in tone. Beautiful sound from a Bösendorfer grand piano.

ALEX JONES AND DOUG CUTLER
- *Kali's Dream* (Alex Jones X-5) VB, NAR. "Unique piano improvisations" written by Jones and played by Cutler. How you "write" improvs they don't explain; what makes them "unique" is also a mystery. But it is a pleasant cross between the Windham Hill sound and the quasi-Eastern sound of New Age music. Cassette only, which means less brilliant sound.

MICHAEL JONES
- *Pianoscapes* (Narada 1001) NAR
- *Seascapes* (Narada 1003) NAR
- *Sunscapes* (Narada 1009) NAR
Jones is a Canadian pianist whose classical training colors his work and gives it a sound that's subtly different from most other solo piano albums. *Pianoscapes* was originally a two-LP set; it's been compressed to one album without the loss of too much significant material. All three albums are certainly a step above the pack. See Lanz and Jones, below.

GEORGIA KELLY
- *Seapeace* (Heru 101) HOS, NAR
- *Birds of Paradise* (Heru 103) VB, NAR
Kelly's harp music has become quite popular. Rather than trying to do something about the harp's image as a purveyor of airy, tinkling tunes, Kelly has taken that as a given and has worked at making gentle solos that need not put you to sleep.

Definitely background music, though. Tony Selvage, electric violin, on the first recording; Richard Hardy, flute, on the second. See Lloyd and Kelly, below.

MITCHELL KORN
- *The Natural Sciences* (OBM-101; OBM Network, 88 University Place, 4th Floor, New York, NY 10003). Korn plays solo twelve-string acoustic guitar. He has developed a tricky fingering technique wherein he plucks only one of each pair of strings, letting the other vibrate sympathetically. This very Central Asian technique is combined with some agreeable music based on American blues and Western classical styles.

LEO KOTTKE
- *Six and Twelve String Guitar* (Takoma C-1024)
- *Mudlark* (Cap. ST-682)
- *Greenhouse* (Cap. ST-11000)
- *My Feet Are Smiling* (Cap. ST-611164)
- *Leo Kottke* (Chrysalis CHR-1106)
- *Burnt Lips* (Chrysalis CHR-1191)
- *Balance* (Chrysalis CHR-1234)
- *Live in Europe* (Chrysalis CHR-1284)
- *Guitar Music* (Chrysalis CHR-1328)
- *A Shout toward Noon* (Private 1701) PRI

Kottke, along with John Fahey and Robbie Basho, must be considered one of the precursors of the Windham Hill sound. A self-taught guitarist, he has been making records since the late 60s, and is one of the two or three undisputed masters of the twelve-string guitar, pulling off runs of harmonics with no apparent effort, alternating plucked and slide guitar passages, etc. Kottke's finest pieces are his instrumentals—a few of these recordings have some vocals, which can be a distraction. *Guitar Music* (1981) is a compendium of guitar techniques; *My Feet Are Smiling* (1972) and *Burnt Lips* (1978) are old favorites, too. The live album has a little singing, and some terrible miking problems. The eponymously titled 1976 collection confounds the purists by using amplification and a back-up band, something Kottke does on occasion elsewhere. His most recent LP makes sparing use of synthesizer or cello, but leaves the guitar in its natural state; it's one of his best albums in years.

KRAMER/EVENSON/VERDEAUX
- *Alive Tree-O* (Soundings of the Planet). Pasteurized music-flavored product. New Age–type trio (tree-o/trio, get it?) music for flute, cello, and piano or organ. Actually, you could probably do worse, but these fellows ought to know better.

ALAIN KREMSKI
- *Megalithes I: Carnac, porte du temps* (Auvidis AV 4720). Fragile, mysterious piano solos, inspired by the ancient civilization that erected the dolmens in Europe. Kremski has also recorded Gurdjieff/de Hartmann music (Chapter 5) and some Asian-derived works (see Chapter 6).

JOACHIM KUHN
- *"New Feeling" "Housewife Song,"* from the LP/CD *Piano One* (Private 1401) PRI. Solo piano; not nearly as good as the Jobson and Sakamoto contributions to this recording (listed under these artists' names).

DAVID LANZ
- *Heartsounds* (Narada 1003) NAR
- *Nightfall* (Narada 1006) NAR
Lanz, both pianist and composer, is not bad at either, without being really distinctive.

DAVID LANZ AND MICHAEL JONES
- *Winter Solstice* (Narada 1008) NAR. Jones does "Good King Wenceslas" and "Carol of the Bells." Lanz does "What Child Is This" and you-know-who's *Canon in D*. Extended improvs appropriate for the Christmas season.

GAIL LAUGHTON
- *Harps of the Ancient Temples* (Laurel 111) HOS. 1969 release, reissued in 1979. Solo harp, and very typical of this genre.

GABRIEL LEE
- *Seasons* (Narada 1002) NAR
- *Impressions* (Narada 1005) NAR
Although his name is barely mentioned in the album notes, Don Slepian helped produce and perform these records of guitar music with subtle electronics. Lee may or may not be a good guitarist—it's hard to tell in this music—but he's as good as he needs to be. Slepian's electronics cunningly imitate the sounds of acoustic instruments and blend in quite nicely. Slow, atmospheric stuff. (See Chapter 6.)

CHARLES LLOYD AND GEORGIA KELLY
- *Big Sur Tapestry* (Pacific Arts 7-139). It's not weighty, profound music, but it's well played, well produced, and not entirely mindless. Lloyd plays flute, Kelly harp. May be out of print.

PAUL LLOYD-WARNER
- *The Miracle of Dolphins* (Miracle of Dolphins Music 201) NAR, FOR. Liquid piano solos combining equal parts of Debussy and New Age. The most interesting of his solo works (but also see Kindler/Lloyd-Warner in Chapter 3).

MICHAEL MANRING
- *Unusual Weather* (Wind. H. WH-1044) WH. Although a Windham Hill release, this is not an acoustic outing. Manring plays several electric basses (some in different tunings) and uses English horn, percussion, keyboards, and other instru-

ments to fill out the sound. The mood is reminiscent of Pat Metheny's mellower work, but the style is Manring's own, and should hold the attention of listeners who never thought they'd care for a "bass album."

ALLAUDIN WILLIAM MATHIEU
- *Streaming Wisdom* (Cold Mountain 008) NMDS
- *In the Wind* (Cold Mountain 009) NMDS
- *Second Nature* (Vital Body/The Art of Relaxation) VB
- *Listening to Evening* (Sono Gaia LP-137) NAR
Piano, prepared piano, and double-speed piano, and infrequent wordless vocals with some pieces in just intonation. Elements of ethnic music, Minimalism, and jazz are present, but the overall mood is certainly in keeping with this part of the chapter: In fact, one of Mathieu's works appears on the *Windham Hill Piano Sampler.* The last release, for unaltered piano, is somewhat prettified; but the first three are solid, enchanting collections.

WALL MATTHEWS
- *Solo Piano and Guitar* (Clean Cuts CC-708) CC, ROU. Aside from the Beatles' "Across the Universe," this album consists of original works, mostly for piano, though Matthews is a more than competent guitarist, too. For the most part, a commendable record.

RICHARD PIERCE MILNER
- *composer/pianist* (Four Winds RM-001L) NAR. Piano solos by a composer who has managed to keep his own voice, and who is equally adept at bouncy piano boogies and slow, expansive melodies.

HERB MOORE
- *Hinterlands* (Melodius-Sync MSS-1001) NAR. Guitar, piano, and scrapophone ("an ever changing percussion instrument made from scrap materials or found objects"). Copies the Windham Hill sound, but does so more successfully than most. One of the best independently produced albums in this style.

EITHNE NI BHRAONAIN
- *"An Ghaoth O'n Grian (Solar Wind)"* and *"Miss Clare Remembers"* (from the audio-cassette magazine *Touch*) NMDS. Two ravishing piano works, one with synthesizer accompaniment. Ni Bhraonain's name is pronounced Enya Nee Vree-noyne. For obvious reasons, she now uses the name Enya professionally. Based in Dublin, she's currently working on a record for the BBC; if these works are any indication, it will be one worth waiting for.

DAVID ONDERDONK
- *Close Call* (Quaver Q-1005) NAR. Pensive solos for guitar. Fred Simon adds synthesizer on two works.

ONE ALTERNATIVE
- *Greenlawn* (AC-10) NMDS. One oboe/English horn, two classical guitars. Hints of Oregon and Stein and Walder, but overall a very good recording.

ANTHONY PHILLIPS
- *The Geese and the Ghost* (PVC 8905) JEM
- *Private Parts and Pieces: Vol.1* (PVC 7905) JEM
  - *Vol.2/Back to the Pavilion* (PVC 7913) JEM
  - *Vol.3/Antiques* (PVC 8908) JEM
  - *Vol.4/A Catch at the Tables* (PVC 8919) JEM
  - *Vol.5/Twelve* (PVC 8926) JEM
  - *Vol.6/Ivory Moon* (PVC 8946) JEM
Despite occasional electronics, Phillips's music is largely acoustic. He plays guitars of many shapes and sizes, as well as piano, and sings once or twice on the early discs. *The Geese and the Ghost* has a large ensemble, including some orchestral and ancient instruments. *Antiques* is a set of guitar duos with Enrique Berro García. All the rest are solos. Phillips's music often has a wistful, longing quality, but can also be spry and cheerful.

JUDITH PINTAR
- *Secrets from the Stone* (Sono Gaia LP-123) NAR. Solo Celtic harp, without any traditional music. Good album, though whether it's good enough to stick out in a crowd is another matter.

POPOL VUH
- *"Spirit of Peace"* from the two-LP set *In the Gardens of Pharao/Aguirre* (CH CEL-008/009) CH. Florian Fricke, Popol Vuh's leader and pianist, recorded a side of solo improvisations to conclude this album. Like his group pieces, these have a curiously timeless quality.

CHRIS PROCTOR
- *The Delicate Dance* (Fly. F. FF-357) FF. Solo guitar, much like what you'd expect from the Windham Hill gang if they had roots in the folk music of the British Isles as well as American folk and blues. Includes variations on a Bach theme and some Scottish jigs as well as original works.

DAVID QUALEY
- *Soliloquy* (Wind. H. 1011) WH. One less-commonly heard WH album, but a good one. Qualey's solos have a strong classical sound and deserve a wider audience.

PRESTON REED
- *Pointing Up* (Fly. F. FF-224) FF
- *Playing by Ear* (Fly. F. FF-324) FF
American folksy guitar, in the style of Kottke or Fahey.

RAPHAEL RUDD
- *Reflections* (Globe G-1000). Modal, colorful improvs for piano.

RYUICHI SAKAMOTO
- *"Merry Christmas Mr. Lawrence"* and *"Germination"* from the LP/CD *Piano One* (Private 1401) PRI. Although Sakamoto is known mostly for his electronic music, these are mature piano pieces, both thoughtful and attractive.

DAVID SALMINEN
- *From the Silence* (no label or #) VB. A generous (ninety minutes) cassette of ingratiating, flowing piano improvs. Sound quality could be better.

TORKOM SARAYDARIAN
- *Temple Dances, Vol. 1* (Hari Seldon, piano/Padme 101) NAR. Eastern-tinged piano music, apparently trying to capture the spirit of Gurdjieff/de Hartmann—an attempt that does not succeed.

STEVEN SCHOENBERG
- *Pianoworks* (Quabbin 1001) NAR
- *Three Days in May* (Quabbin 1002) NAR
Along with the by-now familiar piano impressions, Schoenberg adds elements of blues, classical, and even ragtime. Both albums are way above the level of most independent releases in this field.

BOLA SETE
- *Ocean* (Lost Lake Arts LLA-82) WH
- *Jungle Suite* (Dancing Cat 3005) WH
An individual guitar stylist from Brazil. Vaguely Latin, very dreamy tone poems for steel-string guitar. George Winston's music contains more than a few echoes of Sete's work.

MARCIA SHERMAN
- *Cycles* (Inner City 102) NAR. Harp, wind-harp, and bells. Simple music, nicely recorded.

BARRY SHULMAN AND GREGORY JAMES
- *Tibet* (Rogue 1277) NMDS. Duets for woodwinds and guitar. With titles like "Calcutta" and "Nepal," you'd expect to hear echoes of Central Asia here. (And you do.) You also get a jazzier version of the Windham Hill sound.

BOB SIEBERT
- *Six Lyric Pieces* (Aerial 482) NMDS. Mostly piano, but the album has a lovely, lyrical work for thumb piano as well called "Inside the Music Box."

JORDAN DE LA SIERRA
- *Gymnosphere/Song of the Rose* (Unity UR-701) NAR. Haunting, hypnotic music for retuned, spatially enhanced piano. Unfortunately, most of the "spatial enhancement" (i.e., artificial echo) is added *after* the actual performance, and the resulting sound is simply atrocious. This music deserves better; wait for the Sono Gaia/Narada reissue, remixed and due shortly.

IRA STEIN AND RUSSELL WALDER
- *Elements* (Wind. H. 1020) WH. Oboe and piano. Their studies with Oregon at the Naropa Institute strongly color the music. Fluid melodies over sweeping piano, echoing Oregon's quieter moments.
- *Transit* (Wind. H. 1042) WH. Adds synthesizer, electronic percussion, some wordless voices. Much more individual sound here, and a much wider array of moods.

LIZ STORY
- *Solid Colors* (Wind. H. 1023) WH
- *Unaccountable Effect* (Wind. H. 1034) WH
Piano solos in a personal style that complements this label's other pianists without being at all derivative. Mark Isham adds synthesizer to the title track of the second album; otherwise it's all Story.

TIM STORY
- *Untitled* (Uniton 224) NAR
- *In Another Country* (Uniton 009) NAR
Story has one solo piano piece on the Windham Hill label (see their Piano Sampler, below), but these other recordings could certainly pass for WH discs. Short keyboard vignettes with some electronics. *In Another Country* is the better of the two.

JOHN THEMIS
- *Atmospheric Conditions* (Landscape NAGE-1) NAR, JEM. Themis makes no bones about it: this is a New Age record. It's not all solo, nor is it all acoustic. And frankly, it may not fit the common description of New Age either. Tepid arrangements and some half-hearted attempts at jazz mar what is otherwise a startlingly virtuosic album. A solo disc by a guitarist of Themis's proficiency might be just what New Age needs.

ERIC TINGSTAD
- *On the Links* (Cheshire CT-101) NAR. Solo guitar; a high level of playing and musicality throughout.
- *Urban Guitar* (Cheshire CT-102) NAR. Another album of friendly, appealing guitar pieces; Tingstad has a knack for catchy tunes.

RICK WAKEMAN
- *Country Airs* (Landscape NAGE-10) NAR, JEM. Rock fans will remember Wakeman as the wild keyboard whiz who played with Yes and early David Bowie, and put out several solo electronic albums. This recording sounds like the result of a complete personality change: It's a delicate, rustic collection of piano solos, combining the reflective sounds of New Age with an occasional glance toward the English folk song tradition. Pure fluff, but somehow interesting because of where it comes from.

KIT WALKER

- *Wind Follows the Tiger* (For. FOR-014) FOR. Competent solo piano. Again one wonders about the wisdom of releasing cassettes of solo piano music when the competition is available on LP and CD, both of which are vastly superior in sound reproduction.

ERIC WATSON

- *"Puppet Flower"* from the LP/CD *Piano One* (Private 1401) PRI. Not at the level of the Sakamoto or Jobson contributions.

WINDHAM HILL ARTISTS

- *An Evening with Windham Hill Live* (Wind. H. 1026) WH. Hedges, de Grassi, Liz Story, Ackerman, and Winston appear alone and in various combinations. Winston does a version of John McLaughlin's "Lotus Feet" and everyone plays live versions of material from their studio albums.
- *The Windham Hill Piano Sampler* (Wind. H. 1040) WH. A response to the frustration of not being able to record all the talented musicians the label comes in contact with. Michael Harrison, a pupil of La Monte Young, has a piece here; so do Cyrille Verdeaux, Tim Story, Philip Aaberg (the only one to subsequently have a solo album on the label), Allaudin Mathieu, and several others.
- *Windham Hill Records Sampler '82* (Wind. H. 1024) WH
  - *'84* (Wind. H. 1035) WH
  - *'86* (Wind. H. 1048) WH

Good money-saving idea for people who want to hear representative works without buying a dozen albums.

- *A Winter's Solstice* (Wind. H. 1045) WH. Some Christmas music and some works that just have a wintry feel to them. Strong performances by David Qualey, Oskay and O Domhnaill, Anger and Marshall, Mark Isham, and several others.

STEVEN WINFIELD

- *Forest Flower* (Sono Gaia 118) NAR. Flute, sax, chimes, with some bird noises and piano. Tranquil, ambient music.

GEORGE WINSTON

- *Ballads and Blues 1972* (Lost Lake Arts LL-81) WH
- *Autumn* (Wind. H. 1012) WH
- *Winter into Spring* (Wind. H. 1019) WH
- *December* (Wind. H. 1025) WH

It's amazing that Winston, with relatively little marketing in the usual areas, has sold so many albums. It's amazing that even with the current deluge of solo piano albums, he manages to remain the standard that the others are judged against (whether that's fair or not). But most amazing is the fact that his albums don't even show how good a musician Winston is. His recorded music is suffering right now from overexposure, but his concerts are always fresh and invigorating.

MICHAEL ZENTNER

- *"Tears and Spheres"* from the LP *Present Time* (Red MZ-One) NMDS. Lovely duet for violin and harp, from an album of jazz-rock fusion.

10
THE OLDEST AND NEWEST INSTRUMENTS

When the human being sings he lends expression to the great wise ways in which the world was made.
Rudolf Steiner

Swans sing before they die—'twere no bad thing
Did certain persons die before they sing.
Samuel Taylor Coleridge

Anyone who remembers Yma Sumac can attest to the validity of one of the quotes at the head of this chapter. *Which* one is strictly a matter of taste. Personally, I found her swooping and caterwauling endlessly, if unintentionally, amusing, though in all fairness it was actually those incredible Mariachi-Music-from-Hell arrangements that did her albums in. But it wasn't the music, it was her voice that made Sumac's career. What an instrument she was blessed with—yet divine providence saw to it that the self-proclaimed "descendant of Inca Kings," with her outlandish and (mercifully) one-of-a-kind vocal technique, was the exception rather than the rule.

In recent years, the rush to use the latest electronic gadgetry or the strangest ethnic instruments has opened the door to all manner of unusual sounds. (Even Sumac might be a new-music favorite if she recorded today.) But with ethnic and electronic instruments now commonplace, some of the musicians in this chapter have looked elsewhere, designing and constructing new or adapted instruments to produce previously unobtainable tone colors. Others have taken another look at the oldest instrument—the voice, which is also responsible for some of the newest sounds being made today. So in a figurative sense, at least, the human voice, which we'll examine first, can be considered just as "new" an instrument as the musical inventions we'll discuss later.

Extending the Voice

In general, the human voice has for many years been the instrument whose boundaries have been least explored. "Extended techniques" have been developed for flutes, clarinets, violins, percussion, even synthesizers, which enable performers to wring unusual and unexpected sounds from their instruments. Flutists have been experimenting with key clicks; violinists used slack bows and two-handed pizzicatos; pianists have attacked virtually every portion of their instruments in a relentless search for new sounds—and singers continued to sing the way they had for centuries. Oh, they could sing higher, or deeper, and "special effects" like falsetto or *Sprechgesang* (the "speech-song" used in Schoenberg's *Pierrot Lunaire,* for example) were explored, but serious investigation of some of the more unorthodox sounds that could be made with the voice is a recent phenomenon in Western music.

The artists in this part of the chapter often use the voice as an instrument in itself rather than simply as the carrier of a text. Much of this music features wordless vocals, either in their natural form or altered in various ways. Elements of Minimalism, electronic music, and ethnic music are often involved, but the compositions we'll examine go beyond any simple combination of styles.

Ironically, it was the evolution of electronic music and *musique concrète* in the 1950s that helped again focus attention on the voice as a source of sound. We have already mentioned Karlheinz Stockhausen's *Gesang der Jünglinge,* his 1956 work that convincingly demonstrates the expressive possibilities of using the voice in an unusual way. Just two years later, Italian composer Luciano Berio completed his *Omaggio a Joyce,* the first of a series of vocal works. *Omaggio a Joyce* was an electronic piece built up from fragments of James Joyce's *Ulysses* read in three languages, and it, too, dealt with the sonic potential of placing the human voice in a new setting.

Berio was married for many years to American soprano Cathy Berberian, a gifted vocalist who became the unparalleled interpreter of his music, and with her he explored the outer reaches of vocal technique. In *Circles* (1960) and *Epifanie* (1961), Berio began to write for the voice in its natural form, choosing texts not only for their literal meaning but for their phonetic sounds and rhythms as well. Since then much of his music has been vocally based. Although, like Stockhausen, his musical idiom places him at the forefront of the postwar classical avant-garde, he is mentioned here because any survey of the treatment of the voice in new-music circles must take into account Berio's historical contributions to this area.

Extended vocal techniques began to appear more frequently in the 1960s, as composers like Pauline Oliveros, Alvin Lucier, and John Cage began experimenting with different ways of using and recording the human voice. Oliveros composed a piece in the mid-60s called *Sound Patterns* that included a remarkable array of vocal sounds: Besides conventional singing, whispers, tongue clicks and lip pops were required. The Canadian composer Harry Somers drew on folk techniques in his *Five Songs of the Newfoundland Outports* (1968). Like Gaelic mouth music (see page 171), the folk style of Newfoundland called on singers to imitate instrumental sounds when, as often happened, the instruments themselves were unavailable. Somers employed several of these effects in this concert piece.

During the 1970s, the range of vocal sounds was pushed to extremes by such artists as Meredith Monk, Joan LaBarbara, and David Hykes and his Harmonic Choir. One of the most innovative and durable vocalists producing new music today, Meredith Monk has been exploring the possibilities of the human voice since her

1966 work *16 Millimeter Earrings* for voice and guitar. During the past twenty or more years, she has evolved a number of extended techniques for her own voice and, going one step further, has tried in her ensemble works to create a glossary of techniques that *any* voice, not just hers, can use. Her handling of glottal clicks, whistles, childlike streams of nonsense syllables, and other vocal noises makes for pieces that are completely unlike conventional vocal music. And when she accompanies her vocal writing with simple, melodic instrumental lines, the results are exciting—and surprisingly beautiful.

Monk, a versatile artist, is an award-winning filmmaker as well as a composer, performer, and choreographer. In at least one respect, her work in film has affected her approach to music: Monk's pieces are often narrative, with the vocal parts suggesting a story or a sequence of settings or emotions. In those works with a definite storyline, like her 1976 opera *Quarry,* the actual text is spoken; the sung portions are comprised of the extended vocal techniques. "I've always been interested in the voice as a kind of language for feeling and texture and color," she explains. "I feel the voice has a much more intrinsic emotional quality than instruments. In a way, it's abstract because I don't use lyrics, but I try never to forget that it's a *human* instrument."

Monk's first recording, *Key* (1971), didn't attract a lot of notice, but it has all the earmarks of later Monk albums: a huge assortment of growls, shrieks, and glides —some humorous, others almost childishly innocent. The accompaniment is simple and repetitive, featuring exotic musical forces like electric organ, Jew's-harp, and bits of percussion played by Oregon's Collin Walcott. Walcott produced the album and eventually appeared on three other Monk recordings.

Because of her pared-down instrumental music, Monk was at first thought to be associated with the emerging Minimalist movement. Fortunately, this misconception didn't last as long as it might have. For one thing, it soon became evident that the simplicity of the accompaniment was intended as a foil for the complexity of the vocal line. In 1975's "Gotham Lullaby," from the *Dolmen Music* album, a delicate pattern of notes on the piano repeats throughout the work, while Monk's voice warbles and chatters through its part. Each shift in technique seems to change the mood of the piece, now bittersweet, now mischievous; Monk believes it's almost impossible for the voice *not* to evoke some kind of emotion: "The voice is a very deep and powerful force. It can really get to emotions we don't even have words for, because it gets in between the cracks of the emotions we do have words for."

At about the time Meredith Monk was building her reputation and her musical vocabulary, two other experimental vocalists, Joan LaBarbara and Jay Clayton, began to make their voices heard. Both LaBarbara and Clayton were aligned with Minimalism early in their careers: LaBarbara appeared on the first Philip Glass Ensemble recordings, and Jay Clayton began a long stint as a vocalist with Steve Reich and Musicians in 1971's *Drumming.* But each soon began working on advanced techniques along the lines of those used by Monk or the performers of Oliveros's *Sound Patterns.* Jay Clayton has worked with such avant-garde composers as John Cage, Kirk Nurock, and Muhal Richard Abrams. Her only solo album, *All Out* (1981), displays a variety of musical interests: In particular, her original composition "7/8 Thing" shows the lyrical melodic potential of her voice, even if the techniques involved are not particularly "extended."

Joan LaBarbara has made a number of solo albums, though she, too, has worked with John Cage, the two Mortons (Subotnick and Feldman), and other avant-garde figures. In terms of actual technique, she is perhaps the most phenomenally talented and accomplished vocalist of her generation. Like Monk, LaBarbara employs a wide array of hums, howls, and flutters. She has also experimented with circular singing (i.e., singing while inhaling as well as exhaling); multiphonics (the production of two or more notes simultaneously); and a rasping, clicking technique that involves singing from the back of the throat with the throat muscles completely relaxed. She also uses electronic processing, though infrequently and very subtly.

LaBarbara's musical style, though, is quite different from that of Meredith Monk as it involves using the voice in a completely abstract manner. LaBarbara likens her piece "Twelvesong," in which she layers twelve recordings of her voice on top of one another, to a painter adding splashes of color to a canvas. Whereas Monk exploits the human qualities inherent in the voice, LaBarbara seems to revel in making it sound as instrumental as possible.

The exploration of the potential of the human voice raises the same questions as did the process music discussed in Chapter 3: The idea of singing while inhaling might be a fascinating concept, but if it didn't have any real musical value it wouldn't remain fascinating for very long. In 1977, Meredith Monk completed a set of solo vocal works called *Songs from the Hill.* Released on a 1979 album, this cycle of ten pieces was a showcase of new vocal resources. But *Songs from the Hill* was no mere glossary of peculiar techniques; each piece made sense musically, from the curious buzzing sound of "Insect" (a sort of latter-day *Flight of the Bumblebee*) to the haunted landscape of "Prairie Ghost." "How many different sounds I can make is only a means to an end," says Monk. "For some others, that might have been the end, in terms of exploring what the voice can do. I'll keep trying to stretch the voice and see what it can do, but for me, it's only an expressive device."

Throughout her career, Monk has undertaken multimedia projects that attempt to break down the boundaries between music, film, and choreography. During the 60s, when the musical avant-garde was threatening to turn itself into a three-ring circus of "happenings" and so-called "artistic statements," Monk got into the act with works that involved troops of volunteers spilling out of the performance space and into the surrounding city. Bemused audience members sometimes had to scramble for public transportation to keep up with the piece. Since then, however, her large-scale works have stayed in one place, even if they've become no less eccentric. The opera *Quarry* is cast for actors who also sing and dance, and a silent film directed by the composer was designed specifically for presentation during the performance.

Monk followed a similar path in *Recent Ruins* (1979), *Turtle Dreams* (1983), and *The Games* (1983). In one respect, *The Games* is a typical Monk composition: It calls for sixteen voices and an assortment of musical oddities, including the Flemish bagpipe, Chinese horn, and rauschpfeife (a Renaissance reed instrument). However, its grim sci-fi setting, with its themes of fascism and nuclear destruction, is atypical, the product of Monk's collaborator, the author and director Ping Chong. In many ways, *Recent Ruins,* with its combination of music and film, is one of Monk's most impressive and characteristic productions. Its opening is derived from her *Dolmen Music,* an inventive suite for six voices with occasional cello or percussion released on an album in 1981.

Even outside of its context in *Recent Ruins,* Monk's *Dolmen Music* is one of her most effective, evocative works. A dolmen is a large standing stone, often found in table-shaped groups of three; they're scattered throughout England and Brittany, Stonehenge being the most famous example. It was the dolmens of Brittany that inspired Monk for this work: "We were driving through the fields and we came upon these incredible rock formations. They had so much energy, I felt like I had to go inside and sing there." The music that came from that experience has a timeless quality, for as Monk explains, "It was like trying to get back to the beginnings of civilization. Seeing those dolmens, it just struck you—what people, or what people from what planet, put these things up? And I think *Dolmen Music* has that quality of ancient civilization, but it could also be from another planet. It's got that futuristic and ancient sound simultaneously."

While *Dolmen Music* has primarily an eerie, ritualistic mood, it also has moments of grandeur and whimsy. "I don't think I would ever do a piece without humor," Monk states. "I believe one can have a form that has both humor and tragedy, and the whole spectrum of emotion in one evening. But that gives people a hard time. If they're going to a tragedy, well, that's it—get the handkerchiefs out; and if they're going to a comedy, it can't have any depth." She cites *Quarry* as an example: The opera is a tragic one, but it's shot through with streaks of humor, which give the sadness a bit more of an edge.

The ambiguities that Monk explores in her music—between ancient and futuristic, between humor and pathos—color the works of another leading innovative vocalist, David Hykes. The music Hykes composes for his Harmonic Choir has its roots in both ancient Asian traditions as well as in the most ultramodern vocal techniques. And though the music usually has an ethereal, even ecstatic quality, it somehow can't avoid also sounding a little ominous at times.

There are a number of other similarities between the careers of Meredith Monk and David Hykes. Like Monk, Hykes has been a filmmaker, a career that brought him to New York in 1974. There he heard the music of La Monte Young, whose use of long, sustained tones and natural harmonics pointed to the direction that Hykes's own development would follow. And like Monk, Hykes sees his music as more than just an abstract exercise in vocal legerdemain: "I feel that Harmonic Music is among the most hopeful fields of musical inquiry today. It includes a deep appreciation of the ancient, sacred values of music, and completely new possibilities, both for musical form and for new depths of listening."

A "new depth of listening" is certainly the key to approaching any kind of new music, but it's especially critical for composers who, like David Hykes, have begun exploring the subtle nuances of a single tone. This notion began with La Monte Young's experiments with sustained drones in the 60s, and can be found today in the instrumental works of Yoshi Wada, Phill Niblock, and others. The music of the

Harmonic Choir is based on Hykes's development with his colleagues of a musical practice he calls Harmonic Chant or singing. Simply stated, Hykes and the other members of his choir can sing two notes at the same time. Like anyone else, they sing a basic note, or "fundamental," but they can also make one of the component overtones of that note audible as well.

Tibetan Buddhist monks and Mongolian *hoomi* ("throat") singers have used this method for centuries, but here in the West, it's considered a recent and radical development. As we saw in Chapter 4, La Monte Young's *Well-Tuned Piano* was able to produce a similar array of harmonics or overtones, but only after being tuned to the just intonation system, which is based on the way notes line themselves up in nature, rather than to the usual Western equal-tempered scale. The voice, however, is naturally adaptable to any kind of tuning; it is at least as easy to sing in just intonation as it is in equal temperament. Meredith Monk uses simple overtone singing in one of her *Songs from the Hill,* and Joan LaBarbara uses it in several works, but the exploration of multiphonics, the different overtones that can be isolated from one basic note, has become the trademark of the Harmonic Choir.

Hykes first began working with this unusual vocal style in 1974, when he heard recordings of Tibetan and Mongolian singing. Although he was struck by the purely technical aspects of these chants, he was also taken with the intention behind the music, which implied a kind of discipline or ritual. "I felt that that kind of music embodies values which we need and have forgotten." Also in 1974, Hykes premiered a film called *Moving Parts* at New York's Whitney Museum. For the soundtrack, he had wanted what he termed a "refracted or prismatic voice." He discovered that the Harmonizer, a recently developed electronic special-effects device, would allow him to produce an unearthly chorus of voices using only one voice on a single track of recording.

Not satisfied with electronic manipulations, however, Hykes set about trying to both reproduce and extend the vocal techniques of the Tibetan and Mongolian sacred chants. He coined the term *Harmonic Music* to describe his work: "I chose the term to encompass both the idea of our musical work with all the implications of the harmonic series, *and* the idea that music can help us relate different levels of experience in ourselves. That is, 'harmonic' in the sense of *harmonious relationship.*"

In 1975, Hykes formed the Harmonic Choir with five other vocalists. Although its first album wasn't released until 1983, the Choir recorded several private cassettes and performed live in various locations. The nature of the singing demanded a resonant space to help the high harmonics ring out clearly, so the Choir began performing in churches and abbeys, including New York's Cathedral of St. John the Divine, an acoustically magnificent building that has long been a favorite of musicians. Hykes's Harmonic Choir became artists-in-residence at the Cathedral in 1979 and recorded part of its 1984 album *Current Circulation* there.

The theory and techniques behind harmonic singing might seem arcane and exotic, since it is in just intonation and what initially seems like one simple tone suddenly divides into two or three different notes. In fact the principles of the harmonic series and just intonation are surprisingly simple, especially when compared to the complex, artificial tuning of the Western scale. A brief look at the harmonic series is helpful not only for understanding what David Hykes and the Harmonic Choir are doing, it also helps explain the music of such diverse artists as La Monte Young, Terry Riley, Glenn Branca, and Arnold Dreyblatt.

Despite the way we perceive it, no instrumental sound is "pure." That is to say, if you hear the note C played or sung, it is not just C that you're hearing. That note is comprised of its starting frequency, or fundamental—C, in this case —and several frequencies, known as overtones, harmonics, or partials, which combine to give the note its rich texture. (The only exceptions to this rule are simple electronic tones and those produced by the tuning fork.) These composite frequencies are organized in a fixed ratio to the fundamental; that ratio remains the same whatever the fundamental. This lineup of a fundamental and its overtones is called the harmonic series, and is described by a simple numerical series—1, 2, 3, 4, 5, etc. For example, let's say you start a series at 1 with a fundamental of low C, which measures 131 Herz. (Herz is a unit that measures the number of vibrations per second.) The next harmonic (number 2 in the harmonic series) is a note that vibrates twice as fast as 1, or 262 Herz, a two-to-one ratio. The third harmonic vibrates at 393 Herz, three times as fast as 1, or a three-to-two ratio to 2. The fourth harmonic will be 524 Herz, $\frac{4}{3}$ higher than number 3; the fifth will be 655 Herz, $\frac{5}{4}$ higher than number 4; and so on. You will notice that not only are these overtones consistently related to each other in a predictable way—overtone 16 will be $\frac{16}{15}$ higher than number 15—they are also multiples of the fundamental. If 131 Herz is number 1 of the series, number 6 will be 6×131, or 786 Herz.

This is a very neat, orderly progression. But what does it mean in terms of notes? Well, for any harmonic series, number 2 is always a note that is an exact octave above number 1. So if 1 (the fundamental) is low C, 2 is middle C. Three is always located a perfect fifth above 2—in this case, the note G. Another octave, here high C, is 4. The simple rule of thumb is: The double of any number in a harmonic series is its octave. In our example, harmonics 2, 4, 8, 16, 32, and 64 are all octaves of C. Since number 3 in this series is G, number 6 will be *its* octave, as will numbers 12, 24, and 48.

Here in the West, we have taken the octave and divided it into twelve convenient, completely equal parts. But the ratio of one note to another is not a nice rational fraction like $\frac{3}{2}$ or $\frac{8}{7}$. Instead, it's an unsightly, irrational fraction, $\sqrt[12]{2}$, which works out to an infinite number of approximately 1.059463. . . . This is an awkward way of building a tuning system, though as artifical systems go it has served quite well. But the harmonic series, and the just intonation tuning that derives from it, is organized with the elegance of basic arithmetic. Naturally, you end up with different notes in these two systems. Harmonic number 7 is $\frac{7}{6}$ higher than number 6, which is, as we've seen, an octave of G. This works out to a note that doesn't exist on a piano or guitar: It's a little lower than B-flat. As you get higher up in a harmonic series, you get more of this type of "unassigned" note. If 32 and 64 are both octaves of C, that means there are thirty-two notes between them. Since the Western scale only has twelve notes to the octave, most of those thirty-two are going to be new, unnamed notes.

The simple beauty of the harmonic series becomes apparent when you see it notated. If you feel like doing a bit of easy multiplication, you can set this up yourself. Or you can take the easy way out and trust my math.

Figure 4.
Harmonic Series of C

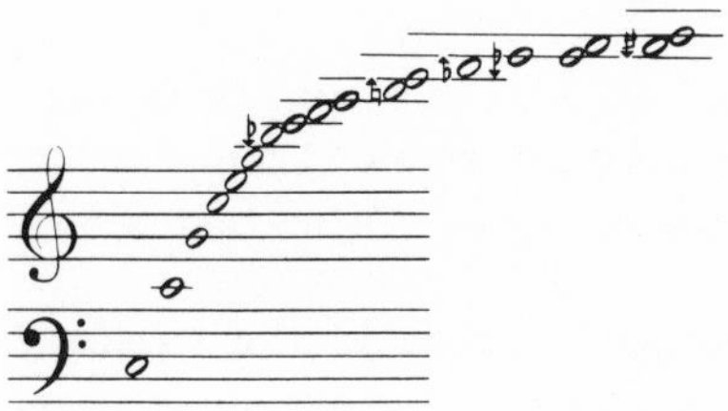

Note	Number in Harmonic Series	Frequency
D	18 (octave of 9)	2358 Hz (18 × 131)
Below C♯	17	2227 Hz (17 × 131)
C	16 (octave of 8)	2096 Hz (16 × 131)
B	15	1965 Hz (15 × 131)
Below B♭	14 (octave of 7)	1834 Hz (14 × 131)
Above A♭	13	1703 Hz (13 × 131)
G	12 (octave of 6)	1572 Hz (12 × 131)
Above F	11	4441 Hz (11 × 131)
E	10 (octave of 5)	1310 Hz (10 × 131)
D	9	1179 Hz (9 × 131)
C	8 (octave of 4)	1048 Hz (8 × 131)
Below B♭	7	917 Hz (7 × 131)
G	6 (octave of 3)	786 Hz (6 × 131)
E	5	655 Hz (5 × 131)
C	4 (octave of 2)	524 Hz (4 × 131)
G	3	393 Hz (3 × 131)
C	2 (octave of 1)	262 Hz (2 × 131)
C	1	131 Herz

This diagram covers only the first eighteen overtones of C, but as David Hykes explains, "a soloist can sing clearly up to the twentieth harmonic. But there are higher harmonics that ring out, as if they were resonances of the lower harmonics. At Bell Labs I heard harmonics up to about 10,000 cycles [or Herz] . . . of course there's sound above that, but this was a real 'note.'"

The harmonic series will eventually take you beyond the threshold of audibility. Hykes's Harmonic Choir does approach that limit, and the higher overtones begin to take on an unreal, almost electronic quality. It takes a bit of effort to remember that all their music is produced by unaltered human voices. The Harmonic Choir's acclaimed first album, *Hearing Solar Winds,* baffled and delighted listeners, many of whom insisted that there had to be a "trick to it" somewhere in the recording process.

Like the harmonic series, the means of producing audible vocal harmonics is completely natural. Speaking itself involves simply changing the overtone structure of whatever "note" at which we happen to be: Saying the vowel sound *oo* uses one set of overtones; saying *ee* uses another. In fact, taking a deep breath and singing a note from deep in your chest while slowly moving your mouth from *oo* to *ee* is a very simple way of producing harmonics.

To bring out the harmonics strongly for the sort of music created by the Harmonic Choir requires a tremendous amount of breath control. Hykes explains how the group produces overtones: "You're holding a steady note, and, changing the shape inside your mouth to be the right size 'room,' so to speak, resonating a particular overtone in that note—just like you can touch a guitar string at different nodal points [e.g., the fifth, seventh, and twelfth frets] along its length to bring out harmonics. So you divide your resonant space, which includes the chest and abdomen. And you have all these possibilities to shape that 'room' while maintaining the fundamental note with the rest of your body, because that note has to be quite stable."

With his colleagues in the Harmonic Choir, especially Timothy Hill, Hykes has developed five levels of Harmonic Chant:

■ Level one, found in Tibetan music, consists of a singer holding a steady fundamental note—"in their case a very low one," Hykes says, "which is in fact a subharmonic of a higher fundamental"—and a chosen harmonic, which continues steadily throughout the chant.

■ "Level two," Hykes continues, "you sometimes hear in passing in Western liturgical music, though I don't know if it's intentional. A simple melody is being heard or recorded in a resonant space, and you can hear, if you're listening carefully, a harmonic moving in parallel."

■ Level three is derived from the *hoomi* singing of Mongolia, in which a steady fundamental note is held while the singer picks out a moving melodic line from the note's overtone series.

■ Level four reverses the process. The harmonic is held steady while the fundamentals move beneath it. One sings a melody in the usual sense, except that a high drone accompanies it. This is accomplished by picking a melody from those notes that have the desired overtone in their harmonic series. A simple example would be singing C and its ninth overtone, D, and then singing G and its third overtone, which is also D. The effect is one of moving from C to G while holding the D constant.

■ Level five involves moving both the fundamentals *and* the overtones at the same time. "That's a mysterious place to make music from," Hykes says, because we're used to listening only to fundamentals, while this technique requires "a balanced listening which is equally able to follow the harmonic movement *and* the fundamental movement."

Like so much music that relies on unusual methods of production, Hykes's Harmonic Music seems particularly susceptible to the "gee-whiz" effect: The listener may be so impressed by the technique that the judgment of whether the music is of value is often ignored. Fortunately, Hykes seems to be aware of the problem, and like Meredith Monk, he is attempting to use extended vocal techniques as a means, not an end. "A step I wait for listeners to move beyond," he says, "is thinking that just because there are harmonics there, it's already something special. I think as more people get interested in this kind of work, we'll see that there are levels of quality in this work just like any other music—both quality of listening and playing. So it's a question of, well, 'I hear harmonics,' or, 'I'm making harmonics'—what now? What's the musical intention?"

Hykes's music is by definition consonant music. It may not always be tonal, in the usual sense, since many of the upper harmonics, especially, lie outside any commonly heard scales; but no matter how complex or dissonant-sounding a particular interval might be, the notes involved are always harmonized: The vibrations always line up. This is one meaning of his term Harmonic Music. The other describes his musical intentions, which goes beyond simply making exotic sounds in unusual places.

"My purpose in music," Hykes states, "is to bring to life both a state of harmony in the listener—a state which is in fact in us, but which we are deaf to—and a more active listening to life just as it is." Although many New Age music fans with their own notions of harmony have been drawn to the Harmonic Choir, Hykes disclaims any connection with the movement: "As a composer or performer, there's no formula to plug into—'New Age' music or 'new music.' There's no formal ground to stand on except a really serious work with our listening." Lest it appear he is taking himself a bit too seriously, remember that while the instrument he uses is an almost universal one, Harmonic Music does require a great amount of training and discipline.

While the oldest instrument is making a remarkable comeback in new music in the work of artists like Meredith Monk, Joan LaBarbara, David Hykes, Kirk Nurock, and Mathias Rüegg, vocal music is also reappearing in some of its more conventional forms. The New Age movement has rediscovered Gregorian Chant; Eastern European chanting, which can be even more arresting, is now fairly well represented on disc. And another type of vocal music has grown up alongside electronics: The various computerized and synthesized methods of altering the sound of the human voice are relatively new, but already several fascinating albums of "processed" natural vocals have appeared.

Many of these altered recordings have been mentioned earlier. Michael McNabb's computer-derived chorus, Scott Johnson's "involuntary songs" produced by tape manipulation, and Paul Lansky's voice-triggered computer music are all examples of process music and are part of Chapter 3. On tour, Philip Glass uses a device known as an Emulator, which multiplies a single voice and achieves choral effects without the logistical (and financial) problems of touring with a whole chorus. And of course Alvin Lucier's *I Am Sitting in a Room* is perhaps the ultimate example of making music by electronically manipulating vocal sounds.

As with electronic music, the exploration of the potential of the voice will ideally benefit amateur musicians as greatly as their professional counterparts. After all, anyone who can talk can sing—perhaps not well, but that's not the point. With training many people can learn to sing a few harmonics and be assured that he or she is always relatively in tune, thanks to the acoustical properties of the harmonic series. With access to a tape deck, even speech can become music, or at least musical.

Why is it only recently that musicians have begun working on extending the range of vocal techniques? Precedents established in rock music may have helped somewhat. Having Enrico Caruso or Bessie Smith or Bing Crosby as vocal role models must have been pretty daunting to anyone not blessed with a strong voice, but if Bob Dylan and Lou Reed can get rich on their voices—which are, quite frankly, nothing to sing about—then it's quite natural for aspiring vocalists to take courage. At any rate, the human voice is finally receiving a good deal of deserved attention, and is being greeted with the enthusiasm due any newly discovered instrument. And for many, that's exactly what it is.

New Sounds from New Instruments

The concern with new sonorities that led some musicians to reexamine the voice has suggested even more unconventional timbres to others. Of course, people have been inventing new ways of producing sound ever since prehistoric man discovered simple percussion. But in the last hundred years or so, with the exception of purely electronic instruments, progress has been fairly slow, as far as new inventions go. The last major instruments to be introduced were Adolph Sax's family of saxophones, first heard in the 1840s.

At the end of the nineteenth and in the early twentieth centuries, late Romantic composers increased the size of the orchestra and added new symphonic instruments, including the Wagner tuba (actually a relative of the French horn) and the heckelclarina (an altered member of the clarinet family built specifically for Wagner's *Tristan und Isolde*). Since then, most innovations have been modifications of pre-existing instruments: Electric guitars and pianos are familiar examples, while Cage's prepared piano is a more specialized adaptation.*

Over the past few decades, however, a number of genuinely new instruments have appeared, thanks to the growing popularity of different tuning systems, the influence of ethnic music, and the accessibility of a wide range of electronic gadgets. This does not mean these instruments depend solely on sophisticated technology: New music can be made with objects as mundane as popsicle sticks and nail files. In fact, Stephen Scott's 1984 release *New Music for Bowed Piano* is produced with exactly these items, and shows just how remarkable such works can be.

Scott began developing his "bowed piano" in 1976, after hearing the music of American avant-garde composer Curtis Curtis-Smith. Curtis-Smith's works featured a number of prepared-piano techniques (see page 95), one of which involved drawing a length of nylon string across the inside of the instrument. Scott realized that Curtis-Smith's innovation could be taken a step further: A regular piano could be transformed into an entirely new instrument if the strings were bowed, like those of a cello, instead of being struck with the standard key-and-hammer mechanism. Unfortunately, you don't make friends and influence people by attacking their grand pianos with cello bows. So Scott set about creating miniature "piano bows," eventually settling on nail files and popsicle sticks with horsehair glued to one or both sides. This technique made possible not only the rich sustained tones that any bowed string is capable of, it also allowed Scott's performers to play quick, interlocking patterns of notes, or hockets (see page 148), which would otherwise require a whole group of string players. Scott's music is at times reminiscent of the rhythmic works of Steve Reich, whom he met in Ghana in 1970 and lists as a major influence.

Stephen Scott's bowed piano is typical of the first of two kinds of new instruments that will be discussed here. Modified or altered instruments also include such things as the electronic, solid-body cellos of David Darling or Tom McVeety and the double-necked violin of L. Shankar. The second type, invented instruments, includes the microtonal constructions of Harry Partch; the large sound sculptures played by Michael Stearns; and innovative designs made from industrial or urban trash by Robert Rutman or Skip LaPlante.

In some instances, the difference in the timbre of these instruments can be very

*The piano, in fact, has been subjected to a great deal of experimentation ever since it was introduced in the late eighteenth century. Inventors concocted such oddities as pianos that plucked strings like a harpsichord instead of hammering them; pianos that used tuning forks instead of strings; piano keyboards attached to a harp; even an instrument that used a revolving wheel on the strings to produce a sustained tone, not unlike the medieval hurdy-gurdy.

subtle and can slip by the inattentive listener; but others demand attention with sounds that stand out. These latter include some striking new instruments that are now, as we'll see, over forty years old.

For over thirty years, until his death in 1974, Harry Partch was the most prolific artist in this field, creating dozens of extraordinary string, percussion, and keyboard instruments. Partch's career was as unusual as his inventions. He was self-taught; he wandered across the United States as a hobo in the 30s, collecting hobo tales and highway graffiti for later use as texts for his music. He was working as a lumberjack when he received the Guggenheim grant in 1943 that allowed him to build twenty of the instruments he had designed. These designs grew out of his need for instruments that were capable of playing in his forty-three-note-to-the-octave scales. These colorful, imaginatively named devices included the "quadrangularis reversum," a large diamond-shaped mallet percussion instrument; "cloud-chamber bowls," a set of different-sized fragile glass bowls; and the "spoils of war," an impossible jumble of metal cans, wooden strips, and glass containers. While they are capable of producing some exhilarating sounds, Partch's devices are precisely tuned to a very specialized scale, and are therefore difficult to adapt to other music.

Instruments have been most often invented or modified by composers who require a particular element in their music, whether a new sonority or simply a greater flexibility in the range of an existing instrument. David Darling, for example, uses a solid-body, eight-string electric cello. "Solid-body" means that the body of the instrument is flat and filled with electronics; it's not hollowed out, because the sound would resonate in the body and feedback would result. The electric cello thus looks like an elongated electric guitar.

Darling developed this instrument, with its two sets of four strings, to produce the same rich effect achieved by a guitarist when he plays a twelve-string rather than a six-string guitar. "It was built because I played with Ralph Towner for so many years," Darling says, "and after hearing him night after night playing all the overtones a twelve-string guitar can produce, I kept wondering—would it be possible to make a cello that would have all those overtones?" The addition of a second set of strings made possible a full, almost orchestral tone that an unaltered cello couldn't match.

Violinist L. Shankar had a more practical reason for creating his solid-body electric instrument. Shankar used to play all of the orchestral string instruments, from violin to double bass. Transporting all of them and having to put one down and quickly pick up another while on stage became a real chore. "So I began thinking about devising one instrument that I could use for all the others," he says. "It was a practical need. I designed it myself over two or three years, and when it was done in 1980, I gave my model to Ken Parker, the luthier. Since then I've used that instrument only."

Shankar's double-violin has ten strings, five per neck. The lower neck corresponds to the double bass and cello range; the upper includes the violin and viola range. With its two separate volume controls and stereophonic pickup, it has a very clean sound. Shankar's album *Vision* was composed to take advantage of the potential of the double-violin. A regular violin is basically a lead instrument; it is not well suited to an accompanying role. But with the double-violin, "you can create so many amazing textures: different types of pizzicato as well as solos and chords. So in *Vision,* I did all the accompaniment."

Yet another solid-body electric string instrument was devised by cellist Tom McVeety, whose decision to amplify an acoustic cello was motivated simply by the desire to try something different: "I had just run out of ideas as far as playing it went," he admits. "It really didn't do much for me anymore. So I taped a pickup to the bridge and plugged that into my stereo—unfortunately for the stereo." McVeety's cello has one set of six strings rather than Darling's two sets of four, giving him an extended range of notes.

It should be pointed out that these electric instruments are much more than just louder versions of their acoustic counterparts. Once the strings have been set vibrating, the entire method of reproducing the sound changes. In a cello, the note bounces around in the resonant body of the instrument; in an electric cello, the vibrations are fed by a pickup to the circuitry inside the instrument. There they create changes in electric current, which can then be amplified, distorted, processed, and finally converted into sound by loudspeakers. By contrast, an instrument like the so-called "electric flute" is not substantially modified at all. If you didn't plug in the pickup, you'd still hear a normal flute sound, for this is simply an amplified instrument, though the sound itself may be modified once it's converted into electric form. If you don't plug in an electric cello, by contrast, all you get is a distinctly unpleasant scratching sound.

While modified instruments allow an artist to "custom design" precisely the sound he or she requires, they do demand a reliance on technology, which means a performer must quickly be able to troubleshoot often sophisticated electronic equipment if something conks out on stage. Fortunately, electronic devices have become more reliable in recent years, and most musicians don't get involved with electric instruments and amplification without at least some knowledge of what they're doing.

These instruments may become as widespread as the electric guitar or electric piano—certainly the principle behind them is the same—but for the moment, the sounds they produce are still new to most ears.

In the face of the technological onslaught, the old acoustic instruments nonetheless continue to have a lot of appeal, even for someone who's as enthusiastic about his modified instrument as is David Darling. "It's an amazing contribution to modern electrified instruments. It can sound like trumpets, and because of the versatility of electric instruments, you can even make it sound Baroque." But, he adds, "they could put me on an island with my acoustic cello anytime and I'd be just fine."

Some musicians, in fact, have come up with new acoustic designs that don't depend on technology at all. In one case, the instrument doesn't even depend on a performer. In the 1950s, American sculptor Harry Bertoia began experimenting with the sonic possibilities of moving pieces of sculpture. The Bertoia Sound Sculptures can produce music in response to changes in air currents, such as those caused by a door opening or by people walking through a room. One typical Sound Sculpture looks like hundreds of long, flexible pipettes growing out of a box. Air movement causes them to strike each other gently, resulting in a cascade of chiming notes, but Bertoia Sound Sculptures can also be played by a musician. Several recordings of these musical curiosities exist.

Perhaps the oddest source of new acoustic instruments is the detritus of modern society, including ordinary household objects and common junk. Prior to a New York concert in the summer of 1985, composer Skip LaPlante sent out flyers announcing the date, time, place, etc. Admission, the flyer said, was five dollars, or an equivalent amount in returnable bottles and cans. At first it seemed like a joke, and a potentially expensive one at that. But LaPlante's ensemble is called Music for Homemade Instruments, and true to its name it turns bottles, cans, and other debris into musical instruments, mostly percussion. The group's performances therefore sound at times quite like the gamelan music of Indonesia.

Another interesting application of the "garbage is in the eye of the beholder" approach is the work of Robert Rutman. His instruments are not, strictly speaking, sound sculptures, but they certainly appear to be pieces of strange, modern sculpture when left unattended. The "steel cello" is a single large sheet of industrial scrap metal that is given a little twist and then bent into a C-shape. It's held in position by a steel wire, running from the top of the C to the bottom. The "bow chimes" consist of a sheet of metal, also contorted into a C-shape, this time on its side, with its open end facing the audience. Instead of being held in place by a wire, a bar runs across the front of the instrument, and coming up from that bar at right angles are two or three long metal rods, which extend past the top of the instrument. Both the steel cello and bow chimes are played with cello bows. The notes on the steel cello can be varied by pressing a finger to different points on the wire; the bow chimes' notes will vary according to which metal rod is bowed, where the bow is along the rod's length, and how hard or soft the bowing action is.

Rutman calls his group the U.S. Steel Cello Ensemble. What kind of music do these curious-looking constructions make? Well, it's not tonal. The instruments can be somewhat unpredictable, and the music is perforce completely improvised. On his album *Bitter Suites,* the sonority is unearthly and, in a harsh, icy way, quite beautiful. The sheets of metal perform the same function as the body of a guitar or cello: They amplify the sound; and because different parts of the sheet vibrate differently according to their distance from the note's source, a whole array of overtones bounces off the curved surface.

The instruments of the U.S. Steel Cello Ensemble are not too difficult to play. In 1981, when Rutman was giving performances at a small museum in Portland, Maine, he invited the audience—all twelve of us—to play the instruments ourselves after the concerts. Rutman's inventions set an excellent example for amateur musicians: Most of us don't have easy access to large sheets of steel, but the simplicity of the instruments' design and the relative ease with which they're played made them very appealing to anyone who took the opportunity to see them.

Probably the best-known source of music among everyday items is the wineglass. As most everyone knows, different levels of liquid in a glass change the pitch that results when that glass is tapped or rubbed around the rim with a moistened finger. An ensemble from Toronto, the Glass Orchestra, has taken this principle to its logical extreme. As its name might imply, this group plays glass instruments almost exclusively. The flute is a rare exception, but even that is played through a glass water basin. The goblets, beakers, pipettes, and bowls of various shapes and sizes in the Glass Orchestra's collection of instruments are more likely to appear in a chemistry textbook than in a musical survey. Yet the ensemble is able to perform in a wide range of styles, from near-Minimalist tonal works to eerie atonal improvisations.

If amateur musicians can take heart in the fact that instruments as simple and accessible as wineglasses can make new music, the good news for professionals is that invented instruments are becoming increasingly more sophisticated. American composer Michael Stearns, who has composed a lot of electronic music, has also worked with the Eikosany vibes, a microtonal (twenty-two notes to the octave) set of chimes, and with the Lyra, a sound sculpture created by sculptor George Landry. The Lyra, another microtonal instrument, is capable of very subtle and beautiful sounds, but unlike the Bertoia Sound Sculptures, it is an electric instrument. It consists of 156 wires, stretched from the floor to the ceiling of the space in which it's installed. Each wire has a pickup, and the sound is electrically routed to speakers at the base of the instrument and to other speakers surrounding it. Because the wires are so long (fifteen to twenty feet), they produce a rich sweep of harmonics when played. Like the sheets of metal in Rutman's instruments, each wire vibrates more quickly at certain points along its length than at others. Thus the base of the wire will produce one overtone, the central part another; because of the pickups, the resulting overtones are discreetly present in the music.

Despite the advances in technology—or perhaps because of them—much new music relies on simplicity of means. The richness of a vibrating string, the expressive potential of the voice, the physical force of even the most basic percussion—these are sounds that will never lose their appeal. Even the application of circuitry and amplifiers to these sounds—as in the Lyra, for example—merely serves to highlight the subtleties inherent in them. This renewed interest in the oldest instrument and the developing new ones is a welcome sign, and the potential for future growth in this area is enormous.

DISCOGRAPHY AND RELATED WORKS

PART ONE: EXTENDING THE VOICE

CHARLES AMIRKHANIAN
- *Lexical Music* (1750 Arch 1779) NMDS. This California-based radio producer and writer knows as much about the voice and how to use it as anyone. Tape and delays create strange acoustic effects; these text-equals-sound-equals-music-of-a-sort pieces are an acquired taste, but it's very interesting work.

- ▲ *Arménie: Chants Liturgiques du Moyen-Age* (Oc. 66) HM. See Chapter 7.

SVEN ERIK BÄCK
- *"Annus Solaris"* from the LP *Stockholm Elektronmusikfestival 1980* (Fylkingen FYLP 1025) FYL. Although heavily processed and synthesized, "Annus Solaris" is primarily a vocal work, or "text-sound composition," as Bäck puts it. Soprano Kerstin Ståhl sings against up to fourteen prerecorded vocal parts with electronic accompaniment. From the same LP as the Charles Dodge work in Chapter 3.

BONNIE BARNETT
- *Trio*
- *Tunnel Hum USA, 1983*
- *Rotunda Hum, 1984*
- *Tunnel Hum, 1984* (Tunnel Hum, 510A Hill Street, San Francisco, CA 94114)
Except for *Trio*, which is Barnett's voice singing overtones played back at half speed, these cassettes are examples of participatory vocal works, involving large groups of people, mostly amateurs, who get together (occasionally by satellite) to sing around a central note. Surprisingly energetic in person, it's one of those "guess you hadda be there" things . . . on tape it's just people humming.

- ▲ *Bulgaria: Le Mystère des Voix Bulgares* (Disques Cellier 008) HOS. While I'm sure Bulgarian men know how to sing, they leave it to the women here. This is a startling, often gripping record of a women's chorus singing mysterious, plaintive melodies.

JAY CLAYTON
- *All Out* (Anima 1J35) NMDS. Highlighted by "7/8 Thing" (see Chapter 4), this disc also includes free jazz improvs, often with unexpected instruments backing up.

- ▲ *Corsica: Coro del Supramonte di Orgosolo* (Cetra IIp244). A truly bizarre LP of male choral music: At least one of the singers seems to be so far off key so consistently that you begin to hear strange harmonic relationships between the voices. Talk about new sounds!

DIAMANDA GALAS
- *Diamanda Galas* (Metalanguage 119) NMDS
- *The Divine Punishment* (Mute STUMM-27)
- *The Saint of the Pit* (Mute, planned for release in late 86–87)
More rumors surround Diamanda Galas than any other figure in (new) music. Rumors that she is in league with the Devil. Rumors that she has been approached about singing conventional opera. (Rumors that she has started all these rumors.) Even a rumor that *Wild Women with Steak Knives* and *Litanies of Satan*, a pair of early works, will be reissued. The facts are these: Galas's stage presence is riveting. Her music, with its shrills and shrieks, whispers and whistles, often amplified and sometimes electronically processed, can be genuinely terrifying. Galas, a prodigiously talented vocalist, needs to be seen as well as heard; her albums, though, are faithful to the mood of her concerts. "Panoptikon," from the Metalanguage disc, is probably an effective introduction to her work.

DAVID GARLAND
- *Control Songs* (Review Records RERE-95) NMDS. Garland's music is certainly friendlier than Galas's, but the Carpenters it's not. Although he does a lot of conventional singing, he also records his voice, cuts it up, and puts the pieces together to create a strange yodeling effect ("I Am

With You"—also released as a single); sings too slow and plays the tape back a bit faster to create a female-impersonating voice ("Keep in Touch"); and plays simple, catchy tunes on everything from toy flutes to Fairlight CMI. Some of the more avant-garde pieces explore the boundary between sound and music. A consistently surprising album.

▲ *Grèce: Chants sacrées de la tradition Byzantine, Vol. 1* (Oc. 558 521) HM
▲ *Grèce: Chants sacrées de la tradition Byzantine, Vol. 2* (Oc. 558 530) HM
▲ *Grèce, Vols. 3 & 4: Liturgies anciennes orthodoxes* (Oc. 558 545/46, 2 LPs) HM
A cappella performances of twelfth to eighteenth-century Greek liturgical music sung by Theodore Vassilikos and his Vocal Ensemble. Most of the music is sung by a unison chorus; it's stately and majestic enough, but some of these pieces call for the chorus to act as a sort of humming drone, changing notes at infrequent and startling points, while Vassilikos takes off on a solo flight.

CLAIRE HAMMILL
■ *Voices* (Landscape NAGE-8) JEM, NAR. An album drawn entirely from the multitracked sounds of Hammill's voice. Even the drum sounds are vocal. Using processing and sampling, she's created incredible textures. But the album ends up sounding like the backing vocal tracks to an album of pop songs.

DAVID HYKES AND THE HARMONIC CHOIR
■ *Hearing Solar Winds* (Oc. 558 607) CH, NAR, FOR, HM
■ *Current Circulation* (CH CEL-010) CH
■ *Harmonic Meetings* (CH CEL-013/014, 2 LPs) CH
If you spend enough time with Hykes or his music, it will change the way you hear vocal music, for the idea of listening closely to a tone, trying to pick out its component parts, is foreign to most people. *Hearing Solar Winds* overcomes the limitations of its imperfect recording and production and is a fine introduction to Hykes's methods. The second LP is a better recording, but seems to tread water, musically. The two-LP set, however, takes a quantum leap forward; Hykes incorporates words from the Abrahamic religions, uses tamboura or drum, and returns to the abbey in Thoronet where the first album was made. His scaled-down choir, a trio, is in good voice, and owing to the multitude of solo or duet passages, the actual production of harmonics by the individual voices can be heard clearly.

RICHARD KOSTELANETZ
■ *Invocations* (Folk. FRS-37902) NMDS. A tape collage of voices from around the world, speaking, chanting, or singing prayers from many religions. It's certainly not easy to listen to, and it may not even be music, but what emerges from the mix is a sense of the spirit and devotion that lies at the heart of all faiths.

JOAN LABARBARA
■ *Reluctant Gypsy* (Wizard 2279) NMDS
■ *As Lightning Comes, In Flashes* (Wizard 2283) NMDS
■ *The Art of Joan LaBarbara* (None. 78029)
Part of her extensive discography. The last album includes Subotnick's *Last Dream of the Beast*, but all the other works are LaBarbara's. Her own compositions tend to be showcases for her extended techniques first, and musical concepts second. Happily, there are times when that tremendous technique and her writing skills come together: "Klee Alee" on the first album, or the nonpareil catalog of vocal effects, "Twelvesong," from the second.

PAUL LANSKY
■ *Six Fantasies on a Poem by Thomas Campion* (CRI 456). See Chapter 3.

MIECZYSLAW LITWINSKI
■ *Garden of Songs/Dusk with Angel* (private tape)
■ *Garden of Songs, Dusk with Angel*, other works (scheduled for release by Music of the World in 1987)
Heartbreakingly beautiful songs by a Polish singer, composer, and multi-instrumentalist. His vocals include overtone chants, sudden falsetto yodels, and techniques of medieval or Jewish cantorial music. His accompaniment is mostly harmonium, which recalls the sounds of Indian devotional music, with some hurdy-gurdy, violin, panpipes, or kazoo. His private tape may be obtained by writing to Source Music, 323 E. 79 St., NY, NY 10021.

ANNEA LOCKWOOD
■ *"Malolo"* from the LP *Sleepers* (Finnadar 90266-1) NMDS. Lullaby for three voices, based on Samoan syllables, from a New Zealand-born composer. See Chapter 5 (Silsbee, et al.) for more from this LP.

MEREDITH MONK
■ *Our Lady of Late* (Labor Records, scheduled for reissue)
■ *Key* (Lovely LML-1501) NMDS
■ *Songs from the Hill/Tablet* (Wergo SM-1022) NMDS
■ *Dolmen Music* (ECM 1197) ECM
■ *Turtle Dreams* (ECM 1240) ECM
If it weren't for the fact that most of her music, the last three albums at least, stands so well by itself, it would be unfair to take Monk's audio work out

of the context of her multimedia productions. Not everyone likes the babyish patter or the unexpected shrillness that are part of her repertoire of techniques; not everyone likes the weird instrumentation or the repetitive accompaniment. I guess there's no accounting for taste. Her ECM records are the best place to start if you're interested in the musical application of extended vocal techniques.

- *"Biography"* from the two-LP set *Big Ego* (Giorno Poetry Systems GPS-012/013). Voice and piano solo by Monk, sort of a poor cousin to the works on side one of *Dolmen Music.* From a collection that also includes Philip Glass, Laurie Anderson, etc.
- *"Candy Bullets & Moon"* from the LP *Better an Old God than a New Demon* (Giorno Poetry Systems GPS-033) NMDS. Reissue of a work recorded in 1967. Monk (voice and bass) is joined by Don Preston (organ, drums) in a wild, spacey piece that definitely uses the late-60s rock sound. If her other stuff intrigues you, check this out.

NIORIN NI RIAIN
- *Caoineadh na Maighdine* (Gael-Linn CEF-084) SHAN. See Chapter 8.

KIRK NUROCK
- *Natural Sound* (Wergo SM-1026) NMDS. Some of this gets pretty far out, but it has an interesting array of unnatural sounds, naturally produced by such performers as Jay Clayton, Skip LaPlante, Rebecca Armstrong, Nurit Tilles, etc. Includes "Overtones & Clusters" and "Rhythm Chants," both self-explanatory.

PAULINE OLIVEROS
- *"Lullaby for Daisy Pauline"* from the LP *Sleepers* (Finnadar 90266-1) NMDS. Choral humming. Short and kind of trancey. See Lockwood, above.

ELIANE RADIGUE
- *The Song of Milarepa* (Lovely LV-2001) NMDS. Lama Kunga Rinpoche speaks/chants the poems/songs of the Tibetan saint Milarepa; then Robert Ashley reads an English translation of same. Both done over a constant electronic drone.

STAR-SCAPE SINGERS
- *Live at Carnegie Hall* (Soundscape KGOM-18). Alphabetically and musically, the Star-Scape Singers belong on the shelf next to the Yma Sumac records. Capable of great vocal acrobatics, they often reach stratospheric heights usually reserved for coloratura sopranos and cats in heat. Unfortunately, the group insists on singing the "spontaneous poetry" of its mentor, Kenneth Mills. Their obvious efforts at "interpreting" his doggerel add a creepy note to the music. This is the least intrusive album in terms of texts; a Fire Mass, based on the sections of the Mass, is due soon. It will be

interesting to see how this group's undeniable vocal talent stands up in this setting.

- *Tibetan Buddhism/Tantras of Gyütö: Mahakala* (None. Explorer H-72055)
- *Tibetan Buddhism/Tantras of Gyütö: Sangwa Düpa* (None. Explorer H-72064) See Chapter 7.

MICHAEL VETTER
- *Overtones—Voice and Tamboura* (Wergo SM-1038/39) CH. Two-LP set of solo performances. Vetter is a German singer, artist, and instrumentalist; he plays the Indian tamboura in an unusual manner (it sounds like an Asian banjo) and sings in a style that recalls the Tibetan Gyütö and Gyüme monks. Since the tamboura is capable of many overtone effects itself, this album has a lot more sound than you might expect from the title.
- *Tamboura Preludes/Pro-Vocationes* (Wergo SM-1041/42) CH. Another two-LP set. First album is solo tamboura, using Vetter's Jew's-harp/banjo techniques; *Pro-Vocationes* is like his drawings: a sort of imaginary proto-language. In both cases, the material is interesting for a few minutes. But a whole album of each is just too much.

YOSHI WADA
- *Lament for the Rise and Fall of the Elephantine Crocodile* (India Navigation IN-3025) NMDS. A pupil of Pandit Pran Nath and an associate of La Monte Young. One side is played on an invented instrument (see Part Two, page 240); the other is wordless overtone singing, recorded in a dry swimming pool in Buffalo.

PART TWO: NEW SOUNDS FROM NEW INSTRUMENTS

LOL CREME AND KEVIN GODLEY
- *Consequences* (Mer. SRM-3-1700, 3 LPs). Ambitious, self-indulgent music by a pair of musicians who founded the rock band 10CC and have become successful and sought-after producers of rock videos. This collection features the "gizmo," a combination "guitar and typewriter keyboard," as they describe it in their album notes. In fact, it's a cleverly designed bowed string instrument, similar in concept to the old hurdy-gurdy and in design to the electric guitar. Text and narration by Peter Cook, and guest appearances by Sarah Vaughan and Mel Collins. Highly experimental, it works only in spots; but after all it was done in 1976–1977, and much of the avant-garde rock of that period has not aged well.

DAVID DARLING
- *Journal October* (ECM 1161). See page 205.

ARNOLD DREYBLATT AND
THE ORCHESTRA OF EXCITED STRINGS
- *Nodal Excitation* (India Navigation 3024) NMDS
- *propellers in love* (Kunstlerhaus Bethanien ST-09)

Dreyblatt studied with La Monte Young, and has developed an interest in overtones. He has created a number of altered string instruments that produce clear, ringing harmonics. The sound is highly repetitive with particularly single-minded rhythms; the *real* music is in the cascading overtones that the repeated striking (or "exciting") of the strings produces. The first album was recorded in New York; the second was made with Dreyblatt's new Berlin-based group. Neither LP really captures the sound of the ensemble in concert, but the second album comes closest.

ELLEN FULLMAN
- *The Long String Instruments* (Apollo AR 11 85 01) NMDS. Using long rubbed strings, Fullman produces an array of overtone effects similar to those in the preceding albums. (Dreyblatt helps perform on one piece.) Percussion is provided by a "water drip drum," consisting of an amplified aluminum pan and a dripping faucet of sorts, both of which can be controlled by the performer. In person, at volumes loud enough for the overtones to ring out strongly, Fullman's instruments/sound installations are quite effective. Here, they sound kind of pointless.

THE GLASS ORCHESTRA
- *The Glass Orchestra* (Music Gallery Editions MGE-10) NMDS
- *Verrillon* (private release, G-002; Glass Orchestra, 81 Portland Street, Toronto, M5V 2M9, Canada)

Glass instruments were common in Baroque times: Mozart wrote for the glass harmonica (a collection of tuned wineglasses) and Benjamin Franklin is often credited with developing the mechanism which made this instrument easy to play and thus very popular in fashionable salons. The Glass Orchestra has brought the eerie, airy sounds of glass instruments back to contemporary music. Whether playing accessible or atonal music, this group will surprise you with the variety of sounds they extract from this medium.

ROBERT GRAWI
- *Solo Gravikord and Kalimba* (White Bear Enterprises, 127 West 78 Street #2, New York, NY 10024). Cassette release of cheerful, Western-sounding music for an African instrument (kalimba) and an invented electric instrument (gravikord) modeled after the African kora.

CHRISTOPHER JANNEY
- *Tone Zone, Percussion Discussion, Heartbeats* (private cassette: C. Janney, 63 Old Rutherford Avenue, Charlestown, MA 02129). "My machine makes mistakes, never music. Please excuse it." So says the computerized voice in one of Chris Janney's amusing, oddball works. Truth is, his machines *do* make music, to the extent that *any* instruments—old, conventional, or new—almost seem unnecessary. *Tone Zone*'s "instruments" are a dancer and a video camera. The dancer's movements trigger different electronic circuits, which in turn produce notes of music. *Percussion Discussion* uses "talking drums"—not African talking drums, but *talking* drums—programmed with words instead of drum sounds and again, controlled by electronic circuitry. *Heartbeats* includes a sax, but pairs it with a human heartbeat. Is it process music? Or audio art? Parts of it need to be seen to be appreciated, but each of these works has passages that stretch our definition of what an instrument is without straining our sense of what is musical.

TOM JOHNSON
- *Nine Bells* (India Navigation 3023) NMDS. Here's an excellent example of a "found" instrument. Johnson fixes nine alarm bells to the ceiling and walks in regular, rhythmic patterns among them, striking each bell as he passes it and following a different pattern for each piece, with his sneakers acting as percussion.

JO KONDO
- *Standing/Sight Rhythmics/Under the Umbrella* (Nexus/CP² 11) NMDS. "Under the Umbrella" is a work for a couple of dozen cow bells. Nexus's performance will convince you that you're listening to "real" percussion, perhaps gamelan instruments.

JACQUES LASRY
- *Chronophagie* (Col. MS-7314). Title translates as "The Time Eaters." The mysterious, alien sounds come from the Baschet Sound Sculptures, aided and abetted by flute, tabla, and bass violin. The Baschet brothers invented a number of glass and metal instruments in the 50s and 60s, which are capable of drone, percussive, and electronic effects. They're tellingly employed in Lasry's album-length work.

ALVIN LUCIER
See Chapter 3, especially *Music on a Long, Thin Wire.*

MACIUNAS ENSEMBLE
- *Music for Everyman 861* (Apollo 028605) NMDS. George Maciunas, founder of Fluxus, "wrote" a "composition" called *Music for Everyman* in the 1960s, which was an open score allowing for any sort of musical sounds. Theoretically, any music is —or can be—part of this score. The Maciunas Ensemble was formed to play this piece in 1968. On this 1986 LP, Holland's Paul Panhuysen (see below) leads the group through two pieces with

computerized rock rhythm tracks and a side-long work called "A wide, white World," which uses long, two-string guitarlike instruments, bowed with cassette-deck motors and rubber bands. The rock pieces are pretty lame; the wall of sound produced by the other work is reminiscent at times of Glenn Branca (Chapter 11), Alvin Lucier, or both.

TOM McVEETY

- *Dream 1 & 2, Music from Home, Fanfare for the Common Man, Meteor Showers* (private tape, see Chapter 3). More music for solid-body electric cello. McVeety's performance of Aaron Copland's *Fanfare* is an exciting one, with surprisingly full sound, that carries on in the tradition of Jimi Hendrix's version of *The Star Spangled Banner.* But his use of chords makes this even more of a knuckle-buster.

DARY JOHN MIZELLE

- *Soundscape/Polytempus II* (Lumina 002) NMDS. Interesting avant-garde textures. Especially good is "Glass," though Mizelle also explores the possible sounds of metal, skin (as in drum heads), wood, and earth on this album.

CONLON NANCARROW

- *Complete Studies for Player Piano, Vols. 1, 2, 3* (1750 Arch S-1768, S-1777, S-1786, respectively). An American maverick who found himself *persona non grata* after fighting in the Spanish Civil War and so moved to Mexico City. He is only recently beginning to appear on the American music scene again. Since the 40s, he has been concerned with subtleties of texture and rhythm that are beyond human performers. His player piano is not the type that appeared in salons and saloons years ago, but a modified instrument capable of incredibly intricate sounds. Somewhat difficult to follow, his music is still witty and absorbing; his earlier works even contain, if you listen *very* closely, echoes of jazz and blues.

NOCTURNAL EMISSIONS

- *"Metal Frames"* from *Touch 33.4: "Lands End."* NMDS. Okay, so the band's name is a little rude. This is a serious piece—even a somber one. Full of metallic sounds that may come from steel pipes, or from some kind of processing trick, it's spooky, arresting, and contains some clearly audible, sharply ringing overtones. Accompanied by unfortunately prosaic electronic percussion.

PAUL PANHUYSEN AND JOHAN GOEDHART

- *Long String Installations* (Apollo AR-088502) NMDS. This is one of the most beautifully produced, lavishly packaged multiple-LP sets ever made. Three records of long wires, either bowed by musicians or controlled by machines. But in both cases, there's little here that can be called music.

HARRY PARTCH

- *Delusion of the Fury* (Col. AL-30577). Partch's music is thorny and unsettling; but no discussion about invented instruments can overlook him. This piece takes up all of two records, and is probably the perfect thing to play at your next break-the-lease party. Once you get past the strange tuning, though, you may be surprised to find actual tunes and rhythms that are not only perceivable but almost pretty, in a twisted way. "Chorus of Shadows," for example, at once recalls both gamelan music and ancient Eastern European chant.
- *The World of Harry Partch* (Col. MS-7207). Probably the best album of Partch's music to start with. "Barstow" has some of his most ingratiating music (if you can call anything with forty-three notes to the octave ingratiating), but the text, consisting of hobo graffiti from a highway railing near Barstow, CA is definitely not something for the family to sing along with.

ROBERT RUTMAN

- *Bitter Suites* (Rutdog 1009) NMDS. Icy, spacey music for bowed metal instruments. Not pretty, but a pretty good showcase for these devices.

TERJE RYPDAL AND DAVID DARLING

- *Eos* (ECM 1263) ECM. See page 211.

STEPHEN SCOTT

- *New Music for Bowed Piano* (New Albion NAL-004) NMDS. A grand piano, with its lid removed, is played by a group of musicians with miniature cello bows. The music alternates between pulsing rhythmic sections and slow sustained passages. One piece, "Resonant Resources," uses a competely different type of bowed piano: An electromagnet bows all the strings at once; the notes are created by pressing a key on the keyboard to allow that note's bowed sounds to be heard. This style requires only one musician, playing in a conventional manner. Either way, this is one of the strangest albums ever made on, or in, a piano. Well worth trying.

ELLIOTT SHARP

- *"Black Rain"* from *Touch 33.4: "Lands End."* NMDS. Uncompromising, forbidding, difficult; you would expect the man behind it to be an ogre. Well, he's not. In fact, he's an original musician whose work, available on a number of LPs (in the NMDS catalog), is based on strict mathematical progressions and abstruse harmonic theories. Sharp usually performs on bizarre instruments like the quartet of hammered electric basses on this short work. It's a good intro to Sharp's music: If the ringing sounds and unsettling tonality appeal to you, you might want to try his other records.

- *The Sounds of Sound Sculpture* (ARC ST-1001). J. B. Floyd, David Rosenboom, and John Grayson perform on Bertoia Sound Sculptures from 1965–1972. Also contains the lush, vacuum- and pressure-operated sculptures of Stephan von Huene, from 1969–70, and more abstract sound sculptures from David Jacobs (1970–1971). (O.P.)

MICHAEL STEARNS
- *Sustaining Cylinders* (Continuum Montage 1002) FOR
- *"Jewel"* from the recording *Morning/Jewel* (Sonic Atmospheres 208) SON, FOR, NAR

Both LPs feature the Eikosany vibes, a twenty-two-note-to-the-octave set of metal tubes. Stearns combines them with women's voices on the latter piece; bells, conches, and ocean sounds on the former. Subtle textures include long, sustained tones made by editing out the initial sound of striking the instrument.

- *Lyra: Sound Constellation* (Continuum Montage 1006) FOR, NAR. The Lyra is an electro-acoustic sound sculpture, consisting of 156 wires, stretched from floor to ceiling in whatever space the instrument is installed. The very few synthesizer effects on this album go by unnoticed; the sound of the Lyra holds your attention throughout, producing deep rumbles, silvery overtones, and everything in between. Like most recordings of sound sculptures or New Age music (this is both), it gets pretty ambient, but it avoids degenerating into experimental muzak.
- *Chronos* (Sonic Atmospheres 112) SON, FOR, NAR. See Chapter 1 for description. Includes "the Beam," a twelve-foot-high acoustic instrument made with airplane struts and piano wires.

JAMES TENNEY
- *"Spectral CANON for CONLON Nancarrow"* from the LP *Cold Blue Sampler* (Cold Blue L-10) NMDS. Music for player piano, with the piano roll punched by Nancarrow himself at his Mexico City studio. Although similar to Nancarrow's work,

Tenney's piece uses a scale derived from the first twenty-four partials of the harmonic series.

ED TOMNEY
- *We* (Reach Out International, no #). Cassette recording of "Guitar Trees," sound sculptures made from electric guitars armed with computer-controlled strummers. Tomney has long been associated with artist Jonathan Borofsky's installations and sound/performance events.

PETER VAN RIPER
- *Whomp Whip Music* (no label, no #). Aluminum baseball bats are cut and suspended in a resonant room, producing a kind of gamelan/chime sound when struck with wooden or metal beaters. Poor sound, interesting idea. (See Chapter 12.)

YOSHI WADA
- *Lament for the Rise and Fall of the Elephantine Crocodile* (India Navigation IN-3025) NMDS
- *Off the Wall* (Free Music FMP-SAJ-49) NMDS

Wada appears in Part One of this discography (page 237). These works, for homemade bagpipes (the "elephantine crocodile" was made from a canvas sack, plumbing pipes, etc.) with reed organ and percussion on the second LP, continue to show his fascination with overtones, undertones, combination or difference tones, and loud, dense blocks of sound. His fascinating blend of modal music seems to draw as much from the Japanese sho as the Scottish bagpipes.

GAYLE YOUNG AND
ROBERT REITZENSTEIN
- *According* (According/WRC 1265) NMDS. Audio portion of a visual installation by Reitzenstein. Young invented a delicate, chiming mallet keyboard instrument called the "columbine," and wrote simple, glowing, but unquestionably offbeat music for that instrument and one or two voices.

11
THE ROCK INFLUENCE(S)

Let me say, although I disagree with some of the statements that you make . . . I have been a fan of your music, believe it or not; and I respect you as a true original and tremendously talented musician.
Senator Albert Gore, Jr. (D–Tenn.) to rock star
Frank Zappa at the 1985 Senate Commerce Committee's hearings on rock lyrics

It's an honor to be able to ask [you] questions. I've been a fan for a long time, Mr. Denver.
Senator Albert Gore, Jr. (D–Tenn.) to "rock star" John Denver
at the 1985 Senate Commerce Committee's hearings on rock lyrics

Excuse me, are you gonna tell me you're a big fan of my music as well?
Dee Snider of the heavy-metal rock band Twisted Sister
to Senator Albert Gore, Jr., etc., etc.

At least one conclusion can be drawn from the often comic proceedings that took place when the Senate and the Parents' Music Resource Center took on the rock industry in an attempt to censor immoral or suggestive lyrics. With the likes of Frank Zappa, John Denver, and Dee Snider of Twisted Sister testifying before the committee, it soon became clear that what did or did not constitute "rock music" was very much a matter of individual taste.

After some thirty years of existence rock has divided and subdivided into so many splinter styles that it's practically impossible to make any sort of blanket statements about it. As just one example, Frank Zappa's Mothers of Invention and Robert Fripp's group King Crimson were both part of the vanguard of "progressive rock" in the early 70s, and stood at the opposite end of the spectrum from the threatening, distorted, only marginally musical din that heavy-metal bands like Black Sabbath produced. But even within so-called "progressive" circles, the differences were often equally dramatic. At the time that King Crimson released *In the Court of the Crimson King, an Observation by King Crimson* (1969), Zappa was preparing *Weasels Ripped My Flesh* (1970). In case the titles aren't a sufficient clue, the serious brow-furrowing compositions by Fripp's group had little in common with

Zappa's sardonic, offbeat music, even though both men shared an interest in avant-garde jazz and classical techniques.

One reason for this diversity is that like jazz, rock has long been open to external influences: Elements of jazz, ethnic, electronic, and classical music have been used, effectively or not, by rock musicians. Some rock musicians—Brian Eno and David Byrne, for example—have even made a name for themselves in the field of new music. And some new music composers—such as Laurie Anderson and Peter Gordon—have borrowed from the language of rock. In either case, the result is music that at least partially derives from rock, without actually being rock itself.

Although rock's influence on new music has come in fits and starts—it's really only since the early 80s that it has had any kind of significant impact—the reverse is certainly not the case, for rock artists have been attempting to escape their particular musical ghetto since the late 60s. Rock may be the most lucrative, glamorous, and ego-gratifying field of music to have yet appeared, yet some rock artists became aware early in their careers that more "serious" musicians in other fields looked down their noses at them. The strategy they used to earn respect as serious performers in their own right was to look beyond the boundaries of rock and to turn to classical music and the jazz avant-garde for inspiration.

The first evidence of this influence, as mentioned in Chapter 1, was the psychedelia movement. Using advanced electronic and tape techniques, Syd Barrett's group Pink Floyd, guitarist Jimi Hendrix, and Tangerine Dream introduced the rock world to a new musical vocabulary. Recordings like the early Pink Floyd albums *Piper at the Gates of Dawn* (1967) and *Saucerful of Secrets* (1968) were at times hardly recognizable as rock music. In California, the Grateful Dead created lengthy, highly experimental musical tributes to the joys of dropping acid. Frank Zappa toyed with *musique concrète* and other advanced tape techniques that inadvertently lent a psychedelic quality to his music.

It was Syd Barrett himself, though, who most epitomized psychedelia in music. His rock songs, always eccentric anyway, soon evolved into electric guitar and electric organ experiments; long, distorted solo lines flowed over a unique combination of both consonant and surprisingly dissonant chords. In an era when songs seldom dared to go beyond three minutes in length for fear of precluding radio play, Barrett's Pink Floyd would devote half an album side to a single work like the typically named "Interstellar Overdrive."

Unfortunately, Barrett lived the psychedelic lifestyle with equal gusto. He suffered two severe breakdowns—the result of allegedly heavy drug use and an apparent inability to handle his sudden notoriety—and was mentally and physically incapable of continuing with the band. He did resurface briefly with a pair of solo albums around 1972–1973, but these recordings, full of charming, quirky songs, didn't include any of the wild, cosmic instrumentals that made his early Pink Floyd records so distinctive.

With Barrett's departure, Pink Floyd began to settle into a more lyrical style, continuing to use progressive sounds and techniques but applying them in a more standard rock context. As the 60s gave way to the 70s, psychedelia gave birth to the "Big Sound" of such British bands as King Crimson, the Moody Blues, Yes, Genesis, and Emerson Lake & Palmer. These groups attempted, with varied results, to infuse the usual rock idioms with a symphonic sound. Emerson Lake & Palmer actually tried playing classical music in a rock format, but they seemed to have trouble remembering to credit the original composers. "Knife-Edge," from their untitled first album (1971), is a note-for-note "borrowing" of Leoš Janáček's 1926 *Sinfonietta;* yet the composer credits read "Emerson/Lake/Fraser." The group's own compositions were occasionally effective (though they were more often simply a pastiche of rock and classical clichés), but the real focus of ELP's music was its instrumentation. Keith Emerson actually took synthesizers on the road—a daring, even foolhardy, step to take, given the sometimes unreliable state of that instrument in 1971—and he was erroneously identified as the first rock musician to use the Moog on a record. (The Beatles had used one on *Abbey Road.*) His undeniable keyboard prowess produced a large, almost orchestral volume (one late ELP tour even included an orchestra to help recreate the band's studio sound), a quality that made ELP's music distinctive and the band one of the most popular groups of its time.

Also working in this style were King Crimson and Genesis. King Crimson sported the sounds of the mellotron, used to simulate the sonority of a string orchestra; a number of reed and wind instruments; and of course, Fripp's guitar. On a song like "I Talk to the Wind," from the first King Crimson album in 1969, the guitar almost disappeared as it blended seamlessly into a shifting layer of oboes, flutes, and other orchestral sounds. Such understated use of a rock instrument was at the time most unusual, and helped establish the group as a leading "classical-rock" ensemble. Although he was the only constant member of King Crimson, Fripp always surrounded himself with first-rate musicians. In whatever configuration, the band would come up with a number of memorable songs, but the focus always remained on musicianship and the deployment of sounds rather than the actual compositions. This was especially true of the later King Crimson albums, which moved away from the lush, neo-Romantic sound of the first three outings to a more contemporary, jazz-inflected style.

Genesis produced a similarly big sound, but given the songwriting talents of vocalist Peter Gabriel, its concern was primarily narrative—the story told in the lyrics. While early King Crimson's oblique lyrics were full of dragons and witches, Gabriel's texts were coherent, miniature fables, drawing on classical mythology, science fiction, and the dislocation of modern life. Like Fripp's group, Genesis used irregular rhythms and complex harmonies, and underwent a number of personnel changes. The group's original guitarist, Anthony Phillips, left after one album and was replaced by the more electrically oriented Steve Hackett. Drummer John Silver was replaced by Phil Collins at about the same time. When Gabriel left Genesis after 1974's two-record parable *The Lamb Lies down on Broadway,* Collins took over as vocalist and front-man for the group, and turned Genesis into a more conventional pop band.

However skilled the members of Genesis and King Crimson were in stretching the sound of rock music, they never, or rarely, strayed beyond rock into a completely different genre. The same qualification applies even more strongly to the group Yes, whose pop and rock roots remained even closer to the surface. These ensembles made genuinely interesting and original music, but they seldom reached listeners outside the rock world.

Fripp disbanded King Crimson in the mid-70s, loudly proclaiming his disgust with the relationship between rock bands and their audience, a relationship he described as "vampiric." The band's quasi-avant-garde aspirations were pretentious to some, exciting to others, but both camps could agree that Fripp and his cohorts were genuinely trying to expand the boundaries of rock. The other English groups, and the even more daring French ensembles like Christian Vander's Magma or Richard Pinhas's Heldon, were perceived similarly. The latter two pushed rock to an avant-garde extreme; but even at their loudest, most threatening, most dissonant moments, all of these bands were still playing, primarily, to a rock audience, however adventurous (and small) that audience might be.

During the 1970s at least two composers were able to remove themselves from the rock mainstream, while retaining their rock fans, by writing an uncategorizable sort of music with skill and imagination. British musicians David Bedford and Mike Oldfield have both had long careers in and out of rock music, and have often appeared on each other's albums. They met in Kevin Ayers's band, The Whole World, in 1970. Oldfield, a bass and guitar player, was a mere seventeen years old at the time, while Bedford, the keyboardist, had already studied for several years with the contemporary classical composer Lennox Berkeley at the Royal Academy of Music, had spent 1960 in Venice studying with Luigi Nono of the Italian avant-garde, and had a number of concert works under his belt. Bedford had also taught music in London's secondary schools throughout the 60s, and had written many pieces for children—including *An Exciting New Game for Children of All Ages,* a 1969 work in which the order of musical events was determined, in the best Cageian manner, by throwing dice. He had thus developed a style that was simple and directly appealing.

Bedford's interests in both rock and classical music led to a number of recordings that went a step further than those of the "classical-rock" groups. Instead of writing rock works that simply appropriated the sounds or techniques of classical music, Bedford fashioned a real synthesis of the two genres. In his albums *Instructions for Angels* (1975) and *The Odyssey* (1976), he freely combined the sounds of a women's choir or a full orchestra with electric keyboards and Oldfield's electric guitar.

Bedford's compositions were often set to the intense, visionary, and almost surreal poetry of Kenneth Patchen, to which his style was especially well-suited. In *Instructions for Angels,* though, the poems are not set in the usual way: They merely provide the titles and serve as the inspiration for the various sections of the piece.

The Odyssey uses its source a bit differently, since its text is adapted from Homer and is actually sung in parts of the work. This is one of Bedford's finest recordings, a glowing album of keyboards, wineglasses, solo voice, chorus, and solo guitar. Less successful is *The Rime of the Ancient Mariner* (1975), after the Coleridge poem. A more complex and perhaps even more interesting piece, its composite parts don't come together quite as neatly.

Mike Oldfield's best compositions, like Bedford's, cannot really be classified as rock. Although his recent recordings have tended to be conventional compilations of short rock songs, in the mid-70s Oldfield produced a number of album-length works that used all kinds of guitars, basses, and keyboards, with percussion, voices, and orchestral strings. (Bedford appears as conductor of the chorus and orchestra on these works.) In works like *Hergest Ridge* (1974), Oldfield effectively combines rock, symphonic, and Celtic folk styles, along with the occasional African drum or electronic effect; on *Ommadawn* (1975) Paddy Moloney of The Chieftains plays uilleann pipes, while an entire African drum ensemble appears on *Incantations* (1977). Fortunately, Oldfield uses his musical forces sparingly, so the music actually sounds lighter than what a trio like ELP might produce.

Oldfield could afford to indulge in such grand forces thanks to the overwhelming success of his 1973 work, *Tubular Bells.* That album sold some ten million copies worldwide, mainly on the strength of the opening two minutes of the piece, a fleet pattern of chimes and piano—the tubular bells themselves don't appear until the end of the side—that became famous as the theme from the movie *The Exorcist.* Anyone who bought *Tubular Bells* expecting to hear the soundtrack to a horror movie must have been surprised by the downright cheery mood of the album. It's a typically pastoral work through much of side one, ending in a flash of droll British humor. Side two is somewhat less serene and more mischievous, but monster music it's not.

Oldfield's albums are constructed with an almost classical logic. Themes are constantly brought back in altered forms, each of which may have a different mood. A moonlit carriage ride through the snow, complete with sleigh bells, on side one of *Hergest Ridge* eventually develops on side two into a dark, stomping piece that sounds like music for an ancient Celtic ritual.

Oldfield has since returned to the rock fold, while Bedford's music, always underexposed, has become almost impossible to find outside England. Although these two composers didn't necessarily write *better* music than King Crimson or Pink Floyd, they were among the first to successfully create *new* music that acknowledged rock's influence without actually falling into the rock category. Later musicians have worked in a similar vein; but Bedford and Oldfield operated on a larger scale than most rock music, while recent trends have included the sound *and* the size of rock.

The mid-to-late-70s was a period of retrenchment; many musicians and fans lost interest in the ponderous pretensions of "classical rock" and the let's-see-how-fast-we-can-play-this-scale-in-unison jazz-rock fusion. Instead, rock music pared down to a leaner, simpler style, which eventually led to the punk, hardcore, and new-wave music of the 80s.

Notably, it wasn't until the excesses of the classical- or jazz-rock styles were stripped away that rock really began to make its influence felt on new music, mainly by way of its rhythmic drive and energy. This shouldn't come as a surprise: The current generation of musicians has grown up on rock music, and has just naturally made it part of its musical vocabulary. Of course, rock music has grown to include a wide variety of styles, a fact reflected in the diversity of the new-music composers who use it. Peter Gordon's Love of Life Orchestra, and such "serious" rock groups as Talking Heads or the re-formed, more tightly knit King Crimson, typify a genre that has come to be known as "art-rock." Quite different is Glenn Branca, whose loud, violent symphonies, some of which use small armies of guitarists, are inspired by the sonorities of so-called "hardcore" punk rock.

The Love of Life Orchestra (or simply LOLO, as it's more often called) was formed in 1977 in New York by sax player Peter Gordon and percussion virtuoso David Van Tieghem. The group has always appeared in different configurations, depending on the requirements for a given performance. Since Gordon's music ranges from concert scores to dance music, LOLO may look like a chamber orchestra one night and a big rock group the next.

LOLO quickly established itself as a showcase for New York's most important "downtown" musicians. It was also regarded as a leader in the "art-rock" movement, although, as Van Tieghem admits, "I don't know if we ever deliberately set out thinking about it that way." Rather, the group was founded simply as a "big band" for downtown musicians: "There was a time between, say, 1979 and 1982, when we tried experimenting with a kind of dance music, playing a lot of clubs and such. We all sort of have rock or rock'n'roll in our roots, so it's hard not to relate to that. But some of Peter's stuff is almost chamber music." Gordon agrees: "I like to think of it as a serious music. It's a composed music, but it uses a lot of languages. Very often it happens to use the language of pop music, or folk and jazz."

This unabashed eclecticism is hardly surprising, considering Gordon's background. He lived in Munich while a teenager, and had a chance to see most of the major British rock acts there. "At that time," he remembers, "all the English groups were coming through to do their club gigs before their big tours, so we heard groups like the Yardbirds, the Kinks, and the Animals. And since it was Munich, there were three or four symphony orchestras and many opera houses, so I got to hear a lot of Webern, Schoenberg, and Penderecki."

Though Gordon's music covers a lot of ground stylistically, LOLO has nonetheless come to be associated most often with a spirited, downtown type of music with a strong rhythmic base. Again, it's not rock music, but it does draw heavily on the rhythms and performance styles of rock. "In traditional orchestral music," Gordon explains, "you have an idealized notion of what the sound should be. [LOLO] is more like the tradition of the Ellington band or a rock band, where people change their parts or bring their own articulations to it. A lot of it is worked out in rehearsals or in the studio. One thing might be strictly notated, but sometimes in the studio I don't know what someone should do and I say, well, just play something." As is true of many rock songs, the actual "composing" consists of how the players' own inventions are put into the final mix.

Both Gordon and Van Tieghem have taken advantage of the opportunities afforded by New York to work with other downtown artists, especially choreographers, including Twyla Tharp, Elisa Monte, Molissa Fenley, and Tricia Brown. Yet Gordon rejects the notion that LOLO is strictly a New York phenomenon. "I try not to think of it as that localized. It's not necessarily a geographical community, but a community of interest. There are people I'm working with who live in London or L.A. or Holland, and they're part of that community as well."

Gordon's conception of a community of ideas has in fact been put into practice in new rock-influenced music today, which is more often than not a collaborative effort. Laurie Anderson has employed both Gordon and Van Tieghem as sidemen on her albums; she has also recorded with Peter Gabriel. Gabriel—whose post-Genesis style is simpler, more basic, and now includes both electronics and West African rhythms—has worked with Robert Fripp, trumpeter Jon Hassell, and violinist L. Shankar. Fripp, Hassell, and Shankar have appeared on various albums by Talking Heads. David Byrne of Talking Heads, along with Laurie Anderson, has contributed lyrics to a set of songs by Philip Glass. Obviously, this is a community that knows how to keep busy.

The David Byrne/Brian Eno record *My Life in the Bush of Ghosts* (1981) is a particularly successful product of the mingling of rock and other styles. Eno had been recruited as producer and unofficial fifth member of Talking Heads for their second album in 1978. He and Byrne started working on other video and musical projects, and *My Life in the Bush of Ghosts,* along with Talking Heads' fourth album, *Remain in Light* (1980), fully explored their mutual interest in African and Near Eastern rhythms and "found sound" techniques. In the 1981 disc, recordings of radio talk-shows, Lebanese and Egyptian singers, and radio evangelists provided the content of each piece, while Byrne and Eno added a strong rhythmic, at times funky, musical accompaniment. The recordings of singers were used as is, as melodic material; the spoken excerpts had to be edited and repeated before taking on a noticeably rhythmic or melodic quality—a process similar to that used by Scott Johnson in his piece *John Somebody* (see Chapter 3), though on a smaller scale.

Preexisting or "found sound" also figures prominently on Van Tieghem's solo album *These Things Happen* (1984), written as a dance score for Twyla Tharp. While *These Things Happen* borrows some ideas from the Byrne/Eno sessions, its "found sounds"—mostly short-wave radio and natural sounds—are incorporated "atmospherically, as raw material, rather than putting an Arabic singer on top of a rhythm track and making that the lead vocal." The album also confronts one of the banes of modern pop music: the onslaught of rhythm boxes and other types of synthetic percussion. You might expect a professional percussionist to feel threatened by these new devices, but Van Tieghem is quite comfortable with them. "I always thought it would be better to make friends with the technology than be afraid of it," he claims. "Rhythm boxes will never replace a drummer; they're just a kind of base on which other things can lay."

Perhaps the new-music career that most fully exploits rock music and its technology is that of Laurie Anderson. While her early pieces involving taped and live sounds, film, photography, sculpture, and storytelling attracted some attention among the avant-garde in the mid-70s, her compositions in the 80s have received enormous publicity. And it's easy to see why when you compare her early recorded works with more recent albums. Two short scores from 1977, "New York Social Life" and "Time To Go (For Diego)," are typically amusing or bittersweet vignettes, built around Anderson's slice-of-life texts. They already reveal Anderson's predilection for rock technology—both pieces feature the common pop practice of overdubbing or multitracking, and Scott Johnson plays pop's signature instruments, electric guitar and organ on the second work—but neither piece actually approaches a "rock sound."

Much of the success of her two subsequent albums, *Big Science* (1982) and *Mr. Heartbreak* (1984), derives from Anderson's unequivocal but shrewd use of rock instruments and rhythms. *Big Science* Anderson describes as "simple and two-dimensional." A recording like *Mr. Heartbreak,* on the other hand, involves the contributions of several well-known rock musicians. Peter Gabriel appears on a number of songs (Gabriel and Anderson collaborated on a video for one of them); guitarist Adrian Belew, from the 80s King Crimson lineup, percussionists David Van Tieghem and Anton Fier, bassist Bill Laswell, and singer Phoebe Snow also show up on various tracks. The record is full of funky rhythms and catchy tunes, but of *Mr. Heartbreak,* Anderson says, "I don't think of it as rock in any way, but it's sitting in the rock bins in record stores, and there are people in it who do rock. After I finished *Big Science,* I probably said several hundred times how much I hated guitars, drums, and bass. Next record: guitars, drums, bass . . . it's all there. Although I can say that I don't think Adrian Belew plays guitar; I don't know what that is he plays—it's some kind of animal. And the way Anton Fier plays drums, those aren't rock'n'roll chops. And I don't know *what* to call Peter's yodeling."

Like most of today's rock artists, Laurie Anderson uses the latest technology —Synclaviers, Lexicons, Harmonizers, vocoders—but she maintains an ironic distance from it all. And like many rock albums, *Mr. Heartbreak* sports a number of instrumental solos ("*I* didn't write them," she says; "I don't know *where* they came from."); but those solos don't stop with the usual—or in Belew's case, *un*usual— electric guitar. The Korean kayagum (a long zither), the Caribbean steel drum, and bits of South American percussion get a chance to step out, too.

Laurie Anderson's music has always been highly original and idiosyncratic. She has the rare ability to combine art and entertainment without any trace of pretension; her works may be "serious music," but they don't take themselves seriously, and they're fun without being trivial. The one word that is continually called upon to describe Anderson's compositions is quirky.

It's not only for her music, though, that Laurie Anderson has achieved such success; she has also become the best-known exponent of that practice known as "performance art." This catchall term was coined in the late 70s to describe (retroactively if need be) the type of multimedia events that avant-garde artists had been engaged in during the 60s and 70s: John Cage, Robert Moran, Meredith Monk, and Robert Ashley were well-known "performance artists" in one form or another. The term remains a nebulous one, and can be applied to virtually any combination of theater, video, music, sculpture, photography, speech, and/or dance. It's probably safe to say that no two people have exactly the same idea of what does or doesn't constitute "performance art." But most of them seem to agree that Laurie Anderson's work fits the bill.

It's certainly true that her work is performance-oriented, and that simply to categorize it as "music" is missing the point. A routine from 1973, for example, saw Anderson armed with her violin and standing on skates on a block of ice. She spoke about balance, a requirement in both skating and bowing the violin, and played the instrument while the ice melted. When the block had melted away, the piece was over. Maybe this could be considered performance art. But then what do you call her two-night, four-part, six-hour epic *United States,* a mixture of comedy, concert music, rock, avant-garde electronics, still and moving visual images, and theatrical touches like a soprano on a diving board or a "tape-bow violin" that actually spoke when played?

Surely you wouldn't place this in the same category as "Duets on Ice." For one thing, the music and the visuals in *United States* are the heart of the work; the earlier piece really concerns Anderson's own skill as a performer. That skill is certainly central to *United States,* too, since Anderson is onstage throughout the entire piece, usually without any visible human accompaniment. But while her earlier conceptual works seemed to involve performing for performing's sake or as an excuse for doing something weird in public, her performance in *United States* served as a vehicle for the piece's narrative.

"I've really tried to stay away from categories in my thinking about the work," Anderson says. "When I was doing *United States,* people who wrote about it would often just analyze my work as some kind of actor. They'd talk about what I wore and how I sounded or what I looked like, instead of as someone who wrote the whole thing and shot the film and composed the music. I think there are other aspects of it—aside from my acting skills, which are pretty marginal I think—that are important to me, and to other people."

In all fairness, Anderson does cultivate a striking stage presence. A slight figure with short, spiky hair, dressed in black, standing alone on a large stage full of hi-tech equipment, and speaking in a variety of natural and processed voices is bound to draw an inordinate amount of attention to itself, so it's entirely understandable that so much was written about her appearance. The term performance art does, all the same, tend to give insufficient due to the music.

That music is very much a product of the same lower-Manhattan community that spawned Philip Glass, a host of punk-rock and new-wave bands, several "performance artists," and the Love of Life Orchestra, whose members frequently appear on her albums. Although born in Illinois, Anderson moved to New York to study art and sculpture; she fell in with the downtown crowd and began working with unusual ways of using and producing sound. One early opus was a kind of sound sculpture, though nothing like the Bertoias mentioned in the previous chapter. The piece looked like an ordinary table; viewers were instructed to rest their elbows on the table and cover their ears with their hands. When they did, they heard music coming from a tape deck concealed within the wood. The sound was audible only when it was conducted up the arms to the listener's ears.

In subsequent pieces, Anderson gave free rein to her native talent for humor and storytelling. Some of these works, "New York Social Life" for instance, are little more than wry observations and light-hearted parodies accompanied by minimal, almost incidental music. One amusing piece from the mid-70s was a reggae song called "It's Not the Bullet That Kills You, It's the Hole." This gently chiding song was aimed at the most extreme performance artist of the period, Chris Burden. "Burden's work is interesting because it involves no metaphor," Anderson declares. "It's not 'one thing is like another thing.' His work is about the thing itself. If he wants to deal with pain, he doesn't talk about pain, or make a song about pain— he is *in* pain. So he shoots himself in the arms, crawls over glass; the masochism is sort of gruesome, but what impressed me was that art doesn't dance around its subject. At a certain point, though, I began to realize he was concentrating more on the caliber of the bullet, on the effects, rather than the sensation itself. I thought that was going too far, so I wrote that song for him."

The turning point in Anderson's career was her 1981 song "O Superman." By this time, she was already at work on her magnum opus, *United States.* The first part of that sprawling, multimedia event had been presented in rudimentary form at The Kitchen in New York in 1979, when Anderson, like many of the downtown poets of the day (Patti Smith, John Giorno, and later Allen Ginsberg), was experimenting with the instruments and language of rock. By temperament, Anderson was less inclined toward the harsh punk-rock sounds that Smith or Giorno used; her texts, full of everyday phrases from television news or telephone-answering machines, as well as word-association games, could be ominous or disquieting at times, but they were never as intimidating or as defiantly obscure as those of her colleagues. This, combined with Anderson's uncanny sense of timing and her sly-but-friendly delivery, gave her works the potential to appeal to a broad range of listeners. And that's just what happened with "O Superman."

In both text and music, this is a characteristic Anderson work. The first line of the song, "O Superman, O Judge, O Mom and Dad," is a corruption of the first line of an aria by French composer Jules Massenet: "O souverain, o juge, o pere" ("Oh sovereign, oh judge, oh father"). From there she develops a series of different personae through the use of electronic filters which change the sound of her voice, and the vocoder, a kind of vocal synthesizer. One cheery voice announces immediately just how contemporary this work is—"Hi! I'm not home right now, but if you wanna leave a message, just start talking at the sound of the tone," while a second (still Anderson, of course) answers, "Hello? This is your mother. Are you coming home?" A third voice now enters and ominously sings/says, "Well, you don't know me. But I know you. And I've got a message to give to you. Here come the planes." At which point the voice, which has become increasingly synthesized and metallic-sounding, settles on the "n" in "planes" and drones off into the distance.

Musically, "O Superman" consists of spare electronics, layers of processed vocals (the sound of a voice whispering "ha, ha, ha" in strict tempo is the first and last sound of the song, and serves as the basic rhythm track throughout), and very brief cameos by flute and sax. Although Laurie Anderson rarely sings, her mastery of the inflections and nuances of American speech turn her delivery into a type of *Sprechgesang,* or speech-song; and through the use of filters and vocoders, these inflections will sometimes take on definite melodic values.

"O Superman" was originally pressed in a limited edition on a private label. But something totally unforeseen happened: People began buying it. In Great Britain, the song not only hit the pop charts—an amazing feat in itself for an "avant-garde" work—but even more astonishingly, peaked at number two.

"I know very little about that part of the music world," Anderson says, "and I didn't even know what the charts were in Britain. People kept calling and saying things like, You're number eight! And it was totally abstract; I just thought, eight on what? I really liked that experience; I liked the fact that other kinds of people than normally would come to my concerts liked that music." "O Superman" sold almost 800,000 copies, and convinced one of the largest pop-music conglomerates,

Warner Bros., to give her a recording contract. This in turn provided Anderson with the resources to complete and produce *United States* at the Brooklyn Academy of Music in February 1983.

United States was an ambitious work, and a puzzling one for critics. It was reviewed as theater, as a music concert, as an "opera" of sorts, and of course, as performance art. Yet, from whatever angle it was approached, *United States* was an impressive achievement, not the least reason for which was the fact that one month before its premiere Anderson had still not completed the work, and admitted to being a bit confused about what went where. "It's an enormous puzzle," she said in an interview then, "not only of songs and tapes, but of hundreds of slides, and it can be really baffling."

The musical portions of *United States* were often quite spare. "The reason for keeping it simple," Anderson explains, "is that if there are pictures, which there almost always are, then it becomes too busy, too overwhelming." Like Robert Wilson, Laurie Anderson has developed a new and original kind of intermedia art. It's a theater of images, both visual and musical. The juxtaposition or sequence of these images is suggestive rather than descriptive, and any kind of narrative logic has to be supplied by the viewer. *United States* is also reminiscent of the work of Robert Ashley, one of the original "performance artists," whose 1980 "video opera" *Perfect Lives (Private Parts)* was one of the earliest combinations of rock-inspired music, video, and narrative.

Even with her slightly skewed views of theater and music, the rock elements in Anderson's music have helped broaden the appeal of her art enormously. To use the term *rock music* to describe what Anderson does, however, is as inaccurate as the term *performance art* is vague. The comparison may seem bizarre, but like Wagner, Anderson attaches equal importance to text, visual presentation, and music. And as with Wagner's later works, a piece like *United States* is too big for the confines of one style or another, and needs to be taken on its own merits.

The success of Laurie Anderson is all the more remarkable because it was accomplished without the easy handle that a musical category provides: Listeners were enjoying the music even if they didn't know just what to call it. But Anderson's art is nothing if not accessible—a word you could never apply to the music of Glenn Branca. Of all the artists combining the sounds of rock with the formal devices of classical music, Branca is, to many ears, the most extreme. Loud, uncompromising, often violent, his work is highly controversial.

Like the LOLO musicians and Laurie Anderson, Branca has long been a part of New York's downtown community; and like them, he has also been commissioned to write scores for dance companies, including those of Twyla Tharp and Elisa Monte. But the similarities end there. Branca makes no bones about his musical background: The walls of sound he unleashes, often from a phalanx of electric guitars, clearly hearken to the abrasive sounds of "hardcore" punk rock.

Volume is one of the foundations of Branca's music, and is certainly the first feature to strike the listener, but it is by no means its sole distinguishing characteristic. "My music is really very formal," he claims. "I'm trying to develop a compositional process which derives from a natural process." The natural process Branca cites is our old friend the harmonic series (see pages 225–28), whose structure has largely determined not only the form of Branca's works, but also their instrumentation (he has had to design new instruments capable of playing the intervals of the series) and notation.

"I have a lot to say about the technical aspects of the music," Branca continues. "Sometimes people will ask me about the acoustic phenomena, and I've thought a lot about that. I've started working with a system of music which is not taught in the schools, which there's no real frame of reference for, necessarily, and I'm not even totally sure of what I'm doing myself. But that's what I work with."

It may be hard to reconcile Branca's loud, brash sonorities with the serious intentions underlying them, but this apparent incongruity only makes his pieces more intriguing. Early Branca works often used massive groups of electric guitars, electric bass, and drums—hardly the battery of instruments you would expect in a symphony, yet his 1981 Symphony #1 *(Tonal Plexus)* was scored for precisely these forces. Even more ambitious was the similarly scored Symphony #2 *(The Peak of the Sacred)* of 1982, a five-movement piece that unleashed a torrent of sound for more than an hour and a half. Anyone expecting a conventional symphonic work at a performance of either work would have been deafeningly disappointed.

Branca's Symphony #3 *(Gloria),* premiered early in 1983, was his first major score to be based on the harmonic series. Subtitled "Music for the first 127 intervals of the harmonic series," the symphony was commissioned by the Brooklyn Academy of Music. As we have seen in Chapter 10, the first 127 intervals, from the first partial to the 128th, cover exactly seven octaves. If you look at Figure 4 on page 227, you'll see that the series becomes fairly complex as early as the fourth octave. It took Branca close to a year to gain some sort of control over this material in order to mount the first production of the piece.

"When I started working with the harmonic series, it was really just an idea about a tuning system," he recalls. "Very quickly it became more than a tuning system: I began to see the compositional potential of the series. That's when it became problematic." Because the intervals of the harmonic series are best produced on "open" strings,* Branca wanted access to seven octaves' worth of them. "It became clear I had to start working with keyboards. I mean, it was ridiculous to have fifty or sixty guitars on stage just to get enough open strings. And I couldn't work with conventional keyboards because I couldn't tune them to some of the octaves in the series. For instance, in the seventh octave, I've got sixty-four intervals (as opposed to the usual twelve). You just can't tune a conventional keyboard like that. So I had to have the keyboards built. So the Symphony #3 was mainly about developing the instruments and approaching a compositional technique. It was really about my discovery of the series."

In both the third and fourth symphonies, *(Physics,* 1983) Branca uses specially tuned keyboards, mallet guitars, and bass and drums. Despite the absence of much electric-guitar noise, these works remain characteristically loud and dense, alternat-

---

*In a given instrument, "open strings" are those that are called upon to play only one note. Piano strings are open strings, except in a prepared piano. Zithers and harps use open strings, too—one string per note, which is why those notes are so resonant and full. Guitar, violin, and bass strings are open at first, but as soon as you require other notes, you must "stop" the string with a finger—and consequently the notes produced aren't as harmonically rich.

ing between ringing, icy brilliance and harsher, more dramatic sections. In the Symphony #5 *(Describing Planes of an Expanding Hypersphere),* Branca returned to the electric-guitar forces of his earlier works because, by 1984, he had completely refretted the guitars so that he could get the intervals he desired.

Since embarking on his solo career in 1979, Branca has always been controversial. The ambiguity of his music, fusing the sounds and stage effects of a rock concert with a serious compositional approach, and the ambiguities of his piece's titles—"Gloria" not only has overtones of religion and classical music, it's also a classic 60s rock song—have caused some misunderstanding. The sight of ten electric guitarists dressed like renegades from the punk-rock clubs is also jarring to some of his audience. But again, the fundamental objection continues to be to the volume.

"It's difficult," he says, "because a younger audience is used to going to rock concerts. It's not a problem there at all. With an older audience that isn't interested in rock, it's a very big problem, because at volume levels that are ridiculously low, many people think it's outrageously loud! Of course it's loud compared to an orchestra or a jazz band, but compared to a hardcore band, it's not loud."

Since the Symphony #3, Branca has worked constantly, almost obsessively, at exploring the potential of the harmonic series. "It really is an incredibly difficult thing to explain from scratch," he says ruefully. "And I hate to be the one saying this because when I discovered the series, I was the first person to say, Why has this been so mysterious? Why have I always had the idea that the harmonic series is so strange and complex? It really isn't. It's arithmetic; it's something very simple that we can all understand. The connotations are another story. If there's been any problem with my music in the past few years, it's that I've been involved in something that has such incredible potential."

Branca had been concerned with form and process even before he started his investigations into the harmonic series. He mentions Philip Glass and Steve Reich as early influences, while he was still doing music/theater pieces in Boston. He moved to New York in 1976 and formed a rock band with Jeffrey Lohn called Theoretical Girls, which very quickly became more than just another punk group. A second band, The Static, was even more austere; each piece was a kind of formal exercise. Branca's early solo works have similar intentions, as titles like *Lesson # 1 for Guitar* might indicate. But the harmonic series has now become the cornerstone of a much more intensive study of musical structure.

"Working with process is almost like coming up with a formula that plays itself out over a period of time. You might say this is a matter of deriving the formula from the harmonic series itself and, in a way, deriving a piece of music completely unintentionally—which relates back to Cage."

Other composers using the harmonic series, like La Monte Young, David Hykes, or Rhys Chatham, work with the overtones themselves—picking upper partials out of a single note's harmonic series and making them audible. Chatham, for example, uses five or six electric guitars to produce blocks of loud, pulsing overtones from a limited number of "source" notes. Branca, however, doesn't so much compose around the harmonics themselves; his music is based on the way the series is set up, and on the relationships within the series. It's a formidable piece of work. "I really feel in each piece as though I want to somehow capture every aspect of the series," he says, "and it's just impossible at this point. It's going to be quite a few years' work for me. I'd love to see a lot of people working on this together, and working off each other—I'm not really such an egomaniac as people might think. A lot of people are working with the harmonic series, but there's so much more room."

Besides the logistical problems of adjusting the tuning and the timbre of the instruments, Branca still faces the difficulty of finding a way to translate the mathematics and geometry of the harmonic series into an actual performance. He claims that the progress he's making on paper with the series has gone far beyond what instruments are capable of doing at the moment, so recent Branca compositions are not necessarily related to his more theoretical work.

In an odd way, Glenn Branca's research is leading him, though by a completely different route, to an approach similar to Morton Feldman's (see page 92). "Up to this point," he explains, "most music, especially 'serious' music, has been linear. My idea is a kind of nonlinear music, which doesn't progress from left to right or up and down. It's not about what happens between one and one hundred; it's not a matter of following it with your finger down the score. I think there *is* a form of nonlinear music, it just hasn't been articulated or described yet, but I think it's something we're going to hear more of."

On the surface, it's patently ridiculous to draw parallels between Feldman's calm, hypnotic compositions and Branca's furiously energetic pieces. But Branca's search for a nonlinear music seems not dissimilar from Feldman's cultivation of a quality of timelessness. It should be fascinating to see where this interest takes him.

In the 1920s, American composer George Antheil stirred up a furor in Europe with works that called for groups of pianos with airplane propellers, car horns, or anvils. The "bad boy of music" was how he became known. Is Glenn Branca the new bad boy of music? "Oh, that'd be great," he laughs, "I'd love to be able to make that claim. Actually, I'm not interested in shocking people simply for the sake of shocking them through any means possible. That's not too difficult to do, really. On the other hand, a little excitement over *anyone's* music is certainly nice."

Understatements aside, it's inevitable that today's most popular musical style would generate some excitement in the new-music arena. Most young composers spent their early years listening to popular music: "When you listen to commercials on TV," says David Van Tieghem, "it's all rock and dance music. It's all over the place; even the muzak in the elevators is rock now. It's just what everyone has grown up with." As that generation comes of age, it is finding that the sounds of rock and concert music are not necessarily incompatible. Scott Johnson's *John Somebody* uses classic tape techniques and has a strong formal quality to it, but it's also a piece filled with electric-guitar solos and chords that are right out of the rock repertoire.

"Growing up in America and studying music in school, you hear one type of music," Johnson maintains, "but you go anywhere else and you hear something quite different. I found myself loving the sounds of American vernacular music, but being a little bored with its lack of structure, and liking the intellectual structure of European music. That became something to try to put together."

Rock, like folk, jazz, classical, ethnic, and electronic music, has made its contributions to the gray area known as new music. Because of its popularity, though, rock will probably become a most effective way of increasing new music's visibility. But rock's virtues are matched by an equal number of drawbacks, and it will be a test of the new-music composers' skills to use the vitality of rock music without resorting to its clichés. True, the most popular rock songs often tend to be the most formulaic, cliché-ridden ones, but the days when "serious" musicians viewed rock simply as Neanderthal noise with nothing of substance to offer now seem to be ending.

DISCOGRAPHY AND RELATED WORKS

AFTER DINNER
■ *Sepiature* (Rec. RRC20) NMDS. A defunct Japanese group. Lovely vocals; avant-garde rock but still melodic. Some Asian influence, too (Indian, actually).

AKSAK MABOUL
■ *"Scratch Holiday," "Un Chien . . ."* from the LP *Made to Measure, Vol. I* (Crammed Discs CRAM-029) NMDS. Excerpts from two film scores. Like the second Aksak Maboul record (see Chapter 9, page 202), this version of the group is much closer to the rock avant-garde. From a compilation that also includes Tuxedomoon (see below) and others.

▲ *American Music Compilation* (Eurock Eurlp-01) EUR. Four ensembles; the most interesting is Anode, which performs three Leimerish works in K. Leimer's Palace of Lights studio using some of his sidemen.

LAURIE ANDERSON
■ *"Time To Go (for Diego)"* and *"New York Social Life"* from the LP *New Music for Electronic and Recorded Media* (1750 Arch S-1765) NMDS
■ *"Three Expediences"* from the two-LP set *Big Ego* (Giorno Poetry Systems GPS-012/013)
■ *"Dr. Miller," "It Was up in the Mountains," "Drums,"* other works, from the Anderson/Burroughs/Giorno LP *You're the Guy I Want To Share My Money With* (Giorno Poetry Systems GPS-033) NMDS
Some of Anderson's contributions to various compilation discs. She also appears on *The Nova Convention* (Giorno Poetry) and *Word of Mouth* (Crown Point Press), but they are textual rather than musical works. Most of these pieces eventually wound up in *United States* (see below).
■ *Big Science* (War. BSK-3674)
■ *Mr. Heartbreak* (War. 25077)
Anderson's finest compositions are contained here. Both albums, especially the first, include parts of *United States*. Both effectively turn rock instruments and technology to Anderson's own ends, resulting in strange, yet accessible, music.

■ *United States Live* (War. 25192, 5 LPs). Quite honestly, this mammoth set is too cumbersome to reflect accurately what *United States* sounded or *felt* like. In bits and pieces it's fine, though the sound is not always the best. But without the visual portion, and without the subtlety of delivery possible only in a live performance, this is an uneven document.
■ *Home of the Brave* (War. 25400-1). Is the thrill gone? This soundtrack to Anderson's concert film has lots of R&B-style vocals, digitally sampled voice sounds, hi-tech musical jokes, and funky rhythms. "Late Show" and "White Lily" are inventive pieces, but the rest are even closer to conventional rock than the previous albums. *Home* doesn't have the power of surprise that made her earlier records so distinctive.

ART BEARS
■ *Winter Songs* (Re 0618) NMDS. Art Bears is an outgrowth of Henry Cow (Chapter 9, page 208), the major difference being the addition of vocalist Dagmar Krause. The fusion of styles is more heavily based on rock, though there are folk song elements here as well. But if you don't like Krause's voice—and many people don't—you may find this tough sledding.
■ *The World As It Is Today* (Re 6622) NMDS. More of the same; this time the political rhetoric, never far from the surface anyway, overpowers the music.

ROBERT ASHLEY
■ *Perfect Lives (Private Parts)—The Bar* (Lovely VR-4904) NMDS
■ *Music Word Fire and I Would Do It Again Coo Coo* (Lovely VR 4908) NMDS
These are the second and third volumes in Ashley's Private Parts series, and the most rock-oriented "serious music" you may ever find. While the music in Chapter 12, both from this video opera and from other projects, is more eccentric and rewarding, these albums, with "Blue" Gene Tyranny and several members of LOLO helping out, prove

that electric instruments and a steady rock beat don't necessarily add up to rock music.

MIKE BATT
- *Tarot Suite* (Epic NJE-36312)
- *Six Days in Berlin* (Epic PE-37665)

Batt likes to combine the sounds of rock musicians with orchestral music. It works, but infrequently. Similar music has been done elsewhere with more success.

DAVID BEDFORD
- *The Rime of the Ancient Mariner* (Vir. 2038). Bedford is one of the composers alluded to in the preceding listing. This album's musical material includes Tielman Susato's *basse danse* "La Mourisque" (from 1561) and "The Rio Grande," a sea shanty. No orchestra here, but a chorus, lots of keyboards, violin, percussion, and narrator. Somewhat more complex and less accessible than the following, but equally interesting.
- *The Odyssey* (Vir. 2070). 1976 setting of Homer's *Odyssey,* though actually there are very few vocals. Bedford plays an impressive number of keyboards, including church organ, and is joined by guitarist Mike Oldfield, a women's choir (especially effective in "The Sirens," perhaps his most radiant piece), and several others.
- *Instructions for Angels* (Vir. 2090). Magnificent collection of works for keyboards, electric guitar, and the Leicestershire Schools Symphony Orchestra, conducted by Eric Pinkett. Uses a five hundred-year-old melody as a basis for a set of variations, each inspired by a Kenneth Patchen poem.

BIRDSONGS OF THE MESOZOIC
- *Magnetic Flip* (Ace of Hearts AHS-10018) WAY. Rock-inflected instrumentals. Lots of electric guitar, synthesizer, drums, and percussion; but a couple of unexpected Satie-esque pieces also. "Terry Riley's House" cues you in to one of this Boston group's main influences. A nifty arrangement of Stravinsky's *Rite of Spring* (the opening only) shows another. Other albums are more conventional.

DAVID BOWIE
- *Low* (RCA CPL-1-2030)
- *"Heroes"* (RCA AFL-1-2522)

Recorded in Berlin in the late 70s, well before Bowie's current fixation on pop music. Between the dual influences of Brian Eno and the Berlin Wall, Bowie was inspired to create his moodiest, most atmospheric works on the second sides of these records. Almost ten years later, these LPs, *"Heroes"* especially, still have not received the credit they deserve.
- *Lodger* (RCA AQL-1-3254). Away from the Wall and in the less insular city of Montreux, Bowie, Eno, and company lightened things up a bit, though the African and Near Eastern ingredients add a bit of color to this album, too.

GLENN BRANCA
- *The Ascension* (99 Records 01LP). Like much of Branca's early work, this album is still obviously linked to the post-punk bands of the late 70s and early 80s. But the transition to music full of drama and substance is underway here, too: This album's title track is still one of Branca's most intense works. And pairing the Robert Longo cover art with the album's title was a stroke of genius.
- *"Bad Smells"* from the John Giorno/Glenn Branca album *Who You Staring At?* (Giorno Poetry Systems 025) NMDS. Stinks. Heh heh, just kidding. This is not one of Branca's better scores, though. Written for Twyla Tharp, it *is* beautifully recorded, but this is not the Branca record to start off with.
- *Symphony #1: Tonal Plexus* (Neutral ROIR-125) NMDS. Cassette only. Loud, aggressive, with huge blocks of sound crashing into one another. The sound is just okay; the work itself represents a significant development in the field of new music.
- *Symphony #3: Gloria* (Neutral 04) NMDS. Symphonies 2, 4, and 5 have not yet been recorded. Even if they are released, this may still stand as Branca's finest album. The truly orchestral sound, the weird tuning and instruments, the sense of power and grandeur in the music—all are marks of an accomplished artist. But this 1983 LP is still the most recent from Branca: He has yet to follow up the work presented here, at least on record.
- *"Acoustic Phenomena, Introduction"* (from the audio-cassette magazine *Tellus,* Vol. 10). NMDS. Poor sound quality, and just a short excerpt, but still a remarkable piece with some striking harmonic effects. For mallet guitar, harmonics guitar, and adapted harpsichords.

CAMEL
- *The Snow Goose* (Passport PB-9856). David Bedford's arrangements lift this album above the level usually achieved by this "progressive rock" band.

CAPTAIN BEEFHEART AND HIS MAGIC BAND
- *The Legendary A&M Sessions* (A&M SP-12570)
- *Trout Mask Replica* (RPS 2MS-2027)
- *Top Secret* (ACD SN-7217)
- *Doc at the Radar Station* (Vir. 13148)

These albums by Captain Beefheart (Don Van Vliet) are still in print; *Shiny Beast, Safe As Milk,* and *Unconditionally Guaranteed* are apparently not. Like Frank Zappa, with whom he was briefly associated, C. B. is an eccentric and original musician. In fact, if Zappa had been as heavily influenced by the blues as Van Vliet (and if he'd had the latter's wonderfully grating voice), his music might have sounded like this. As it is, Captain Beefheart occupies his own little niche in the rock field.

CARMEN
■ *Fandangos in Space* (ABC DSDP-50192). David Allen, John Glascock, and others combine rock and gypsy/Spanish styles. Some very nice flamenco guitar work here. (O.P.)

RHYS CHATHAM
■ *Factor X* (Moers 2008) NMDS. Music for brass, with some electric guitar works. Olu Dara, George Lewis, and Anton Fier head a talented cast. The album is loud and bruising; the excellent deployment of brass and the cascading harmonics of the guitars make it worth hearing.

▲ *Clearlight Symphony* (Vir. 2029). 1976 record from Cyrille Verdeaux, Steve Hillage, et.al. Self-indulgent, but has its moments.

CLUB FOOT ORCHESTRA
■ *Wild Beasts* (Ralph CF-8699) NMDS. This rock band plays just about everything except rock music. Tango, klezmer, big band, funk, and other styles are given a fractured, distorted, but highly musical treatment by Richard Marriott (trombone, flute, synthesizer), Beth Custer (clarinet, voice), Residents' cohort Snakefinger (guitar), and others.

LINDSAY COOPER
■ *Rags* (Rec. Re/arc) NMDS. Good album for fans of Henry Cow or Art Bears. For everyone else, the instrumentals are best. Cooper plays reeds and keyboards.

HOLGER CZUKAY
■ *Movies* (EMC 3319). Czukay was one of the founding members of the experimental group Can, and worked with *musique concrète* and found sound long before the celebrated Byrne and Eno album. This record has some moments of tedium and some of brilliance—one of the latter being "Persian Love," incorporating the sounds of Iranian singers taken off a short-wave radio with the sounds of lyrical pop music.

DELAY TACTICS
■ *Out-Pop Options* (Multiphase DT-002) NMDS
■ *Any Questions* (Multiphase DT-005) NMDS
Delay Tactics is Carl Weingarten's rock band. (See Chapter 1.) Still, Weingarten's other musical interests surface occasionally here, and each album has a couple of works that are less easily pigeonholed.

JOEL DUGRENOT
■ *See* (Eurock EDC-13) EUR. Dugrenot, a well-known bassist in avant-garde jazz-rock circles in France, is also a solo artist. This cassette has a spacey sound with occasional hints at Near Eastern music. Piano, acoustic and electric violins, flute, bass, percussion.

THE DURUTTI COLUMN
■ *The Return of* (Factory FACT 14c). Neat packaging—this cassette looks like a good book. Vini

Reilly, electric guitarist, is the core of the group. "In 'D'" is a series of arpeggiated chords with a lovely introspective aura, played on solo guitar; the rest are harder-edged rock instrumentals.
■ *Tomorrow* (Benelux Fbn-51). A 45-rpm disc, with a lyrical, wistful rock song on one side, and a muted instrumental track on the other. Electric guitar, with sax, violin, some others.

EMERSON, LAKE & PALMER
■ *ELP* (Atco/Cotillion 9040)
■ *Trilogy* (Atlantic 9903)
■ *Brain Salad Surgery* (Manticore 66669)
■ *Works, Vol. 1* (Atlantic SD2-7000)
Emerson's favorite composers are obviously Prokofiev, Bartók, perhaps Janáček, among others. Palmer perhaps shared his enthusiasm for Prokofiev: His side of the *Works* collection includes an arrangement of part of the *Scythian Suite.* Lake's favorite composer is apparently Greg Lake. Toward the end of this trio's career, his pop pablum single-handedly ruined their albums. Much of the group's music doesn't sound too exciting today, although each of these records has some interesting works. On the first album, "The Three Fates" and "Knife's Edge" display the group at its best and worst, respectively. Besides the occasional original, some of their classical arrangements (i.e., where the composer was actually given credit) came off rather well—the Parry and Ginastera pieces on the *Brain Salad Surgery* LP, for example.

BRIAN ENO
■ *Here Come the Warm Jets* (Island ILPS-9268)
■ *Taking Tiger Mountain (By Strategy)* (Island ILPS-9309)
Aside from two compilation discs, *Desert Island* and *More Blank Than Frank* (both on the EG label), these are the only two Eno records that can really be termed rock music. Even here, though, you have to expect the unexpected. The first album, Eno's first solo record, has a couple of instrumental or almost-instrumental pieces that presage his later ambient phase.

FONDATION
■ *Sans Etiquette* (Eurock EDC-03) EUR. Jazz-rock from France. The eerie vocalises lend an otherworldly aura at times; the more conventional accompaniment includes keyboards, guitars, bass, and simple-minded electronic percussion.

ROBERT FRIPP
■ *Exposure* (Poly. PD-1-6201). Explores several rock styles, but the two "Water Music" excerpts are closer to the Fripp and Eno material.

ROBERT FRIPP AND
THE LEAGUE OF CRAFTY GUITARISTS
■ *Live* (EG EGED-44) JEM. This recent album (1986) features Fripp and his sixteen "Guitar Craft" seminar students. There's some Fripper-

tronics, but much of it is acoustic. As you might expect, even the acoustic works sound electric. With moods ranging from funky to ambient, this is everything the Fripp/Summers records should've been, but weren't.

- *The Lady or the Tiger?* (EG EGED-43) JEM. Now *this,* on the other hand, is quite annoying, if I may be so bold. Credited to "Toyah and Fripp, featuring the League of Crafty Guitarists," it places the guitars in a purely background role while relentless (and not entirely professional) readings take up both sides.

ROBERT FRIPP AND
THE LEAGUE OF GENTLEMEN

- [Untitled] (Poly. PD-1-6317). A quartet: guitar, keyboards, bass, and drums. Speedy rock instrumentals with the flair and bite of Fripp's guitar.

ROBERT FRIPP AND ANDY SUMMERS

- *I Advance Masked* (A&M SP-4913)
- *Bewitched* (A&M SP-5011)

Two fine guitarists, but two uneven recordings. Both have moments when the guitars blend convincingly, but Fripp seems uncomfortable with Summers's pop-inflected style and Summers appears unable to follow Fripp's more experimental ideas.

FRED FRITH

- *Gravity* (Ralph 8057) NMDS
- *Speechless* (Ralph 8106) NMDS

The first album is almost completely rock; the second is more daring, and has some pretty way-out pieces.

PETER FROHMADER

- *Nekropolis* (RP 10 122) EUR
- *Nekropolis 2* (Hasch KIF-002) EUR
- *Nekropolis Live* (Schneeball 1037) EUR

Mixing equal parts of Carl Orff, Magma, Glenn Branca, and Black Sabbath, Frohmader makes highly processed musical nightmares that occasionally attempt to recreate the violence and harmonic effects of Branca's recent work. Interesting in the same way a Gothic horror film might be.

GENESIS

- *The Lamb Lies down on Broadway* (Atco SD2-402, 2 LPs)
- *Wind and Wuthering* (Atco 36-144)

Genesis's discography is considerably larger than this, but these albums have a couple of instrumentals that combine electronics, classical guitar, and others in a style that's closer to "space music" than to the so-called "progressive rock" that Genesis championed until their recent pop records.

GHOSTWRITERS

- *Objects in Mirrors Are Closer Than They Appear* (Red 001) NMDS. From the electronic music duo listed in Chapter 1, an album of electronic rock.

"Reference to Rota" is a strange blend of Nino Rota's pensive quality and the sounds of technopop; "Tarpit" echoes gamelan instruments and ethnic drums.

JERRY GOODMAN

- *On the Future of Aviation* (Private 1301) PRI. As usual from this label, stellar recording and production. Goodman is a virtuoso violinist, and he ain't too shabby on guitar, either. The title track is the best; the rest becomes a busy sort of New Age music.

PETER GORDON

- *Innocent* (CBS FM-42098). This album was originally going to be called *Love of Life,* and it features the members of that all-star downtown band. Includes a work cowritten by Gordon and Laurie Anderson, as well as excerpts from *Secret Pastures* and *Geneva* (see below). From the twelve-tone experimentalism of "The Announcement" to the unbridled rock energy in "St. Cecilia (or, The Power of Music)," an appealing example of Gordon's art.

PETER GORDON AND
THE LOVE OF LIFE ORCHESTRA

- *Extended Niceties* (Lust/Unlust JMB-227)
- *Geneva* (Lust/Unlust JMB-233)
- *Casino* (Expanded Music/Italian Records)
- *Star Jaws* (Lovely LM-1031)

These albums date from 1977 through 1982, and with the exception of the last, are almost impossible to find now. Varying degrees of big-band rock, jazz, and experimental music. Some of these are credited to Gordon only, but they are basically LOLO albums.

- *Secret Pastures* (Artservices cassette, no #) NMDS. Gordon's finest work to date, written for Bill T. Jones and Arnie Zane's dancers. LOLO has never sounded better (except in person, of course).

JOHN GREAVES AND PETER BLEGVAD

- *Kew. Rhone.* (Europa 2004) NMDS. 1977 LP from two members of the Art Bears/Henry Cow crew. Extraordinarily packaged jazz-rock concept album. Avant-garde but not self-important. Vocals by Lisa Herman.

STEVE HACKETT

- *Defector* (Charisma CL-3103). The Genesis guitarist has several solo albums, this one probably the best. The instrumentals are spacey but not without energy. Odd meters and forceful electric guitar characterize these works. Some rock songs as well.

JAN HAMMER

- *The First Seven Days* (Nemperor NE-432). 1975 record from this well-known musician. Though now known as the fellow who penned the *Miami Vice* theme, he was a highly regarded keyboardist in the 70s, working with John Abercrombie, Jeff

Beck, and others. Some of the instrumentals here are quite good, others are plainly derivative.

BO HANSSON
- *The Lord of the Rings* (PVC 7907)
- *Ur Trollkarlens Hatt* (Silence SRS-4615)

The first thing you notice about this Swedish composer's work is the incredibly dated organ sound—right out of the mid-60s, though these albums are from the mid-70s. The music, a mix of rock, spacey electronics, and a tinge of jazz here and there, is also dated, though you can find a few interesting things if you look hard enough.

WAYNE HORVITZ
- *Dinner at Eight* (Dossier 7514) NMDS. A figure on NY's downtown scene, Horvitz is much closer to the formal, unpredictable music of Elliott Sharp (see Chapter 10, page 239) than to the LOLO contingent. Still, there's some catchy music here, as well as some real ear-stretchers, mostly for keyboards.

LINDA HUDES
- *Lasting Effect* (Power & Glory cassette, no #). Music written for the dance by another LOLO member. David Van Tieghem and other folks from the band play behind Hudes's keyboards; the music is tightly knit and intelligently planned.

JADE WARRIOR
- *Floating World* (Island ILPS-9290)
- *Waves* (Island ILPS-9318)
- *Kites* (Island ILPS-9393)

Primarily a duo, but with many guests, Jade Warrior has been around since the early 70s. Their combination of rock, jazz, Asian, and experimental sounds works best on the third album, from 1976, only occasionally on the first album, and hardly ever on the second. At its best, though, it's unusual and distinctive music.

SCOTT JOHNSON
- *John Somebody* (None./Icon 79133) NMDS. For more on *John Somebody*, see Chapter 3. Behind the formal concerns and often complex scoring is a guitarist who likes to kick out the jams and *play*. There's nothing rigid or prettified about his music; it's a convincing combination of seemingly incompatible styles.

KALAHARI SURFERS
- *Own Affairs* (Rec. GNP-333) REC. Don't let the paradoxical name of this group (the Kalahari is one of the driest and most inhospitable deserts in the world) fool you—these white South African musicians make loud, angry music that had to be shipped out of the country to be pressed onto vinyl. Unafraid of their own repressive government, they have released two highly political rock albums. "Crossed Cheques," off this LP, uses electronics

and found sound (mostly street recordings), and is reminiscent of David Van Tieghem's music.

KING CRIMSON
- *Discipline* (War. WB-3629)
- *Beat* (War. 23692)
- *Three of a Perfect Pair* (War. 25071)

This is the second edition of King Crimson, which lasted for several years in the early to mid-80s. Fripp's earlier Crimson outfits, from 1969–1976, were among the leaders of the progressive rockers; a few cuts from LPs like *In the Court of the Crimson King* (Atlantic 8245) and *Lizard* (Polydor UK 2302 059) have a chamber music quality that stands them in good stead even now. These records have a harder edge; the instrumentals often have a Near Eastern sound, and side two of the last album has a fine set of atmospheric works.

KRAFTWERK
See Chapter 1.

MANNHEIM STEAMROLLER
- *Fresh Aire I* (American Gramaphone AG-365) NAR
- *Fresh Aire II* (American Gramaphone AG-359) NAR
- *Fresh Aire III* (American Gramaphone AG-365) NAR
- *Fresh Aire IV* (American Gramaphone AG-370) NAR
- *Interludes* (American Gramaphone AG-373) NAR
- *Fresh Aire V* (American Gramaphone AG-385) NAR
- *Christmas* (American Gramaphone AG-1984) NAR
- *Saving the Wildlife* (Original Soundtrack) (American Gramaphone AG-2086) NAR

Mannheim Steamroller's "Best of" collection would probably be a tremendous album. But taken individually, these albums can be pretty frustrating. Using acoustic and electronic keyboards, guitar, bass, drums, and symphony orchestra, this Omaha-based group puts embarrassing, hackneyed muzak next to some swinging orchestral rock numbers and lovely piano pieces. Spectacular production.

RON COOLEY
- *Daydreams* (American Gramaphone AG-368) NAR. This is basically a Mannheim Steamroller album, with guitarist Ron Cooley up front. As usual, beautiful production and packaging, but to what purpose? The album comes off sounding like Mantovani on uppers.

RAY MANZAREK
- *Carmina Burana* (A&M 4945). Produced by Philip Glass, whose musical fingerprints can be easily spotted in only a few excerpts, this rework-

ing of Carl Orff's masterpiece is a real klinker. If you're an old unrepentant Doors fan, get it if you must—but by all means get a *real* recording of this piece, too.

BILL NELSON
- *The Love That Whirls/Beauty & the Beast* (PVC/Cocteau 101) JEM. Since breaking up his rock band Be Bop Deluxe, Nelson has become a musical split personality. He makes above-average synthipop on the first of this two-LP set, and does some uneven, atmospheric keyboard instrumentals on the second disc.
- *Das Kabinet/La Belle et la Bête* (Cocteau JCD-4) JEM. Two LPs; a reissue of *Beauty and the Beast,* and more incidental music for a stage production of *The Cabinet of Doctor Caligari.* More proof that perfectly competent incidental music often makes lousy recordings: These scores do not stand alone well.
- *The Summer of God's Piano* (Cocteau JC-6) JEM. The finest of Nelson's solo electronic albums. With twenty-three short pieces, you get the same self-indulgence and lack of development that mar his other records, but a number of these compositions are worth hearing. Mostly simple, almost naive, these are mostly keyboard solos, with occasional drum machine or electric guitar to remind you of Nelson's glam-rock past.

- *New Music from Antarctica* (various artists/Antarctica 6201) NMDS. All your downtown favorites: David Van Tieghem, Peter Gordon, "Blue" Gene Tyranny, Rhys Chatham, and many others. Wildly uneven, but so weird it's hard not to like.

STEFAN NILSSON
- *Music for Music Lovers* (Breakthru BRS-5) SCA. Well, music for Stefan Nilsson lovers, anyway. Despite the presence of Palle Danielsson, Björn J:son Lindh, Janne Schaeffer, and Per Lindvall, this jazz-rock LP never gets going. The only exception is "Yaqui," which is presumably based on a Yaqui Indian melody.

MIKE OLDFIELD
- *Hergest Ridge* (Vir. VI-2013) NAR. Perhaps Oldfield's best work—a completely successful blend of rock, Celtic, and symphonic music. Each of the work's six sections has a different mood, but they're related thematically, and the work maintains its coherence throughout the length of the album.
- *Tubular Bells* (Vir./Epic PE-34116). Following in the vein of the preceding album, *Tubular Bells* once again sees Oldfield playing dozens of guitars, keyboards, winds, and percussion instruments.
- *Ommadawn* (Vir. V2043). After the commercial success of *Tubular Bells,* Oldfield put more emphasis on the rock element in his sound. Still, this album has some fine music, especially the duet with uilleann piper Paddy Moloney.
- *Incantations* (Vir. VDT-101). Two-LP set, with David Bedford leading the orchestra and chorus; African drums by Jabula, and several other talented musicians. Lively, ambitious music.
- *Airborne* (Vir. VA-13143)
- *QE2* (Vir./Epic FE-37358)
- *Five Miles Out* (Vir./Epic ARE-37983) Later, more rock-oriented recordings. A limited number of *Airborne* releases include live recordings of compressed versions of *Tubular Bells* and *Incantations.* Even when he's making straightforward rock music, Oldfield's knack for mixing and matching instrumental colors is enjoyable.

**MIKE AND SALLY OLDFIELD,
WITH PEKKA POHJOLA**
- [Untitled] (Happy Bird 90096). Dutch release from 1981. Despite a promising lineup (includes percussionist Pierre Moerlen), the album is only sporadically effective.

- *The Ordinaires* (Dossier ST-7509) NMDS. They record at CBGB's, which is certainly a rock haunt; they use electric guitars, bass, and drums, like most rock bands; the album is full of three- to five-minute pieces like any good rock LP. But this is no ordinary rock group. The violins and cello are reminiscent of some of Michael Nyman's string writing, and the saxes add an improvisatory edge to the proceedings. It's not rock, not jazz, not Minimalism, and—despite an arrangement of "Ramayana" that is virtually unrecognizable—not Indonesian. But they sound like they're having fun, and it's contagious.

PINK FLOYD
- *Piper at the Gates of Dawn* (Tower ST-5093)
- *Saucerful of Secrets* (Tower ST-5131)
- *Ummagumma* (Cap. STBB-388, 2 LPs)
- *Meddle* (Harvest SMAS-832)
- *Dark Side of the Moon* (Harvest SMAS-11163) Even the earliest Pink Floyd records are still basically rock music. But works like *Saucerful of Secrets* used classical techniques of tape manipulation, and can certainly qualify as avant-garde. The instrumentals on *Ummagumma* and *Meddle* are vintage psychedelia, a step or two removed from mainstream rock. With the classic *Dark Side of the Moon,* Pink Floyd began moving back into the mainstream, but the album still sounds good and is still selling well today.

PRINCIPAL EDWARD'S MAGIC THEATRE
- *The Asmoto Running Band* (Dandelion DAN-8002). The three LPs by this post-psychedelic British band now seem hopelessly dated, but this second album, from 1971, has at least one interesting cut: "Autumn Lady Dancing Song," for African percussion, guitar, voice, and others, is based on a

story from the Noh theater of Japan. The lady of the song is a demon; the music is appropriately ominous.

PETER PRINCIPLE
- *Sedimental Journey* (Crammed Discs MTM-4) NMDS. Quirky rock instrumentals; includes some film score material. A member of Tuxedomoon (see below).

RAGNARÖK
- *Ragnarök* (Silence 4633)
- *Fjärilar i Magen* (Silence 4655)
- *Fata Morgana* (Silence 4666)

Ragnarök is the Swedish equivalent of the German *Götterdämmerung,* the Teutonic Apocalypse. This group plays dark, sometimes heavy-handed rock. Their second album, apparently written for a theater production, contains a couple of acoustic tracks that provide welcome relief.

- ▲ *Recommended Records Sampler* (Rec. RR8/9) NMDS. A collection of *Sturm-und-Drang* rock, new wave, post-punk, and noise-rock, taken from such exotic locales as Algeria, Barcelona, Berlin, Switzerland, and New Jersey. Rockish works by Aksak Maboul, Univers Zero, and Art Zoyd, as well as chamber-style pieces from Feliu Gasul, Conventum, and Hector Zazou (see Chapter 9 discography). Not for the faint of heart.

RENAISSANCE
- *In the Beginning* (*Prologue & Ashes Are Burning,* reissue) (Cap. SWBC-11871)
- *Turn of the Cards* (Sire 6015)
- *Scheherezade and Other Stories* (Sire 6017)
- *Novella* (Sire 6024)
- *Live at Carnegie Hall* (2Xs 6029, 2 LPs)

This group's talent was exceeded only by the seriousness of its self-image. Too ambitious for its own good, the group tried to blend classical guitar and piano styles with operatic singing and electric bass and drums. These albums, from 1972 to 1977, have some genuinely interesting pieces; but like ELP, musical material is often "borrowed" from the classics, and the blend of styles sounds contrived. Later albums went for a more commercially viable sound.

THE RESIDENTS
- *Meet the Residents* (Ralph 0677)
- *Eskimo* (Ralph, no #)
- *The Residents' Commercial Album* (Ralph 8052)
- *George and James* (Ralph 8402)
- *Whatever Happened to Vileness Fats?* (Ralph 8452)

Found sound, toy instruments, and a carefully cultivated sense of the grotesque can't hide the fact that the Residents' amateurish sound is a put-on. These are four (we think) *real,* if very silly, musicians. Unfortunately, their desire to be strange just for the sake of being strange sometimes gets in the

way of the music; the albums listed here are representative of the amusing and disturbing sides of their work. *Eskimo* is perhaps their most striking record: We're left to guess about what instruments are being used, but the album is highly evocative, in a bizarre way. The *Commercial Album* is forty works, each sixty seconds long (about as much of the Residents' music as commercial radio stations or record stores are likely to play); some of these are quite inventive and entertaining, others are (suitably?) inane little ditties. *George and James* is a set of George Gershwin and James Brown songs in arrangements that can only be described as twisted.

DAVID ROSENBLOOM
- *"Departure"* from the LP *Souls of Chaos/Departure* (Neutral N8) NMDS
- *"Flowers"* (from the audio-cassette magazine *Tellus,* Vol. 2). NMDS

"Flowers" is a part of "Departure" that didn't make it onto the album version of the piece. Using texts drawn from the apocryphal Gospel of Thomas and others, Rosenbloom has created a gripping work with highly rhythmic vocals (chanted rather than sung) and densely textured instrumental passages. As you would expect from a Branca associate, his music is often amplified to great volume; in "Souls of Chaos," the result is noisy and chaotic, but in "Departure" it allows subtle instrumental lines to be easily heard.

NORMAN SALANT
- *Saxaphone Demonstrations* (Alive AEP-101) NMDS. My initial reaction to this album was negative, for two reasons: one, an album title should never be misspelled, especially if the offending word is your featured instrument; and two, the bright day-glo cover hurt my eyes. Inside is a short album of Salant layering sax on sax, with rhythm box and some guitar. A few pieces sound like LOLO; others are arrangements of music by Bowie, Blondie, etc. An expressive, multifaceted record of pieces that sound like music first, and demonstrations second.

SAVANT
- *Stationary Dance/Sensible Music* (Palace of Lights PoL 09/2000) NMDS
- *The Neo-Realist (At Risk)* (Palace of Lights PoL 15/2000) NMDS

K. Leimer's rock group. Lots of percussion, both live and taped, synthesizers, electric guitars, some vocals, lots of found sound. Similar at times to some of Eno's transitional rock albums, though a bit heavier on the ethnic sounds.

17 PYGMIES
- *Jedda by the Sea* (Resistance 1948) NMDS. From the NMDS catalog: "One reviewer said the Pygmies are the greatest thing to hit Christendom

since chili fries, which makes us want to try chili fries." Stirring, emotional music from a California rock band that also tries acoustic music, ethnic sounds, and psychedelic electronic effects. Vocals, electric guitar, and electric bass, of course, but also flute, piano, and quasi-tribal drums.

SKY
■ *Sky 3* (Ariola ASKY-3). Classical guitarist John Williams's attempt at a classical, or at least classy, rock band is actually pretty lame. Along with the usual insipid originals, though, this album includes a lovely arrangement of a Handel Sarabande.

MARC SLOAN
■ *Yeow* (Little Animals LAR-1001) NMDS. Sloan is a bass and keyboard player, and perhaps a multiple personality as well. His album runs from jazz to quirky rock to spacey bass harmonics, and even includes a lyrical piano solo. A curious disc: "Be careful when you play this album," say his liner notes, though he doesn't explain why.

TAG·YR·IT
■ *Predator Score* (After Hours ARCK-106) NMDS. Tag·Yr·It seems to be a one-man band consisting of Ohio's Dale Stevens. Mostly electronic, with a good deal of electronic percussion, it's like an accessible version of the Residents.

▲ *Tellus, Vol. 12: "Dance"* (NMDS). Some of NY's best-known downtown composers perform here: Brooks Williams (Chapter 1) and Hearn Gadbois (Chapter 2) have already been covered. Also appearing are Bill Obrecht, A. Leroy, Lenny Pickett, and others. Some were written for choreographers, some were recorded in dance clubs, some are just eminently danceable.

STEVE TIBBETTS
■ *Steve Tibbetts* (Frammis BZZ-77)
■ *YR* (Frammis 1522-25)
■ *Northern Song* (ECM 1218) ECM
■ *Safe Journey* (ECM 25002-1) ECM
■ *Exploded View* (ECM 1335) ECM
Tibbetts is a fine guitarist who plays both acoustic and electric versions with equal facility. His long-time accompanist, percussionist Marc Anderson, plays tabla, other ethnic percussion, and Western drums. Also a major part of the texture here are the kalimba and various tape sounds. When he picks up an electric guitar, Tibbetts gets into some heavy-duty rock; a surprising amount of this has crept into his ECM records. *Northern Song* is an exception: It's primarily an acoustic album, with spare, ambient textures. But "Going Somewhere," from *Safe Journey*, shows that Tibbetts can make equally atmospheric music with electronics. Of the Frammis albums, the second is much the better; but both are out of print.

TIREZ TIREZ
■ *"Set the Timer"/"Uptight"* (Sire 20445). Nothing out of the ordinary here . . . this is straight dance-oriented rock. But the band is Mikel Rouse (see Chapter 4) and his Broken Consort bassist Jim Bergman.

DAVID TORN, MARK ISHAM, BILL BRU-FORD, AND TONY LEVIN
■ *Cloud about Mercury* (ECM 1322) ECM. How about that for a lineup. Truly progressive rock with a healthy spicing of jazz. For old King Crimson fans who've been looking for something new to latch on to, this may be it. First-rate musicianship, fine production.

▲ *Triangulus and Björn J:son Lindh* (Breakthru BRS-6) SCA. This group, an offshoot of Ragnarök (above), sticks mostly to jazz-rock fusion, but adds the eerie, thereminlike sounds of the musical saw and a bit of harmonic singing to the usual synthesizers, guitar, and drums. So the sound, at least, is inventive, and a couple of the shorter tracks effectively create a mood, but mostly this is an album for fans of European jazz-rock.

TUXEDOMOON
■ *Half Mute* (Ralph TX-8004)
■ *"Verdun"* from the LP *Made to Measure, Vol. 1* (Crammed Discs CRAM-029) NMDS
Steven Brown (sax, synthesizer, voice), Blaine Reininger (violin, synthesizer, voice), and Peter Principle (bass, electric percussion). Despite the vocal pieces, which don't always work, *Half Mute* is their best album, and the least easily classified, though all of it is murky and gloomy. "Verdun" is a set of excerpts from a Dutch film, very much in the same vein.

DAVID VAN TIEGHEM
■ *These Things Happen* (War. 25105-1).
■ *Safety in Numbers* (Private Music, 1987 release) PRI
Most of Van Tieghem's music is written for the dance—Elisa Monte and Twyla Tharp specifically. These LPs include a huge assortment of percussion, including random bits of metal, stools, ashtrays, and electronic percussion. Van Tieghem also plays synthesizer, so there's a good deal more melodic content than you might expect from a drummer going solo. In fact, some of his most effective excerpts have very little percussion, relying instead on moody electronics and prerecorded tapes.

YOUNG MARBLE GIANTS
■ *Colossal Youth* (Rough Trade US-6) NMDS. Never caught on with the public, though the critics loved them. A couple of the instrumentals here straddle the border between rock and ambient music.

ZAMLA

- *Zamlaranamma* (Urspår URS-10) SCA. Swedish progressive rock band that has undergone several personnel changes and has recorded under several similar names. Best for fans of Gong, National Health, and Soft Machine. Like those groups, Zamla uses a jazz-rock style they rarely depart from.

FRANK ZAPPA

- *Studio Tan* (Discreet DSK-2291)
- *Sleep Dirt* (Discreet DSK-2292)

With garish cover art and absolutely no credits, these barely look like professional jobs; Zappa apparently did them in 1978 and 1979 to fulfill contractual obligations. But while neither record is particularly inspired, each contains one work of interest: "Revised Music for Guitar and Low Budget Orchestra" is a typically offbeat piece from *Studio Tan;* and the title track from *Sleep Dirt* is a ravishing guitar duet that simply grinds to a halt —as one of the musicians explains, "my fingers got stuck."

ZIRBEL

- *"Black Snow"* from *Anatomy of a Pig* (Pteranodon Limited 2047) IMP. Engaging music for synthesizer, electric violin, and bass. Lyrical but not schmaltzy. The rest of this cassette seems designed to drive you to do impromptu dissections of barnyard animals—very close to free-form noise-rock, though (I think) better performed.

12
MUSICELLANEOUS

This is a selection of musical miscellany: works that just don't fit anywhere else. Even in a book with the scope of this one, some music resists being placed under a heading that asks it to help illustrate a specific theme. Sometimes a piece is so unusual that you don't know what to make of it. In one sense, of course, all the music discussed in this book can claim to belong in this chapter, but practically that would have made for some very difficult reading.

DISCOGRAPHY AND RELATED WORKS

JOHN ADAMS

- *Songbirdsongs* (Opus One 66) NMDS. From the Alaska-based John Adams, who's both a composer and environmentalist, comes a unique, lovely album for piccolo, ocarina, and percussion. More a re-creation of the tone and mood of bird songs than a scientific, note-by-note transcription, this is graceful and quiet music, relaxing but not insignificant.

- ▲ *Amarcord Nino Rota* (Hannibal 9301) HAN. The first of three albums in this chapter devoted to the music of a single composer in arrangements by many artists from various musical styles. (*Lost in the Stars* (Kurt Weill) and *That's the Way I Feel Now* (Thelonius Monk) are listed below.) This 1981 release includes excerpts from many of Nino Rota's greatest film scores, written for Federico Fellini's *Amarcord, Juliet of the Spirits, Satyricon,* etc. Guitarist Bill Frisell, David Amram's Quintet, Michael Sahl, Muhal Richard Abrams, and members of the rock band Blondie head the cast.

ROBERT ASHLEY

- *Automatic Writing* (Lovely 1002) NMDS. Highly amplified vocal sounds, both semantic and nonsemantic, backed by a soft track of electronics. Though the vocals include words, they are used in such a way that they lose any meaning and have to be taken as pure sounds. The mouth noises (you can hear the sounds of lips and tongues quite clearly) can be disagreeable; this is not a record for everyone.
- *"Interiors with Flash"* from the two-LP set *Big Ego* (Giorno Poetry Systems GPS-012/013). One final excerpt from this eclectic compilation. With its whispering voices and electronic noises, it sounds like a study for the preceding.
- *Private Parts* (Lovely LM-1001) NMDS. Unlike the later rock-based albums from this "opera," which are listed in the preceding chapter, this album cannot be said to grow out of any recognizable musical tradition. Ashley's text consists of an inspired potpourri of camera directions, scene descriptions, and a quietly troubled, touching stream-of-consciousness monologue. He is joined by "Blue" Gene Tyranny playing some of his most effective keyboard music, and a tabla player named Kris. This is one of those albums that will either draw you in completely, or leave you cold. Hear it at least once.

- *Perfect Lives* (Lovely LMC-4913/4947) NMDS. Cassette-only release with three excerpts from the TV opera. Falls halfway between the preceding album and the later albums mentioned earlier.
- *Atalanta (Acts of God)* (Lovely 3301–3303) NMDS. Three-LP set documenting the Rome performance of Ashley's "opera." If you saw one of the early versions of this piece and were disappointed, you may be surprised by the finished product. As with most of Ashley's music, it's definitely out there, by anyone's standards; but with its operatic vocals (in Italian) and Ashley's soft, raspy narration (in English), not to mention the almost Romantic musical score, it's also a highly melodic piece.

DONALD ASHWANDER

- *Turnips* (Upstairs Upst-1). Catchy, sometimes silly, tunes for piano, electric harpsichord, chordiana, and/or rhythm box. (O.P.)

DAVID BOWIE

- *Bertolt Brecht's "Baal"* (RCA CPL-1-4346). A mini-LP of Bowie doing five Brechtian ballads from this early play. Dominic Muldowney (see *Lost in the Stars,* below) turns in some fine arrangements, and if Bowie's singing isn't completely convincing, it's not embarrassing either; his performance of "The Drowned Girl" is dramatic and engrossing.

- ▲ *Caravaggio* (Cherry Red ACME-6). Original music by Simon Fisher Turner. Subtitled "Sound Sketches for Michele of the Shadows," this is the soundtrack to the film about the turbulent life of Michelangelo Caravaggio, one of the last great Italian Renaissance painters. "Sound sketches" is a good description: This LP consists of short (one- to four-minute) excerpts of sound recordings made

266

in Italy (street noise, sounds of a country carnival, barroom noise), electronics, small choral works, and ensemble pieces for dulcimer, harpsichord, bowed psaltery, strings, gongs, and found objects. A very strange recording that will certainly keep you guessing—about what's coming next, and, often, about what you're listening to at the moment.

PASCAL COMELADE
- *Sentimientos* (Dys 05) NMDS. Comelade plays keyboards, synthesizer, guitar, percussion . . . but his characteristic sounds are those of toy pianos and toy saxes. David Cunningham joins here in works by Eno, Satie, Kevin Ayers, Bizet, and Comelade originals dedicated to Syd Barrett, Robert Wyatt, Mozart, etc.
- *Slow Musics* (Eurock EDC-06) EUR. Another recording, this one cassette only, of quiet, almost inadvertently avant-garde works for toy instruments, tapes, etc. Works for K. Leimer and John Cage have appropriately murky and industrial sounds, respectively. Also a mambo, and a number of short, almost Minimal pieces. Even at its most brooding and obscure, Comelade's music is always charming. Poor sound quality, though.

STUART DEMPSTER
- *In the Great Abbey of Clement VI* (1750 Arch S-1775). As much a recording of the space as the musician. Dempster launches his trombone notes into the abbey, where they hang suspended for up to fourteen seconds. Since Dempster is capable of multiphonics and curious "extended" sounds on his instrument anyway, the result is a rich, pleasantly baffling experience. May, unfortunately, be out of print.

HILDEGARD VON BINGEN
- *A Feather on the Breath of God: Sequences and Hymns* (Hyperion A66039) CH
- *Ordo virtutum* (HM/Germany HM-20395/96, 2 LPs)

The best description I've yet heard of this music, by a German abbess, diplomat, writer, mystic, sometime physician, and composer (born 1098, died 1179), came from Bob Hurwitz of Nonesuch Records, who termed it "Medieval space music." The first album features Emma Kirkby and the Gothic Voices, with "symphony" (a type of hurdy-gurdy drone) and reed drones. The second set, by the Ensemble Sequentia, has a tough act to follow, but is equal to the task. Hildegard's music represents an early evolution from plainchant to later Western polyphony; the use of instrumental drones under the mobile vocal lines precedes the *organum* of the Notre Dame composers of the twelfth and thirteenth centuries. More than 800 years old, this music has been overlooked and is still genuinely "new."

▲ *Keys of Life* (CH CEL-017) CH. A piano sampler, with music by Florian Fricke (Popol Vuh), Terry Riley, Peter Michael Hamel, Hans Otte, Herbert Henck playing Gurdjieff/de Hartmann, and Cecil Lytle playing Scriabin. Except for the latter excerpts, all of these pieces can be found under their individual listings in previous chapters.

GUY KLUCEVSEK
- *Blue Window* (Zoar ZCS-08) NMDS. Klucevsek, probably the accordion's most accomplished virtuoso, plays a work based *very* loosely on Strauss's "Blue Danube Waltz," and compositions by John Zorn, Pauline Oliveros, his own "Toronto (Sevenths)" for four accordions, and Lois V. Vierk's "Manhattan Cascade," a wall of sound created by four amplified accordions. A real ear-opener to anyone who thought the accordion was strictly for weddings, polkas, and large ladies with blue hair.

▲ *The Late Fourteenth Century Avant-Garde* (one record from a three-LP set: *The Art of Courtly Love*, by David Munrow and the Early Music Consort of London/Seraphim SIC-6092). Put this in the same group as Hildegard of Bingen—old music that's still new. No matter how often you hear these works, they're still capable of surprise. Some of them, written by composers who took advantage of the extravagance of European courts competing for artistic, as well as political, prestige, are so harmonically daring and just plain weird that they could have been written ten years ago. Munrow's Consort was, as always, superb on this recording.

▲ *Lost in the Stars: The Music of Kurt Weill* (A&M SP-9-5104). The third of the Hal Willner–produced albums devoted to multiform arrangements of one artist's music. Like *Amarcord Nino Rota* (above) and *That's the Way I Feel Now* (below), the roster of artists here is nothing short of amazing. Ever wonder what "September Song" would sound like if Lou Reed did it? It's here. Dagmar Krause finally gets to use her Lotte Lenya voice in a sympathetic setting. Tom Waits sings "What Keeps Mankind Alive." John Zorn, Dominic Muldowney, Marianne Faithful, Sharon Freeman, and Carla Bley are just a few of the other stars and near-stars here.

▲ *Music from Mills* (Mills College-1) NMDS. Three-LP set celebrating the centennial of the chartering of Mills College. Past and present Mills luminaries featured here include: Robert Ashley, Terry Riley, David Behrman, Luciano Berio, Steve Reich, Pandit Pran Nath, Pauline Oliveros, Darius Milhaud, Anthony Braxton, Dave Brubeck, Lou Harrison, Morton Subotnick, David Rosenboom, and "Blue" Gene Tyranny. Shorter, often less-important pieces, but how can you resist that lineup?

PHILL NIBLOCK

■ *Niblock for Celli* (India Navigation IN-3027) NMDS. Joseph Celli plays woodwinds. Niblock's music, divorced from its usual visual component, is an uneasy listening experience for many. But if you're interested in La Monte Young, David Hykes, Yoshi Wada, or anyone else who deals in the possibilities of tuning and harmonics, his work is worth close listening.

PENGUIN CAFE ORCHESTRA

■ *Music from the Penguin Cafe* (Editions EG EGED-27)
■ *Penguin Cafe Orchestra* (Editions EG EGM-113)
■ *Broadcasting from Home* (Editions EG EGED-38)
A couple of hundred pages ago, I listed Penguin Cafe Orchestra in the Minimalism chapter. I've been feeling guilty ever since. Though this British group's music *is* simple and repetitive, perhaps the best way of describing it is as a type of purely imaginary folklore, drawing on classical music, pop styles, and the folk heritage of East Africa, Venezuela, and other spots around the globe.

▲ *Portraits: A Selection from the New Albion Catalogue* (New Albion NAL-009) NMDS. Compact disc only. A beautiful package; see the individual listings for details: Stephen Scott (page 89), Sōmei Satoh (pages 25, 110), Paul Dresher (pages 61, 83), John Adams (page 83), Daniel Lentz (pages 62, 85), and Ingram Marshall (page 46).

MICHEL REDOLFI

■ *Sonic Waters* (Hat Art 2002, 2 LPs) NMDS. Two versions of each chamber work: One is "dry," the other is "wet"—i.e., it's played underwater. I'm not sure what it all means—it suffers from the "gee-whiz" effect somewhat, but the concept is intriguing and there's some engaging music here, if you can get past the bubbles.

ARTHUR RUSSELL

■ *Tower of Meaning* (Chatham Square 145) NMDS. A large group, conducted by Julius Eastman. Some lovely music that's definitely not in a hurry.
■ *Instrumentals* (Crepuscule TWI-8401) NMDS. More mood music for a big band of NY downtowners: Rhys Chatham, Peter Gordon, Jon Gibson, Garrett List, David Van Tieghem, and others.

BRIAN SLAWSON

■ *Bach on Wood* (CBS 39704). Bach, Handel, Vivaldi, Corelli, and Pachelbel (guess which work) all arranged for multitracked percussion: vibes, marimba, chimes, bells, crotales, ratchet, whistles, and the sounds of plywood being sawed. Gourmet stuff it's not—even lapses into mushy background music at times—but at least it is well played, and heck, sometimes you just get in the mood for junk food, you know?

JAN STEELE

■ *Steele & Cage: Voices and Instruments* (Antilles/Obscure AN-7031). "All Day" features text by James Joyce, with Fred Frith on guitar. "Distant Saxophones" has no sax, but does include a viola solo by Dominic Muldowney. "Rhapsody Spaniel" is a piano duet. While they grew out of Steele's work with F&W Hat, a trio of improvising rock musicians, these works are not quite improvised, not completely composed, and closer to chamber music than to rock or jazz-rock. Typically uncategorizable music from Eno's Obscure series.

▲ *Tellus Vol. 14: "Just Intonation"* (NMDS). The title is self-explanatory. Nice collection of works in different styles, all very poorly recorded. Given better sound reproduction, highlights would include Jody Diamond's "In That Bright World," for vocals and gamelan; James Tenney's "Septet for Electric Guitars"; and a couple of pieces by Other Music. David Hykes, Lou Harrison, and Harry Partch are also included.

BOB TELSON

■ *The Gospel at Colonus* (War. 25182-1). With text by Lee Breuer, this joyous setting of the Oedipus legend to Gospel-inspired music is unlike anything else on disc. (That's partly because an even better Telson/Breuer production, *The Warrior Ant*, hasn't been commercially recorded yet.) Telson has played with Philip Glass and numerous salsa bands, in addition to writing pop songs for the likes of Joe Cocker. Even if Gospel music isn't your thing, these works, full of life and charm, are hard to resist.

▲ *That's the Way I Feel Now: A Tribute to Thelonius Monk* (A&M SP-6600). In which many musicians, from the jazz, rock, avant-garde, and pop arenas, join in performing Monk's music. Steve Khan and Donald Fagen do a lovely version of "Reflections" for guitar and synthesizer; Dr. John does "Blue Monk"; Sharon Freeman has a quintet of French horns playing on "Monk's Mood." Also NRBQ, Barry Harris, Was (Not Was), Peter Frampton, and lots of others.

▲ *Touch 33: Ritual.* NMDS. As you may have noticed, this audio-cassette magazine sometimes uses a number (33 or 33.4), sometimes not. This edition is accompanied by a lavishly produced booklet, and includes Regular Music (see Chapter 4), interesting music from Biting Tongues, more indefinable sounds from Nocturnal Emissions, post-punk noise from Einstürzende Neubauten, and other new, strange, ugly, and/or fascinating works. Most ascertainable pieces include David Cunningham's cross-cultural "Two Different Places" and Touch 33's own "North Star" (an ambient, Enolike piece).

PETER VAN RIPER

- *Room Space* (VRBLU 1) NMDS
- *Sound to Movement* (VRBLU 12) NMDS

Van Riper (see Chapter 10) deals here with the sounds of an instrument (specifically, saxes and other reeds) in various spaces. Echo, overtone reflection, and sonic Doppler effects are some of the phenomena he explores. Production values are not good; but the music intermittently overcomes the technical limitations.

▲ *Vor der Flut* (Eigelstein 17-6025/26, 2 LPs) WAY. The title translates as "Before the Flood." Some German musicians happened upon an emptied drinking-water reservoir under the city of Cologne; the tank had been drained for repairs, and these fellows found that the place had an incredible acoustic property: It could sustain notes for up to forty-five seconds. So, they invited musicians from Europe, and North and South America to record in the tank before it was flooded again. Pauline Oliveros, the Trio Basso Köln, panpiper Dario Domingues, and others perform, using an array of instruments that take on some uncharacteristic aspects in this cavernous space. A remarkable record.

REESE WILLIAMS

- *Whirlpool* (Tanam Press 7901) NMDS. Williams tries to conceive what an alien's perception might be of the record of music from around the world that was sent out to space on Voyager II. He takes excerpts from Mississippi John Hurt's "Talking Casey," shakuhachi player Goro Yamaguchi's performance of "Cranes in Their Nest," music for Indian vina, and works by Bach and Satie, presents short snippets from each piece, then puts those snippets together in different ways. He doesn't mix one piece with the other; but he freely combines different parts of one work in unexpected

ways. An interesting look at the process of listening to music.

HECTOR ZAZOU

- *Geographies* (Crammed Discs/Made to Measure Vol. 5) NMDS. Don't really know what to make of this one. But I like it. Works for chamber orchestra—but also with synthesizer and electric guitar. Works for voice in a wide assortment of styles, from children's chorus to impassioned quasi-Romanticism. A lyrical, propulsive album that won't sit still. One minute it sounds like a Nino Rota score, the next like Verdi's heaven-storming *Requiem.*

JOHN ZORN

- *The Big Gundown: Zorn Plays Morricone* (Icon/None.) NMDS. Yes, that's right. John Zorn, NY's master of the truly strange—his primary instruments include various game- and duck-calls—has rounded up the likes of Anton Fier, Arto Lindsay, Bill Frisell, Fred Frith, even Toots Thielmans to perform outlandish arrangements of Morricone's film music for various spaghetti Westerns. Wild results, with one or two more quiet excerpts just to let you catch your breath. Imagine Morricone put through a Vegomatic and you'll get the idea.

PETER ZUMMO

- *Zummo with an X* (Loris LR-001) NMDS. Angular, severely repetitive—but not Minimal. Zummo, whose career has included stints with LOLO and the Lounge Lizards, can make his trombone sound like one or two trumpets, and cellist Arthur Russell (see above) provides an equally unusual array of sounds from his instrument. Side one seems more like an exercise in putting sound together than a series of musical compositions; but side two, a lengthy piece called "Song IV," is a subtle, more impressive work.

IN CONCLUSION: A FEW LAST THOUGHTS

I don't feel new works invalidate old works. We're not toothpaste manufacturers, where a new brand of toothpaste will make the old one obsolete.
Philip Glass

If you look at the motorcycle market, there are all these ads for fancy new motorcycles that are replacing each other every few months. The music market is like that too.
David Behrman

Music does not exist in a vacuum. The field of new music is expanding so rapidly that composers of any given persuasion are likely to find themselves more and more often rubbing elbows with musicians who have completely different aims and methods. As we saw in the chapter on ethnic music, it is such contact between diverse styles that keeps music vital and growing—musicians ignore what's going on around them at their own risk.

But the growth of new music carries risks of its own. One concern that has been voiced frequently in this book is that unusual techniques and strange sounds can sometimes mask a paucity of real musical content. To claim that all the musicians currently exploring new music are high-integrity, highly talented, musically literate artists would unfortunately be naive. When a field opens up and and begins to move into areas that aren't yet well defined, there is as much room for the superficial and opportunistic as there is for the genuinely talented.

The critical judgment that I've brought to this book is based on the assumption that new music is finally little different from the more-established styles in terms of quality. Much of it is undistinguished note-spinning. A larger group of works (which account for most of the music discussed here) have some points of interest or display some promise. A select handful stands above the rest.

Though *New Sounds* covers a wide range of styles, one basic attitude is common to them all: Music must be able to "speak" to its listeners. The most serious among new-music composers haven't ignored the dry, academic styles of the avant-garde; they have reacted to them by adopting the avant-garde's musical values, but have chosen to express them in a different, more accessible language. The musical inbreeding that results from writing works that only other avant-garde musicians can understand is not healthy, and fortunately, the trend now seems to be toward expanding the musical vocabulary once again. Increasingly, composers are finding that it is possible to appeal to more listeners without having to compromise their musical standards. David Del Tredici's series of orchestral pieces based on Lewis Carroll's *Alice's Adventures in Wonderland,* for example, has been a notable artistic *and* commercial success.

A number of other basic principles are common to much of this music. The concept of working "between" the usual styles has been mentioned quite often, and you probably have noticed that alternate tunings have appeared in most of the chapters. Whether one uses the term *microtonality* to refer to a scale consisting of more than twelve notes (as with Easley Blackwood or Tui St. George Tucker), Asian modes (Lou Harrison, Ravi Shankar), or a scale built from the harmonic series (Terry Riley, Glenn Branca), it adds up to the same thing: It is music that approaches the basic concept of tonality in a novel way. It asks the listener to adopt a wider view of what tonality is and accept the music on its own terms.

"What is needed," claims David Hykes, "is not new sounds, but new listening." Stretching our perception of tonality is one way of interpreting that statement, but many musicians have also discussed new listening in less technical terms. Robert Fripp used to talk a lot about "active listening" when he was touring as a solo artist with his tape-loop system, and he performed only in small spaces before a limited number of people in an effort to bring a sense of immediacy to the music. Alvin Lucier's pieces ask you to actually consider the process of listening itself. New Age artists, in particular, seek to reach a "deeper" level of listening as a means of making the music more effective, or affective. Though I've mentioned some reservations about the way this idea is currently being exploited, it may well be the single greatest contribution of the New Age movement. Too many of these recordings urge passivity on the listener ("relax and let the music flow through you") and are consequently little better than the Easy Listening pablum found in shopping malls. But a number of them do ask you to bring something to the music—namely, your attention—and while they may be just as relaxing, they are ultimately more rewarding.

One of the most heartening developments in new music has been the encouragement it has given to the amateur tradition. Amateur music making is a venerable practice; in medieval times, French noblemen amused themselves by composing poetry and setting it to music. King Henry VIII of England was a talented composer, and in Germany, *Hausmusik* ("house music") was a familiar type of family entertainment until the nineteenth century. In recent generations a rift had formed between the professional music community and the average listener. A modern style like Serialism needs to be studied closely, and as much of the interest of the piece lies in its written score as in its eventual sound. But, if it's difficult to be an amateur Serialist, people understand tonality almost instinctively. The resurgence of tonal music has caused that gap between professional and amateur to shrink somewhat. Today, by asking its audience to become more aware of music's possibilities and to appreciate a variety of styles, new music has once again stirred up a keen interest in making music as well as hearing it.

If the increasing availability of inexpensive electronic instruments has been the most obvious benefit to amateurs, we should not discount the workshops now being offered, to anyone who is interested, by artists like Pauline Oliveros, Terry Riley, Paul Winter, David Darling, and others. Ensembles that use common instruments like the voice or instruments made from found objects are also setting useful examples for amateur musicians; and the success of Windham Hill has certainly drawn more people to the acoustic guitar and piano, despite the ever-growing popularity of electric instruments.

One final point needs to be made about the field of new music—its inclination toward direct communication doesn't, or shouldn't, make the music any less serious in its artistic intentions. Since Beethoven's time, "popular" music has been distinguished ever more strongly from "classical." But today music like that of Philip Glass is luring rock fans to the opera house, while Scott Johnson, Glenn Branca, and Paul Dresher are introducing that most "popular" of instruments, the electric guitar, to the concert hall. Of course, there is still much resistance on both sides, and while it's unlikely that any new-music artist will ever achieve the success of the Bruce Springsteens and Michael Jacksons of the pop music world, the attention being paid by both critics and audiences to music that doesn't stay put in one category or another is an inspiring sign.

All of which raises an interesting question. The next generation of musicians is already growing up on electronics, Minimalism, Windham Hill; and they're taking for granted the collision of styles that is still often so exotic to us. What will *their* new music be like? Will they find even more new categories between which to work? Or will they throw up their collective hands in exasperation and mutter: It's all been done before?

Music has always had the potential for the unexpected, and there's no reason to think that we've exhausted it. As long as life continues to change, the music it shapes will change too. Unable to stay in one place, musicians will *have* to look forward. Or, they'll have to look back; even then, the result will be another generation of *new* music, because, as the song says, "Everything old is new again."

APPENDIX 1: RECORD LABEL ABBREVIATIONS

The following abbreviations have been used in the discographies to indicate the record labels that appear most frequently.

Ang.	Angel
Bär.	Bärenreiter
CH	Celestial Harmonies
ChM	Chante du Monde
Col.	Columbia
DG	Deutsche Grammophon
Fly. F.	Flying Fish
Folk.	Folkways
For.	Fortuna
Gram.	Gramavision
Gr. L.	Green Linnet
HM	Harmonia Mundi
Living	Living Music
Lovely	Lovely Music
Mer.	Mercury
None.	Nonesuch
Oc.	Ocora
Ph.	Philips
Poly.	Polydor
Private	Private Music
Rec.	Recommended
Roun.	Rounder
Van.	Vanguard
Vir.	Virgin
War.	Warner Brothers
Wind. H.	Windham Hill

APPENDIX 2: KEY TO RECORD SOURCES

Throughout the discographies, you'll notice two- to four-letter codes after many entries. These are intended to give you an idea of where this music can be found. Except where indicated, each of the following sources can provide you with a catalog for mail/phone orders, either free or at nominal ($1, $2) cost.

ALC
Silo/Alcazar Ltd.
Box 429
Waterbury, VT 05676
802-244-5178
Specializes in folk and New Acoustic Music

ARH
Arhoolie Records
10341 San Pablo Avenue
El Cerrito, CA 94530
Acoustic and traditional North American styles

CAL
Callisto Records
5909 North 6 Street
Philadelphia, PA 19120

CH
Celestial Harmonies
Box 673
Wilton, CT 06897
203-762-0558
Small but select group of electronic and acoustic LPs

CMC
Canadian Music Centre/Centrediscs
20 St. Joseph Street
Toronto M4Y 1J9, Canada

CRI
Composers' Recordings Inc.
170 West 74 Street
New York, NY 10023
212-873-1250

DMP
Digital Music Products
Box 2317
Rockefeller Center Station
New York, NY 10185

ECM
ECM records are available in many stores. The company is currently in transition, and their present address (for American ECM releases only), ECM/Warner Bros. Records, Box 6868, Burbank, CA 91510, may not apply much longer. Polygram, which imports the German ECM releases, is listed under PSI, below, and may soon prove to be the source for domestic issues as well.

EUR
Eurock
PO Box 13718
Portland, OR 97213
503-281-0247
Electronic music, from Europe and points further afield. Also a newsletter detailing recent albums, interviews, etc.

FF
Flying Fish Records
1304 West Schubert
Chicago, IL 60614
Acoustic music: folk, bluegrass, NAM, string jazz, etc.

FOR
Fortuna Records
Box 1116
Novato, CA 94947
Fortuna presents New Age music for the most

part, but also includes ethnic- and Celtic-harp records. Extensive catalog of other labels as well— some otherwise hard to get.
1-800-841-5556
1-800-367-8862 in CA

FYL
Fylkingen
Box 4514
S-102 65 Stockholm
Sweden
Electronic music, mostly avant-garde, on this Swedish label. May also have records on other Swedish labels (Caprice, etc.)

GLT
Green Linnet Records
70 Turner Hill Road
New Canaan, CT 06840
Folk and near-folk music, from the British Isles, U.S., and occasional others

GP
Global Pacific Records
139 East Napa Street
Sonoma, CA 95476
800-545-2001;
707-996-2748 in CA
Electro-acoustic and New Age

GRAM
Gramavision Records
260 West Broadway
New York, NY 10013
212-226-7057
Jazz, new jazz, World Music, some Minimalism

HAN
Hannibal/Carthage Records
PO Box 667
Rocky Hill, NJ 08553
609-466-9320
Richard Thompson, African music, a few surprises

HM
Harmonia Mundi
PO Box 64503
Los Angeles, CA 90064
213-474-2139
Ocora and Chant du Monde labels, as well as German, French, and American Harmonia Mundi releases

HOS
Music from the Hearts of Space
Box 31321
San Francisco, CA 94131
"Space" music

IMP
Important Records
149-03 Guy R. Brewer Boulevard
Jamaica, NY 11434
718-995-9200
Relativity label, other electronic works; lots of imports

JEM
JEM Records
JEM is a distributor to retail stores. Records marked JEM should be available in stores; or stores can order from JEM at: 3619 Kennedy, South Plainfield, NJ 07080

KM
Kicking Mule Records
PO Box 158
Alderpoint, CA 95411
Large list of acoustic LPs, including lots of guitar music

LADY
Ladyslipper
PO Box 3130
Durham, NC 27705
919-683-1570
Feminist music, literature, etc.; many women artists not particularly associated with the movement included too

MED
Medien-Service
Postfach 1165
D-3108 Winsen
West Germany
IC and Inteam labels; Schulze and similar electronics

MHS
Musical Heritage Society
1710 Highway 35
Ocean, NJ 07712
Operates like a book club; a few ethnic or folk-derived LPs, the rest classical

MOW
Music of the World
Box 258
Brooklyn, NY 11209
Ethnic and World music

MULT
Multiphase Records
Box 15176
St. Louis, MO 63110
Electronics from St. Louis; some rock, some not

NAR
Narada Productions
1845 North Farwell Avenue
Milwaukee, WI 53202
800-862-7232
One of the largest catalogs in the field: New Age,
electronics, ethnic, Windham Hill, etc.

NMDS
New Music Distribution Service
500 Broadway
New York, NY 10012
212-925-2121
Hundreds of labels, including New Albion and
Palace of Lights, and *thousands* of records—lots of
jazz, some classical, avant-garde music of every
conceivable type

NOR
Northeastern Records
17 Cushing Hall
Northeastern University
Boston, MA 02115
617-437-2826
Composers in Red Sneakers; classical records

OAO
OAO/Celluloid
155 West 29 Street
New York, NY 10001.
African, NY "downtown" jazz, some ethnic and
World Music

ORI
Oriental Records
PO Box 1802
Grand Central Station
New York, NY 10017
212-557-7851
Indian music—north and south

PAJ
Palo Alto Records
755 Page Mill Road
Palo Alto CA 94304

PHI
Philo Records
70 Court Street
Middlebury, VT 05753
Acoustic music, some New Agey, some folksy, a
few ethnically-flavored

PRI
Private Music
220 East 23 Street
New York, NY 10010
800-382-4052

PSI
Polygram Special Imports
Like JEM, PSI supplies retailers.
ECM and European labels are specialties. Many
PSI albums *are* available through mail order from:
North Country Distributing
Cadence Building
Redwood, NY 13679
A catalog is free when you buy a sample issue of
Cadence magazine.

REF
Reference Recordings
Box 77225X
San Francisco, CA 94107
Audiophile discs in many styles

RIS
Rising Sun Records
PO Box 524
Mill Valley, CA 94942
New Age, acoustic, and electro-acoustic

ROU
Rounder/Roundup
1 Camp Street
Cambridge, MA 02140
617-354-0700 in MA;
212-477-4600 in NY
Roundup is mail order; Rounder is retail: large
catalog of acoustic music

SBMG
Suite Beat Music Group
3355 West El Segundo Boulevard
Hawthorne, CA 90250
213-973-8800
U.S. distributor for German IC label

SCA
Scan-Am/Breakthru Records
2 Lincoln Square
#24E
New York, NY 10023
212-362-1689
Scandinavian jazz, rock, jazz-rock, and others

SHAN
Shanachie Records
DaleBrook Park
1 Hollywood Avenue
Ho-Ho-Kus, NJ 07423
201-445-5561
Extensive catalog of folk, including Irish Gael-
Linn, Tara, etc.

SM
Smithsonian Collection
955 L'Enfant Plaza
Suite 2100
Washington, DC 20560

SON
Sonic Atmospheres
14755 Ventura Boulevard
Suite 1776
Sherman Oaks, CA 91403

TRI
Triangle Publishing
PO Box 452
New York, NY 10021
If you're at all interested in Gurdjieff's work, or the
Gurdjieff/de Hartmann music, contact Triangle.

VB
Vital Body Marketing
Box 1067
42 Orchard Street
Manhasset, NY 11030
800-221-0200;
516-365-4115 in NY
Slimmed down catalog is mostly New Age

WAY
Wayside Music
Box 6517
Wheaton, MD 20906
Imports, cut-outs, other curios; constantly chang-
ing catalog

WH
Windham Hill Records
Box 9388
Stanford, CA 94305
In many stores, but a mail order catalog is still
available in the unlikely event you need one

Also: Recommended Records
387 Wandsworth Road,
London SW8
Great Britain
(European source for all Recommended discs; see
NMDS for American source)

INDEX

(Note: Numbers in **boldface** type indicate main entries in discographies.)

Aaberg, Philip, **213**, 214, 219
Abercrombie, John, 132, **202**, 206, **209**, 259
Abrams, Muhal Richard, 83, **202**, 222, 266
Ackerman, William, *xi, xiii,* 185, 196–200, **214**, 219
Adam, Margie, **214**
Adams, John, 35, 65, 66, 70
  concert music of, 91, 92, 99, 100, **102**
  Minimalism and, 65, 66, 70, 81, **83**, 87
Adams, John (Alaska-based composer), **102**, **266**
Addy, Obo, **151**
Ade, King Sunny, 147
Aeoliah, **40**
Aeolian Chamber Players, 104
Affektenlehre, Die (Mattheson), 38–39
Afghanistan, music of, **153**
Africa
  Central and Southern, music from, 147, **151–152**
  discography for music from, **151–153**
  as jazz source, 188–189
  North, music from, 37*n*, 90, 125, 147, **152–153**
  Reich and music from, 78, 147, 149
  West, music from, 95, 125, 147–150, **151**
  World Music and, 117–118, 123–133 *passim*
  see also entries for specific countries
Afrobeat, 147
After Dinner, **256**
Ahmed, Mahmoud, **123**
Ailana, **123**
Ajemian, Maro, 103, 106
Aka pygmies, **151**
Akhbari, Djalal, 160
Akkerman, Jan, **210**
Aksak Maboul, 45, 132, 193–194, **202**, **256**, 262
Albert, Thomas, **102**
Albion Band, **174**, 181
Albion Country Band, **174**, 176, 181
Albion Dance Band, 169, 172, **174**, 176, 181
Albright, William, 103
Aldridge, Robert, 103
Alexandros, **17**
Allen, Bernoff, Bell & Smith, **40**

Allen, David, 258
Allen, Marcus, **40**, **214**
Allen, Susan, 103, 110
Almqvist, Thomas, 177, **202**
Ambient Music series (Eno), 12–13, 37, 43, 45
Amerlan, **17**
Amirkhanian, Charles, **61**, **235**
Amram, David, 116–117, 119, **123**, 265
An Triskell, **174**
Ancient Future, 119, **123**
Anders, Ursula, 207
Anderson, Jon, 8*n*
Anderson, Laurie, *xii, xv,* 15, 44, 236, 242, 247–251, **256**, 259
  on *Einstein on the Beach,* 69–70, 78–79
  lyrics by, 81, 85
  "O Superman," 250–251
  United States, 248–251, 256
Anderson, Marc, 263
Anderson, Ruth, **17**, 23
Andes, music of, **161**, 184
Andrews, Joel, **214**
Android Sisters, The, **17**
Anger, Darol, 199–200, **212–213**, 214, 219
Angola, music of, **151**
Animals, 246
Anna Själv Tredje, **17**
Anode, 256
Anonymus, 122
Antheil, George, 254
Apetrea, Coste, **202**, **211**
Aphrodite's Child, 8
Aqsak Maboul, *see* Aksak Maboul
Ar Bras, Dan, 170, 172, **174**, 179, 183
Arctic Chamber Orchestra, 102
Archer, Violet, 19
Arditti Quartet, 103
Ardley, Neil, **17**, **102**
Armenia, music of, **153**
Armstrong, Randy, 125
Armstrong, Rebecca, 237
Armstrong, Louis, 185
Art Bears, 208, **256**, 258

279